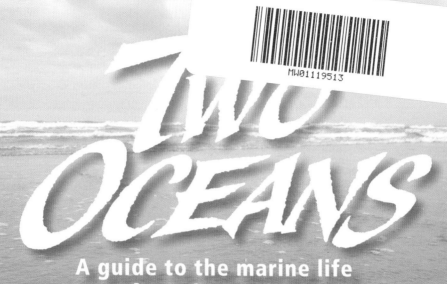

TWO OCEANS

A guide to the marine life of southern Africa

GM Branch, CL Griffiths,
ML Branch, LE Beckley

Principal photographers:
George Branch, Charles Griffiths, Dennis King

Published by Struik Nature
(an imprint of Random House Struik (Pty) Ltd)
80 McKenzie Street, Cape Town 8001
PO Box 1144, Cape Town 8000
South Africa

Company Reg. No. 1966/003153/07

Visit us at www.randomstruik.co.za

First published in 1994 by
   David Philip Publishers

This revised edition 2010
10 9 8 7 6 5 4 3 2 1

Publishing manager: Pippa Parker
Managing editor: Helen de Villiers
Editor: Emily Bowles
Design director: Janice Evans
Design assistant: Jennifer Addington
Illustrator: Margo Branch
Proofreader: Tessa Kennedy

Reproduction by Hirt & Carter Cape (Pty) Ltd
Printed and bound by Kyodo Printing Co (S'pore) Pte Ltd

ISBN 978 1 77007 772 0

Front cover: Batsata Maze, False Bay (Geoff Spiby).
Back cover: *Clockwise from top* humpback whale, green-
eyed fiddler crab, dwarf spotted-anemone, powder-blue
surgeonfish, split disc-weed, sour fig, African Penguins.
Spine: Spine-tipped star. **Title page:** Plough snails devouring
a stranded jellyfish. **Contents page:** Cape fur seal.

PHOTOGRAPHIC CREDITS

Most of the invertebrate and plant
photographs were taken by Charles
Griffiths and George Branch, and
most of the fish photographs by
Dennis King. Many other people
gave, generously and freely,
magnificent photographs that lifted
the calibre of the book. Special
mention must be made of Peter Ryan
(most of the bird photographs) and
Mike Schleyer (many of the sponges
and soft corals).

Alberts, Sharon 29.4
Anderson, Rob 178.9, 185.5
Argus, The 168.2
Ballesta, Laurent & Bahuet, Eric,
   Androméde Collection 156.6
Barkai, Amos & Findlay, Ken 86.5a
Beasley, Isabella p. 360
Berjak, Pat & Pammenter, Norman
   201.1a, 201.2a
Breytenbach, Johan 43.3, 49.3, 107.2
Buchel, Paul 50.5
Chater, Simon 121.1, 121.4, 137.5
Cliff, Geremy 113.3, 114.1, 115.3,
   126.8, 141.3, 143.6, 143.7
Coetzee, Phillip 9.1, 13.1, 149.4,
   149.10
Compagno, Len, Save Our Seas
   Foundation 117.5
Connell, Allan 33.4, p. 444
Currie, Jock 168.5
De Waal, Greg 45.5, 45.6, 47.8,
   95.8, p. 443
Durham, Ben 168.6
Edwards, Lloyd,
   Raggie Charters p. 4

Elwyn, Simon, Namibian Dolphin
   Project 18.5
Ezemvelo KZN Wildlife 157.1,
   157.1a, 157.2a
Gerneke, Dane 97.7
Gershwin, Lisa-Ann 18.1
Griffiths, Melinda 31.7, 38.2
Griffiths, Roberta p. 456
Grobler, Kolette 18.4
Hardenberg, Morné, Shark Explorers
   114.7, 115.2, 116.5
Harris, Jean 99.5, 99.5a–c
Horstman, Deon 42.1
Jørgensen, Morten 167.1a
Kennedy, Fergus 166.2, back
   cover top left
Mackinnon, Jeannie 156.5
Malan, Pierre 162.5, 166.2a–b,
   167.1, 167.5, 168.7
MIKOMTEK map on p. 7
Mittelmeyer, Mike 168.1
Navarro, Rene 161.4
Oceanographic Research
   Institute 151.4
Ogden, Colin 96.2
Painting, Sue 18.3
Pedemors, Vic 168.4
Penry, Gwenith 166.3
Peschak, Tom 114.3
Prochazka, Kim 150.1, 151.8
Randall, Jack 115.7, 120.2, 141.2,
   144.2, 146.1
Reeb, Desary, MRI Whale Unit 166.1
Reisinger, Ryan 167.3
Riegl, Bernhard 3.1, 14.9, 15.5, 16.6a,
   17.5, 17.6, 17.6a, 42.2
Ruis Viladomiu, Marc 110.6
Roeleveld, Martina 97.1

Rutzen, Michael, Shark Diving
   Unlimited 114.2, 114.4
Ryan, Peter 158.1–158.6, 159.1–159.5,
   160.1, 160.2, 160.3a, 160.5,
   161.6, 162.2, 162.6, 163.2, 163.3,
   164.1–164.8
Samaai, Toufiek 2.5, 3.3, 3.4, 4.4
Schleyer, Mike 1.4, 1.7, 2.8, 2.9,
   3.2, 3.5, 3.9, 4.1, 4.3, 4.5–4.9, 5.2,
   9.6, 10.1–10.3, 10.7, 10.10, 11.1a,
   11.2–11.6a, 12.1a, 12.3–12.6, 13.7,
   14.1, 14.3, 14.3a, 16.1, 17.1, 17.2,
   101.2, 110.10, 111.4, 111.7, 111.8
Sink, Kerry p. 12, 1.10, 8.10, 13.3,
   15.6, 16.6, 64.10, 99.3, 99.7, 100.2,
   100.8, 102.2a, 102.3, 107.6
Smale, Malcolm 98.4
Southward, Peter 96.6
Spiby, Geoff front cover
Stevens, Russell 7.4
Steyn, Peter 161.3, 161.5
Tarr, Rob 81.3a, 82.9a, 82.11
Taylor, Jonathan 43.2
Timm, Peter & Eve, Triton Dive,
   Sodwana 7.6, 9.5, 11.1, 12.1,
   12.2, 13.5, p. 76, 45.2, 105.1,
   106.1a, 113.5
Trimble, Alan 109.2, 109.2a
Van der Elst, Rudy 120.6, 121.2, 143.5
Velasquez Rojas, Claudio 5.4, 6.4,
   161.1, 161.2, 161.2a, 163.5
Verhoog, Peter 165.5
Vestheim, Hege 151.6
Wahl, Zelda, Cape Nature
   Conservation 165.4
Whitfield, Alan 120.1, 121.7
Williams, Gary 21.4, 64.9a

SPONSOR'S SUPPORT

The Green Trust (a partnership between WWF-South Africa and Nedbank) has a proud record of initiating and supporting projects that further conservation. This revised and expanded edition of the award-winning book *Two Oceans* has been facilitated by a grant from The Green Trust.

The book is designed to heighten appreciation for, and allow accurate and ready identification of, the extraordinary diversity of marine life for which we are responsible. It contributes directly to many of the marine conservation projects already supported by The Green Trust and WWF, including increasing public and retailer awareness of threatened linefish via the South African Sustainable Seafood Initiative (SASSI); monitoring and recording of marine life by involving divers in the Fish and Invertebrate Monitoring Network and Reef Atlas programmes; provision of protection to bathers and employment to impoverished communities in the Shark Spotters Programme; and wise use of resources through the Responsible Fisheries Programme, which promotes Marine Protected Areas and an Ecosystem Approach to Fisheries.

The Green Trust supports this outstanding publication, which vividly illustrates the richness of our coast and will promote wise use and conservation in the spirit of WWF-SA's 'network of positive change'.

ACKNOWLEDGEMENTS

In addition to our debt to WWF-SA and The Green Trust, the authors and publishers deeply appreciate a grant from Syfrets Charitable Trust, and donations from Mr and Mrs AJ van Ryneveld and an anonymous donor 'in memory of those who loved these shores', which helped launch the first edition. Research grants from WWF-SA, the National Research Foundation and the Andrew Mellon Foundation funded much of the background research reported in this book, including the costs of the tens of thousands of photographs from which the final selection was culled. We also gratefully acknowledge the support of our institutions, the University of Cape Town, the Oceanographic Research Institute and the School of Environmental Science, Murdoch University. Special thanks to technical staff, who produced bizarre items of collecting and photographic equipment. Ezemvelo KZN Wildlife and Triton Dive Lodge arranged accommodation at Sodwana, as did the Inhaca Research Station at Inhaca Island. Willem and Sharon Prinsloo, kindred free spirits, provided friendship, potjiekos and accommodation for impoverished biologists. The shell plates were dependent on the collections of the Iziko Museum and help from Michelle van der Merwe and Liz Hoenson. Bronwen Currie (MFMR) arranged a spectacular research trip to the Skeleton Coast, and access to unpublished distributional records for Namibia.

Many people helped collect animals and plants, including Georgina Jones (SURG), Wendy Robertson (ORI), Anton McLachlan, An de Ruyck and Gary Dobkins (Nelson Mandela Metropolitan University), Graham Brill (Irvin & Johnson), Janda Maybank (Struisbaai), Mike Mittelmeyer (De Beers Marine), and Jenny Ruesink (University of Washington). A crate of beer acknowledges an enthusiastic and special group of people: past and present students at the University of Cape Town, particularly Lara Atkinson, Laura Blamey, Rodrigo Bustamante, Liz Day, Lucy Kemp, Jan Korrubel, Lisa Kruger, Yves Lechanteur, Steven Mayfield, Angela Mead, Kim Prochazka, Bernhard Riegl, Tammy Robinson, Kerry Sink, Nina Steffani, Claudio Velasquez Rojas and Evie Wieters.

Several authorities gave their time and expertise to check identifications or sections of the text of this or earlier editions: Toufiek Samaai (sponges), Naomi Millard (hydrozoans), Jan Heeg and John Ryland (zoanthids), Bernhard Riegl (corals), Gary Williams and Mike Schleyer (octocorals), Mark Gibbons (jellyfish and hydroids), Leslie Newman (flatworms), Dick Kilburn and Dai Herbert (shelled molluscs), Bill Newman (barnacles), Andy Cockcroft and Dave Pollock (rock lobsters), Winks Emmerson, Wendy Robertson and Pat Backwell (decapods), Marek Lipinski and Martina Compagno-Roeleveld (cephalopods), Terry Gosliner (nudibranchs), Wayne Florence (bryozoans), Marc Ruis Viladomiu (ascidians), Len Compagno, Geremy Cliff, Alison Kock (sharks), Simon Chater, Sean Fennessy, Bruce Mann and Phil Heemstra (fish), Ronel Nel (reptiles), Phil Hockey (birds), Peter Best and Eva Plaganyi (cetaceans), Patti Wickens (seals), John Bolton and Rob Anderson (seaweeds), Yvonne Chamberlain, Derek Keats and Gavin Maneveldt (coralline algae), the South African National Biodiversity Institute, John Manning, Dee Snijman and Roy Lubke (flowering plants). Special thanks to our families for their support, love and participation in many adventures.

Every page of this book is marked by the caring leadership of Pippa Parker and her team, particularly the exceptional patience and meticulous ministrations of Emily Bowles and the design genius of Janice Evans. It is a joy to be back in the Struik family.

Contents

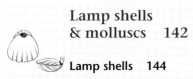

Introduction

This new edition of *Two Oceans* is a complete revision that incorporates 522 additional species, updates biological information, distribution records and scientific names, and has benefited from the digital era, with more than half the photographs being replaced and improved.

About 900 species of birds are found in southern Africa and more than 15 guidebooks are available to identify them. By contrast, there are over 12 000 described species of marine plants and animals in the region, but this is the only field guide currently available that can be used to identify species for the entire region across all major groups of this diverse biota. JH Day's *A guide to marine life of South African shores* broke new ground when it was published in 1974, but it is no longer available. *The living shores of southern Africa*, first published in 1981 to communicate the exciting research done on marine life in the region, was not designed as a field guide. *Two Oceans* serves precisely this purpose: to allow the ready identification of the most common forms of marine life that inhabit our coasts – including invertebrates, fish, reptiles, birds, mammals, algae and flowering plants.

Southern Africa (defined here as stretching from northern Namibia to central Mozambique) has a particularly rich marine fauna and flora, with over 12 000 species, or almost 6% of all the coastal marine species known worldwide. About 33% of these are endemic, occurring nowhere else. Given this rich assemblage, it is impossible to cover every species in one book. Instead, we have focused on the most frequently encountered species, particularly those that live in the intertidal zone and in shallow waters readily accessible to beachcombers and scuba divers – in estuaries, and on beaches, rocky shores and dunes. Similarly, not all groups of animals or plants are covered in the same depth. The emphasis is placed on those groups that are diverse, frequently encountered, and poorly covered in other field guides. The coverage of birds is limited to those seen near the coast or in estuaries. Selecting which fish to feature was another difficult task and we have focused on those species commonly seen in tidal pools, by divers, or frequently caught by anglers. Special attention has been given to the smaller rock-pool fish that have been under-represented in other popular field guides.

HOW TO USE THIS BOOK

The outline of contents on pp. 4–5 includes a pictorial guide to the major groups of animals and plants featured in the text. In the sections dealing with each of these groups there is also a brief introductory paragraph outlining the characteristics and key features used to identify the species. We have kept technical terms to a minimum, but where these are necessary they are defined in the introductory paragraphs, and the Glossary (p. 440).

Almost all of the species are illustrated with a colour photograph. In some cases, line drawings show details necessary for species identification. On the page facing the photographs, each species is described, paying particular attention to the key features used to identify it.

Also given are:
Size: An indication of the size a species normally achieves (in millimetres, centimetres or metres, depending on how big the species is).
Biology: Notes on where the species can be found, its diet, any relationships it has with other species, and other interesting aspects of its biology.
Maps: These accompany the text for most species and show their geographic range. Those that reach the northeastern limit of the map almost all extend into the tropical Indo-Pacific, whereas relatively few reaching the northwestern limit extend into tropical Angola. The word 'Alien' on a map indicates an introduced species.
Similar species: Where there are two or more easily confused species we use this section to provide information on how to distinguish them, or to give brief notes on species that could not be accommodated as full entries.

To identify an animal or plant, first compare the specimen with the photographs: species with similar features have been grouped together to simplify such comparisons. Having matched the specimen with a photograph, read the accompanying text to check if it fits the description. Also check the 'Similar species'. Resist the temptation to 'force' a name onto an animal or plant if it does not conform to the description: sometimes you will have found species that are not included in the guide, or that may be new to the region or even to science. For those enthusiasts wishing to pursue such rarities further, detailed scientific monographs on particular groups are listed in the References (p. 442).

Satellite photograph of the coast of southern Africa

The mighty Agulhas Current drives down the east coast of southern Africa, bringing nutrient-poor warm water (orange-red) from the tropics. On the west coast, upwelled nutrient-rich cold water (blue-black) drifts northwards.

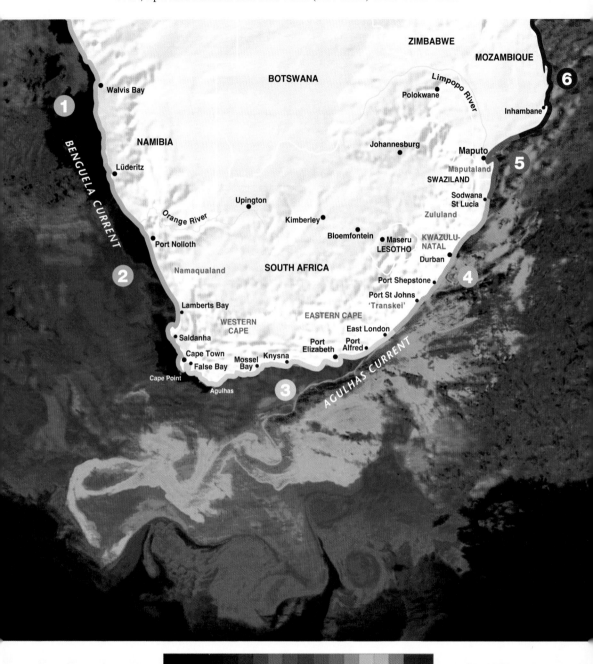

<10 10 11 12 13 14 15 16 17 18 19 20 21 22 23 24 25 >25
Sea surface temperature in °C

Six biogeographic provinces can be recognised in this region, the ❶ Namib (cool temperate), ❷ Namaqua (cool temperate), ❸ Agulhas (warm temperate), ❹ Natal (subtropical), ❺ Delagoa overlap (subtropical), and ❻ Indo-West Pacific (tropical) provinces.

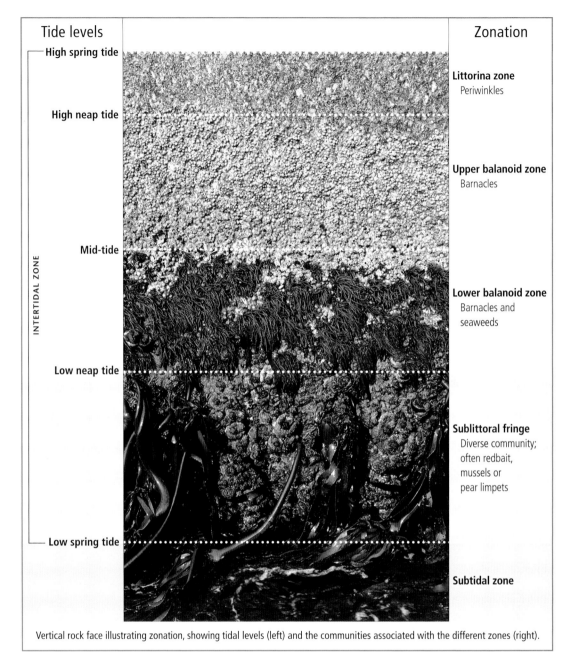

Tide levels		Zonation

High spring tide

High neap tide

Mid-tide

Low neap tide

Low spring tide

INTERTIDAL ZONE

Littorina zone
Periwinkles

Upper balanoid zone
Barnacles

Lower balanoid zone
Barnacles and
seaweeds

Sublittoral fringe
Diverse community;
often redbait,
mussels or
pear limpets

Subtidal zone

Vertical rock face illustrating zonation, showing tidal levels (left) and the communities associated with the different zones (right).

Currents and tides

One reason for southern Africa's exceptionally rich and varied marine fauna and flora is the extreme contrast between the oceans on the east and west coasts. The Agulhas Current, one of the most powerful ocean currents in the world, sweeps warm water from the tropics down the east coast. In the region of East London, the continental shelf widens, forcing the Agulhas Current further offshore, so that the coastal waters become slightly cooler. Eventually, the Agulhas Current swings back on its tracks (retroflects) to flow eastwards.

The west coast is very different. It is chilled by northward-drifting cold water and the predominant southeasterly winds blow surface water offshore, causing cold, deep water to well up near the coast to replace it. Because this water comes from depths where it is too dark for plant life to grow, it retains its rich nutrients. On reaching the sunlit shallows, this water fertilises microscopic floating plant life or phytoplankton. Both phytoplankton and seaweeds are far more productive on the west coast than on the south and east coasts, and fuel more productive food chains, culminating in the lucrative commercial fisheries that are concentrated in the west. Although highly productive, the west coast supports far

8 Introduction

fewer species than the east coast, which is particularly diverse because of the large suite of tropical Indo-Pacific species that contributes to its fauna and flora.

With the changes in temperature around the coast come accompanying changes in the composition of marine life. For example, the east coast boasts large arrays of crabs and corals that are poorly represented in cooler waters. The west coast, by contrast, has prolific kelp forests that are absent from the warmer, less productive south and east coasts. Because of these faunal and floral changes, we recognise six distinct biogeographic provinces in the region, as illustrated on p. 7.

One of the most frequent questions asked is where the influence of the warm Indian Ocean ends and that of the cold Atlantic begins. Even scientists disagree on this issue, because the retroflection of the Agulhas Current moves back and forth, resulting in a broad transition zone that lies between Cape Point and Cape Agulhas; it is difficult to define precisely. However, if we believe what the animals and plants are telling us, Cape Point is the main dividing line, for there is a major difference between the fauna and flora on either side of the Cape Peninsula. Further offshore the boundary is less defined and shifts towards Cape Agulhas.

Another factor affecting the distribution of seashore plants and animals is the tidal cycle. Twice a day the tide rises and falls, reaching its greatest range during spring tides, which occur during full and new moons. At this time, the gravitational forces of the sun and moon act together to drive the tide both higher and lower than normal. Neap tides, when the tidal range is at its smallest, occur during the first and third quarters of the moon, when the gravitational pull of the sun and moon act in opposition. The best time to visit the shore is at about 10h00 on the day following either full or new moon: predictably (and obligingly), the lowest spring tides always fall at these times in southern Africa.

The high-tide level of the shore is seldom submerged; the low-tide level is almost continually underwater. Between these extremes lies the **intertidal zone**, and below it the **subtidal zone**. Within the intertidal zone there is a strong gradient of physical stress. Solar heating and water loss impose their greatest stresses on the high shore, and few species survive there. Tiny snails (*Afrolittorina*) are often the only abundant animals here, and give their name to this region of the shore – the **littorina zone**. Below that is a zone dominated by barnacles and named the **upper balanoid zone**, after the barnacle genus *Balanus*. Lower still, seaweeds or mussels (or both) become important, in the **lower balanoid zone**. These zones, or their equivalents, are found on shores in most of the world. In southern Africa there are, additionally, three unique zones. The east coast has a high-shore band of oysters; the south and northwest coasts have low-shore belts dominated, respectively, by the limpet *Scutellastra cochlear* (the cochlear zone) and the limpet *Scutellastra argenvillei* (the argenvillei zone). These zones are of special interest, as the organisms that create them powerfully influence other life: the oysters provide shelter and food to many species, and the limpets prevent seaweeds from becoming established in 'their' zones.

Exploitation and conservation

Southern Africa has a 3 100 km-long coastline that, by global standards, is still relatively pristine. Its shores offer a wide range of renewable natural resources that can, and should, be shared and enjoyed by fishermen, collectors and nature-lovers for generations to come. Each of these resources is, however, limited, in that it can provide only a certain yield. Repeated removal of catches in excess of a maximum sustainable yield will inevitably lead to the collapse of the resource – as history has all too frequently demonstrated. Marine species in southern Africa, as elsewhere, are under increasing exploitation pressure. This results not only from growth of the human population (South Africa already has less than 10 cm of coastline per person), but also from the growing mobility of the population and the popularity of such sports as angling and diving. Rural people also depend heavily on the sea for subsistence. As the number of individuals exploiting any resource increases, it is imperative that each person's catch be restricted, so that the total take remains below the sustainable limit. Various control measures have been instituted to achieve this. These regulations are compiled on the basis of available information on both the biology of the species concerned and current catch rates. Regulations are thus subject to periodic change, both as better biological data become available and as the number of resource users changes. Readers can obtain current information on marine recreational regulations from the Department of Environmental Affairs, Marine and Coastal Management Branch, or download a brochure listing these regulations from their website **http://www.deat.gov.za/Services/booklets.html**.

Ezemvelo KwaZulu-Natal Wildlife also distributes free pamphlets listing marine regulations. These are available at post offices, KZN coastal reserves and permit offices, or from their website **http://www. kznwildlife.com/site/ecotourism/activities/fish/**. Readers should also familiarise themselves with local by-laws and the locations of any marine reserves in the areas where they wish to fish or collect.

The intention of these regulations is not to spoil the enjoyment of resource users, but rather to conserve the shore, so that it can continue to be enjoyed and used to the full into the future.

The classification and naming of species

Each species in this volume is accorded both its formal scientific or 'Latin' name and a common name. Both systems have their assets. On the one hand, well-established common names exist for most familiar forms, and many users find these more descriptive and easier to pronounce and remember than scientific names. Paradoxically they also tend to be more stable over time. On the other hand, common names lack any formal status, and different names are applied to the same animal not only in each of many languages, but often also from region to region, even within one country, making them an inaccurate means of communication. Worse still, the same common name has sometimes been applied to a number of (sometimes unrelated) species, while no common names exist for thousands of smaller or less abundant species. Unique scientific names, by contrast, are established for every described species and these are universally recognised – even in Arabic, Russian and Japanese texts. Although we have attempted to allocate standard common names to each species, we encourage users to adopt the more powerful scientific terminology, which is briefly explained below.

Scientific names

The system of scientific names, or scientific nomenclature, is best thought of as a hierarchical 'address' system in which each species is positioned according to its relationship with others. At the broadest level, all life is divided into seven kingdoms. Each kingdom is split into phyla, or groups, that share a similar overall body plan (p. 11). Each phylum is then subdivided into more closely related classes, which, in turn, contain progressively more closely related orders, families, and lastly genera and species. Every species is finally allocated a pair of names (these equate to a person's first name and surname, while the phylum, class and family are similar to that person's family connections). The first word of this binomial, which is always written with an initial capital letter, identifies the genus, while the second, which appears in lower case, identifies the individual species. Closely related species will thus share the same generic name. The names of the genus and species are always printed in italics or, if handwritten, are underlined. For example, the classification of the well-known pear limpet is as follows:

Phylum:	Mollusca
Class:	Gastropoda
Order:	Patellogastropoda
Family:	Patellidae
Genus:	*Scutellastra*
Species:	*cochlear*

Note that this scientific name, like many others, is descriptive of the species, the term *Scutellastra* (*scutella* is a 'flat dish' or 'saucer' in Latin) referring to the typical shell shape of limpets, and *cochlear* (*cochleare* is a 'spoon') to the shape of this particular species. A further name and date are sometimes given after the binomial to identify the person who first named the species and when they did this. If the name and date appear in brackets, this indicates that the original generic name has changed. In the above example, the full description is thus *Scutellastra cochlear* (Born, 1778).

Occasionally variants within a species are recognised, and these may be given a third, or subspecific, name. Names may also be abbreviated,

De Hoop Marine Protected Area.

most commonly by reducing the generic name to an initial when the same name is used repeatedly (thus *Scutellastra cochlear* subsequently becomes *S. cochlear*). Members of a genus may also be referred to inclusively by the notation 'spp.' (e.g. *Scutellastra* spp.), or a single unidentified species as 'sp.' (*Scutellastra* sp.).

Sometimes the name of a species may be preceded by 'cf.': for example, specimens of the divided flatworm collected in southern Africa (Plate 22) are named *Pseudoceros* cf. *dimidiatus*. This indicates that although the material examined is close to the species *Pseudoceros dimidiatus*, allocation of the name is provisional and needs to be resolved.

Why scientific names change

One of the most frustrating and misunderstood aspects of scientific nomenclature is that scientific names may change over time. The reasons for this relate both to the hierarchical nature of the 'address' system and to strict rules of precedence, which dictate that each species may have only one valid name, which must be the earliest one given to the species. As additional species are discovered and more is learnt about their relationship to one another, scientists may decide to amalgamate existing genera (resulting in replacement and loss of the younger generic names), subdivide existing genera (resulting in erection of new generic names for those species split off from the original group), or simply to transfer a species from one genus to another. Research (particularly genetic data) may equally reveal that two or more existing species are in reality simply variants of a single species, resulting in the invalidation of the more recent name and application of the older one to both forms. Alternatively, a single name may have been applied to what in fact turn out to be separate species, necessitating the creation of a new name for one of these.

CLASSIFICATION SYSTEM

*Groups not covered in this book

The world's organisms are divided into two Domains:
- **Prokarya** (not dealt with in this book), which comprises unicellular organisms that lack nuclei and mitochondria and includes Kingdom Bacteria.
- **Eukarya** incorporates organisms with nuclei and mitochondria and embraces five Kingdoms: the three listed below that are covered in this book, plus unicellular organisms in the Kingdom Protozoa and the moulds and mushrooms in Kingdom Fungi, which are not covered.

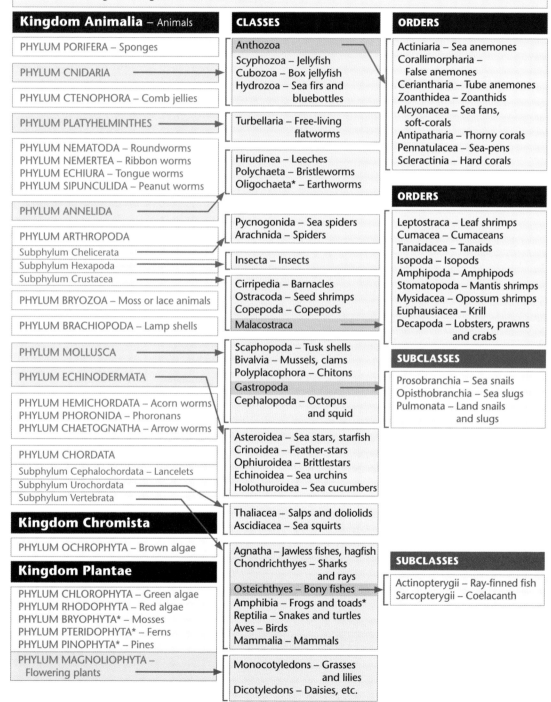

Kingdom Animalia – Animals

PHYLUM PORIFERA – Sponges

PHYLUM CNIDARIA

PHYLUM CTENOPHORA – Comb jellies

PHYLUM PLATYHELMINTHES

PHYLUM NEMATODA – Roundworms
PHYLUM NEMERTEA – Ribbon worms
PHYLUM ECHIURA – Tongue worms
PHYLUM SIPUNCULIDA – Peanut worms

PHYLUM ANNELIDA

PHYLUM ARTHROPODA
Subphylum Chelicerata
Subphylum Hexapoda
Subphylum Crustacea

PHYLUM BRYOZOA – Moss or lace animals

PHYLUM BRACHIOPODA – Lamp shells

PHYLUM MOLLUSCA

PHYLUM ECHINODERMATA

PHYLUM HEMICHORDATA – Acorn worms
PHYLUM PHORONIDA – Phoronans
PHYLUM CHAETOGNATHA – Arrow worms

PHYLUM CHORDATA
Subphylum Cephalochordata – Lancelets
Subphylum Urochordata
Subphylum Vertebrata

Kingdom Chromista

PHYLUM OCHROPHYTA – Brown algae

Kingdom Plantae

PHYLUM CHLOROPHYTA – Green algae
PHYLUM RHODOPHYTA – Red algae
PHYLUM BRYOPHYTA* – Mosses
PHYLUM PTERIDOPHYTA* – Ferns
PHYLUM PINOPHYTA* – Pines

PHYLUM MAGNOLIOPHYTA –
  Flowering plants

CLASSES

Anthozoa
Scyphozoa – Jellyfish
Cubozoa – Box jellyfish
Hydrozoa – Sea firs and
  bluebottles

Turbellaria – Free-living
  flatworms

Hirudinea – Leeches
Polychaeta – Bristleworms
Oligochaeta* – Earthworms

Pycnogonida – Sea spiders
Arachnida – Spiders

Insecta – Insects

Cirripedia – Barnacles
Ostracoda – Seed shrimps
Copepoda – Copepods
Malacostraca

Scaphopoda – Tusk shells
Bivalvia – Mussels, clams
Polyplacophora – Chitons
Gastropoda
Cephalopoda – Octopus
  and squid

Asteroidea – Sea stars, starfish
Crinoidea – Feather-stars
Ophiuroidea – Brittlestars
Echinoidea – Sea urchins
Holothuroidea – Sea cucumbers

Thaliacea – Salps and doliolids
Ascidiacea – Sea squirts

Agnatha – Jawless fishes, hagfish
Chondrichthyes – Sharks
  and rays
Osteichthyes – Bony fishes
Amphibia – Frogs and toads*
Reptilia – Snakes and turtles
Aves – Birds
Mammalia – Mammals

Monocotyledons – Grasses
  and lilies
Dicotyledons – Daisies, etc.

ORDERS

Actiniaria – Sea anemones
Corallimorpharia –
  False anemones
Ceriantharia – Tube anemones
Zoanthidea – Zoanthids
Alcyonacea – Sea fans,
  soft-corals
Antipatharia – Thorny corals
Pennatulacea – Sea-pens
Scleractinia – Hard corals

ORDERS

Leptostraca – Leaf shrimps
Cumacea – Cumaceans
Tanaidacea – Tanaids
Isopoda – Isopods
Amphipoda – Amphipods
Stomatopoda – Mantis shrimps
Mysidacea – Opossum shrimps
Euphausiacea – Krill
Decapoda – Lobsters, prawns
  and crabs

SUBCLASSES

Prosobranchia – Sea snails
Opisthobranchia – Sea slugs
Pulmonata – Land snails
  and slugs

SUBCLASSES

Actinopterygii – Ray-finned fish
Sarcopterygii – Coelacanth

Sponges

Phylum Porifera (Plates 1–4) contains the sponges, which are the most primitive animals, lacking internal organs and consisting of just a few types of cells supported by a skeleton of spicules. Water carrying oxygen and food particles enters the sponge through tiny pores dotting the surface and exits via larger openings (oscula) on turrets that act as chimneys, drawing water through the colony. Collar cells lining the body cavity beat their hair-like flagellae to generate a current, and filter out food particles through their net-like collars. Many sponges contain toxic chemicals, and are exquisitely and vividly coloured to advertise their unpalatable nature.

PLATE 1

Sponges   Porifera

The shape and composition of the spicules in the skeletons of sponges are the only sure means of identification, and they can be separated by dissolving the tissues in a solution of bleach (sodium hydroxide) and examining the spicules under a microscope. Class Calcarea (1.1–1.4) has calcium carbonate (lime) skeletons. Class Demospongiae (1.5 onwards) has glass-like silicon spicules or fibrous spongin – familiar as 'bath sponges'. As this book is a field guide, we have relied on photographs and external features to distinguish the species.

1.1 Hairy tube-sponges   *Sycon* spp.
Small, erect, tubular or vase-shaped. Surface white, coated with hair-like lime spicules. Osculum crowned by long, stiff spicules. **Size:** 10 mm. **Biology:** Grows in gullies and caves or on vertical rock-faces, often on top of seaweeds or other animals.

1.2 Branching ball-sponge   *Leucosolenia* sp.
Small, white hemispherical to spherical sponges with a net-like surface pattern; send out 'roots' or extensions from which other balls bud. **Size:** Diameter 10–20 mm. **Biology:** Usually under loose rocks near low-tide level. The solid appearance is deceptive, as sponges of this genus are formed of a network of tubes that fuse.

1.3 Tube-sponges   *Leucosolenia* spp.
Small, elongated whitish tubes with a large osculum at the end of each. Bases fused to form a colony. **Size:** Tubes 20 mm long. **Biology:** Grow in groups among algae or encrusting animals on the walls of pools or under overhangs.

1.4 Net-sponges   *Clathrina* spp.
Tall yellow or pink tubes with a large, apical osculum; tubes interconnected by side branches, sometimes forming a complex net. **Size:** Tubes 15–20 mm long. **Biology:** Grow in clusters on the upper surfaces of rocks, intermingled with other organisms.

1.5 Encrusting turret-sponge   *Haliclona oculata*
Encrusting purple, pink or vivid blue sheets with large oscula on raised turrets that are tubular in sheltered areas (1.5) but short on intertidal rocks (1.5a). **Size:** 500 mm across; turret 10–100 mm tall. **Biology:** In intertidal pools and subtidally to 15 m.
SIMILAR SPECIES:
1.6 *Haliclona stilensis* (Namibia–south coast of South Africa) has small, lobular turrets with apical, pale-rimmed oscula; beige to purple.

1.7 Tuberculate turret-sponge   *Haliclona tulearensis*
Conical, tubercle-like turrets or ridges; oscula are about one-third the diameter of the turrets. Surface pocked. Bright mustard yellow. **Size:** 200 mm tall. **Biology:** Coats upper surface of rocks among corals on deep reefs.

1.8 Crumb-of-bread sponge   *Hymeniacidon perlevis*
Thick, encrusting, ochre-yellow sheet with a rough, lumpy surface. Oscula surmount low turrets. **Size:** 100–200 mm across; 10 mm tall. **Biology:** The most abundant intertidal sponge on the south and west coasts, found in crevices and on shaded surfaces.

1.9 Chilli pepper sponge   *Tedania anhelans*
Forms crusts like those of the previous species, but is bright red. **Size:** Develops large colonies, up to 500 mm across, but less than 10 mm tall. **Biology:** Intertidal; grows larger and faster on vertical surfaces. Abundant on east coast and widespread around the world.

1.10 Sulphur sponge   *Aplysilla rosea*
Crustose, but thrown into vertical ridges with well-defined, regularly spaced pimples. Upper edges of ridges with small, slightly raised oscula. Colour distinctively sulphurous yellow. Firm to the touch. **Size:** Metres in extent. **Biology:** Subtidal, down to 25 m. Previously known as *A. sulphurea*.

PLATE 2

2.1 Golf-ball sponge   *Tethya aurantium*

Easy to identify to genus because of the spherical body form, seen on the left side of this photograph. Surface usually warty; several oscula on upper surface. **Size:** Typically 50–100 mm diameter. **Biology:** Often occurs in large groups on shallow, subtidal reefs. Sharp spicules project from the surface and cause irritant rashes if touched.

2.2 Nodular sponge   *Clathria hooperi*

Shown in same photograph as previous species – to the right of the golf-ball sponge. Forms irregular lobes and ridges with oscula on upper edges. Delicate pink; soft to the touch. **Size:** 100–250 mm diameter, 50–100 mm tall. **Biology:** Develops large colonies on subtidal reefs at 5–25 m. Often torn free by storms and deposited on beaches.

2.3 Fanned kelp sponge   *Isodictya frondosa*

From a small, disc-like attachment, fans out into upright branches and fans. Always bright orange. Lacks any obvious oscula. **Size:** 100 mm tall. **Biology:** Always subtidal at depths of 3–25 m; abundant in kelp beds on the west coast. **SIMILAR SPECIES:** *I. elastica* (Lüderitz–Cape Point) is also branching or fan-like, but beige.

2.4 Tree sponge   *Echinoclathria dichotoma*

Tree-like, dividing more-or-less dichotomously into regular, round, orange digits. Oscula tiny, scattered on sides. **Size:** 150 mm tall. **Biology:** Found on shallow reefs 15–43 m, and occasionally in deep pools or under overhangs in the low intertidal zone. Often overgrown by the zoanthid *Parazoanthus* sp. (8.2).

2.5 Scroll sponge   *Chondropsis* sp.

Upright, twisted, ochre-orange walls, with tiny pores on the sides and oscula mounted flush with the surface of the upper ridges of the walls. **Size:** 150 mm tall, forming patches up to 350 mm across; oscula 1 mm in diameter. **Biology:** Occurs on relatively deep reefs among soft corals.

2.6 Stellar sponge   *Crambe acuata*

Thinly encrusting, orange-red, with a smooth surface. Hard, almost stony texture, but easily torn. Oscula not obvious, but surrounded by a radiating, star-like network of grooves. **Size:** 50 mm wide, 2 mm thick. **Biology:** Subtidal; 0–180 m. Consumed by the nudibranch *Berthellina granulata*, visible on the left of this photograph. Previously known as *C. chelastra*.

2.7 Tar sponge   *Iotrochota purpurea*

Easily recognised, tar-like black patches. No surface texturing or oscula evident, but frequently with embedded sand grains on upper surface. **Size:** 50–100 mm across; 2 mm thick. **Biology:** Abundant in the intertidal zone, often mixed with zoanthids.

2.8 Crustose suberite-sponge   *Suberites kelleri*

Forms extensive crusts that are usually thin and flat (left of photograph) with regularly spaced, raised ridges surmounted by oscula, but sometimes thicker and almost smooth. Greenish yellow to yellow-brown. **Size:** Forms extensive mats up to 1 m across and 40 mm thick. **Biology:** Abundant in subtidal, tropical reefs on flat surfaces. Zooxanthellate – contains microscopic, algal cells in its tissues.

2.9 Walled suberite-sponge   *Suberites globosus*

Develops thick, upright, chunky, grey to greenish-yellow walls and ridges (right of photograph). Side walls smooth, but upper surfaces eroded and irregular. Oscula not obvious, but concentrated on upper surface. **Size:** Walls up to 300 mm long and 200 mm tall. **Biology:** Subtidal; on flat surfaces. Like the preceding species, also zooxanthellate.

2.10 Black stink sponge   *Ircinia arbuscula*

Forms a thick, flat, black mat with slightly raised, rounded edges. Firm, but slippery to the touch, leaving a strongly pungent smell on the fingers. Texture tough due to coarse spongin fibres. Oscula small and positioned on slightly raised dimples. **Size:** 100–200 mm across; 10 mm thick. **Biology:** Encrusts deep pools or caves low on the shore or on shallow reefs. The smell is a reliable means of identification.

2.1

2.2

2.3

2.4

2.5

2.6

2.7

2.8

2.9

2.10

PLATE 3

3.1 Cupped suberite-sponge · *Suberites* sp.

A very large grey-brown sponge that is goblet-shaped but can be much more irregular. Inner surface smooth; outer surface with rough sculpturing. **Size:** Up to 1 m across. **Biology:** Conspicuous on horizontal surfaces in deeper tropical reefs. The 'goblet' shape may concentrate food particles that settle in it, and may also serve to deposit silt at the bottom, so that the whole colony is not smothered.

3.2 Nodular cup-sponge · *Ircinia* sp.

Another very large cup-sponge with a pinkish-purple wall that is thinner and taller than the previous species and has very obvious flattish projections on the outer surface. **Size:** 600 mm in diameter. **Biology:** Builds large colonies on flat, subtidal reefs at 10–25 m.

3.3 Sand cup-sponge · *Psammocinia* cf. *arenosa*

A relatively small cup-sponge with a smooth, white outer surface and a rough inner surface that is often overgrown by other encrusting organisms. Oscula scattered on the upper and inner edges. **Size:** 150 mm in diameter. **Biology:** Subtidal; often on surfaces that are lightly dusted with sand.

3.4 Pocked cup-sponge · *Agelas mauritiana oxeata*

Forms large, often irregular, cups. External surface pocked with deep indentations. Tough; not compressible. Greenish brown, with olive tints. **Size:** 300 mm tall. **Biology:** Found on shallow and deep reefs, 10–50 m.

3.5 Elephant-ear sponge · *Hemiasterella vasiformis*

A large sponge that forms upright lobes and often develops a vase-like shape, but may be more irregular. External surface smooth to rough and delicately dimpled; internal surface with numerous oscula. Colour pale purple. **Size:** 300–500 mm tall. **Biology:** Found in a depth range of 10–40 m; abundant in subtropical waters.

3.6 Teat-sponge · *Polymastia mamillaris*

A tough, orange-brown encrustation covered in regularly spaced, teat-like projections that carry both the inhalant and exhalant apertures: their tips are dotted with tiny holes. The flesh is firm and leathery. **Size:** Up to 300 mm across, and 25 mm thick. **Biology:** Spreads over flat rock surfaces in gullies and sandy pools, and often grows beneath rocks.

3.7 Atlantic teat-sponge · *Polymastia atlanticus*

Forms thick, butterscotch-yellow or orange-brown pancake-like encrustations with irregular, low-growing ridges and short warts that are flattened at the top and surmounted by tiny holes. **Size:** Colonies 80–100 mm wide, 30 mm tall. **Biology:** Intertidal to subtidal, in a depth range of 1–24 m; often grows in sandy gulleys, and the surface frequently has a sprinkling of sand.

3.8 Vented sponge · *Latrunculia spinispiraefera*

A massive sponge with an orange-to-red exterior 'skin' and yellow 'flesh'. Forms a smooth, fairly regular wall and has numerous large exhalant openings on the upper surface, which project to form short, thin-walled columns. **Size:** 200–300 mm wide, and as much as 2 m long. **Biology:** The largest and most conspicuous sponge on reefs 10–30 m deep in the Western Cape. Chemical extracts from this sponge show promise for cancer drug development and are undergoing clinical tests. The specimen photographed here carries a nudibranch, *Jorunna fuenebris* (95.9). Previously placed in the genus *Spirastrella*.

3.9 Boring sponge · *Cliona celata*

Most of the sponge is embedded in rocks or shells, but it surfaces to form flat, circular, inhalant siphons that are flush with the substratum and covered by a sieve-like mesh that excludes sand particles, and a smaller number of larger, projecting oscula. Bright golden yellow. **Size:** Can be massive – up to 1 m across. Oscula 10 mm tall. **Biology:** Bores into limestone and shells in the low-shore and shallow subtidal zones, down to 15 m.

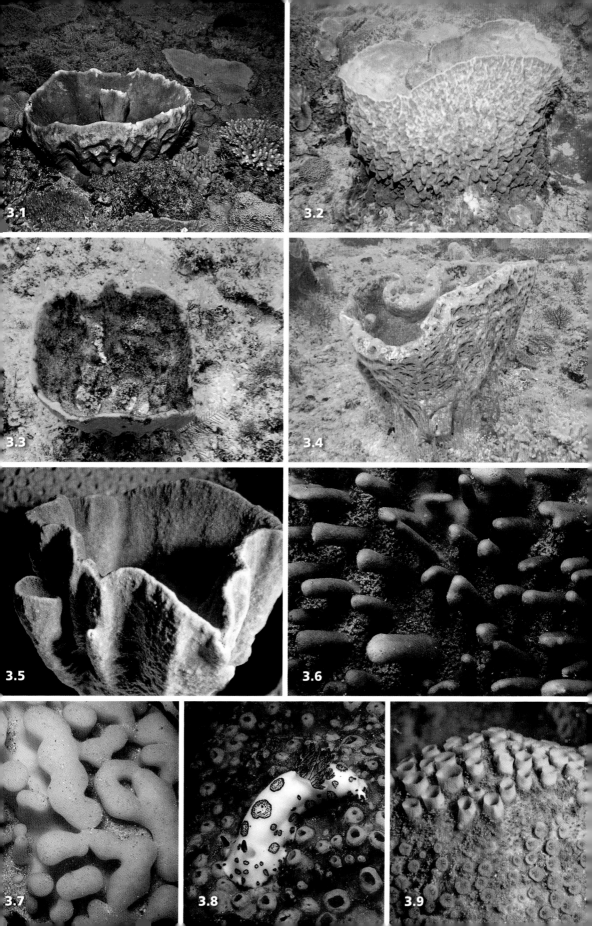

PLATE 4

4.1 Reticulate sponge — *Acanthella* sp.
Varying from encrusting to tree-like, with a lumpy surface of small, rounded domes that are arranged in rows or circles. Oscula few in number and borne on projections. Radiating white canals converge on oscula. **Size:** 200–250 mm wide; crust 10 mm thick. **Biology:** Common on subtidal, tropical reefs.

4.2 Crumpled sponge — *Axinella weltneri*
A very hard, almost woody, blood-red sponge with a strongly ridged surface, a rough, spiny surface texture and no oscula. Forms upright sheets that resemble crumpled, corrugated cardboard. **Size:** 50–100 mm across. **Biology:** Occurs on shallow, tropical reefs and in gullies. Tends to grow on vertical surfaces, possibly to avoid the effects of siltation. **SIMILAR SPECIES:** A recently described species of *Axinella* is soft, purple-brown and flat-bladed, but otherwise similar to *A. weltneri*.

4.3 Spiky tube-sponge — *Callyspongia confoederata*
Several species of *Callyspongia* occur in southern Africa. All are upright and tubular, with a spiky external surface. They range in shape from single barrels to branching tubes. The one shown here is most likely *C. confoederata*, the most common and widespread species. Colour variable: bright orange, yellow or grey with purple tinges apically. **Size:** 50–100 mm tall. **Biology:** Always subtidal; grows on rocky reefs and in sandy areas.

4.4 Vagabond sponge — *Spheciospongia vagabunda*
Lumpy, irregularly shaped sponges with groups of large, crater-like depressions lined internally with fibrous striations. Colour bright but variable; commonly yellow or powder blue. **Size:** 250 mm wide, 100 mm tall. **Biology:** Subtidal, 10–35 m.

4.5 Goose bump sponge — *Fascaplysinopsis reticulata*
Irregular, rounded lumps with numerous pimples and a smaller number of oscula that are often aligned in rows on slightly elevated crests. Orange-beige with yellow pimples. **Size:** 300 mm wide, 100 mm thick. **Biology:** Abundant on tropical reefs; grows at depths ranging from 8–35 m.

4.6 Cratered ball-sponge — *Cinachyrella* sp.
Easily recognised by its yellow colour, ball-like shape and numerous, deep craters. Surface covered with a fine layer of spiky, projecting spicules. **Size:** 100 mm in diameter. **Biology:** Grows on subtidal reefs, 5–30 m depths. Caution: Spicules are an irritant.

4.7 Candyfloss sponge — *Jaspis digonoxea*
Diffuse, lumpy colonies with large oscula on the tops of the tallest ridges. Vivid orange-yellow. **Size:** 250 mm across, 200 mm tall. **Biology:** Grows on horizontal surfaces intermingled with soft corals on tropical reefs at 10–50 m depths.

4.8 Conical sponge — *Theonella conica*
Forms large round lobes that, to variable degrees, extend upwards as conical towers, each surmounted by a single, very large osculum. Colour blue, but often appearing brown due to an overgrowth of microscopic algae. **Size:** 500 mm wide, 150 mm tall. **Biology:** Abundant, large and conspicuous on subtidal tropical reefs, at depths of 5–35 m.

4.9 Chimneyed football sponge — *Oceanapia seychellensis*
A large, football-shaped sponge with multiple tall chimneys that terminate in obvious oscula. Purple-black in colour, although another undescribed, related species is bright red. **Size:** 100–150 mm in diameter. **Biology:** Grows on subtidal reefs only. Frequently colonised by brittlestars.

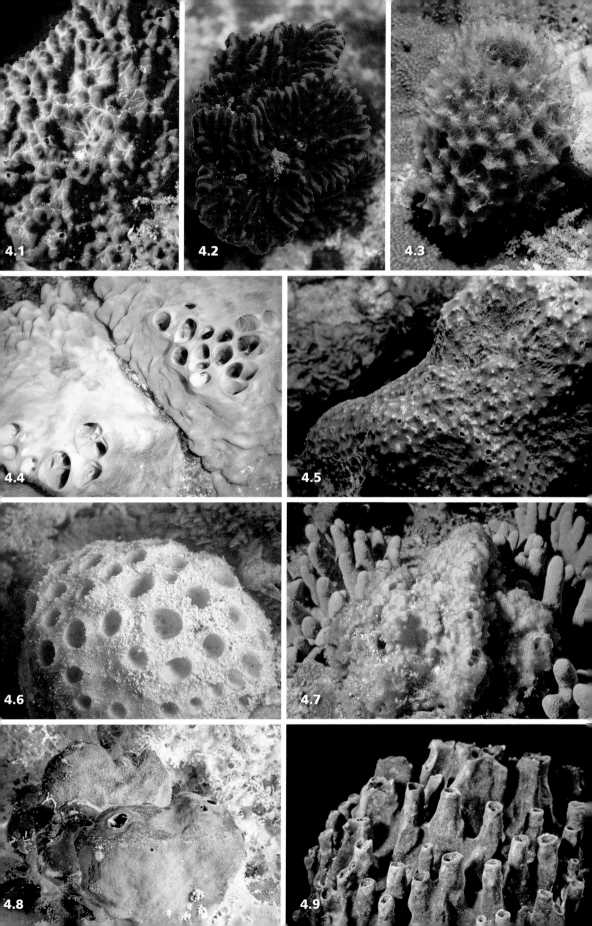

Cnidarians & comb jellies

Phylum Cnidaria includes anemones, corals, jellyfish and hydroids. All have a simple, radial body plan, with tentacles encircling a mouth that is the only opening to a sac-like gut cavity. The body wall comprises only an outer skin or epidermis, and an inner gut lining or gastrodermis, between which is sandwiched a jelly-like 'mesoglea'. Cnidarians occur in one of two basic forms – a swimming, bell-like medusa or an upright, attached polyp. Polyps often form colonies supported by chitinous or lime skeletons. Unique to cnidarians are their stinging cells (nematocysts), which house a coiled, thread-like sting that can explosively inject a toxin. There are no organs for respiration or excretion and only the simplest nervous system. Despite their apparent simplicity, cnidarians are diverse and abundant. Phylum Cnidaria is divided into four classes:

- **Anthozoa** have an upright polyp stage and no medusa, and include the solitary anemones and colonial sea fans and corals (Plates 5–17).
- **Scyphozoa**, the jellyfish, and **Cubozoa**, the box jellyfish, have developed the medusa stage at the expense of the polyp (Plate 18).
- **Hydrozoa** are small, less familiar, and have a complex life cycle alternating between a sexual medusa and a colonial polyp (Plates 19–21).

Phylum Ctenophora comprises the comb jellies (Plate 21).

PLATE 5

Anthozoans

Sea anemones

Simple, solitary animals lacking a hard skeleton. Body cylindrical and hollow; usually attached by a flat, adhesive basal disc. A few species are burrowing, tube-dwelling or unattached. Mouth ringed by tentacles armed with stinging cells, but the stings are harmless to humans. Prey are digested in the central body cavity and excreted through the mouth.

Anthozoa

Actiniaria & kin

5.1 Strawberry anemone   *Corynactis annulata*

The exquisite, semi-transparent pink colour and white knobs on the tips of the tentacles of this small colonial species are distinctive. A member of the order Corallimorpharia, more closely related to corals than true anemones. **Size:** 10 mm diameter. **Biology:** Clusters under ledges in low-shore pools and on shallow reefs.

5.2 Elephant-ear corals   *Discosoma* spp.

Flat; oral disc carpeted with short tentacles, fringed with longer tentacles. Column squat and ridged. **Size:** 150 mm. **Biology:** Occur in shallow waters. Being corallimorphs, they are more closely related to corals than anemones, but have abandoned building a skeleton and hence achieve much larger polyps. Name uncertain: provisionally called *Discosoma*.

5.3 Tube anemone   *Ceriantheopsis* sp.

One of the anemone-like order Ceriantharia, typified by an inner circle of short tentacles and an outer ring of elegant, longer ones. Body worm-like, enclosed in a long mucous tube buried in sand or mud. Colour white, blue or purple. **Size:** Body 150 mm, tubes up to 1 m. **Biology:** Lives in subtidal sandbanks. Retracts rapidly into tube if disturbed.

5.4 Striped anemone   *Anthothoe chilensis*

Delicate green, pink, brown or pale cream. Column smooth and vertically striped. Shoots sticky white defensive threads through the body wall when disturbed. **Size:** 20 mm diameter. **Biology:** Abundant in rock pools, under boulders and in harbours and lagoons. Its tissues contain symbiotic algae. Fed upon by the sea slug *Aeolidiella indica* (93.8). Very variable: may constitute more than one species. Previously named *A. stimpsoni*.

Alien

5.5 Rooted anemone   *Sagartia ornata*

Column often tapering; base off-white, upper portion green or brown, with adhesive discs to which gravel or shells may be attached; oral disc greenish, paler around mouth. Ejects sticky threads if disturbed. **Size:** 15–20 mm. **Biology:** Introduced from Europe. Attaches to shallowly buried intertidal stones, the oral disc and tentacles level with the sand surface. Broods its young and gives birth to fully developed baby anemones.

5.6 Plum anemone   *Actinia mandelae*

Plum red with a glossy, smooth column and a row of bead-like, bright blue spherules hidden under the outer row of tentacles. **Size:** 20 mm. **Biology:** Survives high on the shore by closing up tightly when exposed at low tide, trapping water in the body cavity. Hangs like ripe fruit in shady gullies and overhangs. Young brooded within the body cavity and born fully developed. Previously misnamed *A. equina*, a European species.

5.7 Natal anemone   *Anemonia natalensis*

Column smooth and red-brown, with one row of spherules beneath the 70–100 cream-to-brown tentacles. Upper surface plum-coloured with pale lines radiating onto tentacles. **Size:** 20 mm. **Biology:** Common in rock pools. Like many anemones, undergoes asexual division of the body, leading to clusters that are clones of identical individuals.

5.8 Symbiotic anemone   *Calliactis polypus*

Most often seen on hermit crab shells. Lower part of column has pink to orange vertical stripes, upper portion blotched. Tentacles white to pink. **Size:** 50 mm across. **Biology:** Hermit crabs of the genus *Dardanus* (49.4) may carry up to eight of these anemones on their shells. The hermits derive protection from predators; the anemones gain scraps of food.

5.1

5.2

5.3

5.4

5.5

5.6

5.7

5.8

PLATE 6

6.1 False plum anemone — *Pseudactinia flagellifera*

Column smooth, orange to red, tentacles red or yellow, often mauve-tipped. Cannot readily retract tentacles or close up; 3–5 rows of bubble-like, orange vesicles and one row of spherules just outside tentacles. **Size:** 50–100 mm diameter. **Biology:** Large and conspicuous, found singly or in small family groups in pools or on shallow reefs. Moves about slowly and is aggressively territorial, inflating its vesicles and raking them across unrelated, intruding individuals to sting and repel them. Preys mostly on molluscs and crustaceans. Has the most potent venom known for an anemone. **SIMILAR SPECIES**: *P. varia* (Cape Town–East London) closely resembles it, but is smaller (20 mm), has only 1–2 rows of vesicles, and is usually confined to intertidal pools.

6.2 Knobbly anemone — *Bunodosoma capensis*

Column streaked with small, non-adhesive knobs (papillae) that are usually darker and brighter than the background colour, which can be white, pink, orange, red, blue or purple. Spherules present. **Size:** Generally 20–40 mm diameter. **Biology:** A strikingly variable species, abundant in sand-free pools and reefs; often attached to mussels or redbait (110.1). Sand never adheres to the column (compare with 6.3 below).

6.3 Sandy anemone — *Aulactinia reynaudi*

Column covered in flattened, sticky knobs, to which shell and gravel particles adhere. Over 300 short tentacles, no spherules. Colour very variable – including brown, green, pink and blue. **Size:** Up to 80 mm. **Biology:** Abundant, especially on the west coast, often crowded into sandy gullies, around the bases of boulders or in pools. Feeds on dislodged mussels, sea urchins, whelks and other animals tumbled by the waves. Juveniles common in mussel beds. Previously named *Bunodactis reynaudi*.

6.4 Violet-spotted anemone — *Anthostella stephensoni*

Column peachy, dotted with bright, irregularly spaced violet spots. Scarlet lines radiate from the mouth to the 48 short, blunt tentacles. **Size:** 30 mm diameter. **Biology:** A strikingly coloured but little-known species usually found singly, or in small groups, in sandy sites near or below low-tide level. Previously placed in the genus *Anthopleura*.

6.5 Dwarf spotted anemone — *Anthostella* sp.

Similar in appearance to *A. stephensoni*, but has regularly spaced rows of mauve spots on the column, mauve tips to the tentacles and no radiating lines across the oral disc. **Size:** 20 mm. **Biology:** Feeds by engulfing other reef organisms. Currently being described and named.

6.6 Trumpet anemone — *Aiptasia parva*

Thin column widening distally into broad oral disc surrounded by about 70 long, tapering tentacles; colour light olive with white spots. **Size:** Column 60 mm. **Biology:** Gregarious, emerging from crevices in sheltered pools into which it rapidly retracts when disturbed.

6.7 Brooding anemone — *Halianthella annularis*

A pale, transparent and slender anemone distinguished by having only 24 elongated, tentacles. **Size:** Reaches only about 10 mm diameter. **Biology:** Found in sheltered areas, particularly under boulders. A fold in the skin partway up the column is used to brood the young, which emerge as fully formed young anemones.

6.8 Candy-striped anemone — *Korsaranthus natalensis*

A spectacular and unmistakable species with distinctive red and white stripes radiating across the inflated, unattached foot and oral disc; column dark red or striped. **Size:** Up to 100 mm long. **Biology:** A mobile, unattached, species that feeds on sea fans in reef habitats. The stomach is everted through the mouth to digest the prey externally. Previously known as *Condylactis natalensis*.

6.9 Crevice anemone — *Anthopleura michaelseni*

Column with large sticky pads, to which shells and gravel adhere. Dark stripes usually radiate across the oral disc from the mouth to the 96 long, pink-to-brownish tentacles. Spherules present. **Size:** Reaches about 70 mm diameter. **Biology:** Lives partially buried in sand in rock crevices and sandy pools from the mid shore downwards. Unlike *Aulactinia reynaudi* (6.3 above), usually occurs singly.

6.1

6.2

6.3

6.4

6.5

6.6

6.7

6.8

6.9

PLATE 7

7.1 Ring-tentacle anemone   *Isanthus capensis*

A small, inconspicuous but common anemone. Column smooth, pale basally but becoming darker below the 48 shortish tentacles. Oral disc with brown streaks and each tentacle traversed with two or three brown bands. The two tentacles at either end of the mouth are often distinctly darker. **Size:** Up to 15 mm diameter. **Biology:** Attached to stones; often partially buried in sand or gravel in sheltered areas.

Alien

7.2 Feather-duster anemone   *Metridium senile*

Introduced from Europe and easily recognised by the lobed oral disc fringed by extremely abundant, short, feather-duster-like tentacles, unlike those of any local species. Column smooth and pink to white. **Size:** Can reach at least 100 mm in height. **Biology:** An abundant northern hemisphere species first reported in Table Bay Docks in 1996, where it was introduced by shipping. Recently reported from deeper reefs on the Agulhas Bank.

7.3 Burrowing anemone   *Halcampa capensis*

An unusual, pale sand-coloured anemone with an elongate, worm-like body and no attachment disc. The column is often covered in flake-like white patches. There are only 20 very short tentacles, each of which ends in a distinct round knob. **Size:** About 50 mm long. **Biology:** Lives buried in sheltered sand with the tentacles radiating in a circle on the sand surface. When disturbed, contracts beneath the surface, the tentacles leaving behind a distinctive, daisy-like impression on the sand.

7.4 Hedgehog anemone   *Preactis millardae*

This unique floating species is the only representative of the endemic family Preactidae. Column pink to orange, tapering from the base and irregularly covered in short, stubby vesicles. Oral and pedal discs with 24 radiating orange stripes. **Size:** Up to 200 mm long. **Biology:** A very unusual species found unattached on vertical reefs, where it appears to engulf and feed on sea fans.

7.5 Colonial anemone   *Gyractis excavata*

Column pale and dotted with purple papillae, to which coarse gravel adheres. Outer row of tentacles white with brown tips. Oral disc green, often brilliantly so around the mouth, from which brown lines radiate. Short brown tentacles sprout irregularly from the disc surface. **Size:** About 20 mm diameter. **Biology:** Colonies form sheet-like expanses in intertidal pools along the KwaZulu-Natal coast. Easily mistaken for zoanthids, but differ in that the individuals are not joined at their bases. Previously called *Actinoides sultana*.

7.6 Giant anemone   *Heteractis magnifica*

Forms flat sheets covered with hundreds of uniform tentacles, each longer than 30 mm, that typically waft in the current. Column bright red, purple or green with longitudinal rows of papillae that are the same colour as the column or slightly lighter. **Size:** Often reaches 500 mm diameter. **Biology:** Attaches to rocks or dead coral heads and characteristically displays itself very prominently. Plays host to anemone or clown fish (145.4 & 145.5). Previously called *Radianthus ritteri*. **SIMILAR SPECIES: *Stichodactyla mertensii*** (Sodwana northwards) is gigantic, up to 1 m across, flat and sprawling. Upper surface densely covered with hundreds of uniformly short (10–30 mm) tentacles. Underside with diagnostic purple and orange spots. Buries itself in sand among coral debris or in seagrass beds and hosts anemone fish and commensal shrimps. ***Entacmaea quadricolor*** (Sodwana northwards) has distinctive long tentacles, each ending in a small onion-like bulb. ***H. aurora*** (Sodwana northwards) has tentacles with distinct swollen crossbars.

Zoanthids   Zoanthidea

Anemone-like, with columnar polyps crowned by tentacles around the mouth. Unlike anemones, they are colonial, being united by a basal, sheet-like coenenchyme that carpets subtropical and tropical shores. Zoanthids capture tiny prey but, like corals, most also gain nutrition from microscopic symbiotic algae (zooxanthellae) in their tissues.

8.1 Cape zoanthid   *Isozoanthus capensis*
Orange to pink; column coated with coarse sand; about 30 tentacles. **Size:** 12 mm tall. **Biology:** Seldom abundant, forming small colonies of 20–50 individuals; occurs under overhangs in shallow water. Lacking zooxanthellae, it feeds on plankton.
SIMILAR SPECIES:
8.2 *Parazoanthus* sp. (Cape Peninsula) is never sand-coated and usually grows on sponges. Its mouth is mounted on a central, finger-like projection of the oral disc.

8.3 Knobbly zoanthid   *Isaurus tuberculatus*
Column tall, curving to one side and usually distinctly knobbly; grey to brown. Tentacles seldom visible. **Size:** Polyps 30 mm tall, 7 mm diameter. **Biology:** Occurs in deep pools and in the shallow subtidal zone. Forms extensive colonies, but is seldom common. Previously known as *I. spongiosus*.

8.4 Columnar sandy zoanthid   *Palythoa nelliae*
Polyps tall and only thinly connected at their bases. Column brown, embedded with fine sand grains, giving a sandpapery texture; trumpet-shaped when expanded. Disc at the top ranges from bright green to brown. **Size:** 30 mm tall, 10–15 mm wide. **Biology:** Abundant in low-shore pools, especially in areas periodically covered by sand.

8.5 Squat sandy zoanthid   *Palythoa natalensis*
Polyps short and squat, united by a thick basal sheet that forms grooves between adjacent colonies. Tissues sand-embedded, rough to the touch. Over 40 tentacles. **Size:** 15 mm tall, 10 mm wide. **Biology:** Absent from exposed rocks, but occupies even high-shore pools.

8.6 Violet zoanthid   *Zoanthus sansibaricus*
Polyps 2–3 times taller than wide, connected by a thin coenenchyme. Like all *Zoanthus* spp., column smooth, never embedded with sand. Column violet to grey, disc often vivid green, tentacles violet to dull green. **Size:** Polyps 10 mm tall, 4 mm wide. **Biology:** Common on the low shore, usually around pools. Intolerant of sand. SIMILAR SPECIES: *Z. parvus* is also tall but distinctly smaller: 8 mm tall and 3 mm wide. Disc bright green, column pink.

8.7 Durban zoanthid   *Zoanthus durbanensis*
Very similar to *Z. natalensis*, being short and squat (height roughly equal to width), but never sand-embedded. Column powdery grey; tentacles any grade between green and chocolate brown; oral disc green to grey. **Size:** Polyps 10 mm tall, 8 mm diameter. **Biology:** Same as *Z. sansibaricus*.

8.8 Green zoanthid   *Zoanthus natalensis*
Polyps short and squat, smooth-textured and joined by a relatively thick basal coenenchyme. Grass-green, with darker green tentacles; colour darkening when the polyps contract. **Size:** Polyps 5 mm tall, 8 mm diameter. **Biology:** Grows on exposed intertidal rocks, often higher on the shore than other zoanthids.
SIMILAR SPECIES:
8.9 *Zoanthus eyrei* has lime-green rim to column and disc; bright green to khaki-green tentacles and grey pharynx.

8.10 Leathery zoanthid   *Palythoa tuberculosa*
Polyps large, with 18–24 tentacles. Disc funnel-shaped with stripes from the tentacles to the mouth. Pale brown, with green tentacles and 'funnel'. **Size:** Polyps 1–10 mm. **Biology:** Subtidal; forms leathery tuberculate sheets when polyps contract. Contains the chemical palytoxin and should not be handled. Scientific name requires confirmation.

PLATE 8

30 Cnidarians & comb jellies

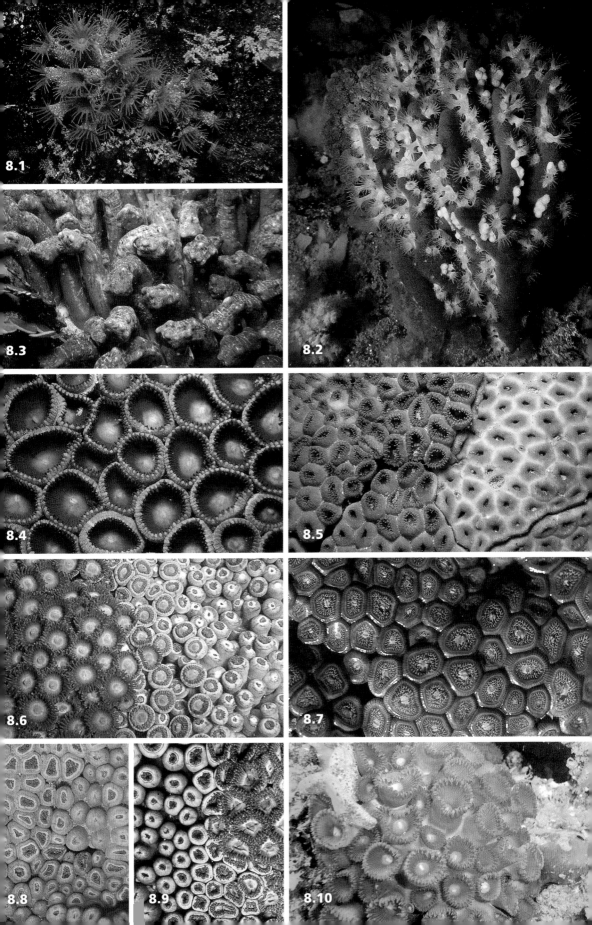

PLATE 9

Sea fans

Alcyonacea

Sea fans (or gorgonians) form branching, fan-shaped colonies. They are distinguished by a stiff central rod of gorgonin (a horn-like protein), covered with small polyps, each with eight feathery tentacles.

9.1 Sinuous sea fan
Eunicella tricoronata

Branches characteristically flattened, sinuous, and lie in one plane. Vivid orange-yellow. When expanded, the polyps impart a fuzzy appearance. **Size:** 300–400 mm tall, branches 7–10 mm wide. **Biology:** Grows on rocky reefs at depths of 10–40 m, below wave surge.

9.2 Nippled sea fan
Eunicella papillosa

Forks at fairly regular intervals, forming a flat fan, although often branches project at irregular angles. Branches cylindrical, covered with nipple-like protuberances from which polyps extend. Pale orange or creamy. **Size:** 15 mm tall; branches 2 mm wide. **Biology:** Common at 2–360 m depths, in wave-sheltered caves or on boulder-sides.

9.3 Flagellar sea fan
Eunicella albicans

Colony divides into very long, thin, whip-like branches, conspicuously flattened near the base and often with longitudinal lines. **Size:** Colonies 300–650 mm tall, branches 3–5 mm wide. **Biology:** Profuse on deeper reefs (10–30 m) where wave action is minimal.

9.4 Palmate sea fan
Leptogorgia palma

Stem with numerous flat side branches that lie in one plane. White polyps adorn the bright red colony (9.4a), but can withdraw into slits. **Size:** 2 m tall; branches 3–10 mm wide. **Biology:** Forms fantastic underwater forests at 10–100 m. Large colonies are over 100 years old and prone to extermination by souvenir-hunting divers. Eaten by sponge-crabs (57.6) and topshells (76.1). Previously named *Lophogorgia flammea*.

9.5 Warty sea fan
Homophyton verrucosum

Sparsely branched, thin round stems, covered on all sides with polyps. Colours red, orange, yellow, pink or white. **Size:** 300 mm tall. **Biology:** Grows attached to rocks, often in sand-inundated areas.

9.6 Ropy sea fan
Rumphella sp.

Many-branched cylindrical stems that fork irregularly. Stem grey or pale beige, covered with polyps in neat spiral rows. When the polyps emerge, they turn the colony brown and fuzzy in appearance. **Size:** Colony 1 m; branches 10 mm wide. **Biology:** Occurs down to about 20 m; the stems are flexible and bend with water movements.

9.7 Multicoloured sea fan
Acabaria rubra

Stems cylindrical, forked in all directions, often fused and tangled. Surface dotted with knobs into which the polyps withdraw. Colours diverse: white polyps on red stems, yellow on white, orange on yellow, or plain red. **Size:** 100–200 mm tall; branches 1 mm wide. **Biology:** Abundant beneath overhangs; often tangled with bryozoans; 1–150 m.

9.1

9.2

9.3

9.4

9.4a

.5

9.6

9.7

PLATE 10

Soft-corals

Alcyonacea

Soft-corals have no internal skeleton and form colonies of polyps, called autozooids if they carry eight distinctive, feathery tentacles, or siphonozooids if they are tiny, lack tentacles and serve only to pump up the colony with water. Autozooids use their tentacles (which contain stinging cells) to capture planktonic animals. Definite identification demands a microscopic examination of spicules in the tissues, but many species can be recognised by external features.

10.1 Thistle soft-corals
Dendronephthya spp.

Tree-like, with soft branches ending in bunches of bright pink, yellow or red polyps that are non-retractile and all of one type. Polyps often supported by bundles of spicules that impart a spiky feel and appearance, resembling exploding fireworks. **Size:** Colony 200 mm. **Biology:** Occupy reefs spanning 12–50 m. Several species occur in southern Africa. The name is derived from *dendron*, 'tree', and *Nephthys*, an Egyptian goddess.
SIMILAR SPECIES:
10.2 *Scleronephthya* spp. (Mozambique northwards) are sparsely branched, vividly coloured and highly contractile, capable of 90% reduction in size; stems wrinkled when the colony contracts. Polyps limited to the ends of branches and extremely contractile.
10.3 *Stereonephthya* spp. (Sodwana northwards) form small, bush-like colonies that are stiff and prickly. Polyps are non-retractile and distributed over the entire colony. Colour never as vivid as in *Dendronephthya*; muted, pastel shades.

10.4 Cauliflower soft-coral
Drifa thyrsoidea

A large, soft, floppy colony with a central stalk and side branches terminating in bunches of polyps. Colour variable, often translucent whitish-cream with transverse opaque white 'stretchmarks'. **Size:** Colonies 300 mm, polyps 2 mm. **Biology:** Hangs from vertical rock-faces in depths of 10–240 m; often seen by divers. By day, especially in clear water, it contracts to resemble an elongate cauliflower. Formerly named *Capnella thyrsoidea*.

10.5 Cave-dwelling soft-coral
Carijoa arborea

Pinkish orange, with a long, narrow stalk that divides into short side branches, each ending in a white, yellow or pink polyp with eight pinnate tentacles. Resembles a bunch of orange grapes when the tentacles withdraw. **Size:** Colony 30–50 mm long, polyps 50 mm. **Biology:** Hangs from the roofs of caves or rock overhangs in shallow, wave-beaten situations. Commonly fouls wrecks and jetties.
SIMILAR SPECIES:
10.6 *Clavularia* sp. (Durban northwards), intertidal pools to shallow subtidal zone, has root-like stolons with upright branches ending in tiny (2 mm) bright blue polyps that withdraw into their bases if touched.

10.7 Stalked soft-coral
Xenia crassa

Upright stalk with swollen head covered with identical polyps that cannot withdraw. Polyps slender, pale, with eight feathery tentacles; stem blue-banded. **Size:** Colony 80 mm, never forming extensive stands; polyps 10 mm. **Biology:** Exclusively subtidal, most common on shallow, sheltered reefs and in lagoons.

10.8 Blue soft-coral
Sansibia flava

Forms small, flat carpets. Polyps tall and cannot withdraw, even when disturbed. Tentacles soft, floppy, royal blue to grey-blue. **Size:** Polyps 10 mm. **Biology:** Common in intertidal pools. Previously named *Anthelia flava*.
SIMILAR SPECIES:
10.9 *Anthelia glauca* (Sodwana northwards) is twice the size, pale creamish grey to light brown, with 1–2 rows of pinnules on the tentacles; recorded at 0–19 m.

10.10 Pulsating soft-coral
Heteroxenia fuscescens

Single, unbranched, white stalk with swollen convex head, densely carpeted by tiny siphonozooids that are concealed by the profusely feathered cream or pale brown autozooids. Tentacles with 4–5 rows of pinnules. **Size:** Colony 150 mm tall; polyps 50 mm long. **Biology:** Occurs on shallow reefs down to 15 m. In calm conditions, it pulsates its tentacles open and shut.

PLATE 11

11.1 Lobed leather-coral   *Sinularia gravis*

All *Sinularia* spp. are leathery in texture and have monomorphic polyps, comprising autozooids only. *S. gravis* forms flat crusts with thumb-sized, unbranched lobes, covered by short polyps (11.1a) that emerge by night. Some lobes diagnostically stretch into narrow walls, notably at the perimeter. Dull beige to grey, tinged pink. **Size:** Up to 1 m across; polyps 1 mm. **Biology:** Subtidal, at 10–30 m. Previously called *S. gyrosa*.

11.2 Finger-branched leather-coral   *Sinularia leptoclados*

Encrusting, with well-defined, finger-like lobes and knobs. Colour brown, with paler polyps. **Size:** Colonies 500 mm across. **Biology:** Unlike other species in the genus, its polyps are often expanded by day, giving it a less leathery, more fuzzy, appearance.

11.3 Spiky leather-coral   *Sinularia heterospiculata*

Relatively small colonies, but easily recognised because it is stalked and has small, crowded lobes that are covered with spiny knobbles. **Size:** 300 mm. **Biology:** Grows on flat surfaces at moderate depths.

11.4 Abrupt leather-coral   *Sinularia abrupta*

Forms huge, flat crusts with irregular, twisted, wall-like knobs that are larger and taller than those of other members of the genus. Well-defined walls mark the edges of the colonies, hence the name *abrupta*. **Size:** Up to 1 m across. **Biology:** Common on surge-exposed, shallow reefs.

11.5 Cabbage leather-coral   *Sinularia brassica*

Colony shape highly variable. Most often forms flat crusts that resemble the previous species, except that the radiating, twisted 'walls' are smaller, form slightly branched folds and are dotted with 'pimples' marking the position of retracted polyps. Some colonies have more obvious, finger-like branches. **Size:** 500 mm across. **Biology:** Often grows at the edge of reefs abutting on areas of sediment. Colonies growing where sand-inundation takes place tend to have upright branches, rather than forming flat crusts. The species includes leather-corals previously called *S. dura*.

11.6 Blanching soft-coral   *Cladiella kashmani*

Colony leathery, attached by a broad, creeping base that forms a carpet with numerous short, blunt lobes up to 40 mm tall, which are flattened from side to side. Dark chocolate brown or dark khaki-coloured when undisturbed (11.6). Dramatically turns almost white when touched (11.6a), due to the withdrawal of the polyps. All the polyps are similar in size and structure. **Size:** Colony 300 mm in diameter, 100 mm tall. **Biology:** Common in moderately deep water (10–20 m). **SIMILAR SPECIES:** *C. australis* is very similar in colour and form but is smaller and has attenuated, finger-like lobes often taller than 40 mm, making it more 'bush-like'. *C. krempfi* is even smaller, its lobes being less than 15 mm tall. All three species blanch when disturbed. They are difficult to tell apart based on external morphology, but *C. kashmani* has spicules that are about 0.36 mm in length whereas those of *C. australis* do not exceed 0.25 mm.

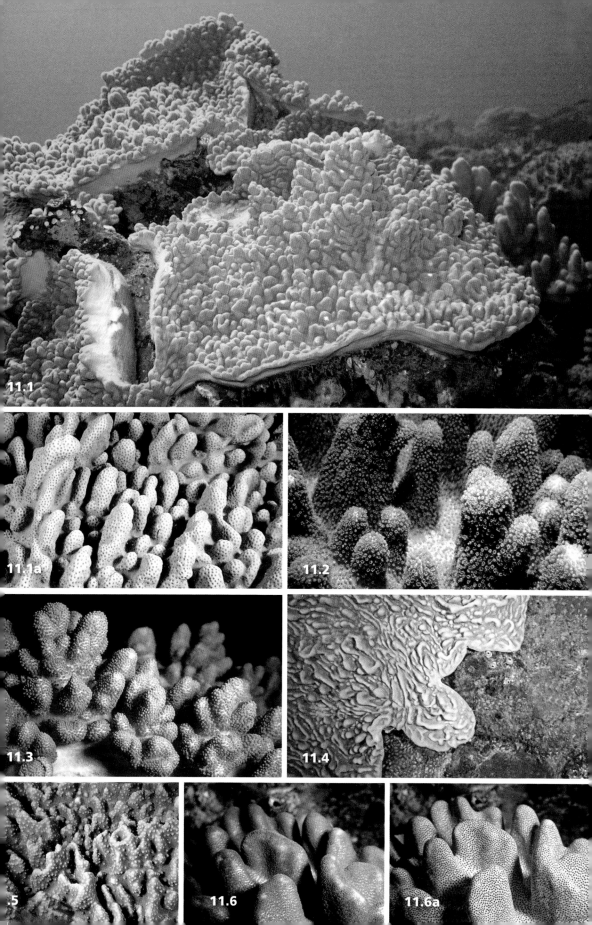

PLATE 12

12.1 Mushroom soft-corals *Sarcophyton* spp.

Attached by a broad stalk that mushrooms into a fleshy, funnel- or cup-shaped head that is soft and has two types of polyps: large, tentacled autozooids, and tiny siphonozooids that lack obvious tentacles and dot the surface (12.1a). Small colonies are mushroom-shaped, larger ones are more funnel-shaped and the edge is thrown into lobes. **Size:** Colonies 200–500 mm; large polyps 5 mm. **Biology:** Abundant at Sodwana, 2–30 m. Long-lived: giants metres across are centuries old. **SIMILAR SPECIES:** At least three species occur in southern Africa. *S. ehrenbergi* is rare in South Africa but common from central Mozambique northwards, and has an amber-coloured stalk and a strongly folded rim. *S. trocheliophorum* is common from Sodwana northwards, has a stalk that is pale, almost white, and its upper surface is grey to light green. *S. glaucum* is the most abundant species and has the same distribution. It is extremely large (up to 1 m), and differs in that its polyps are unable to retract fully, it has a dark brown head and the stalk is pale to yellow (pollen yellow internally).

12.2 Dimorphic soft-coral *Lobophytum venustum*

Like *Sarcophyton*, but unlike *Sinularia* and *Cladiella*, *Lobophytum* spp. have two or more types of polyps: large autozooids and tiny siphonozooids, but the polyps are much smaller than those of *Sarcophyton* and it is never stalked. *L. venustum* forms crusts with smooth, upright lobes, or its edges are raised, flaring upwards like a crumpled cup. Characteristically silver-grey, almost white. Often dotted with tiny, green microalgal balls. **Size:** Up to 1 m. **Biology:** Common on exposed reefs down to 35 m.

12.3 Dimorphic soft-coral *Lobophytum crassum*

Low and creeping, with strongly radiating ridges; soft. Yellow-brown with pale yellow or lime-green polyps. **Size:** Colony 500 mm. **Biology:** Subtidal, 5–40 m. Often grows in areas that are sand-inundated, and the elevation of the vertical ridges allows the colony to shed sand and avoid smothering.

SIMILAR SPECIES: Several other species in this genus share the same distribution:

12.4 *Lobophytum latilobatum* is an encrusting grey species that develops huge colonies up to 5 m across. It is characterised by large, vertical, flattened, radiating lobes. Being flat in profile, it is tolerant of surge and occurs on wave-exposed crests of reefs.

12.5 *Lobophytum patulum* is also grey and easy to confuse with *L. latilobatum*, but its smooth, flat colonies are interrupted only by low radiating mounds. It, too, forms giant colonies up to 5 m across, which may be centuries old, judging by their slow growth.

12.6 *Lobophytum depressum* is also smooth and encrusting, soft, with a completely flat surface that lacks mounds, ridges or lobes. Purple-grey, but densely covered with dark dots that mark positions of withdrawn polyps. Sediment-tolerant and often grows at the interface between rock and sand.

12.7 Sunburst soft-coral *Malacacanthus capensis*

A tough, cylindrical, brown stalk crowned by a radiating ball of bright yellow polyps (autozooids), in between which are tiny, dot-like siphonozooids that serve to re-inflate the colony after it contracts. **Size:** Colony 150 mm tall when expanded. **Biology:** Occurs subtidally, in relatively deep water (10–40 m). When disturbed, the entire crown can fold inwards and be withdrawn into the top of the stalk.

12.8 Purple soft-coral *Alcyonium fauri*

Most commonly a uniform, vivid purple; less often yellow, pink, or red and orange, or some combination of these colours. Colonies encrust the substratum, but thrust out lobes covered with polyps. **Size:** Colony 30 mm tall, polyps 5 mm. **Biology:** Abundant in shallow subtidal zones. Previously named *Parerythropodium purpureum* (meaning 'equal-sized red legs' and 'purple').

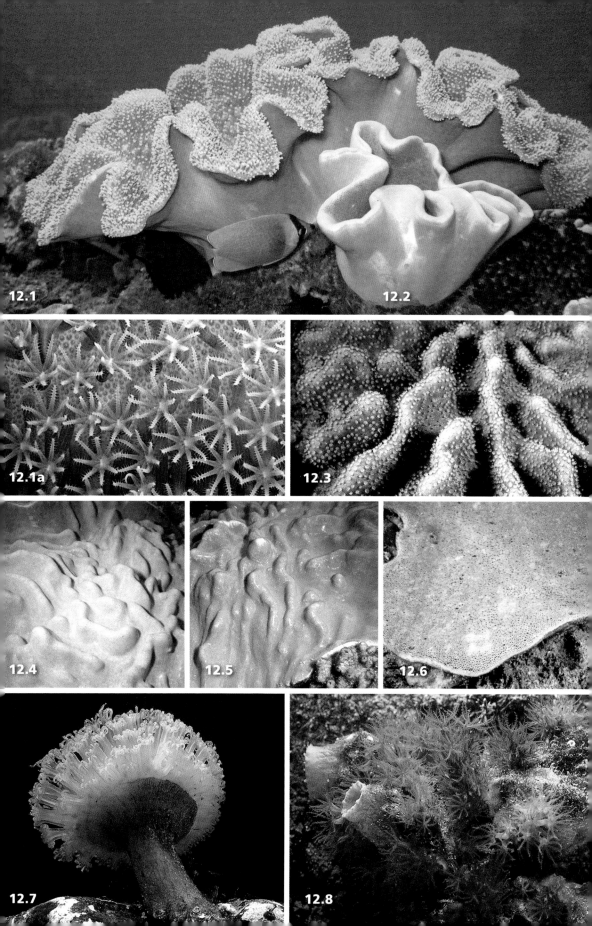

12.1

12.2

12.1a

12.3

12.4

12.5

12.6

12.7

12.8

PLATE 13

13.1 Variable soft-coral — *Eleutherobia variabile*

Shaped like a mushroom bud, with a short stalk and a round, unbranched head covered with polyps. Background colour extremely variable: red, purple, orange, yellow, pink or white, or combinations of these. **Size:** 50 mm tall. **Biology:** One of the most common soft-corals, regularly seen by divers; occurs at depths of 13–468 m.

13.2 Valdivian soft-coral — *Alcyonium valdiviae*

Conspicuous, stout trunk with stubby, banana-shaped branches that become almost globular when contracted. Colour extremely variable: white, pink, or brick red, with white polyps; usually bright orange on the west coast. **Size:** 90 mm tall. **Biology:** Common on rock walls and reefs at 14–18 m depths. Polyps open at night.

13.3 Golden soft-coral — *Eleutherobia aurea*

Plump and sausage-shaped; peduncle fleshy, thick. White polyps evenly distributed around the central axis, which is always yellow. Colony covered with soft, prickly protuberances when the polyps withdraw. **Size:** 12–150 mm. **Biology:** Occurs at 12–300 m, often in sandy crevices among rocks. **SIMILAR SPECIES**: *E. vinadigitaria* (Durban only) has wine-red fingers.

13.4 Organ-pipe coral — *Tubipora musica*

Despite being an alcyonacean soft-coral, *Tubipora* builds a bright red skeleton in the form of parallel, upright tubes (13.4a), from which project daisy-like grey polyps with eight flattened tentacles. **Size:** Colonies 250 mm tall, 'organ pipes' 1.5 mm in diameter. **Biology:** Dead skeletons are a familiar sight washed up on tropical shores, but live animals are seldom seen, though strikingly beautiful. Subtidal, down to 50 m.

Thorny corals — Antipatharia

Bushy, much-branched colonies with a central thorny black skeleton.

13.5 Black coral — *Antipathes* sp.

Forms large, upright, repeatedly branching colonies resembling miniature trees. The central core of the 'trunk' and the branches form a hard black skeleton that is bedecked with tiny spines and coated with yellow or lime-green polyps that have six tentacles, like all members of the Antipatharia. **Size:** Colonies up to 2 m tall, polyps 2–3 mm. **Biology:** Occurs from 25 m down to depths as great as 1 km. The skeleton is sought for use in jewellery, and some species of *Antipathes* have been badly depleted.

Sea-pens — Pennatulacea

Sea-pens have a soft, unbranched, root-like peduncle that anchors the colony in mud or sand, and an upright 'stem' or rachis that has feather-like side branches carrying rows of polyps. Most have a stiff central rod.

13.6 Elegant sea-pen — *Virgularia gustaviana*

Long and thin. Brittle central rod covered by orange tissues. Vivid purple polyps arranged in groups of 80–200 on flat, leaf-like expansions on both sides of the central 'stem' (13.6a). **Size:** 300 mm long, 10 mm wide. **Biology:** Stands upright, with base embedded in clean sand. Commensal brittlestars, *Ophiothela danae* (103.4), attach to its stem. **SIMILAR SPECIES**: *V. schultzei* (entire coast) is similar in structure, but is uniformly white to cream-coloured and has 15–35 polyps on each 'leaf'.

13.7 Rotund sea-pen — *Pteroeides isosceles*

Main 'stalk' inflated, standing stiffly erect, with about 25 paired, bristly leaflets that carry the polyps. White to beige. **Size:** 250 mm long. **Biology:** Lives embedded in sand near reefs at about 40 m. Swivels on its axis as waves surge over it. **SIMILAR SPECIES**: *Actinoptilum molle* (see 96.6) is about 180 mm long, sausage-shaped, and the 'stalk' is covered entirely with rows of polyps; longitudinal lines of small fleshy lobes (calyces) that shield the polyps appear when the polyps withdraw. Colour variable: yellow, white, mauve, pink or brown. Often washes ashore, but lives at depths of 12–300 m, rooted in soft sediment between Cape Columbine and Inhaca Island.

13.1

13.2

13.3

13.4

13.4a

13.5

13.6

13.6a

13.7

PLATE 14

Hard corals
Scleractinia

Corals have anemone-like polyps that produce a limestone skeleton. A few are hydrozoans and fall in the order Milleporina, but 'true' corals are anthozoans and belong to the order Scleractinia. Most form colonies with massive skeletons that have small craters or projections (corallites), each housing one polyp and usually divided by vertical radiating septa, sometimes joined by tiny bridges (synapticula) that are revealed by cleaning and bleaching. Colonial corals house single-celled algae (zooxanthellae) that gain fertilising nitrogen; in return they supply food and help build the skeleton. This symbiosis limits most reef corals to sunlit warm waters.

14.1 Fire coral
Millepora tenella

Irregularly branching into slightly flattened forks. Mustard yellow; tips always pale. Tiny white dots mark withdrawn polyps. **Size:** Branches 5–10 mm wide. **Biology:** A milleporine hydrozoan. Possessing zooxanthellae, it is limited to shallow tropical waters. Inflicts an irritating, persistent sting. **SIMILAR SPECIES:** *M. platyphylla*, the flat-leafed fire coral, has flat, upright, knobbly blades with the same mustard yellow colour and pale tops.

14.2 Noble coral
Allopora nobilis

A single, thick 'trunk' with cylindrical branches. Tiny polyps project from star-shaped pinpricks in the skeleton. Bright pink, often with pale tips. **Size:** Colony 200 mm, polyps 1 mm. **Biology:** Also a milleporine hydrozoan. Lacks zooxanthellae, so it is not dependent on light. Spans depths 5–100 m, and often occurs in caves or under overhangs. Large colonies are over 100 years old. Protected: permit required for collection.

14.3 Staghorn corals
Acropora spp.

Corallites small and porous, projecting as distinct cups; a large, apical corallite always caps each branch. Colony form varies with species: some, such as *A. clathrata* (14.3), form tables or plates like flat-topped trees, but most are branching or bushy (14.3a). Colour variable: brown, whitish pink, pale green or purple-tipped. **Size:** Colonies 300–400 mm, corallites <3 mm. **Biology:** 30 closely related species occur here. The brittle branches restrict them to calm water. Skeleton light, colonies fast-growing: early colonisers of disturbed areas.

14.4 Knob-horned corals
Pocillopora verrucosa

Upright, hemispherical colonies; branches flattened, with knob-like projections. Corallites small, sunken into skeleton. Skeleton not porous. Projecting tentacles make live colonies appear fuzzy. Colour rich brown to light purple, often with a beautiful blue-brown sheen. **Size:** Colony 250 mm, corallites <2 mm. **Biology:** Common, from intertidal pools down to 40 m. Branches may form tiny caves, encapsulating commensal crabs.
SIMILAR SPECIES:
14.5 *Stylophora pistillata*, the 'tramp coral', has flat branches but no knobs.
14.6 *Pocillopora damicornis* has much larger knobs, half the branch width.

14.7 Mushroom coral
Fungia scutaria

Solitary, comprising a huge, single, flat, oval to elongate polyp. Skeleton resembles an upturned mushroom, having a central groove and radiating, vertical, finely toothed septa. Live animals bright yellow, green or brown, with yellow stripes. **Size:** 150–200 mm. **Biology:** Juveniles attached by a short stalk, but soon break free; adults lie loose on the bottom, 4–30 m. Often collected by divers; illegal removal from Sodwana reserve is a recognised problem. **SIMILAR SPECIES:** *Herpolitha* spp. are like larger, thinner, 'stretched-out' versions, up to 400 mm long. *Halomitra pileus*, the helmet coral, is domed, hollow underneath, and up to 500 mm. *Cycloseris* spp. are circular, with neatly equal septa, and quite small: 70–100 mm.

14.8 Cup coral
Balanophyllia bonaespei

Solitary, but often lives in groups. Bright orange, tentacles almost transparent and beaded in appearance. Skeleton columnar, upper surface divided by radiating septa that have prickly, toothed inner edges (14.8a). **Size:** 10 mm diameter, 15 mm height. **Biology:** Often in caves or under dark overhangs, in depths of 1–150 m.
SIMILAR SPECIES:
14.9 *Caryophyllia* spp. are larger (15–20 mm diameter), with longitudinal stripes on the column, and obvious central pali (finger-like projections) on the disc.

14.1

14.2

14.3

14.3a

14.4

14.5

14.6

14.7

14.8

14.8a

14.9

PLATE 15

15.1 Honeycomb-corals — *Favites* spp.

Hemispherical and boulder-like; completely covered with moderately large corallites, which are sunken into the surface. The polyps do not project and have short tentacles, which are seldom visible by day. Colour extremely varied, including bright green, brown, grey, russet. The walls of touching corallites are fused together, forming a honeycomb pattern (15.1a). Adjacent polyps thus share a common wall. The septa are well developed but lack synapticula (tiny bridges). **Size:** Colony width 300 mm, corallites 12 mm wide. **Biology:** Abundant, intertidal to 15 m. Several species in the genus, all difficult to separate. **SIMILAR SPECIES:** *Goniastrea* spp. very similar, but corallites smaller and septa have thickened lobes near the centre, lacking in *Favites*. Rare in South Africa but common in Mozambique.

15.2 False honeycomb-corals — *Favia* spp.

Similar to *Favites*, with hemispherical colonies, but distinguished because the walls of adjacent corallites are distinctly separated from one another by a gap or, if they are touching, by at least a groove (15.2a). Colours again extremely variable. **Size:** Colony diameter 300 mm, height 150 mm, corallite diameter 12 mm. **Biology:** As for *Favites*.

15.3 Irregular honeycomb-coral — *Anomastrea irregularis*

Forms creeping hummocks covered with corallites that are similar to those of *Favites* but half the size, and their septa are joined by synapticula (tiny bridges). The polyps form a thin coating, so that the shape of the skeleton is clearly visible. Living colonies usually brown, sometimes dull green. **Size:** Colony 150 mm, corallites 6 mm. **Biology:** One of the most common corals in intertidal pools.

15.4 Spiny honeycomb-coral — *Acanthastrea echinata*

Colonies irregular but generally domed and boulder-like. Corallites heavily spined, especially on the inner edges of the septa (15.4a). Typically the surface of live animals is thickly fleshy, concealing the skeleton, and textured with tiny bubbles (15.4). Colour variable, often khaki-green with paler centres. **Size:** Colony 250 mm, corallites 20 mm. **Biology:** Never abundant, but occurs from intertidal pools down to 25 m.

15.5 Labyrinthine brain-coral — *Platygyra daedalea*

Forms large, flat slabs or hemispherical mounds; surface convoluted like a brain. The polyps are joined in rows, the corallites housing them forming long grooves separated by ridges with projecting septa (15.5a). Live animals can have a striking network of green grooves and brown ridges, or green ridges on a pale background. Tentacles not evident. **Size:** Colonies 50–1 000 mm, corallite grooves 5 mm wide. **Biology:** Subtidal. Named after the mythical Daedalus, inventor of the labyrinth housing the Minotaur.

SIMILAR BRAIN-LIKE CORALS:

15.6 *Oulophyllia crispa* is similar to *Platygyra daedalea*. Its tentacles are also not evident, but it is often more convoluted and its corallites much larger (10–12 mm groove width) with sharp ridges and finely toothed septa (15.6a).

15.7 *Coscinaraea* spp. have a skeleton that is less obviously brain-like, the corallites being almost separate from one another, the grooves less distinct and the ridges gently rounded. The septa are densely packed, giving the impression of a sieve (*koskinon* is Greek for 'sieve').

15.8 *Gyrosmilia interrupta* also has wide grooves (12 mm) but can be distinguished by its extended tentacles and the large, smooth, skeletal septa, which are alternately large and small (15.8a).

15.9 *Symphyllia valenciennesii* is a giant brain-coral, forming massive colonies: its corallites are 30 mm wide, convoluted and sinuous, and coarsely toothed on their inner edges (15.9a). All brain-corals are tropical, extending from Zululand northwards.

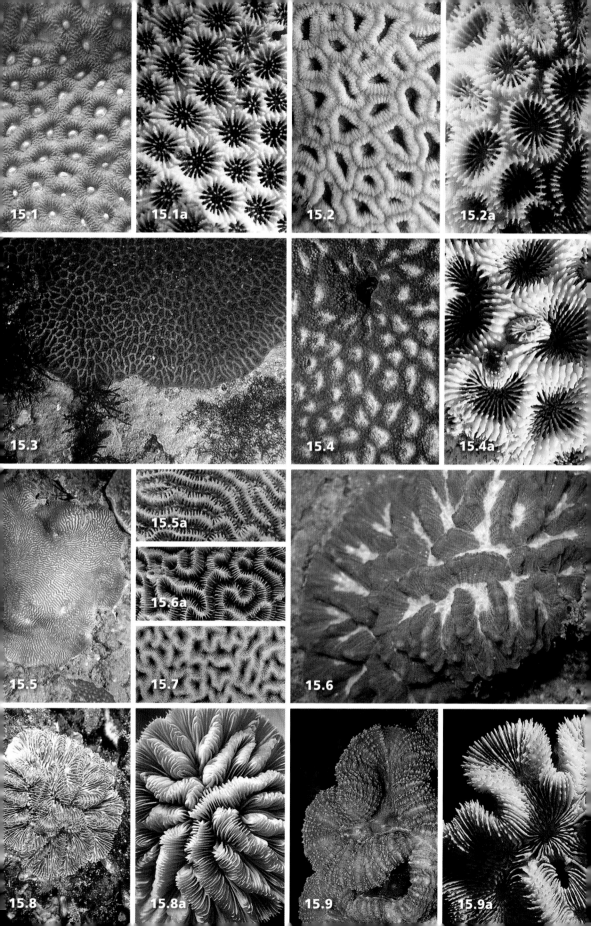

15.1　15.1a　15.2　15.2a　15.3　15.4　15.4a　15.5a　15.6a　15.7　15.6　15.5　15.8　15.8a　15.9　15.9a

PLATE 16

16.1 Daisy coral
Goniopora djiboutiensis

Forms low, boulder-shaped or encrusting colonies. Polyps have conical oral discs and 24 tentacles, and are large and project boldly (by as much as 20 mm), resembling bunches of pale flowers. Skeleton completely covered by corallites that are closely positioned but still separated by a groove (16.1a), similar to the arrangement in *Favia*, but much smaller. **Size:** Colony 250 mm, corallites 4 mm. **Biology:** The only coral that fully expands its polyps by day. Aggressively stings other corals to death. **SIMILAR SPECIES:** *Alveopora* spp. have dark brown polyps with 12 tentacles and a very soft skeleton.

16.2 Porous corals
Porites spp.

Massive, boulder-like colonies, covered densely with small, sunken corallites (16.2a) that have well-developed septa (unlike *Montipora*, which can develop colonies superficially resembling those of *Porites*). Polyps with tiny brown tentacles, scarcely emerging from their corallites by day, but giving the colony a fuzzy appearance even though the skeletal structure is always evident. **Size:** Colony up to several metres, corallites 1–2 mm. **Biology:** Form massive heads that are centuries old; lay down annual growth rings that contain information about past climatic conditions.

16.3 Peacock coral
Pavona decussata

Forms flat, thin blades from which twisted secondary plates jut at right angles. This may produce a structure a little like a peacock's tail, hence the name (*pavo* is Latin for 'peacock'). The corallites (16.3a) are distinctive, lacking definite boundaries because the septa extend uninterrupted from one corallite to the next. **Size:** Colony 150 mm diameter, plates 2 mm thick. **Biology:** Abundant at Inhaca Island in shallow, sheltered lagoons. Plates often break off, settle on the bottom, and sprout fresh upright plates. **SIMILAR SPECIES:** Several other species occur in southern Africa.

16.4 *Pavona clavus* (Maputaland northwards) has a massive, boulder-like skeleton (700 mm diameter), and the septa on its corallites radiate in a daisy-like manner.

16.5 Warty corals
Montipora spp.

Large, flat, undulating colonies, sometimes growing in tiers. If the skeleton is examined closely (16.5a), the corallites are poorly defined, very simple in structure, and their septa rudimentary. However, the surface is distinctive, being dotted with irregular warty protuberances that distinguish the genus. **Size:** Colony up to 300 mm diameter, 'warts' 2–3 mm. **Biology:** Subtidal; very common in our region.

16.6 Many-eyed star coral
Astreopora myriophthalma

Forms encrusting, hillock-like sheets or massive colonies; densely covered with polyps that are slightly conical but recessed in the skeleton. Usually creamish-brown or pale purple. Superficially like *Porites* (16.2), but the skeleton is highly porous, the surface covered with fine spines, and the corallites are conical and consist of simple holes that either lack septa or have very reduced, simple septa (16.6a), so that the colony resembles 'putty peppered with birdshot'. **Size:** Colony very large, up to several metres across, corallites 2 mm. **Biology:** Only subtidal, 2–40 m depths.

16.7 Plate coral
Leptoseris sp.

Develops flat, plate-like sheets with concentric grooves and septa that are clearly visible on the upper surface and radiate outwards. Individual polyps separated and distinct from one another, so that the concentric grooves in which they lie are interrupted, in contrast to *Pachyseris* spp. Like *Pavona*, the septa extend from one corallite to the next so that the boundaries between corallites are undefined. However, the corallites protrude and are much larger and more spaced out than those of *Pavona*. **Size:** Plates 400 mm diameter, corallites about 10 mm apart. **Biology:** Occurs only in deeper waters (20–40 m) below heavy wave surge; abundant in deeper water at Sodwana Bay.

16.8 Disc coral
Pachyseris speciosa

Irregular, flat or upward-folded plates, with continuous, regular, concentric grooves, imparting the appearance of a crumpled, old-fashioned, vinyl music disc. The polyps merge into one another, hence the continuous grooves. Chestnut to chocolate brown; edges pale. **Size:** Plates 400 mm diameter; grooves 7 mm wide. **Biology:** Forms huge expanses on flat reefs at 10–40 m.

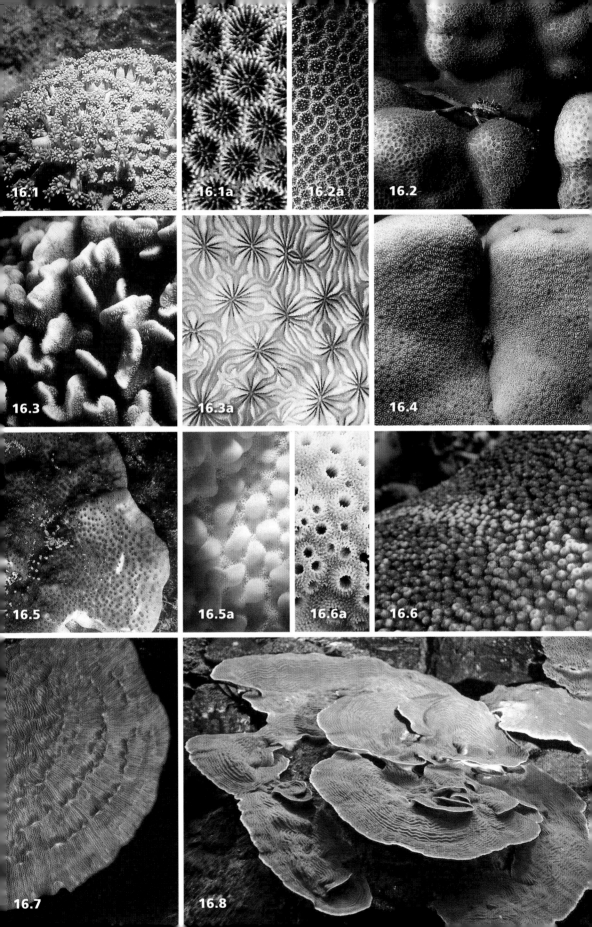

16.1

16.1a

16.2a

16.2

16.3

16.3a

16.4

16.5

16.5a

16.6a

16.6

16.7

16.8

PLATE 17

17.1 Turbinate coral · *Turbinaria mesenterina*

Colony attached by a distinct 'trunk' that expands into a flat table or bract-like plate, often spiralling or funnel-shaped. Corallites (17.1a) widely spaced and sunken into the skeleton. Septa simple, smooth and all of similar size. **Size:** Colony 300 mm, corallites 3–4 mm. **Biology:** Subtidal, 10–40 m. The shape may serve to concentrate silt at the bottom of the funnel rather than letting it smother the whole colony; in turbulent waters the funnel voids silt. The name is derived from *turbo*, Latin for 'whirlpool' or 'spinning top'.

17.2 Spiky coral · *Galaxea fascicularis*

Colony rounded, surface distinctly spiky because the corallites are elevated on columns and their septa project sharply outwards from the apex (17.2a). The tentacles range from brown to bright green and are flattened and tapering, usually with a distinct terminal white knob. They extend well beyond the septa. **Size:** Colonies 150–200 mm, polyps 10 mm. **Biology:** Occurs subtidally in depths of 1–15 m. An aggressive species that stings competitors with long 'sweeper' tentacles. **SIMILAR SPECIES:** *G. astreata* has smaller polyps (5 mm across) and encrusting brown colonies.

17.3 Small-coned coral · *Hydnophora microconos*

Colony flat and encrusting. The corallites are unusual in that the costae project from the surface and taper abruptly to a central ridge, forming tiny, cone-like structures (17.3a). In the living animals the cones are surrounded by polyps that lie in the valleys between the cones, their mouths being flanked by short stubby tentacles. **Size:** Whole colony up to 400 mm, corallites 7 mm. **Biology:** Subtidal, at depths of 1–25 m.

17.4 Star-like coral · *Plesiastrea versipora*

Colonies encrusting and relatively small, densely covered with pale grey polyps with darker tentacles. Mouth field often white, surrounded by bluish or greenish polyp tissue. Skeleton distinctive: corallites (17.4a) almost circular and projecting slightly, crowded but clearly separated by small gaps. **Size:** Colonies 150–200 mm, corallites 5–7 mm. **Biology:** In intertidal pools and down to 20 m subtidally. Previously called *Solenastrea*.

17.5 Prickly-pored coral · *Echinopora hirsutissima*

Colony encrusting, the surface misshapen and rough because the corallites are irregularly scattered, differ in size and vary in the extent to which they project. Corallites of dead specimens resemble snowflakes, their outer surfaces covered with delicately spined ridges. Septa toothed on their inner edges (17.5a). **Size:** Colony 100–200 mm, corallites 8 mm. **Biology:** Subtidal, but tolerant of a wide range of conditions. Grows well in sheltered areas where it is often covered by a thin film of silt, but survives equally well in very exposed situations.

17.6 Turret-coral · *Dendrophyllia robusta*

Colony comprising a few cylindrical branches ending in large corallites, each mounted by a single, very large, golden polyp. **Size:** 50 mm tall; branches 10 mm wide. **Biology:** Polyps often withdrawn by day (17.6a), when they appear flat-topped, and are coated with a thin film of tissue, giving a green sheen over an orange-brown background colour. At night, they expand to 30 mm across the tentacles: big enough to be confused with anemones. Often found in caves and beneath overhangs. **SIMILAR SPECIES:** *Dendrophyllia* spp. have pairs of their septa fused together along their inner margins – a feature never seen in adult *Tubastraea* spp., which are otherwise very similar. Both genera feed voraciously on zooplankton and lack zooxanthellae. *Tubastraea micranthus*, the green tree coral, is a tree-like, deep-water species found from 15–50 m, and is deep black-green. It can grow to a metre in height and is much admired by divers for its stunning beauty.

17.1

17.1a

17.2

17.2a

17.3

17.3a

17.4

17.4a

17.5

17.5a

17.6

17.6a

PLATE 18

Jellyfish   Scyphozoa & Cubozoa

Bell-shaped, gelatinous creatures with a radial body plan that swim by pulsing water from their bells. Small species mostly fall in class Hydrozoa, whereas larger and more familiar jellyfish belong in the classes Cubozoa and Scyphozoa, which spend most of their lives as planktonic medusae. All are carnivorous, stunning prey with stinging cells on their tentacles. Jellyfish are important food for some turtles, and are even eaten by great white sharks.

18.1 Box jellyfish   *Carybdea branchi*

Bell almost cube-shaped, with a single tentacle at each of the four lower corners. **Size:** Bell 40 mm; tentacles up to 700 mm long. **Biology:** Often forms swarms. Inflicts a painful sting, but not as virulent as its potentially lethal relative, *Chiropsalmus*, which has up to nine tentacles at each corner and has been anecdotally reported in KwaZulu-Natal and Mozambique.

18.2 Frilly-mouthed jellyfish   *Chrysaora* sp.

Bell shallow, transparent blue with an opaque, white edge, 24 long marginal tentacles and 16–32 short stubby tentacles. Manubrium frilly, forming four trailing 'arms' when expanded. **Size:** 120 mm diameter. **Biology:** Feeds on relatively large planktonic animals.

18.3 Night-light jellyfish   *Pelagia noctiluca*

Bell hemispherical; the surface is characteristically warty. Margin with eight tentacles. Manubrium with four long frilly lobes. **Size:** Bell 100 mm. **Biology:** Abundant in the Mediterranean, probably affecting fish stocks. Likely to occur elsewhere in our waters.

18.4 Compass jellyfish   *Chrysaora hysoscella*

Pink with radiating rusty red-brown 'spokes'. Up to 24 red tentacles that break off easily. **Size:** 400–800 mm. **Biology:** Often abundant; consumes significant numbers of fish larvae. Commensal hyperiid amphipods (38.3) live embedded in its tissues. Enormous increases in Namibia may signify a long-term ecosystem shift.
SIMILAR SPECIES:
18.5 *Chrysaora fulgida* (Namibia–Cape Peninsula) is white with purple 'spokes'. Up to 40 long purple tentacles that don't break easily. Previously named *C. africana*.

18.6 Blue blubber   *Catostylus mosaicus*

Almost hemispherical; bell margin with multiple scallops but no tentacles; translucent blue to brown. Eight 'mouth-arms' jut abruptly at the top but taper to their tips, and have net-like veins. **Size:** Bell 100–350 mm. **Biology:** Occurs in sheltered bays and occasionally in estuaries. Harvested in the Far East for human consumption. **SIMILAR SPECIES:** *Rhizostoma pulmo* is superficially similar, but the 'mouth-arms' end in fleshy, club-like appendages; bell with a bright purple to brown edge. Commonly washed ashore.

18.7 Root-mouthed jellyfish   *Eupilema inexpectata*

Bell smooth and domed, lacking tentacles; usually translucent white or blue. The manubrium is dotted with numerous, pore-like entrances into the gut. **Size:** Very large, averaging 300 mm; up to 1.5 m. **Biology:** Commonly washed ashore. Lacking tentacles, rhizostomid jellyfish feed by filtering tiny prey through pores in the manubrium.

18.8 Moon jellyfish   *Aurelia aurita*

Roughly hemispherical; densely fringed with about 200 thin, delicate tentacles. Branching canals radiate from the centre to the edge. Four characteristic opaque semicircles mark the gonads near the top of the bell. Manubrium with four frilly arms about as long as the bell radius. **Size:** Usually 20–40 mm, but can reach 600 mm. **Biology:** Widespread, but only recently recorded in South Africa.

18.9 Crystal jellyfish   *Aequorea forskalea*

Relatively flat and saucer-shaped. Central portion thick and transparent; edge thin, with 40–80 fine, radiating, unbranched canals. Margin with multiple, relatively short, delicate tentacles. Manubrium short and small. **Size:** Diameter 30–60 mm. **Biology:** This jellyfish is a hydrozoan and has an unusually large medusa stage for this class. Rare much of the time, but appears in periodic swarms.

18.1

18.2

18.3

18.4

18.5

18.6

18.7

18.8

18.9

PLATE 19

Hydroids   Hydrozoa

Hydroids form colonies of numerous individuals (polyps), and are often fern-like or feathery. Stinging tentacles around the mouth are used for defence and to capture tiny animals. In some species the colony has an external skeletal sheath (perisarc) and each polyp is housed in a cup-like hydrotheca. The numbers of teeth on the margin and the shape of the hydrothecae distinguish species, and line drawings of these microscopic features are provided. Some polyps are reduced to a single long stinging tentacle, housed in a tubular nematotheca. Sac-like reproductive structures (gonothecae) may form miniature jellyfish (medusae) that reproduce sexually, yielding larvae that settle to initiate the next generation of polyps. About 286 species occur in southern Africa.

19.1 Estuarine commensal-hydroid   *Hydractinia kaffraria*
Polyps naked, tubular and yellow, and grow on shells of *Nassarius kraussianus*, the tick shell. Side branches form orange-red gonophores that produce medusae. **Size:** Polyps 2–3 mm tall. **Biology:** Living exclusively on *N. kraussianus,* it is restricted to intertidal estuarine sandbanks, from the Breede River to Durban Bay. It provides protection to its host against some predators, and benefits from scraps of food and a firm substratum on the surface of estuarine sediments.

19.2 High-spined commensal-hydroid   *Hydractinia altispina*
Forms an orange fuzz on shells of the whelk *Nucella squamosa.* Polyps (19.2a) naked (not sheathed or housed in hydrothecae) and interspersed with chitinous spines and tiny, ball-like reproductive gonozooids. **Size:** Polyps 2 mm. **Biology:** Occurs only on *N. squamosa* and repels some of its predators. Found down to 24 m. SIMILAR SPECIES: *H. marsupialia* (Saldanha–Port Elizabeth) coats *Nassarius speciosa* shells.

19.3 Sea-fern hydroid   *Pennaria disticha*
Colony fern-like, with a central stem that branches alternately on the left and right, each branch bearing about six polyps on the upper surface. Polyps naked (not housed on hydrothecae) but attached by a short stalk; a ring of tentacles circles the base and knobbed tentacles are scattered over the surface (19.3a). **Size:** Colony 60 mm tall. **Biology:** Attaches to rocks in pools and down to 20 m. Common on ships' hulls and wrecks.

19.4 Bushy hydroids   *Eudendrium* spp.
Colony branches haphazardly, forming a small bush. Stem enclosed in a sheath that is ringed (annulated) at the origins of branches. Polyps (19.4a) not housed in hydrothecae. Fewer than 40 tentacles, forming a single whorl around the mouth. **Size:** Colony 170 mm tall. **Biology:** The seven species in the genus are difficult to tell apart. They grow on rocks, ships' hulls, algae, or other hydroids.

19.5 Tubular hydroid   *Ectopleura crocea*
Stems long, unbranched and upright, encased in a skeletal sheath and ending in a single apical polyp. Polyps spectacular: pink and white with short tentacles ringing the mouth and a second ring of much larger tentacles, below which hang yellow, grape-like bunches of reproductive sporosacs. **Size:** Stems 100 mm long, polyps 10 mm across. **Biology:** Common on ships' hulls and dock piles. Feeds on tiny planktonic crustaceans. Previously called *Tubularia warreni.* A giant variety, 250 mm tall, occurs in False Bay. SIMILAR SPECIES:
19.6 *Zyzzyzus warreni* (Saldanha–Mozambique) is only 15 mm tall, solitary and lacks a sheath around its stem; grows embedded in sponges. Previously called *Z. solitarius.*

19.7 Thin-walled obelia   *Obelia dichotoma*
Creeping, root-like base with upright, unbranched stems; pale pink to white. Polyps protected by hydrothecae, which have ringed stalks and arise directly from the stem; margins of hydrothecae smooth or undulating, never toothed. Reproductive bodies flask-shaped and three times the length of hydrothecae (19.7a). **Size:** Stems 10 mm long. **Biology:** Common worldwide on ships, dock piles and seaweeds. SIMILAR SPECIES:
19.8 *Obelia geniculata* (Lüderitz–Cape Agulhas) has a markedly thickened stem below each hydrotheca. Common on kelp and on ships' hulls; introduced species.

19.1

19.3

19.4

19.2

19.2a

Gonophore

19.3a

19.4a

19.5

19.6

19.7

19.7a

Hydrotheca

19.8

PLATE 20

20.1 Smoky feather-hydroid   *Macrorhynchia filamentosa*

Upright feathery stems; mottled black, smoky-grey and white. Reproductive bodies protected in flat, circular structures. Hydrothecae roughly cup-shaped and have a projecting tooth above a central, tubular nematotheca (20.1a). **Size:** Colonies 150 mm. **Biology:** Common in KwaZulu-Natal; often grows on algae, such as the red coralline shown here.

20.2 Rusty feather-hydroid   *Lytocarpia formosa*

Creeping 'rootlets' give rise to densely packed, undivided, feathery stems that are rusty red-brown. Hydrothecae (20.2a) with several blunt teeth around the margin, a long projecting spur, a short nematotheca on both sides, and a tubular one below the spur. Reproductive gonothecae (20.2a) gathered in a slender, pinecone-like structure (corbula). **Size:** Stems 10–30 mm. **Biology:** The most frequently seen hydroid in KwaZulu-Natal; often grows on seaweeds and can penetrate their tissues with its rootlets.

20.3 Fire hydroid   *Macrorhynchia phillippina*

Colonies branching, pale white, feathery. Hydrothecae similar to those of *M. filamentosa*, but lack the projecting tooth above the central, tubular nematotheca (20.3a). **Size:** 15 mm tall. **Biology:** Associated with coral reefs. Capable of inflicting a fierce, fiery sting.

20.4 Plumed hydroid   *Plumularia setacea*

A low, creeping base, with pale, upright, unbranched, plume-like stems. Hydrothecae goblet-like, with a smooth margin, and flanked by two lateral nematothecae and a lower, central nematotheca (20.4a). Gonothecae (reproductive individuals) resemble smooth sacs with curved necks. **Size:** Stems 20 mm tall. **Biology:** Widespread and very common in shallow water; one of 11 species.
SIMILAR SPECIES:
20.5 *Kirchenpaueria pinnata* (Namibia–KwaZulu-Natal) has the same appearance, but lacks lateral nematothecae, and its gonothecae have ridges and a spiky apex. Widespread, and the most common intertidal hydroid in the SW Cape.

20.6 Toothed feather-hydroid   *Aglaophenia pluma*

Base root-like, with upright plumed yellow stems. Usually unbranched, but a branching variety does exist. Hydrothecae (20.6a) with nine strong marginal teeth, a projecting, frontal nematotheca, and two lateral nematothecae. Reproductive individuals protected in a corbula resembling a tiny pine cone (20.6a). **Size:** 30 mm, but much longer in the branching variety. **Biology:** Very common; intertidal to 100 m.

20.7 Jointed hydroid   *Thuiaria articulata*

Upright stems with paired side branches that jut out laterally in a single plane. Hydrothecae carried on both sides of the stem and side branches, and are distinctively sunken into them (20.7a). Gonothecae urn-shaped. **Size:** Colony 50 mm. **Biology:** Lives in sheltered pools; common on the SW Cape coast. Previously named *Salacia articulata*.

20.8 Planar hydroid   *Sertularella arbuscula*

Stem bright yellow and branched repeatedly in one plane so that the whole colony is flat. The hydrothecae alternate on either side of the branches, have four marginal teeth and three internal teeth, and are closed by a four-sided, pyramid-shaped operculum (20.8a). **Size:** 50 mm. **Biology:** Grows on vertical, subtidal rocks, aligned at right angles to the water-flow; catches plankton. One of 21 species in the genus.
SIMILAR SPECIES:
20.9 *Symplectoscyphus* spp. are very similar, but their hydrothecae have only three marginal teeth and their opercula have three valves.

20.10 Wiry hydroid   *Amphisbetia operculata*

Thin wiry stems that divide repeatedly into pairs that diverge at an acute angle, creating a thin straggly bush. Hydrothecae arranged in opposite pairs on the stems and are long and thin, their lips extending as two sharp teeth, one often longer than the other (20.10a). The gonothecae resemble elongate figs (20.10a). **Size:** Colonies 50–90 mm tall. **Biology:** Intertidal to 100 m.

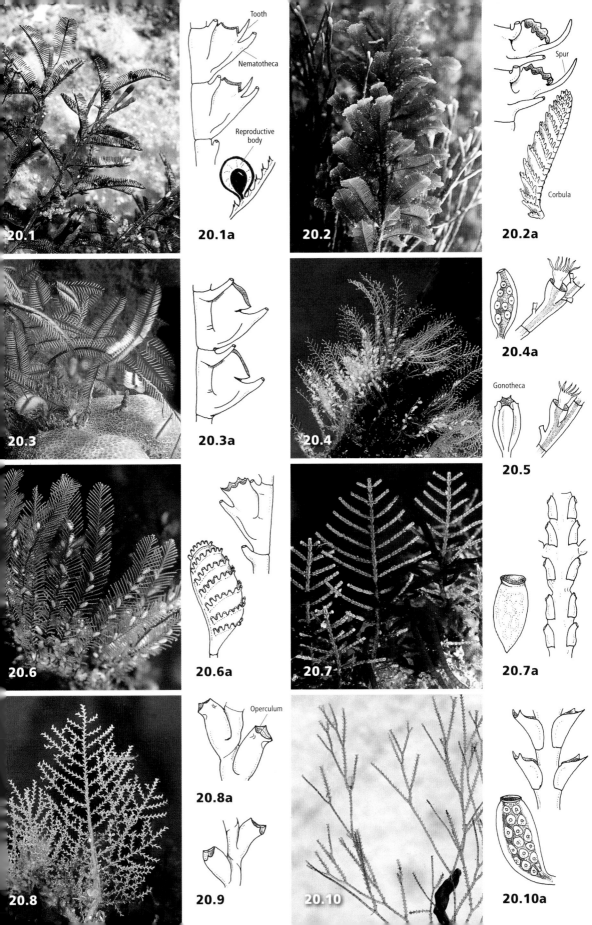

20.1

20.1a Tooth · Nematotheca · Reproductive body

20.2

20.2a Spur · Corbula

20.3

20.3a

20.4

20.4a

20.5 Gonotheca

20.6

20.6a

20.7

20.7a

20.8

20.8a Operculum

20.9

20.10

20.10a

PLATE 21

Bluebottles & their kin   Hydrozoa

The most unusual of the hydrozoans are the bluebottles, which form colonies of highly specialised individuals. One individual is modified into a float with a gas gland that inflates it with a mix of nitrogen and carbon monoxide. Gastrozooids (tubular individuals with a mouth) take in and digest food, and distribute it to the rest of the colony. Dactylozooids comprise a single massive tentacle for defence and prey capture, while gonozooids are solely reproductive.

21.1 **Bluebottle or Portuguese man-of-war**   *Physalia physalis*

Unmistakable with its inflated, blue-green float and long, trailing tentacles. **Size:** Float 50 mm long, tentacles up to 10 m long, but contracting to about 300 mm. **Biology:** Floats on the surface of the sea and is vulnerable to being cast ashore by onshore winds. Because of differences in the shapes of their floats, 'left-handed' and 'right-handed' individuals are blown to port or starboard respectively. On the west coast of South Africa there are more left-handed individuals, because they are less likely to be stranded by the prevailing southeasterly winds. Bluebottles inflict painful stings, best treated by rinsing off with sea water (not fresh water, which increases the discharge rate of the stinging cells) and applying hot water (which is more effective than ice, and also effective for jellyfish stings). Use of vinegar is no longer recommended. Severe cases are rare, but can lead to lethal cardiovascular and respiratory collapse. Such cases should be treated by a medical practitioner with intravenous antihistamines and steroids. Despite their venomous stings, bluebottles are regularly eaten by the sea swallow (94.3), plough snails (88.4) and loggerhead turtles (157.2). There is argument about the identity of the species that occurs in the Indo-Pacific and southern Africa, with some calling it *P. utriculus* on the grounds of its smaller size and single long tentacle; but the most recent view is that the two species are one and should be called *P. physalis*.

21.2 **Blue button**   *Porpita porpita*

The flat, circular, gas-filled float is distinctive, and is surrounded by a short, thin 'skirt'. Beneath the float hang a single, central gastrozooid and rings of short tentacles dotted with minute spheres carrying stinging cells. The float is silvery because of the gas it contains, and the skirt and tentacles a translucent blue colour. **Size:** 30 mm diameter. **Biology:** Floats on the surface and feeds on planktonic animals. Its sting is mild and has no effect on humans.

21.3 **By-the-wind sailor**   *Velella velella*

Float oval and carries a kinked, vertical 'sail'. Beneath the float are a central mouth and a large number of short, simple tentacles. **Size:** 35 mm float length. **Biology:** Like *Porpita*, *Velella* is harmless to humans, but can use its stinging cells to stun and capture tiny planktonic animals. It floats on the surface of the water and is driven by prevailing winds. Being a warm-water species, it is most common on the east coast, but is regularly washed ashore further south during the summer months.

Comb jellies   Ctenophora

Comb jellies are gelatinous and usually spherical or cucumber-shaped, with rows of hair-like, propulsive cilia. They also have complex sticky cells analogous to the stinging cells of the Cnidaria.

21.4 **Cigar comb jelly**   *Beroe cucumis*

Shaped like a rugby ball with an opening at one end for the mouth. Transparent and bedecked with eight longitudinal bands of hair-like cilia that beat continually, passing rhythmic waves of movement down the bands to propel the animal, creating stunningly beautiful, flickering, iridescent colours. **Size:** 30 mm. **Biology:** Planktonic, carnivorous, feeding on quite large, shrimp-like prey and other comb jellies. **SIMILAR SPECIES**: *Pleurobrachia* spp., sea gooseberries, have a spherical body about 10 mm in diameter and two very long trailing tentacles that are feathery when fully expanded. *Cestum veneris*, Venus' girdle, is flattened into a long thin ribbon up to a metre long, which swims using both its rows of cilia and muscular undulations. Luminescent when disturbed.

21.1

21.2

21.3

21.4

Worms & kin

Several unrelated phyla share a long, tubular, unsegmented worm-like body: **Platyhelminthes** (flatworms) (Plate 22), **Nematoda** (roundworms), **Nemertea** (ribbon worms), **Sipunculida** (peanut worms) and **Echiura** (tongue worms) (Plate 23).

Phylum Annelida comprises worms with a segmented body and includes two marine classes:

- **Hirudinea**, the leeches (Plate 24) lack appendages; many are external parasites and attach to their hosts with suckers.
- **Polychaeta**, the bristleworms (Plates 24–29) take pride of place, with about 800 species in southern Africa. They display a wide range of body form, from simple and earthworm-like, to the complex and exquisitely beautiful fanworms. Characteristically, each segment is flanked by clusters of stiff bristles (setae) born on lobe-like parapodia.

PLATE 22

Flatworms   Platyhelminthes

Only free-living flatworms are dealt with here, although the phylum includes many parasitic flukes and tapeworms. Flatworms have simple, flat, leaf-like bodies, and either glide along on a bed of tiny cilia ('hairs'), or by ripples of muscular contraction. A flexible, tubular or ruffled proboscis traps small invertebrates. The gut ends blindly, without any anus. Flatworms are hermaphroditic and cross-fertilise each other by hypodermic insemination; partners then lay strings of large, yolky eggs. The southern African fauna is poorly known and few local species are formally named.

22.1 Sunbasker flatworm   *Convoluta macnaei*

Tiny, elongate, photosynthetic worms, lacking a proper digestive tract (order Acoela). Coloured bright green by symbiotic algae, from which they obtain nutrition. **Size:** Up to 2 mm. **Biology:** Live in large colonies in waterlogged sand, concentrating in seepage channels, where they can colour the sand bright green. Migrate to the surface during the day to allow their symbiotic algae to photosythesise.

22.2 Skittleworms   Order Tricladida

Flatworms of the order Tricladida are small and taper towards the head, which bears two small triangular tentacles with an eyespot at the base of each. They glide along using cilia, rather than the muscular undulations of the larger flatworms of the order Polyclada (all remaining species below). **Size:** Generally 2–4 mm. **Biology:** Triclads are abundant under intertidal boulders but remain unnamed.

22.3 Carpet flatworm   *Thysanozoon* sp.

A large and spectacular polyclad flatworm. Body pink with a frilly margin, dorsal surface covered with distinctive pink to purple finger-like projections, which both camouflage the animal and increase the surface area available for oxygen exchange. **Size:** 20–30 mm. **Biology:** Common under boulders in the intertidal zone. Consumes small crustaceans.

22.4 Gilchrist's flatworm   *Planocera gilchristi*

Mottled brown with irregular black speckles. Margin frilly, but dorsal surface smooth except for two short, pointed tentacles towards the front end. **Size:** 20–30 mm. **Biology:** Preys on small worms, crustaceans and molluscs. Found under boulders near low tide.

22.5 Lightning-strike flatworm   *Pseudobiceros fulgor*

Dorsal surface smooth, with a distinctly ruffled margin. Background colour light brown with a darker brown margin, overlaid with numerous fine wavy white lines, either in parallel rows, or radiating like starbursts. **Size:** 20–30 mm. **Biology:** One of many tropical species in this genus. *Pseudobiceros* spp. feed on small invertebrates, such as gastropods and crustaceans, which they engulf whole.

22.6 Limpet flatworm   *Notoplana patellarum*

A flat, oval, grey-brown species without any dorsal projections, associated with large limpets. **Size:** 10 mm. **Biology:** Lives in the gill cavity between the side of the foot and the shell of large limpets, particularly *Cymbula oculus* (73.4). Feeds on small crustaceans, including tiny commensal copepods that share its specialised habitat.

22.7 Ink-spot flatworm   *Pseudoceros indicus*

Dorsal surface smooth and yellow, becoming pink towards the centre. Margin ruffled and edged with alternating purple and white spots. **Size:** 30 mm. **Biology:** One of many species in this tropical genus, distinguished by unique colour patterns. *Pseudocerus* spp. feed exclusively on colonial ascidians.

22.8 Divided flatworm   *Pseudoceros* cf *dimidiatus*

Margin ruffled and edged in yellow, dorsal surface variably but symmetrically striped in black and white (two very different specimens shown here). **Size:** About 30 mm. **Biology:** *Pseudoceros* spp. all feed on compound ascidians.

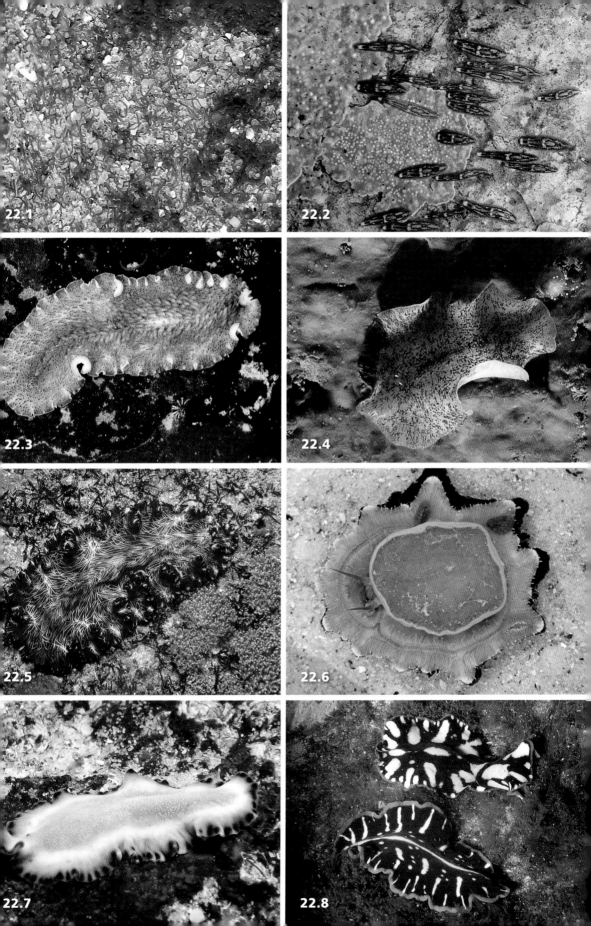

22.1

22.2

22.3

22.4

22.5

22.6

22.7

22.8

PLATE 23

Unsegmented worms

Nematoda, Nemertea, Echiura & Sipunculida

Unsegmented worms incorporate the following four phyla that are not closely related but for convenience are grouped together.

Roundworms   Nematoda

Very slender, elongate, cylindrical and tapering at both ends; covered in a tough cuticle. Widespread and numerous but often overlooked because they are tiny. Many are parasitic, especially in fish. Snoek (143.1) are densely infected by the nematode Anisakis *sp.*

23.1 Mussel-bed roundworm

Unidentified but common in the byssal threads of mussels, and typical of the phylum.

Ribbon or proboscis worms   Nemertea

Thin, very elongate, unsegmented worms with a soft, elastic, flat body that can vary enormously in length. All are carnivorous, capturing small invertebrates with a flexible proboscis that is shot out from the front of the head. One estuarine species, the 300 mm long Polybrachiorhynchus dayi *(recognised by its branching proboscis), is used as bait.*

23.2 Black-back ribbon worm   *Baseodiscus hemprichii*

White, with two dark bars on the head and a longitudinal dorsal stripe. **Size:** 0.5–1 m long; 4 mm wide. **Biology:** Hides under boulders and in coral rubble.
SIMILAR SPECIES:
23.3 *Lineus ornatus* (Western Cape) is blue-grey, with characteristic white lips and a broad white band across the back of the head. Found under intertidal boulders.
23.4 *Lineus lacticapitatus* (False Bay–East London) is similar, but mauve, with a distinct white front part to the head, and is found under stones in sandy pools. *Cerebratulus fuscus* (entire region) is flattened and a uniform yellowish white; 50 mm long. Head triangular and pointed. Burrows in sand on exposed beaches.

Tongue or spoon worms   Echiura

Soft, sac-like, unsegmented body; proboscis very extensible and tongue-shaped.

23.5 Opaque tongue worm   *Ochetostoma capense*

Sausage-shaped, with an opaque wall and numerous minute papillae. 'Tongue' pale yellow. **Size:** 40 mm. **Biology:** Burrows in mud and consumes surface detritus. SIMILAR SPECIES: *O. formulosum* (Durban northwards) has a translucent body and few papillae.

Peanut worms   Sipunculida

Tough, unsegmented and bulbous, with an elongate, tubular, anterior process (the introvert) that can be squeezed out by muscular contraction and then retracted. The mouth at the tip of the introvert is surrounded by a frill of short tentacles, used to gather detritus.

23.6 Common peanut worm   *Golfingia capensis*

Surface lacking papillae, yellowish brown. Introvert longer than the body and smooth, with a single ring of short, evenly spaced tentacles. **Size:** 20–40 mm. **Biology:** Clusters under stones on rocky shores, especially where gravel accumulates. SIMILAR SPECIES: *Phascolosoma* spp. have small, scaly papillae on the body surface. *Siphonosoma* spp. have a short introvert and simple papillae.

23.1

23.2

23.3

23.4

23.5

23.6

PLATE 24

Segmented worms
Annelida

Leeches
Hirudinea

Segmented worms with no setae and 33 body segments, the first and last of which form suckers. Most are parasites, sucking blood from fish and crustaceans.

24.1 Warty leech
Pontobdella sp.

Easily recognised by the ring of wart-like tubercles on each body segment. **Size:** 20 mm. **Biology:** A free-living species found under boulders. **SIMILAR SPECIES:**
24.2 *Helobdella* sp. (Namibia–Agulhas) parasitic on rock lobsters; 4 mm long.

Bristleworms
Polychaeta

Head with a snout-like prostomium and a cylindrical front segment (peristomium) surrounding the mouth. Some have beautiful fans or tufts of feeding tentacles. The segmented body has pairs of lateral, leg-like parapodia carrying one or two tufts of bristles (setae). Fertilisation is external, and the larvae are tiny and planktonic.

24.3 Feather-star myzostomid
Myzostoma fuscomaculatum

Flat and oval; often yellow with brown-ringed, black bars. **Size:** 5 mm. **Biology:** Variously coloured to blend in with its host, the feather-star *Tropiometra carinata* (102.2).

24.4 Milky scaleworm
Antinoe lactea

Body completely covered by 15 pairs of dorsal scales, which are smooth, and coloured white with a grey crescent (24.4a). **Size:** 30 mm. **Biology:** Burrows in sandbanks in lagoons and estuaries. Eats small invertebrates. Often lives commensally in the burrows of the sandprawn *Callianassa kraussi* (47.1).
SIMILAR SPECIES:
24.5 *Harmothoe aequiseta* (Walvis Bay–Durban) has 15 pairs of scales with dark spines.

24.6 Common scaleworm
Lepidonotus semitectus

Twelve pairs of flat, bean-shaped scales, roughened by blunt, conical tubercles (24.6a). **Size:** 20 mm. **Biology:** Common, low-shore and subtidal zones. Carnivorous.
SIMILAR SPECIES: 58 species of scaleworms occur here.
24.7 *Lepidonotus durbanensis* (Mossel Bay–Mozambique) has 12 pairs of scales that are textured with low, spherical tubercles.

24.8 Two-tone scaleworm
Hemilepidia erythrotaenia

Front half of body covered with scales, which are half chocolate brown and half pale pinkish brown. **Size:** 60 mm long. **Biology:** Lives under low-shore boulders. Carnivorous. Previously named *Polynoe erythrotaenia*. **SIMILAR SPECIES:** *P. scolopendrina* (Lüderitz–False Bay) also has scales only in the front half of the body, but they are speckled uniformly grey.

24.9 Plump bristleworm
Euphrosine capensis

Body plump, oval and bright orange-red, with rows of short spines running transversely across each segment. **Size:** 20 mm. **Biology:** Found under stones on rocky shores. Often associated with sponges, upon which it may feed. Sluggish: scarcely moving when disturbed, apart from a tendency to curl up.

24.10 Fireworm
Eurythoe complanata

Body long and thin, flattened; colour grey-green with lateral tufts of white bristles and short red gills. **Size:** 140 mm. **Biology:** Very common in pools on tropical and subtropical rocky shores and among coral. Spines sharp; break off and release a fiercely irritating poison.

24.11 Bamboo worms
Euclymene spp.

Cylindrical, segments extremely long, bamboo-like. Head has a flat plate with a raised rim (24.11a). Anus sunken into a frilly funnel. **Size:** 120 mm. **Biology:** Burrows head down in sand, feeding on organic particles. Forms long, fragile, sandy tubes.
SIMILAR SPECIES:
24.12 *Nichomache* spp. build sandy tubes on boulders; head with an arched crest but lacking the flat plate that distinguishes *Euclymene* spp.

24.1

24.2

24.3

24.4

24.4a

24.5

24.6a

24.7

24.6

24.8

24.9

24.11a

4.10

24.11

24.12

PLATE 25

25.1 Mussel worm　　　　　　　　　*Pseudonereis variegata*

Cylindrical, robust, dark khaki-green. Like all of the family Nereidae, its prostomium has two short tentacles and a pair of swollen palps capped with tiny, nipple-like segments (25.1a). Four pairs of slender, tentacle-like cirri flank the prostomium. Parapodia large and lobed, with two tufts of bristles. Identification of nereids requires examination of the pharynx, which has two rings and is armed with two large jaws and dotted with tiny teeth (paragnaths) that distinguish the species. Often the pharynx must be dissected or everted by gentle squeezing to reveal the paragnaths. *P. variegata* has only two bar-like paragnaths on the basal ring of the pharynx (25.1a). **Size:** 150 mm. **Biology:** Common on rocky shores, among seaweeds, reef-worms or mussels. Popular as bait, but its collection destroys large areas of mussel bed. Eats small animals and seaweed.

25.2 Estuarine nereid　　　　　　　*Ceratonereis erythraeensis*

A slender, delicate worm that resembles *P. variegata* but is smaller, white, and completely lacks paragnaths on the basal ring of the pharynx (25.2). **Size:** 30 mm. **Biology:** Burrows in sandbanks in lagoons and estuaries.

25.3 Comb-toothed nereid　　　　　　*Platynereis dumerilii*

Brown; intermediate in size. Its paragnaths form characteristic, comb-like rows of teeth (25.3). **Size:** 45 mm. **Biology:** Herbivorous; abundant in rocky shore seaweeds, forming mucous tubes that bind the seaweed. Forms swarms during spawning, when its body is modified into a 'heteronereid' stage to improve swimming ability, the parapodia becoming paddle-like and the eyes enlarged.

25.4 Bar-toothed nereid　　　　　　*Perinereis nuntia vallata*

Fairly large and slender; body dull brown. Distinguished by the single row of bar-like paragnaths stretching across the basal ring of the pharynx (25.4). **Size:** 70 mm. **Biology:** In sheltered sandbanks or among rocky-shore seaweeds. **SIMILAR SPECIES:** 25.5 *Nereis* spp., all with groups of tiny conical paragnaths on both rings of the pharynx, occur around the coast in rock pools; seldom abundant.

25.6 Gilled nereid　　　　　　　　*Dendronereis arborifera*

Distinguished from most other species of the family Nereidae by its pale colour and the feathery red gills that lie on either side of the central part of the body (25.6a). It also lacks any paragnaths on either of the rings of the pharynx (25.6). **Size:** 60 mm. **Biology:** Almost completely restricted to black mangrove muds, where it can be very common. Probably feeds on detritus, as its gut often contains mud particles.

25.7 Beadworms　　　　　　　　　　　Syllidae

Small, thin, thread-like worms with long, tentacle-like cirri projecting from the sides of each segment of the body. As is the case in most members of the family Syllidae, the cirri are beaded in appearance (annulated). The head has two swollen palps that jut forwards, and three annulated tentacles. **Size:** 30 mm. **Biology:** Very common in tufts of seaweed. **SIMILAR SPECIES:** There are over 60 species in the family Syllidae, most being difficult to identify without microscopic examination of the teeth on the pharynx. *Typosyllis armillaris* (Namibia–Mozambique) has a long (35 mm), very thin body with short cirri that have only 8–12 annulations. *T. variegata* (whole coast) has 30 annulations in each cirrus, and broken brown bars across the anterior segments.

25.8 Glycerine worm　　　　　　　　*Glycera tridactyla*

Elongate, slender and cylindrical, tapering at both ends. Pink when alive, becoming white if preserved. Prostomium narrow and acutely pointed. Proboscis cylindrical, very long, tipped with four sharp jaws (25.8a). **Size:** 60 mm. **Biology:** Burrows in sandbanks; very active and lashes about when dug out. Proboscis can be shot out, extending almost half the body length when fully everted. Predatory: eats other worms and small crustaceans.

25.9 Nephtys' sand-worms　　　　　　*Nephtys* spp.

Body white, square in cross section. Parapodia with broad flat lobes and two tufts of bristles with a curled gill between them (25.9b). Prostomium small, stubby, with four tiny antennae. Proboscis eversible (but usually withdrawn in the body), lined with rows of soft prickles and a ring of finger-like papillae (25.9a). **Size:** 65 mm. **Biology:** Actively burrows in lagoons and sandy beaches. Named after the Egyptian goddess Nephthys.

25.1

25.1a
ynx
cle
Prostomium
Palp
Cirri
Parapodium

25.2
Jaws
Outer ring
Basal ring

25.3
Paragnaths
Proboscis

25.4

25.5

25.6

25.6a
Gill
Parapodium

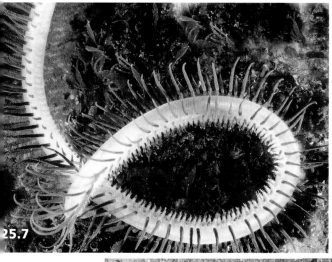

25.7

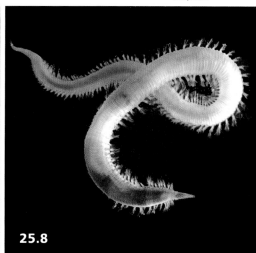

25.8

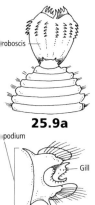

25.9a
roboscis

25.9b
podium
Gill

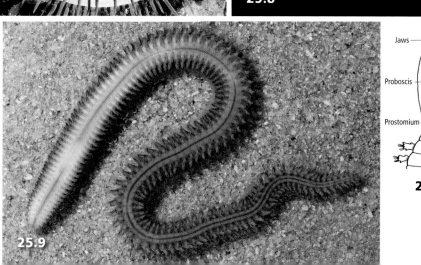

25.9

25.8a
Jaws
Proboscis
Prostomium

PLATE 26

26.1 Wonder-worm *Eunice aphroditois*
Prostomium flanked by rounded palps and five finger-like antennae. Next two segments lack parapodia but two tentacular cirri project upwards and distinguish all *Eunice* spp. from *Marphysa* spp. Cylindrical, mottled purple-brown with an iridescent blue-green sheen. Pale bar across segment 4 (most obvious in juveniles). Feathery gills arise above the parapodia from about segment 8. **Size:** 350 mm, reaching up to 1 m. **Biology:** Common in gravel under boulders. Carnivorous; large jaws inflict a painful bite. Used as bait.
SIMILAR SPECIES:
26.2 *Eunice antennata* (East London–East Africa) has beaded antennae. *E. tubifex* (Durban–Mozambique) has gills from segment 20; forms branching tubes.

26.3 Case-worm *Diopatra cuprea*
Head with two short thin antennae and five much longer ones arising from beaded cylindrical bases (ceratophores). Central ceratophore with 9–12 rings. Large, bushy gills sprout from segment 5 onwards (26.3). Front of body uniformly brown. Lives in a robust mucous tube to which shell fragments are attached. **Size:** 200 mm. **Biology:** Lives in sheltered sandy areas, its tubes embedded with just the shell-decorated top projecting.

26.4 Banded case-worm *Diopatra neopolitana*
Occupies a shell-decorated mucous tube like *D. cuprea*, and its body structure is similar, but its front segments have a central, dark oval patch (or five short bars). **Size:** 80 mm. **Biology:** Its tubes punctuate sandbanks in sheltered bays and estuaries.
SIMILAR SPECIES: *D. monroi* (Walvis Bay–Cape Point) forms tubes of hardened mud without shell fragments, has broad, dark bands across the full width of the anterior segments, a dark spot behind the central tentacle, and only 6–8 rings on its central ceratophore.

26.5 Estuarine wonder-worm *Marphysa elitueni*
Prostomium with two swollen palps and five antennae. Next two segments lack tentacular cirri (unlike *Eunice* spp.). Body distinctly flattened (26.5a). All its bristles are slender and jointed (spinigerous setae). **Size:** 250 mm. **Biology:** Burrows in sheltered sandbanks or in gravel under boulders. Used as bait by fishermen. Previously misnamed *M. sanguinea*.
SIMILAR SPECIES: Other *Marphysa* spp. are distinguished by their microscopic bristles.
26.6 *Marphysa macintoshi* (Port Alfred–East Africa, in muddy sandbanks) has a rounded body and spinigerous setae.
26.7 *Marphysa corallina* (Transkei–Mozambique, under boulders and coral rubble) has a flattened body and only falcigerous setae (stocky, slightly hooked and with a flanged tip).
26.8 *Marphysa depressa* (Saldanha–Durban, burrowing in sandbanks) has a rounded body and both falcigerous and spinigerous setae.

26.9 Three-antennaed worm *Lysidice natalensis*
Head with three finger-like antennae, about the same length as the two swollen palps (26.9). Reddish brown, speckled with white dots. No tentacular cirri on the first two segments of the body. No gills anywhere on the body. (Juveniles of *Marphysa* spp. sometimes also have three antennae, but possess gills.) **Size:** 75 mm. **Biology:** Lives on rocky shores among seaweed, in dead coral or in sand.

26.10 False earthworm *Lumbrineris tetraura*
Earthworm-shaped, long, cylindrical, pale brown; lacking gills. Parapodia stubby, with a single tuft of a few unjointed bristles. Prostomium conical, lacking eyes or antennae (26.10). **Size:** 60 mm. **Biology:** Burrows in sand-covered pools or sandbanks.
SIMILAR SPECIES:
26.11 *Lumbrineris coccinea* (Walvis Bay–Mozambique) has a smoothly rounded prostomium; anterior parapodia with jointed bristles (26.11). Orange-brown when alive. *L. cavifrons* (whole coast) has rounded prostomium; jointed bristles absent.

26.12 Iridescent worm *Arabella iricolor*
Prostomium bluntly pointed; four tiny eyes at its base (26.12a), sometimes concealed if the prostomium is contracted. Body long, cylindrical; iridescent bronze in life. No gills. Parapodia with few bristles. **Size:** 80 mm. **Biology:** Burrows in sand among rocks.

26.1

26.2

Antenna

Cirrus

Gill

26.3

26.4

26.5a

26.5

26.6

Gill

26.7

26.8

Seta or bristle

26.9

Prostomium

Parapodium

Unjointed
bristle
(seta)

26.10

Jointed
bristle
(seta)

26.11

26.12a

26.12

PLATE 27

27.1 Shell-boring spionids   *Polydora* spp.

Tiny worms that burrow in shells or limestone. The head has a pair of slender, grooved palps (characterising the family Spionidae). The fifth segment is swollen, with enlarged, hook-like bristles (27.1). Gills begin on segment 6 or 7. **Size:** 10 mm. **Biology:** Some are pests because they drill into oyster and abalone shells, creating unsightly 'mud-blisters', weakening or even killing these molluscs.

SIMILAR SPECIES:

27.2 *Boccardia polybranchia* (southern Namibia–Maputaland) also has a modified fifth segment, but gills from the second segment.

27.3 *Aquilaspio sexoculata* (Namibia–Zululand) has six eyes, feathery gills on segments 2 and 3, and a normal fifth segment. Previously named *Prionospio sexoculata*.

27.4 *Scolelepis squamata* (Lüderitz–Inhambane) has simple, strap-shaped gills from the second segment to the end of the body, and its fifth segment is not swollen.

27.5 Black boring worm   *Dodecaceria pulchra*

Small pitch-black worms. Prostomium blunt and rounded, flanked by a pair of grooved palps, which are followed by four pairs of long, thin, thread-like gills. **Size:** 10 mm. **Biology:** Occurs on intertidal rocky shores. Gregarious, living colonially and burrowing into encrusting corallines, their gills and palps projecting from burrow openings to obtain oxygen and to catch detrital particles for food.

27.6 Orange thread-gilled worm   *Timarete capensis*

Bright orange. Prostomium blunt. Numerous yellow tentacles on segments 1–3; long, tangled, thread-like orange gills over the rest of the body. **Size:** 90 mm. **Biology:** Lies buried in sediment or between mussels, only the long gills and tentacles visible. Previously placed in the genera *Audouinia* and *Cirriformia*. **SIMILAR SPECIES:** *T. tentaculata* (whole coast) has brown body and red gills; prostomium pointed. *T. punctata* (KwaZulu-Natal–Mozambique) is brown, flecked black; tentacles striped.

27.7 Woolly worm   *Orbinia angrapequensis*

Slender, with a pointed prostomium. No appendages on the head. Body divided into two regions. The anterior region has 18–24 flattened segments in which the parapodia form lateral ridges, behind each of which lie rows of small, conical, fleshy projections (foot-papillae). Posterior to that, the parapodia project dorsally, imparting a 'woolly' appearance. **Size:** 50 mm. **Biology:** Abundant in sandbanks in lagoons and estuaries, where they are often the predominant organisms. There are four species, but only *O. angrapequensis* is common. **SIMILAR SPECIES:** *Scoloplos johnstonei* (NW Cape–Mozambique) co-occurs with *Orbinia* and can be confused with it, but is smaller, proportionally more slender, and lacks foot-papillae.

27.8 Club worm   *Notomastus latericeus*

Resembles a miniature bloodworm. Club-shaped, with a swollen front end; two pairs of bristle-tufts per segment, excluding the first segment. **Size:** 15 mm. **Biology:** Burrows in mud and sandflats; feeds on organic matter and bacteria attached to sand grains. **SIMILAR SPECIES:** *Capitella capitata* (Cunene–East Africa) has bristles on all of the anterior segments. It is abundant in organically rich sediments and a useful indicator of organic pollution.

27.9 Bloodworm   *Arenicola loveni*

Large, dark brown, with tufts of pale bristles and branched red gills in the centre of the body. Tail thin and lacking gills or obvious bristles. Proboscis balloon-like and can be inflated or withdrawn. **Size**: As thick as a thumb; 800 mm long. **Biology:** Occurs in estuaries and lagoons and on sheltered, sandy beaches. Digs deep, U-shaped burrows, one end forming a funnelled depression. Water is drawn through the tube, oxygenating the sediment and encouraging bacterial growth. The 'farmed' microflora decomposes detritus and contributes to the worm's diet. A popular bait, but overexploited in some estuaries. Contains haemoglobin and 'bleeds' red blood when damaged.

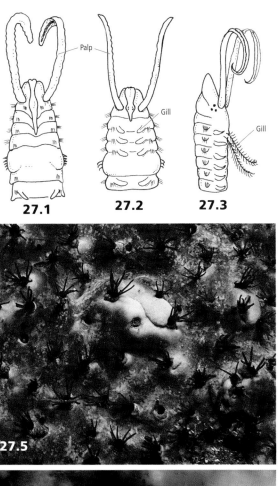

27.1

27.2 Palp Gill

27.3 Gill

27.4

27.5

27.6

27.7

27.8

27.9

PLATE 28

28.1 Flabby bristleworm — *Flabelligera affinis*
Body soft and floppy, covered with a pale green mucous sheath. Thin, simple bristles project directly from the body; parapodia poorly developed. Head surrounded by a cage of long, annulated bristles. **Size:** 30 mm. **Biology:** Lives under boulders in silty pools.

28.2 Cone-tube worm — *Pectinaria capensis*
Head with two comb-like arcs of 11–15 golden bristles. Builds a tapering, cylindrical tube made of sponge spicules, arranged in beautiful brick-like rows. **Size:** 90 mm. **Biology:** Lives in sandbanks, head buried downwards to feed on organic matter. SIMILAR SPECIES: *P. neopolitana* (Lüderitz–East London) makes tubes of coarse sand grains.

28.3 Cape reef-worm — *Gunnarea capensis*
Gregarious, forming massive intertidal reefs of sandy tubes (28.3). Head crowned with numerous short, unbranched, blue-black feeding tentacles (28.3a), which conceal a double row of 40–50 stiff golden bristles (28.3b) that form an operculum used to block the tube when the worm withdraws. Abdomen much thinner than the rest of the body and bends forwards towards the head so the faeces can be voided at the entrance of the tube. **Size:** 50 mm long; reefs span metres. **Biology:** Uses its tentacles to feed on particles. Cements sand grains to its tubes, which are flanged and designed so that passing waves suck out faeces but concentrate food in the entrance. *Gunnarea* is an aggressive competitor for space and cleans its tubes by scraping off settling organisms with its operculum. Sometimes accused of 'invading' or 'taking over' the shore, but fluctuations in its numbers seem natural; storms periodically decimate old colonies.
SIMILAR SPECIES:
28.4 *Idanthyrsus pennatus*, the Natal reef-worm (Durban–Mozambique), has feathery outer bristles in its operculum. It is often solitary or forms small aggregations.

28.5 Chaetopterus — *Chaetopterus variopedatus*
Anterior with nine flattened segments; middle region with a white cupule and three dorsal 'paddles'; posterior with two-branched yellow parapodia serving as gills. Occupies a parchment-like, sand-coated tube. **Size:** 80 mm. **Biology:** Amazing filter-feeding mechanism: wing-like limbs on segment 10 arch upwards and create a mucous net that is drawn backwards to form a bag by the pumping action of the 'paddles' and traps tiny particles. The end of the bag is caught by the cupule, cut into small pieces and passed forwards to the mouth in a central groove. The highly differentiated limbs give the animal its name: *varieopedatus* means 'variable legs'.
SIMILAR SPECIES:
28.6 *Mesochaetopterus minutus* (Durban–central Mozambique) is a miniature version that forms dense colonies of erect, 1 mm wide, sandy tubes.

28.7 Tangleworms — *Thelepus* spp.
Soft, floppy body; head highly modified and completely obscured by a tangled mass of thin, grooved white tentacles. Behind these lie shorter, unbranched red gills. Bristles appear from the third segment backwards (28.7a). **Size:** 50 mm. **Biology:** Like almost all members of the family Terebellidae, *Thelepus* spp. live in mucous tubes, often decorated with sand or pieces of shell. The grooved tentacles extend considerably to capture food particles that deposit on them. SIMILAR SPECIES: There are 44 species in the family, all difficult to distinguish once preserved because the gills and tentacles tangle and drop off.

28.8 Lobed tangleworm — *Telothelepus capensis*
This species also has unbranched gills but is distinguished by a long, tentacular lobe with a frilly margin (28.8). **Size:** 40 mm. **Biology:** Common in sheltered, intertidal sandbanks in lagoons and estuaries.
SIMILAR SPECIES:
28.9 *Nicolea macrobranchia* (Namibia–Durban) has two pairs of branched gills. Tips of bristles smooth, not spiny. Common under boulders and on sheltered sandbanks.
28.10 *Terebella pterochaeta* (Walvis Bay–Zululand) also has two pairs of branched gills, but has microscopic spiny tips to its bristles (28.10).
28.11 *Loimia medusa* (Cape Point–East Africa) has three pairs of branched gills and makes sandy tubes in rock crevices. The tips of its bristles are smooth. Feeding tentacles enormously extensible, stretching over 1 m, resembling pieces of string on the bottom of pools – only to instantly withdraw and disappear into the tube if disturbed.

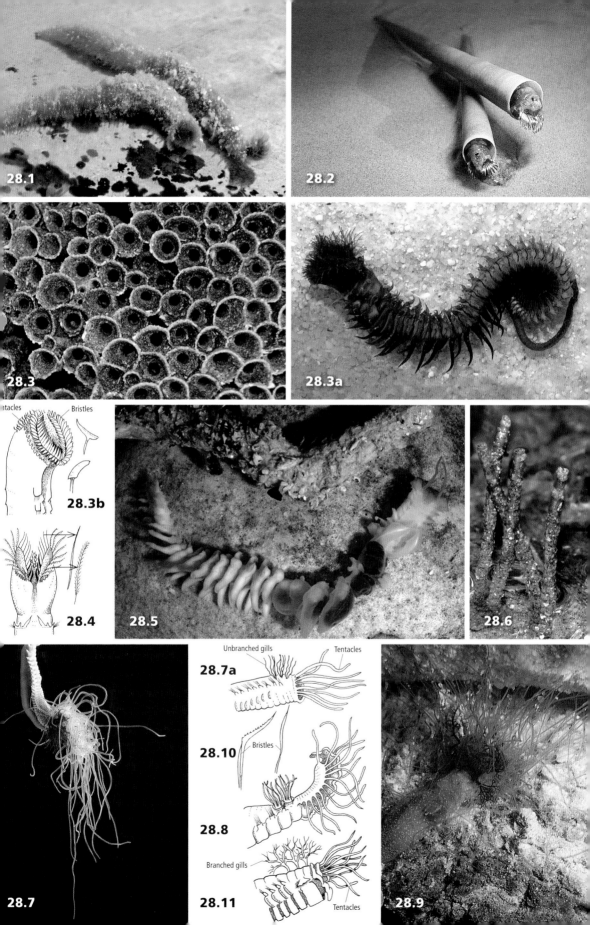

28.1

28.2

28.3

28.3a

Tentacles — Bristles

28.3b

28.4

28.5

28.6

28.7

Unbranched gills — Tentacles

28.7a

Bristles

28.10

28.8

Branched gills — Tentacles

28.11

28.9

PLATE 29

Branchlet / Branch of crown / Lappet

29.1 Feather-duster worm — *Pseudobranchiomma longa*

Two magnificent purple, white or orange spirals crown the head. No lappets (outer flaps) on branches of crown. Tube parchment-like (typifying family Sabellidae). **Size:** 120 mm. **Biology:** Solitary filter-feeder. Previously named *Sabellastarte longa*. **SIMILAR SPECIES:**
29.2 *Sabellastarte sanctijosephi* (Durban–tropical Indo-Pacific) also lacks lappets; its crown forms two semicircles that are partly bent forwards and folded over.
29.3 *Sabellastarte pectoralis* (Durban northwards) similarly lacks lappets, but its crown is orange-brown with dark flecks and forms an irregular 'mop', not a spiral. *Branchiomma* spp. all have lappets; the crown forms two spirals in ***B. natalensis*** (Lüderitz–Cape Point, not KwaZulu-Natal as name suggests!) and two semicircles in ***B. violacea*** (Walvis Bay–Durban). *Megalomma quadrioculatum* (whole coast) has an eye near the tip of most branches.

29.4 Pencil worm — *Sabella penicillus*

Stands erect and is housed in pencil-thin mucous tubes. Head with a single, almost completely circular crown that is usually pale with bands of darker rings. **Size:** 150–250 mm tall. **Biology:** Subtidal; lives at moderate depths, often in dense clusters in sandy areas among rocks, with the tubes projecting vertically upwards.

29.5 Gregarious fanworm — *Potamilla reniformis*

Crown forms two arcs of feathery branches, with small eye dots on their mid-outer surfaces. **Size:** Crown 10 mm. **Biology:** Lives in groups, forming mucous tubes that roll up like a scroll when the animal withdraws, protecting it from predators.

29.6 Red fanworm — *Protula bispiralis*

Head with two bright orange or red spirals of feathery branches. No operculum. Front of body with an obvious collar. Tube white and calcareous. **Size:** Body 65 mm. **Biology:** Grows singly under boulders or in crevices. Catches tiny particles with its crown.

29.7 Operculate fanworm — *Serpula vermicularis*

Head with two semicircles of feathery feeding appendages. Operculum funnel-shaped, with obvious longitudinal ridges that scallop the edge of the cone. Lives in a pinkish-white calcareous tube. Colour variable, usually red-pink but can be orange, purple or brown. **Size:** Body 15 mm, crown 10 mm. **Biology:** Solitary; attached to boulders.

29.8 Christmas-tree worm — *Spirobranchus giganteus*

Crown of two lobes with 4–6 whorls: pink, red, bright blue or white. Operculum ending in a flat plate with 2–4 short, blunt, spiky processes. Tube calcareous. **Size:** Up to 120 mm in length, but smaller locally, where the crown width is about 20 mm. **Biology:** Lives embedded in corals or rocks, often in spectacular multicoloured groups.

29.9 Blue coral-worm — *Pomatoleios kraussii*

Builds massive blue colonies of interwoven tubes, which are calcareous (a feature of the family Serpulidae). Head with two rows of feathery branches and a stalked operculum that has two pointed 'wings' and a flat calcareous cap. **Size:** Body 15 mm, tubes 2 mm diameter. **Biology:** Abundant on moderately exposed shores, often fringing pools.

Alien

29.10 Estuarine tube-worm — *Ficopomatus enigmaticus*

Builds colonies of entwined calcareous tubes, each with a trumpet-shaped mouth and rings down its length. Head with feathery branches and a cone-like operculum ending in short, dark spines. **Size:** Tubes 1 mm wide. **Biology:** Forms thick, jagged growths on jetties in areas of low salinity in estuaries. Harmless, except for snagging unwary bathers.

29.11 Spiral fanworms — *'Spirorbis'* spp.

Minute coiled worms with spiral shells. Head with a small number of feathery branches and a stalked operculum. **Size:** 2 mm. **Biology:** Abundant, dotting rocks and shells. South African species originally in this genus have now been reclassified.

29.12 Filigreed coral-worm — *Filograna implexa*

Tiny, gregarious, forming delicate, lacy, white calcareous tubes. Head with eight feathery orange branches. **Size:** Tubes 0.5 mm diameter. **Biology:** Exclusively subtidal; common in sheltered areas. Capable of reproducing asexually by splitting the body.

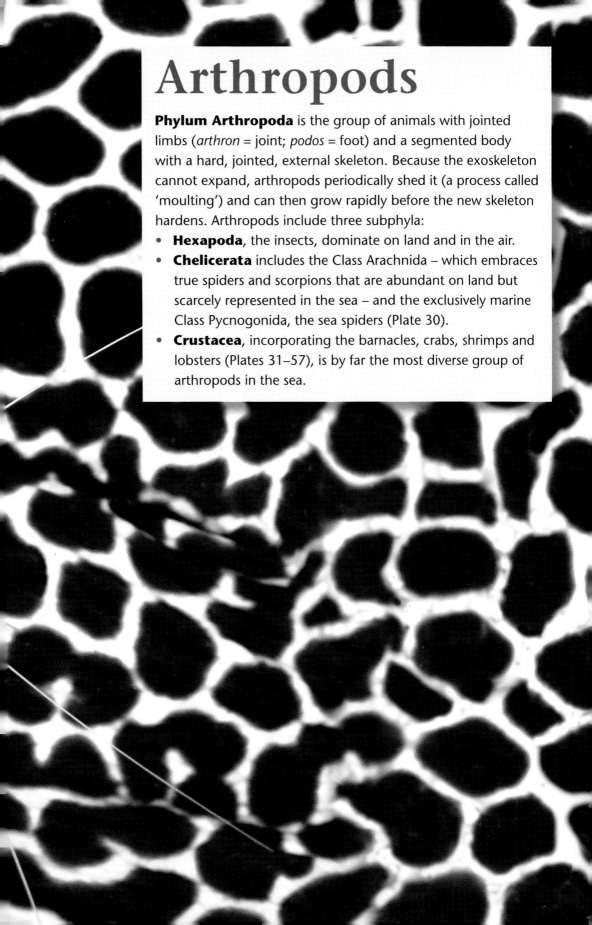

Arthropods

Phylum Arthropoda is the group of animals with jointed limbs (*arthron* = joint; *podos* = foot) and a segmented body with a hard, jointed, external skeleton. Because the exoskeleton cannot expand, arthropods periodically shed it (a process called 'moulting') and can then grow rapidly before the new skeleton hardens. Arthropods include three subphyla:

- **Hexapoda**, the insects, dominate on land and in the air.
- **Chelicerata** includes the Class Arachnida – which embraces true spiders and scorpions that are abundant on land but scarcely represented in the sea – and the exclusively marine Class Pycnogonida, the sea spiders (Plate 30).
- **Crustacea**, incorporating the barnacles, crabs, shrimps and lobsters (Plates 31–57), is by far the most diverse group of arthropods in the sea.

PLATE 30

Sea spiders   Pycnogonida

Sea spiders have four pairs of long legs, but are not true spiders. The head has a tubular proboscis and often two jointed sensory palps and a pair of pincer-like feeding appendages (chelifers). Slender, ovigerous legs hang below the head and the male uses them to carry fertilised eggs.

30.1 Compact sea spider   *Tanystylum brevipes*
Body off-white, short, compact; almost circular, legs quite short. Head with only a pair of palps. Proboscis a large, forward-pointing cylinder. Ovigerous legs present only in male. **Size:** About 10 mm. **Biology:** Abundant intertidally, often under boulders; pierces anemones with its suctorial proboscis.

30.2 Yellow sea spider   *Queubus jamesanus*
Bright yellow, with white bases and tips to the legs. Slender, with a long, tapering and downward-pointing proboscis, palps absent. **Size:** About 12 mm across. **Biology:** Details unknown, but common on rocky shores.

30.3 Scarlet sea spider   *Nymphon signatum*
Body bright pink to red, elongate and slender, with long spindly legs. Head with two pairs of appendages (palps and chelifers). Ovigerous legs present in both sexes. **Size:** 40–50 mm across. **Biology:** A striking species, usually found among hydroids.

True spiders   Arachnida

Body comprises an anterior prosoma, equivalent to a fused head and thorax, and a posterior opisthosoma or abdomen. The prosoma carries poison fangs, leg-like feelers (pedipalps) and four pairs of walking legs. The abdomen contains the lungs, reproductive organs and silk glands. Most spiders are terrestrial, but two occur on local shores.

30.4 Formidable shore spider   *Desis formidabilis*
Brown with a furry grey abdomen; fangs huge: about one-third of body length. **Size:** 20 mm. **Biology:** Common under boulders in the upper to mid-intertidal zone. Traps bubbles of air in silk-lined crevices or shells in which it shelters during high tide. At night and when the tide is out, it emerges to hunt for isopods and amphipods, especially *Hyale* (39.1).

30.5 Chevron shore spider   *Amaurobioides africana*
Distinctive chevron pattern on abdomen; fangs relatively small. **Size:** 15 mm. **Biology:** Occurs higher on the shore, emerging at night to feed on isopods, particularly *Deto* and *Ligia* (35.3 & 35.4) and on amphipods, especially beach hoppers (40.2).

Insects   Insecta

Insects have a distinct head, a thorax with three pairs of legs, usually one or two pairs of wings, and a limbless, segmented abdomen. They abound in terrestrial and freshwater habitats, but few occur in the sea.

30.6 Marine springtail   *Anurida maritima*
Minute, dark grey, six-legged, wingless creatures covered in short, waxy hairs. **Size:** 2–3 mm. **Biology:** Shelters in air pockets under rocks and shells, or in crevices during high tides. Emerges at low tide to scavenge, sometimes congregating around dead or dying animals. Often seen floating in clusters on the surface of rock pools.

30.7 Kelp-fly   *Coelopa africana*
A flat fly with a black thorax and bristly legs. Wings clear with a brownish tinge. Best recognised by its characteristic association with rotting kelp. **Size:** 10 mm. **Biology:** Not found inland, but abundant around decaying kelp, where it can reach pest densities. The white maggots are important decomposers of drift seaweed. When disturbed, typically flies a short distance ahead, remaining close to the sand. **SIMILAR SPECIES:** *Fucellia capensis* (Orange River–Port Elizabeth) is another grey kelp-fly with similar habits, which differs in having four stripes down the thorax.

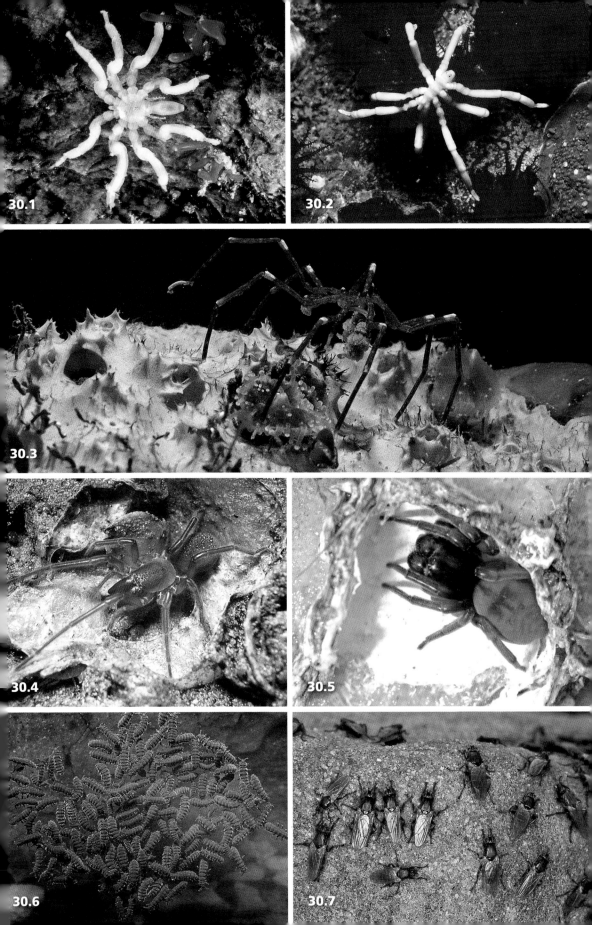

30.1

30.2

30.3

30.4

30.5

30.6

30.7

PLATE 31

Crustaceans   Crustacea

Crustaceans characteristically have two pairs of antennae and at least some limbs have two branches (biramous). The exoskeleton may form a shield (the carapace) that covers various segments of the body. The classes include the barnacles, seed shrimps, copepods and the huge class Malacostraca, comprising the crabs, shrimps and lobsters (Plates 33–57).

Barnacles   Cirripedia

Barnacles are highly modified crustaceans. The adults are permanently attached and encased in a series of shell plates, and the legs have become long, hairy cirri that are extended through an opening between the shells and comb the water for food. Eggs are brooded and expelled as tiny, shrimp-like planktonic larvae. Two very different forms exist: stalked barnacles (order Pedunculata), which live on floating objects or on other animals, and sessile acorn barnacles (order Sessilia), which have a conical shell and are attached to rocks or similar surfaces by a flat base. During low tide, or when threatened, sessile barnacles withdraw their legs and seal the opening with an operculum of four shell plates.

31.1 Yellow-rimmed goose barnacle   *Lepas anatifera*

Exclusively attached to floating objects by a tough, fleshy stalk. Body laterally flattened and enclosed by five shiny white shell plates. Stalk long and dark purplish brown. Margins of the smooth white shell plates outlined with yellow to orange border. **Size:** 30–100 mm tall. **Biology:** Dense colonies found on ships or floating objects, most commonly seen on driftwood cast ashore. The common name originates from the medieval myth that these barnacles grew into Barnacle Geese!

SIMILAR SPECIES: Most goose barnacles, including the following two, are cosmopolitan.
31.2 *Lepas pectinata* is smaller (20 mm) and has a very short stalk and distinct radiating ridges on the bright white shell plates. It has been found attached to a variety of smaller floating objects, such as feathers and *Spirula* (97.1) shells.
31.3 *Lepas testudinata* has a very long, pale, transparent stalk and a relatively small body. The shell plates are white and there is a slight yellow margin to the aperture. Commonly cast ashore attached to floating objects, especially kelp.

31.4 Crab barnacle   *Poecilasma crassa*

A small stalked white barnacle found growing on the shells of large crabs. Stalk short and naked, the three shell plates being in close contact with one another and completely covering the body. **Size:** 15 mm. **Biology:** Attached externally to the shells of large crustaceans, particularly crabs. Usually in deeper water, in this case on the giant spider crab *Neolithodes capensis*. **SIMILAR SPECIES:** *Octolasmis* spp. also commensal on crabs, but tiny (5 mm) and grow internally on the gills. The shell plates are greatly reduced and do not nearly cover the body.

31.5 Buoy barnacle   *Dosima fascicularis*

A thin-shelled barnacle with a short naked stalk and translucent blue plates and body. Most easily recognised by its unique, yellowish flotation ball. **Size:** 40 mm tall. **Biology:** Small individuals may occur on floating objects, but later secrete the characteristic polystyrene-like flotation ball from modified cement glands in the base of the stalk. Other barnacles attach to the float so that colonies form.

31.6 Rabbit-ear barnacle   *Conchoderma auritum*

This yellowish to brown stalked barnacle has lost almost all its calcareous plates, giving it a fleshy appearance. Two distinctive, fleshy, ear-like siphons project backwards from the top of the body and give it its name. **Size:** 50 mm. **Biology:** Found on whales and ships' hulls. Relies on the host to generate a water current and filters food passively from the current, the filtered water exiting through the 'ears'.

31.7 Whale barnacle   *Coronula diadema*

A large spherical species most easily identified by its habitat and unusual globular shape. **Size:** Up to 50 mm diameter. **Biology:** Lives partially embedded in the skin of whales, particularly humpbacks, but also fin, blue and sperm whales. The barnacle benefits from this association by escaping from predators and as an 'energy parasite' that filters food passively from the current generated by the swimming whale!

31.1

31.2

31.3

31.4

31.5

31.6

31.7

PLATE 32

32.1 Grey volcano barnacle — *Tetraclita serrata*

Unmistakable: tall, dark grey and volcano-shaped, with only four strongly ribbed shell plates, the edges of which are difficult to distinguish. **Size:** 20 mm. **Biology:** A dominant invertebrate in the mid-intertidal zone. Prefers moderately sheltered shores and usually replaced by *Octomeris angulosa* in wave-exposed locations.

32.2 Rosy volcano barnacle — *Tetraclita squamosa rufotincta*

Rosy pink with four vertically ridged shell plates; the plates are more easily distinguishable than in *T. serrata*. **Size:** 20 mm. **Biology:** An important component of the upper intertidal community on rocky subtropical shores.

32.3 Eight-shell barnacle — *Octomeris angulosa*

Moderately large with eight distinct dirty white shell plates. **Size:** 10–25 mm. **Biology:** A dominant species on mid- to low-intertidal rocks, forming extensive, often closely packed sheets; characteristic of wave-beaten areas. Feeds by passively holding its legs extended in the waves, while the water passes through them.

32.4 Toothed barnacle — *Chthamalus dentatus*

A small, flat, dirty white barnacle with a membranous (not calcareous) base, helping to distinguish it from *Balanus glandula* (32.8), which is similar in looks and habits. The projecting finger-like ridges on the six shell plates produce the characteristic star-shaped outline. **Size:** 5–10 mm. **Biology:** Common in the upper intertidal zone in southeast South Africa, Namibia and Angola, but extremely rare on the South African west coast.

32.5 Giant barnacle — *Austromegabalanus cylindricus*

Very large with six tall white-to-pink shell plates and a calcareous base. Tips of the opercular plates are modified into long and distinctive 'fangs' that project up through the aperture. **Size:** Typically 30–40 mm, but can reach 150 mm. **Biology:** Usually subtidal, sometimes forming thick mats on floating structures, where it can be a pest.

32.6 White dwarf barnacle — *Notomegabalanus algicola*

A small white species with six shell plates and a calcareous base. The flanges on the sides of each shell plate are perforated by transverse canals (a useful identification feature). **Size:** 5 mm. **Biology:** A short-lived and very fast-growing barnacle that can reach maturity in a few weeks. Typically overgrows mussel shells and low-shore rocks or encrusts floating structures. Can be a serious pest, fouling marine structures.

32.7 Striped barnacle — *Amphibalanus amphitrite*

Six smooth white shell plates with vertical purple stripes. Base calcareous; flanges on sides of shell plates solid. **Size:** 10–15 mm. **Biology:** Usually found in lagoons, estuaries and other similar wave-sheltered sites. Previously *Balanus amphitrite*. **SIMILAR SPECIES:** *A. venustus* (Hermanus–Mozambique) is easily confused with it, but is smaller (5 mm), has pink stripes, and is usually found under low-shore boulders. An introduced species.

Alien

32.8 Pacific barnacle — *Balanus glandula*

A conical off-white to mustard-coloured barnacle with six vertically ridged shell plates; lacks stripes (unlike 32.7 above) and leaves a calcareous base on the rocks when displaced. The junction between the four upper shell plates forms a distinctive M-shaped line. **Size:** 5–10 mm diameter. **Biology:** An introduced species originating from the Pacific coast of North America and first recognised from South Africa only in 2008. Now the most common intertidal barnacle along the southern west coast.

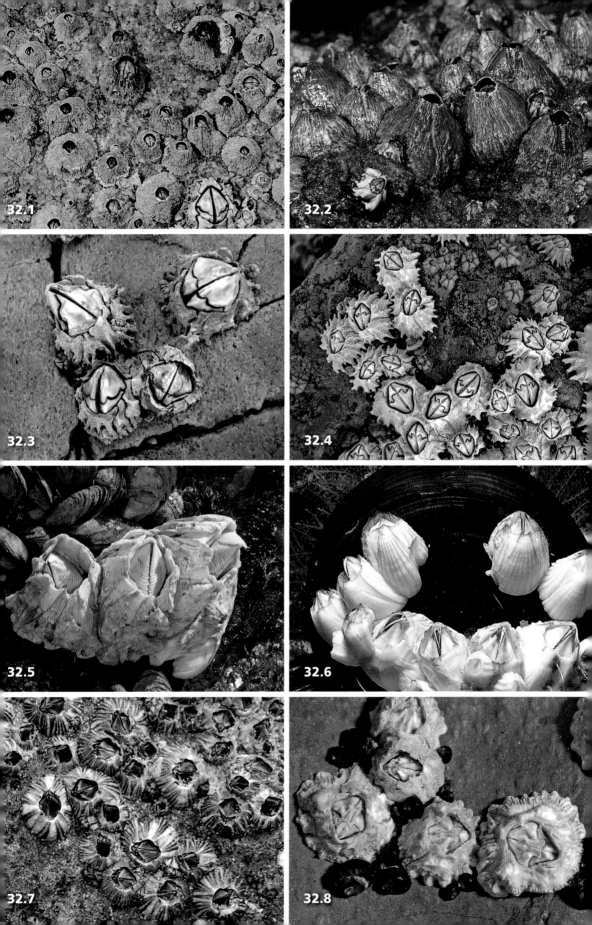

PLATE 33

Seed shrimps   Ostracoda

Head and body completely enclosed by a hard, bivalved, oval carapace, hinged along the centre of the back. Limbs project for burrowing or swimming.

33.1 Larger ostracods (2–4 mm) usually have a notch in the front of the shell, through which the hairy antennae project, while smaller ones are smoothly oval. Some are planktonic, but most plough through the surface layers of sand or mud, propelled by their antennae. The group includes carnivores, herbivores, scavengers and filter-feeders.

Copepods   Copepoda

Extremely abundant, small-bodied crustaceans of variable shape, which all lack a carapace. A major component of planktonic communities and a vital food source for pelagic fish. Some are bottom dwelling and others are parasitic (particularly on fish), with degenerate, sac-like bodies and trailing egg-strings.

33.2 Pelagic copepods   *Centropages brachiatus*
One example of the order Calanoida, typified by tapering cylindrical bodies, very long antennae projecting sideways, and a single, central eye. **Size:** 2 mm. **Biology:** Calanoids dominate the plankton and are a major link in the food chain from phytoplankton to fish.

33.3 Benthic copepods   *Porcellidium* sp.
A representative of the bottom-dwelling copepods (order Harpacticoida) that have short antennae and include broad flattened forms that colonise seaweeds, and elongated cylindrical ones that live between the sand grains on coarse sandy beaches. **Size:** 1 mm. **Biology:** Harpacticoids are ubiquitous bottom-dwellers that eat detritus and microalgae.

33.4 Glitter-bugs   *Sapphirina* spp.
A stunningly beautiful planktonic member of the order Cyclopoidea, most of which are oval and flat. All have small antennae and are distinguished by the fact that none of their antennae divide into two branches. **Size:** 2 mm. **Biology:** Planktonic; glitters in the water.

Malacostracans   Malacostraca

Shrimp-like or crab-like, with eight thoracic segments.

Leaf shrimps   Leptostraca

Thorax and part of the abdomen enclosed by a large bivalved carapace. Abdomen diagnostically has eight segments, unlike all other Crustacea.

33.5 Cape leaf shrimp   *Nebalia capensis*
Eyes stalked, separated by a characteristic, visor-like rostrum. **Size:** 10 mm. **Biology:** The only southern African representative of this group. Feeds on detritus under loose stones on rocky or mixed shores. Easily mistaken for an amphipod, but possesses a carapace.

Cumaceans   Cumacea

Small, distinctively shaped crustaceans with an enlarged, swollen carapace and a very narrow elongate abdomen, ending in a pair of long slender uropods.

33.6 Sandbank cumacean   *Heterocuma africanum*
Carapace inflated, length twice width; texture smooth. **Size:** 20 mm. **Biology:** One representative of 82 South African cumaceans. Burrows in sand or mud; filter-feeds or scrapes organic matter from sand grains; may emerge to swim in the water column.

Tanaids   Tanaidacea

Small cylindrical crustaceans with unstalked eyes. First two thoracic segments fused to head and covered by a short carapace, the other six segments remaining free. First pair of legs bears distinctive, strong nippers.

33.7 Slender tanaid   *Anatanais gracilis*
First antennae with one flagellum; abdomen has six segments. **Size:** 7 mm. **Biology:** Like most tanaids, builds mucous tubes among algae or under boulders. Feeds on pieces of detritus or small organisms, which it grasps with its nippers.

33.1

33.2

33.3

33.4

33.5

33.6

33.7

PLATE 34

Isopods   Isopoda

Isopods are a diverse group of small crustaceans abundant in virtually every marine habitat, from the intertidal zone to the deepest oceans. The body is typically flattened, but can be cylindrical. Head with unstalked eyes. The thorax (peraeon) bears seven pairs of similar legs (hence the name: isos = 'same', and podos *= 'foot'). The abdomen (pleon) usually has five segments, beneath each of which is a pair of flap-like pleopods, used for swimming and as gills. The tail fan has a central telson and lateral uropods. Some or all of the abdominal segments may fuse with the telson to form a pleotelson, or the uropods may be folded beneath the telson to form a chamber protecting the delicate pleopods. Eggs are incubated in a brood pouch under the thorax of females, and develop directly into the adult form. About 300 species occur in southern Africa.*

34.1 Keeled isopod   *Glyptidotea lichtensteini*
Body elongate and strikingly camouflaged with brown or pink blotches. A pronounced keel on the centre of the back ends in a spike on the front of the head. Pleon segments fused to telson. **Size:** 40 mm. **Biology:** Found intertidally under boulders. Herbivorous.

34.2 Metallic isopod   *Idotea metallica*
Body elongate and parallel-sided with an unusual, shiny metallic-silver colour. Two of the pleon segments are fully divided and a third partially divided from the rectangular telson. **Size:** Up to 30 mm. **Biology:** Cosmopolitan; usually found on drifting seaweeds. Sometimes large numbers are recorded swimming in the shallows of sheltered bays.

34.3 Reticulate kelp louse   *Paridotea reticulata*
Large, elongate, with net-like markings on a yellow-brown background. Pleon segments fused to the rectangular telson, which has a thick, grooved margin and ends in two sharp points (34.3a). Uropods folded under the telson. **Size:** 55 mm. **Biology:** Grazes on the spore-bearing parts of kelps, which are heavily defended by anti-herbivore polyphenolic chemicals. Its gut contains surfactants and a chitinous lining to combat these defences.

34.4 Green weed-louse   *Paridotea ungulata*
Green; never reticulated. Lateral margins of telson not thick and grooved; corners project as sharp points (34.4a). **Size:** 40 mm. **Biology:** Common on *Ulva*.
SIMILAR SPECIES:
34.5 *Paridotea rubra* (Kunene–Cape Point) grows to 45 mm, is usually red-brown and found on the fronds of red algae. Corners of telson not pointed.
34.6 *Paridotea fucicola* (Lüderitz–Cape Point) is a smaller, narrow-bodied species. Telson slightly tapering, with a small notch at apex. Abundant on eelgrass.

34.7 Fish louse   *Anilocra capensis*
A smooth-bodied slate-grey species parasitic on fish. Head triangular with short antennae. Legs end in strongly hooked claws that grip the host. Pleon has five segments; telson is rounded. Uropods often extend well beyond body. **Size:** Up to 60 mm. **Biology:** An external parasite on fish, such as the hottentot (133.1). Usually found on the side of the head. Opens up small wounds and feeds on the blood and body juices.
SIMILAR SPECIES:
34.8 *Cymothoidae:* There are many species of fish lice, including 'tongue-replacement isopods' of the family Cymothoidae, which occur in the gill cavity or mouth of the host, and end up withering and replacing the tongue! Female substantially larger than the male, as shown here after removal from the mouth of the host.

34.3a
Pleon
segments

Telson

Grooved
margin

34.4a

34.5

34.6
Notched apex

34.1

34.2

34.3

34.4

34.7

34.8

PLATE 35

35.1 Slender checkered isopod　　　　　　　*Mesanthura catenula*

Body very long and cylindrical, strikingly patterned by a wide black border around the margin of each segment. Antennae very short. Pleon segments fused. **Size:** 20 mm. **Biology:** Found under rocks or among shell gravel. **SIMILAR SPECIES:** *Cyathura estuaria* (Saldanha–Mozambique) is a uniform off-white, and common on estuarine sandbanks.

35.2 Giant beach pill-bug　　　　　　　　　　*Tylos granulatus*

Large, heavy-set, air-breathing isopods, resembling giant woodlice. Roll into a ball when disturbed. First antennae minute. Body surface granular, and pleon of five separate segments. **Size:** 50 mm. **Biology:** A nocturnal species that spends the day buried up to 40 cm below the surface above the driftline of sandy beaches, emerging in rhythm with the nocturnal low tides to feed on washed-up kelp. Entrance holes are covered by tiny 'molehills' of sand, but exit holes are open and flush with the surface, resembling pockmarks left by a walking-stick tip. Locally abundant, but numbers declining: the species is endangered by off-road vehicles travelling on sandy beaches. **SIMILAR SPECIES:** *T. capensis* replaces it from Cape Point to Port Elizabeth, and is recognised by its smooth body surface and smaller size (up to 34 mm).

35.3 Horned isopod　　　　　　　　　　　　　*Deto echinata*

An air-breathing isopod easily recognised by the pair of long curved 'horns' arising from the back of each thoracic segment. These are much longer in males than in females. **Size:** Up to 30 mm. **Biology:** Associated with kelp and other drift algae washed up on rocky shores. Feeds mainly on these algae, but also takes carrion or live prey. Usually mixed with the similar-looking *Ligia*, to which it is only distantly related.

35.4 Sea-slater　　　　　　　　　　　　　　　*Ligia dilatata*

An air-breathing species with a broad, flattened, smooth body. First antennae greatly reduced, second antennae shorter than thorax. Pleon segments not fused, and end of telson rounded. Uropods rod-like and projecting well beyond body. **Size:** Up to 22 mm. **Biology:** Occurs in vast congregations among drift kelp on rocky shores in the western and southwestern Cape, and is a major contributor to the decomposition of drift kelp. **SIMILAR SPECIES:** *L. glabrata*: similar range and habits, but its antennae reach the end of the thorax. *L. natalensis* (east coast) has a rounded telson. *L. exotica* (east coast) has one central and two lateral points on the telson.

35.5 Hairy isopod　　　　　　　　　　　　　　*Iathrippa capensis*

Flattened white isopods, with an elongate, oval body and long antennae and legs. Body and limbs covered with scattered spines. Pleon of one short separate segment, plus a rounded pleotelson. Uropods elongate and cylindrical, projecting well beyond tip of the pleotelson. **Size:** About 5 mm. **Biology:** Common under rocks in low-shore pools. Previously placed in the genera *Janira* and *Notasellus*.

35.6 Stebbing's isopod　　　　　　　　　　　*Joeropsis stebbingi*

Small, parallel-sided isopods with very short antennae. Abdominal segments all fused into a rounded pleotelson. Uropods minute. **Size:** Up to 5 mm. **Biology:** Found under intertidal boulders. One of many similar-looking elongate, short-limbed species in this and related genera. **SIMILAR SPECIES:** *Janiropsis palpalis* (Saldanha–Transkei) has long second antennae, prominent eyes, a speckled body and long, setose legs like those of *Iathrippa capensis*.

35.1

35.2

35.3

35.4

35.5

35.6

PLATE 36

36.1 Right-angled beach louse — *Eurydice kensleyi*

First segment of first antenna projects forward, but the rest of antenna is bent sharply at right-angles to the side. Second antenna almost as long as thorax. Pleon of five free segments; telson rounded, with a central depression. Off-white, speckled black. **Size**: 9 mm. **Biology**: Common on sandy beaches at the mid-tide level. A voracious scavenger; rapidly strips flesh from fish trapped in gill nets. Breeds year-round; lives for one year. **SIMILAR SPECIES:** *Eurydice barnardi* (west coast, intertidal) has shorter antennae (extending to peraeon segment 3) and an almost triangular, pointed telson that lacks a central depression. *Eurydice longicornis* (Table Bay, subtidal) has very long antennae (reaching pleon segment 5). Previously all three species were pooled under this name. Records for the southeast coast are probably an undescribed species.

36.2 Wide-foot beach louse — *Pontogeloides latipes*

Antennae not bent at right angles; both pairs about one-third the length of thorax. Upper lip (epistome) forms a sharp spike projecting up between bases of antennae. Pleon of five separate segments, the first covered laterally by last thoracic segment. Uropods and telson fringed with long hairs. **Size:** Up to 9 mm. **Biology:** A scavenger common on sandy beaches from the mid-intertidal zone to a depth of about 13 m.

36.3 Natal beach louse — *Excirolana natalensis*

Antennae not bent at right angles, first pair half the length of thorax, second pair two-thirds length of thorax. Pleon of five separate segments, the first overlapped on the sides by last thoracic segment. **Size:** 9 mm. **Biology:** A scavenger found in the mid-to-high intertidal zone of sandy beaches. Despite its name, uncommon in KwaZulu-Natal.

36.4 Tube-tail isopod — *Cymodocella magna*

Body smooth, pleon segments fused, but lateral grooves mark their position. Telson smooth: sides curved downwards and inwards to form a tube, directed slightly upwards at its tip. **Size:** 10 mm. **Biology:** Under intertidal boulders. **SIMILAR SPECIES:** The genus is characterised by the tubular telson; five other southern African representatives all have knobs or ridges on the telson, including *C. sublevis* with two rounded tubercles; *C. pustulata* with six, and *C. eutylos* with eight strong tubercles and additional granules.

36.5 Hairy-legged cirolanid — *Cirolana hirtipes*

A large, smooth-bodied species with hairy legs and setae fringing the telson and uropods (36.5a). A groove runs across the head between the eyes. **Size:** 20 mm. **Biology:** Found in sheltered sandbanks from Lüderitz to East London.

36.6 Crimped cirolanid — *Cirolana undulata*

Smooth off-white isopod with five separate abdominal segments. Posterior margins of thoracic segments finely crimped and those of abdominal segments finely toothed. Telson pointed, with a central ridge and crimp marks along margin (36.6a). **Size:** Up to 15 mm. **Biology:** Occurs in pools and crevices on rocky shores.

SIMILAR SPECIES: More than 23 other *Cirolana* spp. occur in southern Africa, many of which are common. Among the most frequently seen are:

36.7 *Cirolana fluviatilis* (Knysna–Maputaland) has rows of small tubercles on the hind margin of last thoracic segment and of pleon segments 3–5; telson has two pairs of tubercles. Reaches 12 mm. Found in estuaries.

36.8 *Cirolana venusticauda* (Lambert's Bay–East London) has tuberculate hind margins on the last thoracic segment and pleon segments 3–5; telson has dorsal projections. Inhabits rocky shores.

36.9 Spike-back isopod — *Parisocladus perforatus*

Male with a single distinctive curved 'horn' on the last thoracic segment, arching back over the pleon. Telson with keyhole-shaped notch at tip (36.9a). Female has practically no 'horn' and lacks the notch in the telson, but its telson has two pairs of low knobs (36.9a). **Size:** 6 mm. **Biology:** Intertidal, under stones or in seaweeds.

SIMILAR SPECIES:

36.10 *Parisocladus stimpsoni* (Lüderitz-East London) has a much smaller horn on the last thoracic segment and a narrow keyhole in the telson (36.10a); female has a very short horn, and no notch on telson (36.10a).

36.1

36.2

36.3

36.4

36.5

36.6

36.5a

Telson

Uropod

36.6a

36.7

36.8

36.9

36.9a

♂ Horn

Keyhole

♀

36.10a

♂

Keyhole

♀

36.10

PLATE 37

37.1 Variegated spherical isopod — *Exosphaeroma varicolor*
Body flattened and mottled pink or black and white. Pleon formed of a single fused segment (with lateral grooves showing where the original segments are joined). Telson triangular, with two small ridges near base. **Size:** 10 mm. **Biology:** Intertidal or shallow water, under stones or in weeds. **SIMILAR SPECIES:** The genus *Exosphaeroma* is characterised by a single fused pleon segment and an unnotched telson, and includes 14 southern African species that are distinguished mainly by the shape of the telson and uropods.

37.2 *Exosphaeroma hylecoetes* (Cape Point–East London) is a purely estuarine form, with a slightly furry body and hair-fringed uropods.

37.3 *Exosphaeroma planum* (Lüderitz–Port Alfred) is a strongly flattened species with slight ridges along the thoracic segments. Telson large and triangular. Uropods broad, the outer branch oval and the inner squared off.

37.4 *Exosphaeroma porrectum* (Lüderitz–Port Elizabeth). Head, thoracic and pleon segments each with a row of 4–6 rounded knobs. Telson long and pointed, with several rows of knobs and a keel near the tip. Occurs on rocky shores.

37.5 *Exosphaeroma truncatitelson* (Swakopmund–Cape Agulhas). Body smooth. Telson broadly oval with squared tip. Uropods pointed (37.5a). One of the most common isopods in lagoons, sandy beaches and sand-inundated rocky shores.

37.6 *Exosphaeroma kraussi* (Swakopmund–Cape Point). Body speckled. Tiny granules on hind margins of thoracic and pleon segments in male. Telson triangular and pointed with small dorsal ridges. Uropods broad and inner lobe rounded. Occurs on rocky shores.

37.7 *Exosphaeroma laeviusculum* (Lüderitz–Cape Point). Like *E. varicolor* but has a speckled body and a semicircle of tiny tubercles on the telson.

37.8 Hump-tailed isopod — *Cymodoce valida*
A large, heavy-set and slow-moving isopod that is often attractively mottled in reds and browns. Telson with a pair of large dorsal humps. **Size:** 22 mm. **Biology:** One of the largest isopods found under boulders or on shallow reefs. **SIMILAR SPECIES:** More than 20 *Cymodoce* spp. occur in southern Africa, many with strongly sculptured telsons.

37.9 Button isopod — *Sphaeramene polytylotos*
Unmistakable – head and body covered in flat-topped, button-like tubercles. Tip of telson with keyhole-like slit in the male, but not notched in female. **Size:** Up to 17 mm. **Biology:** Commonly found among mussels and barnacles on rocky shores and shallow reefs. Herbivorous; feeds on delicate, filamentous algae and simple green algae.

37.10 Roll-tail isopod — *Dynamenella huttoni*
Body smooth and parallel-sided; sides of telson rolled down forming a gutter at tip. **Size:** Up to 18 mm, but usually much smaller. **Biology:** The most common isopod among tufts of algae in the intertidal zone.

SIMILAR SPECIES: One of 10 *Dynamenella* spp. with similar habits. All are characterised by having the apex of the telson notched, or with a narrow slit.

37.11 *Dynamenella ovalis* (Lüderitz–East London) resembles *D. huttoni*, but the body is flatter and oval, not parallel-sided.

37.12 *Dynamenella scabricula* (Lüderitz–Knysna) has a slit at the tip of the telson that widens anteriorly (like a keyhole). Body finely furry with transverse rows of tubercles. Two broad humps on the pleotelson.

37.13 *Dynamenella dioxus* (Lüderitz-Cape Point) has a slit in the telson that widens anteriorly, and is roughly heart-shaped. The body is smooth except for the last peraeon segment of the male, which has two large, sharp, triangular processes.

37.14 *Dynamenella australis* (Lüderitz–Cape Agulhas) has a notch in the telson, with a knob at its base; inner branch of uropod slender and curved. Often shelters under limpets.

37.2

Uropod · Telson

37.4

Keel

37.5a

37.3

37.6

37.7

37.1

37.5

37.8

37.9

37.10

37.11

37.13

37.12

37.14

Inner branch of uropod

PLATE 38

Amphipods   Amphipoda

Amphipods are small but diverse and abundant in most marine habitats. Body compressed sideways (unlike the flat isopods); often protected by large side-plates. Eyes not stalked. First two pairs of thoracic legs (gnathopods) usually form nippers; the remaining five (pereiopods) end in simple claws (amphi = 'both', podos = 'foot'). First three abdominal limbs termed pleopods, the remaining three uropods. Amphipods occupy seaweeds or burrow in sediment; many build tubes. Eggs held in a brood pouch below the body and hatch into mini adults. Over 300 species in our region.

38.1 Skeleton shrimp   *Caprella equilibra*

Highly modified, extremely elongate, cylindrical body. Second pair of legs large, powerful nippers. Last three pairs of legs strongly clawed to grasp the substratum. Abdomen reduced to a tiny stub. **Size:** 10–20 mm. **Biology:** Clings to hydroids or algae, reaching out to grasp passing food items. Occasionally moves, inchworm-fashion, to a new perch. One of many similar species in the family *Caprellidae*.

38.2 Whale-louse   *Cyamus boopis*

Highly specialised amphipods adapted to a parasitic mode of life. Body flattened, with enormously strong legs tipped by powerful, grasping claws. **Size:** 12 mm. **Biology:** Feed on the skin of whales and may cause considerable tissue damage. Often associated with whale barnacles (31.7). Different species of whale and dolphin host separate species of whale lice, this species being from the humpback whale.

38.3 Bubble-eyed amphipod   *Themisto gaudichaudi*

Recognised by its one greatly elongated pair of legs, this is one of many members of the suborder Hyperiidea, which are semi-transparent and usually have huge bulbous eyes. Many have very elongate limbs and elaborate body ornamentation. **Size:** 10 mm. **Biology:** A common planktonic predator, consuming zooplankton and fish larvae. An important food source for sei whales and horse mackerel. Abundant in Antarctica.

38.4 Pram bug amphipod   *Phronima sedentaria*

Another hyperiid amphipod, recognised by its transparent body, huge eyes divided into two parts, crab-like claws and powerful abdominal appendages (pleopods). **Size:** 25 mm. **Biology:** *Phronima* eats out the internal organs of doliolid salps and, as evident in this photograph, uses the hollowed-out test as a mobile home.

38.5 Pocket amphipod   *Amaryllis macrophthalmus*

Sturdy, compact, with large side-plates. Eyes elongate. Antennae short, stout and equal in length. Second leg lacks nippers. Side-plate of third abdominal segment characteristically upturned, with a small 'pocket' above the corner. Brown with blue-grey side-plates. **Size:** 10 mm. **Biology:** A common scavenger in seaweed holdfasts or under loose boulders.

38.6 Compact amphipod   *Lysianassa ceratina*

Body sturdy and compact; limbs protected by long side-plates. Eyes elongate; antennae short and stout. Second pair of legs lacks nippers. Colour white to brown. **Size:** 10 mm. **Biology:** Scavenges under stones, among algae, or in sand or gravel. **SIMILAR SPECIES:** The most common of over 30 easily confused local species in the family Lysianassidae, most of which have a compact body, short antennae and enlarged side-plates.

38.7 Red-striped amphipod   *Ceradocus rubromaculatus*

Recognised by its distinctive, striped, pink-to-red pattern. First antennae much longer than second. First two pairs of legs with nippers, the second pair enlarged in adult males. Posterior edges of first three abdominal segments and their side-plates cut into a characteristic series of teeth. Last pair of uropods with two long, equal-sized projecting branches. **Size:** 20 mm. **Biology:** Usually found under stones on coarse sand or gravel.

38.8 Big-eyed amphipod   *Paramoera capensis*

Delicate and shrimp-like, with long, equal antennae. Eyes unusually large, almost meeting on top of the head. First and second legs both with small nippers. Uropods uniformly elongate. Colour very variable, most often pale, with a red 'saddle' across the back, sometimes mauve. **Size:** About 10 mm. **Biology:** Frequently the most abundant amphipod among seaweeds; also common in the plankton, particularly at night.

38.1

38.2

38.3

38.4

38.5

38.6

38.7

38.8

PLATE 39

39.1 Seaweed amphipod — *Hyale grandicornis*

First pair of antennae much shorter than second. Second pair of legs with powerful nipper in males, weaker in females. Last pair of uropods very short and with only a single branch. Colour green or brown, usually with circular white dots on the thoracic segments. Preserved specimens turn bright orange. **Size:** 10 mm. **Biology:** The most abundant amphipod on rocky shores. Survives high in the intertidal zone by nestling among seaweeds, on which it grazes. The most common of seven similar-looking local *Hyale* spp.

39.2 Brack-water amphipod — *Melita zeylanica*

Colour uniform pale green or yellow. Second pair of nippers large and unusual in that 'finger' closes against the inner surface, rather than the edge of the hand. Third uropods long, reaching well beyond first two pairs, and of characteristic form, the inner branch being only one-fifth the length of outer. **Size:** About 10 mm. **Biology:** Abundant in estuarine weedbeds.

39.3 Sponge amphipod — *Leucothoe spinicarpa*

Colour uniform pale pink to mauve. Nippers extremely large, the first pair characteristic in that the 'finger' is formed by the last two segments, which close against a long, spine-like projection arising from the third-last segment. **Size:** 10 mm. **Biology:** Lives commensally within the body cavities of sponges and ascidians. Believed to filter particles from the stream of water pumped by the host.

39.4 Louse amphipod — *Temnophlias capensis*

Highly unusual amphipods in that the body is flattened and isopod-like, with reduced side-plates. The legs lack nippers and are splayed to the sides, and the uropods are greatly reduced. Colour green to chocolate brown with characteristic rows of fluorescent blue spots along the back. **Size:** 4–7 mm. **Biology:** Common clinging to sponges and ascidians on the undersides of boulders in intertidal pools and gullies.

39.5 Spade-foot amphipod — *Griffithsia latipes*

Distinguished by a pointed hood that projects from the head like a 'nose', and a spiny, spade-like tip to the first pereiopod. **Size:** 7 mm. **Biology:** Abundant on exposed, sandy beaches. Previously named *Mandibulophoxus latipes*, but the current name honours the contributions of one of the authors of this book for his research on amphipod taxonomy. **SIMILAR SPECIES:** *Basuto* sp. (west coast) shares its appearance and habitat, but lacks the spade-foot.

39.6 Burrowing amphipod — *Urothoe grimaldii*

Short, chubby amphipods with wide, hairy legs. Colour off-white. **Size:** 4–6 mm. **Biology:** Superbly adapted for burrowing. The wide legs and broad body create a channel through which water and sand are driven by the powerful pleopods, propelling the animal forwards, while the mouthparts search the sand for food particles. Males have greatly enlarged eyes and elongate second antennae. One of eight similar local *Urothoe* spp.

39.7 Ornate amphipod — *Cyproidea ornata*

A small, but common and conspicuous species, best identified by its brilliant yellow and black colour pattern. The back is humped and the side-plates of segments 3 and 4 enormously enlarged, shielding the limbs. When the abdomen is tucked under the body, the animal is almost spherical. **Size:** 3–4 mm. **Biology:** Particularly common under the sea urchin *Parechinus* (105.6), but also moves around openly on rocky reefs, suggesting that the bright colours may warn predators that it is distasteful.

39.8 Ridgeback amphipod — *Ochlesis lenticulosus*

Unmistakable by virtue of its spectacular mauve and yellow colour pattern. The body is rounded and compact, with a distinct 'keel' or ridge running down the centre of the back. This is cut into a triangular tooth on each of the first three abdominal segments. **Size:** 4–8 mm. **Biology:** A conspicuous species found on bryozoans and sponges on rocky reefs. Thought to obtain protection by ingesting toxic chemicals from the bryozoan *Alcyonidium nodosum* (58.6).

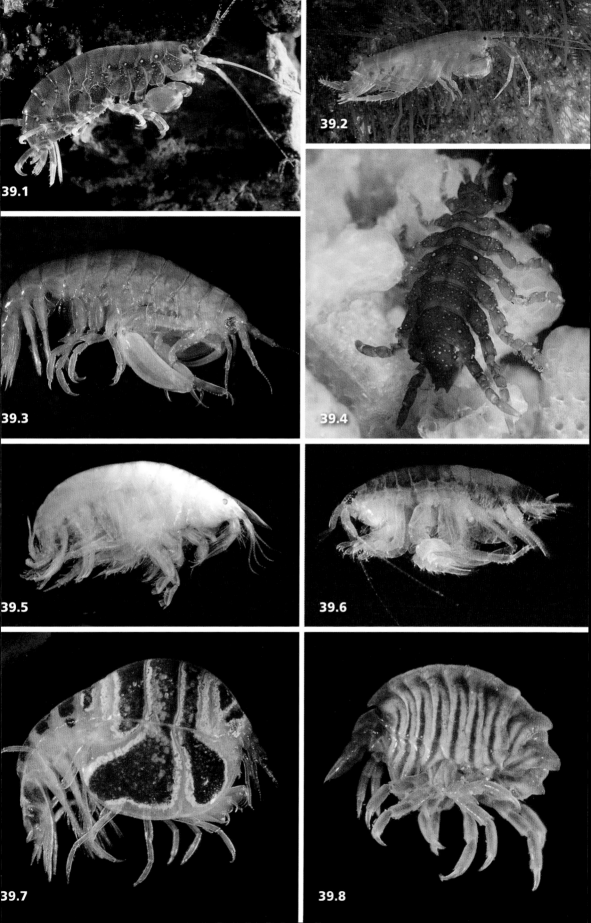

PLATE 40

40.1 Hunchback amphipod
Iphimedia gibba

Top of the first body segment humped, such that the head is directed downwards. First four side-plates elongate and pointed. Brown, with vertical yellow stripes and numerous fluorescent blue spots. A bright yellow stripe runs down the centre of the back. **Size:** 5 mm. **Biology:** Found in coarse sediments and moving openly on rocky reefs. Has been seen feeding on the toxic bryozoan *Alcyonidium nodosum* (58.6) and obtains protection from predators as a result.

40.2 Beach hopper
Talorchestia capensis

Body off-white. First pair of antennae much shorter than second. Second pair of legs of male with large nippers, the palm of the hand with a deep semicircular excision. Last three pairs of legs elongate and splayed sideways to support animal upright. **Size:** 10–20 mm. **Biology:** A familiar, air-breathing scavenger found in vast numbers at or above the driftline of sandy beaches. Often concealed under drift material, exploding into activity if disturbed. At night, hops clumsily about the beach in search of freshly deposited seaweeds. Shortly before dawn, returns up the beach and burrows into the dry sand. Consumed by many shorebirds and by galjoen (135.7).
SIMILAR SPECIES:
40.3 *Talorchestia quadrispinosa* (northern Namibia–False Bay) has white margin to eyes. Males have base of fourth and fifth legs expanded and a prominent pair of spines on the back of each of the first two abdominal segments. Habits similar to *T. capensis*.

40.4 Four-eyed amphipod
Ampelisca palmata

Head with two pairs of small red eyes, each bearing a bead-like lens. Antennae long and hairy, legs without nippers. **Size:** 5 mm. **Biology:** Constructs fragile tubes of fine sand or mud, and extends its antennae to filter food particles from the water. One of 13 *Ampelisca* spp. found in southern Africa, distinguished mainly by differences in the structure of the last pair of legs.

40.5 Hitchhiker amphipods
Jassa spp.

Adult males with very large second nippers that have a large 'thumb' projecting from the palm of the hand. Outer branch of third uropod with characteristic upturned tip and two triangular teeth on upper surface. **Size:** 5 mm. **Biology:** Build open-ended mud or silt tubes attached to rocks and other solid objects in areas of high water flow. Common fouling organisms on piers, buoys and ships' hulls. Filter-feed and prey on small crustaceans. Several closely related species occur in southern Africa, most of them introduced by shipping.

Alien

40.6 Fat-feeler amphipod
Monocorophium acherusicum

Body cylindrical, with the last pair of legs much longer than the others. Second antennae of males greatly inflated and toothed on the lower margin. First pair of legs with a weak claw, second pair very hairy but not clawed. Last three abdominal segments fused. **Size:** 4 mm. **Biology:** Abundant in sheltered, muddy areas, especially in estuaries and lagoons. A burrow is excavated by the anterior legs and the spoil ejected by rapid beating of the pleopods. The animal then propels water through the burrow with the pleopods, and filters particles from the current with its hairy legs. Previously called *Corophium*.
SIMILAR SPECIES:
40.7 *Aora kergueleni* (Namibia–Mozambique). All *Aora* spp. have a long, thin extension jutting out from the fourth-last segment of the second gnathopods (see left).

40.7

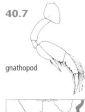

gnathopod

40.8 Nesting amphipod
Cymadusa filosa

Antennae elongate, eyes white, body mottled brown with large side-plates. Last pair of uropods with characteristic short, pad-like branches, the outer with two strongly curved hooks. **Size:** 10 mm. **Biology:** Weaves tubular nests out of fragments of algae or seagrass leaves. Herbivorous.

40.1

40.2

40.3

40.4

40.5

40.6

40.8

PLATE 41

Mantis shrimps   Stomatopoda

Highly specialised predators, recognised by massive raptorial second thoracic limbs, resembling those of praying mantids. Eyes large, stalked and incredibly sophisticated, with trinocular vision and better detection of colour than any other animal. Anterior half of thorax covered by a short carapace. Abdomen with powerful paddle-like swimming pleopods, and ending in an armoured telson and a pair of uropods. Mantis shrimps live in burrows that they defend territorially. There are two functional groups: 'spearers' impale soft-bodied prey, such as shrimps and fish, with a rapid thrust of the barbed finger; 'smashers' seldom have barbed fingers, but strike with the 'heel' of the raptorial limb to disable hard-shelled prey, including crabs and molluscs. Strikes have a force approaching that of a small-calibre bullet and can easily crack the glass of an aquarium. Twenty-five species occur in southern Africa, most in tropical waters.

41.1 Cape mantis shrimp   *Pterygosquilla armata capensis*

A 'spearer' with 6–8 teeth on the finger of the raptorial claw (41.1a). Telson keeled, with six large teeth and a central notch. Pale pink with metallic eyes (41.1b). **Size:** 200 mm. **Biology:** The only west coast stomatopod. Burrows in soft sediments; congregates in large swarms near the surface; eaten by seals, hake, birds and dolphins.
SIMILAR SPECIES:
41.2 *Lysiosquilla capensis* (Cape Town–Port Elizabeth) has 15–17 small claw-teeth.
41.3 *Harpiosquilla harpax*, the robber mantis shrimp, is a tropical sand-burrower; has barred abdomen; raptorial claw with 8–9 teeth. Telson lacks a central notch.

41.4 Sickle mantis shrimp   *Gonodactylus falcatus*

A 'smasher' with an untoothed, sickle-like 'finger' to the raptorial appendage. Usually bright green, but dark, almost black animals also found. Acute median keel on sixth abdominal segment. Five rounded bumps on telson (41.4a). **Size:** About 60 mm. **Biology:** Found under stones in the tropics.
SIMILAR SPECIES: There are several related tropical species.
41.5 *Gonodactylus chiragra* has three humps on the dorsal surface of the telson.
41.6 *Gonodactylus lanchesteri* has numerous small tubercles and spines dotted over the telson in addition to 3–5 larger bumps.

41.7 Peacock mantis shrimp   *Odontodactylus scyllarus*

Another 'smasher' with 2–9 teeth on the 'finger' and a strongly developed 'heel'. Unmistakable colours – green with red legs and claws, blue eyes, and navy-blue, red-fringed uropods. **Size:** 300 mm. **Biology:** Excavates holes in coral rubble and defends them aggressively. The outer limb of antenna 2 is flat, oval and brightly coloured and is flashed at intruders, repelling them with the impression of giant eyes.

Mysids or opossum shrimps   Mysidacea

Small, shrimp-like crustaceans with stalked eyes. A carapace covers the thorax but (unlike true shrimps and euphausids) is not fused to the last four thoracic segments. None of the thoracic limbs bears nippers. The abdomen is slender, with reduced pleopods and ends in a tail fan formed of a central telson and a pair of large branched uropods, with a characteristic round statocyst (a balancing organ) at the base of each uropod. Mysids are detritus feeders and form large swarms. The eggs are brooded in a marsupium or brood pouch, hence the common name.

41.8 Surf mysid   *Gastrosaccus psammodytes*

Telson deeply notched at the tip with 6–7 conspicuous spines along each margin (41.8a). **Size:** 12 mm. **Biology:** Abundant in the surf zone of exposed sandy beaches. Burrows by day, but emerges into the water column by night. Populations often segregated, with brooding females closest inshore and males and juveniles further offshore. SIMILAR SPECIES: Replaced in Namibia by *G. namibensis* (41.9) and in northern KwaZulu-Natal by *G. bispinosa* (41.10) and *G. longifissura* (41.11). *Mesopodopsis wooldridgei* (41.12) forms dense swarms beyond the breaker line and *M. africanus* (41.13) is estuarine. These species are distinguished by the shape and spines of the telson. *M. major* is familiar to Western Cape divers, forming dense swarms in kelp beds.

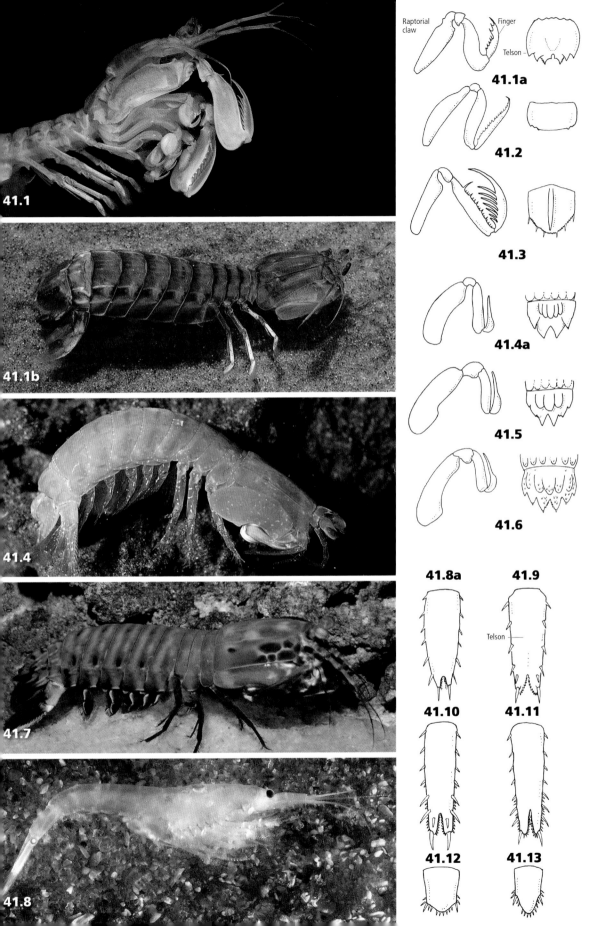

41.1

41.1a

Raptorial claw   Finger

Telson

41.2

41.3

41.1b

41.4a

41.4

41.5

41.6

41.7

41.8a   41.9

Telson

41.10   41.11

41.12   41.13

41.8

PLATE 42

Krill
Euphausiacea

Euphausids, or krill, are shrimp-like, with stalked eyes and a carapace covering the thorax. They swim almost continually, using their hairy abdominal appendages (pleopods) for propulsion. The slender thoracic limbs are fringed with stiff hairs and together form a funnel-shaped basket, through which water is sieved. Many species form huge swarms, and are an important food for fish, whales and other predators.

42.1 Light euphausid *Euphausia lucens*

First six pairs of thoracic limbs similar in size and shape, seventh and eighth pairs greatly reduced. Carapace has a single tooth midway on its lower margin. No dorsal teeth on abdomen. A conspicuous triangular tooth projects from the base of the first antenna. **Size:** 15 mm. **Biology:** Forms dense swarms near the surface during daylight along the south and west coasts. One of many euphausid species in southern Africa.

Lobsters, prawns & crabs
Decapoda

A huge, diverse order of crustaceans, typically with 10 'walking' legs.

ROCK LOBSTERS
ACHELATA (=MACRURA)

Robust large crustaceans with a long tail ending in a well-developed tail fan. The thorax and head are covered with a single shield, or carapace. None of the walking legs ends in nippers. Popularly called crayfish, they are correctly termed 'spiny lobsters' or 'rock lobsters'. Rock lobsters have an elaborate life cycle involving 13 larval stages and many months floating in the sea before metamorphosis into the adult stage.

42.2 West coast rock lobster *Jasus lalandii*

Orange-brown body; tail fan orange, blue and green. Thorax covered with spines; the front of the carapace has two large spines and a smaller central projection (rostrum) between the eyes. **Size:** 30 cm. **Biology:** The most important commercial rock lobster in southern Africa, 1 842 tonnes being harvested in 2007. Past catches of up to 10 000 tonnes steadily eroded the supply of animals of legal size (initially 89 mm carapace length). Growth is slow: males of 80 mm are 5–7 years old; females about 12 years old. Stunted growth from about 1990 has severely reduced catches. To spread the fishing effort over a wider size range and reduce mortalities of discarded undersize animals, the size limit was reduced to 75 mm for commercial fisheries in 1993. *Jasus* is intolerant of low-oxygen levels and, on the northern west coast, regularly becomes concentrated inshore to avoid low-oxygen waters. Occasionally hundreds of thousands become stranded on the shore. *Jasus* feeds on mussels, urchins and even barnacles, and eliminates many species where abundant. A recent shift of distribution has resulted in 'invasion' of the coast southeast of Hangklip, eliminating urchins that provide vital shelter to juvenile abalone. Rock lobsters are eaten by bank cormorants, octopus, catsharks and seals, but have a low natural mortality rate, making them susceptible to overfishing.

42.3 South coast rock lobster *Palinurus gilchristi*

Body orange, with alternating pinkish-orange and white bands on the legs and antennae. A broad plate between the eyes is flanked by outer horns and has about 11 shorter spines on its front edge. Abdominal segments 2–5 have anterior and posterior transverse grooves, which are filled with fine hairs and linked together near the mid-line by two longitudinal grooves, creating an 'H' pattern. The outer surface of the fourth-last joint of the legs is flat and hairy. **Size:** 300 mm. **Biology:** The second-most important commercial species in South Africa, being caught in lobster pots in deep rocky areas (50–170 m). Larvae drift with the Agulhas Current and settle in the south of the Agulhas Bank; juveniles migrate against the current back to the adult grounds.

42.4 Natal deep-sea rock lobster *Palinurus delagoae*

Very similar to the previous species. Reddish mauve with irregular ivory white patches, and banded legs and antennae. The fourth-last joint of each leg is almost cylindrical and lacks hairs. Abdominal segments 2–5 have only a trace of an anterior groove, which is not linked by medial grooves to the posterior groove. **Size:** 400 mm. **Biology:** Prefers open areas of mud and rubble at 180–300 m, and is caught mainly by trawling. Settles offshore and migrates inshore as it ages.

PLATE 43

43.1 East coast rock lobster
Panulirus homarus

Two sharp horns project forwards between the eyes. A transverse, scalloped groove spans each of abdominal segments 2–5. Colour brown to brick-red (or olive-green in one variety), with orange spines and blue and green markings on the head. **Size:** 250 mm. **Biology:** Occurs on surf-zone reefs at 1–36 m, coinciding with brown mussels, their major food. Feeds at night, hides in holes by day. As in other southern African rock lobsters (excluding *Jasus*), the ventral surface of the third segment of the antenna has a rasp (the stridulating organ) that is rubbed against the skeleton to produce squeaky or rattling sounds when the animal is threatened. *P. homarus* readily sheds some of its legs to distract predators, but they can regrow. Moray eels often share holes with *P. homarus*, and attack one of its main predators, the octopus. Male lobsters plaster the undersurface of females with a sperm packet (spermatophore), which hardens in seawater, and is broken open later by the female when she extrudes her eggs. The fertilised eggs are then attached to the pleopods on her abdomen, remaining there until the larvae hatch.

43.2 Longlegged spiny lobster
Panulirus longipes

Conspicuous large white spots down the sides, and a profuse scattering of small yellow-white spots all over its abdomen. Horns between the eyes flattened and oval in section. Grooves cross the abdominal segments, but are not scalloped. Orange stripes run down the legs, although some have spotted legs. **Size:** 350 mm. **Biology:** Shallow water, 1–18 m. SIMILAR SPECIES: *Panulirus penicillatus*, the penicillate spiny lobster (Maputaland northwards), is dark brown to olive-black, with orange spines and thin white lines down the length of the legs. Its horns are rounded in section.

43.3 Ornate spiny lobster
Panulirus ornatus

Blue-green carapace with orange spines. Antennae white in juveniles, turning pink. Transverse bands on legs. A dark band but no grooves across the abdominal segments. The spurs on the sides of each abdominal segment have a conspicuous, diagnostic white spot. **Size:** 50 cm. **Biology:** A shallow water species, 1–12 m, and the most abundant species in East Africa, where it is commercially fished.

43.4 Painted spiny lobster
Panulirus versicolor

Strikingly coloured, the carapace green with a black and white pattern on the sides, and the abdomen dull green with a characteristic white bar across each segment. The legs are black, with longitudinal blue or white stripes. Juveniles have bizarrely obvious white antennae, but they develop a pink base and grey flagella with age. Some individuals are blue instead of black. **Size:** 300 mm. **Biology:** Juveniles are common, hiding in holes with only their extraordinarily long, bright white antennae projecting.

43.5 Shoveller crayfish
Scyllarides elisabethae

Unmistakable, with its short, broad, flattened antennae. The body is dull brown, with a rough texture and orange pattern. The legs are strikingly banded vermilion. **Size:** 250 mm. **Biology:** Occurs most commonly in relatively deep water (about 150 m) on gravel, but sometimes found in the shallows. Shovels its way through the surface layers of sediment; feeds on worms and molluscs. Also called the slipper crayfish or shovel-nosed crayfish.

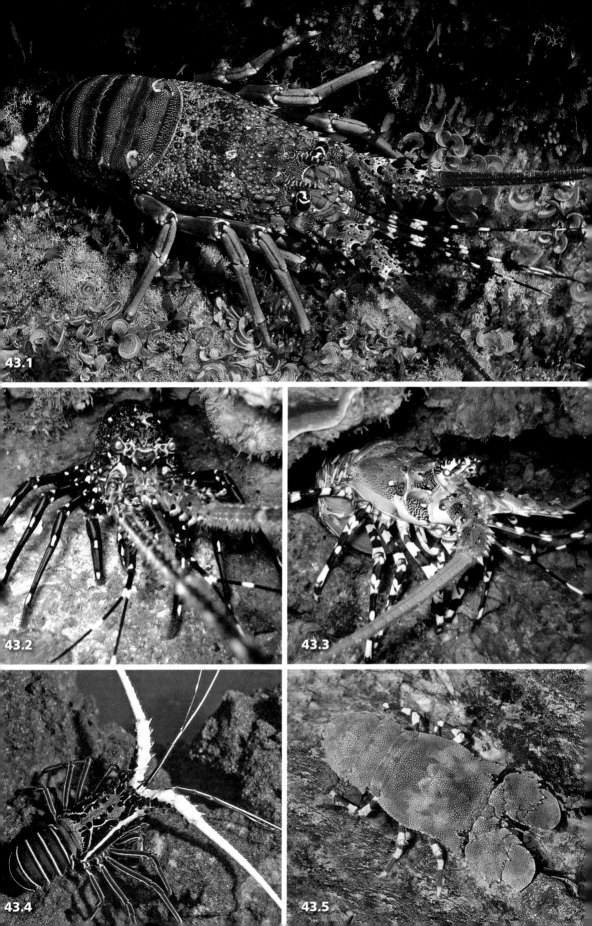

43.1

43.2

43.3

43.4

43.5

PLATE 44

SWIMMING PRAWNS   PENAEIDEA

Swimming prawns are distinguished from other prawns by the sides of the first abdominal segment overlapping the sides of the second segment, the last abdominal segment having a dorsal keel, and the first three pairs of walking legs ending in nippers. Species are distinguished by the shape of the long rostrum projecting forwards between the eyes, and the number of rostral teeth, as indicated by a 'rostral formula' (e.g. 9–11/1 indicates 9–11 teeth on the upper edge and 1 on the lower edge). Swimming prawns breed at sea, but their juveniles develop in nursery areas in estuaries.

44.1 Tiger prawn   *Penaeus monodon*

Rostrum moderately long, about twice as long as the eyestalks. Upper surface of rostrum with seven teeth, lower surface with three. Grooves on either side of the rostrum extend back for about three-quarters of the carapace length. Top of carapace ridged behind the rostral teeth, but this ridge is not grooved. Abdomen barred when the animal is fresh. **Size:** 90 mm. **Biology:** Commonly netted in estuaries and shallow water. With *Metapenaeus monoceros* it makes up 75–95% of the commercial catch in Mozambique and KwaZulu-Natal.

SIMILAR SPECIES:

44.2 *Fenneropenaeus indicus,* the white prawn (Transkei northwards), is plain white. Rostral formula 7–8/4–5. The dorsal ridge on the carapace is not grooved.

44.3 *Penaeus semisulcatus,* the zebra prawn (Durban–central Mozambique), has a rostral formula of 6–7/3 and the ridge on the top of the carapace behind the rostral teeth is characteristically grooved. The fifth pair of walking legs has a small outer appendage (an exopod), which helps distinguish it from *P. monodon.*

44.4 *Penaeus japonicus,* the bamboo prawn (False Bay–Natal), has a rostral formula of 9–11/1, its tail fan is mottled yellow and brown, and the central portion of the tail fan (the telson) has three spines on either side among the marginal hairs.

44.5 *Penaeus canaliculatus,* the striped prawn (East London northwards), is very similar to *P. japonicus,* with a rostral formula of 9–11/1, but its body is greenish brown with faint bands, and its telson has no spines on its margins.

44.6 *Metapenaeus monoceros,* the brown prawn (East London northwards), has a rostrum twice the length of the eyestalks that projects well beyond the eyes. Rostral formula 9–10/0. One of the commonest estuarine and shallow-water prawns, contributing substantially to commercial catches in Mozambique and KwaZulu-Natal.

44.7 Surf shrimp   *Macropetasma africana*

Smaller, more slender and active than most swimming prawns. Distinguished by the possession of a small outer appendage (an exopod) on the first pair of walking legs. Rostrum same length as eyestalks, upper edge strongly convex. Rostral formula 9–10/0, with a distinctive gap between the last two rostral teeth. **Size:** 50 mm. **Biology:** Found almost exclusively in, or just behind, the surf zone of exposed sandy beaches.

CLEANER SHRIMPS   STENOPODIDEA

The cleaner shrimps are similar to swimming prawns, except for the possession of large nippers on the third pair of walking legs.

44.8 Cleaner shrimp   *Stenopus hispidus*

Strikingly coloured, with red and white bands on the body and legs, tinges of blue, and long white antennae. The third pair of walking legs is obviously larger than the other walking legs, spiny, and ends in nippers. **Size:** 50 mm. **Biology:** Occurs on tropical coral reefs. Removes parasites and infected bacterial growths from the surfaces of fish, which will queue for the attentions of cleaner shrimps. Cleaner fish fulfil a similar function (see *Labroides dimidiatus* (147.4).

44.1

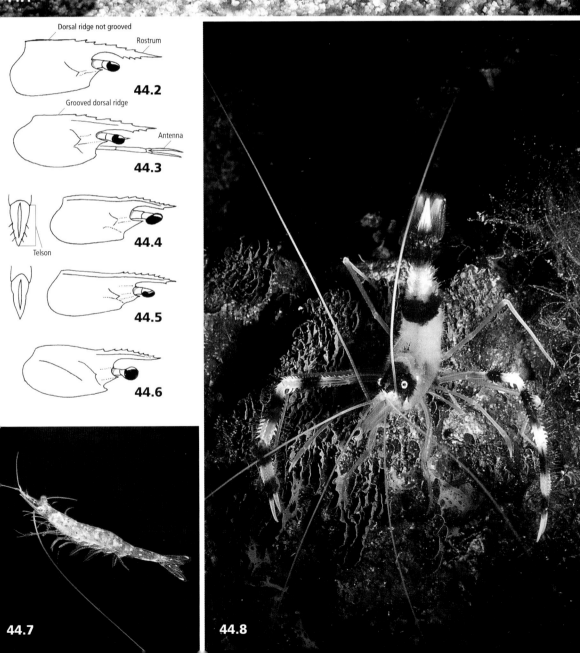

Dorsal ridge not grooved

Rostrum

44.2

Grooved dorsal ridge

Antenna

44.3

Telson

44.4

44.5

44.6

44.7

44.8

PLATE 45

BENTHIC PRAWNS CARIDEA

Bottom-dwelling (benthic) prawns, ill-suited to swimming, fall in the group Caridea, distinguished by the fact that the sides of the second abdominal segment overlap those of the first and third segments, the dorsal surface of the last abdominal segment is rounded, not keeled, and the third walking legs lack nippers. Females attach their eggs to the swimming appendages of the abdomen. Some species occur in estuaries, but none depends on estuaries as nursery grounds, and none is of commercial importance. Several form intimate relationships with other species.

45.1 Blood shrimp *Lysmata debelius*
Bright red, with white antennae and legs and a few white spots on the thorax. **Size:** 25 mm. **Biology:** Associated with coral reefs. Strongly territorial, attacking intruders. Occurs in pairs that form long-term bonds, each individual being capable of distinguishing its partner from strangers.

45.2 Skunk cleaner shrimp *Lysmata amboinensis*
Unmistakable: yellow-bodied with a red back and a white (or occasionally yellow) dorsal stripe. **Size:** 40 mm. **Biology:** A cleaner shrimp that sidles up to fish and removes parasites and dead or diseased tissues. Like the previous species, it undergoes sex change, initially being male when small (and hence incapable of producing more than a few energetically expensive eggs), and then becoming a simultaneous hermaphrodite with both male and female capabilities. Occurs in pairs or small groups.

45.3 Camel shrimp *Rhynchocinetes durbanensis*
Abdomen distinctly humped. Body red, with broad white bands at irregular angles, flanked with narrower white bands and spots. Eyes blue. **Size:** 35 mm. **Biology:** Hides in caves or under overhangs; often in pairs, but aggregates in large numbers to scavenge on dead animals.

45.4 Feather-star shrimp *Hippolyte catagrapha*
Most easily identified from its association with its crinoid hosts. Red with orange stripes or spots. Highly variable in patterning and colour, as it blends with its host. **Size:** 30–40 mm. **Biology:** Exclusively associated with the feather-star *Tropiometra carinata* (102.2), being found on about 20% of individuals, usually 1–3 shrimps per host.

45.5 Snow-capped anemone shrimp *Periclimenes brevicarpalis*
Difficult to distinguish from the background (a purple and green zoanthid in this case), because most of the body is transparent, but with blobs of white – a white bar between the eyes, a white bulb with pale, net-like patterning on the thorax, and white patches on the abdomen and tail, which is orange with a black border to all the lobes. **Size:** 35 mm. **Biology:** Obligate commensal with anemones or sometimes zooanthids. Experiences greater growth, survival and reproduction when associated with anemones than in isolation, but the anemone suffers, as it has pieces of its tentacles snipped off.

45.6 Harlequin shrimp *Hymenocera elegans*
Nippers very broad and flat and held in front of the face. Body pinkish white, with darker pink, blue-rimmed blotches. Legs with blue stripes. Antennae end in leaf-like lamellae. **Size:** 45 mm. **Biology:** Nearly always found in pairs, between which long-term bonds are formed. Consumes starfish, ripping pieces off the arms with its powerful nippers.

45.7 Zebra shrimp *Gnathophyllum americanum*
Stubby, barrel-shaped, with striking black and white stripes. Legs white with yellow and black bars. Rostrum short, pointed: no teeth. **Size:** 12 mm. **Biology:** Found on tropical shores in the shallow subtidal zone, hiding under stones. Slow-moving but territorial; chases away other individuals of the same sex. Previously named *G. fasciolatum*.

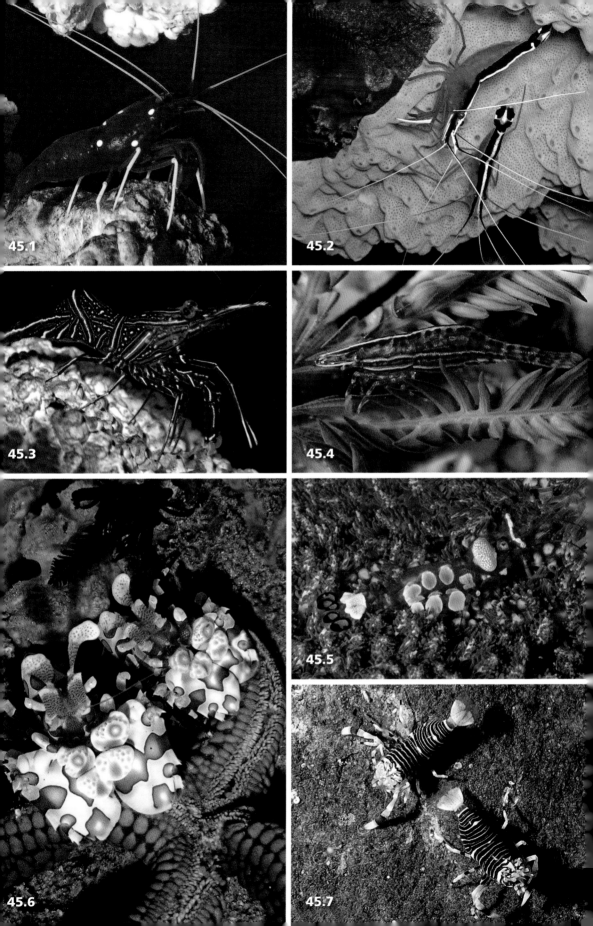

45.1

45.2

45.3

45.4

45.5

45.6

45.7

PLATE 46

46.1 Sand shrimp   *Palaemon peringueyi*

Transparent, with vertical bars across the body; opaque when preserved. Front legs with slender nippers and yellow spots at the joints. Rostrum well developed, toothed and almost saw-like. **Size:** 25 mm. **Biology:** Lives in intertidal pools and shallow areas with a sandy bottom. Scavenges fragments of dead animals. Forms huge swarms in calm-water areas. Previously named *P. pacificus*.

46.2 Broken-backed shrimp   *Hippolyte kraussiana*

Abdomen bent near the middle, giving a hunchbacked appearance. Rostrum long, tipped with three tiny projections; rostral formula 1–2/4–5. **Size:** 15 mm. **Biology:** Lives among estuarine weedbeds, particularly in seagrass. Colour varies with that of the background, but is commonly yellow, dull green or almost black.

46.3 Commensal shrimp   *Betaeus jucundus*

Small, equal-sized nippers on first walking legs. Body almost transparent. Carapace lacks a rostrum, but extends forwards to cover the eyes (46.3a). **Size:** 15 mm. **Biology:** Burrows in sheltered sandbanks in estuaries and lagoons. Often commensal in burrows of the sandprawn *Callianassa kraussi* (47.1), but the nature of the interaction is unknown.

46.4 Oriental shrimp   *Alope orientalis*

Body pale green, mottled brown; rostrum short, rostral formula 4–5/0. A large spine immediately above and behind each eye; second pair of walking legs with a small nipper, and the 'wrist' divided into about seven tiny joints. **Size:** 25 mm. **Biology:** Occurs among weed-covered rocks in intertidal pools; very common in warmer waters.

46.5 Cracker shrimp   *Alpheus macrochirus*

Left nipper huge, with almost parallel sides. Tips of walking legs 3–5 with two claws. Central rostrum either minute or absent, and no horns on the front edge of the carapace (46.5a). **Size:** 30 mm. **Biology:** Lives in kelp holdfasts or burrows among stones or coral rubble. The larger nipper emits a sharp click when snapped closed (familiar to divers in kelp beds), spurting out a high-powered jet of water. Both the sound and the jet of water stun small prey, and play a role in territorial defence, communicating the size and strength of a territory owner.

46.6 Snapper shrimp   *Alpheus lobidens*

First walking legs with strong nippers, one much larger than the other. No spines above the eyes, but a sharp, pointed, central rostrum (46.6a). Front of carapace keeled dorsally. **Size:** 30 mm. **Biology:** Common in sandy or muddy areas, forming burrows that it defends. Emits loud snapping sound. Previously called *A. crassimanus*.

SIMILAR SPECIES: Several species of *Alpheus* burrow in estuarine weedbeds or among coral branches. Often they share burrows with gobies, aiding in burrow construction and benefiting from the gobies' alert reactions to predators.

46.7 *Synalpheus anisocheir* (Knysna–Inhambane) is similar, but has no outer branch to the walking legs. Its carapace extends forwards over the eyes like a hood, and it has a short, but distinct, central rostrum, with a projecting horn on either side of it.

46.1

46.2

46.3

46.4

46.5

46.6

46.3a   46.5a   46.6a   46.7

Rostrum   Eye

PLATE 47

SANDPRAWNS & MUDPRAWNS

THALASSINIDEA

Sandprawns and mudprawns burrow in sediment.

47.1 Common sandprawn

Callianassa kraussi

Pink, fragile and translucent; internal organs visible. Nippers well developed; one much larger than the other (particularly in males). The 'wrist' of the nipper (third joint from the tip) is longer than broad, telson (central part of the tail fan) wider than long. **Size:** 60 mm. **Biology:** Abundant in estuaries, even those closed to the sea for years. Builds deep burrows; sifts sediment for food, ejecting particles from the burrow entrance to create miniature volcanoes. Oxygenates and turns over tons of sediment. This 'bioturbation' profoundly affects other organisms, diminishing bacteria, depleting sediment, consolidating bacterial films of mucus, burying diatoms, reducing meiofauna (animals <1 mm long) and inhibiting larval settlement of many species. Its effects on the environment are so profound that it is termed an 'ecosystem engineer'. Trampling and pumping prawns for bait collapse the prawns' burrows, harming the entire ecosystem. Females carry eggs on the abdomen; offspring dig tiny side-tubes off the parental burrow. **SIMILAR SPECIES:** *C. rotundicaudata*, the round-tailed sandprawn (Saldanha Bay–Durban), has a wrist that is longer than broad and its telson is as wide as it is long. It burrows in sand under stones on the open coast.

47.2 Estuarine mudprawn

Upogebia africana

Green-brown and robust. Nippers equal-sized and subchelate ('thumb' almost absent, 'finger' bending back to meet it). The first two walking legs have no spine at their bases. **Size:** 40 mm. **Biology:** Intertidal in estuarine muddy sands; absent from closed estuaries. Pumps water through U-shaped burrows; filters out particles on its hairy mouthparts. Gut laden with symbiotic bacteria, which may supplement its food. **SIMILAR SPECIES:** *U. capensis*, the coastal mudprawn (Walvis Bay–Mossel Bay), lives in mud under stones on the open coast, and subtidally in lagoons. The first two walking legs have a spine at the base, pointing inwards.

MOLE & PORCELAIN CRABS

ANOMURA

Mole crabs and porcelain crabs resemble true crabs, but are related to hermit crabs (Plate 48): they possess a tail fan, thin, upwardly bent fifth legs, and their second antennae arise outside the eyes.

47.3 Mole crab

Emerita austroafricana

Barrel-shaped body; abdomen tightly tucked under the thorax, and ending in a tail fan. Legs stubby and spade-like. Antennae as long as the body but usually rolled up and hidden. **Size:** 25 mm. **Biology:** Buries itself on exposed sandy beaches, extending its hairy antennae to filter particles from the waves. Moves up and down the shore with the tides. Collected as bait, and often called 'sea lice', a misnomer. **SIMILAR SPECIES:** *Hippa adactyla* (Transkei–Zanzibar) lives in the same habitat. Its body is flatter and broader, and its antennae only a third of the body length.

47.4 Lamarck's porcelain crab

Petrolisthes lamarckii

Crab-like, body flat and circular; nippers very large. Antennae long and thin, but often concealed. Brown or mottled green. Front margin with three low projections between the eyes; 'wrist' of nipper longer than broad. **Size:** 25 mm. **Biology:** Hides under stones high on rocky shores. Voluntarily sheds its nippers when threatened – the abandoned limb merrily snaps away to distract predators.

47.5 *Pachycheles natalensis* (south of Durban–Mozambique) has smoothly rounded margin between eyes; 'wrist' about as broad as long. Pink to red.

47.6 *Pisidia dehaanii* (East London–Maputo) has three obvious teeth on front margin between eyes, all of which are smooth. Body pink.

47.7 *Pisidia streptocheles* (Namaqualand–Port Elizabeth) has three teeth on margin between the eyes; central tooth finely serrated. White or pink.

47.8 Spotted porcelain crab

Neopetrolisthes maculatus

Nippers very large and flat. Body creamish to yellow-brown; covered with regularly spaced dark red-brown dots that are largest on the nippers and the dorsal surface of the body. **Size:** 35 mm. **Biology:** Lives among the tentacles of large anemones. A suspension-feeder, it also gleans mucus from its host.

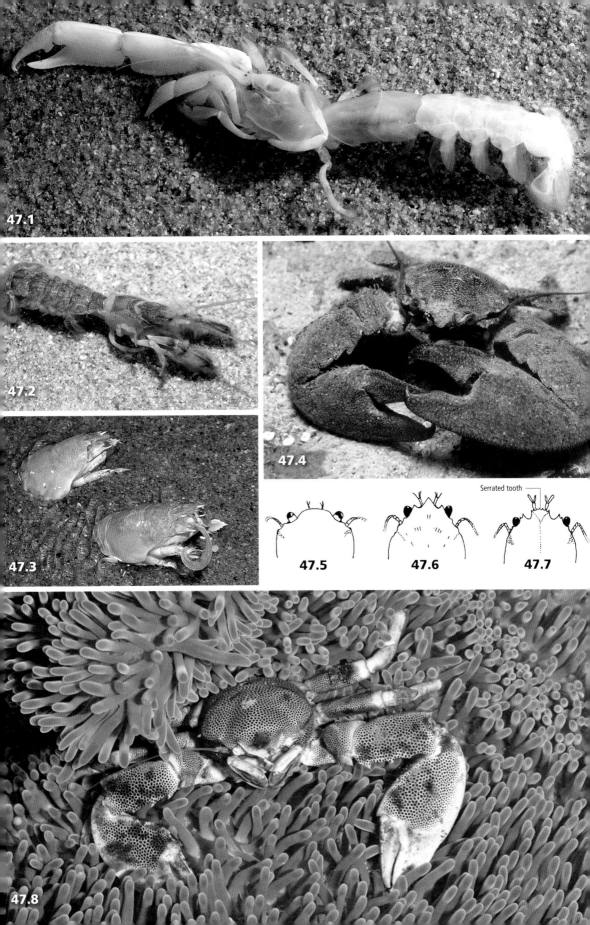

47.1

47.2

47.3

47.4

Serrated tooth

47.5   **47.6**   **47.7**

47.8

PLATE 48

HERMIT CRABS
ANOMURA

Hermit crabs are well known for occupying empty gastropod shells to protect their soft-skinned abdomens. To fit this adopted home, the abdomen and the appendages on the inside of the curve are reduced. The first pair of legs bears nippers, the left one often being enlarged to seal the shell when the crab withdraws. The second and third pairs of legs are for walking, while the last two pairs are reduced and grip the shell. As hermit crabs grow, they move into progressively larger homes, and often fight for shells. Most are scavengers, but some filter particles from the water using their antennae. Southern Africa hosts about 45 species.

48.1 Long-fingered hermit
Clibanarius longitarsus

Blueish to green, spotted with yellow setae. Claws equal, with black-tipped fingers. Walking legs with blue stripes along the length of each segment, last segment very elongate, black-tipped. Eyestalks long and yellowish, with black eye. **Size:** 25 mm. **Biology:** A scavenger common among mangroves in estuaries and calm lagoons.

48.2 Yellow-banded hermit
Clibanarius virescens

Body olive-green to brown, nippers about equal in size, spotted with yellow, the fingers yellow with black tips. Walking legs green to brown with the last segment banded with yellow. Eyestalks long; conspicuous white ring around the eye. **Size:** 10–20 mm. **Biology:** A very abundant scavenger in mid-to-high shore pools or shallow water.

48.3 Common land hermit
Coenobita cavipes

Terrestrial. Body cream to brown; left nipper large. **Size:** 30–40 mm. **Biology:** An air-breather that buries itself above the high-water mark by day, scavenging on land at night, penetrating well inland. Returns to sea only to wet the body and breed. **SIMILAR SPECIES:** *C. rugosus* (KwaZulu-Natal northwards) has a row of tubercles on the outer surface of the left hand, which it uses to produce a rasping noise.

48.4 Blue-eyed hermit
Calcinus laevimanus

Nippers dark brown, with characteristic white 'fingers'; left nipper greatly enlarged to block the shell when the crab withdraws. Eyes distinctively bright blue; eyestalks and first antennae banded brilliant blue and orange. Legs brown, last segment with striking white bands. **Size:** 10–30 mm. **Biology:** Common in tidal pools. Prefers low-spired shells, especially those of *Turbo* and *Nerita* (78.2, 78.4). **SIMILAR SPECIES:** *C. elegans* eyestalks long, thin and blue, nippers purple-brown with white tips.

48.5 Pink hermit
Paguristes gamianus

Body pink, limbs hairy and spiny, left and right nippers equal in size. Fourth leg ends in a simple spine (unlike the minute claw found in all other southern African genera). **Size:** 10–20 mm. **Biology:** The most common hermit on west coast rocky shores, often congregating under boulders in low-tide pools. **SIMILAR SPECIES:** *P. barnardi* (southern Cape) lacks spines on the last joint of the second walking leg.

48.6 Common sand hermit
Diogenes brevirostris

Rostrum between eyes replaced with a movable spine. Body dirty white, with darker speckles and spines; brown stripes on last segments of legs. Left nipper thorny, much larger than the right. **Size:** 30 mm. **Biology:** Abundant in sheltered sandbanks and sandy pools. Buries itself during low tide, emerging when submerged to scavenge. **SIMILAR SPECIES:**

48.7 *Diogenes senex* (Mozambique; abundant at Inhaca Island) has eyestalks longer than basal peduncle of antenna 2; both nippers finely hairy. ***D. extricatus*** (Saldanha–Port Elizabeth) common in slightly deeper waters and recognised by a red spot at the base of the claw. ***D. costatus*** (Cape Point–Maputo) abundant in dredgings; lacks the red spot on its claw and has about seven conspicuous serrations on the sides of the carapace.

48.1

48.2

48.3

48.4

48.5

48.6

48.7

PLATE 49

49.1 Giant spotted hermit — *Dardanus megistos*

A very large and bright red to orange hermit, decorated with spectacular black-bordered white spots. Surface of nippers and walking legs covered with comb-like rows of red and brown bristles. Left nipper is larger than the right. Eyestalks red and eyes black. **Size:** Up to 100 mm. **Biology:** An uncommon but spectacular species found on shallow reefs and sandbanks. Both a scavenger and a predator of molluscs, breaking open their shells with its powerful claws.

49.2 Striated hermit — *Dardanus arrosor*

A large species, easily recognised by its uniform brick red colour and the marked, spiky, horizontal ridges or striations that cover the claws and legs. Eyestalks ringed with red and white, eyes black. **Size:** 50–80 mm. **Biology:** Like most hermit crabs will scavenge, but also captures and feeds on live prey such as crabs.

49.3 Teddybear hermit — *Aniculus aniculus*

Limbs with distinctive golden to orange bands. Very bristly, with striations of short, white hairs across the legs, and bunches of extremely long hairs. Eyestalks blueish with longitudinal black dorsal stripe. **Size:** 50–100 mm. **Biology:** Intertidal to shallow subtidal zone in pools and on coral reefs. Easily recognised but uncommon.

49.4 Anemone hermit — *Dardanus pedunculatus*

Colour pale pinkish, with light-coloured bristles and rows of large sharp spines on the claws. Eyes a distinctive green with red and white striped stalks. **Size:** Up to 50 mm. **Biology:** Forms a commensal relationship with the sea anemone *Calliactis polypus* (5.8), which it deliberately places on the shell. The anemones provide both protection and camouflage for the hermit and, when disturbed, expel sticky threads (acontia) that provide additional defence. In return, the anemones feed on food particles released by the crab.

49.5 Blue-faced hermit — *Pagurus liochele*

A small but pretty species, readily recognised by the bright fluorescent blue bands on the bases of the antennae, eyestalks and mouthparts and on the basal joints of the claws. Eyestalks orange at the base, blue distally, eyes white with red markings. Claws and walking legs dark reddish brown, with conspicuous long pale hairs. Palm of claw conspicuously toothed. **Size:** 20–30 mm. **Biology:** Intertidally and on shallow reefs on the south coast. Less common than many of the other species reported here, but a popular photographic subject due to its attractive coloration. Previously named *Pylopagurus liochele*.

49.6 Cloaked hermit — *Sympagurus dimorphus*

Body pinkish, with red patches on the claws and legs. Claws unequal, the right one much larger and longer than the left. Right claw also sexually dimorphic – that of the male greatly elongated and unable to retract into the 'shell'. **Size:** 50 mm. **Biology:** One of the most common and conspicuous components of the fauna of sandy substrata on the continental shelf and slope, down to 600 m. Has a symbiotic relationship with the zoanthid *Epizoanthus paguriphilis*, which settles on the original shell and then extends to cloak and protect the growing hermit.

49.7 Hairy-clawed hermit — *Parapagurus pilosimanus*

Similar to *Sympagurus dimorphus*, but the right claw is very hairy and is not reduced in females, being large and elongate in both sexes. **Size:** 50 mm. **Biology:** Inhabits deeper water than *S. dimorphus*, occurring down to over 1 000 m depth. Like *S. dimorphus*, its shells are covered by a zoanthid.

49.1

49.2

49.3

49.4

49.5

49.6

49.7

PLATE 50

TRUE CRABS   BRACHYURA

Crabs are highly specialised crustaceans. The abdomen is tucked beneath the thorax, and the abdominal limbs have lost their swimming function and serve only to hold eggs in the female or transfer sperm in the male. The tail fan has disappeared. The first pair of legs (chelipeds) bears nippers; the remaining four pairs are for walking. Crabs scuttle sideways, thus lengthening their stride without entangling their legs. The head and thorax are covered by a shield-like carapace, housing the gills. Eggs hatch into planktonic larvae (recognised by a long dorsal spine), which metamorphose into miniature adults. About 300 species occur here.

Shy-faced crabs
Faces shielded with knobbly or spiny nippers; slow-moving and inactive.

50.1 **Reef box crab**   *Calappa hepatica*
Nippers strongly crested and held like a mask. Best recognised by lobes on the sides of the carapace that cover and hide the legs. **Size:** 40 mm. **Biology:** Hides beneath boulders in the intertidal zone. Slow-moving and 'shams' dead if disturbed.

50.2 **Moon crab**   *Ashtoret lunaris*
Carapace almost round, with a sharp, protruding mid-lateral spine. Cream, with tiny red dots; legs yellow, last pair with paddle-shaped tips. Nippers spiny, and folding neatly to mask the 'face'. **Size:** 40 mm. **Biology:** Burrows in sheltered sandbanks down to 50 m; feeds on worms. Previously called *Matuta lunaris*.

50.3 **Masked crab**   *Mursia cristiata*
Carapace roughly oval, pale pink with red tubercles. About eight short blunt marginal teeth and a single, much larger tooth projecting from the side of the carapace. Cheliped broad and spiky. **Size:** 50 mm. **Biology:** Hides beneath subtidal boulders, down to 400 m. Nippers characteristically held close to the 'face', hence the name 'masked crab'.

Pelagic & marsh crabs
Active, fast-moving crabs with a square or oblong carapace, mostly in the family Grapsidae. Many occupy rocky shores; others are estuarine or even pelagic.

50.4 **Columbus' crab**   *Planes minutus*
Unmistakable: soft, smooth, uniformly blue. **Size:** 30 mm. **Biology:** Widely distributed; often washed ashore with bluebottles; forms part of a 'blue community' near the surface of the sea. First noted by Columbus on voyage to the West Indies. **SIMILAR SPECIES:** *P. major*, the flotsam crab, replaces it in KwaZulu-Natal and Mozambique.

50.5 **Red-clawed mangrove crab**   *Neosarmatium meinerti*
Carapace almost square; 4–5 short lateral grooves, a strong tooth at the front corners, and two small marginal teeth. Eyes fold outwards and fit into depressions on the front of the carapace. 'Chest' strongly granular. Body dark, almost black. Nippers granular, roughly equal-sized; bright red, shading to yellow. **Size:** 50 mm. **Biology:** Estuarine, particularly among mangroves. Builds deep, high-shore holes, with 'hooded' openings. Scavenges, but particularly fond of mangrove leaves, racing for them as they fall. **SIMILAR SPECIES:** *Perisesarma guttatum* (Transkei–Mozambique) has uniformly bright red nippers and a distinctive sharp tooth on the fourth joint of the front legs.

50.6 **Marsh crab**   *Parasesarma catenata*
Carapace square, with lateral grooves; yellow to brown. Nippers yellow-brown, equal-sized, with a characteristic furry lining around the hinge. **Size:** 25 mm. **Biology:** Abundant; burrows in estuarine salt marshes and mudflats in the upper shore. Sucks mud particles to remove organic matter and microorganisms and scavenges on dead animals. **SIMILAR SPECIES:** Two very similar species lack the hairy hinge-lining on the nippers. *Chiromantes eulimene* (estuarine, Bashee–East Africa) has dull yellow-blue nippers. *C. ortmanni* (rare; occupies tropical estuaries) has brilliant orange nippers.

50.1

50.2

50.3

50.4

50.5

50.6

PLATE 51

Rock crabs
Rocky-shore Grapsidae that have a square carapace and are fast moving.

51.1 Cape rock crab · *Plagusia chabrus*
Carapace smooth and velvety in texture, with two notches between the eyes that house the first antennae, and three marginal teeth. Colour red-brown, with orange-yellow ridges on the legs, and rows of yellow tubercles on the nippers. Fourth joint of walking legs with numerous teeth on upper margin. **Size:** 50 mm. **Biology:** Occurs in pools and on shallow reefs. Frequently observed cropping low-growing seaweeds with its nippers, but also feeds on small animals caught up with the seaweed.

51.2 Tuberculate crab · *Plagusia depressa tuberculata*
Very similar to *P. chabrus* except for its pale brown colour, the numerous tubercles on its back, and the fact that the upper margin of the fourth joint of the walking legs has only a single sub-apical tooth. **Size:** 40 mm. **Biology:** Occurs on exposed rocky shores and in the shallow subtidal zone. Also clings to driftwood and attaches to ships.

51.3 Green rock crab · *Grapsus fourmanoiri*
Very similar to the Natal lightfoot crab in structure, but dull khaki-green tinged with yellow, and with pale nippers. The sides of its carapace are almost straight, not obviously convex as in the Natal lightfoot crab. **Size:** 35 mm. **Biology:** Hides in rock crevices and emerges to feed during low tide, particularly at night. Eats algae and small animals incidentally caught up with the algae. Juveniles of the Natal lightfoot crab can easily be confused with this species because they are also drab, but the shape of the sides of the carapace is a reliable distinguishing feature.

51.4 Natal lightfoot crab · *Grapsus grapsus tenuicrustatus*
Carapace black, usually speckled with green; sides obviously convex. The posterior part of the carapace has about eight fine grooves that run outwards to the edge. Legs red-brown and yellow; nippers dark red; 'hand' weakly ridged. **Size:** 50 mm. **Biology:** Abundant in KwaZulu-Natal and southern Mozambique, scurrying around in groups on rocks above the water level, plucking seaweeds and picking up small animals. Males particularly gaudy when mature; juveniles and females more drab and often a dull mottled green. **SIMILAR SPECIES:** A subspecies that closely resembles it, with the boringly repetitive name of *G. grapsus grapsus*, occurs in northern Namibia and Angola.

51.5 Shore crab · *Cyclograpsus punctatus*
Body very smooth, except for a granular 'chest'. Sides of carapace convex, lacking marginal teeth, although a single low tooth lies just outside each eye. Hands smooth. Body black or dark brown near the front, blending into a grey-green network towards the back. Legs orange to brown, flecked red. **Size:** 30 mm. **Biology:** Lives high on the shore, often aggregating densely under boulders. Scavenges by night during low tide, feeding mostly on drift seaweeds, but also animal matter.

51.6 Estuarine rock crab · *Metopograpsus thukuhar*
Distance between the base of the eyes more than half the width of the carapace; no lateral teeth on the carapace except for one that flanks each eye. Sides of carapace very straight, but delicately notched with about six short grooves. The legs have stiff, spiky hairs. 'Hand' of nipper with a single ridge. **Size:** 35 mm. **Biology:** Confined to estuaries, where it is most common on rocky banks; often climbs mangrove trees. **SIMILAR SPECIES:** *M. messor* (East London–East Africa) is similar, but extends further south, and its nippers are purple-red to violet.

51.7 Flat-bodied crab · *Percnon planissimum*
Body flat, with two notches on the front of the carapace and three teeth on each side; mottled green-brown and with narrow bright green bands. At least the lower half of eyes vivid red. Front edge of the largest leg joints strongly serrated. Nippers of the male swollen, resembling tiny balloons. **Size:** Body 35 mm. **Biology:** Very common in KwaZulu-Natal, scuttling secretively around boulders in pools and in shallow water.

51.1

51.2

51.3

51.4

51.5

51.6

51.7

PLATE 52

Swimming crabs

Carapace oval, with a toothed edge. Back legs end in a flat or paddle-shaped joint. Active swimmers, though many spend much time buried in sand or mud. Most fall in the family Portunidae.

52.1 Blue swimming crab · *Portunus pelagicus*

Carapace broad, with long, drawn-out spines mid-laterally and eight smaller marginal teeth. Nippers ridged and usually blue. Body a dull variegated brown; acquires a spectacular pink-brown mottling when the crab matures. **Size:** 120 mm. **Biology:** Lives in sandy bays. Scavenges on dead animals and preys on molluscs and crustaceans. Fights viciously if cornered; can inflict painful wounds. Sold in markets in Mozambique.

52.2 Blood-spotted swimming crab · *Portunus sanguinolentus*

Similar to the previous species, but smaller, and its carapace has three characteristic white-ringed red-brown spots. **Size:** 80 mm. **Biology:** An aggressive and even cannibalistic species that lives off sandy beaches in shallow water.

52.3 Three-spot swimming crab · *Ovalipes trimaculatus*

Carapace triangular, but with rounded corners; five marginal teeth on either side. Sandy-coloured; carapace flecked with red-brown dots and three larger markings resembling the eyes and mouth of a 'sad face'. Like most swimming crabs (family Portunidae), its last pair of legs ends in an oval, paddle-shaped joint (52.3). Nippers ridged and with strong cutting teeth (52.3a). **Size:** 40 mm. **Biology:** An aggressive predator on bivalves and gastropods (particularly *Bullia*) and lives on surf-beaten sandy beaches. It can use its paddles to swim, but more often it scuttles over the sand, digging backwards if threatened. Recently shed moults are often washed up on beaches in large numbers. Larvae of the alien mussel *Mytilus galloprovincialis* settle on the eyestalks and mouthparts of this crab, causing mass mortalities. Previously known as *O. punctatus*.

52.4 Heller's swimming crab · *Charybdis hellerii*

Carapace transversely ridged, and much wider than the distance between the front pair of marginal teeth. Six blunt teeth between the eyes; five marginal teeth on either side. Nippers ridged and spiny. **Size:** 50 mm. **Biology:** Occurs in rock pools and bays. Eats small molluscs, crustaceans and worms. There are several species in the genus.

52.5 Scalloped swimming crab · *Thalamita crenata*

Frontal margin with six low equal-sized lobes. Five equal-sized lateral teeth outside the eye-orbit tooth. As with all *Thalamita* spp. the carapace is scarcely wider than the distance between the first marginal teeth. **Size:** 40 mm. **Biology:** Buries itself in sand or hides under boulders in shallow water. Eats molluscs, worms and crustaceans. **SIMILAR SPECIES:** Two other common, related species have the same geographic range. *T. admete* has two broad lobes between the eyes; base of second antenna serrated. *T. woodmasoni* has four lobes between the eyes; base of second antenna smooth.

52.1

52.2

52.3

52.3a

52.4

52.5

PLATE 53

53.1 Smith's swimming crab *Charybdis smithii*

Carapace smooth, front edge with four pairs of short teeth, sides with four broad, peg-like marginal teeth and a single, pointed tooth. Outstretched nippers easily four times the carapace width. Nippers with 5–6 longitudinal rows of tubercles. **Size:** 120 mm. **Biology:** Pelagic, mostly above 150 m; episodically forms huge offshore swarms, but breeds inshore. Normally tropical, where it is an important food source for tuna, but penetrates south when the sea is unusually warm. First described from False Bay in 1838 but not seen again until 1978, when enormous numbers appeared – and again in 1983 and 1993.

53.2 European shore-crab *Carcinus maenas*

Carapace oval, mottled khaki-green, with five marginal teeth on each side. Legs robust, with flattened but pointed tips. Nippers strong, outer surface smooth-textured, 'finger' and 'thumb' with about 12 teeth. **Size:** 50 mm. **Biology:** Alien to South Africa, probably introduced on oil rigs. First recorded in Table Bay docks in 1983, but has spread to Hout Bay. Capture of a single pregnant female in Saldanha Bay in 1990 may fortuitously have halted its invasion of the bay. Confined to reefs or bays protected from direct wave action. A voracious predator. Poses a threat to many local molluscs, including some used in aquaculture. When it invaded the east coast of America, it caused millions of dollars of damage to the shellfish industry. **SIMILAR SPECIES:** An almost identical species, *C. aestuarii*, may also occur here, as genetic hybrids between the two species have been detected. Its male reproductive pleopods are crescent-shaped and touching, whereas those of *C. maenas* are straight, parallel, and not touching.

53.3 Mud crab *Scylla serrata*

Carapace oval; nine pairs of equal-sized marginal teeth. Nippers massive, with smooth hands. Colour green-brown, but limbs (particularly the paddle-shaped last pair) with a net-like pattern. **Size:** The giant of the swimming crabs: 300 mm. **Biology:** Adults burrow in estuarine mud, but migrate to sea to reproduce. Predatory, but feeds on surprisingly tiny prey, including small molluscs. At least one unwary captor has lost a finger to its powerful nippers. Often inappropriately called the Knysna crab, it occurs in many tropical areas. Commercially fished; slow growth makes it vulnerable to overfishing.

53.4 Harlequin crab *Lissocarcinus orbicularis*

Distinctive but highly variable pattern of white spots on a dark purple-brown background. Sides of carapace with five lobes, the first four larger than the fifth. **Size:** 15 mm. **Biology:** Occurs exclusively attached to large sea cucumbers, the white marking blending in with the sand attached to the sea cucumber and its white-tipped tubefeet. When threatened, disappears into the mouth of the sea cucumber. Nearly always found in pairs, the male being minute compared to the female, as shown here. **SIMILAR SPECIES:** *L. laevis* is almost identical morphologically, except that the first and fifth lateral lobes on the side of the carapace are smaller than the rest; but it is easily distinguished by being associated with ceriantherid anemones (5.3), not sea cucumbers.

53.5 Swimming rock crab *Varuna litterata*

Carapace square, smooth but pitted, steely-blue; one tooth just outside eyes, and two lateral teeth. Last three joints of legs flat, fringed with hairs to aid swimming. **Size:** 70 mm. **Biology:** A member of the family Grapsidae, rather than a true swimming crab, but highly adapted to swimming; spends much time in the water column. Penetrates estuaries, even into fresh water, and occurs offshore, often attached to floating timber.

Land crabs

These crabs spend almost all their time on land, returning to sea only to release larvae. They fall in the family Gecarcinidae, with only one species in our region.

53.6 Giant land crab *Cardisoma carnifex*

A sizable beast with a domed carapace and swollen sides covering the gills. Brown to violet; nippers brown to yellow or creamish-red. Walking legs very hairy. **Size:** Up to 100 mm. **Biology:** Digs deep burrows at the upper edge of mangroves or inland. Emerges by night to feed. Depleted by subsistence fishers as a source of food, and becoming rare.

53.1

53.2

53.3

53.4

53.5

53.6

PLATE 54

Ghost & fiddler crabs

The family Ocypodidae includes ghost crabs – fast-running, nocturnal, sandy-beach scavengers – and fiddler crabs, with one enormous nipper in the males.

54.1 Horn-eyed ghost crab · *Ocypode ceratophthalma*

Distinctive 'horns' cap its eyes (although absent in juveniles). Robust and grey-green. One nipper larger than the other, with a wide hairy ridge across the palm: a rubbing motion of this ridge (stridulation) produces a rasping sound during courtship or aggression. **Size:** 40 mm. **Biology:** Digs deep holes high on sandy beaches; emerges during low tide at night to scavenge on a range of animals, including newly hatched turtles.

54.2 Pink ghost crab · *Ocypode ryderi*

Similar to the previous species, but pale pink, with distinctive mauve joints to the legs, and eyes lacking 'horns'. The larger of the two nippers has a stridulating organ on the palm, which consists of a single row of granules. **Size:** 35 mm. **Biology:** Abundant on wave-exposed, tropical beaches. Burrows deeply by day, emerging by night to feed on deposited carrion and small animals. **SIMILAR SPECIES:** *O. madagascariensis* (Durban–Mozambique) is almost identical, but sandy-coloured, and its legs do not have mauve joints.

54.3 West coast ghost crab · *Ocypode cursor*

Easily distinguished by its distribution and the tufts of hair-like setae extending from the tips of the eyes. **Size:** 35 mm. **Biology:** An active, nocturnal scavenger that speeds up and down open-coast sandy beaches and digs deep holes near the top of the shore.

54.4 Urville's fiddler crab · *Uca urvillei*

Males of all fiddler crabs have one greatly enlarged nipper that, in this species, has a granular outer surface and is bright yellow to orange, sometimes grading to pale blue. Both 'finger' and 'thumb' have a series of low teeth, but there is usually a larger tooth near the midpoint of each. Carapace and legs blue-black, and may have pale blue spots, although mature males can be pure royal blue. Females have two small nippers. Eyestalks very long and slender and arise close together, the distance between their bases being only about twice the eyestalk width. **Size:** 25 mm. **Biology:** Common on mangrove sandbanks. Feeds during low tide on surface sediments, rolling small neat balls (pseudofaeces) to extract organic particles and microorganisms. Males defend their holes, and wave their nippers vertically up and down to attract females. **SIMILAR SPECIES:** *U. vocans* (Transkei–East Africa) has similar, closely spaced eyestalks. It differs in having a brownish-yellow carapace and, in the male, a golden nipper with an obvious tooth near the tip of the 'thumb'; a spine on the fourth joint of the nipper is also unique to the species. Previously called *U. marionis*; some authors prefer to call it *U. hesperiae*.

54.5 Pink-clawed fiddler crab · *Uca annulipes*

Males have a black to grey carapace, with a white network. Nipper bright salmon-pink, outer surface scarcely textured, curving smoothly to its upper margin; inner surface with two marked, oblique ridges. Several equal-sized, weak teeth on the 'thumb' and 'finger'. Eyestalks widely spaced, the distance between them being about three times the eyestalk diameter. Legs black. **Size:** 20 mm. **Biology:** Abundant: forms huge aggregations on open sandflats in estuaries and lagoons. Thousands emerge almost simultaneously at low tide to feed on surface sediments, darting into their holes if alarmed. Courting males extend the large nipper laterally, swinging it inwards in a 'come-hither' gesture.

54.6 Tropical fiddler crab · *Uca inversa*

Also has widely spaced eyestalks, but has two white patches on the male's carapace. The male's large nipper is red, with a prominent tooth just inside the tip of the movable 'finger'. Legs deep red to black-red in both sexes. **Size:** 24 mm. **Biology:** Occupies sand and mudflats just above mangroves.

54.7 Green-eyed fiddler crab · *Uca chlorophthalmus*

Like the previous species, the eyestalks are widely spaced, but the legs are distinctively red. Male's nipper pink to red; the upper edge has a fine ridge and a groove; the inner surface has only one faint ridge. **Size:** 20 mm. **Biology:** Occurs relatively low on the shore in mangroves. Previously incorrectly called *U. gaimardi*.

54.1

54.2

54.3

54.4

54.5

54.6

54.7

PLATE 55

55.1 Army crab
Dotilla fenestrata

Sandy-coloured; the shape and size of a pea, with grooves on the dorsal surface. Nippers small and equal-sized. Walking legs with a distinct oval 'window' on the sides of the fourth joint. **Size:** 10 mm. **Biology:** Lives in dense aggregations on sheltered sandbanks, burrowing shallowly and emerging to feed during low tide, sucking organic material from the sediment and depositing pellets of processed sand. Most abundant in the tropics.

55.2 Long-eyed crab
Macrophthalmus grandidieri

Body width twice the length; the back of the carapace has two parallel shallow grooves running from near the mid-line to the sides. Eyestalks very long: much longer than the distance between their bases. Spine outside the eye orbits bends back to cross over the single lateral spine on carapace edge. **Size:** 25 mm. **Biology:** Burrows in moist, sandy mud near the mid-tide level in sheltered lagoons and estuaries. Retreats sideways down its burrow if disturbed, and sits at the mouth of the burrow with just one eye peering out to survey the world. Feeds on fine particles of detritus. SIMILAR SPECIES: *M. depressus* (Mozambique northwards) has body width 1.5 times length. Nippers pale blue, red spots on either side of the mouth, shaggy hairs on the legs and two parallel rows of granules on the sides of the carapace. Lives in mangrove mud.

55.3 Squat long-eyed crab
Macrophthalmus boscii

Much more squat than the previous species, its carapace only slightly wider than long; the length of its eyestalks is about equal to the distance between their bases. Nipper light brown. **Size:** 10 mm. **Biology:** Lives under loose stones on sandy and muddy sheltered beaches and estuaries. Feeds on fine detritus sieved from sand grains.

55.4 Three-legged crab
Spiroplax spiralis

Unmistakable because it has only three pairs of walking legs (in addition to the nipper-bearing chelipeds). All other crabs have four pairs of walking legs. (They may shed legs when attacked, but, if they do so, the stumps of the discarded legs are clearly evident.) The body is smoothly oval in outline, flat and mottled grey-brown. **Size:** 8 mm. **Biology:** Lives in temporary burrows low on the shore, on sheltered sandbanks. Often found in the burrows of the sandprawn *Callianassa kraussi* (47.1), and may be commensal with it.

55.5 Sandflat crab
Paratylodiplax edwardsii

Small, with a sandy-coloured, flat, almost circular body, the outline being broken by a single tooth near the front corners of the carapace. Eyestalks smooth. **Size:** 8 mm. **Biology:** Scuffles under the surface of the sand in waterlogged areas in lagoonal and estuarine sandbanks. Feeds on fine particles of detritus. SIMILAR SPECIES: *P. algoensis* has a similar distribution and habitats, and differs only in having hairy eyestalks. Both species previously placed in the genus *Cleistostoma*.

55.6 Pea crab
Pinnotheres dofleini

Pea-shaped, soft-bodied, and straw-coloured or yellow. Eyes stunted and minute. **Size:** 10–20 mm. **Biology:** Females are always found inside the shells of bivalves, parasitising their hosts by stealing food from the mucous strings on their gills. The tiny eyes and flimsy legs reflect the crab's sheltered, parasitic life. Males are minute and rarely seen, but can move between hosts seeking females. There is probably more than one species in southern Africa; a large form is found in the horse mussel *Atrina* (63.10) and a small version inside the black mussel *Choromytilus meridionalis* (62.2). (Occasionally they horrify diners who discover them in their meal of mussels, although any seafood gourmet should delight in the unintended supplement to the meal.)

55.7 Coral crab
Tetralia glaberrima

Carapace shiny, roughly oval, with a single, marginal tooth. Eyes extend outwards to reach almost the outer edge of the carapace. Nippers large; outer surface of one of them is faintly woolly. Colour bright orange. **Size:** 20 mm. **Biology:** Lives in coral heads. Aggressively attacks encroaching crustaceans, and defends its host against other competitive corals. SIMILAR SPECIES: Several trapesiid crabs live among branching corals. *Trapezia* spp. have a toothed frontal margin: *T. cymodoce* is red or orange with a black 'finger' and 'thumb'; *T. guttata* is pink with tiny red dots, and *T. rufopunctata* is pink with large red spots.

55.1

55.2

55.3

55.4

55.5

55.6

55.7

PLATE 56

Xanthid crabs

The family Xanthidae comprises heavy-set, slow-moving crabs with an oval carapace and massive nippers. They are important predators on tropical shores.

56.1 Smith's xanthid — *Eriphia smithii*

Carapace oval, brown; front half dotted with tubercles, but not hairy; at least five marginal teeth. Nippers large and robust, the smaller of the two with spiny tubercles whereas the larger is scarcely tuberculate. Eyes orange. **Size:** 50 mm. **Biology:** Slow-moving and sluggish, but has massive powerful nippers with which it crushes molluscs. It is the most abundant xanthid crab on rocky shores in KwaZulu-Natal, wedging itself in holes.

56.2 Red-eyed xanthid — *Eriphia sebana*

Carapace brown, often mottled with grey on the sides, dotted with small knobs and armed with at least five small lateral teeth on each side. Nippers very strong but smooth, not tuberculate. Eyes bright red. **Size:** 40 mm. **Biology:** Less common than *E. smithii*, but with similar habits. Previously called *E. laevimanus*.

56.3 Hedgehog xanthid — *Eriphia scabricula*

Similar in shape, but smaller, and has a sparse coating of short, stout hairs on its carapace and nippers, which have salmon-pink 'fingers'. Body reddish, with yellow-brown mottling. **Size:** 35 mm. **Biology:** Hides in crevices by day, feeds at night.

56.4 Kelp crab — *Pilumnoides rubrus*

Carapace oval, orange to purple-orange. Upper surface densely tuberculate; margins lined with both small and large teeth. Nippers of similar size, heavily dotted with knobs, with a black 'finger' and 'thumb'. **Size:** 30 mm. **Biology:** Lives under stones, among mussels or in kelp holdfasts. Feeds on small molluscs. Previously misidentified as *P. perlatus*, a South American species, but now recognised as a separate, endemic species. **SIMILAR SPECIES:** Several xanthid crabs have carapaces that are not knobbly but are hairy. *Pilumnus minutus* (Saldanha Bay–Durban) has three marginal teeth and a fine fur of short hair through which longer bristles project; previously named *Pilumnus hirsutus*. *Serenepilumnus pisifer* (St Helena Bay–Cape Vidal) is similar, but has four, large tubercles on the second-last joints of its walking legs.

56.5 Nodular xanthid — *Cyclodius obscurus*

Carapace satiny brown, oval, smooth, but with radiating low nodules. Central part set apart from sides by a distinct groove. Nippers smooth, with a pattern of reddish spots, merging into black 'finger' and 'thumb'. **Size:** 35 mm. **Biology:** Intertidal to shallow subtidal, among loose rocks or coral rubble. Previously named *Phymodius monticulosus*.

56.6 Variable xanthid — *Xantho hydrophilus*

Extremely varied in colour and pattern: pure yellow, grey with black blotches, or white with brown blotches, making it very cryptic. The larger nipper is smooth; 'fingers' dark black-brown. Front of carapace with two square-cut lobes; sides with four low teeth plus a tooth outside the eyes. Centre of carapace with two large mounds, separated by an inverted 'V'. **Size:** 30 mm. **Biology:** Intertidal, down to 2 m depth, under loose boulders or buried in mangrove sediments. Previously named *Leptodius exerata*. **SIMILAR SPECIES:** *Etisus electra* (Mozambique northwards) has a bumpy carapace with three marginal teeth; four prominent lobes on front of carapace between the eyes; shaggy fringes to the legs.

56.7 Chocolate crab — *Atergatis laevigatus*

Carapace chocolate-coloured above and pink below, smoothly oval when viewed from above, completely lacking marginal teeth. Eyes small and close-set. Nippers smooth, except for a faint ridge; 'finger' and 'thumb' black, armed with knob-like white teeth. **Size:** 60 mm. **Biology:** A relatively scarce, but handsome crab that hides beneath boulders. Predatory, although its exact diet is unknown. Previously misnamed *A. roseus*.

56.8 Shaggy xanthid — *Pilumnus verspertilio*

Entire body, except for portions of the nippers, covered in a shaggy grey-brown coat. Lower part of nipper white, with red-brown fingers. **Size:** 35 mm. **Biology:** Hides beneath stones on the low shore. Moves agonisingly slowly and 'shams' when disturbed.

56.1

56.2

56.3

56.4

56.5

56.6

56.7

56.8

PLATE 57

Crown, sponge- and decorator-crabs

57.1 Crown crab
Hymenosoma orbiculare

Body round and flat. Small triangular projection (rostrum) between eyes. Hinge of nippers smooth, not hairy; 'finger' and 'thumb' sharply pointed. Pale mottled brown, but often overgrown by microalgae. **Size:** 15 mm. **Biology:** Lives in estuaries and lagoons, shuffling into sand to feed on small crustaceans. Two unnamed *Hymenosoma* spp. replace it in KwaZulu-Natal. **SIMILAR SPECIES:** *Rhynchoplax bovis* (KwaZulu-Natal and Mozambique estuaries) is smaller (5 mm); nippers with furry hinge and spoon-shaped tips.

57.2 Masked crab
Nautilocorystes ocellata

Antennae distinctive: almost as long as body. Carapace longer than broad, with four marginal teeth and four grey blotches ('ocelli'). Tips of legs flat. **Size:** 35 mm. **Biology:** Digs backwards into sheltered sandbanks, extending its long antennae to form a tube of interlocking hairs down which water is drawn.

57.3 Cape long-legged spider crab
Macropodia falcifera

Body small relative to the bizarre long thin legs; nippers thicker than legs, spiny and armed with short, spiky hairs. Rostrum very long: longer than antennae. Carapace longer than broad, with two pairs of long erect spines; fourth joint of walking legs ends in a long spine. **Size:** Body 10 mm. **Biology:** Slow-moving; occurs in deep, calm waters.

57.4 Cryptic sponge-crab
Platydromia spongiosa

Body soft, slightly furry, yellow or cream; carapace broader than long; fifth legs small and bent upwards. Tips of legs knobbly. **Size:** 25 mm. **Biology:** Found under subtidal stones. Like all Dromiidae, it carries a protective cloak of unpalatable sponge or ascidian. Pieces are cut off the rocks, held in position by tiny nippers on its modified fifth legs, and grow to cover the crab almost completely. Previously called *Cryptodromiopsis spongiosa*.

57.5 Shaggy sponge-crab
Dromidia hirsutissima

Densely covered with a magnificent shaggy coat of stiff hairs. Carapace broader than long, with two or three marginal teeth; fifth legs about equal in size to fourth, but twisted up over the carapace. **Size:** 40 mm. **Biology:** Carries a cloak of sponge, ascidian or seaweed. **SIMILAR SPECIES:** *D. unidentata* (Mozambique northwards) has short brown or reddish-brown fur; single tooth at mid-margin of carapace.

57.6 Cloaked sponge-crab
Pseudodromidia latens

Recognised because its body is longer than it is wide, and its fifth leg is much longer than the fourth. A close, yellowish fur covers the body. From above, only two teeth are visible on the rostrum between the eyes. **Size:** 30 mm. **Biology:** Almost completely enclosed in a ball-shaped, ascidian cloak. Often climbs on sea fans, which it may consume.

57.7 Long-legged crab
Philyra punctata

Carapace rounded and swollen, almost circular in outline; apparently smooth but minutely pitted and granular. Uniformly off-white to grey. Arm of nipper triangular in cross section. **Size:** 15 mm. **Biology:** Common on subtidal sandbeds in sheltered lagoons and offshore down to 200 m.

57.8 Shield decorator-crab
Acanthonyx scutellatus

Carapace shield-shaped, with no spines immediately outside the eye, but two large lateral spines on the carapace. **Size:** 20 mm. **Biology:** Like all decorator-crabs, it carries bits of seaweed, but as its carapace is smooth, it is seldom enveloped by them. **SIMILAR SPECIES:** *A. undulatus* (Durban northwards) is also shield-shaped, but has one small tooth outside the eyes and one large and three small marginal teeth.

57.9 Four-toothed decorator-crab
Acanthonyx quadridentatus

Carapace longer than broad, covered with hooked hairs. Two horns between the eyes, a small tooth just outside the eyes, and four marginal teeth. **Size:** 20 mm. **Biology:** Cuts fragments of seaweeds and attaches them to its hairy back, where they continue to grow, camouflaging the crab, which changes colour to match the algae. **SIMILAR SPECIES:** *A. dentatus* (Columbine–southern KwaZulu-Natal) has two large marginal teeth.

57.1

57.2

57.3

57.4

57.5

57.6

57.7

57.8

57.9

Bryozoans

Phylum Bryozoa includes creatures commonly known as moss or lace animals, which are abundant and exquisitely beautiful, but seldom recognised, as they resemble other organisms such as seaweeds, hydroids and corals. They can be encrusting, coral-like or bushy, but all build colonies of tiny individuals, each enclosed in a minute skeleton and crowned by filter-feeding tentacles. Some individuals may be specialised into beaked or rod-like structures that snap or thrash at predators or intruders.

PLATE 58

Moss or lace animals   Bryozoa

Bryozoans form colonies of minute (1 mm) individuals (zooids), each housed in a tiny coffin-like lime or chitin skeleton (zooecium). Tentacles extend through an opening (orifice). Some zooids are specialised into beak-like avicularia, resembling a bird's head, which snap at creatures that threaten the colony. Classification depends on microscopic details of the zooecia, but based on colony form, bryozoans can be divided artificially into: (1) crusts on rocks and other organisms (Plate 58); (2) upright, bushy, leafy or cactus-like colonies (Plate 59); (3) species with heavy lime skeletons, resembling small corals (Plate 60).

58.1 Red-rust bryozoan   *Watersipora subtorquata*
Zooecia in concentric rings, forming flat crusts. Orange-brown with reddish edges and black dots. Zooecia urn-shaped, pitted with pores; orifice notched (58.1a; see also 35.6). **Size:** Colony 40 mm. **Biology:** Common under boulders down to 15 m.
SIMILAR SPECIES:
58.2 *Calyptotheca nivea* (Cape Point–East London). Encrusting, or forms scroll-like twisted plates; creamy or off-white. Zooecia straight-sided, separated by thin raised sutures. Front rough; numerous small round pores. Orifice as wide as long, with a shallow U-shaped notch. A pair of small round avicularia flanks the orifice. *C. porelliformis* (Cape Point–Port Elizabeth) is similar but bright peach to orange. Orifice wider than long; anterior margin gently concave, with a central knob.
58.3 *Escharoides contorta* (Cape Town–KwaZulu-Natal) is grey-white; zooecia oval to rectangular, dotted with pores and scattered avicularia. Orifice with a median point, a pair of avicularia and four distal spines (lost with age). Grows on rocks and mussels, 0–20 m.
58.4 *Steginoporella buskii* (Port Nolloth–Durban) is also pale, but has a thin membrane over the front of each zooecium, beneath which is a lime sheet peppered with pores. Avicularia large and have an inverted 'Y' marked on the operculum.

58.5 Sand-sausage   *Cryptopolyzoon concretum*
Tubular zooecia, arising in groups from a central stem, are soft and not calcified, but so encrusted with sand that they are invisible. Resembles strings of sandy mini-sausages. **Size:** Strings 1 mm wide. **Biology:** Attaches to seaweeds. Protected by the sand coat.

58.6 Nodular bryozoan   *Alcyonidium nodosum*
Lives solely on the whelk *Burnupena papyracea*, forming an orange or purple lumpy cloak. **Size:** 30 mm. **Biology:** Contains highly toxic chemicals; protects its host against predators such as rock lobsters. Benefits of the association for the bryozoan are unknown.

58.7 Membranous lace animal   *Jellyella tuberculata*
Forms lace-like sheets. Zooecia hexagonal, with a pair of rounded tubercles on their anterior corners (58.7a). **Size:** Colonies 100 mm. **Biology:** Covers extensive areas on flat-bladed algae, but apparently harmless. Previously named *Membranipora tuberculata*.

58.8 Rustic lace animal   *Membranipora rustica*
Forms flat, lacy circles. Zooecia rectangular, with tiny knobs at the corners. Walls rustically pitted. **Size:** Patches 20–50 mm. **Biology:** Abundant on kelp. The nudibranch *Corambe* (93.2) feeds on and mimics it. Previously misidentified as *Membranipora membranacea*.

58.9 Hairy lace animal   *Electra pilosa*
Long, narrow, hairy colonies with oblique or transverse rows of narrow zooecia (58.9a) with a dark orifice flanked by one long and four short spines. **Size:** Colonies 50 mm long. **Biology:** Grows on narrow-bladed algae, at 0–20 m. Previously named *E. verticillata*.

58.10 Magellanic lace animal   *Beania magellanica*
Delicate, lacy crusts. Zooecia linked by tubes. Two stalked anterior avicularia (58.10a). **Size:** Colony 30 mm. **Biology:** Coats algae, rocks or other bryozoans.
SIMILAR SPECIES:
58.11 *Beania vanhoeffeni* (Cape Peninsula only) is similar, but zooecia have about 7–10 pairs of short spines projecting inwards from the lateral margins (58.11a). *B. minuspina* (Cape Peninsula only) has longer marginal spines, in 4–5 pairs.

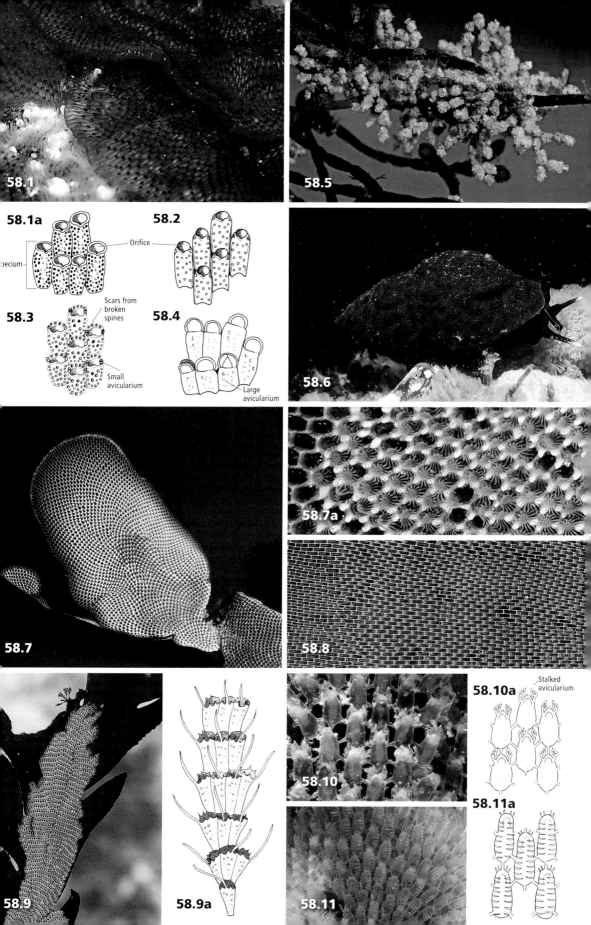

58.1

58.1a

Orifice

ecium

58.2

58.3

Scars from broken spines

Small avicularium

58.4

Large avicularium

58.5

58.6

58.7

58.7a

58.8

58.9

58.9a

58.10

58.10a

Stalked avicularium

58.11a

58.11

PLATE 59

Alien

59.1 Dentate moss animal — *Bugula dentata*

Forms bushy tufts that hang downwards; grey but becoming deep blue when sunlit. Zooecia rounded at their upper ends and armed with about four long spines. Avicularia commonly flank each zooecium and resemble birds' heads (59.1a). **Size:** Colony 50 mm in length. **Biology:** Extremely common in the warmer waters of the east coast, hanging down from the vertical walls of subtidal gullies at depths of 1–400 m.

Alien

59.2 Fouling moss animal — *Bugula neritina*

Stiff, regularly branching colonies: reddish purple or purple-black. Zooecia alternate up the branches and have sharp points (59.2a). Spines and avicularia absent. Ovicells (reproductive bodies) pearly, globular. **Size:** Colony 30 mm long. **Biology:** Almost worldwide; probably spread by shipping – commonly fouls ships and prevalent at localities that have harbours.

59.3 Bird's-head moss animal — *Bugula avicularia*

Colony straw-coloured and much more sparsely branched; zooecia (59.3) have a sharply pointed upper corner and most are armed with a bird's-head avicularium. Mature colonies dotted with pearly round reproductive bodies (ovicells).

Alien

59.4 Fan-shaped moss animal — *Bugula flabellata*

Upright, bushy, orange colonies in which the branches curve inwards. Zooecia in rows of 3–5, almost rectangular, with sharp outer corners. Avicularia present and larger on the margins; rounded reproductive bodies (ovicells) are frequent (59.4a). **Size:** Colony 30 mm tall. **Biology:** Grows on rocks or attached to seaweeds; often abundant on wharfs and underwater pylons. Can seriously foul the hulls of ships. Spans depths of 2–400 m.

59.5 Bonsai bush — *Bicellariella bonsai*

Resembles a miniature willow-tree, with much-divided, drooping branches. Pale, often white. Zooecia (59.5a) rounded, projecting outwards from the branches, and ending in 4–7 very long, curved, eyelash-like spines. Frontal window wider at outer end, tapering inwards. A single bird's-head avicularium lies at the base of each zooecium. **Size:** Colony 60 mm tall. **Biology:** Grows beneath rocky overhangs low on the shore and in the subtidal zone down to 10 m. Previously incorrectly named *B. ciliata*.

59.6 Spiral moss animal — *Menipea triseriata*

Upright, bushy, with flat branches that divide regularly and are usually spirally arranged. Straw-coloured, or orange if growing in dark caves. Zooecia almost rectangular, arranged in pairs or threes; four stubby distal spines near the orifice and a single minute basal avicularium (59.6a). **Size:** Colony 40 mm tall. **Biology:** Often grows among sponges or larger bryozoans, deriving protection against predators from them. Abundant in deeper water, but extends into intertidal pools, spanning depths of 0–100 m. **SIMILAR SPECIES:** *M. ornata* (South African endemic) is dichotomously branched; zooecia in rows of two (three at nodes). No long spines, but a stubby outer spine at distal corners of zooecia.

59.7 Curled moss animal — *Menipea crispa*

Forms upright yellow-brown tree-like colonies with incurving branches; zooecia oval, with a pair of long spines that curve at their tips, and a single tubular avicularium at the base. Occasional larger, triangular avicularia occur on the edges of the branches (59.7a).

59.8 Busk's moss animal — *Onchoporella buskii*

Colony forming flat, leafy blades, white or pale blue to green. Zooecia only lightly strengthened with lime, and form a network on the blades. Each zooecium shaped like an elongate hexagon, with two short spines on either side of the orifice, one large central pore and 1–4 smaller pores below the orifice. **Size:** Colony 50 mm, blades 2–3 mm wide. **Biology:** Usually grows on algae or attached to other bryozoans, at depths of 4–60 m.

59.9 Cactus-bush bryozoan — *Margaretta levinseni*

Short upright cylindrical branches with side-stems, like a miniature cactus. Zooecia resemble Grecian urns, and have a delicate net-like pattern (59.9a). **Size:** Colony 50–80 mm tall. **Biology:** Occurs subtidally at 4–20 m in sites sheltered from strong wave action; mixed with low-growing seaweeds. Previously incorrectly called *M. triplex*.

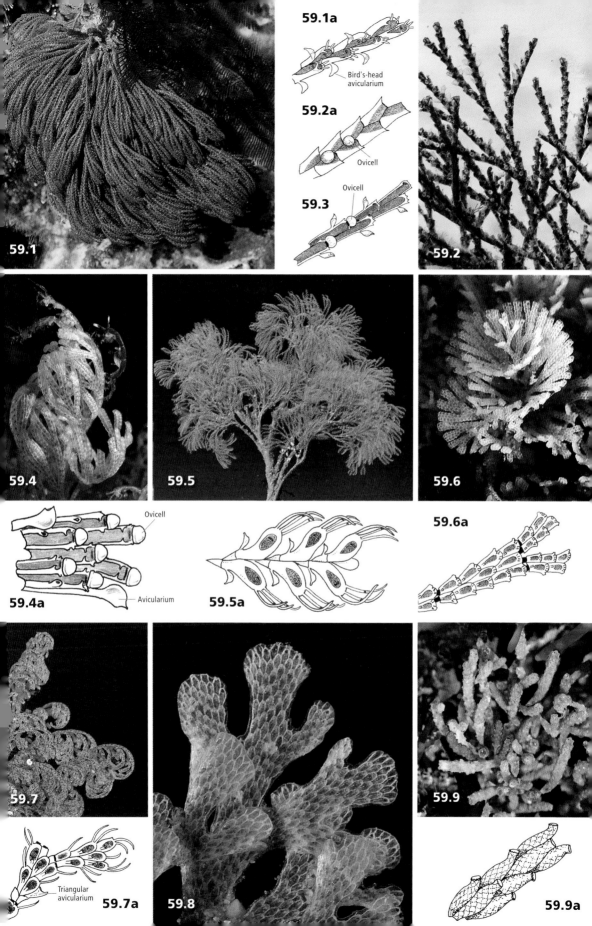

59.1a

Bird's-head avicularium

59.2a

Ovicell

59.3

Ovicell
Ovicell

59.1

59.2

59.4

59.5

59.6

Ovicell

Avicularium

59.4a

59.5a

59.6a

59.7

59.9

Triangular avicularium

59.7a

59.8

59.9a

PLATE 60

60.1 Soft false-coral   *Alcyonidium rhomboidale*

Soft, almost gelatinous, irregular leafy yellow lobes. Zooecia roughly diamond-shaped and very simple in structure, with a smooth gelatinous frontal membrane and a small oval anterior orifice (60.1a). **Size:** Colony 150–250 mm across; 'blades' 10 mm wide. **Biology:** Grows on rocks at 4–20 m. Attachment weak: often ripped off and washed ashore after storms.

60.2 Scrolled false-corals   *Chaperia* spp.

Rigid, encrusting or often projecting, scroll-like twisted plates; beige to orange. Zooecia (60.2a) diamond-shaped with round, soft, frontal membrane. Visible avicularia and spines frequent, imparting a bristly 'unshaven-chin' texture. **Size:** Colony up to 200 mm wide. **Biology:** Several species in the genus: all grow on the sides of rocky overhangs. Often associated with the sea fan *Acabaria rubra*, which stings predators.
SIMILAR SPECIES:
60.3 *Chaperiopsis multifida* (Cape Town–Durban) forms a similar colony but is maroon, and the front of each zooecium has large sessile and stalked avicularia, pairs of straight spines, and antler-like spines that hide the zooecium and impart a characteristic hairiness.

60.4 Pore-plated false-coral   *Laminopora jellyae*

Twisted, irregularly united plates; usually purple-brown, less often orange. Zooecia diamond-shaped, lacking spines and thus not hairy. A pair of triangular avicularia flank the round orifice (60.4a). Scattered large avicularia. **Size:** Colony 100 mm. **Biology:** Grows on silt-free overhangs at 2–50 m. Previously named *L. biminuta*. **SIMILAR SPECIES:**
60.5 *Adeonellopsis meandrina* (East London–Durban) almost identical, but dark purple-brown. Zooecia hexagonal with an oval anterior aperture, one or two tiny triangular avicularia and a central pore.

60.6 Lacy false-coral   *Schizoretepora tesselata*

Brittle, twisted, upright interconnected plates that are often punctured by regularly spaced holes, giving a lacy appearance. Zooecia (60.6a) oval to hexagonal; four long spines around the orifice (usually evident in young zooecia only). Orifice oval, with hind notch. Isolated avicularia with triangular 'beaks' that resemble tiny barnacles. **Size:** Colony 40–120 mm. **Biology:** Grows in rock gullies, from low-tide level to 100 m. **SIMILAR SPECIES:**
60.7 *Reteporella lata* (Cape Town–East London) also forms lacy colonies, but they are off-white and the front surface of the zooecia is dotted with papillae.

60.8 Staghorn false-coral   *Gigantopora polymorpha*

Upright, stubby-lobed, robust, coral-like; dull orange. Zooecia rectangular; dotted with coarse pores. Orifice with a narrow arch carrying two tiny triangular avicularia (60.8a). **Size:** Colony 6 cm. **Biology:** Low shore to 600 m, usually on vertical rock surfaces.

60.9 Spiny false-coral   *Celleporaria capensis*

Forms thick nodular crusts with projecting spikes. Purple to almost black. Zooecia with an oval aperture flanked by a pair of spikes (60.9a). **Size:** 20–40 mm across; 5–10 mm tall. **Biology:** Grows on rocks or kelp holdfasts over a depth range of 1–100 m.

60.10 Forked false-coral   *Adeonella* spp.

White to purple, flat, regularly forked branches. Zooecia in diagonal rows, diamond-shaped or rectangular; front perforated. Primary orifice kidney-shaped, separated by a bridge from an oval secondary orifice (60.10a). Long-beaked avicularia flank the orifice or colony edge. **Size:** Branches 4 mm wide. **Biology:** Several delicate calm-water species; 3–400 m.

60.11 Beauteous bryozoan   *Navianipora pulcherrima*

Exquisite, delicately branched colonies with tubular zooecia that curve away from the branches and have a simple round terminal orifice. **Size:** Colonies 10 mm. **Biology:** Grows only in sheltered places, often beneath boulders. The name *pulcherrima* is Latin for 'most beautiful'. Previously placed in the genus *Tubulipora*.

60.12 Cylindrical false-coral   *Turbicellepora cylindriformis*

Forms irregular finger-like salmon-pink colonies. The surface is dotted with knobbly zooecia that are irregularly oriented. **Size:** Colonies 20–50 mm tall. **Biology:** Grows under large boulders in the lower intertidal and shallow subtidal zones.

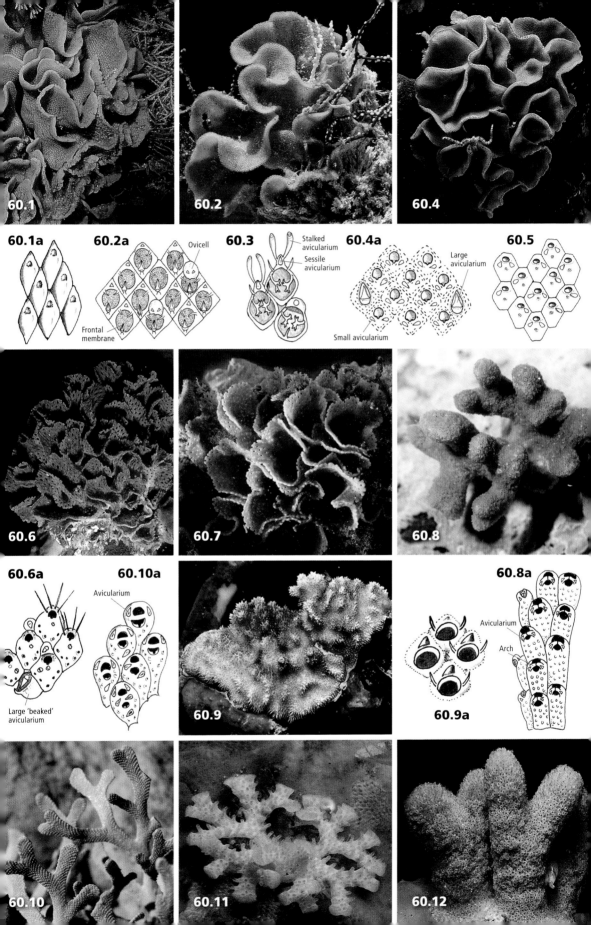

60.1

60.2

60.4

60.1a

60.2a
Ovicell
Frontal
membrane

60.3
Stalked
avicularium
Sessile
avicularium

60.4a
Large
avicularium
Small avicularium

60.5

60.6

60.7

60.8

60.6a
Large 'beaked'
avicularium

60.10a
Avicularium

60.9

60.8a
Avicularium
Arch

60.9a

60.10

60.11

60.12

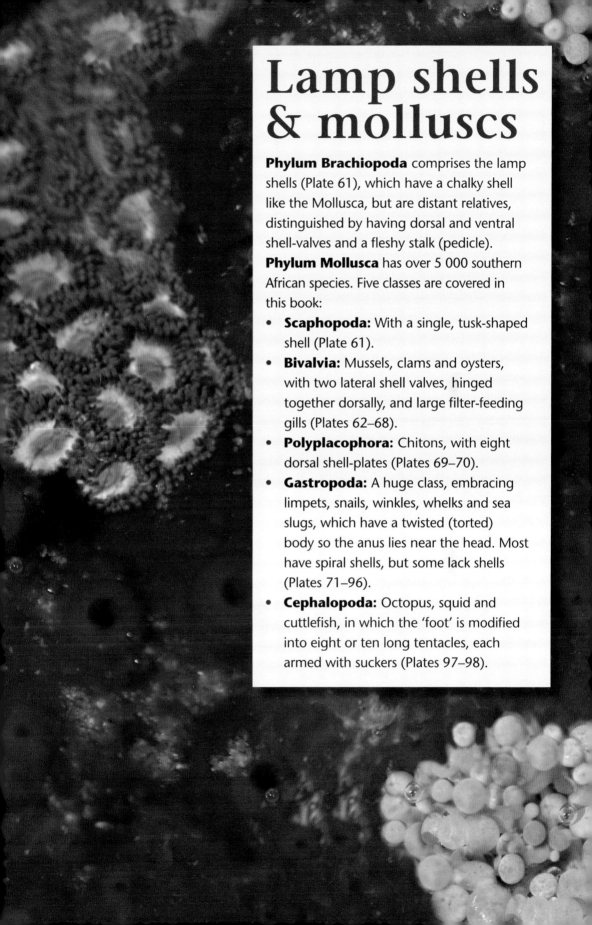

Lamp shells & molluscs

Phylum Brachiopoda comprises the lamp shells (Plate 61), which have a chalky shell like the Mollusca, but are distant relatives, distinguished by having dorsal and ventral shell-valves and a fleshy stalk (pedicle).

Phylum Mollusca has over 5 000 southern African species. Five classes are covered in this book:

- **Scaphopoda:** With a single, tusk-shaped shell (Plate 61).
- **Bivalvia:** Mussels, clams and oysters, with two lateral shell valves, hinged together dorsally, and large filter-feeding gills (Plates 62–68).
- **Polyplacophora:** Chitons, with eight dorsal shell-plates (Plates 69–70).
- **Gastropoda:** A huge class, embracing limpets, snails, winkles, whelks and sea slugs, which have a twisted (torted) body so the anus lies near the head. Most have spiral shells, but some lack shells (Plates 71–96).
- **Cephalopoda:** Octopus, squid and cuttlefish, in which the 'foot' is modified into eight or ten long tentacles, each armed with suckers (Plates 97–98).

PLATE 61

Lamp shells   Brachiopoda

Sessile, filter-feeding animals with calcareous, two-valved shells superficially resembling those of bivalve molluscs, but enclosing the body dorsally and ventrally, instead of laterally. Ventral valve normally the larger, and pierced posteriorly by a short stalk, or pedicle, which anchors the animal to the substratum. The shape of the shells and the wick-like pedicle give these animals the name 'lamp shells'. Internally, the major organ is a large, feathery, horseshoe-shaped filter-feeding organ (the lophophore), often supported by a delicate internal skeleton (brachidium). Brachiopods are relatively uncommon today, but thousands of fossil species testify that they once dominated the seafloor.

61.1 Ruby lamp shell   *Kraussina rubra*

Pink, with 20–30 prominent radiating ridges. The internal skeleton supporting the lophophore (brachidium) resembles a delicate pair of horns. **Size:** 20 mm. **Biology:** The commonest brachiopod on the shore, attached in small groups beneath rocks (61.1a).
SIMILAR SPECIES:
61.2 *Kraussina crassicostata* (Cape Point–Mossel Bay) is similar, but has 10–12 relatively coarse ribs.
61.3 *Terebratulina abyssicola* (Port Alfred–East London) has a brachidium that forms a complete loop; shell longer than broad, pointed to pear-shaped, only faintly ribbed.
61.4 *Terebratulina meridionalis* (Cape Peninsula) also has a brachidium that forms a complete loop, but shell more smoothly rounded, with fine branching ridges on its surface.

61.5 Disc lamp shell   *Discinisca tenuis*

Shell a pair of flat, semitransparent, horny brown discs with concentric growth ridges and a hairy fringe (61.5a). Lophophore visible through the shell. Brachidium absent. **Size:** 20 mm. **Biology:** Attached one on top of another in rafts; frequently washed up on the driftline in Namibia. An important source of food for oystercatchers. A recent arrival in Saldanha and Knysna; probably accidentally introduced from Namibia via mariculture.

Molluscs   Mollusca

All molluscs have an unsegmented body divided into a head, a visceral mass with the gut and gonads, and a foot. Most have a rasping 'tongue' (radula) – unique to molluscs – and a shell.

Tusk shells   Scaphopoda

A small group of molluscs with long tapering tubular shells, open at both ends, living buried upright in sand or mud, usually in deep waters. The narrow posterior end projects from the sediment and is used for water exchange. At the broader, lower opening, long sticky tentacles spread from the head, searching for food particles in the sand.

61.6 Regular tusk shell   *Dentalium regulare*

Shell relatively short and white to pink with 20–30 longitudinal ribs, which may become eroded in older specimens. **Size:** Up to 32 mm. **Biology:** Rarely found alive, but shells fairly commonly cast ashore.
SIMILAR SPECIES:
61.7 *Dentalium strigatum* (Cape Point–East London) is white and strongly curved with 13–14 strong longitudinal ribs.
61.8 *Schizodentalium plurifissuratum* is a larger (60 mm) species. The shell comes to a sharp point and has about 18 primary longitudinal ribs, interspersed with finer ridges.
61.9 *Fissidentalium salpinx* has a large (70 mm) solid shell with a broad aperture. The apex of the shell is finely ridged, becoming smooth towards the aperture. Found in deep water off the Western Cape.

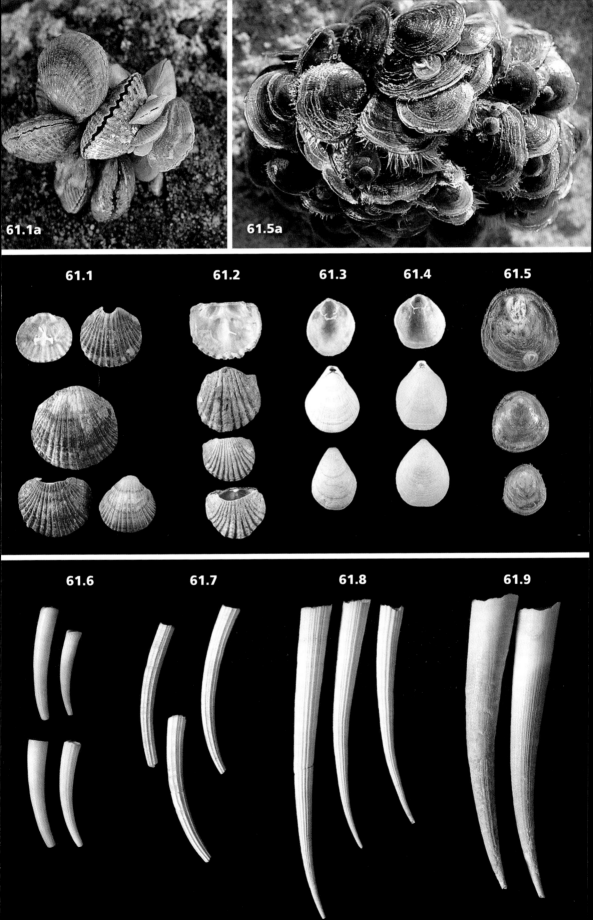

61.1a

61.5a

61.1   61.2   61.3   61.4   61.5

61.6   61.7   61.8   61.9

PLATE 62

Bivalves
Bivalvia

As the name implies, bivalves are enclosed by a pair of shell valves, hinged together along the back by an elastic ligament and extending down on either side of the body. The hinge stretches when the valves are clamped together and springs them apart when the animal relaxes. Bivalves have limited mobility and most cement one valve to the rocks, fasten themselves down with a 'beard' of byssal threads, or burrow into sand, mud, wood or even rock. Nearly all are filter-feeders, sucking water in through an inhalant siphon, sieving it through large, sheet-like gills, and expelling waste water via an exhalant siphon. Much of the body is packed with gonads; most species shed enormous amounts of sperm and eggs, and have planktonic larvae. A few brood their eggs.

62.1 Ribbed mussel
Aulacomya ater

Distinctive strong wavy ridges run the length of the shell, which is brown in juveniles, but becomes blue-black in larger individuals. Eroded areas are white. **Size:** Up to 90 mm. **Biology:** Forms extensive beds low in the intertidal zone and on rocky reefs to a depth of about 40 m. Slow-growing: takes at least 10 years to reach maximum size. An important source of food for the rock lobster *Jasus lalandii* (42.2). Water drawn in through frilly inhalant mantle edge (62.1a).

62.2 Black mussel
Choromytilus meridionalis

Shell smooth and shiny black, eroding to blue. Distinguished from *Mytilus galloprovincialis* by its narrower cross section and absence of pits in the resilial ridge (the narrow white band alongside the hinge ligament on the inner surface of the shell). The flesh of females is coloured dark chocolate by the gonads, which permeate the body, while that of males is pale yellow. **Size:** Up to 150 mm. **Biology:** Common on low-shore rocks and on shallow, flat reefs in the Cape, particularly in areas subject to sand cover or abrasion (62.2a). Grows rapidly, reaching 60 mm within a year. Popular with seafood lovers, but like other bivalves can become poisonous following toxic red tides (which are normally restricted to the west coast).

Alien

62.3 Mediterranean mussel
Mytilus galloprovincialis

Smooth, typically black or blue (62.3a), often shading to brown on lower surface; rarely light brown. Broad, and usually widest at base. Distinguished from *Choromytilus* by presence of pits in the resilial ridge (see above). Flesh of females orange; males off-white. **Size:** 60–140 mm. **Biology:** Introduced from Europe, but now the dominant west coast mussel, forming a dense mid- to low-shore band in wave-exposed areas. Rare below low water and absent from sand-inundated areas. Farmed commercially. Outcompetes other mussels, having a faster growth, higher reproductive output and greater tolerance of desiccation. Ousts rock-dwelling limpet species that are too large to live on its shells, but supports smaller limpets (62.3a). Peaks in areas of strong but not extreme wave action, where food concentration and supply are optimal. Oystercatcher breeding success has increased since its arrival as it boosts their food supply. Shell heavily eroded and weakened by the blue-green alga *Mastigocoleus* and the lichen *Pyrenocolema*.

62.4 Brown mussel
Perna perna

Smooth, yellow-brown, sometimes tinged green or with a chevron pattern. In crowded intertidal beds, often elongate and almost rectangular in cross section. Submerged, fast-growing specimens are taller and narrower. Resilial ridge pitted (see 62.2 above). Flesh of females bright orange; males off-white. **Size:** 80–125 mm. **Biology:** The dominant mussel in the southeast, forming dense beds (62.4a) from the intertidal to a few metres' depth. Important resource for east-coast subsistence fishers. Shells extensively bored by *Phoronis* (109.2) in Namibia. Prone to parasitism, putting it at a disadvantage relative to the parasite-free *Mytilus*. Co-exists with *Mytilus* on the south coast because it survives lower on the shore, where *Mytilus* is excluded by more intense wave action.

62.5 Bisexual mussel
Semimytilus algosus

A small elongate species with a delicate smooth brown or blackish-green shell that bulges below the apex. Resilial ridge narrow, not pitted. **Size:** Up to 50 mm. **Biology:** Probably an alien species, previously being known only from South America. Most specimens are hermaphroditic with male gonad on one side, female on the other.

62.1a

62.2a

62.3a

62.4a

62.1

62.2

62.3

62.4

62.5

PLATE 63

63.1 Brack-water mussel — *Brachidontes virgiliae*

Shells small and brown; both the inner and outer surfaces ribbed, but clean and lustrous: almost never eroded or overgrown. **Size:** 25 mm. **Biology:** Attached to rocks and other hard substrata in the upper reaches of estuaries.

63.2 Semistriated mussel — *Brachidontes semistriatus*

Also small and brown, but smooth or ribbed only externally. **Size:** 22 mm. **Biology:** Forms closely packed groups in intertidal rock crevices, especially in wave-exposed areas in KwaZulu-Natal. Often small, deformed and eroded from crowding and rubbing. Previously called *B. variabilis*.

63.3 Ledge mussel — *Septifer bilocularis*

Shell thick and may be brown, green or orange; external surface covered by radiating ridges. An interior shelly ledge bridges the anterior (pointed) end of each shell valve. **Size:** Up to 43 mm. **Biology:** Found singly or in small groups under rock ledges from mid shore downwards.

63.4 Estuarine mussel — *Arcuatula capensis*

An attractive mussel with a thin, glossy, greenish shell that is smooth, but marked with radiating reddish-brown lines. Inner surface of shell smooth. **Size:** Up to 76 mm. **Biology:** Restricted to estuaries, where it may bury itself in mud among seagrass beds, or attach to rocks, seaweeds or wood.

63.5 Half-hairy mussel — *Gregariella petagnae*

A small reddish-brown mussel in which the anterior end is swollen, the midpoint humped, and the posterior half of the shell covered by fibrous hairs. **Size:** Up to 18 mm. **Biology:** Occurs singly in rock crevices and clumps of seaweed.

63.6 Ear mussel — *Modiolus auriculatus*

Shell broad, with dorsal margin raised and narrowed to form a low, ear-like hump. Colour generally reddish brown; juveniles with a posterior, tufted, outer layer. **Size:** Usually less than 50 mm. **Biology:** Fairly common in low-shore pools and crevices along the east coast; abundant in Mozambique, where it can grow to over 80 mm in length.

63.7 Oblique ark shell — *Barbatia obliquata*

Lower margin of shell concave. Shells sculptured with fine radiating ridges, and covered with a velvety black fur, which is often eroded except along the edges. Eroded areas white. Inner surface shows brown markings posteriorly. **Size:** Up to 58 mm. **Biology:** Attached by byssus in crevices or under rocks in sandy pools.

SIMILAR SPECIES:

63.8 *Striarca symmetrica* (East London northwards) is small, squat and parallel-sided, with a velvety surface. The external ligament is diamond-shaped.

63.9 *Arca avellana* (Port Alfred northwards) has a very rectangular shape and long straight hinge. The exterior surface is fibrous.

63.10 Scaly horse-mussel — *Atrina squamifera*

Very large, with a fragile translucent-brown shell that is open at the wide, posterior end. A series of 6–12 ribs runs the length of each valve and bears conspicuous scale-like cusps. A bunch of long golden byssal threads projects from the ventral margin. **Size:** Up to 390 mm. **Biology:** Lives partially buried vertically in sheltered mud or sand, with the wide posterior end projecting above the surface. The commensal crab *Pinnotheres dofleini* (55.6) commonly lives inside the shell and steals food from the mussel's gills. The byssal threads of the mussel were reputedly woven into Jason's golden fleece of Greek mythology.

63.11 Furrowed horse-mussel — *Pinna muricata*

Almost square-cut posteriorly, has smaller cusps externally on 12–26 fine, radial riblets, and a longitudinal furrow running down the middle of the inner surface of each valve. **Size:** 160 mm. **Biology:** Lives close to the low-tide mark in sandy or gravelly areas among rocks.

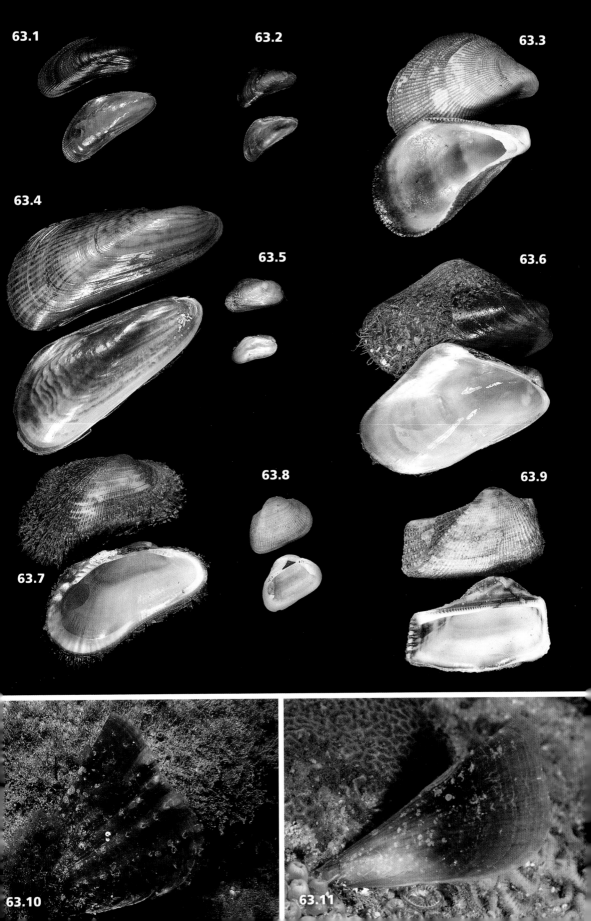

63.1

63.2

63.3

63.4

63.5

63.6

63.7

63.8

63.9

63.10

63.11

PLATE 64

64.1 Cape pearl oyster — *Pinctada capensis*
Large, squarish; attached by byssal threads. Valves equal-sized, with radial bands and projecting concentric wavy growth ridges. **Size:** 130 mm. **Biology:** Intertidal or on shallow reefs. The genus produces pearls, but few by this species. **SIMILAR SPECIES:** *P. nigra* (Transkei northwards) is very similar, but more fragile, and outer surface smooth except for concentric growth rings near the margin. Harvested in Mozambique. *Isognomon nucleus* (East London northwards) is small (5–20 mm), oval, with an obliquely truncated hinge; black, with concentric growth rings, but older parts eroded to chalky white. Abundant in high-shore crevices. Previously named *Parviperna rupella*.

64.2 Cape rock oyster — *Striostrea margaritacea*
Large, heavy-shelled. Deep, multi-layered, cupped lower valve cemented to substratum; upper valve thin, flat, often bearing fine, radial threads. **Size:** 180 mm. **Biology:** Common on rocky reefs from low tide to 5 m. Excellent eating; about 500 000 sold in KwaZulu-Natal each year. Marketable size (60 mm) reached in 33 months. Once named *Crassostrea margaritacea*.

64.3 Brooding oyster — *Ostrea atherstonei*
Large, flat; lower valve shallow, not hollowed below hinge. Often pink-edged. **Size:** 60 mm. **Biology:** Occurs on shallow reefs; often overgrown by fouling organisms and difficult to see. The eggs are brooded in the gill chamber. Fossil deposits of its shells line parts of the floor of Langebaan Lagoon, but there are no living individuals in the lagoon.

64.4 Pacific oyster — *Crassostrea gigas*
Length twice breadth. Strong concentric corrugations and wave-like scallops. White inside; no lustre. One valve slightly indented below apex. **Size:** 200 mm. **Biology:** Introduced for cultivation; wild populations established in three estuaries. Fast-growing. Alien

64.5 Natal rock oyster — *Saccostrea cuccullata*
Lower valve deeply hollowed below the hinge and cemented to the rock; upper valve relatively flat. Margins form a series of neatly interlocking zigzag folds; often tinted mauve. **Size:** 70 mm. **Biology:** The dominant KwaZulu-Natal oyster, forming a distinct band in the high shore (64.5a). Small, but good eating. Previously called *Crassostrea cuccullata*.

64.6 Saddle oyster — *Anomia achaeus*
Small, transparent oyster-like shells that resemble fish scales. Easily recognised by the hole in the lower valve, through which a calcified byssal plug extends to cement the bivalve to the substratum. **Size:** Usually under 20 mm. **Biology:** Common under stones, on algal fronds and on shells of larger molluscs.

64.7 Dwarf fan shell — *Talochlamys multistriata*
This small scallop has a single 'ear' and comes in a wide variety of colours, including orange and violet. Shell valves equal in size, with 50–70 fine, prickly, radiating ridges. **Size:** Up to 37 mm. **Biology:** Found under rocks or in algal holdfasts. Swims if disturbed.

64.8 Edible scallop — *Pecten sulcicostatus*
Right (lower) valve convex, left one flattened; ears equal in size; 12–15 ridges on each shell. Colour pink to brown, darker above. **Size:** 106 mm. **Biology:** Lies on the surface of clean sand or mud, and swims by clapping the valves together. The mantle edges have a series of brightly coloured simple eyes (64.8a). Has potential for commercial culture.

64.9 File shell — *Limaria tuberculata*
Valves equal-sized, translucent white, with small 'ears' and radiating ribs. Animal prominently fringed with mobile, segmented tentacles (64.9a). **Size:** 42 mm. **Biology:** Lives unattached under boulders or in algal holdfasts; can swim clumsily by clapping the shells. The tentacles secrete sticky, repugnant mucus and can be shed to distract attackers.

64.10 Coral scallop — *Pedum spondyloideum*
Mantle edge variable; usually vivid pink to red, rimmed with many small, shining, yellow or red eyes. Inner lip blue with yellow stripes. **Size:** 50 mm. **Biology:** Can be free-living, but usually embedded in corals (particularly *Porites* spp.). Helps repel the crown of thorns starfish *Acanthaster planci* (100.1), an avid coral predator, by squirting exhalant jets of water at it.

150 Lamp shells & molluscs

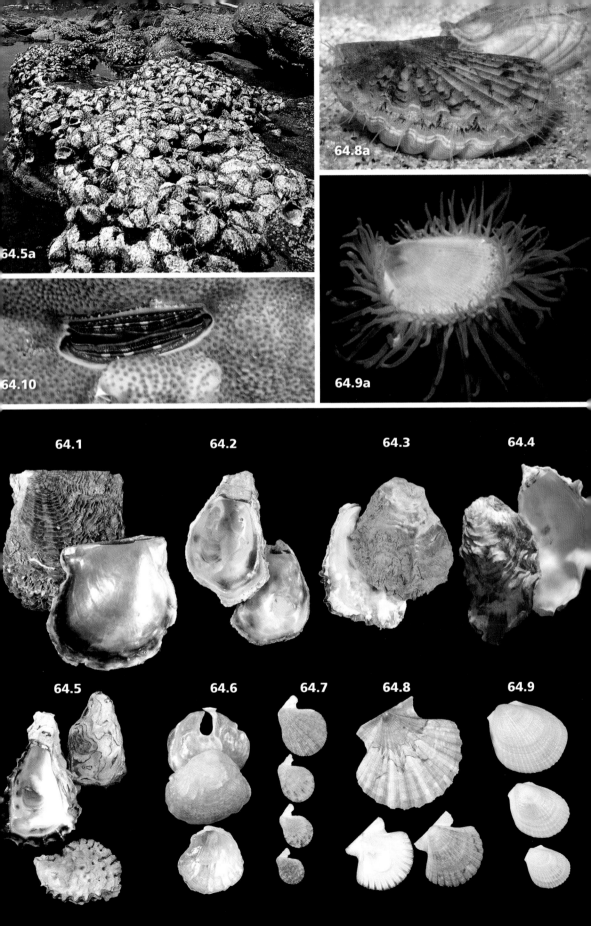

64.5a

64.8a

64.10

64.9a

64.1

64.2

64.3

64.4

64.5

64.6

64.7

64.8

64.9

PLATE 65

65.1 Yellow cockle   *Trachycardium flavum*
Shell taller (hinge to aperture) than long (side to side), with 26–29 radiating ribs; anterior ribs with semicircular scales, posterior ones with erect scales. Colour mottled-brown. **Size:** 64 mm. **Biology:** Buries itself shallowly in muddy sand using its large muscular foot.

65.2 Red-rimmed cockle   *Trachycardium rubicundum*
More elongate than the previous species, with a greater number of ribs (35–38); the shell is flecked with pink or brown and has a red margin internally. **Size:** 60 mm. **Biology:** Buries itself in sand.

65.3 Smooth trough shell   *Mactra glabrata*
Large, fat, oval, smooth and glossy. Creamy, with darker edges; juveniles often with radiating lines. Siphons fused. **Size:** 114 mm. **Biology:** Burrows shallowly in fine sand. Good eating, but the legal limit is eight per day. Once abundant in Langebaan Lagoon, but has disappeared.

65.4 Angular surf clam   *Scissodesma spengleri*
Large, almost equilateral; posterior margin with a distinctive angular, flattened surface. Smooth and off-white, with a thin, brown surface 'skin' (periostracum). **Size:** 113 mm. **Biology:** Burrows shallowly in sandy-beach surf zones and in lagoons. Abundant in False Bay; washes up after storms and is eaten by seagulls. Also recorded in northern Namibia.

65.5 Otter shell   *Lutraria lutraria*
Valves elongate, gaping widely at both ends. Hinge with a prominent spoon-shaped depression internally. White to dirty yellow with brown 'skin'. **Size:** 137 mm. **Biology:** Digs deeply in muddy sands, and extends its long, non-retractile siphons to the surface.

65.6 Pencil bait   *Solen capensis*
Very elongate, almost cylindrical shells, with widely gaping ends. Anterior (upper) end bent outwards to form a lip. Siphons short and fused (65.6a), leaving a keyhole-shaped opening on the sand surface when retracted. **Size:** 160 mm long. **Biology:** Burrows deeply in firm, clean sand in estuaries and lagoons. Good eating, and prized as bait. **SIMILAR SPECIES:** *S. cylindraceus* (Transkei northwards, also found in estuaries) is smaller (50 mm) and lacks a lip around the anterior end. Previously named *S. corneus*.

65.7 Papery cockle   *Fulvia papyracea*
Thin-shelled, with numerous flat-topped radial ribs; interior suffused reddish purple. **Size:** 20–50 mm. **Biology:** Occurs in muddy, shallow, subtidal sediments in calm bays and estuaries. Abundant in Maputo Bay, but less common to the south.

65.8 Rectangular false cockle   *Cardita variegata*
Small; shell almost rectangular, with 20–25 coarse ribs radiating from the hinge, which is displaced to the anterior corner. Colour off-white. **Size:** Up to 35 mm. **Biology:** Lives attached to the underside of rocks on reefs.

65.9 Dead man's fingers   *Thecalia concamerata*
Similar, but ventral margin of the shell folded in to form an internal brood chamber, within which young are incubated. **Size:** 25 mm. **Biology:** Lives under boulders and occurs in groups. Lacks a larval stage: miniature versions of the adults develop in the brood pouch.

65.10 Rough false cockle   *Carditella rugosa*
Small triangular cockles with 16–18 bumpy ribs radiating from the hinge. Colour off-white, flecked with brown. **Size:** Up to 10 mm. **Biology:** Common on sheltered sandbanks. **SIMILAR SPECIES:** *C. capensis* occurs on the west coast and is almost equal-sided.

65.11 Giant clam   *Tridacna squamosa*
Massive. The beautifully coloured mantle lobes project from the wavy aperture. Outer surface of shell white, with pronounced leaf-like projections (scutes). **Size:** 400 mm. **Biology:** Filter-feeds and 'farms' microscopic algae in the brightly coloured mantle lobes; hence confined to shallow clear waters, mainly on coral reefs. Rare in South Africa. **SIMILAR SPECIES:** *T. maxima* (common in Zululand) has much smaller scutes.

65.6a

65.11

65.1

65.2

65.3

65.6

65.4

65.5

65.7

65.8

65.9

65.10

PLATE 66

66.1 Smooth platter shell — *Loripes clausus*

Shell valves smooth, thick and flat, almost perfectly circular. White, with faint growth rings. Ligament internal and cuts obliquely across the hinge plate. **Size:** Up to 34 mm. **Biology:** Estuarine; burrows deeply in muddy sand near low tide. Feeding unusual in that water enters through a mucus-lined tube secreted by the foot (instead of through the inhalant siphon), then exits through an elongate exhalant siphon.

66.2 Toothless platter shell — *Anodontia edentula*

Shell valves thin and deeply concave, with a 'beak' bulging beyond the hinge, which is very thin and toothless. Surface white and smooth, with faint growth rings. **Size:** Up to about 50 mm. **Biology:** Estuarine, burrowing just below the surface of soft muds.

66.3 Dwarf rusty clam — *Lasaea adansoni turtoni*

A tiny globular clam with smooth white or pink valves, often stained red-brown around the hinge. **Biology:** Abundant, nestling among byssal threads of mussels (66.3a) or among barnacles high on rocky shores. Hermaphroditic, starting life as a male, then changing to female. Eggs and larvae brooded in the shell and emerge fully developed. Formerly misidentified as *Kellia rubra*.
SIMILAR SPECIES:
66.4 *Kellia rotunda* (Cape Town–Durban) is egg-shaped, with a smooth oval glossy white shell. **Size:** 8 mm. **Biology:** Also nestles in crevices on rocky shores, but is commonly found in Durban Bay in sandy sediments.

66.5 Dwarf triangular clam — *Tellimya trigona*

A tiny, smooth, off-white and distinctively triangular species, with no texture to the shell other than very faint concentric growth rings. **Size:** 4 mm or less. **Biology:** Abundant and burrows shallowly in west coast lagoonal sandbanks. Name still uncertain.

66.6 Port Alfred tellin — *Tellina alfredensis*

Valves smooth and laterally compressed, posterior end tapering and bent slightly to the right. Colour a lovely pink, vivid on the inner surface, especially when alive. **Size:** 85 mm. **Biology:** Buries itself left side down in shallow water off clean sandy beaches. Long, inhalant siphon moves around on the sand surface, 'vacuuming' up light detrital particles.

66.7 Gilchrist's tellin — *Tellina gilchristi*

Valves of the shell slightly extended posteriorly, but not bent to the side. Colour white or pink, usually with distinctive pink rays (66.7a) that distinguish it from other small species of tellin in the Cape. **Size:** Up to 28 mm. **Biology:** Burrows in sand in the subtidal zone on sandy beaches, but also found intertidally in sheltered bays and lagoons.

66.8 Trilateral tellin — *Tellina trilatera*

Shell delicate and smooth, apart from slight concentric growth rings; glossy white. Anterior end broadly rounded and much shorter than the tapering posterior end. **Size:** Up to 49 mm long. **Biology:** Common on sandy beaches, burrowing in fine sand down to depths of 8 m. Shells often drilled by octopus bite-marks.

66.9 Coated tellin — *Tellina capsoides*

Shell relatively thick, chalky-white, and sculptured with numerous concentric growth ridges. Right valve larger than left. Posterior end angular; hinge line long and straight. **Size:** 58 mm. **Biology:** Burrows in muddy sand. Once abundant in Durban Bay; now rare.

66.10 Ridged tellin — *Gastrana matadoa*

Valves white to fawn and etched with strong, sharp, concentric growth ridges. Hinge of left valve with one wedge-shaped tooth, that of the right valve with two diverging teeth. **Size:** Up to 44 mm. **Biology:** Burrows in sheltered sandbanks and estuaries.

66.11 Littoral tellin — *Macoma litoralis*

A small species with delicate flattened cream-to-white shells. Surface smooth and silky. **Size:** Up to 33 mm. **Biology:** Burrows a few centimetres below the surface of muddy sandbanks in estuaries and lagoons.

66.3a

66.7a

66.1

66.2

66.3

66.6

66.4

66.5

66.7

66.8

66.9

66.10

66.11

PLATE 67

67.1 Shipworm — *Bankia carinata*

Extremely elongate, cylindrical bivalves that occupy burrows cut deep into submerged wood with their reduced, rasp-like shells. Burrows lined with chalky shell material; open end can be closed off by a unique feather-like segmented pallet. **Size:** 200 mm long. **Biology:** Notorious pests: can riddle and destroy wooden structures. Shipworms remain filter-feeders, but are also able to digest wood, aided by symbiotic bacteria in the gut.

67.2 White mussel or wedge clam — *Donax serra*

Wedge-shaped. Coarse wavy ridges run across the truncated, posterior end. Inner surface tinged purple. Ligament large and external, about one-third from hind end. Inhalant siphon stubby, capped with a sieve of tentacles; exhalant siphon long and thin (67.2a). **Size:** 88 mm. **Biology:** Abundant on wave-exposed beaches. Extensively exploited for bait and eating (legal limit 50 per day). In the southeast, adults concentrate at mid-tide and juveniles at low water, but on west coast adults are mainly subtidal and juveniles intertidal. Minimum legal size of 35 mm reached after 20 months; lives up to five years.

67.3 Ridged wedge-shell — *Donax madagascariensis*

A triangular shell easily recognised by the parallel ridges that run diagonally across the entire outer surface. **Size:** Up to 26 mm. **Biology:** Common on sandy beaches in KwaZulu-Natal. The ridges on the shell are thought to facilitate burrowing.

67.4 Butterfly wedge-shell — *Donax sordidus*

Very similar in shape and size, but the shell is smooth, apart from a few fine ridges on the truncated, posterior end. **Size:** 32 mm. **Biology:** Abundant in the Eastern Cape, where it migrates up and down the beach with the tide. Grows rapidly and lives for about two years.

67.5 Slippery wedge-shell — *Donax lubricus*

Anterior end long, posterior end truncated. Surface smooth, white or flesh-coloured, sometimes with purple rays. Sides flanking the hinge lie almost at right angles to each other. **Size:** Up to 35 mm. **Biology:** Seldom found alive, but shells often wash ashore.

67.6 Rayed wedge-shell — *Donax faba*

Resembles *D. lubricus*, but wider, and front proportionally longer. Smooth, apart from growth lines. Variable, but usually with radiating rays, particularly internally. Siphons quite short (67.6a). **Size:** 20 mm. **Biology:** Abundant on semi-exposed sandy beaches.

67.7 Violet-tipped wedge-shell — *Donax bipartitus*

Recognised by the violet coloration of the inner surface of the truncated, posterior end of each shell valve. **Size:** 23 mm. **Biology:** Occupies coarse sand on wave-exposed shores from the low-tide mark down to 25 m.

67.8 Oval wedge-shell — *Donax burnupi*

Elongate, fragile and compressed; both ends rounded and tapering. Surface smooth and glossy, pink or cream to brown, often with dark rays. Interior with a violet mark behind the hinge. **Size:** 36 mm. **Biology:** Burrows in subtidal sands; shells commonly wash up.

67.9 Fragile wedge-shell — *Siliqua fasciata*

Fragile, oval, slightly pointed valves, gaping anteriorly. Internal reinforcing strut runs from the hinge to the margin, made obvious by its white colour, which contrasts with the purple background colour. Three to four pale rays. **Size:** 30 mm. **Biology:** Found in coarse sand down to 30 m, but also abundant in fine sands in Maputo Bay.

67.10 Sunset clam — *Hiatula lunulata*

Elongate oval shells that gape posteriorly. Ligament external, attached to a distinct, projecting platform. Hinge near middle of shell valves. Pale violet with darker rays. **Size:** 35 mm. **Biology:** Estuarine; common in fine, clean sand in shallow water.

67.11 Sand tellin — *Psammotellina capensis*

Almost oval, but hinge nearer front. Outer surface yellow with violet rays, or violet with yellow rays. **Size:** 21 mm. **Biology:** Burrows shallowly in sandbanks in estuaries and lagoons. Most common just inside mouths of estuaries, but tolerant of lowered salinities.

67.1

67.2a

67.6a

67.2

67.3

67.4

67.5

67.10

67.6

67.8

67.9

67.11

67.7

PLATE 68

68.1 Ribbed Venus — *Gafrarium pectinatum alfredense*

Oval with well-developed radial ribs, which branch towards the margins of the shell. Colour pale, speckled or blotched with brown. **Size:** Up to 26 mm. **Biology:** Burrows in coarse sand. Shells frequently washed up on KwaZulu-Natal beaches.

68.2 Mottled Venus — *Sunetta contempta bruggeni*

Shells oval, with a deep depression spanning the joint just behind the hinge. Colour very variable: usually cream mottled with pink or brown, interior tinged with pink. **Size:** Up to 38 mm. **Biology:** Common in coarse sand and gravel below 20 m depth, but shells often cast up on KwaZulu-Natal beaches.

68.3 Warty Venus — *Venus verrucosa*

Shells oval and extremely heavy. Outer surface sculptured with strong concentric ridges that break up into rounded knobs near the margins. **Size:** Up to 60 mm long. **Biology:** Common in clean sand and gravel from low shore downwards.

68.4 Greater heart-clam — *Dosinia lupinus orbignyi*

A heavy, almost perfectly circular white shell with a heart-shaped depression spanning the valves just in front of the hinge. Outer surface with fine, concentric growth lines. **Size:** Up to 53 mm. **Biology:** Burrows in clean subtidal sands. Siphons up to three times the shell length, and are fused except at their tips.

68.5 Lesser heart-clam — *Dosinia hepatica*

Similar-shaped but smaller, with a smooth brown exterior and violet markings internally. **Size:** Seldom exceeds 25 mm. **Biology:** Entirely estuarine. Abundant in substrata ranging from coarse sand to muddy silt. Can clamp its shell shut to survive fresh water for a few weeks during floods.

68.6 Streaked sand-clam — *Tivela compressa*

A large, fat, triangular bivalve with a smooth shiny shell marked by concentric brown lines and radiating brown streaks. **Size:** Up to 61 mm. **Biology:** Burrows in clean sand below low-tide level. Washes up frequently in False Bay.

68.7 Brown sand-clam — *Tivela polita*

Smaller than streaked sand-clam, pointed, with very straight triangular posterior edge. Interior usually edged with purple. **Size:** 46 mm. **Biology:** Common on wave-washed beaches. Shells common in beach-drift, and often drilled by gastropods.

68.8 Beaked clam — *Eumarcia paupercula*

A smooth, swollen clam with the posterior end produced into a 'beak'. Colour very variable, usually cream to brown with brown zigzags, flecks or rays. **Size:** Up to 42 mm. **Biology:** Burrows 20–30 mm below the surface of sheltered sand or mudbanks. Abundant in Mozambique, where it is sold in markets.

68.9 Zigzag clam — *Pitar abbreviatus*

Shells like inflated commas: fat, round, and with a large oval depression just in front of the hinge. Pale, usually with areas of brown zigzag markings. **Size:** Up to 38 mm. **Biology:** In clean sand, especially in KwaZulu-Natal and Mozambique, where it is eaten.

68.10 Corrugated Venus — *Venerupis corrugatus*

Shell elongate, oval, with hinge towards anterior end. Surface usually cream, with fine, wavy, concentric growth ridges, sometimes attractively rayed in juveniles, but becoming dull and corrugated in adults. Siphons short (68.10a). Interior purple towards margin. **Size:** Up to 77 mm. **Biology:** Commonly nestles among mussels in sandy areas, or burrows shallowly in sheltered sandbanks.

68.11 Thick-shelled clam — *Meretrix meretrix*

Shell very thick, equal-sided, with a smoothly rounded base. Extremely variable, but usually pale to dark brown, often with darker bands. **Size:** 25 mm. **Biology:** Abundant in calm lagoons and estuaries. Large numbers sold in Maputo markets.

PLATE 69

Chitons   Polyplacophora

Oval, flattened molluscs, with eight overlapping shell plates, or valves, along the back – polyplacophora means 'bearer of many plates'. The plates are surrounded by a tough, flexible girdle, often armed with protective scales, hairs or spines that are useful aids to identification. Head completely hidden beneath the girdle, and lacks both eyes and sensory tentacles. The remainder of the underside consists of a broad muscular foot rimmed with small gills. Chitons are sluggish creatures, and usually shelter in crevices or beneath rocks. When active, usually at night, they creep slowly about, rasping encrusting plants or animals from the rock surface with a powerful file-like radula. There are some 26 southern African species, most of which occur intertidally.

69.1 Textile chiton   *Ischnochiton textilis*

Shell valves usually pale yellow or grey, central sections minutely pitted, lateral areas and end valves with fine, radiating ridges. Girdle covered in small oval scales; when viewed under the microscope each scale is crossed by 12–24 fine ridges. **Size:** 20–40 mm. **Biology:** Common in groups on the undersides of boulders in rock pools along the Cape coast. May detach and roll into a ball when the boulder is overturned.

69.2 Dwarf chiton   *Ischnochiton oniscus*

Colour often white, but can occur in a wide variety of patterns and colours. Valves textured with fine pits, which are often arranged in rows, but lack radiating ridges. Girdle narrow, covered in tiny scales that appear smooth to the naked eye, but reveal fine ribs under microscopic examination. **Size:** Usually about 10 mm. **Biology:** The smallest southern African chiton. Generally occurs in small groups on the undersides of rocks in sandy pools.

69.3 Ribbed-scale chiton   *Ischnochiton bergoti*

Colour usually off-white to brown, valves finely pitted, sometimes with vague radiating ridges or growth marks. When viewed under the microscope, girdle scales each have 3–8 coarse radiating ribs. **Size:** Small, usually 10–20 mm. **Biology:** A rather drab species occasionally found under stones at low tide along the cold Atlantic coastline. Thought to brood its eggs beneath the girdle. Previously named *I. hewitti*.

69.4 Python chiton   *Chiton salihafui*

Closely resembles *C. tulipa*, the girdle being similarly covered with overlapping scales, but the central portions of the valves have fine yet clear longitudinal striations, and there is an elongate dark triangle on each valve, off-centre of a pale area. **Size:** 40 mm. **Biology:** Occurs relatively high on the shore in shady overhangs. Hunted for its traditional putative medicinal properties, and becoming scarce as a consequence. Also recorded in Tanzania and Somalia.

69.5 Tulip chiton   *Chiton tulipa*

An attractive chiton with smooth pink valves streaked and flecked with a wide range of brown patches and zigzags. Central portion of valves smooth, but often with a striped pattern. Girdle striped, covered with large, smooth, overlapping scales. **Size:** Typically 30–40 mm. **Biology:** A common and well-known, brightly coloured chiton found under rocks near low tide; usually solitary.

69.6 Brooding chiton   *Chiton nigrovirescens*

Valves dark brownish black with vague radiating ridges. Girdle rufous with black band, covered with large, conspicuous, smooth scales, sometimes with a coppery sheen. **Size:** 10–25 mm. **Biology:** Found in tightly packed groups under stones from the mid-intertidal zone downwards. Unusual in that the eggs are retained under the girdle, where they develop into fully formed baby chitons.

69.1

69.2

69.3

69.4

9.5

69.6

PLATE 70

70.1 Broad chiton — *Callochiton dentatus*
Broad and very flat with minutely granular, shiny, dark brown to orange valves. Girdle wide and densely covered with tiny, elongate, spine-like scales, giving it a velvety texture. If the girdle is pulled away from the second to seventh valves, four characteristic slits are revealed in the margin of each shell valve. **Size:** 20–50 mm. **Biology:** Uncommon and found singly under stones at low tide. Previously named *C. castaneus*.

70.2 Spiny chiton — *Acanthochitona garnoti*
Shell valves dull brown with oblique pale stripes, largely concealed by the wide girdle. Girdle dotted with small spicules and nine characteristic paired tufts of long glassy spines. **Size:** 30–45 mm. **Biology:** Unusual in that it is abundant on exposed rock surfaces high in the intertidal zone, rather than under rocks. Active at night. Handle with care, as the spines cause irritation if they become embedded in the skin.

70.3 Black chiton — *Onithochiton literatus*
Shell valves usually brownish black, sculptured with wavy radiating lines, often badly eroded in larger specimens. Girdle broad, brown to black, velvety, with minute embedded spicules. **Size:** 25–50 mm. **Biology:** One of the few common chitons in KwaZulu-Natal, found in the open on wave-exposed rocks or around the margins of intertidal rock pools.

70.4 Natal giant chiton — *Dinoplax validifossus*
Similar to *D. gigas*, but with the girdle hairs uniformly distributed, not concentrated into distinct tufts. **Size:** 50–70 mm. **Biology:** In sandy gullies on subtropical shores, often in small groups.

70.5 Giant chiton or armadillo — *Dinoplax gigas*
Shell large with steeply arched grey or brown valves, usually badly eroded. Girdle brown and dotted with distinct tufts of small brown hairs. **Size:** 70–100 mm. **Biology:** Usually found partially or totally buried in sand on flat, rocky reefs. Sometimes used as bait by fishermen and eaten by some people, although tough and leathery.

70.6 Orange hairy chiton — *Chaetopleura pertusa*
Shell valves sculptured with numerous beaded ribs, usually pink or orange. Girdle wide, often bright orange or pink and bearing both branched bristles and short simple hairs. **Size:** May reach 40–50 mm. **Biology:** A relatively uncommon but brightly coloured species found under rocks at low tide or below.

70.7 Hairy chiton — *Chaetopleura papilio*
Shell valves smooth and shiny, attractively marked with alternating light and dark brown stripes, sides often flecked with light blue. Girdle wide and brown with a sparse covering of long unbranched black bristles. **Size:** 40–70 mm. **Biology:** A distinctive but uncommon west coast species, usually found singly under rocks in low-tide pools.

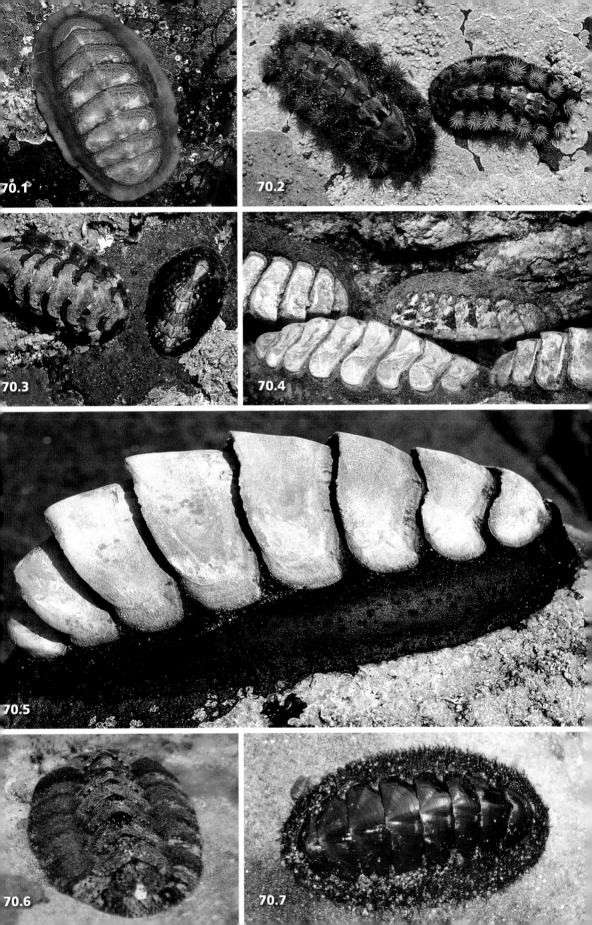

PLATE 71

Snails & their kin

Gastropods typically have a single, usually spiral, shell.

Sea-snails & limpets

Gastropoda

Prosobranchia

Most marine gastropods fall in the large subclass Prosobranchia, have a spiral shell, a well-developed head with tentacles, and a large flat foot used for locomotion; although limpets have cap-shaped shells. Primitive members are herbivorous, rasping seaweeds and micro-algae, and have a characteristic round shell aperture. Advanced forms are predators, have a long proboscis and a cylindrical siphon, and their shell aperture has an anterior canal or groove to house the siphon.

Abalone

The shells of abalone form a very flattened spiral with an enormously enlarged aperture and a row of small holes along the left side. Water enters the gill cavity under the front shell margin and exits through the holes. As the shell grows, new holes are created and old ones filled in. The large muscular foot (which is much sought-after as a seafood) grips tightly to the rock and allows for rapid locomotion. Abalone are herbivorous. They shed their eggs and sperm into the water, where the larvae undergo a brief planktonic development.

71.1 Siffie or Venus ear
Haliotis spadicea

Shell ear-shaped with a concave outer lip (or growing edge). Interior mother-of-pearl, with a red stain beneath the spire; exterior fairly smooth, blotched reddish brown. Margins of mantle lobed. **Size:** Up to 80 mm long. **Biology:** Common but cryptic: found in rock crevices or among redbait close to the level of low tide. Feeds on red algae. Collection is legally limited to 10 per person per day and a minimum diameter of 32 mm.

71.2 Beautiful ear-shell
Haliotis speciosa

The outer lip of the shell is smoothly convex, and there is no red stain under the spire. The outer surface of the shell is mottled grey and red-brown with fine, spiral ridges. **Size:** Up to 86 mm. **Biology:** An extremely rare species, about which little is known. Occurs in shallow waters but is seldom found in the intertidal zone.

71.3 Spiral-ridged siffie
Haliotis parva

Small, with a conspicuous spiral ridge running around the middle of the last whorl of the shell. Holes on low humps, which arise from a second, less distinct marginal ridge. External colour brown or orange, sometimes mottled. Head with two orange-red tentacles; mantle with multiple tubercles and intervening smooth tentacles of various sizes (71.3a). **Size:** Up to 45 mm. **Biology:** Never abundant; lives under stones in rock pools or on shallow reefs.

SIMILAR SPECIES:

71.4 *Haliotis queketti* (Port Alfred–Zululand) replaces *H. parva* to the east, but is rare. The holes in the shell are raised on prominent turrets and there is usually one well-marked and several weaker spiral ridges. Grows to 46 mm.

71.5 Perlemoen or abalone
Haliotis midae

Shell large and heavy with strong, irregular corrugations parallel to the growing edge. Margins of mantle with a dense fur of fleshy, frilly projections, surmounted by longer simple tentacles (71.5b). **Size:** Up to 190 mm. **Biology:** Juveniles (71.5a) lack the corrugations and occur under boulders or beneath spiny sea urchins. Decline in urchins east of Cape Hangklip following 'invasion' by rock lobsters in the 1990s has led to a collapse in the recruitment of abalone there. Adults occupy crevices or exposed positions on shallow reefs, particularly in beds of kelp, *Ecklonia maxima*. They consume pieces of drift weed, notably kelp and red algae, which they trap beneath the foot. Sexual maturity is reached only after 8–10 years and minimum legal size (shell width 114 mm) after 13 years. Collection by recreational fishers was banned in 2006, and a total ban on harvesting imposed in 2008 as a consequence of depletion by poaching. A substantial commercial fishery for abalone previously occurred in the southwestern Cape, conducted by divers using 'hookah' equipment from small boats. Most of the catch was frozen or canned and exported to the Far East.

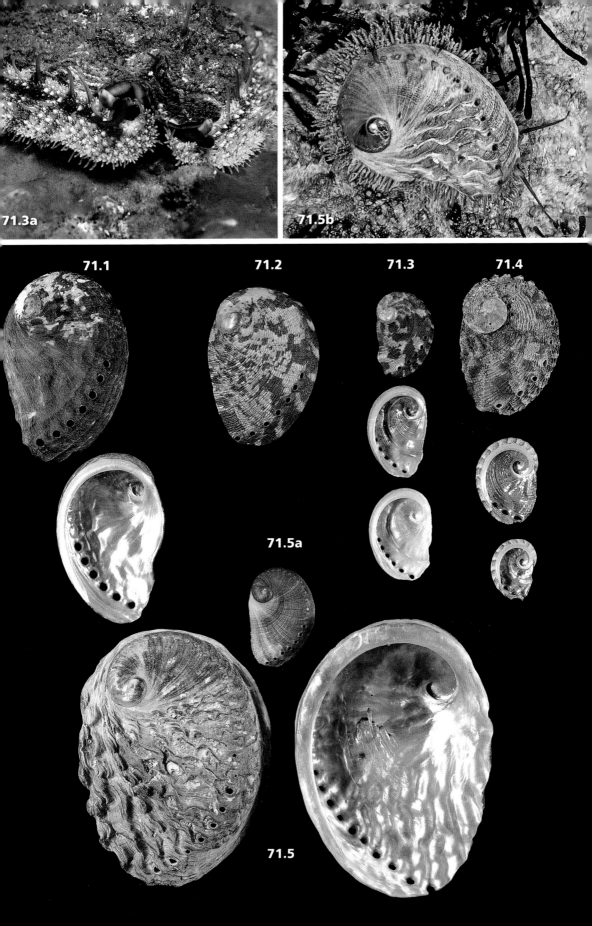

71.3a

71.5b

71.1

71.2

71.3

71.4

71.5a

71.5

PLATE 72

Limpets

Limpets have a cap-shaped shell. They include both 'true' limpets in subclass Prosobranchia, with a ring of gills around the foot, and 'false' limpets, subclass Pulmonata, which have a lung and are related to land snails. All are herbivorous and use a rasping, ribbon-like tongue to graze on algae.

72.1 Argenville's limpet   *Scutellastra argenvillei*

Large, tall and almost oval, with fine, radiating riblets and distinct teeth beneath the margin; inner surface porcelain white. **Size:** 90 mm. **Biology:** Occurs low on moderately exposed shores. Reaches extraordinary densities on the west coast, but is being displaced by the alien mussel *Mytilus galloprovincialis* (72.1a). Traps and feeds on kelp, 'mushrooming' the shell upwards and slamming it down to capture fronds (72.1b).

SIMILAR SPECIES:

72.2 *Scutellastra aphanes* (Transkei–Cape Vidal) is like a miniature *S. argenvillei* being oval, ribbed and pale, with slightly darker rays, but margin lacks teeth. Common on mussels; eats encrusting corallines. Territorial; aggressively pushes other individuals away.

72.3 Bearded limpet   *Scutellastra barbara*

Highly variable, but typically tall, with strong spiky ribs. Sides of foot white, speckled grey. **Size:** 80 mm. **Biology:** Occurs on the low shore and subtidally. On the southeast coast it defends 'gardens' of filamentous red algae, thrusting away intruding grazers. On the more productive west coast it lacks gardens and is not territorial.

SIMILAR SPECIES:

72.4 *Scutellastra pica* (Zululand–Mozambique) has a slightly pear-shaped shell with radial ridges that throw the edge into irregular serrations, giving it a crumpled appearance. Often overgrown by algae. Sides of foot never flecked with grey.

72.5 Pear limpet   *Scutellastra cochlear*

Distinctively pear-shaped, often encrusted by coralline algae; inner surface white, tinged blue and often mottled with black; muscle scar U-shaped and blue-black. **Size:** 70 mm. **Biology:** Lives in dense aggregations low on exposed shores, forming a 'cochlear zone'. Very slow-growing, living 25 years. Associated with a paint-like coralline alga, *Spongites yendoi* (192.4), on which it grazes. Narrow gardens of fast-growing, fine red algae fringe and sustain larger individuals (72.5a), and are territorially defended and fertilised by the limpets.

72.6 Duck's foot or long-spined limpet   *Scutellastra longicosta*

Shell star-shaped, with about 11 very long projecting ribs. Interior white or blue-white, with a black edging. **Size:** 70 mm. **Biology:** Juveniles live on other shells, feeding on the encrusting alga *Ralfsia* (175.2), then move to the rock-face and eat encrusting coralline algae until they establish gardens of *Ralfsia* (72.6a), which they defend against other grazers. The limpets cut regular paths through the *Ralfsia*, increasing its growth rate and reducing the amounts of anti-herbivore chemicals produced by the alga.

SIMILAR SPECIES:

72.7 *Scutellastra obtecta* (Transkei–Kosi Bay) is like a small *S. longicosta*, but has less obvious ribs, lacks black edging, and is always predominantly white inside. It is easily confused with specimens of *S. longicosta* from KwaZulu-Natal, which are stunted and have short spines.

72.8 Giant limpet   *Scutellastra tabularis*

The largest of African limpets. Shell with about 30 roughly equal-sized ribs that project slightly at the margin. Interior white, with an attractive pink margin. **Size:** 180 mm. **Biology:** Lives and feeds on large flat sheets of *Zeacarpa leiomorpha* in the shallow subtidal zone; territorially defends its 'gardens' by violently thrusting against intruding grazers.

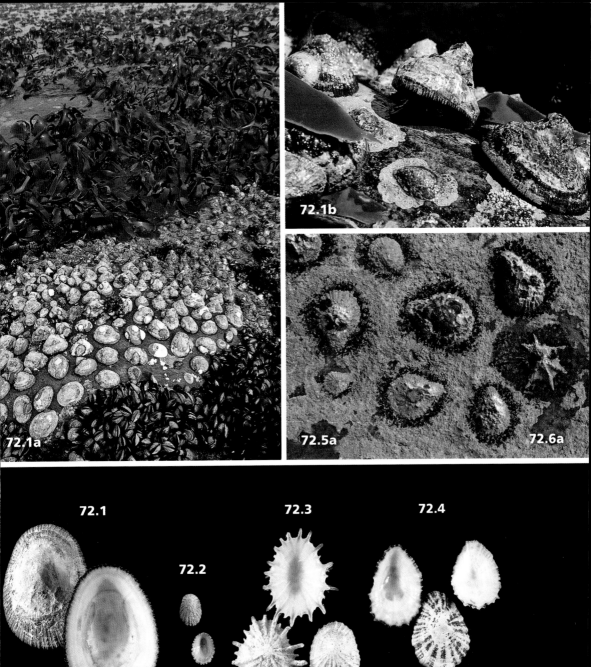

72.1a

72.1b

72.5a   72.6a

72.1   72.3   72.4

72.2

72.5   72.6   72.7   72.8

PLATE 73

73.1 Pink-rayed limpet
Cymbula miniata

Shell thin, flat and nearly oval, with about 80 fine riblets that alternate in size and are slightly prickly. Pale, shot with numerous beautiful pink rays; interior pale in the centre and with a bluish sheen over the pink rays. **Size:** 80 mm. **Biology:** Lives low on the shore and in the shallows; feeds exclusively on encrusting coralline algae.

73.2 Giant pink-rayed limpet
Cymbula sanguinans

Shell more robust and narrower than that of *C. miniata*; almost smooth, and has broad, radiating purple-brown rays. **Size:** 110 mm. **Biology:** Creates and defends territorial patches of an encrusting red alga *Hildenbrandia rubra*.
SIMILAR SPECIES:
73.3 *Cymbula safiana* (northern Namibia–Angola) is closely related, but with coarser ribs, broader internal rays. Usually about 70 mm, but dull white giants reach 120 mm.

73.4 Goat's eye limpet
Cymbula oculus

Shell flat, dull brown above. About 10 major ribs. Interior with a broad black margin and a pink-brown centre. Juveniles yellow, flecked iridescent green (73.4a). **Size:** 100 mm. **Biology:** Occupies the mid-shore zone and controls algal growth there. Large individuals aggressively attack predators, slamming the shell down to damage them. Changes sex: initially male, becoming female in the second or third year. Overexploited in Transkei, where it is consumed. The flatworm *Notoplana patellarum* (22.6) lives under its shell.

73.5 Granite limpet
Cymbula granatina

Similar to *C. oculus*, but taller, with about 15 major ribs. Granite-like chevron pattern on upper surface (although often eroded away). Interior pale, with a narrow edging that varies from granite-patterned to uniformly dark; centre shiny, dark red-brown. Juveniles flecked green. **Size:** 80 mm. **Biology:** Reaches huge densities in Namaqualand, where its shells are tall and domed because of crowding. Dense aggregations rely on drift seaweeds (mainly kelp) for food, and occur in sheltered boulder-bays that accumulate drift weeds.

73.6 Kelp limpet
Cymbula compressa

Elongate. Opening concave, fitting a cylindrical kelp stem (73.6a); shell 'rocks' on a flat surface. Brown, finely ribbed; interior blue-white to brown. **Size:** 90 mm. **Biology:** Lives on the kelp *Ecklonia maxima*. Instantly drops off if its host kelp is detached and floats away. Adults form scars on the 'stem' and territorially thrust away intruding limpets. One of the first South African shells named – by Carl von Linné in 1758.

73.7 Granular limpet
Scutellastra granularis

Roughly oval; about 50 fine ribs, textured with white granules. Often eroded, smoothing the ribs and exposing a brown cap. Interior blue-white with a central brown patch and a dark border that is wider in west coast (73.7a) than in southeast coast specimens (73.7b). **Size:** 60 mm; larger on the productive west coast. **Biology:** Abundant high on the shore, where it regulates algae, maintaining bare rock (73.7). Calcium carbonate in the shells varies with temperature: aragonite predominates in warm seas and calcite in cold water. Their ratios in prehistoric shells track sea temperatures.
SIMILAR SPECIES:
73.8 *Scutellastra natalensis*, the black-grained limpet (KwaZulu-Natal), is almost identical, but the granules are black on a brown background.
73.9 *Scutellastra miliaris* is broadly oval, brown with black granules; interior white with brown centre and narrow dark rim. The dominant high-shore limpet in Angola.

73.10 Variable limpet
Helcion concolor

Shell flat, finely ribbed (but not granular); egg-shaped in outline. Colour extremely varied, but radiating streaks and dots are common. **Size:** 50 mm. **Biology:** Occurs in the mid shore; very common in KwaZulu-Natal. Previously named *Patella variabilis*.

73.11 Lustrous limpet
Cellana capensis

Co-exists with *Helcion concolor*, and the two are easily confused. *C. capensis* has a more oval shell. Its interior has a lustrous silky yellow or pearly sheen, shot with broad dark bands or spots; the outer surface is finely granular when not eroded. **Size:** 50 mm. **Biology:** Rolls its mantle over its shell to deter predators such as whelks (73.11a).

73.4a

73.6a

73.7

73.11a

73.1

73.2

73.3

73.4

73.5

73.8

73.6

73.7a

73.7b

73.9

73.10

73.11

PLATE 74

74.1 Prickly limpet — *Helcion pectunculus*

Shell tall, oval in outline, apex positioned very close to the anterior end; brown, with about 26 black ribs that are distinctively prickled. **Size:** 30 mm. **Biology:** Lives very high on the shore, concealed in crevices or beneath boulders.

74.2 Broad rayed-limpet — *Helcion pruinosus*

Shell low, fragile, oval; apex about one-quarter from front margin. Surface smooth, pale brown, shot with beautiful iridescent green spots and rays (74.2a). **Size:** 35 mm. **Biology:** Hides under low-shore boulders; emerges by night. Often eaten by the rocksucker (151.8).

74.3 Slim rayed-limpet — *Helcion dunkeri*

Similar, but narrower, with fine, radial ribs. West coast specimens are white to yellow, with broad black rays; south coast examples are brown, with darker rays and sometimes green flecks like *H. pruinosus*. **Size:** 25 mm. **Biology:** As for *H. pruinosus*.

74.4 Dwarf limpet — *Patelloida profunda albonotata*

Small, but tall for its size; oval and with a central apex. Usually uniformly white, but interior with a greenish cast, and sometimes marginal spots or blotches. **Size:** 10 mm. **Biology:** Very common on the mid to high shore, among barnacles or on the Natal rock oyster.

74.5 Cape false-limpet — *Siphonaria capensis*

Apex almost central. Oval; slightly swollen on right where a siphon extends from the lung cavity. About 40–50 low, flat, roughly equal ribs. Margin smooth or gently scalloped. Interior shiny brown or blotched; narrow dark brown rays cross the pale margin. **Size:** 25 mm. **Biology:** Occupies mid-shore pools and exposed rocks. Like other *Siphonaria* spp., tolerant of sand: on rocks intermittently sand-covered, it replaces *Scutellastra granularis* (73.7) as the commonest mid-shore limpet. Returns to fixed home scar after feeding. Attachment weak: feeds during low tide to avoid detachment by waves. Tissues laden with toxic, milky mucus that repels predators. Lays gelatinous egg strings that festoon pools (74.5a).

74.6 Serrate false-limpet — *Siphonaria serrata*

Shell tall, with an obvious siphonal lobe on the left (when the shell is viewed from below); ribs prickly and project from the serrated margin. Interior pale white to brown, with pale rays radiating through the darker rim. Dark flecks on sides of foot. Previously called *S. aspersa*. **Size:** 25 mm. **Biology:** A mid-shore inhabitant.

74.7 Ribbed false-limpet — *Siphonaria concinna*

Ribs well-spaced, never prickly; 20–25 large ribs alternating with smaller ribs. Interior with a large white central patch; margin black, with narrow white rays. Sides of foot with fine, white spots. Shells of juveniles flecked iridescent blue-green. **Size:** 34 mm. **Biology:** Occupies mid-shore home scars. Lays coiled egg masses (74.7a).

74.8 Eyed false-limpet — *Siphonaria oculus*

Shell ribs number 46–58, raised and projecting slightly from the margin, alternately small and large. Inside, dark brown with pale rays around the edge and (usually) a diffuse white 'eye-spot' bar across the apex; foot dotted with fine, white spots. **Size:** 30 mm. **Biology:** Most common on sheltered rocks in the mid shore.

74.9 Blotched false-limpet — *Siphonaria nigerrima*

Shell low, slightly pear-shaped, with 30–60 fine ribs. Often shot with radiating iridescent blue-green flecks. Interior brown or brownish orange; inner margin dark brown with pale patches and white rays. **Size:** 25 mm. **Biology:** Four varieties once called *S. tenuicostulata* (74.9) with 50–60 ribs, *S. anneae* (74.9a) with 30–40 ribs, *S. dayi*, and *S. nigerrima* (74.9b), which has a uniformly dark brown or black interior and lives high on the shore, now all merged as one species on genetic grounds. Can be confused with *S. concinna*.

74.10 Eelgrass false-limpet — *Siphonaria compressa*

Tiny, narrow, and lives exclusively on eelgrass *Zostera capensis*. **Size:** 4 mm. **Biology:** Small size, direct development and localised distribution make it South Africa's most rare and endangered marine invertebrate. Intolerant of low salinities, and prone to siltation and flooding; population collapses to less that 1% have been recorded.

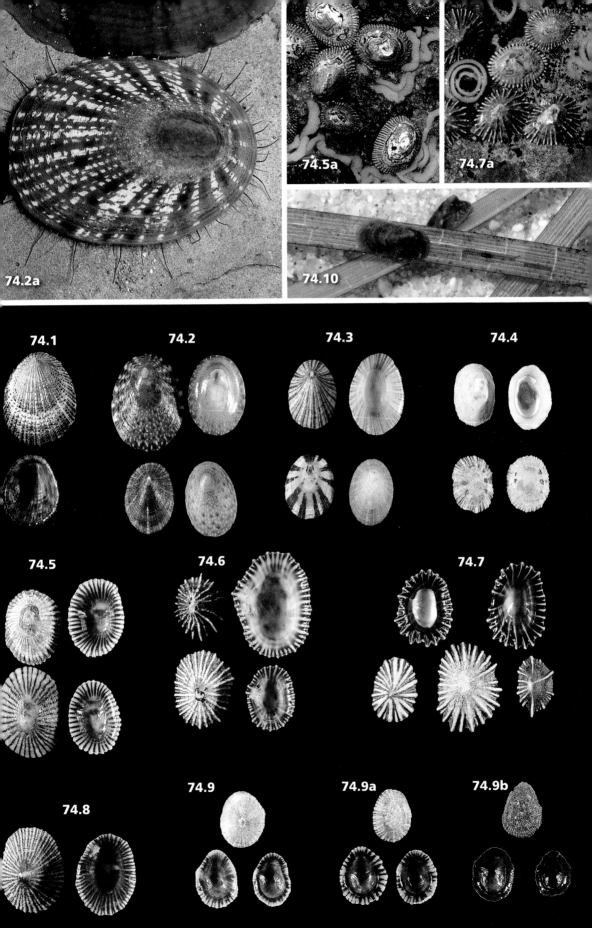

74.5a

74.7a

74.2a

74.10

74.1

74.2

74.3

74.4

74.5

74.6

74.7

74.8

74.9

74.9a

74.9b

PLATE 75

Keyhole- & slipper-limpets

Keyhole-limpets have oval shells with a central hole through which a siphon carrying the anus protrudes, so faeces are voided well away from the gills, which are hidden under the shell. Slipper-limpets have a partial shelf inside the shell, so that the empty shell resembles a slipper.

75.1 Saddled keyhole-limpet   *Dendrofissurella scutellum*
Shell much smaller than body. Saddle-shaped: rocks on a flat surface. 'Keyhole' smoothly oval. Foot very large; frilly, branching protuberance at front (75.1a). **Size:** 40 mm. **Biology:** Body cannot withdraw into the shell. Probably contains toxins: when threatened by a predator, the mantle expands to cover the shell. Lives under boulders and in sheltered sandy areas. Herbivorous: an important consumer of the commercial seaweed *Gracilaria*.

75.2 Conical keyhole-limpet   *Diodora parviforata*
Shell white, roughly oval, with radiating riblets; animal completely covered by the shell. 'Keyhole' small and round, close to the front of the shell. **Size:** 25 mm. **Biology:** Seldom common; lives under boulders and in caverns low on the shore. Eats sponges and detritus.

75.3 Cape keyhole-limpet   *Fissurella mutabilis*
Shell flat, almost large enough to cover the body, with attractive rays and scallops, and is smooth or has delicate radial ridges. 'Keyhole' narrow, with undulating sides. **Size:** 20 mm. **Biology:** Common under boulders or among mussels. Herbivorous.
SIMILAR SPECIES:
75.4 *Fissurella natalensis* (Port Alfred–Mozambique) has a heavier, dark brown shell with paler rays and coarse radial ridges.

75.5 Mantled keyhole-limpet   *Pupillaea aperta*
Shell small relative to body, with white rim and large, bevelled, oval 'keyhole'. Shell covered by mantle, so the animal looks slug-like (75.5a). Body grey, striped or mottled black; foot bright orange. **Size:** Shell 35 mm, body 80 mm. **Biology:** Solitary and subtidal.

75.6 Slipper-limpet   *Crepidula porcellana*
Teardrop shaped, with a concave internal shelf. Surface smooth, usually brown. **Size:** 15 mm. **Biology:** Lives on other shells, frequently in stacks, one on top of another (75.6a). Changes sex as it matures: the larger (lower) individuals are female, the smaller, younger ones male. Females brood yellow eggs beneath the shell (75.6a). Gill enlarged and filters plankton from the water.
SIMILAR SPECIES:
75.7 *Crepipatella capensis* (Mossel Bay–Lambert's Bay) has a smooth oval shell with a convex shelf, and attaches to rocks. Previously incorrectly called *Crepidula dilatata*.
75.8 *Bostrycapulus odites* (Namibia–KwaZulu-Natal) is sculptured with curved rows of scales. Previously named *Crepidula aculeata*.

75.9 Chinese hat   *Calyptraea chinensis*
Shell flat, smooth and round; internal shelf spirals from apex to margin. **Size:** 15 mm. **Biology:** Hides under rocks and seldom seen, but shells of dead animals often washed ashore. Like the slipper-limpet, it undergoes sex change and is a filter-feeder. SIMILAR SPECIES:
75.10 *Calyptraea helicoidea* (Port Elizabeth–East London) has radiating ridges.

75.11 Horse's hoof   *Sabia conica*
Shell conical but apex slopes backwards; ribs usually scallop the edge of the shell. **Size:** 5 mm. **Biology:** Attaches itself beneath other gastropods, eroding a depression in the shell. Gathers mucus and faeces from the host. Male smaller than female (shown here attached to the left of a female on a hermit-occupied shell). Previously called *Hipponix conicus*.

75.12 Congregating limpet   *Trimusculus* spp.
Circular, very tall white shells with roughly equal-sized radial ridges (often eroded away). **Size:** 20 mm. **Biology:** Hangs upside down in caves or under large boulders, in aggregations so dense that their margins interlock. Uses a mucus curtain to filter-feed. Contains chemicals that inhibit predatory fish. SIMILAR SPECIES: *T. costatus* has strong ribs and occurs on the south and east coasts. *T. ater* is taller, less obviously ribbed, and occurs from Angola northwards.

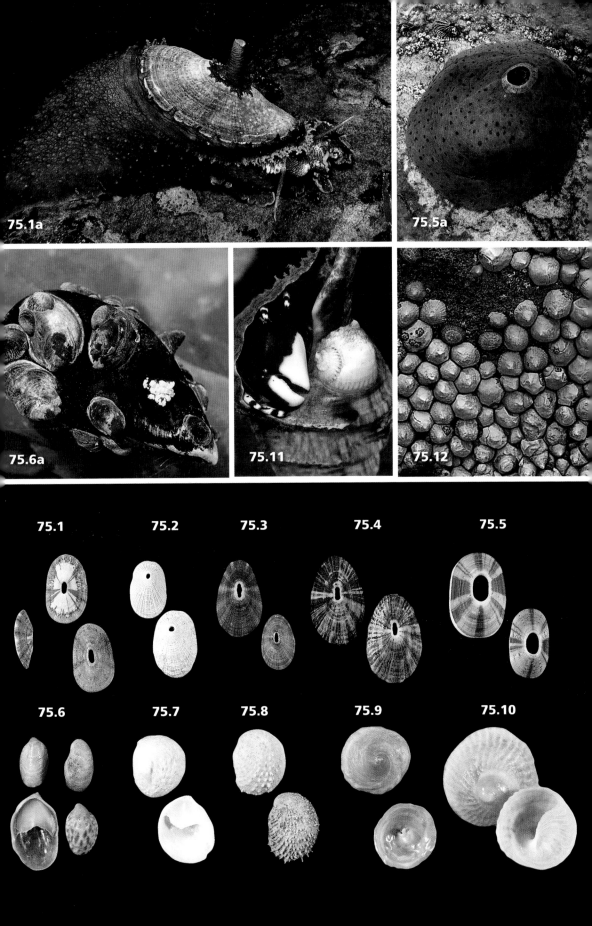

75.1a

75.5a

75.6a

75.11

75.12

75.1

75.2

75.3

75.4

75.5

75.6

75.7

75.8

75.9

75.10

PLATE 76

Winkles

Winkles (or topshells) fall in the families Trochidae and Calliostomatidae, and have round squat shells, with a circular or semicircular mouth (aperture) blocked by a flexible horny 'door' (operculum). Nearly all are herbivorous.

76.1 Ornate topshell   *Calliostoma ornatum*

Top-shaped, the base sharply set off from the sides by an acute angle. About 2–3 strong granular ridges spiral around the lower whorls, alternating with weaker ridges. Aperture smoothly round, lacking teeth or nodules. Operculum round, thin and flexible. Shell brown to orange-red or violet; foot and head bright orange (76.1a). **Size:** 20 mm. **Biology:** The commonest of several *Calliostoma* spp., spanning the low shore down to 50 m. Often attaches to gorgonians (sea fans) and possibly feeds on them.
SIMILAR SPECIES:
76.2 *Calliostoma africanum* (Port Elizabeth–Transkei) is similar, but not as broad at the base, and has about 6–8 thin, very finely granular spiral ridges, all of similar strength.

76.3 Black-chained topshell   *Clanculus atricatena*

Shell conical, much wider than tall, and with convex sides. Background colour grey-brown. Each whorl has about two well-developed spiral granular ridges with darker oblong spots. Between these ridges lie weaker ridges that lack this decoration. Operculum round, thin and flexible. The inner lip of the aperture has a strong tooth, and the outer lip a ridge-like tooth near its posterior edge. Viewed from below, the shell has a narrow tunnel (the umbilicus) that runs up its centre. **Size:** 20 mm. **Biology:** Live animals are seldom seen, hiding beneath boulders in sandy areas.
SIMILAR SPECIES: All *Clanculus* spp. have a toothed inner lip and an umbilicus.
76.4 *Clanculus puniceus* (KwaZulu-Natal–tropical Indo-Pacific) is vivid red, with darker spots and white dots on the spiral ridges.
76.5 *Clanculus miniatus* (Cape Point–Transkei) is obviously top-shaped, a sharp keel separating base from sides. Brown to reddish pink, usually with spots around the keel.

76.6 Multicoloured topshell   *Gibbula multicolor*

Shell small, wider than tall. Aperture rounded; lacks teeth. Shell whorls with 2–3 spiral ridges. Umbilicus shallow or closed completely. Colour variable, but always bright, usually a background of red decorated with white bands and tiny green dots. **Size:** 10 mm. **Biology:** Lives under boulders and in rock pools, as well as in the shallow subtidal zone.
SIMILAR SPECIES: All *Gibbula* spp. have small shells (10 mm) that are wider than tall, an aperture that lacks teeth and a flexible horny operculum. The umbilicus is developed to differing degrees.
76.7 *Gibbula capensis* (Saldanha–Agulhas) has a relatively flat shell; the sides form an acute angle with the base and have fine, spiral threads. Shell pink to red with regularly spaced white blotches or bars. Tentacles white with thin black bars (76.7a).
76.8 *Gibbula cicer* (Lüderitz–Transkei) is globular, only slightly taller than wide, the lowest whorl being smoothly rounded; 4–5 spiral ridges on each whorl. Usually pale cream with drab olive-brown to grey spots.
76.9 *Gibbula zonata* (central Namibia–Agulhas) has rounded and pale shell with distinctive dark spiral lines. Tentacles white with longitudinal pink stripe (76.9a).
76.10 *Gibbula beckeri* (Namaqualand–Cape Point) is dark grey, with irregular paler flames, and usually has 2–3 major spiral ridges as well as finer intermediary ridges.
76.11 *Cinysca dunkeri* (Lüderitz–eastern Transkei) has a thick rounded shell; uniformly pale on the west coast, speckled on the south coast. Umbilicus large and obvious. About eight strong, equal-sized ridges spiral around each whorl and corrugate the outer lip. Operculum horny and flexible, but has spiral rows of minute calcareous beads. Related to turban shells (Plate 78) although superficially resembling winkles.

76.1a

76.7a

76.9a

76.1   76.2   76.3   76.4   76.5

76.6   76.7   76.8   76.9   76.10   76.11

PLATE 77

77.1 Black-spotted topshell   *Trochus nigropunctatus*

Top-shaped; triangular when viewed from the side, wider than tall, with granular spiral ridges. Base with about five spiral ridges that run into the aperture; umbilicus shallow but has three spiral ridges encroaching into it. Colour dull brown with darker spots, most obvious on the base. **Size:** 25 mm. **Biology:** Hides in crevices or among seaweeds in tidal pools. Like many topshells, swivels its shell violently when touched by a predator.

77.2 Toothed topshell   *Monodonta australis*

Recognised by its thick shell, rounded whorls, obvious spiral ridges, the single, stubby tooth that projects inwards from the inner lip of the aperture, and the absence of an umbilicus. Usually pale brown with darker rectangular spots, but tints of green and pink often brighten the shell. Operculum round, flexible and horny. **Size:** 30 mm. **Biology:** A very common intertidal species, usually found in pools; grazes on microalgae.

77.3 Variegated topshell   *Oxystele variegata*

Shell rounded, about as tall as wide, smooth or with very gentle spiral ridges. No trace of an umbilicus. Colour extremely variable, but typically tabby patterned with irregular dark bands that run obliquely across a pale yellow or greenish background. Inside of aperture pearly, with a narrow margin that repeats the variegated tabby pattern. As in all *Oxystele* spp., the operculum is horny and flexible, yellow-brown, with spiral growth rings. **Size:** 25 mm. **Biology:** Abundant on intertidal rocky shores. Grazes on microalgae and encrusting algae. Juveniles live low on the shore, shifting upshore as they become more tolerant of the greater physical stresses experienced there. Upshore movement apparently shifts adults away from intense predation by starfish and whelks. If adults are experimentally transplanted downshore they navigate accurately and return to their original zone within a day.

77.4 Beaded topshell   *Oxystele impervia*

Almost identical to *O. variegata*, but has bead-like dots that spiral around the whorls. **Size:** 25 mm. **Biology:** Similar to *O. variegata*, but tends to occur in more sheltered areas and slightly higher on the shore. Chemoreceptive tentacles extend when it is active (77.4a). For years considered a variety of *O. variegata*, but is genetically distinct from it.

77.5 Striped topshell   *Oxystele tabularis*

Similar to the previous two species, but has clearly defined grey-brown to grey-green bands that run radially across each whorl and alternate with thinner red and green lines. **Size:** 22 mm. **Biology:** An abundant mid- to low-shore species.

77.6 Pink-lipped topshell   *Oxystele sinensis*

Larger than the previous three species; shell round and blunt-spired, with fine, spiral sculpturing. Dark purple-black above; aperture with a distinctive pink inner lip. **Size:** 45 mm. **Biology:** Lives low on the shore, down to about 5 m. Grazes on encrusting algae and microalgae. Harvested together with *O. tigrina* as a source of food in Transkei.

77.7 Tiger topshell   *Oxystele tigrina*

Shell similar, with a dark (almost black) upper surface, sometimes with scattered white dots. Aperture white, with a narrow black border, lacking any traces of pink. **Size:** 43 mm. **Biology:** As for *O. sinensis*.

77.8 Variegated sundial shell   *Heliacus variegatus*

Shell flat, height less than half the width, with four beaded spiral ridges per whorl. Umbilicus well developed and lined with nodules. Colour grey-white, speckled with brown-to-black rectangular spots. Operculum calcareous and conical. **Size:** 15 mm. **Biology:** Slow moving. Parasitises the zoanthid *Palythoa nelliae* (77.8a), boring into it with its proboscis, which is protected against the zoanthid's stinging cells by a rough cuticle. *Heliacus* resembles winkles, but falls in a different family: Architectonicidae.

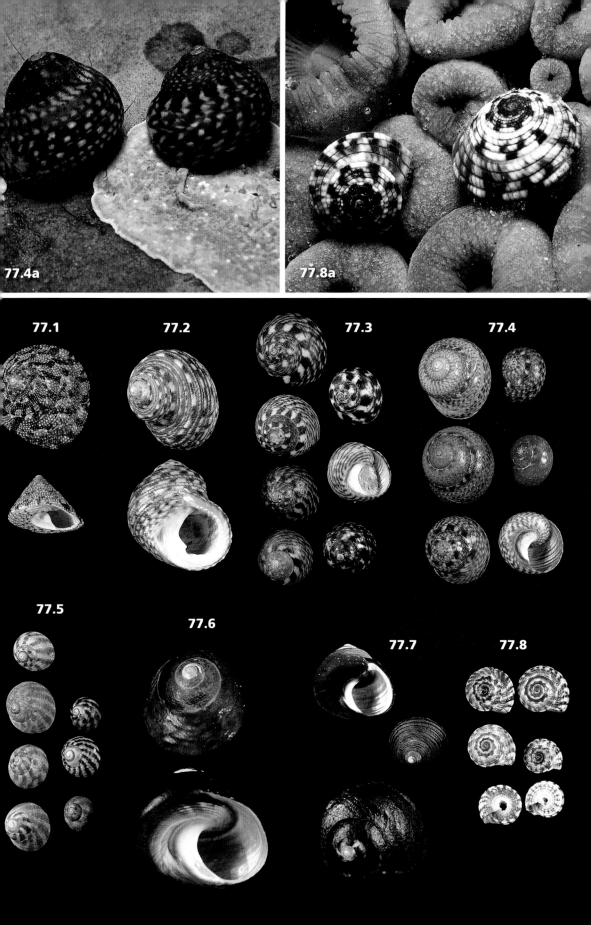

77.4a

77.8a

77.1

77.2

77.3

77.4

77.5

77.6

77.7

77.8

PLATE 78

Turban shells & nerites

Turban shells (family Turbinidae) and nerites (family Neritidae) have a hard, calcareous operculum that blocks the shell when the animal withdraws. The aperture and operculum are round in turban shells, but semicircular in nerites. Both groups are herbivorous.

78.1 Smooth and ridged turban shells   *Turbo cidaris*

Two distinctly different subspecies exist. The smooth turban shell, *T. cidaris cidaris* (Cape Peninsula–Port Elizabeth), has an attractive, smooth, glossy shell, usually purple-brown to red-brown with paler radial flares (78.1a). Its operculum is sparsely granular and has a groove that spirals towards a central pit. *T. cidaris natalensis*, the ridged turban shell (Port Elizabeth–north of Durban), has 6–11 well-defined spiral ridges, but no nodules (78.1b), and its operculum is completely covered with coarse nodules. **Size:** 50 mm. **Biology:** Herbivorous: grazes on microalgae. Gathered for food on the east coast.

78.2 Coronate moon turban   *Turbo coronatus*

Distinguished by its operculum, which has a greenish tinge and is smooth, or has only a faint granulation. Shell with very strong, spirally arranged nodules, the uppermost row particularly well developed and forming distinct knobs. **Size:** 35 mm. **Biology:** Common in mid-shore pools or under boulders. Placed in the genus *Lunella* by some authors.

78.3 Alikreukel or giant turban   *Turbo sarmaticus*

Large and round, height less than width. About three rows of low nodules spiral around each whorl (though they may erode and disappear). Aperture smoothly round, outer lip dark brown or black, inner lip white to bright orange. Operculum round, thick and calcified; outer surface with densely packed, coarse nodules (78.3a). **Size:** 100 mm. **Biology:** Lives in pools and down to about 8 m. Although still common, it is becoming increasingly difficult to find large specimens in the intertidal zone, except in marine reserves, despite regulations limiting its collection (five per day, per person; minimum size 63.5 mm). Relatively slow-growing, it reaches this size at an age of 3–4 years. **SIMILAR SPECIES**: *T. marmoratus*, the great green turban (central Mozambique–Indo-Pacific), is huge (up to 120 mm), green with blotches of brown, and has a strong shoulder ridge on the basal whorl and blunt tubercles on other whorls. Extensively collected for the button and jewellery trades.

78.4 Blotched nerite   *Nerita albicilla*

Shell semicircular in side view; spire sunken and not protruding. Upper surface smooth or with weak spiral grooves. Commonly black with white blotches; sometimes striped or orange (78.4a). Inner lip of aperture forms a flat, pimpled shelf. Operculum calcareous, semicircular, pale and finely granular. **Size:** 25 mm. **Biology:** Abundant, aggregating in mid-shore pools and under damp boulders. Grazes nocturnally on lichens, encrusting algae and diatoms; cuts into the rock-face with its powerful radula to remove embedded microalgae. Lays oval white egg capsules about 2 mm long, which prominently dot pools and the undersides of rocks (78.4a). Several eggs are housed in each capsule and yield planktonic larvae. Shells used as decorative beads by coastal people.

78.5 Glossy nerite   *Nerita polita*

Upper surface smooth, glossy, usually mottled brown but often with radial bands. Operculum smooth except for fine ridges that run across the outer margin. **Size:** 35 mm. **Biology:** Occurs relatively low on the shore. Emerges to feed by night.

78.6 Textile nerite   *Nerita textilis*

Upper surface strongly ridged; off-white with conspicuous oblong black spots. Outer lip of aperture spotted black. Inner lip with three feeble teeth, the adjacent flat plate granular and usually yellow. **Size:** 30 mm. **Biology:** Scarce. Lives high on the shore. Esteemed by Pondo people as an ornament.

78.7 Plicate nerite   *Nerita plicata*

Shell globular, with about 14 radial ridges, giving a fan-like (plicate) appearance. Inner and outer lips strongly toothed. Colour uniformly pale cream, sometimes with darker spots. Outer lip yellow. **Size:** 30 mm. **Biology:** Occupies rocks above the high-tide mark.

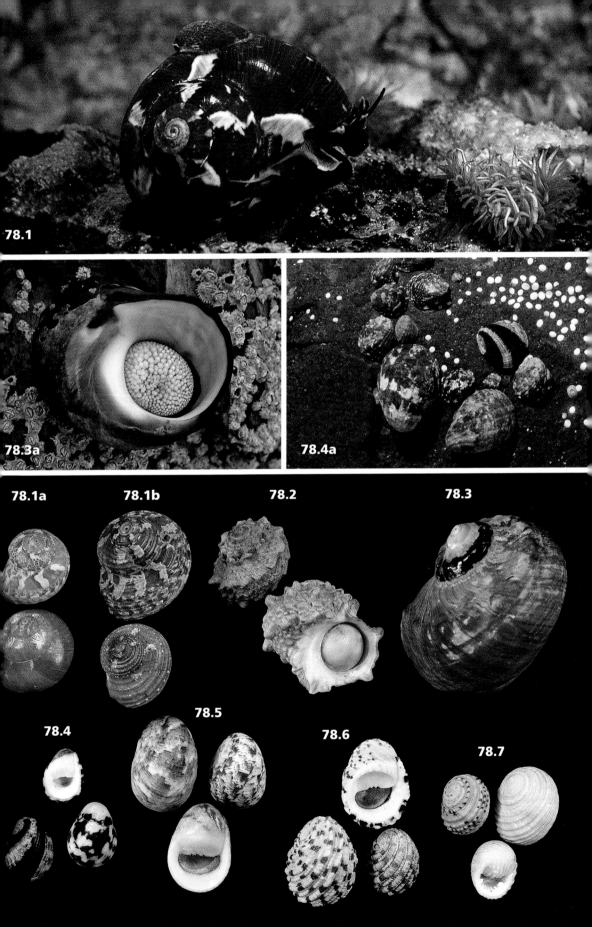

78.1

78.3a

78.4a

78.1a   78.1b   78.2   78.3

78.4

78.5

78.6

78.7

PLATE 79

Periwinkles

Included here are the periwinkles (family Littorinidae), which dominate the tops of rocky shores, and other small round-apertured gastropods. All are herbivorous, feeding mainly on diatoms and microalgae.

79.1 African periwinkle
Afrolittorina africana

Aperture rounded and closed by a transparent, horny operculum. Shell smooth, with a short conical spire. Blue-grey, with a brown aperture. **Size:** 5–8 mm. **Biology:** The dominant species at the top of the shore. Grazes on microalgae and lichens.

79.2 Southern periwinkle
Afrolittorina knysnaensis

Final whorl with slight shoulder. Varies from flecked brown with a dark ring around each coil to almost pure black. **Size:** 5–10 mm. **Biology:** Congregates in high-shore crevices, or hangs from hot rocks by a mucous thread (79.2a) in the heat of the day. Feeds at night or on moist days. Juveniles occur higher on the shore to avoid wave action.

79.3 Striped periwinkle
Littoraria glabrata

Shell smooth with a fairly tall spire, flesh-coloured with oblique pink or brown lines or zigzags. **Size:** Up to 24 mm. **Biology:** An extremely desiccation-resistant species found at, or above, high spring-tide level on subtropical shores. Previously called *L. kraussi*.

79.4 Estuarine periwinkles
Littoraria scabra group

Fine, spiral ribs and irregular lines of dark dashes. Three closely related southern African species: *L. scabra* (white columella), *L. intermedia* (dark purple to pink columella, coarse ribs) and *L. subvittata* (narrow, pink-brown columella, fine ribs). **Size:** 28 mm. **Biology:** Estuarine, often on mangroves and salt-marsh vegetation, well above the high-tide level.

79.5 Nodular periwinkle
Echinolittorina natalensis

Shell blue-grey with fine, spiral lines and about three rows of paler nodules running around each coil. Aperture dark brown. **Size:** Up to 12 mm. **Biology:** In crevices around the high-water mark on subtropical shores. Previously called *Nodilittorina*.

79.6 Tropical periwinkle
Planaxis sulcatus

Shell thick and strong, and decorated with equal-sized spiral ridges. Colour grey-brown, with regular elongate dots on the spiral ridges. **Size:** Up to 20 mm. **Biology:** One of the dominant gastropods low on rocky tropical shores. Characteristic of sheltered shores.

Alien

79.7 British periwinkle
Littorina saxatilis

Globular, with a round aperture that flanges forwards at the front. Variable, from uniformly off-white to pale brown with darker rings. **Size:** 5–8 mm. **Biology:** Introduced from Britain: well established in *Spartina* beds in Langebaan and Knysna, but localised.

79.8 Pheasant shell
Tricolia capensis

Smooth, high-spired, glossy shell. Calcareous, white operculum. **Size:** 5–9 mm. **Biology:** Herbivorous; abundant under rocks (79.8a), among seaweeds and in beach drift.
SIMILAR SPECIES:
79.9 *Trichola kochii* (Cape Agulhas–southern Mozambique) is also high-spired, but larger (8–14 mm), bright red to yellow, usually with bright turquoise spots below suture.
79.10 *Tricolia neritina* (Namibia–Port Alfred) is small (5 mm), globular, and short-spired; operculum smooth, calcareous. Colour pale pink with fine, spiralling pink or purple stripes.

79.11 Globular mud snail
Assiminea globulus

Globular brown shell; spire short, operculum horny. Head broad and truncated, flanked by short tentacles. **Size:** 4 mm. **Biology:** Countless thousands occur high on lagoonal mudflats (79.11a); feeds on diatoms and bacteria. **SIMILAR SPECIES:**
79.12 *Hydrobia* spp. (Langebaan–Knysna) are tiny (3–5 mm). Shell brown, operculum horny, spire acute, with more whorls than *Assiminea*. Head narrow in front; tentacles longer than the head. Abundant in upper levels of estuarine salt marshes.
79.13 *Eatoniella nigra* (Lüderitz–Port Alfred) is minute (1 mm), black; spire acute, operculum calcareous. Abundant in seaweeds but confused with *Afrolittorina knysnaensis*.
79.14 *Assiminea ovata* (Knysna–Mozambique) is chubbier, reaches 7 mm, and usually has one or two pale bands around the whorls. Dominant in east coast estuaries.

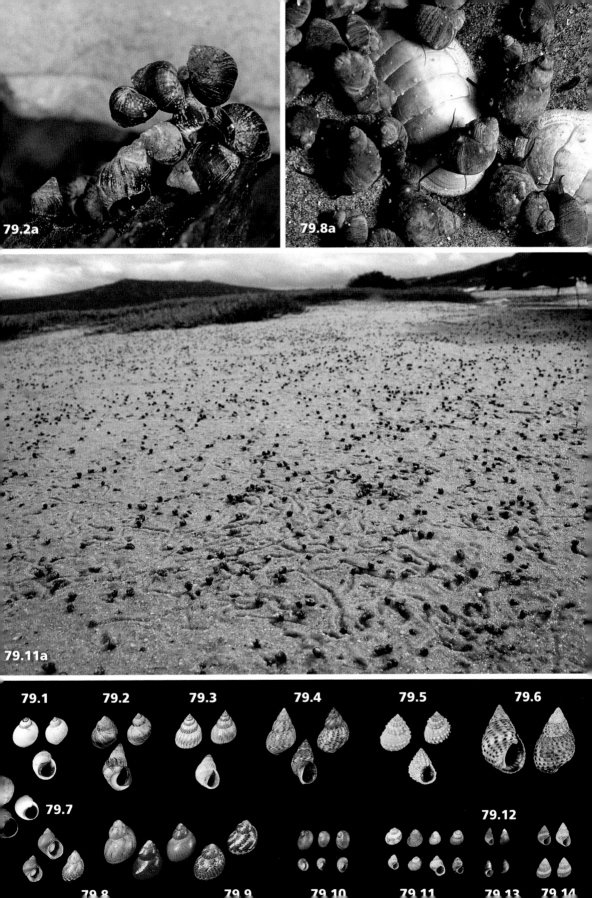

79.2a

79.8a

79.11a

79.1

79.2

79.3

79.4

79.5

79.6

79.7

79.12

79.8

79.9

79.10

79.11

79.13

79.14

PLATE 80

Worm-, screw- & turret shells

A miscellaneous group including the worm-shells, with long, irregularly twisted shells permanently attached to rocks, and other elongate, tall-spired forms.

80.1 Colonial worm-shell   *Dendropoma corallinaceus*

Small and gregarious, forming an intertwining mass of long, worm-like white tubes, often sunken into encrusting coralline algae. Operculum present. **Size:** 10 mm long. **Biology:** A filter-feeder that spins a mucous net to trap floating particles. **SIMILAR SPECIES**: *D. tholia* is almost identical, but replaces it in Transkei and KwaZulu-Natal.

80.2 Solitary worm-shell   *Serpulorbis natalensis*

Solitary. Shell an irregularly coiled white tube, cemented to the underside of rocks. Operculum absent. Animal pink or red. **Size:** 40 mm long. **Biology:** Spins and then eats a mucous net to capture food particles. Eggs laid in capsules attached inside the shell.

80.3 Waxy screw-shell   *Protomella capensis*

Very elongate, with numerous rounded whorls. A pair of fine, spiral ridges frequently present on each whorl. Pink or pale brown, often with fine markings. **Size:** 33 mm. **Biology:** Buries itself shallowly in sheltered sand. Spreads a mucous net and filters water drawn down a tube communicating with the surface. Extremely common in lagoons. Previously called *Turritella capensis* and *T. knysnaensis*.

80.4 Threaded screw-shell   *Turritella carinifera*

Shell long and pointed, with a sharp spiral ridge running up the middle of each whorl. **Size:** 48 mm. **Biology:** Found on the open coast under rocks lying on sand, or embedded among sponges and ascidians.

SIMILAR SPECIES:

80.5 *Turritella sanguinea* (Cape Point–KwaZulu-Natal) has several fine, spiral ribs on each whorl, and they are coloured with red-brown spots.

80.6 Truncated mangrove snail   *Cerithidea decollata*

Aperture notched and with a flanged outer lip. Spire elongate, but apex invariably broken off in adults. Each whorl has about 20 strong cross-ridges. **Size:** Up to 36 mm. **Biology:** Lives high on the trunks of mangroves (80.6a), out of reach of aquatic predators, descending to the mud to feed on detritus during low neap tides. Also found less abundantly in estuaries to the south that lack mangroves.

80.7 Mangrove whelk   *Terebralia palustris*

Large, heavy, dark brown shell with three spiral grooves running up each whorl. Aperture notched, black inside. **Size:** Up to 120 mm. **Biology:** Crawls over wet mud, usually in association with mangrove swamps. Feeds on diatoms and mangrove leaves. The photograph shows a juvenile: adults have a thick lip.

80.8 Ribbed turrid   *Clionella sinuata*

Shell dark brown, apex eroded. Whorls flattened and with about 16–18 coarse ribs across the last turn. Aperture with short anterior canal and a slight bend or notch in outer lip. **Size:** 65 mm. **Biology:** A scavenger found under loose rocks in sandy areas. Congregates to lay masses of purse-shaped egg cases under boulders (80.8a).

SIMILAR SPECIES:

80.9 *Clionella rosaria* (Cape Point–KwaZulu-Natal) also has oblique ribs, but is pinkish orange with brown and white dots along the suture.

80.10 Knobbled horn-shell   *Rhinoclavis sinensis*

Three or four granular ridges on each whorl, the first enlarged and with marked knobs. Anterior canal short, bent abruptly upwards. **Size:** 40 mm. **Biology:** Abundant in tropical sandy pools. Shells often occupied by hermit crabs.

SIMILAR SPECIES:

80.11 *Cerithium crassilabrum* (East London–Mozambique) is smaller, lacks the upturned anterior canal and has about four similar-sized granular spiral ridges. It aggregates in huge numbers around boulders on sandy shores.

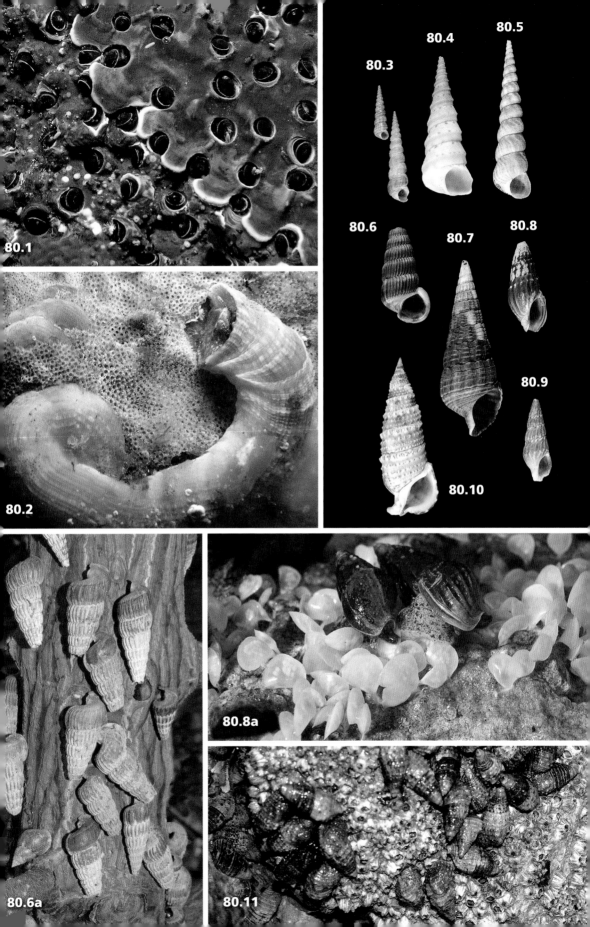

80.1

80.2

80.3

80.4

80.5

80.6

80.7

80.8

80.9

80.10

80.6a

80.8a

80.11

PLATE 81

Cowries

Colourful, glossy shells with an egg-like shape, the spire being enclosed within the last whorl. Aperture forms a narrow slit running the full length of the shell; both lips usually ridged or toothed. Operculum absent. In life the mantle lobes, which are often dramatically coloured and textured, extend over the shell, obscuring it and giving it the brilliant gloss so prized by shell collectors.

81.1 Cape cowry   *Cypraea capensis*

Easily distinguished by the numerous ridges running across the shell, which is light brown with darker blotches dorsally. Mantle orange to black with small white projections and spots. **Size:** 30 mm. **Biology:** Browses on sponges on sandy reefs at 8–110 m.

81.2 Toothless cowry   *Cypraea edentula*

Pink to lilac with speckling of reddish-brown spots; base usually white. Both lips toothless, and aperture relatively wide. Mantle smooth, usually orange, spattered with dark spots. **Size:** 25 mm. **Biology:** On reefs at 12–40 m depth. Probably feeds on sponges.

81.3 Dark-toothed cowry   *Cypraea fuscodentata*

Margin of shell blue, purple or pink; dorsal surface with dense, fused brown dots and dashes. A series of 15–19 prominent brown teeth form ridges that run right across the base. Mantle colour highly variable, usually orange with black spots (81.3a). **Size:** 22–44 mm. **Biology:** Usually found among thick, black sponges on reefs 6–130 m deep.

81.4 Ring cowry   *Cypraea annulus*

Shell pale, easily identified by the orange or yellow ring around the apex. Mantle greyish with paler branching projections (81.4a). **Size:** 15–28 mm. **Biology:** Common in depressions on wave-washed rocks or under stones in pools, as well as on sheltered tropical seagrass beds. Often congregates in small groups.

81.5 Money cowry   *Cypraea moneta*

Shell small but thick, with a rather irregular knobbly outline; colour yellow, becoming purple when eroded. Mantle dark brown. **Size:** 15–28 mm. **Biology:** Abundant intertidally in the tropics, becoming rare in KwaZulu-Natal. Widely used in the curio trade, and formerly employed as currency in the slave and ivory trades.

81.6 Arabic cowry   *Cypraea arabica*

Large, with a flattened base. Dorsal surface pale brown, densely patterned with an irregular network of darker brown markings. Base pale with darker teeth; margins spotted. Mantle grey with small projections (81.6a). **Size:** 51–102 mm. **Biology:** Occurs under rocks and in crevices, intertidally and on shallow reefs. An omnivorous grazer. Previously common, but becoming scarce because of collectors.

81.7 Carnelian cowry   *Cypraea carneola*

Shell elongate and deep; flesh-coloured and crossed by four darker bands. Edges of aperture violet. Mantle dark grey with paler conical projections. **Size:** 27–48 mm. **Biology:** Under rocks or in crevices on shallow reefs. An omnivorous grazer.

81.8 Tiger cowry   *Cypraea tigris*

A large, well-known species with a grey shell densely covered with dark brown spots. Base white. Mantle mottled grey and black, with long, white-tipped processes. **Size:** 66–113 mm. **Biology:** A sponge-feeder common on sandy tropical reefs, but rare in KwaZulu-Natal and seldom seen in Transkei.

81.3a

81.4a

81.6a

81.1 81.2 81.3 81.4 81.5

81.6 81.7 81.8

PLATE 82

82.1 Snake's head cowry — *Cypraea caputserpentis*

Thick, flattened shell with chocolate-brown margin; densely spotted with white dorsally; ends and underside pale. Mantle yellow, with brown spots. **Size:** 20–37 mm. **Biology:** Hidden on wave-washed shores by day, emerging to browse at night.

82.2 Honey cowry — *Cypraea helvola*

Shell brown with numerous tiny white spots; underside orange-brown with lilac ends. Mantle red-brown with branched processes. **Size:** 12–37 mm. **Biology:** Under rocks on protected shores and subtidal reefs. Beach-worn shells are violet and are commonly washed ashore in KwaZulu-Natal.

82.3 Sieve cowry — *Cypraea cribraria*

Top dark chocolate-brown with conspicuous large white spots. Sides and lower surface white. Mantle bright red and covered with simple papillae. **Size:** 20–25 mm. **Biology:** Rare in the region, but more common in the tropics. Subtidal.

82.4 Orange cowry — *Cypraea citrina*

Small and orange-brown, with round grey spots and a few brown ones. Underside orange. Mantle a dense bush of branching off-white processes. **Size:** 12–30 mm. **Biology:** Intertidal to depth of 100 m; feeding habits unknown. Effectively camouflaged by the bush of processes on the mantle.

82.5 Eroded cowry — *Cypraea erosa*

Olive-brown with small white spots, some of which show dark rings; a brown blotch midway along each side. Margin of shell prominent and ridged. Mantle pale brown with dense branched processes (82.5a). **Size:** 19–52 mm. **Biology:** Under intertidal rocks.

82.6 Kitten cowry — *Cypraea felina*

Small, elongate; blue-grey dorsally with dense brown speckles and darker cross-bands. Sides have large black spots. Underside yellowish. Mantle yellow with simple white projections. **Size:** 18–28 mm. **Biology:** Fairly common under boulders and in rock pools, particularly on the zoanthid *Palythoa nelliae* (8.4).

82.7 Stippled cowry — *Cypraea staphylaea*

Shell light grey and usually textured with small raised nodules. Ends of shell orange-brown; teeth lined with orange. Mantle black, with long projections (82.7a). **Size:** 12–23 mm. **Biology:** Found in crevices and under rocks on shallow reefs. Rare in KwaZulu-Natal and Transkei; common in the tropics.

82.8 Baby's toes — *Trivia aperta*

Fat pink shells with pale ridges running right around the shell, but halting at the mid-line. Mantle off-white, yellow or purple-grey, studded with pustules. **Size:** 14–27 mm. **Biology:** Feeds on compound ascidians, which the mantle matches closely in colour. Lays vase-shaped egg cases in cavities excavated in the ascidian colony.
SIMILAR SPECIES:
82.9 *Trivia ovulata* (Cape Point–southern Transkei) has smooth pink shell, white below; 13–20 mm. Mantle astoundingly variable: orange with brown spots, golden with black streaks, blue with white-ringed black spots, or white with dark squiggles (82.9a).
82.10 *Trivia phalacra* (Port Elizabeth–East London) is pink and ridged below, but the ridges disappear halfway up the sides leaving the top smooth; 13–19 mm.
82.11 *Trivia millardi* (Cape west coast) has a broad smooth white shell. Mantle highly variable: often yellow with pale streaks or dark dots; 14–23 mm.

82.12 Teardrops or riceys — *Trivia pellucidula*

Small and white, with 23–28 ridges running uninterrupted right around the shell. Mantle usually brown or green, spotted with short projections. **Size:** 4–8 mm. **Biology:** Feeds on compound ascidians on shallow tropical reefs. **SIMILAR SPECIES:** *T. oryza* (Port Alfred–KwaZulu-Natal) nearly identical, but a mid-dorsal, longitudinal groove interrupts the ridges.

82.3

82.9a

82.5a

82.7a

82.11

82.1

82.2

82.4

82.5

82.6

82.7

82.8

82.9

82.10

82.12

PLATE 83

Necklace-shells, helmet-shells & violet snails

Short-spired, predatory whelks. Necklace-shells (so named because they lay collar-like egg masses) have a large foot (83.3), and plough through sand and drill through the shells of other molluscs. Helmet-shells also occupy sandy areas. Violet snails secrete rafts of bubbles and drift upside down on the ocean surface.

83.1 **Comma necklace-shell** *Natica gualteriana*
Shell colour bluish- or brownish-grey, unmarked or with faint spiral patterning. Umbilicus present and comma-shaped. Operculum calcareous and semicircular. **Size:** 26 mm. **Biology:** Feeds on small bivalves and gastropods in east coast estuaries or shallow marine sandbanks, drilling holes through their shells. Eggs laid in a coiled sandy collar, which lies unattached on the sand.

83.2 **Mottled necklace-shell** *Natica tecta*
Shell brown, densely marked with bands of darker spots or streaks. Umbilicus closed. Operculum smooth and calcareous. **Size:** 41 mm. **Biology:** Lives in clean sand on the open coast or in estuaries. Feeds on bivalves, including mussels, and drills a neat bevelled hole through their shells (83.2a). Egg mass is a flattened, leaf-like strip attached to solid objects by a short stalk.

83.3 **Beaded necklace-shell** *Natica alapapilionis*
Shell longer than broad, with 1–4 spiral white bands that are beaded with brown blocks. Operculum with concentric rings. Foot grey, with darker grey speckles. **Size:** 30 mm. **Biology:** Burrows in fine sand, from the low shore down to 25 m.

83.4 **Moon shell** *Polinices didyma*
Shell smooth and globular. Light brown, with darker callus and aperture. Operculum flexible, horny and brownish, with a spiral groove. **Size:** 50 mm. **Biology:** Burrows just below the surface of sandbanks. Eggs laid in a coiled collar (83.4a).
SIMILAR SPECIES:
83.5 *Polinices mamilla* (Transkei northwards) has a shell that is more elongate and pure white. Lays its eggs in a similar collar, often in several frilly layers.

83.6 **Helmet-shell** *Phalium labiatum zeylanicum*
A shiny globular shell with a very short spire and a thickened outer lip. Last whorl usually with one or more rows of rounded knobs. Colour buff, with rows of paler spots and five pairs of dark bars on outer lip. Operculum smaller than aperture. Foot with a narrow yellow line around margin. **Size:** Up to 78 mm. **Biology:** A slow-moving subtidal predator that bores through the shells of sea urchins and pansy shells. Siphon held erect to 'sniff' the waters for prey (83.6a).

83.7 **Bubble-raft shell or violet snail** *Janthina janthina*
Thin, fragile, rounded shells grading from dark violet around the aperture to much paler at the apex. Aperture squarish, lacking an operculum. **Size:** Up to 34 mm. **Biology:** Hangs upside down from the sea surface, suspended by a raft of mucus-coated bubbles secreted by the foot (83.7a). Often washed ashore in association with bluebottles, *Physalia* (21.1), and by-the-wind-sailors, *Velella* (21.3), upon which it feeds. Eggs are brooded and released as late-stage larvae.
SIMILAR SPECIES: Several species have the same warm-water distribution and habit of suspending themselves by a bubble-raft.
83.8 *Janthina prolongata* is uniform in colour and has an elongate, pear-shaped aperture that is produced to form an anterior 'spout'.
83.9 *Janthina pallida* is a very pale species with a broadly rounded aperture and neither a spout nor a notch.
83.10 *Janthina exigua* is smaller, reaching only 15 mm. The surface is covered in fine ribs angled to meet at mid-whorl, creating a V-shaped notch in the aperture.
83.11 *Janthina umbilicata* is another small species, but is smooth, with a weak ridge at mid-whorl and no notch in the aperture.

83.2a

83.3

83.4a

83.6a

83.7a

83.1

83.2

83.4

83.5

83.6

83.7

83.8

83.9

83.10

83.11

PLATE 84

Whelks

Whelks are all predators or scavengers, capturing prey with a tubular proboscis. Their shells have an oval aperture, which is notched at the front, or even extended into a tubular siphonal canal, to accommodate a cylindrical siphon.

84.1 Granular frog shell   *Bursa granularis*

Outer lip thickened, ridged, armed with small teeth. An anal canal notches the posterior end of the outer lip where it joins the body whorl. Two swollen longitudinal ridges run down the sides of the shell. About 5–7 spiral rows of granules traverse the body whorl. Brown, with pale nodules. **Size:** 50 mm. **Biology:** Found under rocks in mid-shore pools. Eats other gastropods.

84.2 Pink lady   *Charonia lampas pustulata*

Outer lip thickened and decorated with transverse brown bars; inner lip with transverse wrinkles. Fine, spiral grooves, a spiral row of nodules and 2–3 longitudinal ridges decorate each whorl. Foot mottled brown-red; tentacles orange and usually barred. **Size:** The largest whelk in the region, reaching 250 mm. **Biology:** Most common subtidally, down to 40 m. Feeds on sea urchins, starfish and sea cucumbers.

84.3 Furry-ridged triton   *Cabestana cutacea africana*

Variable in shape, some forms being more slender than others. Usually short and squat, barrel-shaped; body whorl with about seven strong grooved ridges. Outer lip corrugated or thickened with blunt teeth. Shells of live animals coated with a brown proteinaceous fur. **Size:** 50 mm. **Biology:** Often found among redbait (*Pyura stolonifera*), on which it may feed.

84.4 Pustular triton   *Argobuccinum pustulosum*

Thick-shelled with two longitudinal ridges; outer lip strengthened with about nine teeth. Inner lip with a strong nodule and 2–3 ridges. Pale brown with darker spiral ridges dotted with pale pustule-like nodules. **Size:** 60 mm. **Biology:** Common in shallow water; feeds on worms, particularly the Cape reef-worm (28.3). Secretes acidic 'saliva' that dissolves the worms' protective tubes (84.4a). Previously named *A. argus*. **SIMILAR SPECIES:**

84.5 *Ranella australasia gemmifera* (Cape Point–Durban) has one row of large nodules, and its outer lip is toothed and white, with dark brown bars.

84.6 Branched murex   *Chicoreus ramosus*

A large handsome shell. Mouth flanked by a row of spiky projections. Each whorl has three longitudinal rows of spikes, between which are lower nodular ridges. More delicate ridges spiral around the shell. The siphonal canal is as long as the aperture and forms an open gutter. **Size:** 180 mm. **Biology:** Lives in shallow water among rock rubble. Feeds on bivalves and other gastropods. Specimens from Durban have stunted spines.

84.7 Short-spined murex   *Murex brevispina*

Unmistakable, with its extremely long siphonal canal and rows of short blunt knobs. **Size:** 60 mm. **Biology:** Lives on protected, intertidal sandbanks among eelgrass. Aggregates to mate, and produces communal balls of egg capsules. A mating pair is illustrated in the photograph (84.7a).

84.8 Stag shell   *Pteropurpura graagae*

Small; white to pale brown. Body whorl with three rows of spines, including one row that edges the aperture. The shoulder spines are narrow, elongate and strongly bent, usually touching and fusing with the whorl above. Other spines all short and blunt. **Size:** 25 mm. **Biology:** Hides beneath stones, and bores through the shells of other gastropods and barnacles to feed on them.

84.9 Hooked murex   *Pteropurpura uncinaria*

Broader, thicker-spined, the shoulder spines rarely bending enough to reach the whorl above. Other spines range from truncated to sharply pointed. **Size:** 27 mm. **Biology:** As for *P. graagae*. Both species have had a troubled nomenclature, receiving various names and even swapping names. **SIMILAR SPECIES:** Six easily confused species fall in the genus.

84.4a

84.7a

84.1

84.2

84.3

84.4

84.5

84.6

84.7

84.8

84.9

PLATE 85

85.1 Fenestrate oyster-drill   *Ocenebra fenestrata*

A spindle-shaped shell, readily recognised by having two spiral ridges that are pitted with oblong 'windows'. **Size:** 15 mm. **Biology:** Lives subtidally beneath boulders, among redbait (*Pyura*) or in the holdfasts of kelp. Diet unknown.

85.2 Mulberry shell   *Morula granulata*

Shell grey-brown with spirals of strong black knobs aligned in nine longitudinal rows. Outer lip with four pronounced teeth. **Size:** 25 mm. **Biology:** Abundant, extending up the shore as high as the oyster band. Drills holes in the shells of barnacles and molluscs; may influence the abundance of oysters by eating newly settled spat.

85.3 Salmon-lipped whelk   *Purpura panama*

Heavy and squat. Lip salmon-pink, armed with numerous low teeth. Body whorl has 3–4 low ridges with darker nodules. **Size:** 70 mm. **Biology:** Found under boulders in pools. Drills barnacles and oysters; also dislodges and consumes limpets. Females aggregate to spawn – the photograph illustrates a mating pair astride a mat of egg capsules (85.3a). SIMILAR SPECIES:

85.4 *Thais bufo* (Transkei–Indo-Pacific) is very similar, but has a shorter spire, and the body whorl often has a smooth callus where the outer lip joins it.

85.5 *Mancinella alouina* (Transkei–Indo-Pacific) is squat, with a low spire and four rows of strong nodules; inner margin of aperture yellow to pale orange.

85.6 Knobbly dogwhelk   *Thais capensis*

Spire almost as long as aperture. Grey, with 3–4 spiral rows of obvious paler tubercles. **Size:** 40 mm. **Biology:** Hides under rocks in low-shore pools or shallow waters. Feeds on sea squirts (ascidians) by pushing its proboscis down their siphons; also eats gastropods. SIMILAR SPECIES:

85.7 *Thais haemastoma* (central Namibia–Angola) has 1–2 rows of knobs on the shoulder and a bright orange aperture. Consume bivalves.

85.8 *Thais wahlbergi* (Saldanha–False Bay) is off-white with fine spiral grooves.

85.9 *Thais savignyi* (Zululand–Indo-Pacific) has four spiral rows of angular tubercles and a mottling of dark flames; the mouth is edged with black.

85.10 Girdled dogwhelk   *Nucella cingulata*

White or blue-grey; usually girdled with 1–4 strong spiral ridges. **Size:** 30 mm. **Biology:** Common among mussels and drills neat cylindrical holes through their shells. The mussels can, however, retaliate by binding the whelks with their byssus threads. Lays pink egg capsules with a narrow stalk and two apical 'wings'.

85.11 Common dogwhelk   *Nucella dubia*

Extraordinarily variable (hence 'dubia'). Body whorl weakly ridged. Colour either grey with black flames, red-brown with dotted bands, plain grey or brown. Aperture usually large and dark, often purple. **Size:** 20 mm. **Biology:** Extends almost to the high-tide mark on rocky shores. Eats limpets, barnacles and periwinkles. Lays egg capsules, from which crawling young emerge. The absence of a planktonic larval stage reduces gene flow between populations, leading to enormous variations between populations.

85.12 Scaly dogwhelk   *Nucella squamosa*

About 15 spiral ridges overlie longitudinal ridges, giving the shell a scaly (squamous) appearance. **Size:** 35 mm. **Biology:** Low shore or subtidal. Lays egg capsules resembling flat clubs. Shell usually coated by the hydroid, *Hydractinia altispina* (19.2), making the shell prickly and orange. The hydroid's stinging cells repel a variety of predators.

85.13 Elongate whelk   *Afrocominella elongata*

Shell long and narrow; aperture about one-third the total length. Numerous fine, spiral ridges. Pale brown, with delicate darker longitudinal streaks. **Size:** 50 mm. **Biology:** Subtidal, sometimes extending into the intertidal zone.

85.3a

85.7

85.1

85.2

85.3

85.4

85.5

85.6

85.8

85.9

85.10

85.11

85.12

85.13

PLATE 86

86.1 Ridged burnupena — *Burnupena cincta*

Robust. Outer surface with coarse spiral ridges, although west coast specimens may lack these. Aperture about 1.5 times longer than the spire. Posterior end of outer lip strongly kinked inwards. Dull brown, often tinged green by algae. Aperture pale violet. **Size:** 40 mm. **Biology:** Scavenges on dead or injured animals low on the shore and subtidally.

86.2 Variable burnupena — *Burnupena lagenaria*

Shorter than *B. cincta* (spire less than half aperture length); often has wavy dark flames. The commonest *Burnupena* on the southeast coast, where it has obvious coarse spiral ridges (86.2a) and a violet-brown or yellow aperture. On the west coast it has an even shorter spire, only a trace of ridges, and a deep-purple aperture (86.2b). **Size:** 35 mm. **Biology:** Intertidal to shallow subtidal. Lays scale-like egg capsules in domed clusters (86.2).

86.3 Flame-patterned burnupena — *Burnupena catarrhacta*

Shell elongate (length twice width), smooth but crossed by numerous fine, spiral ridges. Juveniles often patterned with alternating dark and light flames (later obscured by erosion and algal overgrowth). Inside of aperture dark purple-brown. Outer lip pale, thin and only moderately kinked inwards at its posterior end. **Size:** 30 mm. **Biology:** A common scavenger. Rapidly congregates around dead or injured animals in rock pools.

86.4 Rotund burnupena — *Burnupena rotunda*

Smooth, with fine, spiral ridges like *B. catarrhacta*, but much more robust and squat. Its outer lip is thick and scarcely kinked inwards posteriorly. Shell dull brown; inside of aperture pale. **Size:** 35 mm. **Biology:** Lives low on the shore.

86.5 Papery burnupena — *Burnupena papyracea*

Live specimens are coated by the purple or orange bryozoan *Alcyonidium nodosum*, which throws the surface into tiny bumps (see 58.6). Dead individuals (86.5) lose this coating and are dull brown with fine, spiral ridges, and a papery outer layer that peels off. Outer lip thin; aperture white inside. **Size:** 50 mm. **Biology:** *Alcyonidium* is toxic and protects the whelk against predators. Abundant subtidally, *B. papyracea* can exceed densities of 200 per m², and may 'gang up' to consume rock lobsters (86.5a), excluding them from certain areas, with profound implications for the community composition.

86.6 Pubescent burnupena — *Burnupena pubescens*

Extremely similar to the previous species. In life, it is also covered by *Alcyonidium*. Dead shells differ only in being smaller and having fine, longitudinal ridges that cross the spiral ridges to create a checkered (cancellate) texture, most evident on the spire. Beach-worn shells are patterned with alternating white and brown streaks. **Size:** 30 mm. **Biology:** Exclusively subtidal.

86.7 Long-siphoned whelk — *Fusinus ocelliferus*

Shell elongate. Siphonal canal up to one-third the total length. Whorls decorated by delicate spiral ridges. Sometimes the shoulder ridge is strengthened and may carry nodules. Colour white to brown, sometimes flecked with darker spots. Foot bright orange-red. **Size:** 150 mm. **Biology:** Most common subtidally; feeds on polychaete worms, as evidenced by their bristles in its faeces.

SIMILAR SPECIES:

86.8a *Fasciolaria lugubris lugubris* (Lüderitz–False Bay) is foreshortened, with more delicate ribs and a shorter siphonal canal. The inner lip has two pleats near the siphonal canal, distinguishing it from *F. ocelliferus*.

86.8b *Fasciolaria lugubris heynemanni* is a deeper-water subspecies that extends to Agulhas, with a longer canal, pronounced shoulder knobs and few spiral ridges.

86.9 Forsskål's whelk — *Peristernia forskalii*

Small but solid, with short siphonal canal, low ridges on the outer lip, and 11 bulging longitudinal ribs on the body whorl, crossed by a much finer spiral texturing. Foot orange-red. **Size:** 25 mm. **Biology:** Very common on intertidal and subtidal reefs; often shelters among oysters. Feeds on polychaetes. The darker subspecies *P. forskalii forskalii* (86.9a) is replaced south of Durban by the pure white *P. forskalii leucothea* (86.9b).

86.2

86.5a

86.1

86.2a

86.2b

86.3

86.4

86.5

86.8b

86.9a

86.6

86.7

86.8a

86.9b

PLATE 87

Nassariids, mitres & strombs

Nassariids are scavengers that inhabit sands or muds in sheltered areas. Shells often with strong axial ribs and a large shiny callus alongside the aperture. Mitres are sand-dwelling predators with spindle-shaped shells and 3–6 strong oblique pleats on the inner lip. Wing shells, or strombids, are herbivores with a thickened, flared, outer lip that is notched anteriorly to accommodate the stalked right eye.

87.1 Onion-peel whelk   *Volema pyrum*
Pear-shaped, with a strong shoulder, and spiral grooves near the front. Outer surface brownish yellow with velvety coating; aperture flushed red-brown. **Size:** 66 mm. **Biology:** Occupies mud and sandflats and the fringes of mangroves. Burrows during low tide and emerges to pursue molluscs as the tide rises. Once abundant in Durban Bay.

87.2 Cape dogwhelk   *Nassarius capensis*
Shell narrow with a small, smooth, ventral callus and 12–14 strong axial ribs crossing the body whorl. Usually pale yellow-brown, with a darker spiral band on lower part of whorl, and brown speckles. Foot speckled with white (87.2a). **Size:** Up to 17 mm. **Biology:** Found in sandy rock pools and down to 30 m.

87.3 Shielded dogwhelk   *Nassarius arcularius plicatus*
Whorls swollen, with a distinct step between them. Underside covered by a thick, smooth callus shield; last whorl with about 15 strong axial ridges. Operculum with serrated margin. Colour grey-white with brown bands inside aperture. Body white, flecked grey (87.3a). **Size:** 27 mm. **Biology:** Scavenges on sheltered sandbanks.
SIMILAR SPECIES:
87.4 *Nassarius coronatus* (Durban–Indo-Pacific) has a much more restricted callus and fine ridges on the outer lip.

87.5 Lattice dogwhelk   *Nassarius plicatellus*
Cream to brown. Broad axial ribs and finer radial ribs create a pale lattice-like pattern. Callus reduced. **Size:** Up to 25 mm. **Biology:** Occupies sheltered sandbanks.
SIMILAR SPECIES:
87.6 *Nassarius albescens gemmuliferus* (Transkei–Indo-Pacific) has a shorter spire, wider callus and strong, equal-sized spiral and longitudinal ribs.

87.7 Tick shell   *Nassarius kraussianus*
Shell globular, with a short, smooth spire. Entire undersurface enveloped in a glossy yellow callus. Sometimes coated by hydroids (19.1); otherwise purplish with yellow bands. Body translucent grey, flecked white (87.7a). **Size:** 7–10 mm. **Biology:** Abundant in estuarine or lagoonal mudbanks. Preys on small bivalves or scavenges. Tick shells were used as beads in necklaces over 75 000 years ago – some of the oldest evidence of symbolic behaviour by human beings anywhere in the world.

87.8 Purple-lipped dogwhelk   *Nassarius speciosus*
Shell pale brown, with purple anterior canal at the tip of the aperture. About 11 strong axial ribs on body whorl, crossed by fine, spiral threads to create knobbly ridges. Callus extends about halfway across the underside. **Size:** Up to 30 mm. **Biology:** Common in protected areas, down to depths of 95 m. Scavenges on dead animals.

87.9 Brown mitre   *Mitra picta*
A smooth, spindle-shaped shell with a narrow aperture bearing 3–4 pleats on the inner lip. Off-white, streaked with brown flames, mauve when eroded. Operculum absent. **Size:** 44 mm. **Biology:** A shallow-water predator of sipunculid worms.
SIMILAR SPECIES:
87.10 *Mitra litterata* (western Transkei–Mozambique) has a broader, yellowish shell with brown zigzag markings. It also feeds on sipunculid worms.

87.11 Variable stromb   *Strombus mutabilis*
Has the flared and notched outer lip typical of the family Strombidae. Colour cream with spiral rows of yellow-brown flecks and spots. Aperture ridged and lined with orange. A row of nodules lies close to the suture line. **Size:** Up to 38 mm. **Biology:** In crevices or under stones and in tropical lagoons. Feeds on soft algae.

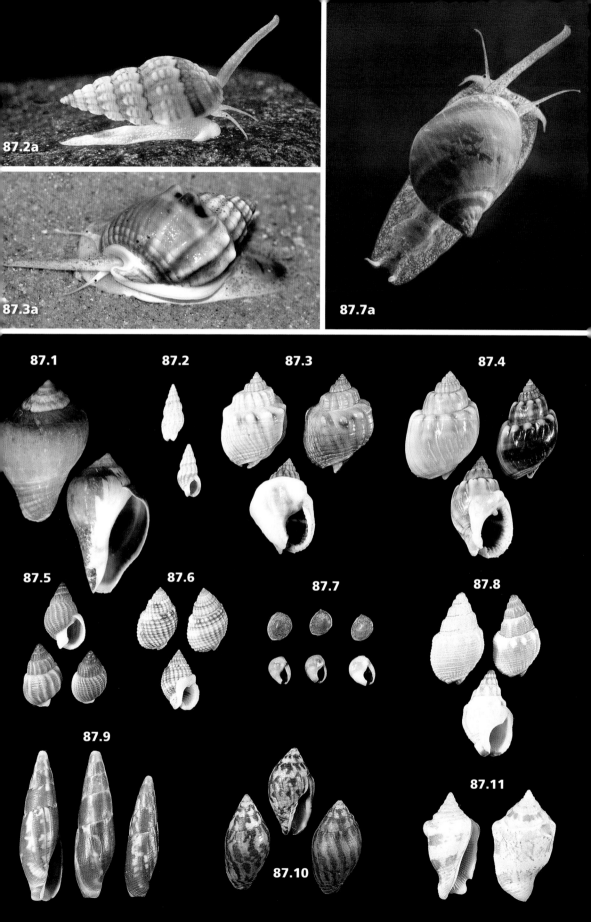

87.2a

87.3a

87.7a

87.1

87.2

87.3

87.4

87.5

87.6

87.7

87.8

87.9

87.10

87.11

PLATE 88

Plough shells

Plough shells of the genus Bullia *are a feature of wave-exposed southern African sandy beaches, and are recognised by the extremely broad flat foot and reduced, often serrated, operculum. All are blind and rely on a keen sense of smell to detect carrion, around which they rapidly congregate. Many use the waves to 'surf' up the beach, and crawl on the wet sand with a characteristic 'rowing' movement in search of jellyfish, bluebottles and other cast-up animals.*

88.1 Annulated plough shell   *Bullia annulata*
Pale brown, with faint spiral ridges and a distinctive 'step' separating the whorls. Operculum oval and not serrated. **Size:** Up to 60 mm. **Biology:** Shells often washed ashore, but live animals are subtidal, extending down to depths of about 100 m.

88.2 Calloused plough shell   *Bullia callosa*
Similarly 'stepped' between the whorls, but the steps, aperture and heavy callus area around it are usually dark brown, and the spiral ridges on the shell vary from weak to absent. **Size:** 50 mm. **Biology:** Scavenges at depths of 7–36 m.

88.3 Fat plough shell   *Bullia laevissima*
A heavy, squat species with a short spire and very large aperture. The large shiny callus area covers most of the underside of the last whorl. Operculum tiny and oval, without serrated margins. **Size:** Up to 55 mm. **Biology:** Extremely common in deeper water below the surf zone, and is harvested by a small-scale commercial fishery. Extends into the intertidal zone in very sheltered bays and lagoons.

88.4 Finger plough shell   *Bullia digitalis*
Narrow, with a long pointed spire and smooth cream shell, often tinged with violet. Operculum with serrated margins. **Size:** Up to 60 mm. **Biology:** The dominant plough shell on Atlantic shores. Lives buried low on the shore, emerging to 'surf' upshore (88.4a) in response to the smell of carrion. Congregates in large numbers to feed, particularly on stranded jellyfish and bluebottles (88.4b). Algae coating the shell supplement the diet.

88.5 Smooth plough shell   *Bullia rhodostoma*
Similar to the previous species, but shell somewhat broader, aperture orange; opercular margins smooth. **Size:** Up to 55 mm. **Biology:** The dominant plough shell on the south and east coasts, congregating in enormous numbers around carrion cast up on exposed sandy beaches. Lighter than *B. digitalis*, and surfs higher up the shore. Slow-growing, reaching 10 mm after one year and 40 mm after 10 years.

88.6 Pure plough shell   *Bullia pura*
Shell pale pinkish brown, sometimes with brown markings on lower whorls; sculptured with fine, spiral ridges. Operculum has smooth margins. **Size:** Up to 34 mm. **Biology:** Usually occurs subtidally, occasionally also around the low-tide level. Broods its young under its foot, releasing them as fully formed juveniles (88.6a).

88.7 Pleated plough shell   *Bullia natalensis*
Shell smoothly tapering, with flattened whorls; each whorl distinctly pleated just below the suture or join line. Light brown in colour, darker between the pleats. Operculum not serrated. **Size:** Up to 66 mm. **Biology:** The most abundant plough shell in the surf zone of sandy beaches in KwaZulu-Natal, scavenging on dead animals.

88.8 Mozambique plough shell   *Bullia mozambicensis*
Very similar to the previous species, but ornamented by shallow spiral grooves in addition to longitudinal pleats, and the pleats also differ in extending further across each whorl than in *B. natalensis*. **Size:** 60 mm. **Biology:** Behaves like *B. natalensis*, but extends further north to northern Mozambique.

88.4a

88.4b

88.6a

88.1

88.2

88.3

88.4

88.5

88.6

88.7

88.8

PLATE 89

Olive shells & marginellas

Marginellas have smooth shiny shells with a narrow elongate aperture three-quarters or more of the total shell length. The spire is correspondingly short. The outer lip is strengthened, and the inner lip has 3–5 ridges or 'pleats'. Olive shells have a similar long thin aperture, but lack these pleats.

89.1 Carolinian olive shell   *Oliva caroliniana*

Cylindrical, smooth and shiny, and attractively decorated with spiral dots and streaks. Spire sharply pointed, but extremely short. Aperture violet; interrupted at its hind end (next to the spire) by a groove for the anus. **Size:** 45 mm. **Biology:** Occurs subtidally in sandy gullies or on sheltered sandbanks. Scavenges on dead animal matter.

89.2 Pinch-lipped marginella   *Marginella rosea*

Ground colour white, exquisitely shot with pink or brown flares that run longitudinally or spirally. Outer lip distinctively 'pinched', being narrowed at its posterior end. Foot grey or cream, with vivid white streaks and red dots (89.2a). **Size:** 30 mm. **Biology:** Lives low on the shore or in the shallow subtidal zone, usually concealed under boulders. Chases small gastropods (89.2a) and captures them with its proboscis, apparently paralysing them with a toxin. Often it will transport its prey attached to the posterior tip of its foot.

SIMILAR SPECIES:

89.3 *Marginella piperata* (Cape Point–KwaZulu-Natal north coast) is smaller, and lacks the 'pinch' on the lip. Colour of shell extremely varied: usually white to cream with flares or bands of brown.

89.4 *Marginella ornata* (Port Elizabeth–Transkei) is more 'chubby', grey to red-brown, with three pale spiral bands. Shells of this species are quite commonly washed ashore, but no live animals have yet been recorded.

89.5 *Marginella musica* (Lüderitz–Cape Agulhas) is easily recognised, being grey to cream with about 10 encircling narrow black bands. The foot is cream-coloured and marked with scarlet lines.

89.6 Cloudy marginella   *Marginella nebulosa*

One of the larger marginellas, recognised by its size, the obviously angular shoulder on its shell, and the longitudinal wavy bands of brown or grey. Foot white, with red spots (89.6a). **Size:** 35–40 mm. **Biology:** Never abundant, but collected live by divers in depths of 5–75 m. It is usually found buried shallowly in sand around rocky outcrops. Eats other gastropods.

89.7 Cape marginella   *Volvarina capensis*

Shell small, oval, with a short rounded apex. Uniformly white to pale buff, occasionally golden. Foot grey, with white spots and blotches (89.7a). **Size:** 10 mm. **Biology:** Lives in sheltered sandy lagoons. Attracted to fish offal but also feeds on bivalves. Has round, domed egg capsules 2.5 mm wide, which it often attaches to other gastropods.

89.8 Zoned marginella   *Volvarina zonata*

A small species with a white shell and either one broad red-brown spiral band (89.8a) or two narrow brown ones (89.8b). **Size:** 8 mm. **Biology:** Forms small aggregations under stones low on the shore or in shallow waters. A micro-predator that eats minute gastropods and polychaetes. Erroneously named *Marginella biannulata* in the past.

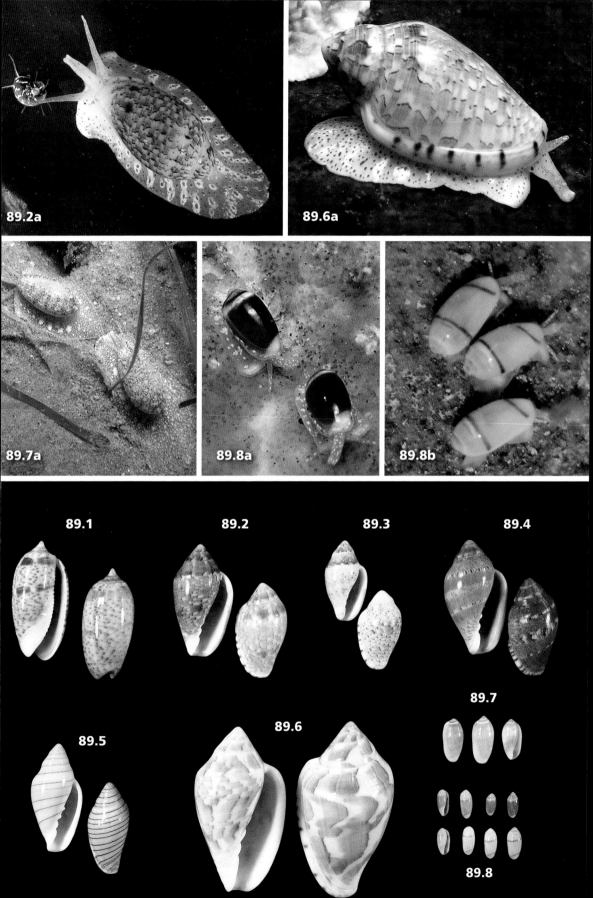

89.2a

89.6a

89.7a

89.8a

89.8b

89.1

89.2

89.3

89.4

89.7

89.5

89.6

89.8

PLATE 90

Cone shells

Members of the family Conidae have conical shells, long narrow apertures, and short blunt spires. Outer lip thin and smooth; inner lip never toothed or pleated. Cones are predators and use hollow, harpoon-like teeth to inject a potent neurotoxin. Conus textile and C. geographus are potentially lethal to humans.

90.1 Hebrew cone — *Conus ebraeus*

White to cream with 3–4 rows of roughly rectangular dark blotches. **Size:** 35 mm. **Biology:** Occurs commonly on rocky shores in low-shore pools, particularly those containing clean sand. Often buries itself in the sand. Feeds on polychaete worms.

90.2 Natal textile cone — *Conus natalis*

White to yellow, with a fine brown network that is concentrated in spiral bands. Diagnostic features are the smoothly rounded shoulder and low largely brown spire. **Size:** 55 mm. **Biology:** Commonly washed up; rarely seen alive. Lives in muddy sand under boulders. Active by night, when it consumes gastropods.

SIMILAR SPECIES:

90.3 *Conus textile*, the textile cone, is tropical but occasionally found in KwaZulu-Natal; has a similar pattern of tent-shaped markings, but the 'tents' are flatter and the spire more acute.

90.4 Livid cone — *Conus lividus*

Readily distinguished by the row of low knobs on the angular shoulder and its almost uniform yellow or brown colour, which is interrupted only by an obscure pale band around the middle of the shell. **Size:** 50 mm. **Biology:** Moderately common in sandy or muddy pools. Eats worms.

90.5 Wedding cone — *Conus sponsalis*

Sides slightly rounded, and shoulder distinctly rounded. Colour white, with scattered orange-brown dots, blotches or flares. Foot coloured red (90.5a). **Size:** 25 mm. **Biology:** Common; aggregates in sandy pools where it buries itself, leaving only the siphon exposed. Feeds on polychaete worms. *Sponsalis* comes from the Latin for 'betrothal' – an allusion to its bridal-white colour.

90.6 Algoa cone — *Conus algoensis*

Shoulder rounded and the spire 'stepped' between the whorls. There are three subspecies. *Conus algoensis algoensis* (west coast) is narrow, chocolate-brown, with white blotches. Its spire is white, flamed with brown (90.6). *C. algoensis simplex* (Cape Point–Hermanus) is yellow with longitudinal wavy brown bands that tend to unite on the shoulder (90.6a). *C. algoensis scitulus* (Hermanus–Cape Agulhas) is smaller, white, yellow or pink with spiral bands of dark dots (90.6b). **Size:** 50 mm. **Biology:** Lives in sand-covered intertidal pools, extending down to 50 m; eats polychaete worms.

90.7 Elongate cone — *Conus mozambicus*

There are two subspecies. *C. mozambicus mozambicus* (90.7) is slender and its spire acute. The shoulder has fine, spiral ridges. Colour drab, plain brown or blotched with darker brown flecks concentrated on the spire and shoulder. *C. mozambicus lautus* (90.7a) has a shorter shell, less acute spire and is red-brown, often with paler spiral streaks or spots. It can be confused with *C. tinianus*, but has a distinctly ridged shoulder slope. **Size:** 65 mm. **Biology:** *C. mozambicus mozambicus* (Lüderitz–Mossel Bay, but not Mozambique!) is the commonest cold-water cone and eats polychaete worms. *C. mozambicus lautus* replaces it east of Cape Agulhas. Lays clumps of rounded egg capsules (90.7b), each containing several eggs. Early-hatching offspring consume the remaining eggs.

90.8 Variable cone — *Conus tinianus*

Sides of shell gently convex – more so than in *C. mozambicus lautus*, with which it can be confused. Shoulder strongly rounded; spire low and blunt. Colour extraordinarily variable – background colour pink, orange, yellow, olive or white, often blotched with brown or ringed with dots and streaks. **Size:** 50 mm. **Biology:** The most common and variable of southern African cones. Feeds on polychaete worms and possibly gastropods.

90.5a

90.7b

90.1

90.2

90.3

90.4

90.5

90.6

90.6a

90.6b

90.7

90.7a

90.8

PLATE 91

Sea slugs & nudibranchs — Opisthobranchia

A diverse subclass, including bubble-shells, sea hares, nudibranchs and sea slugs, and characterised by a reduction or total loss of the shell. With their soft body parts exposed, many opisthobranchs defend themselves by secreting toxic chemicals or reusing stinging cells derived from their prey. Flamboyant colours warn potential predators of their unpleasant nature. Most opisthobranchs have two sensory tentacles, called rhinophores, on top of the head. The original gills are often lost and may be replaced by a plume of secondary gills around the anus, or by finger-like 'cerata' on the back. Opisthobranchs are hermaphrodites, but incapable of self-fertilisation. Eggs are laid in jelly-covered strings or ribbons, and hatch into planktonic larvae. Most are specialised predators, thus difficult to keep in aquaria. Some 300 species occur in southern Africa.

91.1 Shelled sand slug — *Philine aperta*

Smooth, rather featureless, and creamish white. Body wedge-shaped and flattened, with a translucent internal shell. **Size:** Up to 100 mm. **Biology:** A widely distributed, active predator that glides just beneath the sand surface, often covered by a thin film of sand. Feeds mainly on small molluscs, which are swallowed whole and crushed by the muscular gizzard. Secretes sulphuric acid to deter predators.

91.2 Green bubble-shell — *Haminoea alfredensis*

Body flattened, blackish green, mottled with irregular paler spots. Flaps fold upwards over the sides of the relatively small, speckled, translucent external shell. **Size:** 15 mm. **Biology:** Occurs in sometimes dense colonies among algae and seagrass beds in estuaries, sheltered intertidal pools and embayments. Feeds on filamentous green algae or diatoms scraped from rocks or seaweeds. Lays spiral yellow egg masses that are visible in this photograph. **SIMILAR SPECIES:** *H. natalensis* is closely related and replaces it in KwaZulu-Natal.

91.3 Striped bubble-shell — *Hydatina physis*

Shell external, delicate and oval, bearing numerous fine, spiral, brown lines. Foot large and pink with thin wavy margin attractively edged in blue. **Size:** 30 mm. **Biology:** Lives in protected sandflats or rock pools. A specialist predator of burrowing polychaetes. **SIMILAR SPECIES:** *H. amplustre* (Durban northwards) has a white body and broad, black-edged, alternating pink-and-white bands across the shell.

91.4 Mottled bubble-shell — *Bulla ampulla*

Larger than *Haminoea* and with a thicker, opaque shell, which has a mottled, sometimes zigzag, pattern. Body orange with white dots. **Size:** 30 mm. **Biology:** Usually remains buried in soft silt or sand by day, but emerges at night to crawl actively about and to feed on seaweeds. Populations fluctuate, but it can be very common in tidal pools.

91.5 Assassin bubble-shell — *Philinopsis speciosa*

Large and spectacular, with a flattened head and elevated lobed posterior end. Colour extremely variable: usually brown to dark blue with longitudinal yellow to orange stripes and a blue margin. **Size:** 50 mm. **Biology:** Nocturnal, ploughing through sand or mud following the mucous trails left by its prey, notably other bubble-shells. **SIMILAR SPECIES:** *P. capensis* (Cape Town–East London) is similar in shape, but is plain brown with white spots.

91.6 Polka-dot bubble-shell — *Micromelo undata*

Shell external, white with thin wavy brown lines crossed by three thin spiral lines. Body an exquisite blue-green with white spots and a yellow to green margin. **Size:** 15 mm. **Biology:** A photographer's favourite, common in intertidal pools in KwaZulu-Natal, where it buries itself in sandy crevices and feeds on polychaete worms.

91.1

91.2

91.3

91.4

91.5

91.6

PLATE 92

92.1 Spotted sea hare — *Aplysia oculifera*

Typical of smooth-skinned sea hares, with prominent tentacles and ear-like rhinophores. Green-brown in colour, speckled with small white-centred black spots. **Size:** 150 mm. **Biology:** Common in shallow bays and estuaries. Like all members of the genus, it hides by day and emerges at night to eat seaweeds. Swims by flapping its parapodia.
SIMILAR SPECIES:
92.2 *Aplysia parvula* (Cape Town–northern KwaZulu-Natal) is the smallest of the genus (60 mm) and plain green-brown or with tiny white dots. *A. juliana* (Cape Town–Mozambique) has black splashes and a posterior sucker. *A. dactylomela* (Port Elizabeth–Indo-Pacific) has a green or brown ground colour and larger yellow-centred black circular markings and grows to 400 mm.

92.3 Shaggy sea hare — *Bursatella leachii*

Body covered in shaggy tassels, which are short and dense in the darker Cape animals, but much longer and sparser in KwaZulu-Natal specimens, which also have blue circles on the body (two species are possibly confused). East coast juveniles (92.3a) look quite different, with few projections, dark blotches and bright blue spots. **Size:** 100 mm. **Biology:** Common in estuaries and tidal pools. Forms dense breeding aggregations, and lays eggs in long stringy green tangles. Herbivorous. Emits a purple dye if disturbed.

92.4 Wedge sea hare — *Dolabella auricularia*

A very large dull brown sea hare with a shaggy surface. Posterior end is a flat oblique disc; tail absent. **Size:** 150–400 mm. **Biology:** A slow-moving nocturnal grazer found in sheltered pools or weedbeds. By day it lies partially buried in sand or mud, where it is hard to see, despite its large size. Emits a purple dye if disturbed.

92.5 Lemon pleurobranch — *Berthellina granulata*

Body smooth, yellow to orange, often with clusters of white spots; shell fragile and internal; single gill situated under the mantle edge on the right side. **Size:** About 30 mm. **Biology:** Commonly found in pairs under boulders intertidally and on shallow reefs. Believed to be a grazing carnivore, feeding on sponges and other sessile invertebrates. Previously known as *B. citrina*. **SIMILAR SPECIES:** *Doriopsilla miniata*, the scribbled nudibranch (Cape Town–Port Elizabeth), is smooth and yellow, with a ring of anal gills, but is readily recognised by irregular thin white 'scribbles' on its back. It feeds on sponges. A very similar unnamed species in this genus occurs from Cape Town to Saldanha.

92.6 Spotted pleurobranch — *Pleurobranchaea brockii*

A large elongate brown pleurobranch with a dense scattering of white spots and prominent rhinophores. **Size:** 50 mm. **Biology:** Found in silty pools; probably a browsing carnivore. Widespread in the Indo-Pacific, as far afield as eastern Australia.

92.7 Papillate pleurobranch — *Pleurobranchus peroni*

Body a uniform deep red colour and covered in a net-like pattern of small, rounded, simple papillae. **Size:** 35 mm. **Biology:** Thought to be a grazing carnivore feeding on sponges, ascidians and anemones.

92.8 Smooth pleurobranch — *Pleurobranchus grandis*

Similar to the previous species, but much larger and has rings of small tubercles around larger central tubercles. Sometimes pure red, but mottled white and red in South Africa. **Size:** 100 mm. **Biology:** Nocturnal. Found in intertidal pools and the shallow subtidal zone.

92.9 Warty pleurobranch — *Pleurobranchaea bubala*

Rhinophores widely separated on corners of head. Body grey, with elevated warts carrying opaque white markings; shell internal. Single gill present under the mantle edge on the right side. **Size:** 60 mm. **Biology:** Occurs on shallow reefs. Feeds voraciously on large prey, including other opisthobranchs. **SIMILAR SPECIES:** *P. tarda* (Cape Town–Knysna) closely resembles it, but is smaller (25 mm), and has a smooth dorsal surface.

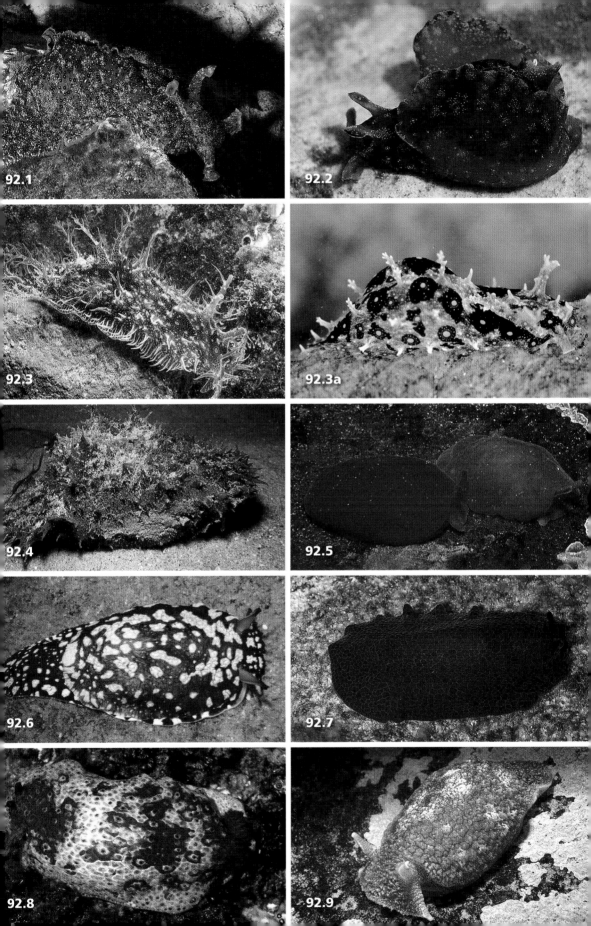

PLATE 93

93.1 Umbrella sea slug   *Umbraculum umbraculum*

Unmistakable, with a large orange foot covered in pale knobs and topped by an unusual, flat external shell, which does little more than protect the gills. **Size:** 40–60 mm. **Biology:** Usually found clinging to rocks in low-shore pools and gullies, but often buries itself in sand or mud during the day. Feeds on sponges.

93.2 Crazed nudibranch   *Corambe* sp.

One of the most cryptic of all nudibranchs, with a simple flat body shape and gills situated in a notch at the back of the body. Brown, with a pattern of crazed white crack-like lines. **Size:** 7 mm. **Biology:** Found on the fronds of kelps and other large algae, where it is associated with, and feeds on, the bryozoan *Membranipora rustica* (58.8), against which it is perfectly disguised. Lays a flat, spiral egg mass, shown on the left of this photograph.

93.3 Gas flame nudibranch   *Bonisa nakaza*

Large, and densely covered with closely packed cerata. Colour highly variable, the cerata being yellow or pink, with or without blue to purple tips. **Size:** 70 mm. **Biology:** Conspicuous on shallow reefs in the Western Cape, where it is a favourite subject of underwater photographers. Feeds on bryozoans. Lays a highly convoluted mass of white eggs.

93.4 Cape silvertip nudibranch   *Janolus capensis*

Back covered with silver-tipped grey club-shaped projections (cerata). **Size:** 15–25 mm. **Biology:** Common intertidally and on shallow reefs. Eats bryozoans, particularly upright bushy species such as *Menipea triseriata* (59.6). Egg mass is a globular, convoluted string of beautiful white egg capsules, each containing 30–40 eggs. **SIMILAR SPECIES:** *J. longidentatus* (False Bay) is almost indistinguishable based on external features, but its head is rounded, not conical.

93.5 Coral nudibranch   *Phyllodesmium horridum*

Recognised by the paired bunches of long bright orange or red cerata with their opaque off-white or luminous blue surface sheen. A white stripe runs along the length of the back and head and along each of the cerata. **Size:** Typically 30–40 mm. **Biology:** Locally common, from the extreme low shore down to about 30 m. Feeds on the soft tissues of sea fans. Previously known as *P. serratum*.

93.6 Four-tone nudibranch   *Godiva quadricolor*

The paired bunches of painted cerata with their very striking bands of brown, orange, blue and yellow readily characterise this beautiful nudibranch. **Size:** 20–30 mm. **Biology:** A voracious predator that feeds on anemones and on other nudibranchs. Occurs intertidally and on shallow rocky reefs, extending down to a depth of about 15 m.

93.7 White-tipped nudibranch   *Cratena capensis*

Cerata arranged in rows across the back. Body white, cerata brown or red with white tips. There are characteristic red or orange patches on the side of the head. **Size:** 10–20 mm. **Biology:** A small but common nudibranch that feeds on a range of hydroid species. The colour of the cerata varies, depending on the prey species that has been consumed.

93.8 Indica nudibranch   *Anteaeolidiella indica*

A pair of orange lines extends backwards from the head, separating on the back to surround white patches. Tentacles short, cerata short and club-shaped, grey or pink, with pale tips. **Size:** 10–40 mm. **Biology:** A common intertidal and shallow-reef nudibranch. Preys on the anemone *Anthothoe chilensis* (5.4).

93.1

93.2

93.3

93.4

93.5

93.6

93.7

93.8

PLATE 94

94.1 Cowled nudibranch   *Melibe rosea*

The unusual hooded or cowled form of the head is unique. Colour ranges from white to orange or red, often with opaque white patches. **Size:** Typically 30–40 mm. **Biology:** The most common intertidal nudibranch in the Cape. The cowl surrounds the mouth and is used like a basket to trap small crustacean prey. Lays a tall, collar-like egg mass on the underside of boulders in rock pools, often high in the intertidal zone.

94.2 Orange-clubbed nudibranch   *Limacea clavigera*

Body white, with scattered orange spots on the back; the gills and club-like marginal projections have orange tips. **Size:** 10–25 mm. **Biology:** Found on the fronds of large algae in shallow waters, where it feeds on encrusting bryozoans of the genera *Jellyella* and *Membranipora* (58.7 & 58.8). Lays white egg masses in the form of flat, spiral ribbons.

94.3 Sea swallow   *Glaucus atlanticus*

Readily recognised by its unusual habits and lateral tufts of silver-blue processes, which all lie in one plane. **Size:** 30 mm. **Biology:** Floats upside down on the surface of the ocean, gulping air bubbles to help keep afloat. Normally occurs in the open ocean, but often cast up on the shore following onshore winds. Feeds on bluebottles and their relatives and can employ the stinging cells of these prey for its own defence. **SIMILAR SPECIES:** *G.marginatus* (east coast) has lateral processes arranged in tufts, not in one plane.

94.4 Blue dragon   *Tambja sp.*

Blue-black background colour with a variable pattern of strong longitudinal pale blue and yellow lines. The rhinophores and gills are edged with blue, as is the foot. **Size:** 35 mm. **Biology:** Occurs in intertidal pools and down to a depth of 15 m.

94.5 Crowned nudibranch   *Polycera capensis*

Head with a fan of six pointed, gold-tipped, finger-like processes. Further gold processes arise on either side of the dorsal tuft of gills. Body white, with a variable pattern of longitudinal black and yellow stripes. **Size:** 25–50 mm. **Biology:** Feeds on bryozoans of the genus *Bugula* intertidally and on shallow reefs. **SIMILAR SPECIES:** *P. quadrilineata*, the fourline nudibranch (Cape Town–Port Elizabeth), differs only in having yellow tubercles on the black dorsal and lateral stripes.

94.6 Black nudibranch   *Tambja capensis*

A tall, elongate nudibranch easily recognised by its blue-black body colour and green or blue outline. **Size:** Typically 30–40 mm. **Biology:** One of the more common nudibranchs seen by divers in the Cape. Feeds on bryozoans, especially the bushy *Bugula dentata* (59.1). Lays a rose-like, spiral ribbon of bright yellow or orange eggs.

94.7 Iridescent nudibranch   *Notobryon sp.*

Brown with iridescent green spots. The two sets of fine, branching, transparent gills and flanking pairs of flattened body lobes are unique. **Size:** 20–40 mm. **Biology:** A common intertidal species, which feeds on hydroids. Swims readily, if disturbed, by thrashing its body from side to side.

94.8 Warty nudibranch   *Phyllidia varicosa*

Black with a series of knobbly white ridges, one running along the mid-line and others forming semicircular patterns down the sides of the body. Tips of knobs and rhinophores yellow. Body very firm to the touch. **Size:** 40–60 mm. **Biology:** Known to produce toxic chemicals from glands in the skin. The bright colours probably warn predators that they are poisonous to eat. **SIMILAR SPECIES:** One of many similar and gaudily coloured species in this genus. *P. coelestris* (previously called *P. varicosa*) has two longitudinal blue ridges on the back. Two other undescribed pink-ridged species also occur in Sodwana.

94.1

94.2

94.3

94.4

94.5

94.6

94.7

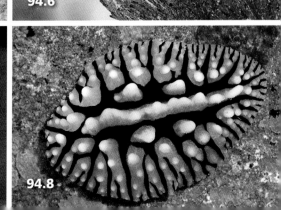

94.8

PLATE 95

95.1 Mottled dorid
Hypselodoris infucata

Extremely variable in colour. Some individuals have a blue-black background with a mottling of bright yellow spots and streaks. Others are much paler (as illustrated here). The rhinophores and edges of the gills are always red. **Size:** 35 mm. **Biology:** Found intertidally and in shallow water on tropical reefs.

95.2 Cape dorid
Hypselodoris capensis

Body pale with white lines along the back and a broken blue margin. Rhinophores and tips of gills orange. **Size:** About 40 mm. **Biology:** Occurs intertidally and on shallow reefs; feeds on the light-blue sponge *Haliclona oculata* (1.5). **SIMILAR SPECIES:** *H. carnea* is very similar but replaces it in KwaZulu-Natal. The purple band around the front of the head is continuous in *H. carnea* but usually broken in *H. capensis*. The radular teeth provide certain identification, *H. carnea* having tiny denticles on most teeth.

95.3 Blue-speckled dorid
Dendrodoris caesia

Body flat, pale pink to blue, densely speckled with small blue dots and with a ruffle of pale to blue gills. Mantle edge distinctively frilled and spotted with larger blue patches. **Size:** 70 mm. **Biology:** Intertidal to 20 m depth. Feeds on sponges.

95.4 Contoured dorid
Dendrodoris denisoni

A distinctive species with a brown ground colour, spotted with bright blue circles. Large pink tubercles on the back are each surrounded with circular 'contour lines'. **Size:** 40–50 mm. **Biology:** Widespread in the Indo-Pacific and probably feeds on sponges.

95.5 Polka-dot chromodorid
Chromodoris annulata

Easily distinguished by its bright yellow spots and the purple rings around the gills and rhinophores. **Size:** 20–30 mm. **Biology:** Found in intertidal rock pools. Habits unknown. **SIMILAR SPECIES:** One of the more than 16 southern African members of this genus.

95.6 Gaudy chromodorid
Chromodoris tennentana

Background colour cream to golden brown, attractively spotted with purple and yellow and lined with a blue to purple margin. Gills and rhinophores brown to purple-blue. **Size:** 20–30 mm. **Biology:** Recorded from KwaZulu-Natal and Tanzania. Subtidal, usually among sponges, on which it probably feeds. Previously called *C. vicina*.

95.7 Large-spotted chromodorid
Chromodoris sp.

Colour pattern very variable over its range (Reunion–South Africa). Body yellow to deep orange, with white and blue marginal bands (sometimes also a yellow band). Large deep purple to black spots on the back are each outlined in white. Gills and rhinophores range from yellow with purple edges to deep purple. **Size:** Up to 60 mm. **Biology:** Thought to feed on sponges. **SIMILAR SPECIES:** *C. geminus* resembles it, but has yellow rhinophores.

95.8 Four-coloured chromodorid
Chromodoris africana

Back black with two pale blue stripes and rimmed with a white stripe. Gills orange to yellow and lateral margins yellow, sometimes with a narrow white rim. **Size:** 30 mm. **Biology:** Common in the tropics. **SIMILAR SPECIES:** *C. hamiltoni* (KwaZulu-Natal–East Africa) has a vivid blue dorsal background colour, with three thin black stripes. Common at 10–20 m; feeds on sponges.

95.9 Dotty dorid
Jorunna funebris

A large white dorid with circular patches of prickly black spots and a prominent plume of black-veined gills. **Size:** 60 mm. **Biology:** A conspicuous resident of rock pools on the KwaZulu-Natal coast, where it feeds on sponges (see 3.8). The egg mass is a tall undulating white collar.

95.10 Warty dorid
Doris granosa

Body is a low, warty, yellow hump with eight gills arranged in a circle around the anus. **Size:** Typically 20–30 mm. **Biology:** Feeds on the intertidal crumb-of-bread sponge, *Hymeniacidon perlevis* (1.8), which it resembles closely in colour. **SIMILAR SPECIES:** One of many rather featureless, humpy dorids distinguished by surface texture and colour pattern.

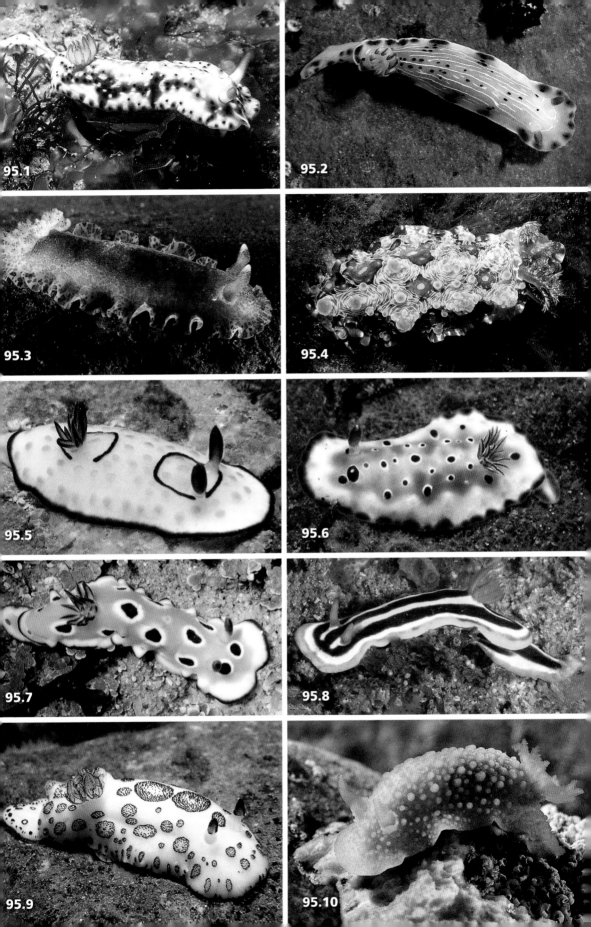

95.1

95.2

95.3

95.4

95.5

95.6

95.7

95.8

95.9

95.10

PLATE 96

96.1 Spanish dancer
Hexabranchus sanguineus

This well-known tropical nudibranch is recognised by its large size and flat orange-to-red body with a thin marginal edge. A daisy-like dorsal tuft of gills surrounds the anus near to the hind end of the body. **Size:** 70–100 mm or more. **Biology:** A non-selective predator found on coral reefs. Noted for its ability to swim using undulating movements of the brightly coloured body margin, which is unrolled when the animal is disturbed.

96.2 Yellow-blocked nudibranch
Halgerda wasinensis

Body firm to the touch, black and divided into regular blocks by a network of elevated bright yellow ridges. A tuft of sparsely branched black-edged gills emerges from the back. **Size:** 40–50 mm. **Biology:** Fairly common on tropical shores, where it feeds on sponges. One of several similar species in the genus. The photograph shows a mating pair.

96.3 Plant-sucking nudibranch
Elysia sp.

A small green nudibranch covered in tiny metallic blue spots. Sides of the body extended into two leaf-like flaps. **Size:** 10 mm. **Biology:** Pierces the cell walls of the alga *Codium* and sucks out its contents, including the chloroplasts. These continue to photosynthesise inside the mollusc's tissues – providing nutrition and colouring it green. **SIMILAR SPECIES:** There are at least 15 southern African *Elysia* spp., many unnamed, including this species, which was originally incorrectly called *E. viridis*.

96.4 Ornate nudibranch
Elysia ornata

Much larger than most other members of the genus. Recognised by the spotted sides to the foot and the orange and black stripes along the margins of the mantle. **Size:** 40 mm. **Biology:** Common throughout the Indo-Pacific; feeds on *Bryopsis* and *Codium*.

Alien

96.5 Sea-fan nudibranch
Tritonia nilsodhneri

Body elongate, plain yellow to orange, with small nodules on surface and eight pairs of dorsal gills. The rhinophores are branched at the tip and surrounded by distinct, cup-like sheaths. **Size:** 30 mm. **Biology:** Always associated with sea fans of the genus *Eunicella*, on which it is perfectly camouflaged. Possibly introduced from Europe. **SIMILAR SPECIES:** Another, apparently undescribed, bright purple species is found associated with the purple soft-coral *Alcyonium fauri* (12.8).

96.6 Striped sand slug
Armina sp.

Flattened sand-dwellers with a single gill on the right side, under the mantle. Body with marked, longitudinal black and yellow stripes. **Size:** 70 mm. **Biology:** Found buried in, or moving over, the surface of sand, where they are specialist sea pen predators.

96.7 Wing-foot
Cavolinia longirostris

Tiny, bubble-like, transparent shell with a curved mouth and three stubby horns. **Size:** 3 mm. **Biology:** Planktonic, swimming by undulation of two flat expansions of the foot that characterise the order Pteropoda. Shells of four species litter sandy beach driftlines. **SIMILAR SPECIES:** *Creseis acicula* has slender, transparent tusk-like shells.

Pulmonate sea slugs
Pulmonata

Pulmonate snails and slugs are largely terrestrial, but a few such as the false-limpets (Plate 74) and the following sea slugs are marine.

96.8 Air-breathing sea slug
Onchidella capensis

Body a small mottled brown hemisphere with a thick, warty skin, resembling a shell-less limpet. The head has two short tentacles, and a lung opens behind the anus. **Size:** 10 mm. **Biology:** Air-breathing; common in upper intertidal zone. Large numbers share communal shelters, emerging to feed on diatoms during moist, low-tide conditions.

96.9 Warty sea slug
Peronia peronii

Similar to *Onchidella*, but larger, and surface distinctly tuberculate, with 3–4 eyespots on most tubercles, and a mat of frilly gills over the posterior third of the body. **Size:** 30 mm. **Biology:** Solitary, except at mating time. Browses on microalgae. **SIMILAR SPECIES:** *Onchidium* sp. (Transkei northwards) is even larger (40 mm), lacks the mat of gills and has secondary tubercules on the tubercles, some with a single central eyespot.

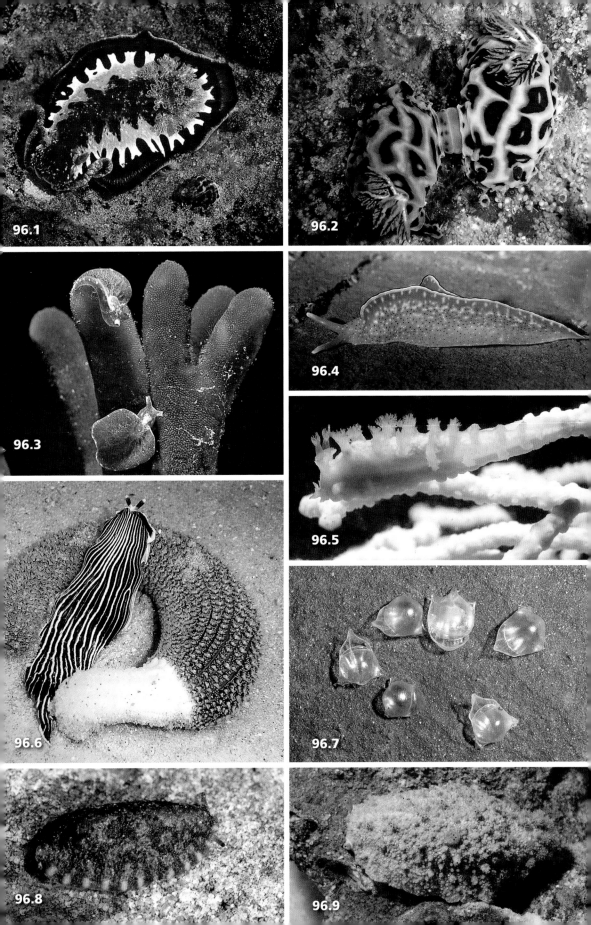

PLATE 97

Octopus, squid and cuttlefish   Cephalopoda

Cephalopods are the most advanced molluscs and among the most sophisticated and largest of invertebrates: the giant squids reach 20 m in total length. In many, the shell is reduced to an internal flotation device or thin internal 'pen', while others have lost it completely. The head and foot are merged, and the foot has become divided into 8 or 10 arms with suckers. The mouth has a strong parrot-like beak that tears into the prey and may inject a toxin. The mantle forms a sheath into which water is drawn and then forcefully expelled, jetting the animal backwards. The ancestral relatives of squid and cuttlefish once dominated the seas and many species still support major commercial fisheries.

97.1 Ram's horn shell   *Spirula spirula*

Live animals squid-like, with eight short arms and two long tentacles (97.1). Shells form an open, flat spire made up of a series of chambers (97.1a). **Size:** Shell 25 mm. **Biology:** Shells frequently wash ashore, but live animals rarely seen; they hang head-down and vary the volume of gas in the shell to regulate buoyancy.

97.2 Paper nautilus   *Argonauta argo*

Body with eight arms, two of which bear large lobes used to secrete and hold the delicate white shell. Shell patterned with wave-like ridges and with two keels around the margins, each studded with low conical knobs. **Size:** 100 mm. **Biology:** Only the female produces a shell, which serves primarily as a brood chamber for her eggs and is not equivalent to those of other molluscs. The ancestors of the paper nautilus lacked a shell. Females float near the surface of the sea and are frequently cast ashore during storms. Males are minute, shell-less, and planktonic. **SIMILAR SPECIES:** Two less common species occur in our region. *A. nodosa* has lumpy radial ridges on its shell. *A. boettgeri* is smaller, with coarser radial ridges and large rounded nodules on the keels, which are usually smoky black.

97.3 Brush-tipped octopus   *Aphrodoctopus schultzei*

Shell-less, with eight arms, each with only a single row of suckers. There are also long brush-like structures at the tips of the arms, but they are not obvious. **Size:** 200 mm. **Biology:** Little is known about this species. It is a local endemic, occurring in shallow water and feeding on small crustaceans. Previously known as *Eledone thysanophora*.

97.4 Common octopus   *Octopus vulgaris*

Octopus species have eight arms, each with two rows of suckers, and no shell. Species are distinguished by the tip of the male's right third or hectocotylus arm, which is sucker-less and transmits sperm to the female. In *O. vulgaris* this is tiny (less than 2% of arm length) and spoon-shaped. Outer half of gills with 9–11 filaments. **Size:** 600 mm. **Biology:** The most common shallow-water octopus, extending down to 200 m. Exploited as bait and for export. Preys on crabs, rock lobsters and shellfish. Hides in cavities, the entrance to the hole often littered with discarded shells. Females lay clusters of eggs, which they tend by blowing water over them. Eggs hatch into miniature octopuses, without any larval stage. They grow rapidly, become sexually mature in a few months and reach a maximum mass of about 6 kg in a year.

SIMILAR SPECIES:

97.5 *Octopus marginatus*, the veined octopus (east coast), has a network of branching dark lines on the body and contrasting white to blue suckers.

97.6 *Octopus macropus*, the white-spotted octopus (Sodwana–East Africa), is a member of a confused species complex of globally distributed, exclusively nocturnal red octopuses, with white dots and long front arms.

97.7 Southern giant octopus   *Enteroctopus megalocyathus*

One of the largest octopuses in the world. Distinguished by its hectocotylus arm ending in a long groove that exceeds 10% of the arm length, and the outer half of its gills having 13 filaments. **Size:** Arms up to 3 m long. **Biology:** A regular by-catch in trawls between Lüderitz and Port Elizabeth. Previously named *Octopus magnificus*.

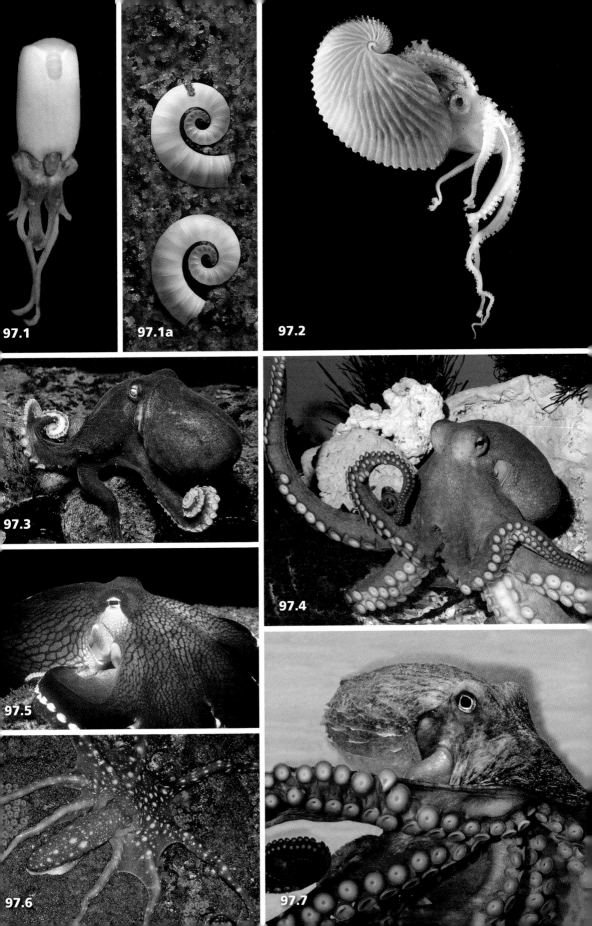

97.1

97.1a

97.2

97.3

97.4

97.5

97.6

97.7

PLATE 98

98.1 Common cuttlefish   *Sepia vermiculata*

Body elongate, with a fin running down each side. Pale below, upper surface with constantly changing, rippling bars of colour. Head with eight short arms and two very long tentacles that can be retracted and concealed in 'pockets' below the eyes. The tentacles end in a club, with about eight oblique rows of suckers, including one row of enlarged suckers. All the suckers on the short arms are similar in size. Shell (98.1a) reduced to an internal, chalky, flat, smoothly oval cuttlebone with a sharp posterior spine. **Size:** Body 150 mm. **Biology:** The largest southern African cuttlefish, particularly common in sheltered lagoons and estuaries. Captures fish by rapidly shooting out its tentacles. Lays small bunches of pea-sized black eggs. The cuttlebone is used to regulate buoyancy by varying the proportions of its gas and liquid contents. **SIMILAR SPECIES:** *S. papillata* has three extremely large suckers on the club of the tentacles, equal in width to the club itself. Its shells are often washed ashore, and resemble those of **S. vermiculata,** except that the spine is reduced to a rounded knob. *S. simoniana* has a similar shell but very long tentacular clubs with numerous minute, equal-sized suckers.

98.2 Pore-bellied cuttlefish   *Sepia typica*

Easily recognised by its small size at maturity and two rows of small pores that run down the sides of the 'belly'. **Size:** 50 mm. **Biology:** Occurs in weedbeds in sheltered bays and is frequently dredged on soft sediments. **SIMILAR SPECIES:** *S. australis,* the southern cuttlefish (Namibia–Port Alfred), is abundant in deeper waters (100–200 m). It has a smooth body, dark purple pigmentation all over the body, and a narrow red-brown band down the base of the fins. The central suckers on the short arms are much larger than those in the rows on either side. The shell tapers very obviously to a sharp spine at the rear end.

98.3 Tuberculate cuttlefish   *Sepia tuberculata*

Upper surface of body roughened by soft papillae and the lower surface by two oval glandular patches. Some of the suckers on the club of the tentacles are enlarged, but only to about half the width of the club. The cuttlebone is oval and has no posterior spine. **Size:** 80 mm. **Biology:** Lives mainly in shallow water, often in intertidal pools or gullies; sticks to rocks with its glandular patches.

98.4 Chokka squid   *Loligo reynaudi*

Squid are slender and delicate, and have reduced their shells to a transparent 'pen' that lies just under the skin of the dorsal surface. Eight short arms and two very long retractable tentacles ring the mouth: all have suckers. The chokka is distinguished by its relatively long diamond-shaped fins, which cover more than half the length of the mantle, and by the fact that the largest of the suckers on the tentacle are smoothly ringed, not finely toothed. Unlike other members of its family, its eyes are covered with a membrane that is continuous with the skin covering the head. **Size:** 200–500 mm. **Biology:** The most abundant squid in southern Africa. Concentrates in bays between Cape Point and Port Alfred in summer to breed. Larvae drift west in the Agulhas Current and adults migrate back eastwards to the spawning grounds. Sustains an important fishery between Plettenberg Bay and Port Alfred. It is caught by 'jigging' with lures, but a significant by-catch is also made by trawlers. Squid are active predators and feed mainly on small fish. Eggs are laid in sausage-like strings on the sea floor. Chokka are immensely important as a food source for sharks, fish, seabirds and marine mammals.
SIMILAR SPECIES: *Uroteuthis duvaucelii,* the Indian Ocean squid (Port Alfred–western Indo-Pacific), has shorter fins, less than half the mantle length, and two light-emitting organs on the ink sac in the mantle cavity. Prawn-trawlers catch it off Durban. *Thysanoteuthis rhombus,* the diamond squid, is one of the larger squid species in our waters, with a body length of 1 m and a mass of 20 kg. Its fins cover the full length of the mantle and have a diamond-shaped outline.

98.1

98.1a

98.2

98.3

98.4

Echinoderms

Phylum Echinodermata includes the starfish, sea urchins, brittlestars, sea cucumbers and feather-stars. As their name implies, they have spicules or spines in their skins (*ekhinos*, 'a hedgehog', and *derma*, 'skin'), and they also share a radial symmetry. There are five classes:

- **Asteroidea:** Starfish, with a flattened central disc that merges imperceptibly into five or more projecting arms (Plates 99–101).
- **Crinoidea:** Feather-stars, which have tiny round bodies with short hook-like limbs, and a handsome crown of feather-like, filter-feeding appendages (Plate 102).
- **Ophiuroidea:** Brittlestars, with slender, brittle arms that arise from a central body and propel the animal with a snake-like undulation (Plates 103–104).
- **Echinoidea:** Sea urchins, which are encased in a hard calcium carbonate test, and have long protective spines (Plates 105–106).
- **Holothuroidea:** Sea cucumbers, which have become sausage-shaped and lie on their sides, but retain a reminder of their ancestral radial symmetry in having five rows of tubefeet with which they attach themselves to rocks (Plates 107–108).

Starfish or seastars Asteroidea

PLATE 99

Familiar echinoderms, recognised by their flattened, star-shaped bodies and the central disc merging imperceptibly into five (sometimes more) relatively stout, tapering arms. The mouth is situated centrally on the undersurface and the anus on the upper side. A groove running along the underside of each arm protects rows of tiny hydraulically operated tubefeet that are responsible for the slow, creeping movement typical of the group. Most starfish are mobile scavengers or predators, though a few are herbivorous. Some 90 species occur around southern Africa.

99.1 Pink sandstar *Astropecten irregularis pontoporeus*

Body off-white to apricot, with fairly long triangular arms becoming mauve at the tips. Each arm is edged by a double tier of large tile-like plates, those in the upper row each bearing a single spine and those on the lower tier 3–4 longer spines. The tubefeet are pointed and lack suckers. **Size:** 90 mm. **Biology:** Lives in sand, into which it shuffles in search of small molluscs or crustaceans.

99.2 Grey sandstar *Astropecten granulatus*

Similar to the previous species, but an attractive grey colour, and has no spines on the upper row of tile-like side-plates, although strong white spines project from the lower series of plates. **Size:** 90 mm. **Biology:** Burrows in sheltered sandbanks and feeds on bivalves.

99.3 Speckled sandstar *Luidia maculata*

An unmistakable large, 7–9-armed star with very long evenly tapering arms, covered in short fine spines dorsally; arms fringed with strong, pointed marginal spines. Colour mottled brown and white. **Size:** Up to 300 mm diameter. **Biology:** Burrows in sand in shallow water in tropical seas. Feeds on other burrowing stars.

99.4 Spine-tipped star *Protoreaster lincki*

Upper surface variable in colour: can be brown, green, yellow or grey, but typically bears large red conical projections that are linked by a network of raised red ridges. Characterised by 2–4 obvious spines or knobs that project from the sides of each arm near the tip. **Size:** 220 mm. **Biology:** Occurs from the low shore down to 10 m, most commonly on seagrass beds but also among coral.

99.5 Beaded starfish *Pentaceraster mammillatus*

Colours very variable, including yellow, green, brown, red, blue and grey (99.5 & 99.5a–c). Centre of body elevated, tapering down to triangular arms. Rows of conical, bead-like knobs, often of contrasting colour, run down each arm and around the body margin. **Size:** 200 mm across. **Biology:** Occurs in seagrass beds in sheltered sandy lagoons.

99.6 Blue star *Linckia laevigata*

Unmistakable, with very elongate, cylindrical, non-tapering arms and usually a distinctive bright blue colour (see also 1.10), although pink and brown individuals are rarely seen. **Size:** Up to 400 mm diameter. **Biology:** Among coral debris and in seagrass beds throughout the tropical Indo-Pacific.

99.7 Fat-armed star *Thromidia catalai*

Arms fat and round in section, relatively short and scarcely tapering; pink, with darker tips. **Size:** 100 mm. **Biology:** Found on rocky tropical reefs. Has expanded its geographic range with global warming.

99.1

99.2

99.3

99.4

99.5

99.5a

99.5b

99.5c

99.6

99.7

PLATE 100

100.1 Crown of thorns starfish
Acanthaster planci

Instantly recognisable by its large size, multiple arms and formidable spiny surface. **Size:** 400 mm. **Biology:** A specialist predator of corals. Should be handled with care as the spines are coated with an irritant poison. Very dense populations can develop, destroying coral over huge areas. Originally it was believed that these outbreaks were caused by pollution, or overexploitation of predators, but examination of marine sediments for spine fragments has shown that periodic population explosions have occurred for thousands of years.

100.2 Granulated star
Choriaster granulatus

A large and inflated star with short thick arms, usually becoming paler or white towards the tips. Dorsal surface mottled with pink or red. Ventral surface smooth, with a granular appearance (hence the name). **Size:** Up to 250 mm diameter. **Biology:** Feeds on corals and other invertebrates on shallow tropical reefs.

100.3 Brooding cushion-star
Pteraster capensis

Large, fat, orange-brown starfish with short blunt arms. Upper surface covered by a unique soft outer skin supported by short, turret-like spines. The cavity created under the skin is ventilated through a central hole on the back and acts as a brood chamber. **Size:** About 100 mm. **Biology:** Found subtidally on both rock and sand. The eggs are brooded in the space under the dorsal skin, and juveniles emerge as tiny starfish. Secretes copious mucus to deter predators. Can be observed 'breathing' in and out to inflate the brood chamber.

100.4 Granular cushion-star
Patiriella dyscrita

Very similar in shape and colour to the next species, but larger and distinguished by having an evenly granular surface texture, rather than clusters of spines. **Size:** 40 mm. **Biology:** *P. dyscrita* and *Parvulastra exigua* have long been confused, but *Patiriella dyscrita* occurs only subtidally and also differs in that its eggs develop into planktonic larvae.

100.5 Dwarf cushion-star
Parvulastra exigua

Tiny, flattened, pentagonal starfish with poorly developed arms. Dorsal surface made up of tile-like plates, each with a cluster of tiny knob-like spines. Uniformly khaki-green on the west coast; variegated patterns of orange, brown, green and white on the Indian Ocean coast. **Size:** 20 mm. **Biology:** Abundant in the intertidal zone, but very well camouflaged. Feeds by extruding the stomach through the mouth and plastering it onto the rock, thus digesting microscopic algae. Eggs are laid under rocks and hatch directly into tiny starfish, without a planktonic larval stage. Previously named *Patiriella exigua*.

100.6 Namibian cushion-star
Asterina stellifera

Larger than either of the two preceding species, and has more distinct, longer arms and mottled charcoal and white coloration. **Size:** 60 mm. **Biology:** Common in the intertidal zone. Feeds on microalgae. Previously named *Patiria stellifera*.

100.7 Pincushion starfish
Culcita schmideliana

Large, plump, blotchy, orange cushion-star with a pentagonal body and virtually no arms. Dorsal surface usually with numerous scattered black tubercles. **Size:** Up to 140 mm across. **Biology:** A tropical form that feeds on both corals and detrital material, and is fairly common on reef flats and seagrass beds.

100.8 Regular star
Halityle regularis

Large fat star with an almost pentagonal shape and short arms. A double row of enlarged plates runs around the perimeter, separating upper from lower surface. Colour brown to bright red, becoming paler at the tips of the arms. Upper surface dissected by a series of faint lines, dividing it into a grid of regular triangular shapes (hence the name). **Size:** Up to 300 mm. **Biology:** Occurs on shallow tropical reefs.

100.1

100.2

100.3

100.4

100.5

100.6

100.7

100.8

PLATE 101

101.1 Spiny starfish — *Marthasterias glacialis*

Body orange or blue-grey, and covered in conspicuous spines, each surrounded by a halo of minute pincer-like organs called pedicellaria that are used to keep the body surface clean. Small red eyespot at the tip of each arm. **Size:** 200–250 mm across. **Biology:** A voracious predator, particularly of mussels, but also taking winkles, limpets, barnacles and even redbait. Hunches over the victim and extrudes its stomach through the mouth to digest the prey externally. Sometimes forms large feeding aggregations. A possible introduction from Europe.

101.2 Blocked starfish — *Fromia elegans*

Colour orange, the surface granules arranged into blocks, defined by black lines (reminiscent of giraffe skin). Arms fairly long, slightly swollen close to base, then tapering evenly. **Size:** About 100 mm across. **Biology:** Found on shallow tropical reefs. Thought to feed on algae and detritus.

101.3 Red starfish — *Callopatiria granifera*

Arms markedly tapering from a broad base and with a distinct break between upper surface and flattened lower surface, giving the arms a semicircular cross section. Colour deep orange to red, with upper surface texture resembling small overlapping tiles. **Size:** Up to 80 mm across. **Biology:** A detritus feeder. Often found together with *Henricia ornata* (101.4), but distinguished by its broader tapering arms. Previously named *Patiria granifera*.

101.4 Reticulated starfish — *Henricia ornata*

Arms long, very gradually tapering and cylindrical in cross section. Orange to maroon, with an irregularly honeycombed surface texture. **Size:** Up to 90 mm across. **Biology:** Thought to feed on sponges by everting the stomach and digesting the sponge tissue in situ, although may also consume detritus. A tiny skeleton shrimp (*Caprella scaura*) is frequently found clinging to the body surface and perfectly matches its host in colour.

101.5 Button star — *Nardoa variolata*

Medium-sized star with evenly tapering slender arms. Ground colour dark brown, densely covered with prominent round button-like yellow plates of variable size. Tips of the arms lighter yellow. **Size:** Up to 130 mm. **Biology:** On shallow tropical reefs.

101.6 Granular starfish — *Austrofromia schultzei*

Surface coated in granules and regularly raised into small humps. Ground colour orange; humps and tips of arms yellow. Arms broaden slightly just beyond base, before tapering evenly to blunt tip. **Size:** About 100 mm across. **Biology:** A resident of shallow reefs in the southern Cape.

101.1

101.2

101.3

101.4

101.5

101.6

PLATE 102

Feather-stars Crinoidea

Graceful echinoderms with small, soft bodies, surrounded by 10 or more elongate, upraised arms, each consisting of a central axis with numerous side branches or pinnules. Food particles trapped by the arms are passed along ciliated grooves to the mouth, which is situated on the upper surface. A simple, U-shaped gut fills most of the body cavity and ends in an anal cone close to the mouth. The gonads are in the pinnules of the arms closest to the body, and these become greatly expanded during the breeding season (102.1a), eventually rupturing to release the eggs or sperm into the water. Crinoids are sedentary, gripping the substratum with a ring of claw-like segmented limbs (the cirri) beneath the body, but they can crawl or even swim using their arms. Attached stalked crinoids, called sea lilies, are abundant in the fossil record, but few survive today, and only in the deep sea. There are 17 species of southern African crinoids.

102.1 Common feather-star *Comanthus wahlbergi*

Colour very variable, from white to pink, blue or orange, often variegated. Arms rather ragged, with 10–22 pinnules, and usually curled above the body (102.1). Basal pinnules swollen with gonads in reproductively mature individuals (102.1a). The anus is central and the mouth off-centre. Cirri number 12–25. **Size:** Arm length up to 80 mm. **Biology:** Abundant under rocks or in crevices at low tide and forms dense clusters coating shallow reefs. Tiny pentacrinoid larvae can sometimes be seen clinging to the adults. **SIMILAR SPECIES:** *Annametra occidentalis* (Saldanha–Knysna) has 35–40 cirri and a central mouth with an off-centre anus.

102.2 Elegant feather-star *Tropiometra carinata*

A striking species with 10 long arms, evenly lined with tapering rows of straight pinnules, reminiscent of a bird's feather. Cape Peninsula specimens have arms that are usually uniformly golden yellow or purple-brown near the base, becoming yellow at the tips (102.2), although the colour varies considerably. Tropical-water individuals are deep red-brown to black, sometimes with overlays of other colours (102.2a). Cirri number 20–30 and have 20–32 segments that are broader than they are long. **Size:** Arm length up to 150 mm. **Biology:** Usually found singly on shallow reefs, but becomes more abundant on deeper reefs, crowding crevices and overhangs. If displaced, may swim with a slow beat of the arms, or fold the arms overhead, dropping elegantly to the bottom. Frequently hosts commensal shrimps (45.4) and myzostomid worms (24.3). It is possible that the Cape Peninsula individuals are a separate species.

102.3 Indicated feather-star *Stephanometra indica*

Arms 18–30 in number, each with large numbers of closely spaced pinnules of uniform length. Basal pinnules sharply pointed and folded inwards over the central disc; remaining pinnules held broadly apart. Variously banded brown and white. **Size:** Arm length up to 150 mm. **Biology:** Common on exposed reefs throughout the tropical Indo-Pacific. Nocturnal, hiding in caves and crevices during the day.

102.1

102.1a

102.2

102.2a

102.3

PLATE 103

Brittlestars

Ophiuroidea

Brittlestars have a flat, circular body (the disc), with five or more long, thin, jointed, flexible arms that break easily, hence 'brittlestars'. The segments of the arms are each covered by 1–3 tiny plates, and their shape and number help distinguish species. The sides of the arms often have spines. Brittlestars move by snake-like undulation of their legs. The mouth lies on the lower surface of the body and is surrounded by five-toothed jaws. The texture of the disc allows division of brittlestars into three groups: those with (1) granules, (2) short spines, or (3) a leathery or scaly texture. Just above the origin of each arm there are usually two enlarged scales on the disc, called radial shields. Most brittlestars have minute planktonic larvae, but a few brood the young in their bodies and give birth to miniature replicas of themselves. There are 120 species in southern Africa, but only about 20 are common.

103.1 Basket star
Astrocladus euryale

Immediately recognisable because the 10 arms branch into ever-finer, delicately striped tendrils. Disc decorated with coarse knobs that stand out because their colour contrasts with the disc and they are often ringed with black. **Size:** 300–500 mm. **Biology:** Holds its arms outstretched like a basket to catch passing animals. Often attaches itself to sea fans.

103.2 Banded brittlestar
Ophiarachnella capensis

Disc granular, arms strikingly patterned with alternating dark grey and pink (or red) bands. Very short spines flank the arms. On the lower surface of the disc, on either side of the base of each arm, there is a single long genital slit. **Size:** 45 mm. **Biology:** Lives under boulders near the low-tide mark. Feeds on detritus.

103.3 Serpent-skinned brittlestar
Ophioderma wahlbergii

Disc granular; arm spines short and closely applied to the arms. Upper surface uniformly black-brown; arms occasionally banded. **Size:** 90 mm. **Biology:** Lives gregariously on subtidal gravel or sand. Very common in certain areas, thousands massing together. On either side of the base of each arm there are two genital slits that lead into chambers in which juveniles are brooded until they emerge as fully formed miniature brittlestars.

103.4 Commensal brittlestar
Ophiothela danae

Commonly six-armed. Centre of disc granular. Arms about six times disc diameter. Colour variable; disc often red-blotched and arms have alternating bands of purple-red and white. Top of arms granular; side spines just shorter than arm width. **Size:** 10 mm. **Biology:** Lives exclusively attached to gorgonians, soft corals and sea-pens.

103.5 Snake-armed brittlestar
Ophiocoma valenciae

Disc granular, with the granules taller than broad near the edge of the disc. Disc mottled, arms usually indistinctly banded. Arm spines project very obviously: about as long as the arm width. **Size:** 100 mm. **Biology:** Very common. Hides in crevices and extends its tentacles to pick up organic particles and dead animal matter or prey on tiny animals. **SIMILAR SPECIES:** *O. erinaceus* (Durban northwards) is black, with tiny black or orange arm tentacles. Arms about 4–5 times the disc diameter. Disc granules shorter than broad. *O. scolopendrina* (Durban northwards) has mottled or banded arms that are more than six times the disc diameter. Disc granules again shorter than broad.

103.6 Hairy brittlestar
Ophiothrix fragilis

Upper surface of disc covered with spines; even the radial shields have spines. Arm length less than six times disc diameter. Arms fringed with long spines that project at right angles and taper towards their tips. **Size:** 50 mm. **Biology:** Very common on rocky shores beneath boulders, and extends down to depths of about 100 m. Often lives in dense aggregations. Holds its arms up in the water to catch detrital particles. **SIMILAR SPECIES:** *O. foveolata* (Maputaland northwards) lacks spines on its radial shields, but is otherwise very similar. *Macrophiothrix hirsuta cheneyi* (Durban northwards) has longer arms (7–10 times the disc diameter) and its arm spines have characteristically expanded and flattened tips. A thin pale line runs down the upper surface of each of its arms, often flanked with blue.

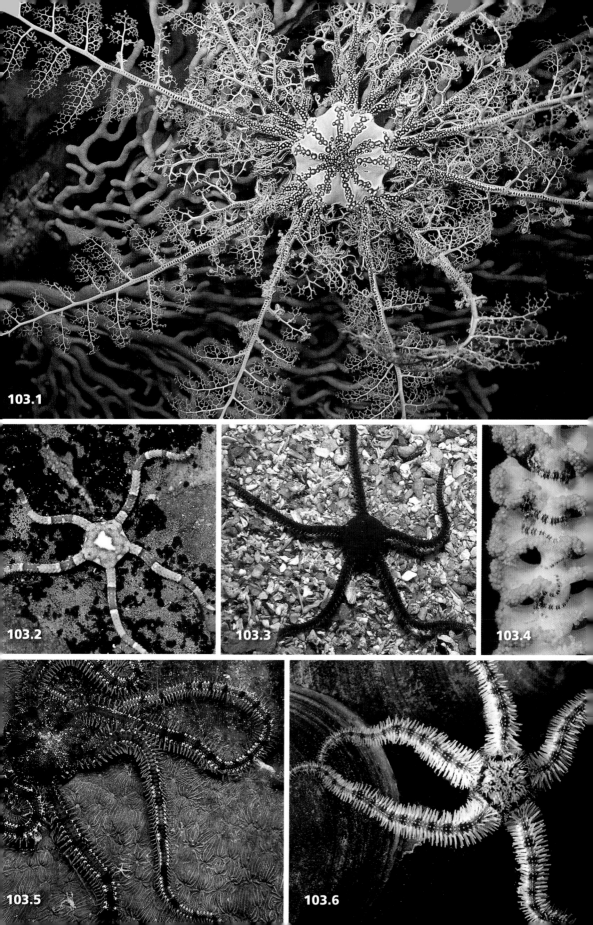

103.1

103.2

103.3

103.4

103.5

103.6

PLATE 104

104.1 Striped brittlestar — *Ophionereis dubia*

Disc appears smooth to the naked eye: scales microscopic. Often a net-like pattern, including irregular 'Y' markings, near the base of each arm. Arms long and narrow, each joint with a central plate and two flanking accessory plates (visible only when magnified). Arms pale, usually white, with a narrow stripe about every fifth joint. **Size:** 70 mm. **Biology:** Seldom abundant; hides in crevices and waves its arms over the rock-face.
SIMILAR SPECIES:
104.2 *Ophionereis porrecta* (Cape Agulhas–East Africa) also has accessory plates on its long thin arms, but its disc is clearly scaly and the bands on its arms broader.

104.3 Equitailed brittlestar — *Amphiura capensis*

Upper surface of disc lacks spines, but is covered with small scales. Radial shields touch one another only at their outermost tips: nearer to the centre of the disc they diverge from one another, resembling a fat 'V' (104.3). Individual joints of the arms covered by a single scale. Disc usually grey to black; arms yellow to orange, sometimes with broken bands. Colour is, however, unreliable for identification, individuals being brown, yellow, red or purple (see 104.3a–c for examples of variability). **Size:** 25 mm. **Biology:** Common under stones in gravel or coarse sand; often aggregates in dense colonies.
SIMILAR SPECIES:
104.4 *Amphioplus integer* (Port Nolloth–East Africa) shares most features with *Amphiura capensis*, but its radial shields contact one another for their full length.

104.5 Scaly-armed brittlestar — *Amphipholis squamata*

Very small, uniformly white or pale grey, distinguished by the arrangement of scales on the upper surface of the arms. In most brittlestars the scales of adjacent segments are in contact with one another for most of their width. In this species, the scales are small, triangular with rounded corners, and either separated or only just touching. Disc scaly. Radial shields arranged in pairs and abut one another for their full lengths. **Size:** 10 mm. **Biology:** Extremely common from the intertidal zone down to 175 m. Most often found in areas with gravel, sand or mud. Feeds on minute detrital particles. If attacked, the arms break off and emit flashing, bioluminescent light to distract the predator.

104.6 Snake-star — *Ophiactis carnea*

Upper surface of disc scaly, with scattered short spines towards the edge. Radial shields triangular and scarcely touch one another. Often red or white, sometimes with irregular bands on the arms. **Size:** 25 mm. **Biology:** Usually found in gravel or shell deposits. SIMILAR SPECIES: *O. savignyi* is closely related, but usually has six arms instead of five, is bright green, and has conspicuous dark patches on its radial shields and a white patch at the outer end of each radial shield. Probably introduced to Durban Harbour, but occurs naturally from Mozambique northwards.

104.7 Hitchhiker brittlestar — *Ophiocnemis marmorata*

Radial shields triangular, very large and bare. Disc scales limited to areas between the shields. Upper arm plates broad, tent-shaped; lower arm plates much broader than long. Colour usually marbled dark and light. **Size:** 40 mm. **Biology:** A filter-feeder that is associated with sandy to gravelly sediments, but large numbers are found associated with rhizostome jellyfish and are often washed ashore attached to the jellyfish.

104.8 Pansy-shell brittlestar — *Ophiodaphne scripta*

Disc coarsely scaled; radial shields large, almost half the disc diameter. Arms four times disc diameter. Arm spines short. **Size:** 25 mm. **Biology:** Found exclusively beneath the pansy shells *Echinodiscus auritus* and *E. bisperforatus*. Male minute and lives permanently attached to the female in a mouth-to-mouth position, arms alternating – as evident in this photograph. Previously named *Amphilycus scripta*.

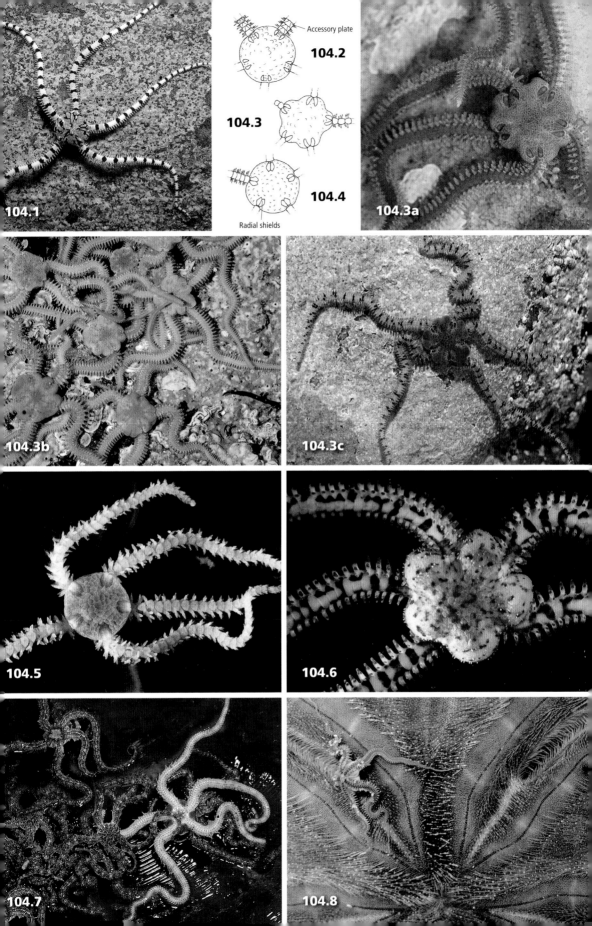

104.2 Accessory plate

104.3

104.4 Radial shields

104.1

104.3a

104.3b

104.3c

104.5

104.6

104.7

104.8

PLATE 105

Sea urchins   Echinoidea

Sea urchins are encased in a calcium carbonate shell, or test, covered with spines, and are usually spherical. The mouth lies centrally on the underside, and the anus is usually on the upper surface. Five double rows of tubefeet run from the apex down the sides of the shell. Minute defensive, stalked pincers (pedicellaria) are dispersed over the body. These are armed with poison glands – mostly harmless to humans, but one species, Toxopneustes pileolus, is potentially lethal. Most rocky-shore urchins are grazers, but flattened, sand-dwelling forms feed on detritus. Some 58 species occur in southern Africa.

105.1 Needle urchin   *Diadema setosum*

Black urchins with extremely long needle-sharp spines that are waved menacingly at intruders. Iridescent, dotted blue lines run down the body between the spines; a red ring surrounds the anus. The spines of juveniles are banded black and white. **Size:** Test diameter up to 70 mm. **Biology:** Grazes algae among rocks or coral. Dangerous to handle: the spines are hollow, penetrate the flesh easily and contain an irritant toxin. **SIMILAR SPECIES:** *D. savignyi* (Transkei northwards) is almost identical, but lacks the red ring around the anus. It is the more common of the two, but they are difficult to distinguish.

105.2 Oval urchin   *Echinometra mathaei*

Test oval when viewed from above, purple to black. Spines fairly long and stout, tapering evenly to a sharp tip; purple, brown or green, sometimes with white tips. **Size:** Diameter 70 mm. **Biology:** The most common urchin in east coast rock pools. A mobile grazer that occupies hollows in exposed reefs, catching drifting algae or emerging to graze at night.

105.3 Pot-hole urchin   *Stomopneustes variolaris*

Test circular in outline; spines about half test diameter, strong, cylindrical and obviously tapering. Colour shiny black or dark purple, with a metallic sheen. **Size:** Width 100 mm. **Biology:** Shelters on wave-swept shores in crevices, or in hollows that it excavates over many generations. Feeds on drift algae. Strong wave action erodes its spines, reducing feeding efficiency, with a consequent decrease in body size.

105.4 Bicoloured urchin   *Salmacis bicolor*

Test circular in outline, with a dense covering of short thin spines, which are markedly flattened around the mouth. Spines red or purple at their bases, becoming attractively banded with yellow or white towards the tips. **Size:** Test diameter up to 70 mm. **Biology:** Found among algae in sheltered lagoons and reefs, but seldom common.

105.5 Short-spined urchin   *Tripneustes gratilla*

A large round urchin evenly coated with short white spines, all of roughly the same length. The tubefeet are long and numerous, often projecting well beyond the spines. **Size:** Test diameter up to 145 mm. **Biology:** Found in weedbeds, often concealed by pieces of algae held over the body by the tubefeet.

105.6 Cape urchin   *Parechinus angulosus*

Test round, densely covered in shortish pointed spines that vary in length but never exceed about one-fifth of the test diameter. Colour variable, most often purple, but also green, red or pale. **Size:** 60 mm. **Biology:** Abundant on rocky shores in the Western and Eastern Cape and in kelp beds. Extends down to 30 m. It is an important grazer that controls the survival of newly settled kelp plants. Uses dead shells as a 'sunshade'.

105.7 Flower urchin   *Toxopneustes pileolus*

Distinctive, easily recognised by its beautiful flower-like pedicellaria, or pincers. Spines very short; tubefeet elongate, reaching well beyond spines. **Size:** Up to 150 mm. **Biology:** Its enormous pedicellaria are equipped with potentially lethal poison glands; they should not be touched with bare hands. *Toxopneustes* is a tropical reef species and often carries seaweeds or shells to shade it from the sun.

105.1

105.2

105.3

105.4

105.5

105.6

105.7

PLATE 106

106.1 Rough pencil urchin   *Prionocidaris pistillaris*

Spines broad and cylindrical, covered with rows of pointed knobs; bases decorated with characteristic longitudinal pink stripes. Spines initially purple, but encrusting algae often obscure the colour except at the base. Juveniles have fewer spines and are more vividly coloured (106.1a). **Size:** Test up to 60 mm across. **Biology:** A tropical grazer. **SIMILAR SPECIES:** *Heterocentrotus mammillatus*, the slate pencil urchin, has massive, smooth, attractively banded spines that are often sold as ornaments.

106.2 Tuft urchin   *Echinostrephus molaris*

A small, easily overlooked urchin with a circular, but peculiarly top-heavy test. Lateral spines short, while those on the top are elongate and needle-sharp, making an erect tuft. **Size:** 28 mm. **Biology:** Excavates a cylindrical burrow from which the long dorsal spines are extended to intercept drift food. Excess food may be stored at the bottom of the burrow.

Alien

106.3 Black urchin   *Tetrapygus niger*

Test round, purplish, somewhat flattened; spines strong, pointed, dark brown, almost black. **Size:** 60 mm. **Biology:** A recent alien arrival in South Africa, so far confined to oyster farms in Namaqualand. Probably introduced accidentally with imported oyster spat. Native to Chile, it is an aggressive consumer of algae and generates bare 'urchin barrens'. Steps should be taken to eliminate it while it is localised. May be confused with *Stomopneustes variolaris* (105.3), but has narrower spines and lacks the metallic black sheen of that species; the two have differing ranges.

106.4 Banded urchin   *Echinothrix calamaris*

Test circular, armed with two distinct types of black-and-white-banded spines: longer, thicker primary spines as long as the test diameter, and shorter, needle-like secondary spines, with downward-pointing barbs. **Size:** Test diameter up to 130 mm. **Biology:** A nocturnal grazer with an irritant toxin in the hollow spines. The eye-like anal cone is often inflated like a balloon and dotted with white spots.

106.5 Heart urchin   *Echinocardium cordatum*

Irregularly oval, fragile test with a well-developed frontal depression leading down to the mouth, which is positioned near the front and has a scoop-like posterior lip. Spines white and arranged around a series of depressed 'petals' containing the tubefeet. **Size:** 40 mm long. **Biology:** A detritus-feeder that burrows in fine sand, using specialised paddle-shaped spines on the underside.
SIMILAR SPECIES:
106.6 *Spatagobrissus mirabilis* (Lüderitz–Agulhas) is a larger, smooth-shelled heart urchin (typically 90 mm long), without a frontal depression. Shells are often found by divers in areas of coarse sand.

106.7 Lamp urchin   *Echinolampas crassa*

A large urchin with a strong, heavy, flat-bottomed shell densely coated with uniformly short yellowish spines. Mouth central. **Size:** Up to 120 mm across. **Biology:** Ploughs along just below the surface of coarse sands, feeding on organic particles, which it ingests along with large amounts of sand. Regularly collected by divers, especially in False Bay, where dense populations can be found.

106.8 Pansy shell   *Echinodiscus bisperforatus*

A flat, biscuit-like urchin with two closed slits in the back half of the test. The short fur-like spines drop off after the animal dies. Tubefeet extend through a petal-like pattern of holes on the upper surface. **Size:** 90 mm. **Biology:** Burrows just below the sand surface in sheltered waters, feeding on fine, organic particles sorted from the sediment. **SIMILAR SPECIES:** *E. auritus* (Maputo northwards) has slots in the test that extend to the edge of the shell, like deep notches.

PLATE 107

Sea cucumbers   Holothuroidea

Sea cucumbers have lost the star-shaped symmetry typical of other echinoderms, evolved elongate, sausage-shaped bodies with soft, leathery skins, and taken to lying on their sides. The mouth lies at one end, surrounded by 10–20 retractable feeding tentacles, while the anus lies at the other. Tentacular structure distinguishes three groups, respectively with 12 feathery tentacles (107.1), 18–20 tufted tentacles (107.4a) or 10 tree-like tentacles (108.3). Up to five bands of tubefeet run the length of the body. The sticky tentacles gather detritus from the seabed, or catch plankton floating overhead. When disturbed, some species eject long sticky threads from the anus. Others disgorge part or all of the gut, subsequently regenerating it.

107.1 Snake sea cucumber   *Synapta maculata*
The 12 feather-like tentacles each consist of a central axis with regular side branches (107.1). Body extremely elongate and rope-like, with a mottled brown coloration (107.1a). Tubefeet absent. **Size:** May exceed 1 m. **Biology:** Lies among seagrass or coral debris on tropical shores, picking detritus from the sand using the sticky tentacles, which are then licked clean. Skin packed with anchor-like spicules that adhere to everything they touch – almost impossible to detach from a diver's wet suit.

107.2 Pineapple sea cucumber   *Thelenota ananas*
Unmistakable, with a firm, loaf-shaped orange body covered in large, soft, branching papillae. There are 12–16 leaf-shaped tentacles surrounding the mouth. **Size:** Up to 700 mm. **Biology:** Found on shallow reefs and on sand, and much sought after in the bêche-de-mer trade in the Far East.

107.3 Banana sea cucumber   *Holothuria parva*
Body pale, mottled brown and white, distinctly bent and tapering to a fairly narrow point at both ends. Dorsal tubefeet scattered. **Size:** Up to 310 mm. **Biology:** Intertidal, usually in fine mud or sand. Often associated with mangrove roots.

107.4 Tufted sea cucumber   *Holothuria cinerascens*
Moderately large, but very cryptic, with a rough, sand-covered, brown-to-pink dorsal surface and scattered tubefeet on the rosy underside. Upper surface with large numbers of pointed papillae that lack tubefeet (107.4). The 18 tentacles have a distinct stem ending in a tuft of short branches (107.4a). **Size:** Average 150 mm. **Biology:** Common in low-shore rock pools and gullies, but not easily seen because of its sand coating.

107.5 Tapering sea cucumber   *Holothuria leucospilota*
Elongate, thin black body tapered towards the head end, and with short thin papillae. Head with 18–20 short tentacles. **Size:** Up to 500 mm. **Biology:** Found in sandy lagoons or on shallow tropical reefs, down to 13 m, often with the posterior end hidden in a crevice. Tends to assume a thin, snake-like shape. Tentacles rake the sand for food particles. **SIMILAR SPECIES:** *H. atra* (Maputaland north) is also large (400–600 mm) and uniformly black, but chubbier, sausage-shaped, smooth-textured, and often completely coated in fine sand, except for circular bare patches in two rows on the back.

107.6 Noble sea cucumber   *Holothuria nobilis*
Large and loaf-shaped, with 4–8 prominent bulges on each side. Colour pattern distinctive: the dorsal surface black with scattered white to yellow spots and the lateral bulges marked with white to yellow patches. Underside white, with scattered tubefeet. **Size:** Up to 500 mm. **Biology:** In seagrass beds and on coral reefs in tropical areas, down to 13 m. One of the most valued species in the commercial sea cucumber fishery. **SIMILAR SPECIES:** *H. scabra*, the sandfish (Durban northwards), is similarly fat and loaf-shaped, but mottled grey above (sometimes with thin transverse dark bands) and white below.

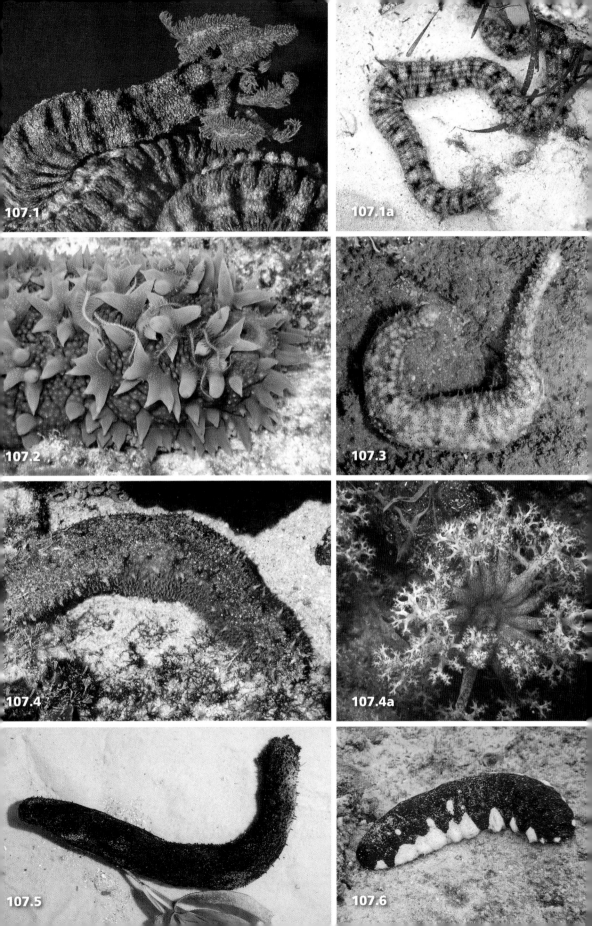

107.1

107.1a

107.2

107.3

107.4

107.4a

107.5

107.6

PLATE 108

108.1 Golden sea cucumber — *Thyone aurea*

A floppy, soft-skinned golden-orange sea cucumber with 10 tree-like (dendritic) tentacles. The tubefeet are weak and scattered randomly over the entire body surface. **Size:** Up to 130 mm long. **Biology:** Lives buried in sand, with only the tentacles visible, or between mussels, redbait, or other holothurians. Regularly washed ashore because of its poor powers of adhesion. Disgorges its gut at the slightest provocation.

108.2 Warty sea cucumber — *Neostichopus grammatus*

Moderately large and uniformly red or cream to brown. The dorsal surface lacks tubefeet, but is covered with obvious pointed wart-like papillae. At least 18 tentacles, which are closely crowded and difficult to count. Each tentacle arises from a short stalk that divides into short horizontal branches. **Size:** Average 150 mm. **Biology:** Found singly in rock pools and shallow waters down to about 5 m. **SIMILAR SPECIES:** *Stichopus chloronotus* (Mozambique northwards) has a distinctive box-shaped black-green body with four rows of tubercles along the longitudinal margins.

108.3 Red-chested sea cucumber — *Pseudocnella insolens*

Colour diagnostic. Intertidal specimens may be dark above with a red 'chest', but subtidal ones are uniformly bright red. Tubefeet scattered dorsally, but in three bands of two or three rows each on the underside. Has 10 irregularly branched tentacles. **Size:** 40 mm. **Biology:** A small species found in dense colonies covering shallow reefs. The young are brooded in pockets in the skin and can often be seen clinging to the surface of the parent. Previously known as *Cucumaria insolens* and as *Trachythyone insolens*.

108.4 Cask sea cucumber — *Pentacta doliolum*

Body tough; upper surface varies from pale mauve to mauve-black, becoming pale grey on the flattened sole. Tubefeet strongly suctorial and restricted to five regular bands, each consisting of a double row. Has 10 irregularly branched tentacles. **Size:** Typically 70 mm. **Biology:** A filter-feeder that forms dense beds on shallow reefs along the west coast. *Thyone aurea* (108.1) often occurs in mixed beds with this species, relying on its stronger powers of adhesion to avoid being washed away.
SIMILAR SPECIES:
108.5 *Aslia spyridophora* (Saldanha–Durban) has similar features, but its sole is not distinct and the body is uniformly grey.

108.6 Black sea cucumber — *Pseudocnella sykion*

Uniformly black, like *Roweia stephensoni* (108.7). Distinct bands of tubefeet are visible on the dorsal surface, but a few tubefeet are also scattered between these bands. The bands on the ventral 'sole' have no more than four rows of tubefeet. The 10 tentacles are each branched in a tree-like fashion. **Size:** 60 mm. **Biology:** Common on rocky shores. Insinuates itself into rocky crevices near the low-tide mark. Previously known as *Cucumaria sykion*.

108.7 Stephenson's sea cucumber — *Roweia stephensoni*

Uniformly black. Upper surface with irregularly scattered tubefeet and soft papillae. Tubefeet on lower surface arranged in distinct bands of six rows each. Has 10 irregularly branched tentacles. **Size:** Typically 60–70 mm. **Biology:** Aggregates around the sides of rocks or in sandy crevices. Previously known as *Cucumaria stephensoni*.

108.8 Horseshoe sea cucumber — *Roweia frauenfeldii*

Body arched into a U-shape, dark above and grey below. Tubefeet grouped into five bands, each made up of 4–6 rows (2–3 rows near the ends of the body). Has 10 irregularly branched tentacles. **Size:** Typically 70–80 mm. **Biology:** A crevice-dwelling species. Cape specimens are usually found under sand with only the tentacles and anus projecting, the remainder of the body being firmly attached to a rock buried beneath the sediment.

108.1

108.2

108.3

108.4

108.5

108.6

108.7

108.8

Sea squirts & kin

Three small phyla in Plate 109 – **Phylum Hemichordata** (acorn worms),
Phylum Phoronida (phoronans) and **Phylum Chaetognatha** (arrow worms)
– are related to the huge **Phylum Chordata**, which has three subphyla:

- **Subphylum Cephalochordata:** Lancelets, resembling simple fish (Plate 109).
- **Subphylum Urochordata:** Salps and doliolids (Plate 109) and sea squirts,
  or ascidians (Plates 110–112), which seem rather featureless, but are highly
  advanced and closely related to vertebrates, as is most evident in the larvae,
  which are tadpole-like, with a tail and a dorsal nerve cord supported by a
  notochord. Adults lose these features and are sessile and sac-like, topped by
  a pair of tubular siphons and enclosed in a cellulose casing (the test or tunic).
  Water is sucked in via the inhalant siphon, filtered through a sieve-like pharynx
  and expelled through the exhalant siphon.
- **Subphylum Vertebrata:** Animals with a vertebral column (see later chapters).

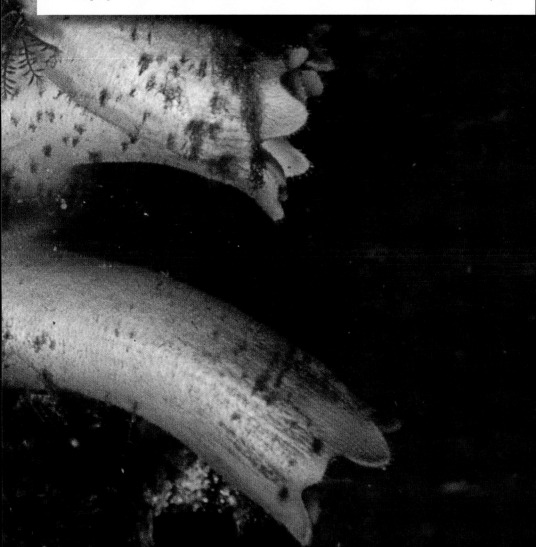

PLATE 109

Acorn worms Hemichordata

Worm-like, with a hollow dorsal nerve cord. Unsegmented body divided into a proboscis, a collar, and a long trunk. About 10 species in southern Africa.

109.1 Cape acorn worm *Balanoglossus capensis*

Soft, yellowish with an acorn-like proboscis, a collar and a long fragile trunk. Front folded upwards over gill slits; posterior with khaki-green hepatic lobes. **Size:** 100 mm. **Biology:** Forms U-tubes on sheltered sandbanks. Eats detritus: ejects coiled castings from the burrow. **SIMILAR SPECIES:** *B. natalensis* (Durban Bay) is about 1 m long.

Phoronans Phoronida

Worm-like. Long unsegmented trunk; head with a horseshoe-shaped set of tentacles (the lophophore). Produce chitinous tubes or drill into shells.

109.2 Mussel phoronan *Phoronis ovalis*

Minute worms that drill into shells, exposing only their tentacles (109.2). Body long, unsegmented and narrow, with a thin, reflected posterior end (109.2a). **Size:** 2 mm. **Biology:** Found exclusively and in enormous numbers boring into shells – particularly those of the brown mussel *Perna perna*, but also low-shore limpets, winkles and whelks.

Arrow worms Chaetognatha

Like larval fish, with small lateral and tail fins; head has two eyes and a characteristic fan of spines used to capture prey. About 30 species in southern Africa.

109.3 Common arrow worm *Sagitta* sp.

Long, thin and transparent white. Head swollen, with tiny eyes and spine-like jaws. Tail narrow, with a flat terminal fin. **Size:** 10 mm. **Biology:** Strong swimmers that dart through the water capturing small prey with a rapid snap of the mouth bristles. Most common prey are copepods, but much larger organisms, including small fish, may be taken.

Lancelets Cephalochordata

Dorsal nerve cord and notochord place them in phylum Chordata. Eel-like, transparent, with muscle bands, gill slits and a tail, but no jaws, eyes or scales.

109.4 Cape lancelet *Branchiostoma capensis*

Laterally flattened, eel-shaped, with a narrow fin around most of the body. Head pointed, with short cirri around the mouth. Obvious V-shaped blocks of muscles. **Size:** 50 mm. **Biology:** Burrows in sand at depths of 20–80 m, with just the head showing. Water is drawn in through the mouth, and food particles filtered out by the gill slits.

Urochordates Urochordata

Salps & doliolids Thaliacea

Planktonic tunicates (sea squirts). Body muscular, enclosed in a jelly-like capsule. Either solitary or forming large colonies.

109.5 Three-tailed salp *Thalia* sp.

Falls in order Salpida: gelatinous, cylindrical, with incomplete, hoop-like muscular bands. Three tails diagnose the genus. **Size:** 20 mm. **Biology:** Water passing through the 'barrel' is filtered by the gills. Solitary stage asexual: buds off metre-long chains of sexual individuals. **SIMILAR SPECIES:** Order Doliolida: also barrel-shaped, but 'hoops' encircle the body. See 38.4.

109.6 Fire roller *Pyrosoma* sp.

Hollow tubular transparent colonies of hundreds of individuals; closed at one end like the finger of a glove. Blue-white; almost transparent. **Size:** 50–500 mm. **Biology:** Often washed ashore. Luminescent when disturbed, hence the name (*pyro* = 'fire', *soma* = 'body').

109.1

109.2

109.2a

109.3

109.4

109.5

109.6

PLATE 110

Sea squirts
Ascidiacea

Large ascidians are solitary and have single inhalant and exhalant siphons, but many smaller species are colonial, comprising numerous tiny individuals (zooids), embedded in a shared sheet of jelly-like tissue. Such individuals may maintain separate siphons, or share common exhalant siphons.

110.1 Redbait
Pyura stolonifera

Very large, well-known, solitary ascidian with a thick, opaque white test covered by a wrinkled dark brown 'skin'. Siphons slightly scalloped, but lacking papillae. The orange or red flesh is used as bait by anglers, hence the common name. **Size:** Typically 150 mm tall, but can be as large as a rugby ball. **Biology:** Forms extensive aggregates on wave-exposed rocks from low tide to 10 m depth. Sometimes forms loose, boulder-like masses on the seabed. Commensal copepods, amphipods and pea crabs (55.6) occur in the pharynx. Harvested as a source of food on the southeast coast.

110.2 Herdman's redbait
Pyura herdmani

Another large solitary ascidian, similar to the previous species, but with large pointed papillae on the tunic, particularly around the siphons. **Size:** 100 mm tall. **Biology:** Not as abundant as *P. stolonifera*, but can form dense aggregates in more sheltered habitats.

Alien

110.3 Microcosmos
Microcosmos squamiger

Brown with an irregular tunic, but hard to recognise in the field as it is always covered with a shaggy coat of other species (hence the name *Microcosmos*). Siphons striped red and orange. **Size:** 40 mm. **Biology:** Aggregates on ropes and pontoons in harbours. Introduced from Australia.

Alien

110.4 Sea vase
Ciona intestinalis

Tall, cylindrical, solitary ascidian. Test soft, floppy, off-white to yellow and transparent – pharynx and digestive organs clearly visible. Inhalant siphon large and terminal; exhalant siphon smaller and projects off the shoulder. **Size:** 50–100 mm tall. **Biology:** Introduced from Europe. Forms dense aggregates in sheltered waters on jetties, piers and culture-ropes in mussel farms.

110.5 Angular ascidian
Styela angularis

Solitary, tall, tough, leathery, six-sided; stalk thin and tapering. Inhalant siphon leans to one side; exhalant siphon terminal. **Size:** Up to 100 mm tall. **Biology:** Occurs singly on rock surfaces where the current is fairly strong. Often partially concealed by seaweeds or other marine growths that cover the test. Previously named *S. costata*.
SIMILAR SPECIES:
110.6 *Styela plicata* (south–east coasts) is squat, with a pale, almost white, tunic; four pairs of brown stripes on each siphon. Introduced from Asia: concentrated in harbours.

110.7 Crevice ascidian
Ascidia caudata

Large, semitransparent, yellow to brown. Attached to rocks by its entire left side; the right, or upper, side is usually covered with large pieces of shell and gravel. Siphons long, diverging: openings not lobed. **Size:** Up to 250 mm long. **Biology:** In crevices or beneath boulders in intertidal pools and on shallow reefs.
SIMILAR SPECIES:
110.8 *Ascidia canaliculata* (Namibia–Mozambique) is very similar in appearance and habits, but has grooved siphons with lobed openings. *A. sydneiensis* (Port Elizabeth and Maputo) resembles *A. canaliculata*, but internally its dorsal tubercle is thrown into irregular folds (pierced by several openings) rather than forming definite spirals. Introduced.
110.9 *Ascidia incrassata* (Saldanha–Mozambique) grows to 100 mm length and has a hard, translucent, purple to red tunic. The siphons each have 6–8 marked lobes with a distinctive orange-red spot between each lobe.

110.10 Choirboys
Pycnoclavella narcissus

Colonial, with clusters of independent zooids attached by a common base. A darker patch between the two siphons is conspicuous against the otherwise almost completely transparent pale test. Colour usually blue or yellow; rarely light blue-green. **Size:** Colony height 50–100 mm. **Biology:** Found along vertical rock-faces and under overhangs.

PLATE 111

111.1 Fan ascidian — *Sycozoa arborescens*

A colonial form with flattened fan-shaped heads arising from a short, often much-branched stalk. The individual zooids are arranged in double rows along the margin of each head. Pink to brown, apertures often ringed in white. Large specimens can be very convoluted. **Size:** Colony up to 100 mm across and 50 mm tall. **Biology:** Found on vertical rock-faces where there is strong water-flow. Several other fan-shaped species, including one that is a spectacular fluorescent blue, have been photographed, but remain undescribed.

111.2 Bell ascidian — *Clavelina lepadiformis*

An unmistakable and beautiful colonial species, transparent except for a white line up the side of each individual and around its siphons. The sieve-like pharynx and orange visceral organs are clearly visible through the body wall. **Size:** About 30 mm high. **Biology:** A European species recently introduced to South Africa and only found in harbours and sheltered lagoons, where it forms small colonies, usually on man-made structures.

111.3 Elephant's ears — *Gynandrocarpa placenta*

A large, colonial form with a short stalk, or peduncle, on which is borne a thick oval pad of fibrous pink tunic. Numerous darker pink zooids are embedded within the tunic. **Size:** Colonies up to 200 mm long. **Biology:** Grows on shallow reefs, but more common in deeper waters. Colonies ripped off and cast ashore in large numbers after storms.

111.4 Strawberries — *Pseudodistoma africanum*

Distinctive stalked lobes, each with a sandy base and a wider, clean, conical head, within which rows of deeply pigmented zooids are embedded. Colour varies from white through pink to deep red. **Size:** Colonies up to 50 mm tall. **Biology:** Small groups of colonies found on reefs up to 35 m depth.

111.5 Blue lollipop ascidian — *Eudistoma caeruleum*

Colonies club-shaped, with a short stout stalk bearing a distinctive dark blue head studded with regular rows of zooids that give the colony a knobbly appearance. **Size:** Colonies about 20–30 mm tall. **Biology:** Common in intertidal rock pools along the east coast, even those that are regularly inundated with sand.

111.6 Bulb ascidian — *Sigillina digitata*

Colonies form soft, cushion-like, often lobed masses. Within these, each zooid forms a separate rounded hump, with independent siphons. Zooids not arranged into patterns or systems. Colour varies from white to pink or pale brown, but zooids usually dusted with opaque white pigment. **Size:** Colonies up to 150 mm across. **Biology:** Common in intertidal pools and down to 15 m. Often colonised by the amphipod *Polycheria atolli*, which excavates a hole in the test, in which it lies upside down and filter-feeds.

111.7 Green urn ascidian — *Didemnum molle*

Forms distinctive urn-shaped colonies, illustrated by the two larger pale individuals in the photograph. Pale greenish white, sometimes blotched grey, with a lime-green exhalant aperture that opens into the large central cavity at the top of the 'urn'. Small star-shaped inhalant siphons dot the colony and lie flush with the outer surface. **Size:** Colony 50 mm. **Biology:** Abundant on coral reefs. Easily mistaken for a vase sponge because of the colony shape. Green colour caused by symbiotic blue-green algae that grow around the inhalant siphons.

SIMILAR SPECIES:

111.8 *Atriolum robustum* – the smaller, more numerous yellow individuals in the same photograph as *Didemnum molle* – has a similar form but the inhalant siphons are slightly larger, less numerous, and raised on mounds. Maputaland northwards.

111.9 *Didemnum* spp. (whole coast). At least 10 other easily confused species within the genus *Didemnum* occur in the region. Unlike *D. molle* these form hard opaque crusts, regularly dotted with star-shaped inhalant apertures. The shared, turret-like exhalant openings are more widely spaced. The species depicted is probably *D. obscurum*.

111.1

111.2

111.3

111.4

111.5

111.6

111.7   111.8

111.9

PLATE 112

112.1 Brain ascidian   *Trididemnum cerebriforme*

Forms thin, smooth encrustations, often with a convoluted surface. Numerous spicules in the test give it a firm texture and an opaque white to grey colour. Regularly spaced, star-shaped inhalant openings reveal the locations of the tiny zooids. The larger, turret-like exhalant siphons are more widely spaced and shared by many zooids. **Size:** Zooids 1 mm, colonies 100 mm. **Biology:** Very common, but often misidentified as a sponge.

112.2 Seaweed ascidian   *Botryllus elegans*

Colonial, with separate, regularly distributed, opaque spherical zooids, usually arranged in the same orientation. Zooids may be white, golden or pink and lie within a transparent or pinkish jelly-like matrix. Granular dots within the matrix form part of a common blood circulation system. **Size:** Zooids 2 mm, colonies up to 100 mm across. **Biology:** Always grows on flat-bladed algae, particularly *Rhodymenia obtusa* (181.4). Common in gullies and on shallow reefs. Previously know as *B. anomalus* – an allusion to the fact that all other *Botryllus* spp. share common exhalant openings (see below).

112.3 White-ringed ascidian   *Botryllus magnicoecus*

Colonial ascidian that often forms large, lobed colonies. The matrix may be red or yellow, but is most commonly pink. Zooids can form circles or rows, but are arranged along a network of common exhalant canals. Inhalant apertures almost always conspicuously circled with white pigment. **Size:** Colonies typically 100 mm across, but can form much larger double-sided hanging sheets in harbours. **Biology:** Common, but bewilderingly variable: easily confused with several other related species.

112.4 Variable ascidian   *Botryllus gregalis*

Colony mat-like. Zooids opaque and lining a branching network of common exhalant apertures; distinctly separated by grooves. Colour incredibly variable (three variations shown here). Certain identification relies on internal anatomy. **Size:** 100 mm. **Biology:** Most common in sheltered waters. Previously misidentified as *Botrylloides leachi*.

112.5 Golden star ascidian   *Botryllus schlosseri*

Variable in colour, but often dark brown to black. Zooids arranged in separated, star-shaped clusters, each around a common exhalant aperture. **Size:** 150 mm. **Biology:** Probably introduced, as it is mostly found in harbours.

112.6 Meandering ascidian   *Botryllus maeandrius*

Long, thin, meandering, sometimes branched, crustose colonies. Zooids in regular rows along each side of long exhalant channels, which have only a few, hardly visible openings. Often uniform pink to reddish (112.6), but highly variable (e.g. 112.6a). Edges of colony spotted with granules that form part of the common blood system. **Size:** Colonies 20–50 mm. **Biology:** Fairly common under intertidal boulders and in the shallow subtidal zone.

112.7 Cushion ascidian   *Aplidium monile*

Soft, cushion-like pale blue to pink colonies, often growing between zoanthids. Apertures pale, inhalant openings being arranged in irregular circles around larger exhalant openings, which form funnel-like projections when the colony is feeding. **Size:** Colonies typically 20–50 mm across. **Biology:** Common in intertidal rock pools in KwaZulu-Natal. Bubbles of oxygen build up on the colony due to photosynthesis by symbiotic algae in its tissues.

112.8 Emerald ascidian   *Trididemnum cyclops*

Colonial, forming thin, meandering cushions or mats within which the tiny zooids are embedded. Characteristic bright green colour due to symbiotic unicellular algae (*Prochloron*) within the body. **Size:** Colonies 100 mm, individual zooids only about 1.5 mm. **Biology:** Common on intertidal reefs in tropical regions; often exposed at low tide.

112.9 Gossamer ascidian   *Diplosoma listerianum*

Thin, soft, fragile gelatinous sheets covering seaweeds or similar objects. Zooids tiny and scattered throughout the sheet, which also includes small yellow pigment bodies. Each zooid has an inhalant pore; larger, shared exhalant openings are inconspicuous. **Size:** Colonies 50–100 mm. **Biology:** Introduced from Europe. Common in harbours and on sheltered shores. Breaks up easily. Frequently overlooked, or mistaken for a sponge.

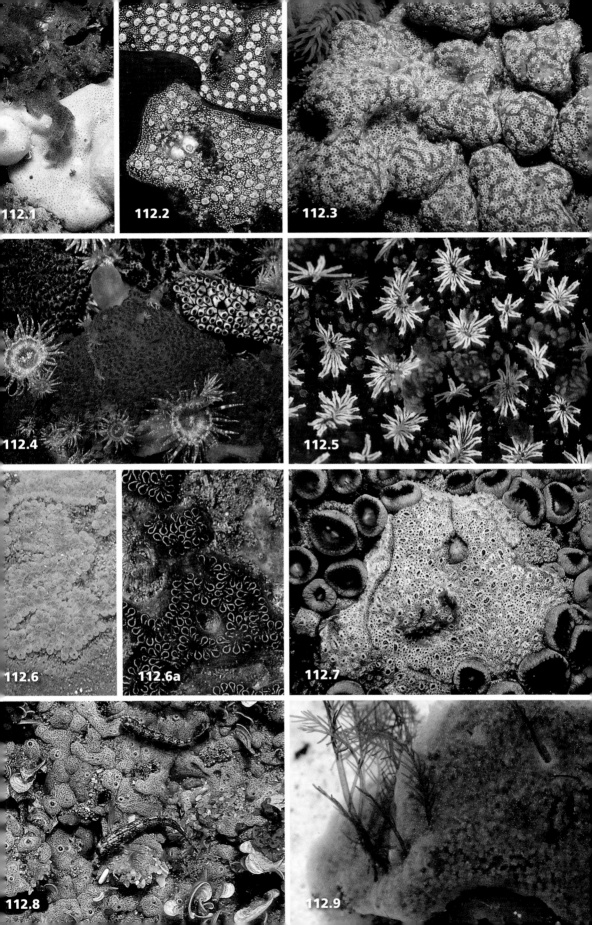

112.1

112.2

112.3

112.4

112.5

112.6

112.6a

112.7

112.8

112.9

Fishes

Over 2 000 species of fish occur in the seas around southern Africa. They comprise both cartilaginous and bony fishes and range in size from tiny cryptic clingfishes to huge, but harmless, whale sharks. The majority are tropical and subtropical Indo-Pacific species but about 16% are endemic, being found only in southern Africa. Fishes are key constituents of coastal ecosystems and many are of great economic importance.

PLATE 113

Classification & identification of fishes

Fishes are diverse. Their classification and the features used to identify them, including the numbering scheme used for ray and spine counts of bony fish, are summarised here.

Jawless fishes
Class Agnatha

Jawless fishes have cartilaginous skeletons and include hagfishes (**113.1**), lampreys (not found in southern Africa) and numerous extinct species.

Cartilaginous fishes
Class Chondrichthyes

Chondrichthyes all have jaws and a cartilaginous skeleton. There are two subclasses.

Sharks and rays
Subclass Elasmobranchii

In addition to a cartilaginous skeleton, elasmobranchs have 5–7 gill slits and lack scales: the skin is sandpaper-like because of tiny embedded, tooth-like denticles. The teeth can be sharp for cutting or flattened for grinding. Adult males have two claspers on the ventral surface. Rays are flat (**113.2** & see Plates 117–118) but sharks are usually cylindrical (**113.3** & see Plates 114–116).

Elephantfish
Subclass Holocephali

Elephantfish (**113.4** & see 116.6) are named after the floppy proboscis on the snout and share many features with the elasmobranches, but have a single gill opening on each side.

Bony fishes
Class Osteichthyes

Osteichthyes (see Plates 119–156) have bony skeletons, a single gill opening on each side, and fins that are either fleshy or have rays.

Fleshy-fin fishes
Subclass Sarcopterygii

A division of the bony fishes with lobed fins that have a fleshy base. Fleshy-fin fishes are largely extinct except for the coelacanth (**113.5** & see also 156.6) and lungfish.

Ray-fin fishes
Subclass Actinopterygii

Ray-fin fishes (or teleosts) are the most diverse vertebrate group. All have a single gill opening on each side, protected by a gill cover. Skin covered by overlapping scales (**113.6**), which can form larger scutes or fuse into an exterior armour (**113.7**). Sexes similar unless they differ in colour. Sensory receptors lie in the lateral line flanking the body.

The number of spines and soft rays in the dorsal and anal fins (diagram below) diagnose most species. Spines are hard and spiky; rays are soft and flexible, usually divided near their tips, and crossed by vein-like stripes. Their numbers and arrangement are given in formulae with Roman numerals for spines and Arabic numerals for soft rays. A formula of DIV + I 8, AIII 8 decodes to mean two dorsal fins (D), one with four spines (IV), the second with a single spine (I) and eight soft rays; the anal fin (A) has three spines (III) and eight soft rays.

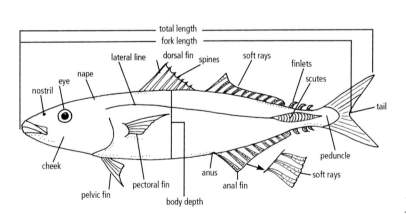

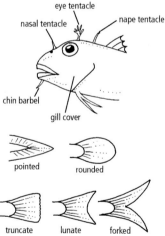

Most common types of tail

Jawless fishes
Agnatha

113.1 Six-gill hagfish
Eptatretus hexatrema

Eel-shaped and grey; no paired fins. Mouth lacks jaws but has two protrusible rows of horny teeth. Six barbels on the head. Two rows of slime pores and 5–8 pairs of gill openings on underside of body. **Size:** 80 cm. **Biology:** Endemic; occurs down to 400 m. Often caught in lobster traps off west coast. Secretes lots of sticky slime when irritated.

113.1

113.2

113.3

113.4

113.5

113.6

113.7

PLATE 114

Cartilaginous fishes

Chondrichthyes

Sharks

About 100 species of shark occur off southern Africa, although many are rarely seen. Most are harmless, but a few can attack bathers. Shark nets do protect bathers (by killing sharks), but have detrimental effects on other sea life.

114.1 Whale shark   *Rhincodon typus*

Large; grey-blue covered in white spots and lines. Large mouth with minute teeth. Tail fin taller than dorsal fins. **Size:** 14 m; 36 tonnes. **Biology:** Circumtropical; migrates long distances. Usually solitary but seasonally abundant in Mozambique and KwaZulu-Natal waters. Feeds on plankton sieved through the gills. Females can produce 300 young in a litter. Harmless, but divers should keep a respectful distance from the largest fish in the ocean.

114.2 Great white shark   *Carcharodon carcharias*

Large, powerful; grey-blue but white below. Snout conical. Teeth triangular; both sides serrated. Pectoral fins long; black patch behind fin. Tail sickle-shaped; anal and second dorsal fins small. **Size:** 6.4 m; 1 208 kg. **Biology:** Worldwide in coastal and offshore areas; often close to seal islands. Ranges between the Cape and KwaZulu-Natal. Dangerous; known to attack swimmers, divers, surfers and boats. Lives up to 27 years. Sexually mature at 3.5–5 m (9–14 years); 7–14 pups per litter. Protected in South Africa.

114.3 Bronze whaler   *Carcharhinus brachyurus*

Bronze to brownish grey; snout broad and bluntly pointed. Upper teeth triangular with narrow pointed cusps. No ridge along back. **Size:** 3 m; 240 kg. **Biology:** Worldwide in temperate coastal waters. Attains age of 30 years and only matures at 2 m (20 years). Gestation period of 12 months; produces up to 20 pups. Feeds on fish and squid. Common in Eastern Cape and often associated with the 'sardine run' into KwaZulu-Natal.

114.4 Zambezi or bull shark   *Carcharhinus leucas*

Grey and robust; snout short and blunt. Broad, triangular, saw-edged upper teeth. High first dorsal fin; no markings on fins. No mid-back ridge. **Size:** 3.2 m; 315 kg. **Biology:** Circumglobal, frequenting estuaries and coastal waters; has even been recorded far upstream in the Zambezi River. Extremely dangerous; several recorded attacks on people. Slow growing; attains age of at least 32 years. Sexually mature at 2 m (about 22 years); bears up to eight pups in summer. Feeds on small sharks, fishes and dolphins.

114.5 Dusky shark   *Carcharhinus obscurus*

Dusky grey with characteristic mid-back ridge. Upper teeth triangular and saw-edged. Second dorsal fin small; juveniles may have dark fin tips. **Size:** 4.2 m; 450 kg. **Biology:** Worldwide in depths to 400 m. Complex coastal migratory patterns. Attains age of 34 years. Sexually mature at 2.5 m (20 years). Bears 6–14 young in autumn off KwaZulu-Natal. Frequently caught in fishing tournaments. Proliferation of juveniles in KwaZulu-Natal possibly due to removal of larger predatory sharks by nets.

114.6 Blacktip reef shark   *Carcharhinus melanopterus*

Brownish grey; short, bluntly rounded snout. No mid-back ridge. Conspicuous black fin tips often accentuated by submarginal whitish band. **Size:** 2 m. **Biology:** Indo-Pacific; particularly shallow coral reefs and lagoons. Bears 2–4 young. Feeds on small sharks, fishes and octopus. Has been known to attack people wading in shallow water.

114.7 Blacktip shark   *Carcharhinus limbatus*

Snout longer, narrower and more pointed than previous species. Trailing edge of tall first dorsal fin and tips of second dorsal and pectoral fins dark; black tips fade with age. **Size:** 2.5 m; 125 kg. **Biology:** Circumtropical; ranges south to the Cape in summer. Sexually mature at 1.6 m (six years). Breeds off Mozambique; has about six young. Eats pelagic fish.

114.8 Blackspot shark   *Carcharhinus sealei*

Slender, grey; long, rounded snout. Large oval eyes. Oblique cusped teeth. Black spot on second dorsal fin. **Size:** 1 m. **Biology:** Indo-Pacific; shallow coastal waters. Bears 1–2 young. Feeds on small fish, squid and prawns.

114.1

14.2

114.3

14.4

114.5

114.6

14.7

114.8

PLATE 115

115.1 Tiger shark
Galeocerdo cuvieri

Short broad head and blunt snout. Dark vertical bars. Large, saw-edged, cockscomb teeth. Ridge along mid-back. Upper tail-lobe long. Low keels on tail peduncle. **Size:** 6 m; 800 kg. **Biology:** Worldwide; coastal and offshore. Voracious predator on fishes, birds, mammals and turtles; implicated in attacks on humans. Sexually mature at around 3 m; bears litters of up to 80 young. Frequently seen by divers at Aliwal Shoal.

115.2 Blue shark
Prionace glauca

Slim, elegant. Snout conical, pectoral fins very long. Dorsal fin arises well behind the pectoral fin. Lustrous blue above (fading on death); white below. **Size:** 3.5 m. **Biology:** Circumglobal; migrates long distances. The most abundant large shark, but rare inshore. Large numbers caught commercially on longlines for their fins. Bears up to 135 pups. Feeds mainly on fish; attacks humans.

115.3 Ragged-tooth shark
Carcharias taurus

Robust, plump-bodied; brown with darker spots on the sides. Snout pointed; teeth fang-like (see 113.3). Dorsal and anal fins equal-sized. **Size:** 3 m; 294 kg. **Biology:** Widespread; common on coastal reefs. Attains 14 years; matures at 2.3 m (5–6 years). Migrates seasonally along the coast: mates off northern KwaZulu-Natal in summer; produces two young nine months later in Eastern Cape. Eats fish, small sharks and crustaceans. Only dangerous if provoked.

115.4 Scalloped hammerhead shark
Sphyrna lewini

Peculiarly flattened head, protruding sideways; front edge scalloped, with central notch (115.4a). Smooth-edged, slanting, triangular teeth. Rear edge of pelvic fin straight. **Size:** 3 m; >100 kg. **Biology:** Pelagic; circumtropical. Matures at 1.6 m. Breeds in summer; about 10 pups in litter. Juveniles form large schools near the surface.
SIMILAR SPECIES:
115.5 *Sphyrna zygaena*, the smooth hammerhead, lacks a central notch on snout.
115.6 *Sphyrna mokarran*, the great hammerhead, has a central indentation on snout, but teeth serrate (not smooth), dorsal fin tall, and pelvic fin with concave hind edge.

115.7 Whitetip reef shark
Triaenodon obesus

Slender, greyish brown. Conspicuous white tips on first dorsal fin and upper tail lobe. Snout short, broad. No ridge between dorsal fins. Tooth cusps oblique. **Size:** 2.1 m; 50 kg. **Biology:** Indo-Pacific coral reefs; often rests in caves. Eats fish, octopus and crustaceans. Matures at 85 cm; females bear 1–5 young. Usually harmless; shy of divers.

115.8 Spotted gully shark
Triakis megalopterus

Robust, greyish brown; covered in irregular black spots. Fins large, with second dorsal fin almost as large as first dorsal fin. **Size:** 2 m; 50 kg. **Biology:** Endemic; found in shallow sandy or rocky areas. Attains age of 21 years. Matures at 1.3 m (about 14 years). Long gestation period of nearly two years and produces litters of 6–12 young.

115.9 Hardnosed smooth-hound shark
Mustelus mosis

Slender and cylindrical. Greyish brown, often with white-tipped first dorsal fin. Adults with hard bone-like growth embedded in snout. Length of tail-fin dorsal lobe 1.7–2 times greater than the distance from the base of the second dorsal fin to the start of the tail fin. Teeth with low rounded cusps. **Size:** 1.5 m. **Biology:** Western Indian Ocean; coastal bays and sandy beaches. Feeds mainly on crustaceans and fish.

115.10 Smooth-hound shark
Mustelus mustelus

Slender and cylindrical. Grey; may have scattered black spots. Length of dorsal tail-fin lobe 1.9–2.4 times greater than the distance from second dorsal fin base to tail-fin origin. Teeth with low rounded cusps. **Size:** 1.7 m; 25 kg. **Biology:** Eastern Atlantic; coastal bays to outer shelf. Feeds mainly on crustaceans and fish. Attains 24 years. Females mature at 1.3 m (12–15 years) and males at 1 m (6–9 years). **SIMILAR SPECIES:** *Galeorhinus galeus*, the soupfin shark, has a smaller second dorsal fin and small blade-like teeth, which are serrated on the posterior edge.
115.11 *Squalus acutipinnis*, the spiny dogfish, has a prominent spine at front of each dorsal fin and no anal fin.

15.1

115.2

115.3

115.4a

115.5

115.6

115.4

115.7

115.8

115.9

115.11

115.10

PLATE 116

116.1 Leopard catshark — *Poroderma pantherinum*

Elongate, with long nasal barbels. Black spots that can vary in size and shape along the body and also on the fins. Some animals have a mix of dots, rings and stripes. Small pointed tricuspid teeth. **Size:** 70 cm. **Biology:** Endemic. Found on shallow rocky reefs to 250 m depth. Feeds on crustaceans, small fish and octopus. Nocturnal. Produces two brown egg cases.

116.2 Pyjama catshark — *Poroderma africanum*

Elongate with short nasal barbels. Longitudinal black stripes extend along body onto head. Small pointed tricuspid teeth. **Size:** 1 m; 8 kg. **Biology:** Endemic. Found in shallow rocky areas. Nocturnal and spends much time lying on the seabed. Tagging shows that it is highly resident. Feeds on small reef fish and octopus. Matures at about 65 cm; females produce two brown egg cases, which are attached to seaweed.

116.3 Puffadder shyshark — *Haploblepharus edwardsii*

Elongate with no nasal barbels. Nostrils connected to mouth by groove. Brown with tan saddles that have dark margins; numerous pale spots. Fins small, marked with brown blotches and pale spots. Eyes narrow. **Size:** 60 cm. **Biology:** Endemic; found in shallow rocky or sandy areas. Females lay two eggs, which are protected by tough egg cases. **SIMILAR SPECIES:** *Halaelurus* spp. have nostrils that are entirely separate from the mouth. *Halaelurus lineatus* (KwaZulu-Natal and Mozambique) and *Halaelurus natalensis* (Saldanha–East London) both have brown saddles like the puffadder shyshark, but differ in having pointed, upturned snouts. *H. lineatus* has many small dark spots that are absent in *H. natalensis*.

116.4 Dark shyshark — *Haploblepharus pictus*

Elongate with no nasal barbels. Deep grooves connect the nostrils to the mouth. Brown with about seven dark saddles extending over the head and body. **Size:** 60 cm. **Biology:** Endemic; lives in shallow inshore areas. Feeds on bottom-dwelling invertebrates. Females produce two egg cases, often called 'mermaid's purses' (116.4a). Shysharks curl themselves into a circle when disturbed, covering the eyes with the tail (hence the Afrikaans name 'skaamoog'). **SIMILAR SPECIES:** *H. fuscus*, the brown shyshark (Agulhas–Durban), is yellow-brown, slightly paler below, and has very indistinct brown saddles that merge with the background colour.

116.5 Spotted sevengill cowshark — *Notorynchus cepedianus*

One of a family of sharks that have 6–7 gill slits instead of the usual five. Head blunt; single dorsal fin. Body silver-grey dorsally, fading to a creamy colour below; covered with small black spots. **Size:** 3 m; 182 kg. **Biology:** Widespread, temperate coastal species; bottom-dwelling to 130 m. Females mature at 2 m (11 years); males earlier. Bears 60–80 young. Feeds on a wide range of invertebrate and vertebrate prey.

116.6 St Joseph shark — *Callorhinchus capensis*

The unusual shape, silvery and scaleless skin, long tail and trunk-like appendage on the snout characterise this curious cartilaginous fish. First dorsal fin has large serrate spine. Males have a spiny knob on the head. The single gill opening typifies the subclass Holocephali, of which this species is the only common southern African representative. **Size:** 1.2 m. **Biology:** Endemic; bottom-dwelling in shallow water, particularly in the southwestern Cape, where it is fished commercially. Feeds on bottom-dwelling invertebrates and small fish. Attains an age of 12 years. Sexually mature at 60 cm (3–4 years). Females deposit spindle-shaped, hairy brown egg cases on the seabed in summer; empty cases often wash ashore (116.6a).

116.1

116.2

116.3

116.4

116.4a

116.5

116.6

116.6a

PLATE 117

Rays, skates & guitarfishes

There are about 60 species of rays and skates in southern African waters and most of these flattened fishes live on the seabed. Their pectoral fins are greatly expanded into wing-like structures and the mouth and gill openings are on the underside of the head.

117.1 Blackspotted electric ray   *Torpedo fuscomaculata*

Rounded and disc-like; numerous black spots on dorsal surface. Two dorsal fins; tail fin rounded. Five pairs of gill openings beneath body. **Size:** 64 cm. **Biology:** Occupies sandy bottoms in coastal waters. Kidney-shaped electric organs at base of pectoral fins generate powerful shocks that are used for defence or to stun prey. **SIMILAR SPECIES:** *T. sinuspersici* (western Indian Ocean–south of Coffee Bay) is brownish red with a yellow reticulated pattern on dorsal surface. *Narke capensis*, the onefin electric ray, is yellow-brown and has a single dorsal fin.

117.2 Lesser guitarfish   *Rhinobatos annulatus*

Guitar-shaped and flattened; snout pointed, translucent. Blunt pavement-like teeth. Colour usually tan with dorsal spots; spots are brown in KwaZulu-Natal but appear as brown and white rings in other areas. **Size:** 1.4 m; 28 kg. **Biology:** Endemic; common in sandy areas, particularly lagoons and surf zone of beaches. Preys on bottom-dwelling molluscs and crabs, which it crushes with its pavement teeth. Matures at about 60 cm; females bear 2–10 young in summer. **SIMILAR SPECIES:** *R. leucospilus*, the greyspot guitarfish, has blue-grey spots on the snout and occurs only in KwaZulu-Natal.

117.3 Giant guitarfish   *Rhynchobatus djiddensis*

Flattened, pointed head with elongate snout. Blunt pavement-like teeth. Tail fin with distinct lower lobe. Grey, with rows of white spots; pair of darker eyespots on bases of pectoral fins. **Size:** 3 m; 227 kg. **Biology:** Indo-Pacific species; inhabits shallow sandy areas down to 30 m. Abundant in summer in KwaZulu-Natal. Feeds on crabs, molluscs and small fish. Matures at 1.5 m; bears four young in summer.

117.4 Biscuit skate   *Raja straeleni*

Flattened disc with wing-like pectoral fins and pointed snout. Tail with two small dorsal fins near tip. Row of thorn-like structures along mid-dorsal region of snout, disc and tail. Brown with many small black spots and two larger eyespots at base of pectoral fins. **Size:** Width 68 cm. **Biology:** Eastern Atlantic species; sandy or muddy areas down to 700 m. Feeds on invertebrates and fishes. Eggs laid in tough dark brown cases.

117.5 Spearnose skate   *Rostroraja alba*

Large angular disc with narrow pointed snout. Large thorns in three rows on tail. Disc greyish with many small white spots, though colour varies with age. **Size:** Width 1.8 m. **Biology:** Eastern Atlantic species; widespread in shallow water, particularly sandy bays. Feeds on fish, crustaceans and molluscs. Eggs laid in large rectangular cases.

117.6 Bluespotted ribbontail ray   *Taeniura lymma*

Oval-shaped disc that is longer than wide. Brown with blue spots on disc and pelvic fins. Spine located towards end of fleshy tail. **Size:** Width 90 cm; 5 kg. **Biology:** Indo-Pacific; sandy areas near coral reefs. Nocturnal; feeds on benthic invertebrates. Produces litters of up to seven young.

117.7 Blue stingray   *Dasyatis chrysonota*

Brown, with mottled blue markings on dorsal surface. Snout pointed. One serrated spine on the whip-like tail. **Size:** Width 75 cm; 25 kg. **Biology:** Endemic; shallow sandy areas down to depth of 100 m. Buries itself under a thin layer of sand. Feeds on small fish and crustaceans. Attains an age of 14 years. Females mature at 50 cm (seven years). Litters of 1–4 young are born in early summer after a gestation of nine months.

PLATE 118

118.1 Manta ray   *Manta birostris*

This charismatic giant of the ocean is an awesome sight. Its very large disc is wider than long. Large mouth at front of head with a fleshy paddle on each side (see also 113.2). Short tail. Usually dark on top, and white with variable black blotches and spots on underside. **Size:** Width 7 m; 3 tonnes. **Biology:** Circumtropical and pelagic. Feeds on plankton. Sometimes seen doing barrel rolls or jumping out of the water. Bears two young at a time. Known to aggregate in specific areas.

118.2 Eagle ray   *Myliobatis aquila*

Diamond-shaped; body wider than long. Projecting snout is continuous with front edge of pectoral fins. Large pelvic fins; long, whip-like tail with two serrated spines at base. Jaws with seven rows of tooth plates. Dark brown dorsally with irregular black spots; underside white. **Size:** Width 1.5 m; 22 kg. **Biology:** Eastern Atlantic species; coastal waters to depth of 95 m. Feeds by crushing molluscs and crustaceans. Bears litters of 4–7 young. **SIMILAR SPECIES:** *Pteromylaeus bovinus*, the bull ray, has a snout like a duck's bill and the brown disc usually has blue-grey crossbars.

118.3 Spotted eagle ray   *Aetobatus narinari*

Diamond-shaped with a distinct duck's bill snout. Tail long and whip-like; 1–3 spines at the base. Dorsal surface dark with numerous white spots; underside white. **Size:** Width 2.5 m; 98 kg. **Biology:** Circumtropical; shallow coastal waters. Feeds on bottom-dwelling invertebrates, which it crushes with its chevron-like pavement teeth. Bears litters of up to four young.

118.4 Honeycomb stingray   *Himantura uarnak*

Large; brown with a pale honeycomb pattern on upper surface and white below. Snout pointed; single spine on long, whip-like tail. **Size:** Width 2 m; 120 kg. **Biology:** Indo-Pacific; estuaries and sandy coastal areas down to 50 m. Feeds on bottom-dwelling invertebrates and fishes. Bears litters of 3–5 young in summer.

118.5 Green sawfish   *Pristis zijsron*

Conspicuous saw-like snout with 23–34 pairs of teeth. Body flattened, with angular pectoral fins. **Size:** 6 m; 276 kg. **Biology:** Indo-Pacific; shallow coastal areas. Uses its saw to dig crustaceans and molluscs from seabed or to strike fish. Females bear litters of 15–20 young, and used to be recorded in St Lucia and Richards Bay in summer. Juveniles occur in estuaries and bays.

118.1

118.3

118.2

118.4

118.5

PLATE 119

Bony fishes
Ray-fin fishes

Osteichthyes
Actinopterygii

Eels

Eels have long snake-like bodies that lack scales and pelvic fins. There are 13 different families of eel in southern Africa. Although the large moray eels are probably the best known, there are many rarely seen deep-water species. Eels have peculiar flattened, transparent larvae called leptocephalus larvae – widely dispersed by currents. Eels of the genus Anguilla live in fresh water, but migrate to the ocean to spawn.

119.1 Serpent eel   *Ophisurus serpens*

Elongate and thin; brown to olive-green; pale below. Snout pointed with fanglike teeth at front of jaws; black spots on head and lateral line (119.1a). Tail tip hard, pointed. Pectoral fins distinct, dorsal and anal fins inconspicuous. **Size:** 2.5 m. **Biology:** Burrows in sandy and muddy areas: often only the protruding head is seen. Feeds on crustaceans and small fishes. **SIMILAR SPECIES: *Strophidon sathete*** (formerly *Thyrsoidea macrura*), the slender giant moray, is common in KwaZulu-Natal estuaries and can exceed 3 m. It has a shorter snout, no pectoral fins and continuous dorsal and anal fins.

119.2 Ocellated snake-eel   *Myrichthys maculosus*

Elongate; cream with a series of black oval spots along the body. Tail tip is hard and pointed. **Size:** 50 cm. **Biology:** Widespread in Indo-Pacific. Usually found buried in sandy areas near reefs. Sometimes mistaken for a sea snake, but easily distinguished by absence of scales and lack of a flattened, paddle-like tail.

119.3 Zebra moray   *Gymnomuraena zebra*

Black with 40–80 encircling white rings. Jaws bear granular teeth but no sharp fangs. Anus well behind midpoint of body. **Size:** 1.5 m. **Biology:** Indo-Pacific; on shallow coral and rocky reefs. Usually concealed in crevices with only its head protruding.

119.4 Floral moray   *Echidna nebulosa*

Creamish with longitudinal double rows of dark blotches along body. Snout is typically white. The jaws lack sharp fangs. **Size:** 70 cm. **Biology:** Indo-Pacific; inhabits shallow coral and rocky reefs. Juveniles often found in tidal pools in KwaZulu-Natal.

119.5 Honeycomb moray eel   *Gymnothorax favagineus*

Dark brown with characteristic creamish-yellow honeycomb pattern. Dorsal and anal fins are connected and lack spines; No pectoral fins. Prominent canines. **Size:** 2 m; 18 kg. **Biology:** Indo-Pacific; lives in caves and holes in coral and rocky reefs. These cryptic predators favour eating octopus. They can inflict a serious bite if threatened.

119.6 Starry moray   *Gymnothorax nudivomer*

Light brown with numerous small close-set white spots that become darker and larger towards tail. Inside of mouth conspicuously yellow; single row of compressed canines with sharp, serrate edges. Gill opening in a dark blotch. **Size:** 1 m. **Biology:** Indo-Pacific; lives in caves and holes in coral and deeper rocky reefs.

119.7 Geometric moray   *Gymnothorax griseus*

Mottled brown with conspicuous lines of black dots on head. Distinct dorsal fin starts on head. **Size:** 65 cm. **Biology:** Western Indian Ocean; coral reefs. Feeds on fish and crustaceans.

119.8 Guineafowl moray   *Gymnothorax meleagris*

Dark brown with many pale spots that become sparser towards tail. Inside of mouth conspicuously white; three rows of fang-like canines. Gill opening in a black blotch. **Size:** 1 m. **Biology:** Indo-Pacific; lives in caves and holes in coral and shallow rocky reefs.

119.9 Moustache conger   *Conger cinereus*

Long and thin; grey with white underside. Pectoral fins well developed; other fins have distinct black edges. A black stripe extends below the eye. **Size:** 1 m. **Biology:** Western Indian Ocean; inhabits crevices in coral reefs down to 30 m.

119.1

119.1a

119.2

119.3

119.4

119.5

119.6

119.7

119.8

119.9

PLATE 120

Sardines & anchovies

The clupeiforms are small, primitive, pelagic fishes that often form huge shoals. About 20 species of anchovies and sardines occur in the waters of southern Africa, but microscopic examination is often necessary to distinguish them.

120.1 Estuarine roundherring   *Gilchristella aestuaria*

D 14–15, A 20. Tiny and translucent; bright silver head and abdominal cavity. Single dorsal fin lacks spines. Mouth terminal. **Size:** 7 cm. **Biology:** Endemic; forms large shoals in estuaries and coastal lakes. Completes entire life cycle in estuaries; tolerates fresh to extremely saline conditions. Spawns throughout year with peaks in spring and summer. Filter-feeds on plankton and is important in the diet of large predatory fishes.

120.2 Goldstripe sardinelle   *Sardinella gibbosa*

D 17–20, A 17–21. Small and silvery; distinguished by a thin gold stripe along sides. **Size:** 20 cm. **Biology:** Indo-Pacific; coastal waters including estuaries. **SIMILAR SPECIES:** At least four easily confused species occur in southern African waters. *S. aurita*, the round sardinelle, extends from Angola into Namibia with southward intrusions of warmer water.

120.3 Pilchard or sardine   *Sardinops sagax*

D 17–20, A 18–22. Silver and blue; 10–15 black spots along sides. Single dorsal fin lacks spines. Belly rounded, with feeble scutes. **Size:** 28 cm. **Biology:** Pelagic, forming vast shoals. Filter-feeds on phytoplankton and small zooplankton; is an important prey item for large fishes, birds and dolphins. Attains age of about five years. Spawns on Agulhas Bank and juveniles recruit in upwelling areas of west coast. Huge tonnages were caught off the west coast in the 1960s, followed by a collapse of the stock. During the famous KwaZulu-Natal winter 'sardine run' they are driven ashore by predatory fishes and dolphins. Previously called *S. ocellatus*. **SIMILAR SPECIES:** *Etrumeus whiteheadi*, the redeye roundherring, is another commercially important clupeid (Walvis Bay– KwaZulu-Natal). It has 12–13 anal fin rays, lacks lateral spots, and its eyes are noticeably red after capture.

120.4 Cape anchovy   *Engraulis japonicus*

D 14–17, A 15–21. Small and silvery. Snout projects past lower jaw. Belly lacks enlarged scutes. **Size:** 13 cm. **Biology:** Widespread; coastal shoaling species. Filter-feeds on zooplankton; important in diet of many fishes, birds and mammals. Attains age of three years. Spawns inshore on the Agulhas Bank in summer; juveniles recruit westwards and are a major component of the purse seine fishery, usually being processed into fish meal and fish oil. Previously named *E. capensis* and *E. encrasicolis*.

120.5 Razorbelly   *Hilsa kelee*

D 16–19, A 17–23. Deep-bodied and silvery; black spot behind the gill cover. Belly compressed into a keel. Tail deeply forked. Juveniles have several black spots on their sides. **Size:** 35 cm. **Biology:** Indo-Pacific, coastal species. Shoals often recorded around Durban. Filter-feeds on plankton; important component of the diet of larger predatory fishes. Spawns in summer.

120.6 Glassnose anchovy   *Thryssa vitrirostris*

D 13–14, A 34–43. Silvery; black spot behind gill cover. Snout blunt, translucent and overlaps the underslung mouth, the interior of which is orange. Sharp scutes along belly. **Size:** 20 cm. **Biology:** Indian Ocean; coastal species common in bays and estuaries. Filter-feeds on plankton. Spawns in winter. **SIMILAR SPECIES:** *T. setirostris*, the longjaw glassnose, has a long posterior extension on the upper jaw.

120.7 Beaked sandfish   *Gonorhynchus gonorhynchus*

D 11–13, A 9–10. Elongate and cylindrical. Pointed snout with barbel; mouth inferior. Jaws toothless; lips with papillae. Dorsal and pelvic fins situated well back on body. **Size:** 60 cm. **Biology:** Widespread circumglobal species; occurs over sand on continental shelf. Has long pelagic larval phase that is often preyed upon by seabirds.

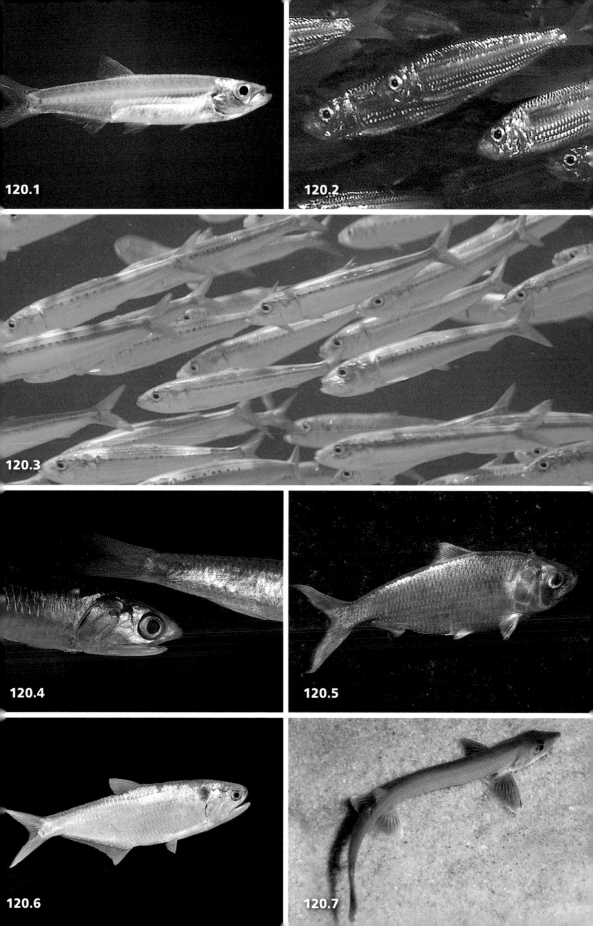

120.1

120.2

120.3

120.4

120.5

120.6

120.7

PLATE 121

Wolfherring, tarpon, silversides, lizardfishes & kin

121.1 Wolfherring — *Chirocentrus dorab*
D 16–19, A 29–36. Elongate and compressed. Silver; back greenish blue. Spineless fins and deeply forked tail. Large mouth with two large canines at front of upper jaw. Scales tiny. **Size:** 1 m. **Biology:** Indo-Pacific; pelagic in coastal waters, particularly near surf zone. Carnivorous, preying on small fishes.

121.2 Ladyfish or springer — *Elops machnata*
D 22–27, A 15–18. Elongate and cylindrical. Silvery with spineless dusky-yellow fins. Tail fin strongly forked. Mouth terminal and large, reaching back past the eye. Fatty adipose eyelids. **Size:** 1 m; 11 kg. **Biology:** Occurs in coastal waters and estuaries. Preys on fishes and crustaceans. Also called 'springer' as it often leaps from the water. Larvae recruit to estuaries in summer, and resemble eel leptocephalus larvae, but have forked tails.

121.3 Oxeye tarpon — *Megalops cyprinoides*
D 17–20, A 24–31. Elongate and compressed. Silver with large scales. Projecting lower jaw; no teeth. Distinctly forked tail; anal fin base much longer than that of dorsal fin. Last dorsal fin ray elongate. Fatty adipose eyelids. **Size:** 1 m. **Biology:** Indo-Pacific; coastal waters, estuaries and even fresh water. Usually solitary, it preys on small fishes. Larvae resemble eel leptocephali but have forked tails.

121.4 Milkfish — *Chanos chanos*
D 13–17, A 8–10. Large and torpedo-shaped. Silver; back greenish blue. Mouth small, terminal and toothless. Fins lack spines; large powerful, scissor-like tail. Fatty adipose eyelids. **Size:** 1.8 m; 18 kg. **Biology:** Indo-Pacific; coastal waters, estuaries and bays. Feeds on detritus and small invertebrates on mud or sandbanks. Spawns at sea; ribbon-like larvae recruit to estuaries, where they metamorphose into juveniles. Attains 15 years.

121.5 Bonefish — *Albula glossodonta*
D 15–19, A7–9. Elongate and cylindrical. Silvery green with lines along body; yellow marks at corners of mouth and bases of pectoral and pelvic fins. Mouth located below conical snout. Spineless fins; forked tail. Adipose fatty eyelids. **Size:** 1 m; 9 kg. **Biology:** Western Indian Ocean; coastal waters in sandy mangroves and estuarine habitats. Preys on crustaceans. Larvae resemble eel leptocephali, but have forked tails.

121.6 Hardyhead silverside — *Atherinomorus lacunosus*
DIV–VII + I 8–11, AI 12–17. Small and translucent; distinct silver stripe along sides. Notch on preopercle edge. Two dorsal fins. **Size:** 15 cm. **Biology:** Indo-Pacific; occurs in large schools in coastal waters. Feeds on zooplankton.

121.7 Cape silverside — *Atherina breviceps*
DV–VIII + I 11–15, AI 15–18. Small, translucent, with an obvious lateral silver stripe. Scales with small black dots. Two dorsal fins. **Size:** 11 cm. **Biology:** Endemic; shoals in surf zones and lower reaches of estuaries. Matures at 4 cm; breeds in spring and summer. Eggs have long sticky filaments for attachment to sand or vegetation.

121.8 Indian lizardfish — *Synodus indicus*
D 11–13, A 9–11. Slender and cylindrical; mouth extends past eye. Body dusky pink with horizontal pale blue stripes and blotches; two short black lines on gill cover. Small adipose fin on dorsal surface before tail. **Size:** 33 cm. **Biology:** Indian Ocean; sandy areas to depths of 100 m. Lies camouflaged on seafloor and ambushes prey.

121.9 Redband lizardfish — *Synodus variegatus*
D 11–13, A 8–10. Slender and cylindrical; mouth with needle-like teeth, and extends past the eye. Red-brown blotches along flanks and some saddle-like blotches. Small adipose fin on dorsal surface before tail. **Size:** 33 cm. **Biology:** Indo-Pacific; coral reefs and sandy areas near reefs. Lies camouflaged on bottom and snaps up small fish and crustaceans as they swim unsuspectingly by.

121.1

121.2

121.3

121.4

121.5

121.6

121.7

121.8

121.9

PLATE 122

Catfishes, kingklip, hakes & anglerfishes

122.1 Natal seacatfish
Galeichthys sp.

DII 7, A17–21. Robust, with dark dorsal surface and flanks. Scaleless body covered in mucus. Head compressed; six barbels on lower jaw. Dorsal and pectoral fins each bear a serrated spine. The Natal seacatfish is a newly recognised, unnamed species. **Size:** 45 cm. **Biology:** Endemic; shallow coastal waters. Spines inflict painful injuries. Male carries fertilised eggs in his mouth until they hatch and lose their yolk sacs. **SIMILAR SPECIES**: *G. feliceps*, the white seacatfish (Swakopmund–East London; common in Eastern Cape estuaries), is paler with a white belly. *G. ater*, the black seacatfish (south coast but not in estuaries), is dark brown; tail less deeply forked, with rounded lobes.

122.2 Striped eel-catfish
Plotosus lineatus

DI 4 + 80–90, A 58–82. Eel-shaped. Black, with 2–3 yellowish stripes from snout to tail. Mouth surrounded by eight barbels. Second dorsal fin and anal fin joined to pointed tail fin. Dorsal and pectoral fins bear a serrated spine. **Size:** 32 cm. **Biology:** Indo-Pacific; shallow coastal waters. Juveniles congregate in dense, ball-like schools. Omnivorous. **SIMILAR SPECIES**: *P. nkunga*, the endemic eel-catfish, lacks horizontal stripes.

122.3 Kingklip
Genypterus capensis

Elongate and eel-like. Mottled pink and brown. Dorsal, tail and anal fins joined; pelvic fin reduced to a pair of rays. Very small scales. **Size:** 1.6 m; 20 kg. **Biology:** Endemic. Bottom-dwelling to depths of 500 m. Preys on fish and invertebrates. Attains 20 years. Sexually mature at 50–60 cm (4–6 years). Favoured table fish, commanding a high price.

122.4 Shallow-water hake
Merluccius capensis

D 10–12 + 38–43, A 37–41. Elongate, silvery-grey, with white belly. Fins lack spines and tail fin truncate. Eyes large; teeth sharply pointed. **Size:** 1.4 m; 19 kg. **Biology:** Endemic; bottom-dwelling to depths of 500 m. Migrates into mid-water at night to feed on fish and crustaceans; cannibalistic on small hakes. Attains age of 15 years. Spawns in spring. An important commercial species trawled on the west coast. **SIMILAR SPECIES**: *M. paradoxus*, the deep-water hake, is almost identical, but has more vertebrae and dark spots on the gill arches. As its name implies, occurs in deeper water than *M. capensis*.

122.5 Sargassum fish
Histrio histrio

DI + I + I 11–13, A 7–8. Globular body. Colour variable, but often mottled brown. Many skin flaps and filaments on head and body. First dorsal spine modified into fleshy fishing lure (called an esca). Pectoral fins have limb-like appearance. **Size:** 20 cm. **Biology:** Circumglobal; usually associated with clumps of floating *Sargassum* seaweed.

122.6 Painted angler
Antennarius pictus

DI + I + I 11–13, A 7–8. Globular body. Colour variable but generally brown, with irregular dark and white patches. Many skin flaps and filaments on head and body; skin has tiny prickles. **Size:** 24 cm. **Biology:** Indo-Pacific; inhabits shallow reefs. Uses modified first dorsal spine as a fishing rod to attract small fishes, which it then swiftly engulfs with its large mouth. Produce rafts of mucus-coated eggs.

122.7 Giant angler
Antennarius commersoni

DI + I + I 12–13, A 8. Globular body. Colour varies, often assuming that of surrounding rocks or sponges. First dorsal spine modified to form fleshy fishing lure (esca); second dorsal spine curved backwards and encased in thick skin. **Size:** 33 cm. **Biology:** Indo-Pacific; inhabits shallow reefs. Uses its bait to attract small fishes, which it swiftly engulfs in its large mouth. Produces rafts of mucus-coated eggs.

122.8 Snakehead toadfish
Batrichthys apiatus

DIII + 18–20, A 14–17. Small; cylindrical and compressed. Buff-brown; irregular blotchy, dark brown vertical bars extending onto the dorsal and anal fins. Skin loosely attached to head, body and fins. Network of fine ridges on head; four spines on gill cover. Small tentacles around mouth. **Size:** 10 cm. **Biology:** Endemic; found in tidal pools. Makes a loud grating noise when intruded upon.

122.1

122.2

122.3

122.4

122.5

122.6

122.7

122.8

PLATE 123

Scorpionfishes & gurnards

123.1 False Jacopever
Sebastes capensis

DXII 13–14, AIII 6. Robust; numerous spines on gill cover and top of head. Reddish brown with 5–6 pale spots along back near dorsal fin. **Size:** 40 cm. **Biology:** Western Cape and the islands of Gough and Tristan da Cunha; deep rocky reefs. **SIMILAR SPECIES:** *Helicolenus dactylopterus*, the jacopever, is reddish with darker vertical bars and has 12 dorsal spines and five anal spines.

123.2 Smallscale scorpionfish
Scorpaenopsis oxycephala

DXII 9, AIII 5. Skin flaps and tentacles decorate the head and body. Colour variable. Upper spine on gill cover is not split. **Size:** 30 cm. **Biology:** Indo-Pacific; coral reefs to depth of 35 m. Usually well camouflaged and preys on small fish and invertebrates. Several similar species in region.

123.3 Popeyed scorpionfish
Rhinopias eschmeyeri

DXII 9, AIII 5. Compressed body. Highly variable in colour. Eyes set high up on head; large skin flap over eye. Snout depressed. **Size:** 20 cm. **Biology:** Indo-Pacific; coral reefs and rocky areas to depth of 30 m. Usually well camouflaged.

123.4 Paperfish
Taenianotus triacanthus

DXII 10–11, AIII 5–6. Compressed head and body; leaflike. Variable in colour; scales reduced. High dorsal fin. **Size:** 10 cm. **Biology:** Indo-Pacific; coral reefs and sandy areas to depth of 135 m. Usually well camouflaged.

123.5 Devil firefish
Pterois miles

DXIII 9–11, AIII 6. Body reddish with many white crossbars; dark spots on soft dorsal, anal and tail fins. Pectoral fins (13–15 rays) and sharp dorsal spines extremely long. **Size:** 30 cm. **Biology:** Indo-Pacific; coral and rocky reefs. Juveniles often in tidal pools. Feeds on crabs, shrimps and fish by extending the pectoral fins like a net and engulfing prey with a lunge. Spines venomous: cause painful wounds. **SIMILAR SPECIES:** *P. antennata*, the antenna firefish, has a pair of long banded tentacles above the eyes and 12 dorsal spines. *P. russellii*, the plaintail firefish, has numerous thin bars on body and no spots on dorsal, anal or tail fins. Note that there is some uncertainty in taxonomy of this genus.

123.6 Radial firefish
Pterois radiata

DXII–XIII 11, AIII 5–6. Reddish body with 5–6 broad dark bars edged with white; horizontal bar on tail peduncle. Pectoral fins (16 rays) and dorsal spines extremely long. No spots on dorsal, anal and tail fins. **Size:** 20 cm. **Biology:** Indo-Pacific; coral reefs. Spines are venomous and can cause painful wounds.

123.7 Bluefin gurnard
Chelidonichthys kumu

DIX–X + 15–16, A 14–16. Elongate; large head encased in bony plates. Pectoral fins large, strikingly blue-edged with three rays that are not united by a web. Row of small spines on each side of dorsal fin. **Size:** 60 cm. **Biology:** Indo-Pacific; bottom-dweller over sand to depth of 150 m. Free pectoral rays act as feelers in the search for prey. **SIMILAR SPECIES:** *C. capensis*, the Cape gurnard, is endemic. It does not have a blue edge to pectorals and is wider between the eyes.

123.8 Stonefish
Synanceia verrucosa

DXII–XIII 5–7, AIII 5–6. Squat, warty body with large head. Row of sharp, grooved dorsal spines with poison sacs located at their bases. **Size:** 35 cm. **Biology:** Indo-Pacific; shallow reefs, rubble and sandy areas. Solitary, sedentary, cryptic predator. Highly venomous and wounds from this fish are often fatal. Immersing the wound in extremely hot water to denature the protein poison is recommended.

123.9 Bartail flathead
Platycephalus indicus

DIX–X + 13–14, A 13. Elongate; very flat head with smooth bony ridges. Mouth large; lower jaw longer than upper. Brownish; tail yellow or white with 2–3 horizontal black crossbars. **Size:** 1 m; 4 kg. **Biology:** Indo-Pacific; estuaries and shallow sandy areas. Lies camouflaged on bottom and lunges at prey. Matures at 45 cm; spawns winter and spring.

123.1

123.2

123.3

123.4

123.5

123.6

123.7

123.8

123.9

PLATE 124

Halfbeaks, seahorses, pipefishes & needlefishes

Syngnathiform fishes include many highly specialised and interesting species. Among them are the pipefishes and seahorses, which are protected by bony plates arranged in a series of rings that encase the body. Their snouts are tubular and their tails are often prehensile.

124.1 Tropical halfbeak   *Hyporhamphus affinis*

D 15–17, A 15–17. Elongate and silver. Long, needle-like lower jaw and scaly, short, triangular upper jaw. Dorsal and ventral fins set far back and lack spines. Tail fin forked with lower lobe longer than upper lobe. **Size:** 26 cm. **Biology:** Indo-Pacific; pelagic around reefs. Feeds on plankton by skimming the open beak along the surface. Eggs have long filamentous strands for attachment to floating objects or seaweed. **SIMILAR SPECIES:** *H. capensis*, the Cape halfbeak, which is endemic, frequents estuaries and has a weakly forked tail. *Hemiramphus far*, the spotted halfbeak, has black spots along its flanks and no scales on the upper jaw.

124.2 Shrimpfish or razorfish   *Aeoliscus punctulatus*

DIII + 10–11, A 12–13. Highly compressed head and body; long snout. Bony plates with sharp ventral edges. Peculiar fin arrangement; dorsal fin located at end of body and tail fin displaced ventrally. **Size:** 20 cm. **Biology:** Western Indian Ocean; shallow coastal waters along edges of reefs. Has characteristic head-down swimming position. Feeds on planktonic crustaceans.

124.3 Knysna seahorse   *Hippocampus capensis*

D 16–18, A 3–4. Ring-like plates cover body; no dorsal crown. Tapering, prehensile tail. Single dorsal fin and no anal or tail fins. **Size:** 8 cm. **Biology:** Endemic; only Knysna, Keurbooms, Swartvlei and Kleinbrak estuaries. Matures at 6 cm (one year) and male bears young in ventral pouch. Feeds on small crustaceans. Several other species of seahorses found in Indo-Pacific region.

124.4 Longsnout pipefish   *Syngnathus temminckii*

D 33–42, A 3. Elongate and slender (124.4). Body covered by 54–64 ring-like plates. Tubular mouth at end of long snout (124.4a). Small fin at end of tapering tail. Colour varies with habitat. **Size:** 32 cm. **Biology:** Endemic; estuaries, often associated with eelgrass or sago pondweed (as in this photograph). Matures at 12 cm; breeds in summer and male carries eggs in an underslung pouch. Feeds on zooplankton and benthic crustaceans. Previously known as *S. ater*.

124.5 Trumpetfish   *Aulostomus chinensis*

DVIII–XIII + III 23–27, AIII 23–26. Elongate and compressed. Long, tube-like snout; small barbel at tip of lower jaw. Row of short, isolated dorsal spines along back. Dorsal and anal fins of equal size; positioned well back on body. Colour variable. **Size:** 50 cm. **Biology:** Indo-Pacific; coral reefs. Usually solitary; feeds on small fish and crustaceans. **SIMILAR SPECIES:** *Fistularia commersonii*, the smooth flutemouth, is more cylindrical, does not have dorsal spines and has a long filament extending from the forked tail.

124.6 Yellowfin needlefish   *Strongylura leiura*

D 18–21, A 22–26. Elongate and cylindrical. Silvery green with black bar on cheek. Both jaws elongated into slender beak with rows of pointed teeth. **Size:** 80 cm. **Biology:** Indo-Pacific; coastal waters. Usually seen at the surface, where it harries small fishes. **SIMILAR SPECIES:** *Tylosurus crocodilus*, the crocodile needlefish, has similarly long upper and lower jaws, but has 21–24 dorsal rays and a fleshy keel on peduncle of tail fin. *Ablennes hians*, the garfish, also has elongate upper and lower jaws, but is distinguished by marked blotches or vertical bars in at least the rear part of the body. Worldwide in tropical and subtropical waters.

124.1

124.2

124.3

124.4

124.4a

124.5

124.6

PLATE 125

Squirrelfishes, flagtail, thornfishes, glassies & kin

125.1 Crown squirrelfish — *Sargocentron diadema*

DXI 12–14, AIV 8–10. Red body with thin horizontal silvery-white stripes. Stout spine on gill cover. Prominent fin spines; black membrane between dorsal fin spines. Large eyes. **Size:** 20 cm. **Biology:** Indo-Pacific; coral reefs to 30 m. Nocturnal; hides in caves during day and feeds at night on benthic invertebrates. **SIMILAR SPECIES:** *S. caudimaculatum*, the tailspot squirrelfish (south to the Eastern Cape), has uniformly red fins and body, and its scales are silver-edged.

125.2 Blotcheye soldier — *Myripristis murdjan*

DXI 12–15, AIV 11–13. Oblong red body with black edge to gill cover. Prominent fin spines; dark red fins edged with white. Rough scales. Large eyes. **Size:** 25 cm. **Biology:** Indo-Pacific; coral reefs to 50 m. Nocturnal; feeds on crustaceans and small fishes. **SIMILAR SPECIES:** *M. berndti*, the bigscale soldier (south to Aliwal Shoal), has a yellow outer half to the first dorsal fin and a pale pink tailfin. *M. kuntee*, the epaulette soldier (south to Aliwal Shoal), has a yellow outer half to the otherwise red first dorsal fin, and a dark red tail fin.

125.3 John Dory — *Zeus faber*

DIX–XI 22–24, AIV 20–23. Compressed and oval; mouth large and protrusile. Prominent black blotch below lateral line. Dorsal spines elongate; large pelvic fin. Spiked plates along base of dorsal and anal fins. Spiny scutes along belly between pelvic and anal fins. **Size:** 90 cm; 8 kg. **Biology:** Circumglobal; continental shelf and slope to depth of 400 m. Feeds on fish and crustaceans. Attains 15 years.

125.4 Barred flagtail — *Kuhlia mugil*

DX 9–11, AIII 9–11. Small and silver; two distinct spines on gill cover. Single dorsal fin; five dark stripes on the tail fin. **Size:** 20 cm. **Biology:** Indo-Pacific; common on reefs in KwaZulu-Natal. Juveniles frequent tidal pools. Feeds on crustaceans.

125.5 Thornfish — *Terapon jarbua*

DXI–XII 9–11, AIII 7–10. Silver with 3–4 curved brown stripes extending from head across body and onto tail. Two prominent spines on each side of gill cover. **Size:** 33 cm. **Biology:** Indo-Pacific; common in estuaries. Characteristically arches body to expose spines when captured. Eats scales off live fish as part of its diet. Also known as 'pest of St Lucia'.

125.6 Crescent-tail bigeye — *Priacanthus hamrur*

DX 13–15, AIII 13–16. Compressed and silvery red. Large eyes, upturned mouth and scales on gill cover. Crescent-shaped tail. Dorsal, anal and pelvic fins dusky. **Size:** 45 cm. **Biology:** Indo-Pacific; coral and rocky reefs to depth of 250 m. Nocturnal.

125.7 Smooth glassy — *Ambassis natalensis*

DVIII 9–11, AIII 9–11. Translucent and silvery. Deeply notched dorsal fin; membrane between anterior dorsal spines blackish. Gill cover smooth except for a few spines at angle. **Size:** 10 cm. **Biology:** Western Indian Ocean; completes life cycle in estuaries. Shoals; feeds mainly on zooplankton. Matures at 4 cm; spawns in spring. **SIMILAR SPECIES:** *A. dussumieri*, the bald glassy, has a serrate lower gill cover, interrupted lateral line and spine below nostril.

125.1

125.2

125.3

125.4

125.5

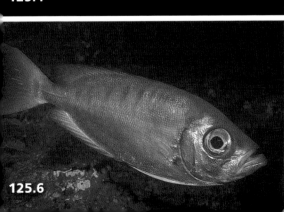

125.6

125.7

PLATE 126

Rockcods

Fishes in the family Serranidae occur worldwide on tropical and subtropical reefs. They include the small colourful anthiine basslets and goldies, and the larger solitary epinepheline rockcods, of which there are about 50 species in the region. Most rockcods have rounded tails. Many are hermaphroditic – some are protogynous, changing sex from female to male, while others are protandrous, being male first and then becoming female. All are slow-growing and vulnerable to overfishing.

126.1 Coral rockcod — *Cephalopholis miniata*

DIX 14–16, AIII 9. Striking red-orange colour with blue spots over body, head and tail, dorsal and anal fins. **Size:** 40 cm. **Biology:** Indo-Pacific; coral and rocky reefs to 150 m. Males maintain harem of females. Preys on fish and crustaceans.

126.2 Duskyfin rockcod — *Cephalopholis nigripinnus*

DIX 14–16, AIII 9. Head and body red with small orange spots. Tail and rear part of pectoral, anal and dorsal fins dark. **Size:** 25 cm. **Biology:** Indian Ocean: coral reefs to 40 m. Little known about biology.

126.3 Tiger rockcod — *Epinephelus posteli*

DXI 16, AIII 9. Head and body covered with small reddish spots. Thick caudal peduncle. Wavy dark stripes on spinous dorsal fin. **Size:** 1 m; 10 kg. **Biology:** Western Indian Ocean; coral reefs to 50 m. Knowledge about its biology is sparse.

126.4 Catface rockcod — *Epinephelus andersoni*

DXI 13–15, AIII 8. Robust and elongate. Body brown with dark spots that extend over the dorsal and tail fins; three distinctive black stripes across head. Large mouth. **Size:** 87 cm; 9 kg. **Biology:** Endemic; rocky areas to 70 m, especially between Durban and Richards Bay. Attains age of 11 years. Matures at 50 cm (four years). Spawns in summer in KwaZulu-Natal; juveniles found in tidal pools.

126.5 Yellowbelly rockcod — *Epinephelus marginatus*

DXI 14–16, AIII 8. Robust; large mouth. Brown with distinct yellow belly; irregular greenish-white blotches on body and dorsal fin. Pale edges to fins. **Size:** 1.2 m; 35 kg. **Biology:** A mainly Atlantic species; rocky reefs down to 200 m. Also occurs from Angola northwards. Attains age of 24 years. Females mature at 60 cm (6–8 years) and change sex to male at 80–87 cm (15–17 years). Spawns in spring and summer; juveniles occur in tidal pools and gullies. Preys on small fishes and bottom-dwelling invertebrates. High site fidelity.

126.6 Brindle bass — *Epinephelus lanceolatus*

DXI 14–16, AIII 8. Large and robust. Adults brown with black spots on fins; juveniles with irregular brown and yellow mottling that extends over fins. Broad head; large mouth. Fin spines shorter than rays. **Size:** Can reach an enormous size: 2.7 m; 300 kg. **Biology:** Indo-Pacific; estuaries, coral and rocky reefs, wrecks and caves to depth of 100 m. Feeds on crustaceans and fishes. Territorial and largest of rockcods.

126.7 Malabar rockcod — *Epinephelus malabaricus*

DXI 14–16, A III 8. Elongate and robust. Grey-brown with broad vertical bars and numerous small black spots over head, body and fins. Head length greater than body depth. **Size:** 1.2 m; 25 kg. **Biology:** Indo-Pacific; widespread through range of habitats to depth of 150 m. Feeds on fish and crustaceans.

126.8 Potato bass — *Epinephelus tukula*

DXI 14–15, AIII 8. Large and robust; grey-brown with dark ovate blotches over body and fins. Mouth huge. **Size:** 2.2 m; 100 kg. **Biology:** Indo-Pacific; rocky and coral reefs to depths of 230 m. Solitary, territorial, top predator that can be aggressive to divers if provoked. Feeds on fishes and crustaceans.

126.1

126.2

126.3

126.4

126.5

126.6

126.7

126.8

PLATE 127

127.1 Yellowedge lyretail   *Variola louti*
DIX 13–14, AIII 8. Striking red-orange fish with purple spots over body and fins. Tail fin lunate; rear margin of all fins yellow. **Size:** 80 cm; 12 kg. **Biology:** Indo-Pacific; coral reefs to depth of 50 m. Preys on reef fishes and crustaceans.

127.2 Whiteblotch koester   *Acanthistius* sp.
DXI–XIII 15–17, AIII 7–8. Body with irregular brown blotches and five white blotches along base of dorsal fin. Many smaller orange spots over body. **Size:** 35 cm. **Biology:** Endemic; lives in rocky areas from shallow subtidal to depth of 25 m. Preys on crabs and small fish. Still to be scientifically described and named. **SIMILAR SPECIES:** *A. sebastoides*, the endemic koester, is very similar but has a beige body covered in bright orange spots. Tail and anal fin dark; pelvic fin yellow.

127.3 Sea goldie   *Pseudanthias squamipinnis*
DX 15–17, AIII 6–7. Females are orange-gold with an iridescent blue stripe below eyes; males reddish with elongated third dorsal spine and two red spots on pectoral fin. Tail fin lunate. **Size:** 10 cm. **Biology:** Indo-Pacific; schools on coral reefs. Changes sex from female to male. Males maintain harems. Feeds on zooplankton. Very popular with marine aquarists.

127.4 Sixstripe soapfish   *Grammistes sexlineatus*
DVII 13–14, AII 9. Similar in shape to rockcods but with fewer spines in fins. Dark brown with horizontal yellow stripes across body. **Size:** 25 cm. **Biology:** Indo-Pacific; inhabits reefs and tidal pools. Solitary and nocturnal in habit. Uses slimy toxic mucus produced by the skin to deter predators.

127.5 Ninestripe cardinal   *Apogon taeniophorus*
DVII + I 9, AII 8. Small and robust; two dorsal fins. Large eyes and mouth. Four horizontal black stripes and one along dorsal mid-line. **Size:** 8 cm. **Biology:** Indian Ocean; coral reefs. Nocturnal. Male carries the fertilised eggs in his mouth until they hatch. **SIMILAR SPECIES:** *A. angustatus*, the broadstriped cardinal, has five stripes and a black tail spot. *A. cookii*, the blackbanded cardinal, has six stripes and an obvious black tail spot.

127.6 Spinyhead cardinal   *Apogon kallopterus*
DVII + I 9, AII 8. Small and robust; two dorsal fins. Large eyes and mouth. Dark stripe from snout through eye to tail; black spot on tail peduncle. **Size:** 15 cm. **Biology:** Indo-Pacific; coral reefs. Nocturnal. Male carries the fertilised eggs in his mouth until they hatch.

127.7 Flower cardinal   *Apogon fleurieu*
DVII + 19, AII 8. Small and robust; two dorsal fins. Large eyes and mouth. Conspicuous blue-edged band across head. Dark band around tail base. **Size:** 10 cm. **Biology:** Indo-Pacific; coral reefs. Nocturnal. Male carries fertilised eggs in his mouth until they hatch. **SIMILAR SPECIES:** *A. aereus*, the bandtail cardinal (Durban northwards), has a black band around tail peduncle, which is hourglass shaped.

127.1

127.2

127.4

127.5

127.3

127.6

127.7

PLATE 128

Rubberlips & grunters

Nineteen species of the family Haemulidae have been recorded from reefs and estuaries in southern Africa. Grunters rub their pharyngeal teeth together after being captured, producing a characteristic sound, from which they acquire their common name. They are an important source of food for people in the tropics.

128.1 Dusky rubberlip   *Plectorhinchus chubbi*

DXI 16–17, AIII 7–8. Robust and oblong. Bronze-grey with paler undersides. Eyes large; lips become fleshy with age. **Size:** 85 cm; 10 kg. **Biology:** Western Indian Ocean; frequents reefs down to 80 m. Feeds on bottom-dwelling invertebrates and small fish. Groups of juveniles often associated with floating seaweed.

128.2 Whitebarred rubberlip   *Plectorhinchus playfairi*

DXII 19–20, AIII 7. Robust and oblong. Dark with four white vertical bars; pale belly. Fins dark; lips pink and fleshy. **Size:** 90 cm; 7 kg. **Biology:** Western Indian Ocean; coral reefs to 80 m. Solitary. Feeds on bottom-dwelling invertebrates.

128.3 Spotted grunter   *Pomadasys commersonnii*

DXI 14–15, AIII 9–10. Elongate with a long sloping forehead, serrated gill covers and small protrusible mouth. Sides and dorsal surface covered with dark spots. No spots on head. Small juveniles lack spots and have only two anal spines. **Size:** 90 cm; 10 kg. **Biology:** Indian Ocean; shallow sandy areas and estuaries. Sought-after by anglers, especially during summer 'grunter runs' in KwaZulu-Natal. Often seen with tails waving out of the water on shallow banks where they feed on sand- or mudprawns. Attains age of 15 years and matures at 33–40 cm (three years). Spawns in KwaZulu-Natal during spring and early summer. Juveniles occur only in estuaries.

128.4 Pinky or piggy   *Pomadasys olivaceum*

DXII 15–17, AIII 11–13. Silvery olive with a distinct dark blotch on gill cover. **Size:** 30 cm. **Biology:** Western Indian Ocean; sand and reefs to depths of 90 m. One of the smallest grunters and is particularly common in inshore waters, where it occurs in large shoals. Important prey item in the diets of large predators such as sharks and dolphins. Spawns all year round. **SIMILAR SPECIES:** *P. maculatus*, the saddle grunter, has several saddle-like crossbars along body, with a particularly noticeable one on the nape.

128.5 Javelin grunter   *Pomadasys kaakan*

DXII 13–15, AIII 7–8. Oblong, becoming more robust with age. Silver with row of dark spots along base of dorsal fin membrane. Juveniles have five dark vertical bars extending down flanks and a dark patch on the gill cover. **Size:** 75 cm; 6 kg. **Biology:** Indo-Pacific; estuaries and offshore to 75 m in sandy or muddy areas. Bottom-feeder. Spawns in winter.

128.6 Striped grunter   *Pomadasys striatus*

DXII 13–14, AIII 6–7. Silvery brown; three distinct horizontal brown stripes, the lowest passing across the gill cover to eye. **Size:** 22 cm. **Biology:** Western Indian Ocean; forms small shoals in sandy areas and reefs down to 40 m. Eats bottom-dwelling invertebrates. **SIMILAR SPECIES:** *P. furcatum*, the grey grunter, has 6–7 stripes along the sides and is also confined to the western Indian Ocean.

128.7 Cavebass   *Dinoperca petersi*

DIX–XI 18–20, AIII 12–14. Oval; truncate tail fin. Dark brown with white specks and black band across cheek. Anterior dorsal and anal rays markedly longer than posterior ones. Scales extend onto head and fins. **Size:** 75 cm; 6 kg. **Biology:** Indian Ocean; under rocky ledges or in caves down to 75 m. Solitary and more active at night. Can make loud drumming noises when disturbed. Feeds on crustaceans.

128.1

128.2

128.3

128.4

128.5

128.6

128.7

PLATE 129

Fusiliers & snappers

The snapper family, Lutjanidae, is represented by 26 species in southern Africa. All are carnivorous. Many are vividly coloured and form shoals. They are important food fishes in the tropics.

129.1 Yellowback fusilier — *Caesio xanthonota*

DX 15, AIII 12. Elongate; vivid yellow and blue. Protrusible upper jaw and forked yellow tail. Yellow dorsal surface extends onto head. **Size:** 30 cm. **Biology:** Indo-Pacific; occurs in shoals over coral reefs. A plankton eater; often sighted by divers at Sodwana.

129.2 Blue-and-gold fusilier — *Caesio caerulaurea*

DX 14–15, AIII 11–13. Elongate; protrusible upper jaw. Dorsal surface blue; conspicuous horizontal yellow stripe across flank to head. Tail fin forked, with dark band on each lobe. **Size:** 35 cm. **Biology:** Indo-Pacific; occurs in shoals over coral reefs. Planktivorous; often seen by divers.

129.3 Green jobfish — *Aprion virescens*

DX 11, AIII 8. Sleek and elongate. Dark green to bluish dorsal surface; paler underside. Strongly forked tail; short pectoral fins. Snout blunt, grooved below nostrils. **Size:** 1.1 m; 16 kg. **Biology:** Indo-Pacific; usually found in the water column above coral or rocky reefs to 180 m. Solitary predator. Matures at 70 cm (3–4 years).

129.4 Twinspot snapper — *Lutjanus bohar*

DX 13–14, AIII 8. Robust; reddish brown with dark fins. Large mouth; prominent canines. Nostrils in a deep groove. Scales above lateral line oblique. Juveniles have two white spots below dorsal fin. **Size:** 90 cm; 13 kg. **Biology:** Indo-Pacific; coral reefs down to 70 m. Usually solitary in caves. Attains age of at least 13 years. Matures at about 45–55 cm (3–5 years). Preys on fish and invertebrates.

129.5 Bluebanded snapper — *Lutjanus kasmira*

DX 14–15, AIII 7–8. Yellow with four horizontal black-edged blue stripes across body. Pale ventrally. **Size:** 33 cm. **Biology:** Indo-Pacific; shoals over coral and rocky reefs to depths of 50 m. Preys on crustaceans, squid and fish. Matures at about 20 cm.

129.6 Speckled snapper — *Lutjanus rivulatus*

DX 15–16, AIII 8–9. Deep body; brown with silvery-blue spots on each scale. Head covered in wavy blue lines. Fins with yellow margins. Mouth with fleshy lips and conical teeth. **Size:** 80 cm; 11 kg. **Biology:** Indo-Pacific; coral and rocky reefs to 50 m. Solitary cave dweller and normally highly resident. Feeds on benthic invertebrates.

129.7 Dory snapper — *Lutjanus fulviflamma*

DX 12–14, AIII 8. Yellow; conspicuous oval black spot on lateral line below the soft dorsal fin. Head often pinkish and fins yellow. **Size:** 35 cm. **Biology:** Indo-Pacific; shoals on coral reefs to 30 m. Juveniles in estuaries, mangroves and seagrasses. **SIMILAR SPECIES**: *L. russellii*, Russell's snapper (Durban northwards), has a spot above the lateral line and usually 7–8 narrow, longitudinal stripes.

129.8 River snapper — *Lutjanus argentimaculatus*

DX 13–14, AIII 7–8. Robust; greenish grey with two blue lines under eye. Fins pinkish; tail fin truncate. Large mouth; prominent canines in both jaws. Juveniles have vertical bars. **Size:** 1 m; 17 kg. **Biology:** Indo-Pacific; estuaries and reefs down to 120 m. Spawns at sea; juveniles recruit to estuaries and frequent mangrove areas. Preys on fish and crabs.

129.9 Humpback snapper — *Lutjanus gibbus*

DX 13–14, AIII 8. Deep-bodied with steep, concave forehead. Bright red; distinct notch on gill cover. Tail, anal and soft dorsal fins dark, and all, except pectorals, fringed with white. Tail fin forked with rounded lobes; upper one larger. **Size:** 50 cm. **Biology:** Indo-Pacific; rocky and coral reefs down to 120 m. Eats invertebrates. Matures at 25–30 cm. Juveniles in seagrass beds. **SIMILAR SPECIES:** There are two other red-coloured snappers: *L. sanguineus*, the blood snapper (Port Elizabeth northwards), is scarlet with a conspicuous bump on the head and a truncate tail. *L. sebae*, the emperor snapper (Durban northwards), is also red, but has a convex head profile and 15–16 dorsal rays.

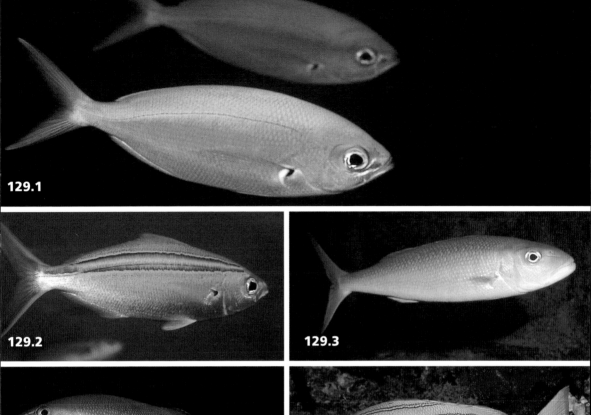

129.1

129.2

129.3

129.4

129.5

129.6

129.7

129.8

129.9

PLATE 130

Sea breams

The family Sparidae is particularly diverse in southern Africa with 41 species in our waters. Of these, 25 species are endemic. Sea breams are extremely important linefish. They often attain ages in excess of 30 years. Many are hermaphroditic: some are protandrous, changing sex from male to female, while others are protogynous, being female first and later becoming male.

130.1 King soldierbream — *Argyrops spinifer*
DXI–XII 10–11, AIII 8. Pink with blue dots on scales. Blunt, angular head with scaling between eyes, ending in a point. First two dorsal spines very small, but third to seventh spines elongate. **Size:** 70 cm; 6 kg. **Biology:** Indo-Pacific; on soft substrata to depth of 400 m. Feeds on invertebrates.

130.2 River bream — *Acanthopagrus vagus*
DXI 10–12, AIII 8. Deep-bodied, with a steep forehead and pointed snout. Silvery grey; anal fin yellow with large second spine. **Size:** 75 cm; 3 kg. **Biology:** Occurs throughout the western Indian Ocean; most commonly seen in estuaries. Spawns in estuary mouths in winter. Feeds on bottom-dwelling invertebrates. **SIMILAR SPECIES:** *A. berda*, the picnic seabream, has a convex head profile and nine rays in anal fin. It was previously confused with *A. vagus*.

130.3 Twobar bream — *Acanthopagrus bifasciatus*
DXI–XII 12–15, AIII 10–12. Deep-bodied; two black bars on head. Tail, dorsal and pectoral fins yellow. Second anal spine distinctly longer than first. **Size:** 50 cm. **Biology:** Western Indian Ocean; shallow coastal waters including estuaries. Usually solitary; little known about biology.

130.4 Fransmadam — *Boopsoidea inornata*
DXI 10–11, AIII 11. Small and deep-bodied. Silvery with bronze sheen; dark fins. Distinct lateral line and large eyes. Snout pointed; mouth small, with many fine, sharp teeth. Juveniles are bright orange in colour. **Size:** 30 cm. **Biology:** Endemic; rocky reefs to depths of 30 m. Juveniles frequent seaweed beds, particularly in summer months. Omnivorous. Regarded as pest by anglers as it nibbles bait intended for larger fish.

130.5 Carpenter — *Argyrozona argyrozona*
DXII 10, AIII 8. Moderately elongate. Silvery pink with horizontal rows of pale blue spots. Prominent canines but no molars. **Size:** 90 cm. **Biology:** Endemic; offshore reefs to depths of 200 m. Preys on fish and squid. Matures at about 30 cm; spawns on the Agulhas Bank during summer. Of commercial importance, though catch declining.

130.6 Santer — *Cheimerius nufar*
DXI–XII 10–11, AIII 8. Oval-shaped. Silvery pink; vertical bars on flanks more obvious in juveniles. Well-developed fins; third to seventh dorsal spines elongate. Anal and pelvic fins have a bluish tinge. Strong, slender canines. **Size:** 75 cm; 7 kg. **Biology:** Western Indian Ocean; reefs to a depth of 100 m. Preys on fish, squid and crustaceans. Attains age of 22 years. Sexually mature at four years (35 cm); spawns in summer. Regularly caught by ski-boat fishermen.

130.7 Englishman — *Chrysoblephus anglicus*
DXII 10, AIII 8. Deep-bodied; forehead blunt. Silvery pink with four vertical red bars. Well-developed pink fins. Mouth small; strong, slender canines. **Size:** 90 cm; 7 kg. **Biology:** Endemic; offshore reefs to depth of 120 m. Feeds on crustaceans, molluscs and fish. Attains age of 17 years. Protogynous hermaphrodite; sexually mature at seven years (40 cm).

130.1

130.2

130.3

130.4

130.5

130.6

130.7

PLATE 131

131.1 Dageraad   *Chrysoblephus cristiceps*

DXII 10, AIII 8. Deep-bodied; steep pointed head. Moderately large mouth bearing enlarged canines and several rows of molars. Red; golden sheen over the gill cover and blue mark under the eye. Characteristic dark spot at the end of the dorsal fin. Juveniles pink with dark blotches. **Size:** 70 cm; 9 kg. **Biology:** Endemic; over reefs to depths of 100 m. Preys on benthic invertebrates and small fish. Attains age of 23 years. Spawning occurs in summer. Undergoes sex change from female to male; fewer males in heavily fished areas. Declining component of commercial and recreational ski-boat catches.

131.2 Red stumpnose   *Chrysoblephus gibbiceps*

DXI–XII 10–11, AIII 7–9. Large head; steep forehead, which develops a conspicuous bump in old males. Silvery pink; 5–7 vertical red bars and numerous irregular black spots over the body. Jaws with 4–6 canines and rows of small molars. Pectoral fins long. **Size:** 75 cm; 8 kg. **Biology:** Endemic; deep reefs down to 150 m. Preys on benthic invertebrates and small fish. Matures at 35 cm; spawns in summer.

131.3 Roman   *Chrysoblephus laticeps*

DXI–XII 10–11, AIII 7–9. Robust. Scarlet-red with prominent white saddle; white blotch on the gill cover and blue line between eyes. Conspicuous canines and several rows of molars in both jaws. **Size:** 50 cm; 4 kg. **Biology:** Endemic; on rocky reefs down to 100 m. Undergoes sex change from female to male at about 30 cm. Spawns in summer; juveniles frequent shallow reefs. Attains age of 17 years. Resident benthic predator with small home range of 0.1–0.3 hectares.

131.4 Slinger   *Chrysoblephus puniceus*

DXII 10, AIII 8. Deep-bodied; steep forehead and small mouth. Silvery pink; conspicuous blue bar below eyes and iridescent blue spots on the body. **Size:** 85 cm; 4 kg. **Biology:** Endemic; shoals on deep reefs to 130 m. Attains age of 11 years. Matures at 25 cm; spawning occurs in spring. Undergoes sex change from female to male. Sex ratio varies, depending on the level of exploitation, with up to 100 females per male in heavily fished areas. Extremely important in the linefisheries of KwaZulu-Natal and Mozambique.

131.5 False Englishman   *Chrysoblephus lophus*

DXI 10, AIII 9. Deep-bodied; steep forehead with a pitted bony area between the eyes. Silvery pink; 5–8 vertical red bars. Third to sixth dorsal spines elongated. Pectoral fins long; tail fin deeply forked. **Size:** 50 cm; 3 kg. **Biology:** Endemic; offshore reefs down to 150 m. Benthic carnivore. **SIMILAR SPECIES:** Distinguished from similar Englishman, *C. anglicus* (130.7), by more vertical bars and longer dorsal spines.

131.6 White karanteen   *Crenidens crenidens*

DXI 10–11, AIII 10. Silvery grey with several faint horizontal stripes. Mouth small; many multi-pointed incisors. Anal fin often yellow. **Size:** 30 cm. **Biology:** Western Indian Ocean; shallow bays and estuaries, especially Durban harbour. Omnivorous, feeding on seaweeds and invertebrates.

131.7 Poenskop   *Cymatoceps nasutus*

DXII 10, AIII 8. Large and robust; snout rounded, becoming white and fleshy with age. Four prominent canines in upper jaw and six in lower jaw; two rows of rounded molars in each jaw. Greyish black; juveniles greenish brown with white blotches. **Size:** 1.2 m; 40 kg. **Biology:** Endemic; rocky reefs to 100 m depth. Grows slowly; attains age of 45 years. Matures at 55 cm (10 years); spawns in winter. Changes sex from female to male at about 70 cm. Adults territorial benthic predators; juveniles frequent shallow weedy areas. Stock depleted.

131.1

131.2

131.3

131.4

131.5

131.6

131.7

PLATE 132

132.1 Zebra
Diplodus hottentotus

DXI 12–13, AIII 11. Oval-shaped. Six conspicuous vertical black bars, one of which runs through the eye. Mouth surrounded by fleshy lips. Single row of sharp incisors and several rows of molars in each jaw. Juveniles have black pelvic fins. **Size:** 60 cm; 6 kg. **Biology:** Endemic; adults resident in rocky areas down to 60 m. Omnivorous. Attains age of 33 years. Sexual maturity at 30 cm (six years). Spawns in spring and summer; juveniles occur in tidal pools.

132.2 Blacktail
Diplodus capensis

DXII 14–15, AIII 13–14. Oval-shaped. Silver with a marked black patch on the tail peduncle. Juveniles have 8–10 thin vertical crossbars. Mouth small; eight incisors and several rows of molars in each jaw. **Size:** 45 cm; 3 kg. **Biology:** Endemic; ubiquitous in a range of shallow habitats. Juveniles common in tidal pools and estuaries. Attains 21 years of age. Spawns from 25 cm (three years). Spawning occurs throughout the year with a peak in late winter and spring. Omnivorous. A fine, light-tackle angling species.

132.3 Janbruin
Gymnocrotaphus curvidens

DX 11–12, AIII 9–10. Robust. Brown with conspicuous blue eyes. Protruding curved incisors and smaller conical teeth in each jaw. **Size:** 50 cm; 3 kg. **Biology:** Endemic; shallow rocky reefs to depth of 30 m. Nowhere abundant and usually solitary; omnivorous.

132.4 White steenbras
Lithognathus lithognathus

DXI 10, AIII 8–9. Large and elongate; long sloping forehead and pig-like snout. Head longer than the length of the pectoral fin. Silver with dark bars along flanks. **Size:** 1 m; 30 kg. **Biology:** Endemic; sandy beaches and estuaries. Preys on sand-dwelling benthic invertebrates. Attains age of 30 years. Spawns at 65 cm (six years). Adults undertake spawning migrations up the east coast during winter. Juveniles recruit to estuarine nursery areas in spring. Stock collapsed. **SIMILAR SPECIES:** *L. aureti,* the west coast steenbras (Namibia and Angola), is a deeper-bodied fish with a proportionally shorter head (equal to, or less than, pectoral fin length).

132.5 Sand steenbras
Lithognathus mormyrus

DXI 12–13, AIII 10–11. Small and elongate. Silver with 12–14 vertical brown bars. Mouth protrusible; small teeth. **Size:** 50 cm; 1 kg. **Biology:** Eastern Atlantic; abundant in surf zones and to depths of 30 m in sandy bays. Feeds on sand-dwelling benthic invertebrates. Spawns in summer; juveniles common in Eastern Cape surf zones.

132.6 Red tjor-tjor or sand soldier
Pagellus bellottii natalensis

DXII 10–11, AIII 10. Pink; rows of small iridescent blue spots. Mouth small; sharp conical incisors and two series of small molars. **Size:** 35 cm. **Biology:** Western Indian Ocean; shoals over deep sandy areas. Juveniles common in shallow south coast bays. Preys on small benthic invertebrates; important in the diet of larger coastal predators. Spawns in spring; larvae common in plankton along the east coast.

132.7 Dane
Porcostoma dentata

DXIII 10–11, AIII 8–9. Plump and oblong. Orange-red; purple band between the eyes and red blotch at the base of pectoral fin. Jaws with 4–6 projecting canines. **Size:** 30 cm. **Biology:** Endemic; over reefs in depths of 20–120 m. Feeds on reef invertebrates. Spawning occurs in spring. Little known about this species.

132.1

132.2

132.3

132.4

132.5

132.6

132.7

PLATE 133

133.1 Hottentot
Pachymetopon blochii

DX–XI 11–12, AII1 10. Bronzy grey with dark fins. Mouth small; five rows of incisors in each jaw but no molars. **Size:** 50 cm; 3 kg. **Biology:** Endemic; small shoals in kelp beds and over reefs. Omnivorous. Attains age of 12 years. Matures at 25 cm (five years); spawning occurs throughout year. Caught by commercial linefisheries in Western Cape.

133.2 Blue hottentot
Pachymetopon aeneum

DX–XI 11–13, AIII 10. Silvery bronze with blue sheen; head blue. Mouth small with no molars; five rows of incisors in each jaw. Scales on gill cover; long pectoral fins. **Size:** 60 cm; 5 kg. **Biology:** Endemic; reefs to 80 m depth. Juveniles occur in shallower areas. Feeds on sessile invertebrates. Attains age of 12 years. Matures at 25 cm and females change sex to male. Spawns in summer.

133.3 Bronze bream
Pachymetopon grande

DXI 11, AIII 10–11. Plump and oval-shaped. Brown with smallish head and bump over the eyes. No molars; five rows of incisors in each jaw. No scales on front of gill cover. **Size:** 70 cm; 5 kg. **Biology:** Endemic; occurs in rough, shallow water along rocky shores. Feeds on seaweeds and associated invertebrates. Attains age of 38 years. Matures at 35 cm (five years); spawning occurs in late summer and autumn.

133.4 German
Polyamblydon germanum

DXI 11–12, AIII 10–11. Greyish blue; snout profile concave. Single row of curved incisors and rows of small molars. **Size:** 50 cm; 2.5 kg. **Biology:** Endemic; reefs to 50 m. Biology little known. **SIMILAR SPECIES:** Often confused with bronze bream, *Pachymetopon grande* (133.3), and blue hottentot, *Pachymetopon aeneum* (133.2), but these have five rows of incisors.

133.5 Red steenbras
Petrus rupestris

DXI 10–11, AIII 8. Large and robust; red to copper-coloured. Mouth large; prominent canines in both jaws. Juveniles orange with red spot on tail peduncle. **Size:** 2 m; 70 kg. **Biology:** Endemic; over deep reefs to 160 m. Powerful predator on octopus and fishes. Long-lived, exceeding 33 years in age. Sexual maturity attained at 60 cm (seven years); spawning aggregations occur in spring off Eastern Cape coast, north of East London. Juveniles occur over shallow reefs. A legendary angling species but stock depleted. Liver is poisonous due to high vitamin A content.

133.6 Scotsman
Polysteganus praeorbitalis

DXII 10, AIII 8. Large; steep forehead and deep body tapering towards the tail. Pinkish red; numerous blue dots on sides and blue lines encircling the small eyes. Large mouth; 4–6 canines in each jaw and several rows of smaller conical teeth. **Size:** 90 cm; 10 kg. **Biology:** Endemic; offshore reefs from 50–120 m. Juveniles on inshore reefs. Exceeds 13 years in age. Sexual maturity attained at 40 cm (six years). Changes sex from female to male. The stock of this powerful solitary predator has been severely depleted.

133.7 Seventy-four
Polysteganus undulosus

DXII 10, AIII 8–9. Pinkish-red; 4–6 iridescent horizontal blue stripes along sides. Conspicuous black blotch above the pectoral fin. 4–6 canines and many small teeth in each jaw. **Size:** 1 m; 14 kg. **Biology:** Endemic; deep reefs to 200 m. Attains age of 20 years. Matures at 65 cm (eight years); spawns in spring. The stock is severely depleted due to overfishing of spawning aggregations in the 1960s and is currently totally protected.

133.8 Panga
Pterogymnus laniarius

DXII 10, AIII 8. Pink; several horizontal lines of fine, blue spots on flanks. Fleshy, furry lips; 4–6 canines in each jaw. **Size:** 45 cm; 1 kg. **Biology:** Endemic; reefs and sand to depths of 230 m. Common on Agulhas Bank. Carnivorous on crustaceans, squid and small fishes. Attains age of 16 years. Matures at 25 cm (five years); spawns throughout year. Important component of commercial line and trawl fisheries.

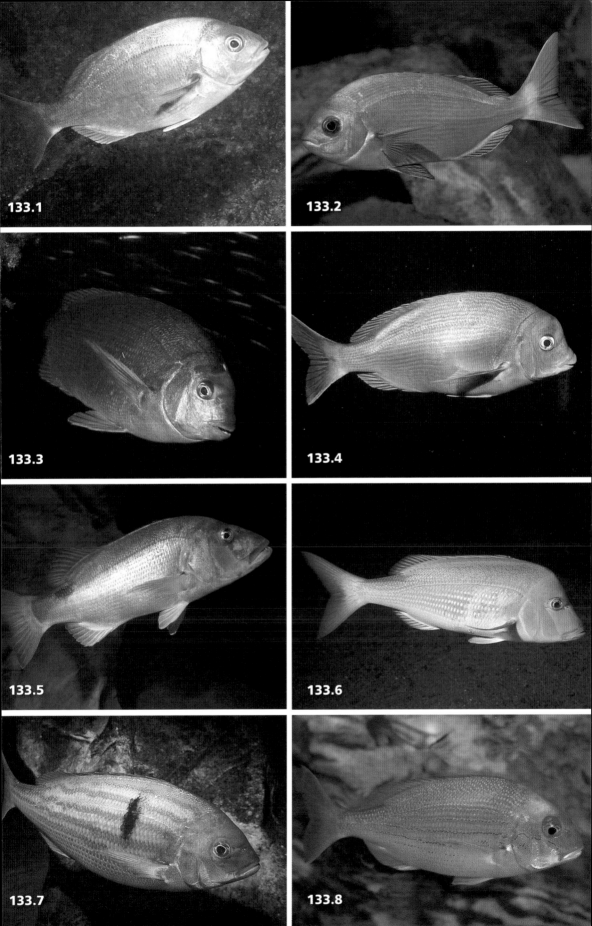

133.1

133.2

133.3

133.4

133.5

133.6

133.7

133.8

PLATE 134

134.1 Musselcracker — *Sparodon durbanensis*

DXI 11–12, AIII 10. Large and robust. Large head with blunt snout; powerful jaws equipped with four prominent incisors and rows of crushing molars. Adults silvery grey; juveniles have bright orange fins. **Size:** 1.1 m; 23 kg. **Biology:** Endemic; rocky shores and shallow reefs. Attains age of 31 years. Matures at 35 cm (five years); spawning occurs in spring and summer. Juveniles are common in Eastern Cape tidal pools. Juveniles feed on algae, but as molars develop they take hard-shelled prey. Adults solitary; feed on molluscs, redbait and crabs. This is a highly sought-after rocky-shore angling species.

134.2 Steentjie — *Spondyliosoma emarginatum*

DXI 11–13, AIII 10. Greyish blue with some horizontal pale yellow lines on flanks; fins dark. Jaws with 4–6 rows of pointed incisors; single row of molars. **Size:** 45 cm; 1 kg. **Biology:** Endemic; occurs in large shoals above reefs to 60 m depth. Feeds on benthic invertebrates. Attains age of eight years. Matures at 25 cm; spawns in spring and summer. Sexually mature males brightly coloured; they construct nests in sand next to reefs and guard eggs until they hatch. Females and immature males more uniformly dull in colour.

134.3 Strepie — *Sarpa salpa*

DXI 14–16, AIII 13–15. Small and elongate. Silver-green with 8–10 horizontal yellow stripes running from head to tail. Upper incisors notched, lower incisors pointed; no molars. **Size:** 40 cm; 1 kg. **Biology:** Eastern Atlantic; shoals are common in rocky and sandy areas. Adults herbivorous, although juveniles feed on small crustaceans. Attains age of six years. Matures at 15 cm (1.5 years); spawns in KwaZulu-Natal during winter and spring. Changes sex from male to female. Popular catch along KwaZulu-Natal coast.

134.4 Natal stumpnose — *Rhabdosargus sarba*

DXI 12–13, AIII 11. Silver-grey with a yellow streak on the belly. Yellow dots on scales form horizontal lines on the body. Jaws have 6–8 compressed incisors and rounded molars. **Size:** 80 cm; 8 kg. **Biology:** Indo-Pacific; frequents estuaries, shallow reefs and sandy areas to depths of 50 m. Preys on benthic invertebrates. Attains age of 16 years. Changes sex from male to female at 20–30 cm. Matures at 25 cm; spawns in winter and spring. Juveniles recruit to estuarine nursery areas.

134.5 Cape stumpnose — *Rhabdosargus holubi*

DXI 12–13, AIII 10–11. Silver with conspicuous mid-lateral yellow stripe from head to tail. Blunt head; jaws have 6–8 compressed incisors and rounded molars. In juveniles, each incisor has three cusps. **Size:** 45 cm; 3 kg. **Biology:** Endemic; sandy bays and inshore reefs. Matures at 20 cm; spawns in winter and spring. Juveniles use estuarine nursery areas where they graze in eelgrass beds. Adults feed on benthic invertebrates.

134.6 White stumpnose — *Rhabdosargus globiceps*

DXI 11–13, AIII 10–11. Silvery with 6–7 dark vertical bars. Head blunt; jaws have 4–8 incisors and rows of strong molars. **Size:** 50 cm; 3 kg. **Biology:** Endemic; sandy and rocky areas to 80 m depth. Attains age of 21 years. Matures at 20–25 cm (four years); spawns during spring and summer. Juveniles found in estuaries and surf zones.

134.7 Bigeye stumpnose — *Rhabdosargus thorpei*

DXI 13, AIII 12. Silver with broad yellow band on belly; several thin horizontal yellow stripes along sides. Anal and pelvic fins yellow. Large eyes. Jaws have six compressed incisors and four rows of molars at the back. **Size:** 50 cm; 4 kg. **Biology:** Endemic; coral and rocky reefs to 70 m. Feeds on molluscs and crustaceans. Juveniles common in northern KwaZulu-Natal estuaries. Biology poorly known.

134.1

134.2

134.3

134.4

134.5

134.6

134.7

PLATE 135

Emperors, galjoens & chubs

135.1 Glowfish — *Gnathodentex aureolineatus*

DX 10, AIII 8–9. Colour varies, but characteristic yellow patch at end of dorsal fin; yellow lines on body. Canines flare outwards. Eyes large. **Size:** 30 cm. **Biology:** Indo-Pacific: under ledges or shoaling on coral reefs down to 100 m. Eats benthic invertebrates.

135.2 Bluelined barenose — *Gymnocranius grandoculis*

DX 9–10, AIII 9–10. Silver-grey with wavy blue lines on cheeks of adults. Juveniles have vertical black bar through eye and several other diffuse vertical bars that fade with age. Strong conical teeth; large eyes. **Size:** 80 cm; 5 kg. **Biology:** Indo-Pacific; over reefs and sandy areas down to 100 m. Feeds on benthic invertebrates.

135.3 Bigeye barenose — *Monotaxis grandoculis*

DX 10, AIII 9. Head heavy; snout becoming increasingly blunt with age. Silvery grey; upper flank darker with four distinct white vertical bars. Eyes large. **Size:** 60 cm. **Biology:** Indo-Pacific; coral reefs and adjacent rubble and sandy areas down to depth of 60 m.

135.4 Spotcheek emperor — *Lethrinus rubrioperculatus*

DX 9, AIII 8. Elongate with pointed snout. Olive to grey-brown; often with irregular dark blotches on flanks. Characteristic red spot on gill cover. Lips usually red. **Size:** 50 cm; 1 kg. **Biology:** Indo-Pacific; coral reefs to depth of 160 m. Eats benthic invertebrates.

135.5 Spangled emperor — *Lethrinus nebulosus*

DX 9, AIII 8. Robust with sloping forehead. Brownish, but each scale has a blue centre. Blue lines radiate forward from eyes. Cheeks without scales; dense scaling on inner base of pectoral fin. **Size:** 75 cm; 8 kg. **Biology:** Indo-Pacific; coral and rocky reefs down to 80 m. Matures at 35–40 cm. Preys on benthic and planktonic invertebrates.

135.6 Banded galjoen — *Dichistius multifasciatus*

DX 21–23, AIII 13–14. Deep-bodied, robust. Grey with about 14 alternating wide and narrow vertical dark bands. Mouth small with curved incisors. Fin spines prominent; small scales cover entire body including the fins. **Size:** 35 cm; 2 kg. **Biology:** Endemic; inhabits turbulent waters off rocky and sandy shores. Eats benthic invertebrates. Matures at 22 cm; spawns off KwaZulu-Natal in winter and spring. Juveniles occur in tidal pools and gullies.

135.7 Galjoen — *Dichistius capensis*

DX 18–19, AIII 13–14. Deep-bodied and robust. Varies in colour from grey to black. Mouth small, with curved incisors. Fin spines prominent; small scales cover the entire fish including the fins. **Size:** 80 cm; 6 kg. **Biology:** Endemic; inhabits turbulent water off rocky and sandy shores. Exceeds an age of 13 years. Sexually mature at 31–34 cm (six years); spawns in summer. Eats benthic invertebrates. Tagging has shown that individuals remain in the same area for several years. South Africa's national fish.

135.8 Stonebream — *Neoscorpis lithophilus*

DVI–VIII 20–23, AIII 23–26. Kite-shaped; silvery grey with dark fins. Anal and dorsal spines short and stout. Small scales cover the entire body. Mouth small, with rows of fine teeth. **Size:** 50 cm; 3 kg. **Biology:** Endemic; occurs in turbulent water along rocky and sandy shores. Eats seaweeds. Attains 10 years. Matures at 30 cm (four years). In KwaZulu-Natal, spawning occurs in spring and summer. Juveniles occupy tidal pools and shallow gullies.

135.9 Grey chub — *Kyphosus bigibbus*

DX–XI 11–13, AIII 11. Robust and oblong-shaped; short pectoral fins. Mouth small with curved incisors. Greyish with brown scale-edges forming horizontal lines on flanks. Brown band from corner of mouth to gill cover. **Size:** 70 cm; 10 kg. **Biology:** Indo-Pacific; shallow reefs. Herbivorous, feeding on seaweeds. Spawns during spring. Juveniles often associated with drifting seaweed and other flotsam. **SIMILAR SPECIES:** *K. cinerascens*, the blue chub (East London northwards), has soft dorsal rays that are obviously longer than the dorsal spines. *K. vaigiensis*, the brassy chub (the Indo-Pacific, southwards to Port Elizabeth), has 13–15 dorsal rays and bronze lines on the scale rows of the body.

PLATE 136

Kobs & knifejaws

136.1 Squaretail kob *Argyrosomus thorpei*

DIX–XI + I 26–28, AII 7. Elongate, silver with bronze sheen; row of silver spots along lateral line. Tail fin with straight edge; long pectoral fins. Scales present behind pectoral fin base. **Size:** 1.2 m; 14 kg. **Biology:** Endemic; reefs and sand to 80 m. Attains 13 years. Matures at 33 cm; spawns in winter off KwaZulu-Natal. Juveniles common on Thukela Bank. **SIMILAR SPECIES:** *Johnius dussumieri*, the small kob, has a pointed tail; plentiful in KwaZulu-Natal estuaries. *Otolithes ruber*, the snapper kob (southwards as far as Port Elizabeth), has two prominent canines in each jaw.

136.2 Silver kob *Argyrosomus inodorus*

DX–XI + I 25–29, AII 7. Elongate. Silver with bronze sheen; row of silver spots along lateral line. Pectoral fins have dark blotch at the base. Tail peduncle narrow and long; peduncle depth 58–74% of peduncle length. Fold of skin at pectoral fin base without scales. Pectoral fin reaches to, or beyond, tip of pelvic fin. **Size:** 1.5 m; 36 kg. **Biology:** Occupies soft-bottom and low-relief areas to 120 m. Attains 25 years. Matures at 30 cm; spawns on south coast in spring. Important in commercial and recreational catches. **SIMILAR SPECIES:** *A. japonicus*, the dusky kob, is usually darker, with a deeper caudal peduncle (peduncle depth 70–92% of penduncle length). Widespread in estuaries and shallow, soft-substrate areas of the Indo-Pacific. Attains 1.9 m, 75 kg and 42 years. Matures at 1 m (five years); spawns in spring in KwaZulu-Natal and juveniles occur in estuaries. Important in commercial and recreational linefisheries.

136.3 Geelbek *Atractoscion aequidens*

DX + I 27–31, A II 8–9. Large and elongate; silver with coppery dorsal surface. Tail fin concave. Interior of mouth and gill cover yellow. **Size:** 1.3 m; 25 kg. **Biology:** Widespread piscivore that occurs over reefs and in water column. Attains age of nine years. Matures at 90 cm (five years). Shoals of reproductively ripe fish migrate from the Cape to KwaZulu-Natal in winter with the 'sardine run' and spawn in spring. Stock depleted.

136.4 Slender baardman *Umbrina robinsoni*

DX + I 22–27, AII 7. Brown; moderately long with curved dorsal profile. Short thick barbel on chin; long tail peduncle. **Size:** 1 m; 13 kg. **Biology:** Western Indian Ocean; sand and reef down to 120 m. Resident with small home range. Eats benthic invertebrates. **SIMILAR SPECIES:** *U. canariensis*, the baardman (Namibia–East London), has more dorsal fin rays (24–30) and its tail peduncle is shorter. Attains 42 cm.

136.5 Cape knifejaw *Oplegnathus conwayi*

DXII 11–14, AIII 11–13. Dark and oblong. Teeth fused to form a parrot-like beak. Small scales cover whole of the body. Juveniles are bright yellow with vertical black band over head and in front of tail (136.5a). **Size:** 90 cm; 7 kg. **Biology:** Endemic; inshore reefs. Attains age of at least 13 years. Omnivorous. Though rarely caught by anglers, frequently seen by divers and shot by spearfishermen.

136.6 Natal knifejaw *Oplegnathus robinsoni*

DXI 20–24, AIII 14–17. Dark and deep-bodied. Teeth fused to form parrot-like beak. Similar to Cape knifejaw but dorsal and anal rays more numerous and tail more forked. Juveniles (136.6a) are bright yellow with five vertical black bars. **Size:** 60 cm; 3 kg. **Biology:** Endemic; reefs down to 100 m. Feeds on reef-dwelling invertebrates. Attains age of at least 10 years. Rarely taken by line, but frequently seen by divers.

136.1

136.2

136.3

136.4

136.5

136.6

136.5a

136.6a

PLATE 137

Batfishes, moonies, pursemouths & smelts

137.1 Longfin batfish
Platax teira

DV–VI 29–34, AIII 21–26. Deep, compressed body with steep forehead. Elongate dorsal, anal and pelvic fin rays; pelvic fins yellow. Body grey-brown with faint dark bar near pectorals. Dark blotch on side of belly. **Size:** 65 cm. **Biology:** Indo-Pacific; found on coral reefs, seaweed beds, shipwrecks and jetties. Can form large shoals. Feeds on zooplankton, benthic invertebrates and seaweeds. **SIMILAR SPECIES:** *P. orbicularis*, the orbicular batfish (southwards to Knysna), has 34–39 dorsal and 25–30 anal fin rays and a more sloping forehead.

137.2 Spadefish
Tripterodon orbis

DIX 19–21, AIII 15–17. Deep, compressed, oblong body with steep forehead. Small mouth with thick lips. Third to fifth dorsal spines are elongate. Juveniles have several dark vertical bands that fade with age. **Size:** 75 cm; 8 kg. **Biology:** Western Indian Ocean; inshore reefs to depths of 30 m. Feeds on planktonic and bottom-dwelling invertebrates.

137.3 Cape or oval moony
Monodactylus falciformis

DVIII 25–30, AIII 25–29. Compressed and kite-shaped; rudimentary pelvic fins. Eyes large; mouth small with rows of tiny, needle-like teeth. Silver; lobes of dorsal and anal fins dusky yellow. Juveniles have about a dozen dark vertical bars that fade with age. **Size:** 25 cm. **Biology:** Western Indian Ocean; shoals in shallow bays and estuaries. Usually seen in mid-water. Feeds on zooplankton. Matures at 15 cm; spawns off beaches in summer. Juveniles abundant in south coast estuaries.

137.4 Natal or round moony
Monodactylus argenteus

DVIII 27–30, AIII 27–30. Shares the same body form, large eyes and small mouth as the Cape moony, but its teeth are flattened and tricuspid. Dorsal and anal fins yellow, but can have dark lobes. Juveniles have two dark stripes over the head. **Size:** 25 cm. **Biology:** Indo-Pacific; shoals in shallow bays and estuaries. Matures at 15 cm. Juveniles common in estuaries and seagrass beds.

137.5 Slender ponyfish
Secutor insidiator

DVIII–IX 15–17, AIII 14. Oval and highly compressed. Silver with dusky fins; series of black dots on upper flanks. Protrusible mouth that points upwards. No scales on cheeks. **Size:** 15 cm. **Biology:** Indo-Pacific; occurs in shoals in shallow coastal waters. Feeds on plankton. Spawns along KwaZulu-Natal coast in summer; juveniles common in estuaries. **SIMILAR SPECIES**: *Leiognathus equula,* the common ponyfish (Indo-Pacific, extending south to Transkei), has a downward-pointing mouth and faint vertical bars. A thick layer of mucus covers the body.

137.6 Smallscale pursemouth
Gerres longirostris

DIX–X 9–11, AIII 7. Small and silvery with series of grey-brown bars along flanks. Snout pointed and mouth protrusible. Tail fin dark; deeply forked with long lobes. **Size:** 25 cm. **Biology:** Indo-Pacific; shoals in estuaries. Feeds on benthic invertebrates. Spawns at sea.

137.7 Silver smelt
Sillago sihama

DXI + I 20–23, AII 21–23. Silvery; cylindrical with long snout. Scales are easily shed. **Size:** 35 cm. **Biology:** Indo-Pacific; estuaries and shallow sandy shores. Often partially buried in the sand. Feeds on sand-dwelling benthic invertebrates.

137.1

137.2

137.3

137.4

137.5

137.6

137.7

PLATE 138

Angelfishes

The family Pomacanthidae are conspicuous and beautiful fishes on coral reefs and a dozen species occur off southern Africa. They are characterised by compressed bodies and bright colours. The conspicuous spine on the margin of the gill cover separates angelfishes from butterflyfishes. They have small mouths with brushlike teeth. Generally active during day, but hide in reef crevices at night.

138.1 Royal angel   *Pygoplites diacanthus*

DXIV 18–19, AIII 18–19. Oblong and compressed; large anal and dorsal fins. Tail fin truncate. Adults are bright yellow, with alternating bluish-white bands. Conspicuous blue spine on edge of gill cover. Tail, pectoral and pelvic fins yellow. Juveniles have black spot on soft dorsal fin. **Size:** 25 cm. **Biology:** Indo-Pacific; coral reefs to depths of 70 m. Feeds on corals and sponges. Solitary or in pairs.

138.2 Old woman   *Pomacanthus rhomboides*

DXI–XII 22–25, AIII 21–23. Oblong and compressed; large anal and dorsal fins. Tail fin truncate. Adults are dull brown, but hind part of body is paler. Small spine on the edge of gill cover. Juveniles are black with 15–20 vertical blue-white bars. **Size:** 45 cm. **Biology:** Western Indian Ocean; coral and rocky reefs to depths of 40 m. Occurs in small groups; feeds on both planktonic and benthic invertebrates. Juveniles in tidal pools.

138.3 Semicircle angelfish   *Pomacanthus semicirculatus*

DXIII 21–23, AIII 20–22. Oblong and compressed; greenish brown with numerous blue spots over body and fins. Tail fin rounded; elongate filaments on dorsal and anal fins. All fins except pectorals with blue edge. Gill cover has a blue margin and conspicuous blue spine (138.3). Juveniles (138.3a) dark with alternating blue and white semicircular lines and pale blue edges on dorsal and anal fins; transforming into adult coloration via an intermediate stage at 10–15 cm (138.3b). **Size:** 40 cm. **Biology:** Indo-Pacific; solitary on coral reefs to depths of 40 m. Feeds on algae and benthic invertebrates. Juveniles in tidal pools and sometimes found far south due to dispersal of larvae by Agulhas Current.

138.4 Emperor angelfish   *Pomacanthus imperator*

DXIV 19–21, AIII 19–20. Oblong and compressed; many yellow and blue stripes across body. Blue-edged dark mask over the eyes; conspicuous spine on the gill cover. Rounded yellow tail; anal fin dark with curved blue lines. Juveniles (138.4a) strikingly different, with concentric blue and white lines on head and body. **Size:** 40 cm. **Biology:** Indo-Pacific; coral reefs to depths of 70 m. Solitary or in pairs. Feeds on sponges and other invertebrates. Juveniles in tidal pools.

138.5 Jumping bean   *Centropyge acanthops*

DXIV 16–17, AIII 16–18. Brilliant blue; golden head, dorsal surface and dorsal fin. Conspicuous blue spine on gill cover. Blue line around eye and edges of dorsal and anal fins. **Size:** 8 cm. **Biology:** Western Indian Ocean; coral reefs and rubble. Solitary; feeds on algae. Changes sex from male to female. Popular aquarium fish.

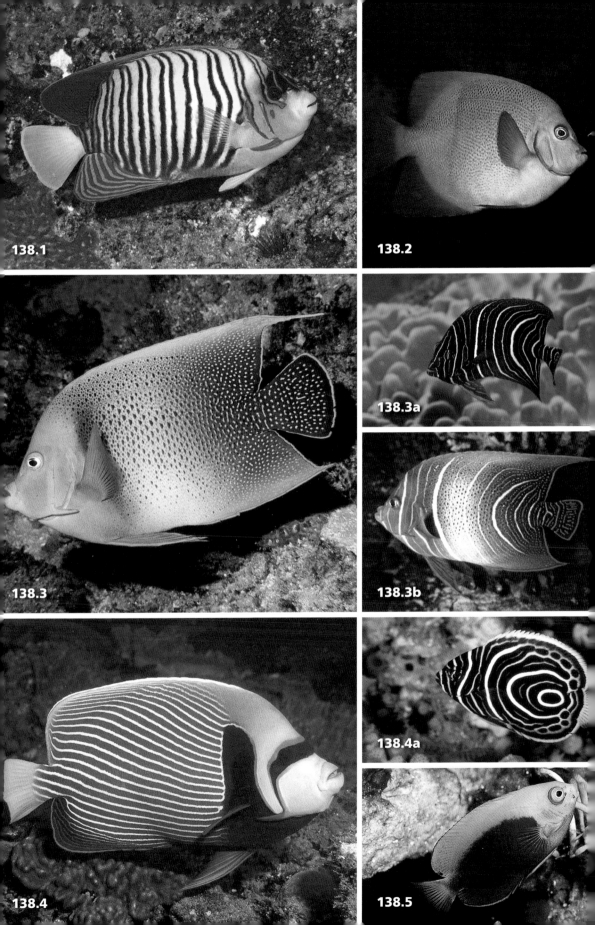

138.1

138.2

138.3

138.3a

138.3b

138.4

138.4a

138.5

PLATE 139

Butterflyfishes

Butterflyfishes of the family Chaetodontidae are conspicuous inhabitants of coral reefs. There are more than 20 species of these colourful, disc-shaped fishes in southern Africa. They are usually active by day and seek shelter close to the reef at night. Most have a dark bar to conceal the eye, and several have conspicuous 'eyespots' on the body that may serve to confuse would-be predators. They lack the sturdy spine on the gill cover found in angelfishes.

139.1 Threadfin butterflyfish — *Chaetodon auriga*
DXIII 23–24, AIII 20–21. Small whitish fish with grey chevron markings on flanks. Tail, anal and dorsal fins yellow. Black bar through eye, and a characteristic black spot on soft dorsal fin. In adults, soft dorsal fin has a trailing filament. **Size:** 20 cm. **Biology:** Indo-Pacific; coral reefs to 40 m. Usually seen in pairs. Feeds on small reef invertebrates. Juveniles often found in tidal pools on the east coast.

139.2 Brownburnie — *Chaetodon blackburnii*
DXVI–XVII 21–23, AIII 16–18. Relatively drab, with most of body and dorsal, anal and tail fins dark brown. Front of body yellow; dark band extends through eye. **Size:** 14 cm. **Biology:** Western Indian Ocean; on coral and rocky reefs to 70 m. Preys on small invertebrates. Solitary or in pairs.

139.3 Gorgeous gussy — *Chaetodon guttatissimus*
DXIII 21–23, AIII 16–18. Pale yellow body; numerous small black spots extending onto, and coalescing on, dorsal and anal fins. Black band extends through eye and tail fin. Dorsal and anal fins are yellow-edged. **Size:** 12 cm. **Biology:** Indian Ocean; on coral reefs to 70 m. Occurs in small groups. Feeds on coral polyps and small invertebrates.

139.4 Blackedged butterflyfish — *Chaetodon dolosus*
DXII–XIII 21–22, AIII 18–19. Grey, with small brown spots. Hind part of the body black; dark vertical stripe through the eye. Tail fin yellow; edge of dorsal and anal fins white. **Size:** 15 cm. **Biology:** Western Indian Ocean; coral and rocky reefs to 200 m. Feeds on coral polyps and invertebrates.

139.5 Raccoon butterflyfish — *Chaetodon lunula*
DXII–XIII 23–25, AIII 17–19. Yellow with darker flanks. Conspicuous black and white bands on head and black crescent extending to dorsal fin give it characteristic raccoon-like mask. Juvenile has black spot on soft dorsal fin and at base of tail fin. **Size:** 25 cm. **Biology:** Indo-Pacific; on coral and rocky reefs down to 30 m. Often found in pairs; juveniles often encountered in tidal pools. Eats coral polyps and small invertebrates.

139.6 Whitespotted butterflyfish — *Chaetodon kleinii*
DXIII 20–23, AIII 18–19. Body yellow, with white spot at the centre of each scale. Black band through eye extends onto chest. Jaws black; dorsal and anal fins yellow. **Size:** 15 cm. **Biology:** Indo-Pacific; on coral reefs down to 40 m. Occurs singly or in pairs. Feeds on coral polyps and small invertebrates.

139.7 Pearly butterflyfish — *Chaetodon madagaskariensis*
DXIII–XIV 20–21, AIII 16–17. Greyish white; broad orange bands across hind part of body and tail fin. About six black chevron marks on sides; black band through eyes, and short black bar in front of dorsal fin. **Size:** 15 cm. **Biology:** Western Indian Ocean; on coral and rocky reefs down to 40 m. Often found on seaward or outer reefs. Eats small invertebrates and seaweeds.

139.1

139.2

139.3

139.4

139.5

139.6

139.7

PLATE 140

140.1 Teardrop butterflyfish
Chaetodon interruptus

DXIII 21–23, AIII 17–20. Bright yellow with conspicuous black spot on flanks. Black bar through the eye. Thin black lines through tail fin base and along trailing edge of soft dorsal and anal fins. **Size:** 20 cm. **Biology:** Western Indian Ocean; on coral and rocky reefs to 90 m. Occurs singly or in pairs. Feeds on small invertebrates.

140.2 Doublesash butterflyfish
Chaetodon marleyi

DXI 22–25, AIII 18–19. Silvery white; two vertical orange-brown bars extend across flanks. Vertical bars through eye, tail peduncle and tail fin. Dorsal, anal and pelvic fins orange. Black spot in middle of dorsal fin that is conspicuous in juveniles. **Size:** 20 cm. **Biology:** Endemic; temperate and subtropical rocky reefs to 120 m. Generally seen in pairs. Attains age of four years. Spawns in winter and spring; juveniles frequent tidal pools and shallow reefs. Feeds on invertebrates.

140.3 Maypole butterflyfish
Chaetodon meyeri

DXII 23–24, AIII 18–20. Striking greyish white with characteristic black lines curving across body and fins. Fins and body margins yellow. **Size:** 20 cm. **Biology:** Indo-Pacific; occurs singly or in pairs on coral reefs. Preys exclusively on coral polyps.

140.4 Vagabond butterflyfish
Chaetodon vagabundus

DXIII 23–26, AIII 19–21. White with hind part of body yellow. About eight thin diagonal lines run towards head across front of body; 14 thin lines run diagonally across flanks towards tail. Black vertical bars through eye, tail fin and from under soft dorsal fin to anal fin. **Size:** 23 cm. **Biology:** Indo-Pacific; coral and rocky reefs down to 30 m. Usually occurs in pairs. Omnivorous.

140.5 Longnose butterflyfish
Forcipiger flavissimus

DXII 22–24, AIII 17–18. Bright yellow with black and white head. Distinctive elongate snout and small black spot on anal fin. **Size:** 20 cm. **Biology:** Indo-Pacific; frequents coral and rocky reefs to 100 m. Specialised mouth enables it to probe small holes and crevices for invertebrate prey. Usually in pairs.

140.6 Coachman
Heniochus acuminatus

DXI–XII 23–26, AIII 17–19. White with two broad black bars across body. Fourth dorsal spine elongated into white filament that extends past tail. Soft dorsal, tail and pectoral fins yellow. Black band between eyes. Adults develop a short stout spine in front of each eye. **Size:** 25 cm. **Biology:** Indo-Pacific; on coral and rocky reefs to 70 m. Preys on small invertebrates. Juveniles sometimes remove parasites from other fish. **SIMILAR SPECIES:** *H. diphreutes*, the schooling coachman (Durban northwards), has a shorter snout and the black band between eyes extends further up front of head. *H. monoceros*, the masked coachman (Cape Vidal northwards), has a dark snout, a short horn in front of each eye, and no long filament on the dorsal fin fourth spine.

140.7 Moorish idol
Zanclus cornutus

DVI–VII 39–42, AIII 31–37. Black and white, with conspicuous yellow marking on flanks. Third dorsal fin spine extends into long filament. Snout pronounced, with yellow saddle. Black tail fin has bluish-white edge. Adult has bony projection in front of each eye. **Size:** 22 cm. **Biology:** Indo-Pacific; on coral and rocky reefs. Belongs to the monotypic family Zanclidae. Feeds on invertebrates. Pelagic larvae are disc-like and often carried south by the Agulhas Current.

140.8 Bluespotted rabbitfish
Siganus sutor

DXIII 10, AVII 9. Oval-shaped and compressed. Prominent fin spines and tiny scales. Mouth small with tiny incisors. Colour variable and often mottled. **Size:** 50 cm; 3 kg. **Biology:** Western Indian Ocean; associated with shallow reefs and seagrass beds. Herbivorous and shoaling. Spines extremely sharp and coated with toxic mucus. Stabs are agonisingly painful, but can be eased by immersion in very hot water.

140.1

140.5

140.2

140.6

140.3

140.7

140.4

140.8

PLATE 141

Kingfishes

Some 54 species of the family Carangidae (known internationally as trevallies) are found off southern Africa. Identification can be difficult and requires detailed examination of the scales and counts of lateral-line scutes (enlarged scales that bear spines or ridges).

141.1 Coastal kingfish   *Carangoides caeruleopinnatus*

DVIII + I 20–23, AII + I 16–20. Deep-bodied, almost oval with long steep forehead. Silvery blue with small yellowish spots; black spot on gill cover. Scaleless chest patch extends from gill cover to pectoral fin and down to pelvic fin; 20–38 small hard scutes along lateral line near tail. **Size:** 50 cm; 4 kg. **Biology:** Indo-Pacific; shoals over deep coastal reefs. Eats crustaceans and fish. One of 12 *Carangoides* spp. in southern Africa.

141.2 Blue kingfish   *Carangoides ferdau*

DVIII + I 26–34, AII + I 21–26. Silver flanks; blue above with small yellow spots often present. Juveniles can have six dusky vertical bars. Snout blunt; long, sickle-shaped pectoral fin; 21–37 small hard scutes along lateral line near tail. Scaleless patch from gill cover to pelvic fin base and another at pectoral fin base. **Size:** 70 cm; 8 kg. **Biology:** Indo-Pacific; inhabits sandy beach surf zones, coastal waters and reefs to 60 m. Feeds on crustaceans and fish.

141.3 Yellowspotted kingfish   *Carangoides fulvoguttatus*

DVIII + I 25–30, AII + I 21–26. Silver flanks; blue-green above with small yellow spots. Adults often have large black blotches on lateral line. Scaleless chest area extends past pelvic fin base; 15–21 scutes along lateral line near tail. Fatty tissue on eyes. **Size:** 1 m; 18 kg. **Biology:** Indo-Pacific; shoals over reefs down to 100 m. Feeds on fish and crustaceans.

141.4 Giant kingfish   *Caranx ignobilis*

DVIII + I 18–21, AII + I 15–17. Deep robust body with steep forehead. Silvery grey with small black spots on flanks. Small scaleless patch between gill cover and pelvic fin; another at pectoral fin base. Pectoral fin sickle-shaped and extends to anal fin; 26–38 prominent lateral-line scutes near tail. **Size:** 1.6 m; 70 kg. **Biology:** Indo-Pacific; on reefs and along sandy shores. Large powerful predator; preys mainly on fish. Attains age of 10 years. Sexually mature at 65 cm (three years); spawns in summer. Juveniles found in KwaZulu-Natal estuaries. A prized game fish, caught from ski-boats and the shore. Largest of seven *Caranx* spp. in region.

141.5 Bluefin kingfish   *Caranx melampygus*

DVIII + I 21–24, AII + I 17–20. Elongate, silvery green; black and blue spots on flanks. Second dorsal, anal and tail fins brilliant blue; 27–42 strong lateral-line scutes near tail. Breast completely scaled. Pectoral fin yellow, sickle-shaped and extends to anal fin. **Size:** 1 m; 10 kg. **Biology:** Indo-Pacific; over coral and rocky reefs to depth of 30 m. Occurs in small groups; preys on fish. Matures at 45 cm; spawns in summer.

141.6 Blacktip kingfish   *Caranx heberi*

DVIII + I 19–21, AII + I 15–17. Silvery green; fins yellow. Tail fin strongly forked; dorsal tip black. Head rounded; body elongates with age. Breast generally lacks scales except for small patch in front of pelvic fin; 30–40 lateral-line scutes near tail. **Size:** 1 m; 12 kg. **Biology:** Indo-Pacific; forms small shoals over coastal reefs. Most common during summer. Preys on small fish.

141.7 Bigeye kingfish   *Caranx sexfasciatus*

DVIII + I 19–22, AII + I 14–17. Silver; blue-green above. Conspicuous large eyes, partially covered by fatty tissue. Black spot on gill cover; white lobes on dorsal and anal fins. Breast covered in scales; 27–36 strong lateral-line scutes near tail. Juveniles have six dusky vertical bars. **Size:** 1 m; 15 kg. **Biology:** Indo-Pacific; adults on reefs. Common in KwaZulu-Natal; preys on fish and invertebrates. Matures at 50 cm. Juveniles in estuaries in summer.

141.1

141.2

141.3

141.4

141.5

141.6

141.7

PLATE 142

142.1 Golden kingfish   *Gnathanodon speciosus*

DVII + I 18–20, AII + I 15–17. Silvery yellow; few black blotches on flanks of adults. Juveniles bright yellow with 7–12 dark vertical bars (142.1). Mouth protrusile; lips thick. No teeth. Breast completely scaled; weak lateral-line scutes. **Size:** 1.2 m; 15 kg. **Biology:** Indo-Pacific; sandy areas near reefs. Juveniles often associated with large sharks. Occurs in small groups. Sucks up bottom-dwelling invertebrates through protrusible mouth.

142.2 Leervis or Garrick   *Lichia amia*

DVII + I 19–21, AII + I 17–21. Elongate and compressed; silvery green. Large mouth and dark fins. Conspicuous curved lateral line lacks scutes. Tiny scales cover body. Juveniles yellow with several black vertical bars. **Size:** 1.8 m; 32 kg. **Biology:** Eastern Atlantic; swift, aggressive piscivore; hunts in the surf backline. Migrates north to KwaZulu-Natal following the winter 'sardine run'. Attains age of 10 years. Matures at 85 cm (four years). Spawns off KwaZulu-Natal in spring; juveniles occur in Cape estuaries. A highly rated game fish.

142.3 Southern pompano   *Trachinotus africanus*

DVI + I 21–23, AII + I 19–21. Robust and deep-bodied; blunt nose. Silvery; lacks spots or scutes on flanks. Fins dusky yellow; tail fin strongly forked. **Size:** 1 m; 25 kg. **Biology:** Indian Ocean; shallow sandy areas near reefs. Eats mussels and crustaceans, which it crushes with strong pharyngeal grinding plates. Grows fast; mature in less than three years. Spawns in spring; juveniles common in sheltered bays. Often caught by surf-zone anglers.

142.4 Largespotted pompano   *Trachinotus botla*

DVI + I 22–24, AII + I 19–21. Oval with blunt snout. Silvery blue; flanks with 1–5 large black spots. Fins blue with elongated dorsal and anal rays; six short separate dorsal fin spines. Tail deeply forked, with long lobes. No lateral-line scutes. **Size:** 75 cm; 3 kg. **Biology:** Indian Ocean; sandy beach surf zones. Feeds on bivalves, crabs and worms.

142.5 Talang queenfish   *Scomberoides commersonnianus*

DVI–VII + I 19–21, AII + I 16–19. Elongate and compressed; large mouth. Silvery; 5–8 large black blotches on flanks. Pectoral fins short; tail fin deeply forked. Dorsal fin preceded by six short separate spines. No lateral-line scutes. **Size:** 1.2 m; 15 kg. **Biology:** Indo-Pacific; coastal, usually near reefs. Eats fish and crustaceans. SIMILAR SPECIES: *S. lysan*, the doublespotted queenfish (Durban northwards), has two rows of dark spots on its flanks. *S. tol*, the needlescaled queenfish (KwaZulu-Natal northwards), has 5–8 oval black spots along lateral line and needle-like scales mid-body.

142.6 Giant yellowtail   *Seriola lalandi*

DVII + I 30–35, AII + I 19–22. Large and elongate. Blue above and silvery white below; horizontal bronze stripe from snout to tail. Base of the tail has moderate keel. Fins yellow. **Size:** 1.5 m; 52 kg. **Biology:** Circumglobal (warm-temperate); shoals in coastal and offshore waters, often associated with reef pinnacles. Voracious predator; migrates annually up east coast following 'sardine run'. Attains age of 10 years. Matures at 65 cm (three years); spawns on Agulhas Bank in summer. Highly prized game fish and important component of commercial linefish catches in the Cape.

142.7 Maasbanker   *Trachurus trachurus*

DVIII + I 30–36, AII + I 24–32. Spindle-shaped and elongate. Silvery; dorsal surface olive green. Eye large with much fatty tissue. Black spot on the gill cover. Lateral line has up to 78 prominent scutes. **Size:** 70 cm; 1.5 kg. **Biology:** Eastern Atlantic; pelagic in large shoals. Eats plankton, migrating vertically to follow its prey. Attains 16 years. Matures at 35 cm (three years); spawns late winter and spring on Agulhas Bank. Lüderitz upwelling cell separates South African and Namibian stocks. Commercially harvested.

142.8 Elf or shad   *Pomatomus saltatrix*

DVII–VIII + I 23–28, AII 23–27. Elongate; silver with greenish sheen. Mouth large; single row of sharp teeth in each jaw. Scales small, easily shed. **Size:** 1.2 m; 15 kg. **Biology:** Circumglobal; coastal waters. Powerful predator; follows 'sardine run' to KwaZulu-Natal. Attains age of 10 years. Matures at 25 cm (one year); spawns in KwaZulu-Natal in spring and summer. Juveniles common in south coast bays. Once severely depleted, but imposition of a bag limit, minimum size and closed season have helped stocks to recover.

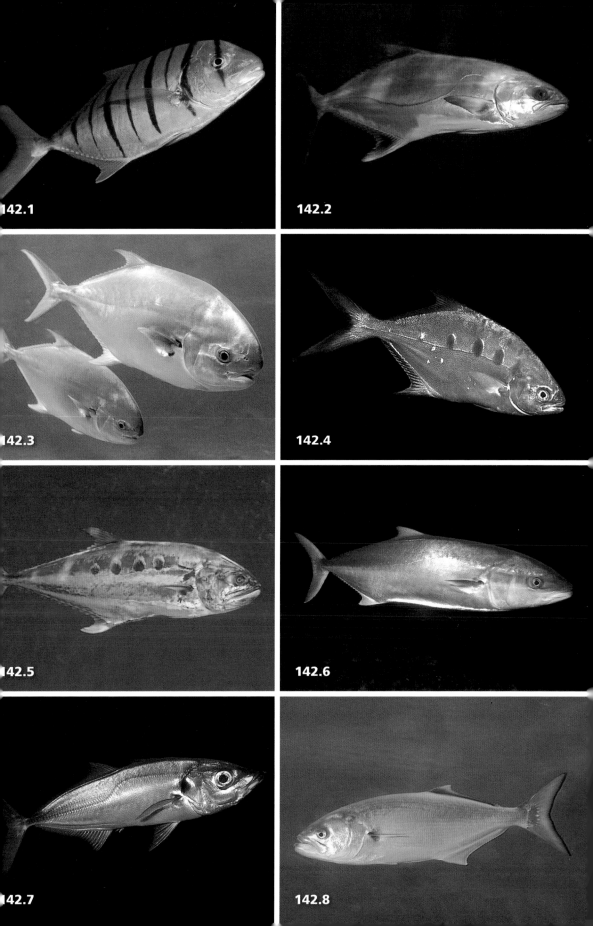

142.1

142.2

142.3

142.4

142.5

142.6

142.7

142.8

PLATE 143

Snoek, mackerel, tuna & billfish

Tunas are wide-ranging and migratory; 18 species occur around southern Africa. Worldwide, some 6 million tonnes are caught each year. Billfish (swordfish, marlin and sailfish) are close relatives of tunas.

143.1 Snoek   *Thyrsites atun*

DXVIII–XXI 10–12 + 5–7 finlets, AI 9–12 + 5–7 finlets. Elongate and compressed. Silvery; bluish grey above. Dorsal spines prominent; pelvic fins small. Lateral line wavy. Large mouth with sharp teeth. **Size:** 1.3 m; 9 kg. **Biology:** A southern hemisphere temperate pelagic predator; forms migratory shoals on west coast. Reaches 10 years; matures at 75 cm (three years). Spawns winter to spring on the shelf break. Caught commercially.

143.2 Chub mackerel   *Scomber japonicus*

DIX–X + 11–12 + 5 finlets, AI + 11–12 + 5 finlets. Torpedo-shaped. Dorsally metallic green with wavy lines. Narrow tail peduncle; two fleshy keels on tail fin base. **Size:** 70 cm; 5 kg. **Biology:** Cosmopolitan; coastal. Pelagic, shoaling fish; a plankton-feeder. Attains eight years; matures at 40 cm (three years); spawns in winter and spring. SIMILAR SPECIES: *Rastrelliger kanagurta*, the Indian mackerel (Durban northwards), is more robust, has black spot under pectoral fin and golden stripes on flanks.

143.3 Eastern little tuna   *Euthynnus affinis*

DXV–XVII + 12–13 + 8 finlets, A 13–14 + 7 finlets. Robust, spindle-shaped. Silvery with dark wavy dorsal lines. Dark spots on chest when fish excited. Row of tiny, conical teeth in each jaw. **Size:** 1 m; 12 kg. **Biology:** Indo-Pacific; shoals in coastal waters. Eats small fish. Matures at 50 cm; larvae on KwaZulu-Natal shelf during summer. SIMILAR SPECIES: *Auxis thazard*, the frigate tuna (worldwide in tropical waters), is more slender, smaller, has 11–12 dorsal spines and lacks black ventral spots.

143.4 Striped bonito   *Sarda orientalis*

DXVII–XIX + 14–17 + 7–9 finlets, A 14–16 + 6–7 finlets. Oblong. Bluish grey; 5–10 slightly oblique dark stripes across back. Short pectoral fins; caudal peduncle with prominent fleshy lateral keel between two smaller keels. Large conical teeth. **Size:** 1 m; 12 kg. **Biology:** Coastal and shelf pelagic predator on fish, crustaceans and squids.

143.5 Skipjack tuna   *Katsuwonus pelamis*

DXIV–XVI + 14–15 + 7–9 finlets, A 14–15 + 7–8 finlets. Spindle-shaped. Blue above; silvery belly with 4–6 horizontal stripes. Mouth large. Keel on tail peduncle. **Size:** 1 m; 20 kg. **Biology:** Cosmopolitan. Abundant off east coast in summer; spawns further north. Eats pelagic fish, squid. Reaches 12 years; matures at 45 cm (two years). SIMILAR SPECIES: *Thunnus albacares*, yellowfin tuna (same distribution), has yellow fins with elongated dorsal and anal fin lobes and no horizontal stripes. *T. alalunga*, the longfin tuna, has long pectoral fins and no horizontal stripes.

143.6 Queen mackerel   *Scomberomorus plurilineatus*

DXV–XVII + 19–21 + 8–10 finlets, A 19–22 + 7–10 finlets. Elongate. Silvery blue; rows of dark dashes on flanks. Lateral line straight. Tail strongly forked; three keels on tail peduncle. **Size:** 1.3 m; 13 kg. **Biology:** Western Indian Ocean; coastal waters. Attains age of six years. Matures at 80 cm (two years); does not spawn off South Africa.

143.7 King mackerel   *Scomberomorus commerson*

DXV–XVIII + 15–20 + 8–11 finlets, A 16–21 + 7–12 finlets. Elongate. Silver with irregular wavy dark bars on flanks. Mouth large; conspicuous teeth. Lateral line distinct, with downward bend after anal fin. Tail fin large; three distinct keels on tail peduncle. **Size:** 2 m; 47 kg. **Biology:** Indo-Pacific; coastal waters. Pelagic predator; migrates south in summer. Matures at 1 m (three years); does not spawn off South Africa.

143.8 Sailfish   *Istiophorus platypterus*

D 42–49 + 6–8, A 12–17 + 5–8. Elongate, streamlined. Long spear. Metallic blue. First dorsal fin very high and blue; middle rays longest. Tail fin large; two keels on tail peduncle. **Size:** 3 m; 100 kg. **Biology:** Oceanic. Common in summer off KwaZulu-Natal. Attains 15 years. Grows fast; matures at 1.5 m (three years); does not spawn off South Africa.

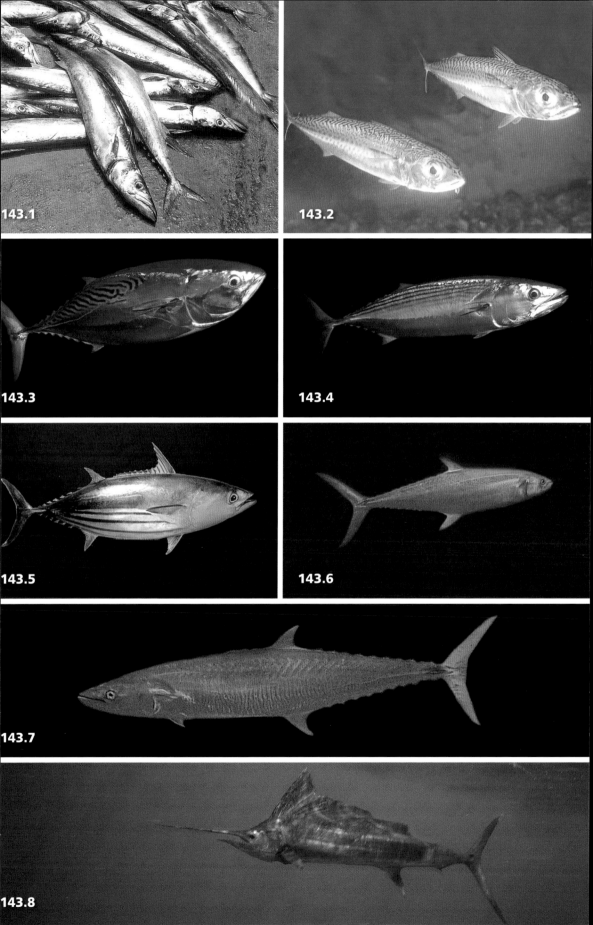

143.1

143.2

143.3

143.4

143.5

143.6

143.7

143.8

PLATE 144

Remoras, hawkfishes, fingerfins & sweepers

144.1 Shark remora
Echeneis naucrates

D 34–42, A 32–38. Slender and cylindrical; flattened head bears a sucking disc with 21–28 grooves. Head white; body grey with white-edged black horizontal stripe from jaw to tail. **Size:** 1 m; 6 kg. **Biology:** Circumtropical; usually attached to sharks, rays and turtles by means of sucking disc. Feeds on pieces of food wasted by the host. **SIMILAR SPECIES:** *Remora remora*, the common remora, has a more robust, uniformly brown body and the sucking disc has 16–19 grooves. *Rachycentron canadum*, the cobia, is brown with a white band and pale belly. It does not have a sucker and the dorsal fin has 7–9 spines.

144.2 Spotted hawkfish
Cirrhitichthys oxycephalus

DX 12–13, AIII 6–7. Small with reddish-brown blotches. Enlarged pectoral fin rays; little tufts on dorsal spines. **Size:** 10 cm. **Biology:** Indo-Pacific; coral reefs to 40 m. Sits on or under corals. Males maintain harems and territories. Preys on small invertebrates.

144.3 Freckled hawkfish
Paracirrhites forsteri

DX 11, AIII 6. Small; reddish brown with numerous red spots on head and pectoral fin base. Variable black and white markings towards tail. Little tuft on each dorsal spine. **Size:** 22 cm. **Biology:** Indo-Pacific; rests on live coral. Darts out to snap up passing crustaceans and small fishes.

144.4 Twotone fingerfin
Chirodactylus brachydactylus

DXVII–XVIII 28–31, AIII 8–10. Reddish brown. Distinct red pectoral fins, with elongated rays. Row of five bluish-white spots on flanks. Fleshy lips surround small mouth. **Size:** 40 cm; 3 kg. **Biology:** Endemic; lives in tidal pools, subtidal gullies and offshore reefs. Feeds on benthic invertebrates. Matures at 25 cm. Compressed silvery juveniles recruit to tidal pools in summer and acquire adult coloration at 5 cm.

144.5 Natal fingerfin
Chirodactylus jessicalenorum

DXVII–XVIII 26–27, AIII 7–8. Reddish brown; dark patch at base of pectoral fin. Pectoral fin rays elongated. Lips fleshy. **Size:** 75 cm; 10 kg. **Biology:** Endemic; found on rocky reefs down to 40 m. Preys on benthic invertebrates. Rarely caught by anglers but frequently speared in KwaZulu-Natal. **SIMILAR SPECIES:** *C. grandis*, the bank steenbras, is dull brown, has 22–24 soft dorsal rays and occurs on rocky reefs to 150 m from Namibia to Eastern Cape.

144.6 Redfingers
Cheilodactylus fasciatus

DXVII–XIX 23–25, AIII 9–11. Offset brown bars extend across body onto dorsal, anal and tail fins. Pectoral fins red with thickened elongated lower rays. Tail fin with spots and stripes. **Size:** 30 cm. **Biology:** Endemic; occupies tidal pools, subtidal gullies and reefs to 25 m. Preys on invertebrates. Juveniles compressed, silvery and lack the extended pectoral rays.

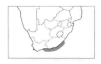

144.7 Barred fingerfin
Cheilodactylus pixi

DXVIII–XX 19–23, AIII 9–11. Continuous vertical bars across body; tail translucent. Pectoral fins with thickened elongated lower rays. **Size:** 18 cm. **Biology:** Endemic; found in subtidal gullies and reefs to depth of 30 m. Preys on invertebrates. Juveniles compressed, silvery and lack the extended pectoral rays.

144.8 Slender sweeper
Parapriacanthus ransonneti

DV 9, AIII 20–23. Small and compressed; large eyes. Pale pink; sides of head and belly silvery yellow. Dark ring on tail peduncle. **Size:** 10 cm. **Biology:** Indo-Pacific; forms shoals in caves and overhangs on coral and rocky reefs to 50 m. Two luminescent organs in belly.

144.9 Blackstripe sweeper
Pempheris schwenkii

DVI 8–9, AIII 35–43. Small and compressed; silvery bronze. Oblique mouth; large eyes. Short dorsal fin; anal fin very long and dusky with black stripe along base. **Size:** 17 cm. **Biology:** Indo-Pacific; forms shoals in caves and overhangs on coral and rocky reefs to 30 m. Nocturnal; preys on planktonic invertebrates.

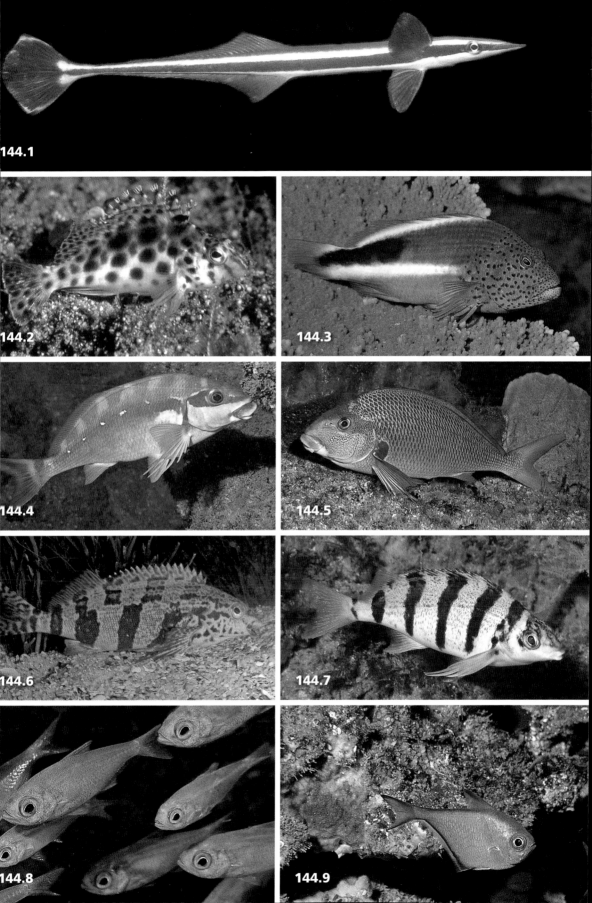

144.1

144.2

144.3

144.4

144.5

144.6

144.7

144.8

144.9

PLATE 145

Damselfishes

Damselfishes are small deep-bodied fishes that are abundant on coral reefs. There are 50 species in southern African waters. They lay demersal eggs and can be herbivores, omnivores or planktivores.

145.1 Spot damsel *Abudefduf sordidus*

DXIII 14–16, AII 14–15. Small and oval. Grey with black saddle on tail peduncle; 6–7 pale vertical crossbars. Fins yellowish; black spot at the base of pectoral fin. **Size:** 23 cm. **Biology:** Indo-Pacific; shallow rocky reefs. Juveniles common in tidal pools in summer. Omnivorous. Adults defend home territories against intruders.

145.2 Sergeant major *Abudefduf vaigiensis*

DXIII 12–14, AII 11–13. Small and pale with yellow dorsal surface; five separate vertical black bars. **Size:** 20 cm. **Biology:** Indo-Pacific; coral and shallow rocky reefs. Juveniles abundant in tidal pools. Omnivorous. Adults defend home ranges and nesting sites. **SIMILAR SPECIES**: *A. natalensis,* the fourbar damsel, has four broad dark bars; the one on the tail peduncle joins dark bands along the tail-fin lobes. *A. sexfasciatus*, the scissortail damsel, has five dark bars; the last is separate from the band along the ventral tail-fin lobe but joins one on the upper lobe.

145.3 Sash damsel *Plectroglyphidodon leucozonus*

DXII 15–16, AII 12–13. Small and robust. Brown with pale vertical bar across the mid-body. Juveniles have black spot on soft dorsal fin. **Size:** 15 cm. **Biology:** Indo-Pacific; coral reefs and shallow rocky areas. Juveniles frequent tidal pools. Herbivorous. Aggressively guards territories.

145.4 Twobar clownfish *Amphiprion allardi*

DX–XI 15–17, AII 13–15. Small. Brown with yellow jaws and chest; two bluish-white vertical bars. Tail fin pale; other fins orange-yellow. **Size:** 15 cm. **Biology:** Western Indian Ocean; coral reefs to 30 m. Usually shelters among tentacles of large sea anemones. Omnivorous. Eggs are attached to the reef during summer and are cared for by the parents.

145.5 Nosestripe clownfish *Amphiprion akallopisos*

DVIII–X 17–20, AII 12–14. Small and oblong. Pinkish orange; pale stripe along dorsal surface from snout to tail peduncle. **Size:** 10 cm. **Biology:** Western Indian Ocean; coral reefs to 25 m. Usually associated with large sea anemones. Changes sex from male to female. If dominant female is removed from its anemone, then one of the smaller males will develop into a female.

145.6 Chocolate dip *Chromis dimidiata*

DXII 12–13, AII 12–13. Front half of body distinctly brown and back half white. **Size:** 9 cm. **Biology:** Indian Ocean; coral reefs down to 40 m. Shelters among branching corals. Feeds on zooplankton and benthic invertebrates.

145.7 Blue-green chromis *Chromis viridis*

DXII 9–11, AII 9–11. Small and pale green; blue line from eye to snout. **Size:** 9 cm. **Biology:** Indo-Pacific; coral reefs to 12 m. Aggregates above corals and rapidly retreats among their branches on approach of danger.

145.8 Domino *Dascyllus trimaculatus*

DXII 14–16, AII 14–15. Small and round. Black; juveniles have white spots on forehead and dorsal flanks but these are lost in adults. **Size:** 14 cm. **Biology:** Indo-Pacific; coral reefs to 50 m. Juveniles sometimes associate with sea anemones or hide among the spines of sea urchins. Feeds on zooplankton.

145.9 Blue Pete *Pomacentrus caeruleus*

DXIII 14–15, AII 15–16. Brilliant blue with yellow ventral surface. Tail, anal and pectoral fins yellow. **Size:** 10 cm. **Biology:** Western Indian Ocean; occupies coral reefs and rubble to 10 m. Feeds on zooplankton. Usually solitary.

145.1

145.2

145.3

145.4

145.5

145.6

145.7

145.8

145.9

PLATE 146

Wrasses

Wrasses are highly variable in size, shape and colour. Many change sex from female to male, altering colour as they mature, sometimes making identification of the 70 species in southern Africa difficult. Most species have pharyngeal teeth with which they crush hard-shelled invertebrates. They use pectoral fins to cruise over reefs.

146.1 Bird wrasse   *Gomphosus caeruleus*

DVIII 13, AIII 11. Compressed and oblong; elongate tubular snout with terminal mouth. Juveniles and females are yellowish grey (146.1); mature males are blue-green with yellowish fin edges (146.1a). **Size:** 30 cm. **Biology:** Indian Ocean; coral reefs to 30 m. Feeds on small benthic invertebrates; uses long snout to extricate prey from crevices.

146.2 Diana's hogfish   *Bodianus diana*

DXII 10, AIII 12. Elongate with sloping forehead. Reddish brown with black spot on tail; 3–4 yellow spots on upper flank. Scales on hind upper flank have black dots. Juveniles are dark with white blotches on body and black spots on fins. Jaws with sharp canines. **Size:** 25 cm. **Biology:** Indo-Pacific; lives on coral and rocky reefs down to 40 m. Solitary. Feeds on hard-shelled benthic invertebrates.

146.3 Saddleback hogfish   *Bodianus bilunulatus*

DXII 10, AIII 12–13. Elongate with pointed snout. Red-edged scales in lengthwise rows. Large black saddle below soft dorsal fin; white band across cheek. Two pairs of protruding canines. Juveniles with large black blotch between dorsal and anal fins. **Size:** 55 cm and 2 kg. **Biology:** Indo-Pacific; occurs on coral and rocky reefs down to 100 m. Feeds on benthic invertebrates.

146.4 Picture wrasse   *Halichoeres nebulosus*

DIX 11–12, AIII 11. Oblong; jaws with conical teeth. Females brownish green with large maroon patch on belly; yellow-edged black spot on dorsal fin. Males primarily green; maroon patch reduced or absent. **Size:** 12 cm. **Biology:** Indo-Pacific; occurs from the surge zone where waves rush up the shore, down to depth of 40 m on shallow reefs. Preys on benthic invertebrates.

146.5 Checkerboard wrasse   *Halichoeres hortulanus*

DIX 11, AIII 11. Elongate; greenish head with pink bands radiating from mouth. Scales dark-edged, giving a checkered appearance. Conspicuous yellow blotch at base of dorsal fin. Males blue-green; females paler. **Size:** 25 cm. **Biology:** Indo-Pacific; occupies coral reefs to 30 m. Usually in pairs, foraging for benthic invertebrates.

146.6 Goldbar wrasse   *Thalassoma hebraicum*

DVIII 13, AIII 11. Oblong with rounded head. Bluish green; several curved blue bands extending across head to pectoral fin. Male has conspicuous vertical yellow bar from front of dorsal fin to belly; tail lunate. Tail truncate in juveniles and females. **Size:** 25 cm. **Biology:** Indian Ocean; coral reefs to 30 m. Solitary; preys on benthic invertebrates.

146.1

146.1a

146.2

146.3

146.4

46.5

146.6

PLATE 147

147.1 Crescent-tail wrasse   *Thalassoma lunare*

DVIII 13, AII 11. Oblong with rounded head. Head pink with irregular blue stripes. Juveniles and females green with blue belly and vertical purple lines on scales; tail emarginate. Adult male greenish blue; yellow lunate tail and pink pectoral fins edged with blue. **Size:** 25 cm. **Biology:** Indo-Pacific; found on coral reefs down to 30 m. Occurs in small groups; active on reef. Feeds on benthic invertebrates.

147.2 Surge wrasse   *Thalassoma purpureum*

DVIII 13, AIII 11. Oblong and sturdy. Males blue-green; irregular pink bars radiate from eyes; three horizontal pink stripes on flanks. Juveniles brown; females have two horizontal rows of vertically elongated green blotches that extend onto head. **Size:** 43 cm; 1.5 kg. **Biology:** Indo-Pacific; lives in very shallow coral or rocky areas exposed to surge. Changes from female to male at about 15 cm. Very active; feeds on wide range of benthic invertebrates. Caught by shore anglers.

147.3 Twotone wrasse   *Thalassoma amblycephalum*

DVIII 13, AIII 11. Elongate. Terminal-stage males have a green head with a yellowish area behind it; red body. Juveniles and females pale with broad dark stripe from snout through eye to tail. Lobes of tail fin orange. **Size:** 15 cm. **Biology:** Indo-Pacific; occupies coral and rocky reefs to 20 m. Occurs in small groups; feeds on zooplankton.

147.4 Bluestreak cleaner wrasse   *Labroides dimidiatus*

DIX 11, AIII 10. Small and elongate. White and bright blue; black horizontal band extends from snout and widens towards tail. Black bars along base of dorsal and anal fins. Small terminal mouth with thick lips and small canines. **Size:** 12 cm. **Biology:** Indo-Pacific; coral reefs to 40 m. Males and attendant harems set up 'cleaner stations' and remove parasites from larger fishes, even venturing into mouths and under gill covers. **SIMILAR SPECIES:** *Spidontus tractus,* the mimic blenny, masquerades as the cleaner wrasse but tears chunks of flesh from its unsuspecting 'clients'. Resembles *Labroides*, but has an underslung mouth and longer dorsal and anal fins.

147.5 Ember parrotfish   *Scarus rubroviolaceus*

DIX 10, AIII 9. Robust with blunt snout. Teeth fused to form beak-like structure. Colour varies with age and sex. Mature male is bluish green with yellowish flanks (147.5); pink and blue bands around mouth that reach the eye. Teeth blue; tail fin lunate. Female is red with greenish-brown mottled flanks (147.5a). Teeth pink; tail truncate. **Size:** 70 cm; 8 kg. **Biology:** Indo-Pacific; widespread on coral reefs to 35 m. Feeds on algae, which are scraped from reef with the beak. Schools common at Sodwana Bay.

147.6 Blue humphead parrotfish   *Chlorurus cyanescens*

DIX 10, AIII 9. Striking, with distinct hump on head. Body dark blue with posterior half green; thin blue margins on tail, dorsal, anal and pelvic fins. Prominent white tooth plates. **Size:** 50 cm. **Biology:** Western Indian Ocean; coral reefs to 30 m. Feeds by biting off coral and associated algae. Occasionally seen by divers at Sodwana Bay.

147.1

147.2

147.3

147.4

147.5

147.5a

147.6

PLATE 148

Goatfishes, mullets & barracudas

148.1 Yellowfin goatfish   *Mulloidichthys vanicolensis*

DVII + I 8, AI 6. Elongate with large scales. Greyish white with yellowish dorsal area; conspicuous yellow horizontal stripe extends from eye to tail. All fins except pectorals yellow. Small mouth with fleshy lips; pair of long chin barbels. **Size:** 40 cm. **Biology:** Indo-Pacific; coral reefs to 25 m. Forms dense shoals. Feeds on benthic invertebrates.

148.2 Rosy goatfish   *Parupeneus rubescens*

DVIII + I 8, AI 6. Elongate, with large scales. Reddish brown with characteristic black saddle blotch in front of tail. Fleshy lips, two long chin barbels. **Size:** 42 cm; 3 kg. **Biology:** Western Indian Ocean; sandy areas around coral and rocky reefs. They use their sensitive movable barbels to detect the benthic invertebrates upon which they feed.

148.3 Southern mullet   *Liza richardsonii*

DIV + I 8–9, AIII 9. Elongate, with pointed snout. Silver with darker dorsal surface; yellow spot on the gill cover. When pectoral fin is folded forwards, it just reaches eye. Teeth feeble. **Size:** 40 cm. **Biology:** Endemic; estuaries and sandy bays. Extremely tolerant of variable salinities. Feeds on phytoplankton and benthic diatoms. Matures at 23 cm; spawns in spring and summer. Juveniles frequent estuaries. Particularly common in Western Cape. Caught by commercial treknetters; salted and dried as 'bokkoms'.

148.4 Groovy mullet   *Liza dumerili*

DIV + I 8, AIII 9. Elongate, with pointed snout. Greyish silver, with a yellow spot on the gill cover. When the pectoral fin is folded forwards it reaches past the eye. Scales have a characteristic groovy pattern, most easily seen on dorsal surface of head. Teeth feeble. **Size:** 40 cm. **Biology:** Eastern Atlantic (Senegal to Angola) and southeast African coast; usually found in estuaries. Spawns at sea in spring and summer. Small juveniles (1–2 cm) recruit to estuarine nursery areas. Feeds on benthic diatoms and small invertebrates. **SIMILAR SPECIES:** *L. tricuspidens,* the striped mullet (Mossel Bay–Kosi Bay), is larger (up to 75 cm), has about eight dark horizontal stripes along the sides, and is characterised by tricuspid teeth.

148.5 Flathead mullet   *Mugil cephalus*

DIV + I 8, AIII 8. Elongate, with blunt snout. Silvery with darker dorsal surface; diffuse stripes on sides. When folded forwards pectoral fin does not reach eye. Eyes almost entirely covered by transparent adipose (fatty) eyelids. Curved, compressed teeth. **Size:** 80 cm; 5 kg. **Biology:** Cosmopolitan; shoals in coastal waters and estuaries. Sometimes enters fresh water. Feeds on diatoms and detritus. Matures at 45 cm; spawns at sea in winter. Juveniles (1–2 cm) recruit to estuarine nursery areas in spring. Large pre-spawning aggregations form in estuary mouths. **SIMILAR SPECIES:** *Valamugil buchanani,* the blue-tail mullet (Indo-Pacific, south to Knysna), is also large (up to 1 m), but has a bright blue tail and lacks adipose eyelids. *Myxus capensis*, the endemic freshwater mullet (False Bay–Kosi Bay), is smaller, has a pointed snout, and flattened teeth in the upper jaw. It frequents rivers and the upper parts of estuaries, but spawns at sea.

148.6 Pickhandle barracuda   *Sphyraena jello*

DV + I 9, AII 9. Cylindrical and very elongate. Large mouth extends to eye; sharp conical teeth. Silvery with about 20 vertical bars. Tail fin yellow and strongly forked; dorsal fins dusky and widely separated. **Size:** 1.5 m; 16 kg. **Biology:** Indo-Pacific; around coastal reefs in small shoals. Preys on fish. Juveniles common off Durban. **SIMILAR SPECIES**: *S. barracuda,* the great barracuda, has irregular dark blotches on sides, dark fins and can attain 2 m. There are eight species of *Sphyraena* in southern Africa.

148.1

148.2

148.3

148.4

148.5

148.6

PLATE 149

Blennies & triplefins

149.1 Snakelet
Halidesmus scapularis

DI 58–63, A 48–52. Elongate and cylindrical. Eel-like, with long dorsal and anal fins; no pelvic fins. Brown with dark spot above gill cover. **Size:** 20 cm. **Biology:** Endemic; intertidal pools and shallow subtidal zone. Lives in crevices; feeds on amphipods and isopods.

149.2 Horned rockskipper
Antennablennius bifilum

DXI–XIII 17–20, AII 17–21. Elongate and slightly compressed. Mottled, with seven dark bands and many small blue dots along flanks; three bands on underside of head. Pair of tentacles (joined at the base) on nape; no tentacles on eye. **Size:** 10 cm. **Biology:** Western Indian Ocean; tidal pools and shallow reefs. Eggs attached to rocks.

149.3 Ringneck blenny
Parablennius pilicornis

DXI–XII 18–24, AII 20–25. Elongate. Dusky, with nine vertical bands; dark spots ventrally. Often two dark bands under head. No tentacles on top of head; tentacles above eyes have several filaments. **Size:** 12 cm. **Biology:** Occurs in the Atlantic and on the southeast African coast. Inhabits tidal pools. Eats seaweed and crustaceans. Eggs attached to rocks and guarded by male. **SIMILAR SPECIES:** *P. cornutus*, the endemic horned blenny, is irregularly banded and its eye-tentacles consist of a central stalk with many side branches.

149.4 Two-eyed blenny
Chalaraderma ocellata

DXII–XIII 19–21, AII 21–22. Mottled, with up to five bands on body; conspicuous dark spot on anterior part of dorsal fin. Tentacles above eyes consist of several filaments arising from a broad base. **Size:** 7 cm. **Biology:** Endemic; tidal pools and subtidal reefs.

149.5 Maned blenny
Scartella emarginata

DXI–XIII 12–16, AII 14–18. Mottled with vertical bands and small spots. Mane-like row of tentacles on top of head. Eye and nostril tentacles have several short filaments. Upper-jaw teeth not movable. **Size:** 10 cm. **Biology:** Lives in pools and shallow rocky areas. Eats algae and invertebrates. Breeds year-round; eggs fixed to rocks; guarded by male.

149.6 Bandit blenny
Omobranchus banditus

DXI–XIII 19–21, AII 21–23. Small, elongate. Body with dark vertical bands; black spot above gill opening. No tentacles above eye or nostril. Enlarged, curved canines on lower jaw. Fleshy head crest in male. **Size:** 6 cm. **Biology:** Endemic. Inhabits tidal pools and gullies. Eggs attached to rocks. Distinct gill-cover spine in larvae and juveniles. **SIMILAR SPECIES:** *O. woodi*, the kappie blenny, found in Eastern Cape estuaries, has irregular dark bands only on the front part of the body.

149.7 Rippled rockskipper
Istiblennius edentulus

DXIII 20–21, AII 21–23. Elongate. Dusky, with alternating dark and pale stripes on sides. Deep notch in middle of dorsal fin. Females often paler than males; fleshy head crest in male. Small tentacles on nostril, eye and nape. Upper jaw teeth freely movable. **Size:** 13 cm. **Biology:** Indo-Pacific; shallow reefs and tidal pools. Eggs attached to rock surfaces.

149.8 Streaky rockskipper
Istiblennius dussumieri

DXII–XIII 19–22, AII 18–22. Elongate. Dusky vertical bands branching ventrally. Branched eye and nostril tentacles; none on nape. Males with fleshy crest. **Size:** 10 cm. **Biology:** Indo-Pacific; found on shallow reefs and in tidal pools.

149.9 Hotlips triplefin
Helcogramma rharharbe

DIII + XII–XIV + 10–11, AI 17–20. Tiny; dorsal fin divided into three parts. Body mottled with interconnected reddish-brown blotches. Male dark, with conspicuous red blotch on side of upper lip; brilliant blue and black cheek and throat. **Size:** 4 cm. **Biology:** Western Indian Ocean; common in weedy tidal pools and shallow subtidal areas.

149.10 Cape triplefin
Cremnochorites capensis

DIV + XIV–XV + 10–11, AII 21–22. Dorsal fin divided into three parts. Body has irregular brown bars. Head covered with small denticle-like scales. Branched eye-tentacles. **Size:** 8 cm. **Biology:** Endemic; occupies shallow subtidal reefs.

PLATE 150

Klipfishes

All 40 species of southern African klipfishes (family Clinidae) are endemic. They are highly cryptic and though most species inhabit shallow rocky areas, a few occur in sandy habitats. The females undergo internal fertilisation and give birth to fully developed juveniles (viviparous).

150.1 Agile klipfish — *Clinus agilis*

DXXXII–XXXVIII 2–4, AII 20–25. Elongate and compressed. Grey-green with dark crossbars. Small tufts of cirri on tips of first 15 dorsal spines; slight notch between third and fourth dorsal spines. Eye-tentacle flattened, with short branches. **Size:** 10 cm. **Biology:** Endemic; hides among weeds in pools and estuaries.

150.2 Bluntnose klipfish — *Clinus cottoides*

DXXXI–XXXVI 4–6, AII 21–25. Elongate, with robust head. Mottled; black blotch on the gill cover. First three dorsal spines shorter than fifth or sixth; no notch in dorsal fin. Pelvic fin rays elongate. Prominent tentacle above eye has numerous filaments. **Size:** 15 cm. **Biology:** Endemic; hides in tidal pools. Breeds throughout the year.

150.3 Super klipfish — *Clinus superciliosus*

DXXXI–XLII 5–10, AII 21–30. Elongate. Highly variable dark-green to red mottling. First three dorsal spines are longer, form a crest and bear clusters of cirri at tips. Distinct notch between third and fourth dorsal spines. Pelvic rays long. Eye-tentacle flat with a few short branches; in adult male it has a long stalk. **Size:** 30 cm. **Biology:** Endemic; abundant in tidal pools and subtidal gullies. Breeds throughout the year. Eats invertebrates; readily takes the bait of budding young anglers.

150.4 Speckled klipfish — *Clinus venustris*

DXXXVII–XLI 2–3, AII 23–28. Elongate; mottled, reddish brown. Cheek flares distinctive. No distinct notch in dorsal fin, although second spine is longer than rest. Tentacle above eye with several short branches at tip. Elongate pelvic rays. **Size:** 12 cm. **Biology:** Endemic; tidal pools and subtidal reefs down to 15 m.

150.5 Westcoast klipfish — *Clinus heterodon*

DXXX–XXXII 6–7, AII 20–22. Elongate; irregular crossbars. Tips of anal and pelvic fins red; tips of dorsal fin pale. Tentacle above eye with several short branches. Pale-edged spot on shoulder; two radiating bands across cheek. **Size:** 13 cm. **Biology:** Endemic; occurs in tidal pools. Feeds on invertebrates.

150.6 Nosestripe klipfish — *Muraenoclinus dorsalis*

DXLI–XLVIII 1, AII 25–31. Elongate and eel-like. Greenish brown; conspicuous white stripe from tip of snout onto dorsal fin. Elongate pelvic fin rays. Flattened tentacle with fine cirri above eye. **Size:** 10 cm. **Biology:** Endemic; under stones in tidal pools. Feeds on benthic invertebrates.

150.7 Grass klipfish — *Pavoclinus graminis*

DXXX–XXXV 4–6, AII 21–24. Elongate. Variable mottled markings. Dorsal fin with low anterior crest, but usually no notch between third and fourth spines. No tentacle above eye. **Size:** 20 cm. **Biology:** Endemic; tidal pools and subtidal gullies. Assumes colour of seaweeds with which it is associated.

150.8 Rippled klipfish — *Pavoclinus laurentii*

DXXIX–XXXIII 4–5, AII 20–22. Elongate. Variable mottled markings. First three dorsal spines form a crest; distinct notch between third and fourth dorsal spines. No tentacle above eye. **Size:** 13 cm. **Biology:** Endemic; inhabits tidal pools. Hides among seaweeds. Feeds on invertebrates.

150.1

150.2

150.3

150.4

150.5

150.6

150.7

150.8

PLATE 151

Gobies & suckerfishes

Gobies are extremely diverse. Most of the more than 100 species are small, dusky and difficult to distinguish, but several brightly coloured species live on coral reefs.

151.1 Barehead goby — *Caffrogobius nudiceps*

DVI + I 11–12, AI 10–11. Head rounded. Dusky and mottled; pale vertical bar at base of pectoral fin. First dorsal fin striped; pelvic fin disc-like. **Size:** 14 cm. **Biology:** Endemic; tide-pool occupant. Breeds year-round; attaches eggs to stones. Omnivorous; eagerly takes the bait of junior 'bent-pin' anglers. **SIMILAR SPECIES:** *C. caffer,* the banded goby, has 12–14 dorsal rays and 8–12 vertical bars. *C. gilchristi*, the prison goby, has 11–12 dorsal rays and 16 thin, broken, dark vertical bars forming two irregular horizontal bands. Common in tidal pools.

151.2 Commafin goby — *Caffrogobius saldanhae*

DVI + I 9–11, AI 9–10. Small; body with many spots. Black spot at end of first dorsal fin; pelvic fin disc-like. **Size:** 12 cm. **Biology:** Endemic; tidal pools. Eats small invertebrates.

151.3 Knysna sandgoby — *Psammogobius knysnaensis*

DVI + I 9–10, AI 9–11. Small with broad head; gill opening extends across throat. Grey-brown with brown spots; pale belly. Pelvic fins disc-shaped. Males have black spot on rear of first dorsal fin. **Size:** 7 cm. **Biology:** Endemic; sandy banks in estuaries. Breeds all year round; feeds on small benthic invertebrates.

151.4 Bigfin mudhopper — *Periophthalmus argentilineatus*

DXIV–XVII + I 10, AI 9–10. Steep forehead; protruding pop-eyes. Pectoral fins large. Dorsal fins have white margin and black stripe. **Size:** 15 cm. **Biology:** Indo-Pacific estuaries, particularly mangroves. Spends periods out of water, retaining oxygenated water in gill chamber. Lays eggs in mud nests defended by males. **SIMILAR SPECIES:** *P. kalolo*, the African mudhopper, has fewer dorsal spines and wider gap between two dorsal fins.

151.5 Fire goby — *Nemateleotris magnifica*

DVI + I 28–32, AI 27–30. Small and elongate; compressed head. Front part of body yellowish grey; rear part and fins red. First spine of dorsal fin elongate and yellow; tail fin sometimes black. **Size:** 10 cm. **Biology:** Indo-Pacific; coral reefs to depth of 60 m. Adults in pairs; dives into burrow at approach of danger. Feeds on zooplankton.

151.6 Pelagic goby — *Sufflogobius bibarbatus*

DVI + I 12–13, AI 12–13. Compressed head; two barbels under chin. Jaw reaches to below eye. Fins dusky. **Size:** 13 cm. **Biology:** Endemic; pelagic down to 200 m. Important in west coast pelagic ecosystem.

151.7 Pennant glider — *Valenciennea strigata*

DVI + I 17–19, AI 16–19. Conspicuous curved blue bar below eye extending to gill cover. Second and third dorsal spines filamentous. **Size:** 18 cm. **Biology:** Indo-Pacific; coral reefs to 25 m. Pairs have burrows in coarse sand and rubble.

151.8 Rocksucker — *Chorisochismus dentex*

D 6–9, A 6–7. Head broad, compressed; teeth strong, conical. Pelvic fins form a suction disc. Colour depends on surrounding habitat. **Size:** 30 cm. **Biology:** Endemic; shallow waters to 10 m. Eats invertebrates, particularly limpets, which it levers off with its strong teeth. Two shown here: one cryptic and 'rock-sucking' (right) and the other attacking a limpet (left). Breeds year-round; eggs attached under rocks and guarded by female.

151.9 Chubby clingfish — *Apletodon pellegrini*

D 5–6, A 5. Head broad and flat. Pelvic fins form an adhesive double disc. Colour variable. **Size:** 5 cm. **Biology:** Atlantic; rocky areas. Associated with seaweeds.
SIMILAR SPECIES:
151.10 *Eckloniaichthys scylliorhiniceps*, the weed sucker (Lüderitz–Transkei); D 5–6, A 5–6. Similarly tiny, cryptic, and attached by a pelvic disc; but colour uniform and body narrower. Usually associated with kelp, and matches its colour.

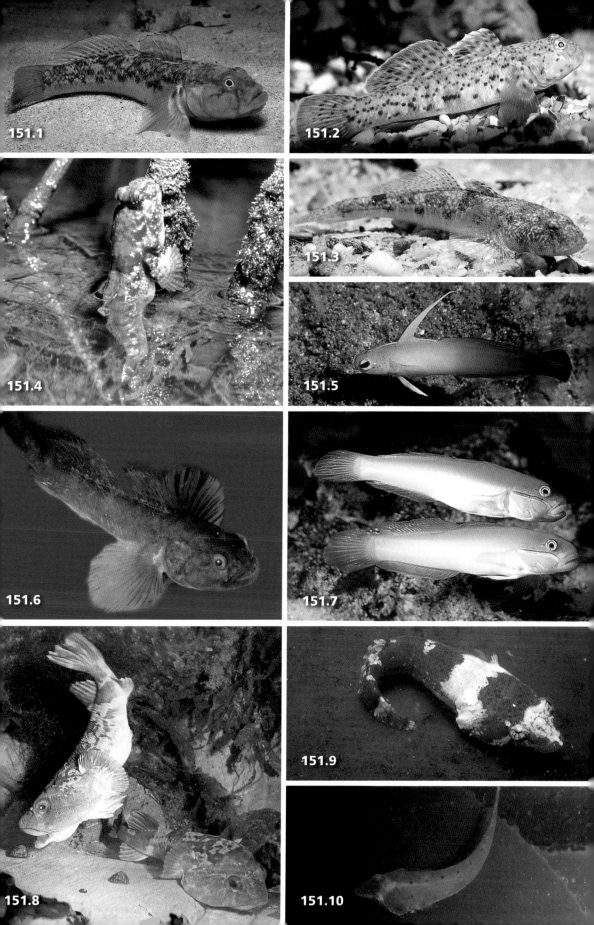

151.1

151.2

151.3

151.4

151.5

151.6

151.7

151.8

151.9

151.10

PLATE 152

Surgeonfishes & unicornfishes

The family Acanthuridae is characteristic of coral reefs. They are oval, brightly coloured and have a scalpel-like spine each side of the tail peduncle. There are 19 surgeonfish species and 12 unicornfish species on reefs off southern Africa.

152.1 Pencilled surgeon — *Acanthurus dussumieri*

DIX 25–27, AIII 24–26. Compressed and oval. Brown with thin horizontal wavy blue lines; yellow band between and around eye. White spine in black socket on tail peduncle. Dorsal and anal fins yellowish, often blue towards tail. Tail fin with black dots and broad blue margin; juveniles with white band on base of tail fin. **Size:** 54 cm. **Biology:** Indo-Pacific; coral reefs to depths of 30 m. Solitary and herbivorous. **SIMILAR SPECIES:** *A. nigrofuscus,* the brown surgeon, is brown, with small orange spots on head and chest; black spot at end of dorsal fin. Tail spine socket and all fins dark.

152.2 Powder-blue surgeonfish — *Acanthurus leucosternon*

DIX 28–30, AIII 23–26. Compressed and oval. Bright blue; black head and white chin. Yellow dorsal fin; anal and pelvic fins white. Tail fin white with black margins. Sharp yellow spine on tail peduncle. **Size:** 25 cm. **Biology:** Indian Ocean; coral reefs to 25 m. Occurs in small shoals; grazes on seaweeds.

152.3 Convict surgeon — *Acanthurus triostegus*

DIX 22–24, AIII 19–22. Compressed and oval. Grey-green; 5–6 vertical black bars, and white belly. Tail spine small. **Size:** 25 cm. **Biology:** Indo-Pacific; coral and rocky reefs to 25 m. Forms large shoals; grazes on algae. Matures at 12 cm; transparent juveniles recruit to tidal pools during summer.

152.4 Bluebanded surgeon — *Acanthurus lineatus*

DIX 27–29, AIII 25–28. Compressed and oblong. Head and upper flanks yellow; belly lavender blue. Horizontal black-edged blue stripes extend from head to tail peduncle. Fins edged in blue; tail fin lunate. Long spine on tail peduncle. **Size:** 38 cm. **Biology:** Indo-Pacific; shallow outer edges of coral reefs. Territorial.

152.5 Palette surgeon — *Paracanthurus hepatus*

DIX 19–20, AIII 18–19. Compressed and oblong. Brilliant blue with dark flanks and yellow belly. Pectorals, tail fin and tail spine yellow. **Size:** 26 cm. **Biology:** Indo-Pacific; coral reefs and sandy areas to 30 m. Feeds on zooplankton; adults also graze on algae.

152.6 Sailfin tang — *Zebrasoma desjardinii*

DIV 27–31, AIII 22–24. Compressed and disc-like. Distinctly elevated dorsal fin. Alternating pale and dark vertical bars overlaid with thin orange lines. Head grey with small pale spots. Curved yellow lines on dorsal and anal fins; tail spine dark. **Size:** 40 cm. **Biology:** Indian Ocean; sheltered coral reefs. Solitary or pairs; feeds on algae and detritus.

152.7 Spotted tang — *Zebrasoma gemmatum*

DIV 27–29, AIII 24–25. Compressed and disc-like. Dark brown; bluish-white spots or streaks on head and body extend onto fins. Elevated dorsal fin. Tail fin yellow; tail spine dark. **Size:** 22 cm. **Biology:** Western Indian Ocean; deep coral reefs. Solitary and herbivorous.

152.8 Orange-spine unicornfish — *Naso lituratus*

DVI 27–30, AII 28–30. Compressed and oblong; head angular. Pair of sharp, orange spines on each side of orange tail peduncle. Olive-brown; nape with orange-yellow area that extends below eye to mouth as thin curved line. Dorsal fin orange-yellow. Tail fin emarginate; pair of bony spines on tail peduncle. **Size:** 45 cm. **Biology:** Indo-Pacific; coral reefs. Herbivorous; feeds primarily on brown algae.

152.1

152.2

152.3

152.4

152.5

152.6

152.7

152.8

PLATE 153

Unicornfishes, triggerfishes & filefishes

Unicornfishes have a pair of bony spines on the tail peduncle and most have a horn on the head. In triggerfishes and filefishes (family Balistidae) the first spine in the dorsal fin can be locked in place by the second spine.

153.1 Spotted unicornfish   *Naso brevirostris*

DVI 27–29, AII 27–29. Oblong and compressed; characteristic long bony horn that projects from forehead. Bluish grey; dark spots on head and irregular vertical lines on body. Pair of sharp bony spines on tail peduncle. Tail fin truncate. **Size:** 60 cm. **Biology:** Indo-Pacific; coral and rocky reefs to 30 m. Often in schools on reef drop-off. Adults eat zooplankton but juveniles are herbivorous.

153.2 Bluespine unicornfish   *Naso unicornis*

DVI 27–30, AII 27–30. Oblong and compressed; characteristic short bony horn that projects from forehead. Brownish grey. Pair of sharp blue spines on each side of tail peduncle. Tail fin lunate; outer rays extended into filaments in adults. **Size:** 70 cm. **Biology:** Indo-Pacific; shallow coral reefs. Grazes on algae.

153.3 Clown triggerfish   *Balistoides conspicillum*

DIII + 25–27, A 21–22. Robust; first dorsal spine can be locked in place by second spine. Black with large round white blotches on ventral part of body. Orange ring around mouth; orange band under eye. Body covered in tough scales; rows of tubercles on tail peduncle. Groove on snout. **Size:** 50 cm. **Biology:** Indo-Pacific; outer coral reef slopes to 75 m. Preys on hard-shelled invertebrates, which it crushes with its strong teeth.

153.4 Redfang triggerfish   *Odonus niger*

DIII + 33–36, A 28–30. Deep body; jutting lower jaw. Body blue; teeth red. Tail lunate with extended lobes. First dorsal spine can be locked in place by second spine. Pelvic fin reduced. **Size:** 50 cm. **Biology:** Indo-Pacific; coral reef slopes. Feeds on zooplankton.

153.5 Picasso triggerfish   *Rhinecanthus aculeatus*

DIII + 23–26, A 21–22. Robust; grey with distinctive stripe pattern. Orange bridle extending from mouth to base of pectoral fin; bright blue band around mouth. Rows of small black spines on tail peduncle. First dorsal spine can be locked upright by second spine. **Size:** 30 cm. **Biology:** Indo-Pacific; reef flats and inshore sandy areas among coral rubble. Sleeps on its side at night. Omnivorous.

153.6 Boomerang triggerfish   *Sufflamen bursa*

DIII + 27–30, A 25–27. Greyish brown; two sickle-like yellow bands behind eye. Covered by tough scales. First dorsal spine can be locked upright by second spine. Pelvic fin reduced to a single spine. **Size:** 25 cm. **Biology:** Indo-Pacific; coral reefs. Feeds on benthic invertebrates. Wedges itself in crevices at night.

153.7 Halfmoon triggerfish   *Sufflamen chrysopterus*

DIII + 26–28, A 23–26. Dark brown; purplish-blue area extends from mouth along ventral surface. Vertical yellow bar below eye; white-edged tail fin. Scales with small spines form dark horizontal lines from tail peduncle. First dorsal spine can be locked upright by second spine. **Size:** 30 cm. **Biology:** Indo-Pacific; coral reefs and lagoons. Usually solitary. Feeds on benthic invertebrates.

153.8 Porky   *Stephanolepis auratus*

DII + 28–34, A 30–34. Compressed; brownish grey with irregular blotches on body and fan-like tail. First dorsal-fin spine barbed; can be locked in upright position by second spine. Pelvic fin reduced to a single barbed spine. Body covered in small spinules. **Size:** 28 cm. **Biology:** Western Indian Ocean; shallow reefs and estuaries. Small juveniles often associated with flotsam.

153.1

153.2

153.3

153.4

153.5

153.6

153.7

153.8

PLATE 154

Flounders, tonguefishes & soles

Flatfish have compressed asymmetrical bodies, with both eyes on the same side of the head. They lie on the seafloor on the nonpigmented side of their bodies, which is without eyes. There are about 50 species in southern Africa.

154.1 Peacock flounder   *Bothus mancus*

D 96–104, A 74–81. Flattened; almost round in shape. Eyes on left side of head; anterior head profile concave. Pectoral fin elongated in males. Tail fin distinct from dorsal and anal fins. Greyish, with numerous small blue spots; 2–3 large dark blotches on lateral line. **Size:** 45 cm. **Biology:** Indo-Pacific; shallow sandy areas or reef flats to 150 m. Feeds on benthic invertebrates. Characteristic transparent, leaf-like larvae are abundant in plankton in the Agulhas Current.

154.2 Leopard flounder   *Bothus pantherinus*

D 84–97, A 61–73. Flattened; almost round in shape. Eyes on left side of head; anterior head profile convex. Pectoral fin elongated in males. Tail fin distinct from dorsal and anal fins. Dusky, with dark spots and blotches; single large dark blotch on lateral line. **Size:** 30 cm. **Biology:** Indo-Pacific; shallow sandy areas or reef flats. Feeds on benthic invertebrates.

154.3 Cape sole   *Heteromycteris capensis*

D 95–102, A 64–75. Flattened and elongate. Eyes on right side of head; snout hooked over mouth. Dorsal and anal fins separate from tail fin; no pectoral fins. Brown with pale and dark spots on body and fins. **Size:** 15 cm. **Biology:** Endemic; shallow sandy shores and estuaries. Spawning peak in summer; juveniles of 1 cm recruit to estuaries.

154.4 Blackhand sole   *Solea bleekeri*

D 61–74, A 46–59. Flattened and oval. Eyes on right side of head. Black pectoral fin; last dorsal and anal rays joined by membrane to base of tail fin. Brown with dark spots on body and fins. **Size:** 17 cm. **Biology:** Endemic; estuaries and muddy or sandy coastal areas. Feeds on small benthic invertebrates, especially siphon tips of bivalves. Matures at 10 cm; spawns in spring. Juveniles recruit to estuaries at about 1 cm. **SIMILAR SPECIES**: *S. fulvomarginata*, the lemon sole (south coast), is larger (up to 26 cm) and has yellow fins with more fin rays.

154.5 Sand tonguefish   *Cynoglossus capensis*

D 103–110, A 81–88. Flat and elongate. Eyes on left side; snout hooked over lower jaw. Continuous dorsal, caudal and anal fins; pectoral fins absent. Mottled grey to brown on upper surface. No lateral line on blind side of body; three lateral lines on eyed side. **Size:** 30 cm. **Biology:** Endemic; shallow sandy areas on continental shelf. Eats benthic invertebrates. Larvae have conspicuous elongated anterior dorsal rays. **SIMILAR SPECIES**: *C. zanzibarensis*, the redspotted tongue-fish (Western Cape–Kenya), has more dorsal and anal rays and conspicuous orange-red spots on the fins.

154.6 East coast sole   *Austroglossus pectoralis*

D 90–110, A 80–95. Flattened and elongate. Eyes on right side of head. Right pectoral fin longer than head. Dorsal and anal fins continuous with tail fin. Brown. **Size:** 60 cm; 1 kg. **Biology:** Endemic; lives on sandy banks down to about 100 m. Preys on benthic invertebrates. Females grow larger than males. Spawning occurs on the Agulhas Bank. The most important commercial flatfish in South Africa. **SIMILAR SPECIES**: *A. microlepis*, the west coast sole (Namibia–False Bay), also commercially important, but now very depleted. Has fewer anal fin rays and the right pectoral fin is shorter than the head.

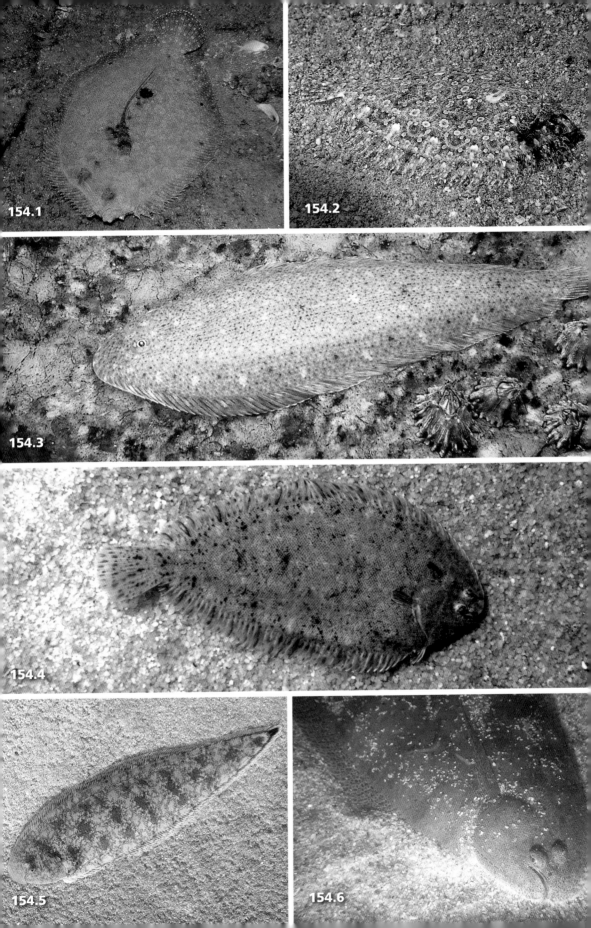

154.1

154.2

154.3

154.4

154.5

154.6

PLATE 155

Boxfishes, cowfishes, puffers, porcupinefishes & sunfish

The bodies of boxfishes and cowfishes are enclosed by modified scales that are fused into a hard bony armour. This has openings for the fins, mouth, eyes, gill slits, nostrils, anus and tail peduncle. Puffers and porcupinefishes are capable of inflating their bodies by swallowing water (or air). Their flesh is very toxic. All are feeble swimmers.

155.1 Longhorn cowfish   *Lactoria cornuta*

D 8–9, A 8–9. Body enclosed by armour of fused bony scales; two prominent horns project forwards from above eyes. Another two horns point backwards from base of anal fin. Belly flat and mouth terminal (see also 113.7). **Size:** 45 cm. **Biology:** Indo-Pacific; coral reefs and weedy areas. Juveniles appear seasonally in KwaZulu-Natal.

155.2 Spiny cowfish   *Lactoria diaphana*

D 9, A 9. Body enclosed by armour of fused bony scales. Short spines over eyes; two spines on back. Ventral ridges with spines; belly rounded. **Size:** 25 cm. **Biology:** Indo-Pacific; shallow coral reefs. Pelagic juveniles can be washed up on Cape coast.

155.3 Boxy   *Ostracion cubicus*

D 8–9, A 9. Body boxlike; enclosed by armour of fused scales. No spines or dorsal ridge. Females yellow with dark-edged white spots on each scale. Males bluish green with pale spots edged with black dots on each scale. Juveniles bright yellow with black spots. **Size:** 45 cm. **Biology:** Indo-Pacific; shallow coral reefs. Juveniles encountered in late summer along east coast; sometimes cast ashore further south.

155.4 Whitespotted puffer   *Arothron hispidus*

D 10–11, A 10–11. Plump grey body with white spots; irregular bars on head and pale belly. Yellow spots on base of pectoral fin. Small fleshy nasal tentacle below eye. Teeth fused into beak. **Size:** 48 cm. **Biology:** Indo-Pacific; coral and rocky reefs to 50 m. Juveniles in weedy areas. Feeds on benthic invertebrates.

155.5 Black-edged puffer   *Arothron immaculatus*

D 9–10, A 9–10. Plump brown body without markings. Tail fin yellowish with black margin; pectoral fin base dark. Small fleshy nasal tentacle below eye. Teeth fused into beak. **Size:** 30 cm. **Biology:** Indo-Pacific; coral, rocky and sandy areas to 50 m. Juveniles found in estuaries. Feeds on benthic invertebrates.

155.6 Blackspotted blaasop   *Arothron nigropunctatus*

D 10–11, A 10–12. Plump grey, brown or yellow body with black blotches. Snout profile concave. Small fleshy nasal tentacle below eye. Teeth fused into beak. **Size:** 30 cm. **Biology:** Indo-Pacific; coral and rocky reefs to 35 m. Feeds on benthic invertebrates.

155.7 Evileye blaasop   *Amblyrhynchotes honckenii*

D 9–10, A 8. Elongate with prominent blunt chin. Teeth fused to form strong beak. Dorsal surface greenish brown with pale spots; yellow lateral band and white belly. Conspicuous green eyes. **Size:** 30 cm. **Biology:** Indo-Pacific; reefs, sandy areas and lower reaches of estuaries. Inflates when provoked. Flesh extremely poisonous. Often buries itself in sand where it awaits prey such as crabs and small fishes. Regarded as a pest by anglers because of its bait-robbing habits.

155.1

155.2

155.3

155.4

155.5

155.6

155.7

PLATE 156

156.1 Spotted toby — *Canthigaster amboinensis*
D 11–12, A 11. Angular head and body slightly compressed. Dark with white spots; numerous pale lines on head. Covered with tiny prickles. **Size:** 15 cm. **Biology:** Indo-Pacific; shallow rocky and coral reefs. Feeds on invertebrates.

156.2 Birdbeak burrfish — *Cyclichthys orbicularis*
D 11–13, A 10–12. Body inflatable; scales modified into short immovable spines. Pelvic fins absent. Teeth fused into beak-like plate in each jaw. Brownish grey with black blotches on back and sides. **Size:** 15 cm. **Biology:** Indo-Pacific; coral rubble and sandy areas. Adults nocturnal and solitary. Pelagic juveniles are sometimes washed ashore along the Cape coast.

156.3 Balloon porcupinefish — *Diodon holocanthus*
D 13–15, A 13–15. Body inflatable; scales modified into long movable spines. Spines longer than eye diameter; no spines on tail peduncle. Pelvic fins absent. Teeth fused into beak-like plate in each jaw. Head and body tawny with small black spots and large dark dorsal blotches including one between eyes. **Size:** 30 cm. **Biology:** Circumtropical; coral, rocky and sandy areas to 100 m. Nocturnal and solitary. Feeds on benthic invertebrates.

156.4 Shortspine porcupinefish — *Diodon liturosus*
D 14–16, A 14–16. Body inflatable; scales modified into short movable spines. Spines on head shorter than elsewhere; no spines on tail peduncle. Pelvic fins absent. Teeth fused into beak-like plate in each jaw. Dark, pale-edged bars below eye, on nape and in front of pectoral fin base; three large black blotches on dorsal surface. **Size:** 50 cm. **Biology:** Indo-Pacific; coral and rocky reefs. Inflates into a round prickly ball when threatened. Feeds on benthic invertebrates. Juveniles are pelagic.

156.5 Sunfish — *Mola mola*
Body oblong and compressed; body depth more than half the length. Truncate, chopped-off appearance with no tail. Dorsal and anal fins long and stiff; pelvic fins absent. Gill opening reduced to small hole at base of pectoral fin. Mouth small; teeth fused to form parrot-like beak. Skin thick and tough with small denticles. Usually blue in colour. **Size:** 3 m; 3 tonnes. **Biology:** Circumglobal; pelagic to 600 m. Sometimes seen basking at surface. Feeds on jellyfish and salps. Larvae have spines and a tail, which are reabsorbed during metamorphosis. **SIMILAR SPECIES:** *Ranzania laevis*, the trunkfish (circumglobal), is smaller (80 cm), has a proportionally longer body that is obviously truncated, and the head and belly have pale, black-edged stripes.

Fleshy-fin fishes — Sarcopterygii
Ancient fish, long considered extinct until their discovery in South Africa. Fleshy bases and lobed shape of the fins are diagnostic features.

156.6 Coelacanth — *Latimeria chalumnae*
Robust, with large overlapping scales. Dark with white spots. All fins, except the first dorsal, are lobed, with characteristic fleshy bases. Caudal fin with central cartilaginous tube (notochord) projecting backwards (see 113.5). **Size:** 1.8 m; 100 kg. **Biology:** 'Living fossil' first discovered off East London in 1938. Now known from canyons off Sodwana Bay. Weak swimmer; feeds on fishes. Bears live 'pups' (36–38 cm); gestation period about a year. (This unique picture, one of the first coelacanth photographs to be secured by a diver, was taken by Laurent Ballesta/Eric Bahuet for the Andromède Collection during a deep dive in Sodwana led by Peter Timm of Triton Dive.)

340 Fishes

156.1

156.2

156.3

156.4

156.5

156.6

Reptiles & birds

Two classes are dealt with here:

- **Class Reptilia:** Reptiles are abundant on land, but only turtles and a few snakes have made the sea their home (Plate 157).
- **Class Aves:** Conquerors of the air, several groups of birds have a specialised association with the sea, but are still tied to land when they breed. Among them, many waders are found almost exclusively on the coast or in estuaries, including some that undertake phenomenal annual migrations across the globe (Plates 158–159). Gulls, terns, cormorants and gannets (Plates 160–163) congregate to breed on coastal islands but feed mainly at sea. Penguins (Plate 163) are the epitome of marine birds, having lost the power of flight and using their wings to 'fly' underwater. Masters of the open sea, the albatrosses and petrels (Plate 164) have perfected gliding and may spend years on the wing without alighting.

PLATE 157

Turtles & snakes
Reptilia

Five species of turtles occur in southern Africa, but only one snake in the region is completely marine. Turtles are adapted to live at sea. Their legs are modified into flat flippers and their bodies are encased in a hard bony carapace. They nest on sandy beaches, returning faithfully to the same beach year after year. In South Africa they nest only on a short stretch of coast in Maputaland, between October and February. Temperature controls the sex of the offspring. Eggs kept at 25–29°C hatch as males, those above 29°C become females. Turtles are vulnerable to disturbance at nesting beaches, capture for meat, strangulation in shark nets and on long-lines, and death due to ingestion of tar-balls or plastic. Since protection of the Maputaland nesting ground was instituted, populations there have slowly increased.

157.1 Leatherback
Dermochelys coriacea

Easily recognised by its leathery back and seven longitudinal ridges, evident even in hatchlings (157.1a). **Size:** Reaching 2 m and a mass of 1 tonne, the leatherback is the heaviest (and fastest-growing) living reptile. **Biology:** About 60–70 breed in Maputaland annually; fewer than 20 nested there in 1963 prior to conservation measures. Feeds largely on soft-bodied prey, such as jellyfish, bluebottles and pelagic tunicates. Attacked by sharks and killer whales. Large size allows it to maintain a constant core body temperature, so it can penetrate cold waters such as the Benguela.

157.2 Loggerhead turtle
Caretta caretta

Upper surface of carapace broken up into a series of plates that do not overlap one another. On either side of the central row of plates there is a row of five plates. Head large relative to body size. **Size:** 1 m. **Biology:** The most common turtle in southern Africa. Breeds in Maputaland. Nesting holes 60–80 cm deep are dug at night above the high-water mark, and about 100 eggs deposited. Over a season, each female may lay almost 600 eggs. Incubation lasts 60–70 days. The hatchlings (157.2a) emerge simultaneously at night and run the gauntlet to the sea, many falling prey to ghost crabs. Currents transport them south, and they spend the next 5–10 years in the gyres of the Agulhas Current, being recorded as far afield as Zanzibar, Madagascar and Cape Agulhas. Reproduction takes place after 15–20 years. Juveniles feed largely on floating soft-bodied creatures, including bluebottles and bubble raft shells. Adults also consume snails, mussels, rock lobsters, crabs, prawns, cuttlefish, starfish and fish.

157.3 Green turtle
Chelonia mydas

Like the loggerhead, the carapace consists of a series of nonoverlapping plates. Distinguished by having only four lateral plates in the row on either side of the central row, one claw on the front flipper; the bill is rounded, and there are two scales between the eyes. **Size:** 90 cm. **Biology:** Resident in southern Africa but never nests here. Breeds on the central Indian Ocean islands, on several of which it has been hunted close to extinction. Juveniles eat small fish and molluscs, but adults subsist almost entirely on marine plants including seaweeds and seagrass.

157.4 Hawksbill turtle
Eretmochelys imbricata

Carapace comparatively broad and flat. Plates on upper surface are imbricated: each one overlaps the plate behind; margin often serrated. Tortoiseshell pattern on upper surface. Bill strongly hooked, hence 'hawksbill'; four scales between eyes. **Size:** 90 cm. **Biology:** Eats invertebrates. Regular visitor; never breeds here. **SIMILAR SPECIES:** *Lepidochelys olivacea*, the olive Ridley turtle, is an occasional migrant to the east coast. Distinguished by having more than five lateral plates and tortoiseshell patterning. In addition, if the ventral surface is examined, there are four pores on each side in the second row of lateral plates. Scattered breeding in the western Indian Ocean, including northern Mozambique.

157.5 Yellow-bellied sea snake
Pelamis platurus

Distinctive black upper surface and a yellow to yellow-brown lower surface. Tail flattened and yellow with black blotches. **Size:** 65 cm. **Biology:** Occurs widely in the Pacific and Indian oceans from the west coast of central America to the east coast of Africa. Found far from the coast and spends its entire life at sea. Gives birth to 3–8 young. Feeds on small fish. Has a potent venom that acts by paralysing muscles. Dangerous to humans, although its bite has never proved lethal.

157.1

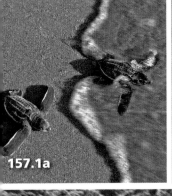

157.1a

157.2

157.2a

157.3

157.4

157.5

PLATE 158

Coastal birds

Aves

Waders

Eight species of waders are common on beaches and rocky shores. Several others frequent estuaries and inland wetlands. Many breed in the Arctic, migrating south for the (southern) summer. Oystercatchers are the largest of the waders and have bills that are markedly flattened from side to side, short legs and only three toes.

158.1 Common Whimbrel
Numenius phaeopus

Long downcurved bill 2 – 2.5 times the head length. Dark cap, with pale central line and pale stripes above the eyes. White back and rump visible in flight. **Size:** 43 cm. **Biology**: Common during summer on coastal lagoons, estuaries and rocky shores. Breeds in Siberia and Russia. Its diet consists mainly of crabs, mudprawns and polychaetes. **SIMILAR SPECIES:** *N. arquata*, the Eurasian Curlew, is larger (55 cm) with a longer bill, and lacks head stripes.

158.2 Bar-tailed Godwit
Limosa lapponica

Long, thin, slightly upturned bill, twice the head length. Brown upper and white lower body. In flight, absence of wing bar and five thin brown tail bars are diagnostic. Legs black-brown. **Size:** 38 cm. **Biology:** Common during summer on coastal lagoons and estuaries. Probes mud for prey, notably polychaetes. First colonised southern Africa about 100 years ago; its numbers have steadily increased since then. **SIMILAR SPECIES:** *Xenus cinereus*, the Terek sandpiper, also has a long, gently upturned bill but is much smaller (23 cm), with short bright yellow-orange legs; occurs in estuaries and lagoons but is scarce.

158.3 Common Greenshank
Tringa nebularia

Long olive-green legs and long slightly upturned bill diagnostic. Body white below, brown above with narrow white edges to feathers. White back and rump visible in flight. **Size:** 32 cm. **Biology:** Common summer visitor; widespread on edges of dams, rivers, estuaries, salt marshes and rocky or sandy shores. Eats crabs, sandprawns, mudprawns and polychaetes; also scythes bill from side-to-side in water to catch small fish.

158.4 Avocet
Recurvirostra avosetta

Unmistakable, with its long, markedly upcurved thin black bill, black cap and black and white wings. **Size:** 43 cm. **Biology**: Occurs in shallow waters in estuaries, lagoons and coastal saltworks. Feeds on invertebrates by pecking or by scything its bill from side-to-side over the surface of the mud.

158.5 Black-winged Stilt
Himantopus himantopus

Long thin pointed bill about 1.5 times head length. Back and wings black, head, neck and belly white. Extremely long bright red legs a key feature; they trail behind the body in flight. **Size:** 37 cm. **Biology**: Wades in shallow standing water in estuaries, lagoons, vleis and marshes. Numbers increasing due to construction of artificial wetlands.

158.6 Common Sandpiper
Actitis hypoleucos

Grey-brown above, white below, with a distinctive white shoulder patch. Bill straight and slightly longer than the head. Legs dull grey-green. Flight fluttering; upperwing has a bold white central bar and a white trailing edge. **Size:** 20 cm. **Biology**: Summer visitor; occurs on river edges and in wetlands and estuaries. Eats invertebrates, especially insects.

158.7 Ruddy Turnstone
Arenaria interpres

Distinctive yellow-orange legs. Bill black, shorter than head. Belly white, foreneck and chest mottled or black. Hunched, head-in-shoulders appearance. Breeding plumage striking, with black bands on the white face; upperparts chestnut and black. Non-breeding plumage more drab: head mottled and wing feathers brown with pale margins. In flight, recognised by a combination of three parallel white lines down the back and conspicuous white wing bar. **Size:** 22 cm. **Biology**: An Arctic migrant, common here in summer. Small flocks feed on rocky shores or tidal sandflats, overturning pebbles and seaweeds to expose invertebrates.

158.1

158.2

158.3

158.4

158.5

158.6

158.7

PLATE 159

159.1 Red Knot — *Calidris canutus*

Grey upperwing and body; undersurface white, flecked grey. Breeding plumage: head and underparts rich rufous colour. Bill black, very slightly downturned; same length as head. Legs grey, tinged green. **Size:** 24 cm. **Biology:** Occupies estuaries, lagoons and rocky shores; locally common on west coast. Migrates to Siberian breeding grounds in April. Feeds on tiny gastropods, bivalves, polychaetes and amphipods.

159.2 Sanderling — *Calidris alba*

White below, pale grey above; dark shoulder patch. Bill stubby, straight, black; as long as head. In flight, conspicuous white bar across top of wings; rump white with blackish central line. Breeding birds suffused yellow-brown; head and neck chestnut. **Size:** 19 cm. **Biology:** Common on west coast beaches. Flocks run up and down beaches ahead of the waves, ploughing their bills through the sand to gather small animals. Migrates >12 000 km to breed in the Arctic. Abundance here inversely correlated with that of Siberian lemmings because Arctic foxes turn to birds' eggs and young when lemmings are scarce.

159.3 Curlew Sandpiper — *Calidris ferruginea*

Pale grey-brown above, white below; breeding birds with dark rufous underparts and face. Bill about 1.5 times head length, curving gently down. In flight, white rump and wing bars visible. **Size:** 20 cm. **Biology:** An Arctic-breeding migrant. Huge flocks feed on pans, vleis and estuaries, probing wet mud for molluscs, crustaceans and worms.

159.4 Grey Plover — *Pluvalis squatarola*

Short-necked, plump. Grey above, with upperwing and head mottled brown. Breeding birds with black throat and chest, spangled black and white above; sides of neck white. Bill half head length. Legs fairly long and black. In flight, a distinctive black 'armpit' is evident. **Size:** 28 cm. **Biology:** Common on tidal sandflats and sheltered shores in summer. Eats molluscs, sand- and mudprawns, crabs and worms.

159.5 White-fronted Plover — *Charadrius marginatus*

Chubby, short-necked; bill also short. Grey-brown above, off-white below. Narrow white neck collar; chest band incomplete. Narrow dark line through the eye. **Size:** 17 cm. **Biology**: Familiar on sandy beaches, singly or in small groups, dodging waves to pick out worms and crustaceans. Nests in sandy depressions above high-water zone.

159.6 Cape Wagtail — *Motacilla capensis*

Grey with a long tail, white throat, and dark band across the upper breast. White brow above the eye. **Size:** 18 cm. **Biology:** Occurs singly or in pairs, usually near water. Common on rocky shores where it pecks insect larvae and crustaceans. Wagtails are among the few passerine (perching) birds to frequent the shore.

159.7 African Black Oystercatcher — *Haematopus moquini*

Unmistakable jet-black body, pink legs and bright orange-red bill and eye-ring. **Size:** 43 cm. **Biology:** Breeding endemic. Usually in territorial pairs, but also roosts in flocks of up to 100. Occupies estuaries and open coast; abundant on west coast islands. Eats mussels, limpets, whelks and worms, scissoring flesh out with its flattened bill. Males have shorter blunter bills than females, and eat more gastropods; females consume more mussels and polychaetes, presumably reducing competition between sexes. Where abundant, oystercatchers transform rocky shores by depleting limpets, allowing algae to proliferate, enhancing the habitat for other invertebrates. The nest is a scraped hollow above the high-tide mark. Eggs and chicks extremely well camouflaged. Juveniles emigrate, many to Namibia where they form large 'nursery flocks', but return after 2–3 years. Rated near-threatened, but numbers increased by 45% between 1980 and 2006, partly due to the arrival of the alien mussel *Mytilus galloprovincialis* (62.3), which supplies additional food – and also because of improved coastal protection. Episodic deaths are caused by consuming mussels contaminated by toxic 'red tides'.

159.1

159.2

159.3

159.4

159.5

159.6

159.7

PLATE 160

Skuas & gulls

Skuas and gulls (family Laridae) have slender wings, webbed feet and robust pointed beaks. Gulls are raucous scavengers around ships, harbours and rubbish dumps.

160.1 Subantarctic Skua — *Catharacta antarctica*

Overall dark mottled brown, with white wing patch on the upper and lower surfaces near wing tips, visible in flight (160.1). Bill with sharply hooked tip (160.1a). **Size:** 60 cm. **Biology:** Oceanic: disperses from its breeding grounds on subantarctic islands during winter, when it concentrates on the west and south coasts. Surface-seizes fish or squid. Steals from other birds and scavenges discards from fishing vessels. **SIMILAR SPECIES:** Three species of jaeger (previously called skuas) have a similar appearance and habits but are considerably smaller, usually with pale throats or bellies. ***Stercorarius parasiticus***, the Parasitic Jaeger, is the most common of these.

160.2 Sabine Gull — *Larus sabini*

Bill black, tipped yellow. Tail shallowly forked. Blackish half collar on neck, and upperwing tricoloured: grey centre, white triangular trailing section and black outer edge. **Size:** 30 cm. **Biology:** A common oceanic summer visitor from its circumpolar breeding grounds. Most abundant on the west coast, but seldom seen from the shore.

160.3 Kelp Gull — *Larus dominicanus*

White, with a black back and wing; trailing edge of wing white. Bill yellow with a red spot. Eye dark, with orange ring. Olive feet and legs. Young birds mottled brown (160.3a) with a paler rump that distinguishes them from all stages of the Subantarctic Skua. **Size:** 60 cm. **Biology:** Scavenges offal and animals cast up by storms. Smashes mussels and turban shells by dropping them from the air onto rocks. Captures white mussels by paddling in wet sand. Eats eggs and chicks of other island-breeding birds if they leave their nests. Its numbers have increased because it scavenges from rubbish dumps. Nests on coastal islands or cliffs.

160.4 Hartlaub's Gull — *Larus hartlaubii*

White, with grey back; upperwing tipped black and white. Head white, but pale grey when breeding. Eyes dark; no orange-red eye-ring. Legs and bill dark reddish black. **Size:** 38 cm. **Biology:** Mainly coastal. Scavenges offal and fish remains, frequents rubbish dumps and follows ploughs to capture displaced insects and worms. Scuffles small invertebrates from sandy beaches by paddling wet sand. Nests on flat parts of coastal islands, often mixed with Swift Terns. Builds nest of vegetation, usually in a natural depression, and incorporates pebbles or snails' shells among its eggs.

160.5 Grey-headed Gull — *Larus cirrocephalus*

Body white; head and most of upper body and wings grey. Wing tips mostly black, with a white inner flash. Legs and bill red. Eyes pale, with red rim. Juveniles have darker upperparts than Hartlaub's Gull, and a dark band at the tail tip. **Size:** 42 cm. **Biology**: Predominantly an inland species, but occurs along the entire coast. Scavenges on dead fish and offal, and hunts insects and crustaceans.

160.1

160.2

160.1a

160.3

160.3a

160.4

160.5

PLATE 161

Terns

Terns (family Sternidae) have slender pointed bills and more delicate bodies than gulls, and their tails are long and often forked. Most plunge-dive to capture fish. Several species are difficult to tell apart: size and bill colour help to distinguish them.

161.1 Swift Tern
Sterna bergii

Fairly large; identified by its long, uniformly chrome-yellow bill, white front to forehead and crested head. **Size:** 48 cm. **Biology:** Resident in southern Africa year-round; nests communally, usually on coastal islands, scraping a shallow depression on the ground. Often breeds in association with Hartlaub's Gull. **SIMILAR SPECIES:** *S. bengalensis*, the Lesser Crested Tern, occurs from KwaZulu-Natal northwards and is smaller, with paler upperparts and a rich orange bill. Forehead black in breeding plumage.

161.2 Caspian Tern
Sterna caspia

Very large, with short tail and massive black-tipped red bill. Diagnostic dusky, almost black, tips to underwing (161.2). Body white, back and upperwings pale grey; cap and legs black (161.2a). **Size:** 55 cm. **Biology**: Locally common, breeding in colonies. Nests in shallow scrapes on the ground. Considered near-threatened.

161.3 Damara Tern
Sterna balaenarum

In combination, small size, pitch-black bill and a grey rump and tail distinguish this species. In breeding plumage, a black cap covers the entire head above the eyes. **Size:** 23 cm. **Biology:** Breeding summer migrant to southern Africa, locally common in Namibia. Nests in dune-slacks and gravel plains up to 5 km from the sea. Vulnerable to disturbance by off-road vehicles. **SIMILAR SPECIES:** *S. albifrons*, the Little Tern, is also small (23 cm), but has a white rump and tail, and yellow-brown (not black) legs at all times. In breeding condition, bill yellow with black tip. Found mainly on the south and east coasts.

161.4 Common Tern
Sterna hirundo

Medium-sized and easily confused with several other terns. Distinguished by its relatively dark grey upperparts, and pale grey rump and tail (visible in flight). Bill quite long (equal to head length); red, with a black tip in the breeding phase. Legs dull red; longer than in Arctic or Antarctic terns. **Size:** 35 cm. **Biology:** Strictly coastal; most abundant in spring and summer. Most common coastal tern: roosts in large groups, regularly numbering tens of thousands, around estuaries or on beaches.

161.5 Antarctic Tern
Sterna vittata

In breeding plumage, distinctly grey underbelly; grey neck separated from black cap by narrow white cheek-stripe. Tail white, deeply forked. Legs shorter than in the Common Tern. Bill and legs bright red. In non-breeding birds, crown distinctively grizzled. **Size:** 37 cm. **Biology:** Locally common visitor in winter. Breeds on subantarctic islands. **SIMILAR SPECIES:** *S. paradisaea*, the Arctic Tern (open sea Namibia–Maputo), has a uniformly red, much shorter thinner bill (although the bill, like that of the Common Tern, is black in non-breeding plumage). Rump white. Common at sea September–January, rarely ashore. *S. dougallii*, the Roseate Tern (Saldanha–Maputo, but mostly in Algoa Bay), has a very pale bill. Breeding birds with chest tinged pink; bill red with a dark tip; legs bright carmine red. In the non-breeding season, the legs fade, the bill is similar to that of the Common Tern – long, thin and dark – but the tail feathers are always pure white and much longer, with protruding tail streamers. Main breeding colony on Bird Island, Algoa Bay. Endangered in South Africa.

161.6 Sandwich Tern
Sterna sandvicensis

Relatively easy to recognise because the long thin bill is black, tipped with yellow. Rump white. Back of the head with slight crest. **Size:** 40 cm. **Biology:** Restricted to the coast; seldom ventures far out to sea. Roosts on beaches in large numbers. A common summer visitor to most of the coast, except Mozambique.

161.1

161.2

161.2a

161.3

61.4

61.5

161.6

PLATE 162

Cormorants, egrets & herons

Cormorants (family Phalacrocoracidae) are predominantly black, with short legs, webbed feet and slender bodies. Their feathers get wet when they enter water, and they often spread their wings out to dry them. Herons and egrets fall in a closely related family (Ardeidae) and are tall slender birds with pointed bills and long thin toes. They frequent shallow water, vleis, grass plains and ploughed land.

162.1 Bank Cormorant — *Phalacrocorax neglectus*

Usually wholly black; rump white during breeding season. Plumper than the Cape Cormorant, and distinguished by its dark bill, totally black head and a small crest. Eye two-tone: upper half orange-brown, lower half green. **Size:** 75 cm. **Biology:** Endemic. Makes seaweed nests on top of large boulders on islands. Dives shallowly; eats klipfish, gobies and invertebrates, including small rock lobsters. Endangered: total numbers down to 3 000 in 2001, a 66% decline from 1972, due to shrinking food supplies and displacement from some islands by expanding seal populations.

162.2 Cape Cormorant — *Phalacrocorax capensis*

Mature birds uniformly greenish black. No crest. Gape of bill bright orange-yellow; eye turquoise, with green eye-ring. Tail short. **Size:** 65 cm. **Biology:** Breeding endemic. The most common cormorant, confined to the coast. In Namibia it nests on artificial floating platforms, placed in the sea to harvest guano. Nests made of sticks and seaweed, frequently stolen from adjacent nests. Often flies in long lines or V-shaped flocks (hence the Afrikaans name 'Trekduiker'). This conserves energy, each bird gaining 'lift' from the one in front. Feeds on pelagic fish, notably pilchards and anchovies. Flocks settle on the sea, and repeatedly dive to catch the fish. Other fish-eating birds are attracted to these feeding frenzies. Considered near-threatened: declined from about a million in the 1970s to 240 000 in 2000, due to a combination of disease, parasites, displacement by seals and food shortages. Abundance correlated with that of anchovies.

162.3 White-breasted Cormorant — *Phalacrocorax lucidus*

The largest of the cormorants, with a distinctive white throat and chest, the rest of the body being brown, or glossy greenish black when breeding. Eyes green. **Size:** 90 cm. **Biology:** Usually nests in colonies on coastal islands or cliffs, often on man-made structures, but does occur inland, wherever water is readily available. Feeds on fish.

162.4 Crowned Cormorant — *Phalacrocorax coronatus*

Glossy green-black; obvious tuft of upright feathers on head. Ruby-red eye. Gape of bill pale yellow. Tail relatively long. **Size:** 55 cm. **Biology:** Endemic. Nests in small colonies on rocky ledges and bushes on islands. Eats small fish and crustaceans, caught by diving in shallow waters. Numbers only 2 500: rated near-threatened.

162.5 Little Egret — *Egretta garzetta*

Body white, bill slender and black. Legs black; feet distinctively pinkish brown (or orange-red during breeding), visible even in flight. **Size:** 65 cm. **Biology:** Common at marshes, dams, estuaries and on open coast. Roosts in groups. Feeds by stabbing shallow fish and crabs. **SIMILAR SPECIES:** Five other egrets occur here, but are rare on seashores. *E. alba*, the Great Egret, is much larger (95 cm); legs and feet totally black, bill black with a yellow base. Forages in estuaries from the Eastern Cape northwards. *E. intermedia*, the Yellow-billed Egret, has yellow upper legs; lower legs and feet black. Bill yellow or red. Feeds in fresh water, in estuarine waters and in grasslands.

162.6 Grey Heron — *Ardea cinerea*

Grey with white neck; front flecked black. Cap white; black streak behind eyes extends as plumes. In flight, undersurface of the wings pure grey. **Size:** 100 cm. **Biology:** Common in or near estuaries, vleis and dams, mangroves and rocky shores. Stands stock-still much of the time. Stalks and stabs fish, amphibians, crabs, insects and even other birds.

162.1

162.2

162.3

162.4

162.5

162.6

PLATE 163

Penguins, ibis, pelicans, gannets & flamingoes

Despite appearing disparate, these birds belong to five closely related families allied to herons and cormorants.

163.1 African Penguin   *Spheniscus demersus*

Flightless, with flipper-like wings. Face and back black, separated by a white stripe. Chest white, with an inverted black 'U'. Bare pink skin above eyes. Pattern of chest spots unique to each individual. Juveniles grey above; chicks uniformly brown and fluffy. **Size:** 60 cm. **Biology**: Occurs on offshore islands and at three mainland colonies. Feeds largely on pelagic fish, diving to 130 m and circling to concentrate the fish. Feathers modified to a scaly cover, trapping air when the birds submerge, 'wet-suiting' the body. Moults once a year; cannot feed when moulting. Monogamous. Numbers have declined over the past 100 years, from about 2 million to about 26 000 breeding pairs. Causes include oil spills, competition with fisheries for food, harvesting of eggs (which ceased in 1967) and collection of guano, which prevents the birds from digging nests, exposing their eggs to heat and predators. Serious declines in 2003–2008 coincided with pelagic fish shifting from the west to the south coast. Seals have eliminated 10 island colonies. After a major oil spill in 2000, about 40 000 adult birds were evacuated from Dassen Island to Algoa Bay, but swam the 1 200 km return journey within 21 days.

163.2 African Sacred Ibis   *Threskiornis aethiopicus*

Head and neck bare and black (adult) or with speckled feathers (juveniles). Massive downcurved black bill. Body and most of wing white; trailing edge of wing black. Breeding individuals have a red flash under the wing. **Size:** 75 cm. **Biology:** Common on margins of marshes, estuaries and lagoons, and at offshore islands. Previously bred only on offshore west coast islands but now breeds throughout its range. Eats insects and crustaceans, and attacks eggs and chicks of other birds on islands.

163.3 Eastern White Pelican   *Pelecanus onocrotalus*

White, flushed with pink when breeding. Trailing edge of wings black. Bill, pouch and facial skin yellow to orange. **Size:** 160 cm. **Biology:** Frequents lagoons, estuaries, rivers and vleis; common near the coast. Coastally, breeds on Dassen Island, at Lake St Lucia and at Walvis Bay. Groups herd fish into shallow water. Has recently turned to cooperatively attacking nesting birds and their chicks on west coast islands. **SIMILAR SPECIES:** *P. rufescens*, the Pink-backed Pelican, is not common; concentrated in KwaZulu-Natal and southern Mozambique. Grey, with pink rump, back and pouch; hind edge of wing grey.

163.4 Cape Gannet   *Morus capensis*

Elegant golden head, black stripe across the eye and down the throat, and broad black trailing edges to the wings. Bill and eyelids pale blue. Young birds brown, flecked white. **Size:** 90 cm. **Biology:** Nests on offshore islands, forming huge colonies on flat areas – most readily viewed at Lambert's Bay. Incoming birds recognise their mates in the crowd, and elaborate greetings follow their return, including 'fencing' of bills, head-bowing and mutual preening. Adults plummet from great heights to catch fish – mainly pilchards, anchovies or pelagic gobies. Feeding flocks associate with seals, sharks and dolphins. Numbers have declined on the west coast with the collapse of Namibian sardine stocks, a shift of pelagic fish to the south coast, and attacks by seals. In 2006 the entire colony abandoned Lambert's Bay Island after land-based attacks by seals, but returned after conservation measures to deter the seals.

163.5 Greater Flamingo   *Phoenicopterus ruber*

White, tinged pink; open wings bright red with black trailing edge. Bill pink with black tip. Legs red. **Size:** 150 cm. **Biology:** Concentrates in coastal lagoons and pans. Breeds most commonly in Botswana and at Etosha Pan, Namibia. Feeds in shallow water, leaving tyre-shaped 'wheelies' in the mud by 'treadling' in circles to suspend small animals that are filtered out with the bill. This profoundly affects the life on the sandflats, decreasing the abundance of most invertebrates. **SIMILAR SPECIES:** *P. minor*, the Lesser Flamingo, is smaller, darker pink, and has a black-tipped deep maroon bill, which appears all-dark in the field. Feeds by filtering the water, never by treadling in circles; eats cyanobacteria (blue-green bacteria).

163.1

163.2

163.3

163.4

163.5

PLATE 164

Albatrosses & petrels

Albatrosses and petrels are open-water species that spend most of their time in the air, seizing surface prey or scavenging from fishing vessels. Consummate gliders, albatrosses spend up to two years continuously on the wing. Long-line fishing is a threat to them, but can be countered by weighted lines, streamers above lines, and setting lines at night.

164.1 Shy Albatross   *Thalassarche cauta*
White, with black tail, dark grey back and upperwing; narrow black border to underwing. Diagnostic black spot on 'armpit'. Bill pale olive, tipped yellow (adult) or black (juveniles). **Size:** 95 cm. **Biology:** Dives shallowly to catch pelagic fish, but obtains 40% of its food by scavenging from fishing vessels. In 2000, long-lining caused up to 10 000 deaths per year in southern Africa, but remedial measures have improved the situation.

164.2 Black-browed Albatross   *Thalassarche melanophrys*
Similar to Shy Albatross, but head has a prominent dark 'eyebrow', bill is yellow with pink tip, and underwing has much broader black border, covering about half the wing. **Size:** 90 cm. **Biology:** Most common albatross in Cape waters, aggregating around fishing vessels, where it gleans 80% of its food from discards and offal. Also dives for fish, crustaceans and squid. Long-lining deaths similar to Shy Albatross.

164.3 Indian Yellow-nosed Albatross   *Thalassarche carteri*
Body white; back and tail blackish brown. Diagnostic black bill with reddish tip and yellow dorsal stripe. Cheeks washed pale grey. **Size:** 95 cm. **Biology:** Breeds on Prince Edward and Gough islands. Most common in winter in the southeast. **SIMILAR SPECIES:** *T. chlororhynchos*, the Atlantic Yellow-nosed Albatross, is almost identical, but whole head and neck covered with darker grey wash; most abundant on west coast.

164.4 Sooty Shearwater   *Puffinus griseus*
Sooty grey-brown, slightly paler below, with pale silvery central panel on the underwing. Bill dark grey (not whitish as in White-chinned Petrel). **Size:** 44 cm. **Biology:** The most abundant oceanic bird here; winter aggregations reach 10 000. Feeds in association with cetaceans, seals, gannets and cormorants. Periodically scavenges from trawlers.

164.5 Wilson's Storm-Petrel   *Oceanites oceanicus*
Small; dark brown, except for white rump and grey patch on top of inner wing. Legs long, toes extending beyond the square-cut tail in flight. **Size:** 18 cm. **Biology:** The most abundant storm-petrel in our waters: about 300 000 concentrated on the west and south coasts. Treadles the water surface while feeding on zooplankton and small squid and fish.

164.6 Pintado Petrel   *Daption capense*
Underside white except for black head, tail and wing edge. Upper surface dark with speckles and four white wing patches, giving a characteristic pied appearance. **Size:** 38 cm. **Biology:** A surface-seizer; feeds on crustaceans and squid; aggregates in groups of hundreds or thousands to scavenge offal from trawlers near the shelf break, especially in winter.

164.7 White-chinned Petrel   *Procellaria aequinoctialis*
Uniformly shiny black, with a white patch on chin and throat. Bill pale, with dark saddle and side-stripe. **Size:** 54 cm. **Biology:** Breeds on subantarctic islands; concentrated on the west coast shelf break, especially in winter, surface-feeding in association with cetaceans and seals. Scavenges from trawlers.

164.8 Southern Giant-Petrel   *Macronectes giganteus*
Heavy, uniformly grey-brown body; head paler. Bill massive, with large flesh-coloured nostril tube, and greenish tip (164.8a). **Size:** 90 cm. **Biology:** Most abundant here in winter. Dives shallowly and scavenges around seal colonies. **SIMILAR SPECIES:** *M. halli*, the Northern Giant-Petrel, is distinguished by its reddish-brown bill tip.

164.1

164.2

164.3

164.4

164.5

164.6

164.7

164.8

164.8a

Mammals

Class Mammalia originated on land. Mammals are air-breathing, viviparous (give birth to live young), suckle their offspring with milk, and have hairy bodies, even if the hairs are sometimes barely evident. A small number of species have made the sea their home, and their bodies are streamlined and their limbs modified into paddles. The supreme mammalian denizens of the sea are the whales and dolphins, which have thick insulating blubber and have lost their hind limbs, relying instead on a flattened tail fluke for propulsion. Some can dive as deep as 2 km and stay underwater for up to two hours. No other animal is as breathtaking as the blue whale, *Balaenoptera musculus*, shown on this page: the largest animal that has ever existed on earth, reaching 33 m and 175 tonnes – and once hunted to the edge of extinction. When Linnaeus named the creature, he was having a private joke, for the word *musculus* means 'little mouse'.

PLATE 165

Seals, otters & dugongs

Carnivora & Sirenia

Seals and otters fall in the order Carnivora. Seals are streamlined, covered with blubber and thick fur or hair to reduce heat loss, and their limbs form flippers. Fur seals (family Otariidae) have external ears and their hind limbs can rotate forwards to walk on land. Harbour seals and elephant seals (family Phocidae) lack external ears; their hind limbs cannot turn forwards, so they wriggle their bodies to move on land. Otters (family Mustelidae) have webbed hind feet and a strongly muscular tail for swimming. Dugongs (order Sirenia) are superficially dolphin-like, in that the hind limbs are replaced by a tail fluke.

165.1 South African fur seal
Arctocephalus pusillus pusillus

Adults chocolate-brown; darker when wet. Pups black. Teeth behind canines cusped, unlike other fur seals. **Size:** Bulls 2.5 m, 300 kg; cows 1.6 m, 75 kg. **Biology:** Consumes mainly anchovies, pilchards, bearded gobies, but also octopus, squid, mantis shrimps and rock lobsters. Adult bulls 'haul out' in October at island or mainland colonies and defend territories for 4–8 weeks, without any time-out to feed. In November, cows arrive and bulls establish harems of 10–40. After mating, embryo implantation into the uterus is delayed for about four months so that the eight-month pregnancy leads to birth at the next haul-out time, a year later. Decimated by sealing in the 1800s, but increased under a controlled harvest of about 2.7 million in the 1900s. Harvesting now restricted to Namibia after being banned in South Africa from 1973. By 2001, numbers recovered to about 2 million, despite Namibian mass mortalities in 'warm years' when fish diminished. Seals do compete with the fishing industry, consuming about 2 million tonnes each year, interrupting fishing operations and damaging gear. However, culling is unlikely to be an effective counter. Trawlers accidentally kill about 4 000 per year. Seals have displaced bird colonies from several islands. **SIMILAR SPECIES:** Subantarctic fur seals, *Arctocephalus tropicalis*, occasionally visit South Africa. They have a cream to burnt-orange chest and face and the bulls have a prominent head crest.

165.2 Leopard seal
Hydrurga leptonyx

Silvery grey, paler below, with darker grey spots and blotches. Head elongate; enormous gape. **Size:** 3.4 m. **Biology:** Predominantly Antarctic, but hauls out onto subantarctic islands in winter; rare vagrants occasionally seen on the South African coast. Aggressively preys on penguins, other seals, fish and krill.

165.3 Southern elephant seal
Mirounga leonina

Enormous size and swollen, proboscis-like snout of the male distinctive. Females chubby, drab brown, and lack the proboscis. Uniquely, only one pair of incisors in the lower jaw. **Size:** Bulls 4.6 m, 3.5 tonnes; cows 2.9 m, 350 kg. **Biology:** Common on subantarctic islands. Feeds mainly on squid and fish. Once heavily hunted for their oil, and eliminated from several islands in the late 1800s, but most populations have recovered. Stragglers occur in South Africa and Namibia. Dives to 1.5 km and stays underwater for up to two hours.

165.4 Cape clawless otter
Aonyx capensis

Sleek; tail robust, tapering. Dark brown with white belly. Chin and throat white – never spotted (unlike the spotted-necked otter, which never occurs in the sea). Hind feet partly webbed. Front legs have grasping, characteristically clawless fingers. **Size:** 1.5 m; 18 kg. **Biology:** Found throughout wetter parts of southern Africa, and also in the sea, where it consumes fish, octopus and crabs. East of Cape Hangklip the rock lobster, *Jasus lalandii*, has become a dominant dietary element since lobsters 'invaded' that area in the late 1980s. Most active early morning and evening.

165.5 Dugong
Dugong dugon

Slate-grey, chubby, with crescent-shaped tail and broad flat flippers. Fleshy lower lip and bloated upper lip both covered with long stiff bristles. **Size:** 3 m; 500 kg. **Biology:** Occurs in shallow sheltered bays and lagoons where seagrasses grow prolifically. Cuts swathes through seagrass beds, consuming about 25% of its body weight per day. Severely depleted by hunting, entanglement in nets, and habitat destruction.

165.1

165.2

165.3

165.4

Whales & dolphins — Cetacea

Whales and dolphins (order Cetacea) have lost their hind limbs and modified the forelimbs into flippers for stability and steering; horizontal tail flukes provide propulsion. Fifty-one species occur in southern Africa. There are two groups: Odontoceti are toothed; Mysticeti lack teeth but have comb-like baleen plates in their mouths to filter seawater for prey. Cetaceans must surface to breathe air, spouting out air and water vapour. Dolphins navigate by echolocation, emitting high-frequency clicks that bounce off solid objects. Dolphins have conical teeth, and usually a 'beak' and a hooked fin; porpoises have spade-like teeth, no beak and a triangular fin. Larger whales were once hunted close to extinction for their meat and oil, but protection has led to partial recoveries.

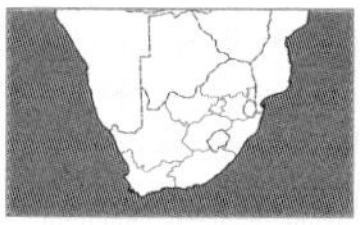

166.1 Southern right whale — *Eubalaena australis*

No dorsal fin or throat grooves. Lower jaw curved to meet the arched snout. Wart-like white callosities bedeck the jaws, forehead and chin. Black above, with white belly blaze; sometimes grey or white patches on back. Spout V-shaped. **Size:** 14–15 m; 47 tonnes. **Biology:** The whale most often seen from the shore, particularly between Cape Town and Port Elizabeth. Breaches with a spectacular leap, then crashes down explosively. Courting males jostle for females. Migrates to subantarctic waters in summer, where it eats mainly copepods and sometimes krill; overwinters on the coast of southern Africa from July–November, where females give birth and rear young in sheltered bays. Heavily overexploited, with about 130 000 killed 1770–1850; reduced to about 300 individuals, approaching extinction. Protected from 1935; now recovering at 7.1% per annum. Named the 'right' whale as it was easy to hunt, rich in oil, had high-quality baleen and floated after being killed.

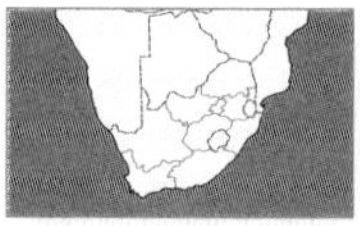

166.2 Humpback whale — *Megaptera novaeangliae*

Distinctive long narrow flippers, about one-third the body length; leading edge with obvious knobs. About 30 throat grooves. Dorsal fin small, and followed by small 'knuckles'. Tail fluke usually white below; edge clearly scalloped. Upper jaw decorated with 3–5 rows of knobs (166.2b): one medial and two down each side – each knob housing a lonely hair follicle. Black, but variably white below. Totally or partially white individuals not unusual. Spout directed upwards and 'bushy' at the top. **Size:** 13 m; 56 tonnes. **Biology:** Worldwide; spends summer eating krill in Antarctica. Circles underwater and releases a 'bubble curtain' that concentrates prey. Overwinters on tropical and subtropical breeding grounds off west and east Africa. Seldom feeds during winter, relying on blubber reserves. Males produce melodious 'songs' on the breeding grounds that slowly change from year to year. Badly overfished. Protected from 1963; recovering at about 9% annually. Breaches spectacularly (166.2), and 'spyhops' (166.2a).

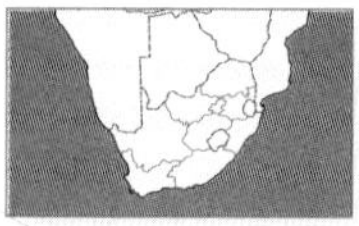

166.3 Bryde's whale — *Balaenoptera brydei*

Upper jaw very pointed, with three longitudinal ridges. Dorsal fin clearly 'hooked'. Dark grey above, grading to white below; throat grooves extend to the navel. **Size:** 13 m. **Biology:** Comes close to shore, and hunted here until 1975. Eats small shoaling fish. Correctly pronounced 'brewder' but anglicised as 'breeder'. SIMILAR SPECIES: Several other baleen whales occur here, but seldom near shore. ***B. physalus***, the fin whale, has single longitudinal ridge on the snout; lower jaw and chin white on the right and dark grey on the left. Dorsal fin small; front edge straight and angled back at 27–40°. Historically caught off Saldanha and Durban. ***B. borealis***, the sei whale, is very similar, but head colour same on both sides – grey above and white below – and fin angled back at 38–51°. Main summer feeding grounds south of South Africa. ***B. acutorostrata***, the dwarf minke whale, is small (7 m); quite common around the coast but seldom seen from the shore. Single ridge on snout. Flipper white with black tip; large white 'shoulder' patch flares upwards into a grey crescent.

166.1

166.2

166.2a

166.2b

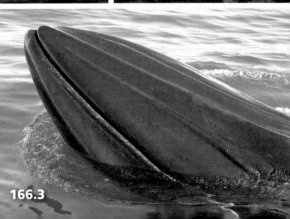

166.3

PLATE 167

167.1 Sperm whale · *Physeter macrocephalus*

The largest toothed whale. Lower jaw narrow, slung under the enormous blunt head; has heavy conical teeth. Dorsal fin a triangular fleshy hump; 3–4 backbone 'knuckles' behind it. Blowhole S-shaped and lies on the left of the snout; spout characteristically directed forwards and left (167.1). Body with longitudinal 'wrinkles'. Flukes huge: one-third the body length; edge straight, with central V-notch (167.1a). **Size:** Males 17 m, 46 tonnes; females 11 m, 14 tonnes. **Biology:** Worldwide but rare near the coast. Females tend to remain in warmer areas (40° S – 40° N); adult males range far into cold waters. Eats mainly squid, especially deep-water species. Capable of prodigious dives: over two hours and deeper than 2 km. Produces clicks that travel at least 11 km underwater. Ambergris, formerly used in perfumes, forms in its rectum. Its head houses spermaceti, speculated to be for buoyancy control or sound propagation, and once used as a high-quality industrial lubricant; a seventeenth-century belief that it was sperm gave the animal its name.

167.2 False killer whale · *Pseudorca crassidens*

Slender. Dorsal fin taller than long; tip rounded. Head round, without beak; body black with grey 'cape' and thin white belly-line. Front edge of fluke S-shaped. **Size:** 4–5 m; 1 tonne. **Biology:** Occurs in groups; feeds on fish and squid. Prone to mass strandings. Possible causes are interference with echolocation by near-shore micro-bubbles, loss of orientation due to inner-ear parasites, or disturbance of geomagnetic fields that may be used for navigation.

167.3 Killer whale · *Orcinus orca*

Black with a white belly, grey saddle behind the very tall dorsal fin, and a distinctive oval white patch behind the eye. Dorsal fin large; juts vertically in adult males, curves backwards in females and young males. **Size:** 7– 8 m; 8 tonnes. **Biology:** Perhaps the world's most widespread mammal, spanning Arctic to Antarctic, surface to 3 000 m. Common in Antarctic and subantarctic, but regularly seen off our coasts. Eats fish, squid, birds, seals, turtles, dolphins and attacks large whales. Hunts in packs. Never known to attack humans. Produces clicks for echolocation and whistles and buzzes for communication. An Antarctic 'type' has a much more obvious grey saddle. **SIMILAR SPECIES:** *Globicephala melas*, the long-finned pilot whale, has bulging, melon-like head: low, stubby, strongly 'hooked' backward-pointing dorsal fin; black with white 'eyebrow' streak, white breast and belly-streak and small grey saddle behind dorsal fin. *G. macrorhynchus*, the short-finned pilot whale, is very similar but pure black dorsally.

167.4 Indo-Pacific bottlenosed dolphin · *Tursiops aduncus*

Body robust. Snout moderate length, abruptly narrower than the head, hence 'bottlenosed'. Lead-grey dorsally; sides paler, belly almost white. No distinct boundaries between these three grades of colour. Belly often spotted grey. **Size:** 2.4 m. **Biology:** Eats mainly fish, but also squid, schools of 20–50 encircling prey. Often joins bathers, and assists newborn or injured dolphins. Shark nets kill about 37 each year, out of a population of at least 16 000. Chlorinated hydrocarbon levels are very high in KwaZulu-Natal individuals, and females 'offload' these toxins to unborn young and in their milk, with unknown effects on suckling young. **SIMILAR SPECIES:** *T. truncatus*, the common bottlenosed dolphin, is larger (3.3 m); offshore, except in Namibia–Angola. Dorsal, lateral and ventral colours clearly distinct; side grey, with a 'tongue' up to the dorsal fin. Belly not speckled. Eats mainly lantern fish (east coast) and mullet (Namibia). Echolocation formidable: can detect a 7 cm ball 113 m away!

167.5 Long-beaked common dolphin · *Delphinus capensis*

Long narrow pointed beak (6.4–8.4% of body length). Characteristic lateral 'criss-cross' figure-of-eight pattern: a buff patch in lower front of body, and a pale grey patch on upper flank behind dorsal fin. Dark stripe from corner of jaw to flipper. Below the dorsal fin, the dark back area dips down in a distinct shallow 'V'. Flippers quite small (13–15.7% of body length). **Size:** 2.5 m; 160 kg. **Biology:** Abundant inshore, forming schools that may number 1 000–5 000 individuals. Feeds on shoaling fish; follows the 'sardine run'. **SIMILAR SPECIES:** *D. delphis*, the short-beaked common dolphin, occurs offshore; seldom seen. Beak shorter (5.2–7% of body length) and flippers larger (15–17% body length).

167.1

167.1a

167.2

167.3

167.4

167.5

PLATE 168

168.1 Heaviside's dolphin — *Cephalorhynchus heavisidii*

Head conical; no obvious beak. Dorsal fin diagnostic: triangular, never curving backwards. Pale grey frontal cape and a dark line from the blowhole to the dorsal fin. Rest of upper surface black. Belly white, with a distinctive white lobe pointing obliquely backwards towards the tail. **Size:** 1.7 m. **Biology:** West coast endemic. Forms small schools from the surf zone to 45 km offshore. Eats mainly bottom-dwelling fish such as hake and kingklip. Occurs inshore in the morning, moving offshore around midnight, when hake move closer to the surface and are easier to catch.

168.2 Dusky dolphin — *Lagenorhynchus obscurus*

Beak very short and black-tipped. Fins, flippers and upperparts black, with dark mid-body 'brush-mark' extending backwards and downwards onto the white belly, and a pale flare from the flank forwards towards the dorsal fin. Dorsal fin two-tone. **Size:** 1.9 m. **Biology:** Coastal. Sometimes forms large schools and often rides the bow-waves of ships. Frequently leaps out of the water, even somersaulting in the air. Feeds cooperatively, herding fish to the surface during deep dives.

168.3 Striped dolphin — *Stenella coeruleoalba*

Dark blue-grey above; grey sides and white belly. Three distinct grey lines run backwards from the eye, one to the anus, a second to the base of the flipper, and a short one between them. Pale flare from eye to dorsal fin. **Size:** 2.5 m; 150 kg. **Biology:** Forms schools of 5–400 off the shelf edge. Feeds on fish and squid. About 80% of the prey have luminous organs, and feeding takes place mainly by night.

168.4 Pantropical spotted dolphin — *Stenella attenuata*

Long narrow beak. Body dark grey-brown above, from the head to behind the dorsal fin, and almost white below. Adults have profuse dark spots and blotches on lower surface and equivalent pale marking on the upper surface. **Size:** 2.3 m. **Biology:** Seldom seen from the shore, but one of the most common dolphins sighted from boats. Usually in schools of about 10–100, but sometimes up to 1 000-strong. **SIMILAR SPECIES:** *S. frontalis*, the Atlantic spotted dolphin (central Namibia–Angola), is more uniformly dark when adult and has much larger white spots – to the extent that the spots merge with each other on the lower half of the body. A distinctive and diagnostic mid-body flare of white spots extends upwards and backwards just below the dorsal fin, and is evident in animals of all ages. Occurs from near the coast out to depths exceeding 1 000 m.

168.5 Spinner dolphin — *Stenella longirostris*

Front two-thirds of body with sharply delineated longitudinal zones: grey-black dorsally, pale grey laterally and off-white ventrally. Dark grey flare from the eye down to the flipper, which is also dark grey. Long beak. **Size:** 2 m. **Biology:** Famous for its twisting leaps, spinning on its axis as it explodes from the water. This may help to dislodge remoras (144.1) that are attached in inconvenient places, but may simply help define the position of the school. Feeds on mid-water pelagic fish and squid.

168.6 Indo-Pacific humpback dolphin — *Sousa chinensis*

All humpback dolphins have a fleshy dorsal hump, bearing a small dorsal fin that is hooked in this species. Dark brown-grey, shading to off-white below. **Size:** 2.8 m; 280 kg. **Biology:** Common inshore, in schools of 5–25. Total southern African population only about 1 000. Threatened by shark nets and pesticides, which concentrate in its fatty tissues and are 'dumped' in the milk: has the highest organophosphate concentration of any marine mammal in the region. **SIMILAR SPECIES:** *S. teuszii*, the Atlantic humpback dolphin (Angola northwards), has fin that forms a backward-facing lobe; not recurved as in the Indo-Pacific species.

168.7 Southern right whale dolphin — *Lissodelphis peronii*

Striking and distinctive. Lack of a dorsal fin and the contrast between its white belly and black back instantly distinguish it. **Size:** 2.3–2.9 m. **Biology:** Circumpolar in subantarctic waters, and periodically recorded off the Namibian coast.

168.1

168.2

168.3

168.4

168.5

168.6

168.7

Seaweeds

Algae include simple unicellular planktonic organisms and large seaweeds. Some are of considerable economic importance. Identification of seaweeds is sometimes difficult because they vary in shape and colour, and phases of the life cycles may differ substantially. Structure, texture and habitat are useful characters.

Seaweeds are separated into three divisions:

- **Chlorophyta** or green algae (Plates 169–173)
- **Ochrophyta** or brown algae (Plates 174–178)
- **Rhodophyta** or red algae (Plates 179–192).

PLATE 169

Green algae   Chlorophyta

The Chlorophyta are easily distinguished by their bright green colour – resulting from the green pigments chlorophyll a and b, which are the same as those found in higher land plants. Chlorophyta have three basic body forms: (1) simple flat sheets one or two cells thick (Plate 169); (2) filaments of cells placed end to end in simple strings, branched or grouped into more complex structures (Plate 170); (3) coenocytic forms – consisting of continuous tubes grouped together (Plates 171–173). The life cycles of Chlorophyta are simple, alternating between an asexual sporophyte and male or female gametophyte generation that are similar in appearance.

Simple green sheets & cushions

Sea lettuces have membranous vivid green blades or tubes, attached by a disc-shaped holdfast. Ulva spp. are two cells thick; some form hollow tubes and were formerly placed in the genus Enteromorpha. Monostroma spp. are only one cell thick. Being tolerant of wide temperature and salinity changes, both flourish in mid- to high-tide pools or estuaries, and are early colonisers on denuded rocks. When cold water enters pools on the rising tide, spores are shed from the edges of the blades, forming a green scum. Ulva and Monostroma are eaten in the Far East and farmed in a number of countries.

169.1 Ribbon sea lettuce   *Ulva fasciata*

Plants pale green, attached by a disc-shaped holdfast. Blades tough, ribbon-like, two cells thick; cells cylindrical. **Size:** Usually about 120 mm long. **Biology:** Mostly on rocks in pools. **SIMILAR SPECIES:** *U. rhacodes* (south coast) has a lax narrow elongate blade with frilled margins armed with double teeth. Occurs in high-shore pools; often epiphytic on other algae.

169.2 Rigid sea lettuce   *Ulva rigida*

Firm grass-green blades irregularly lobed and often forming small rosettes: the margins near the base have minute teeth; blades two cells thick, cells in section rounded to square; holdfast disc-shaped. **Size:** Usually 20–200 mm in diameter. **Biology:** Common on exposed intertidal rocks. **SIMILAR SPECIES:** *U. capensis* (Namibia–Cape Agulhas) has holes and irregular toothed margins, cells bullet-shaped. Occurs in the lower intertidal zone. *Microdictyon kraussi* (Port Elizabeth–Mozambique) has flat green blades that look superficially solid but comprise a net of tubular cells, visible under a hand lens.

169.3 Green sea intestines   *Ulva intestinalis*

Membranous green tubes, with walls one cell thick. **Size:** About 100 mm long. **Biology:** Like other *Ulva* spp. it tolerates temperature and salinity fluctuations and lives in mid- to high-tide pools and estuaries. Flourishes around sewage outfalls. **SIMILAR SPECIES:** There are several related tubular species, all previously placed in the genus *Enteromorpha*. Can be confused with *Scytosiphon simplicissimus* (178.5), but is bright green, not brownish.

169.4 Tangleweed   *Ulva clathrata*

A tangled floating mass of thin tubular axes, richly branched at right angles. **Size:** Tubes 1–5 mm diameter. **Biology:** Tolerant of relatively low salinities but requires sheltered conditions: found in lagoons and estuaries, where it may form extensive tangled mats.

169.5 Mossweed   *Cladophoropsis herpestica*

Compact moss-like green cushions attached by basal rhizoids, often trapping sand. Composed of tangled segmented filaments, branched to the first or second order. **Size:** Up to 200 x 1–2 mm thick. **Biology:** Common in the intertidal to shallow subtidal zones. **SIMILAR SPECIES:** Compare with *Cladophora contexta* (170.5).

169.6 Green ligamentweed   *Chlorodesmis hildebrandtii*

Compact bright to dark green tufts or mats attached by basal rhizoids. Axes branch dichotomously, forming long thin straight branches that are constricted at the base and radiate out but are not tangled. **Size:** Up to 25 mm tall. **Biology:** Intertidal rock pools and shallow subtidal zone. Forms striking green patches on coral reefs.

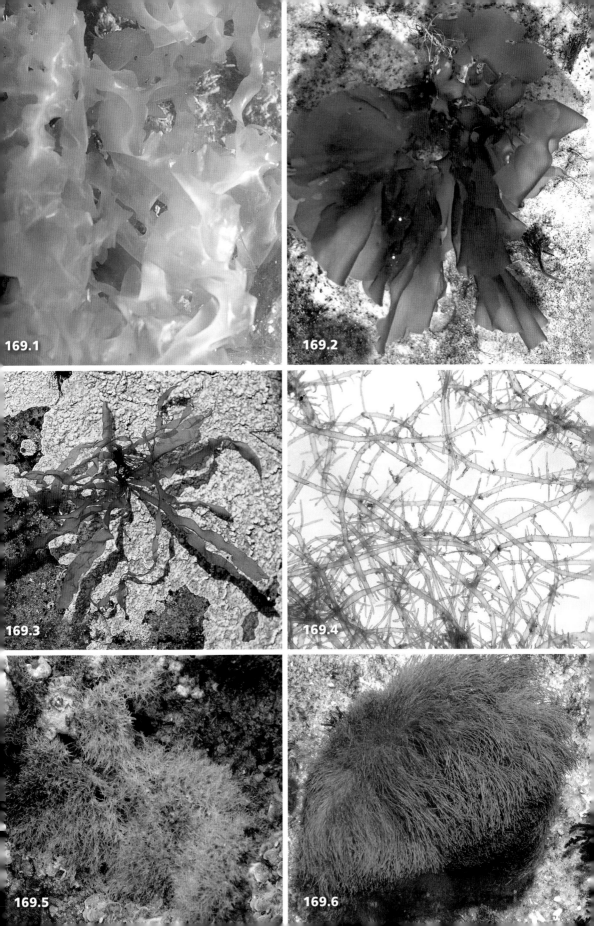

169.1

169.2

169.3

169.4

169.5

169.6

PLATE 170

Simple filamentous green algae

Chaetomorpha *spp. are simple unbranched filaments of cells placed end to end. In* Cladophora *the filaments are branched.*

170.1 Hair weed *Chaetomorpha linum*

Dark green low-growing clumps of long stiff thread-like filaments, attached by a fibrous holdfast. **Size:** Filaments about 50 mm long, less than 0.2 mm wide. **Biology:** Grows in high-tide pools. Formerly known as *C. aerea*.

170.2 Antenna weed *Chaetomorpha antennina*

Grass-green brush-like tufts of low-growing unbranched segmented filaments. The basal cell is very long and stiff, and the flexible terminal portion is made up of short cells that are often transparent because they have released spores. **Size:** Filaments about 20 mm long and less than 0.5 mm wide. **Biology:** Grows in high-tide pools and the shallow subtidal zone.

170.3 Robust hair-weed *Chaetomorpha robusta*

Stiff straight grass-green threads consisting of a single row of large barrel-shaped cells up to 2 mm wide. The penultimate cells are spherical and contain the spores. Transparent empty cells form at the tips when the spores are shed. **Size:** 100 x 2 mm. **Biology:** Grows in mid- to high-tide pools and in the shallow subtidal zone. **SIMILAR SPECIES:** *C. crassa* (East London–Mozambique) has coarse unbranched green filaments comprising barrel-shaped cells, 2–3 mm wide, which characteristically coil around other algae and lack holdfasts. Used as bait in fish traps in East Africa.

170.4 Blue whip cladophora *Cladophora flagelliformis*

Fine, wiry segmented blue-green filaments with untidy whorls of branches at the joints. Widens gradually to the tips, which are dark when filled with spores and transparent once the spores are shed. Holdfast is a small disc. **Size:** 150 mm; less than 0.8 mm wide. **Biology:** Untidy bunches on the sides of mid- to high-tide pools. **SIMILAR SPECIES:** *C. mirabilis* (Saldanha–northern Namibia) also has a disc holdfast, but its coarse dark green filaments are up to 1 mm wide and fork repeatedly, not in whorls.

170.5 Turf cladophora *Cladophora contexta*

A compact grass-green turf a few centimetres high, composed of entangled branched segmented filaments, attached by rhizoids from several points along the filaments. **Size:** Filaments 1–1.5 mm thick. **Biology:** Intertidal. **SIMILAR SPECIES:** Compare with *Cladophoropsis herpestica* (169.5) and *Chlorodesmis hildebrandtii* (169.6).

170.6 Rough cladophora *Cladophora prolifera*

Coarse dark broom-like tufts made up of filaments of a single row of cells, densely branching at the ends. Holdfast fibrous. The lowest segments are long and truncheon-shaped with faint annular constrictions. **Size:** Up to 130 mm, width 0.13–0.7 mm. **Biology:** The most common *Cladophora* low on the shore in KwaZulu-Natal. Formerly called *C. rugulosa*. **SIMILAR SPECIES:** *C. radiosa* (Cape Point–East London) has similar coarse dark green branching filaments but the basal segments are long, smooth and cylindrical, lacking annular constrictions.

170.7 Cape cladophora *Cladophora capensis*

Fine filaments of a single row of cells, with many alternating and fairly short stiff grass-green branches. Holdfast fibrous. **Size:** Up to 300 mm long, width 0.2 mm. **Biology:** Long flexible plants in subtidal gullies, short untidy bushes in tidal pools. **SIMILAR SPECIES:** *Cladophora ordinata* (Port St Johns northwards) forms green tufts up to 80 mm tall with regular branches that lie in a single plane. Branching to the fourth degree, lateral branches arise in opposite pairs, 0.04–0.17 mm width. Common, intertidal to depths of about 35 m.

170.1

170.2

170.3

170.4

170.5

170.6

170.7

PLATE 171

Bryopsis & Caulerpa

These seaweeds are made of continuous branching tubes with numerous nuclei and few or no cross-walls. The plants may be quite complex in structure. Their chloroplasts make the best use of the prevailing light conditions by migrating through the tubes to the surface when it is dull, and away from the surface if the light is very bright. Many species contain chemicals that deter herbivores.

171.1 Sea moss   *Bryopsis myosuroides*

Soft dark green cushions of feathery unsegmented filaments with a bare stalk and short side branches in the upper half. **Size:** Filaments about 50 mm tall. **Biology:** Common in rock pools. Previously called *B. flanaganii*. **SIMILAR SPECIES:** There are several species with varying degrees of branching; all form soft, very dark green cushions of filaments.

171.2 Sea moss   *Bryopsis pennata*

Soft feather-like plants with a short bare stalk at the base and a long plume. Basal rhizoids. **Size:** Filaments about 50–100 mm long. **Biology:** Grows on sand, rock and other plants in tropical areas.

171.3 Berry caulerpa   *Caulerpa peltata*

A mat of rhizomes giving rise to bunches of swollen light green or blue-green berry-like branches. The berries may be club-shaped, round or trumpet-shaped. **Size:** Bunches up to 20 mm tall. **Biology:** Forms carpets on protected rocks at low-tide level. Formerly known as two varieties of *C. racemosa*.
SIMILAR SPECIES:
171.4 *Caulerpa racemosa lamourouxii* (Sodwana northwards) has light green plants with sparse, much larger branches.

171.5 Feathery caulerpa   *Caulerpa holmesiana*

Stiff green feathers arising from a horizontal rhizome. The feathers have a short basal stipe, which is annulated, and a long shaft with many fine, pinnate branches. **Size:** Feathers 30–50 mm long. **Biology:** Common on shallow sheltered subtidal rocks amid kelp, to a depth of 5 m. **SIMILAR SPECIES:** Two other feather-like tropical caulerpas with fewer, larger pinnae are *C. taxifolia*, which has regularly placed flattened pinnae projecting distally at about 30°, and *C. cupressoides*, which has cylindrical cypress-like branches, with short upcurved pinnae.

171.6 Saw-edged caulerpa   *Caulerpa scalpelliformis denticulata*

Tangled rhizomes give rise to flattened erect blades on short cylindrical stipes. The margins of the blades are coarsely serrated with flat incurved teeth. Dark green, sometimes mottled with darker veins. **Size:** Blades 30–50 x 3 mm. **Biology:** Can form dense stands on sand-covered rocks in intertidal pools.

171.7 Toothed caulerpa   *Caulerpa serrulata*

Rhizomes give rise to short stipes bearing stiff, twisted, flattened blades that branch dichotomously and have coarsely toothed margins. Blue-green with a pale midrib. **Size:** Blades 5–15 x 3 mm wide. **Biology:** Grows on rocks to depths of 12 m.

171.8 Strap caulerpa   *Caulerpa filiformis*

Tangled root-like rhizomes give rise to flattened, erect strap-like blades with cylindrical annulated bases. Grass-green, mottled with dark green spots. **Size:** Blades 200 x 5 mm. **Biology:** Forms dense stands in sandy gullies; withstands being partially smothered by sand because the chloroplasts migrate to portions of the blades exposed above the sand.

171.9 Finger caulerpa   *Caulerpa webbiana*

Rhizomes give rise to short, spongy, soft, finger-like uprights composed of an axis surrounded by closely packed small branchlets, which are dichotomously branched 3–4 times, creating a fluffy appearance. Dark green. **Size:** 'Fingers' 10 x 3 mm wide. **Biology:** Grows in sand-covered pools. **SIMILAR SPECIES:** *Dasycladus ramosus* (Sodwana northwards) superficially alike, with finger-like branches 15–30 mm long x 2–3 mm wide, but the branches are firm, not soft and fluffy.

PLATE 172

Spongy green algae

Codiums have thick spongy branches or cushions made up of interwoven tubes, which end in specialised swellings (utricles) that cover the surface. When a Codium *is squeezed, the utricles separate. In* Pseudocodium *(173.1) the utricles adhere to one another.*

172.1 Hairy upright codium   *Codium extricatum*

Plant upright; branches blackish green, cylindrical; tips thinner and have a halo of fine hairs. Utricles cylindrical (172.1a), separate easily and bear several hairs (visible with a hand lens). **Size:** 150 x 3–5 mm. **Biology:** Inhabits sandy rock pools.
SIMILAR SPECIES:
172.2 *Codium tenue* (East London–Durban) has flattened lower region, while the tips are cylindrical and translucent; utricles club-shaped, with one or two hairs.

172.3 Fragile upright codium   *Codium fragile capense*

Thick cylindrical branches. Utricles with small apical spine (172.3a); hairs common. **Size:** 300 x 3–8 mm. **Biology:** Sublittoral fringe and intertidal pools.
SIMILAR SPECIES:
172.4 *Codium isaacii* (Saldanha–Transkei) has uniformly small utricles with round tips. Plants 200 x 3–6 mm (see 96.3).

172.5 Duthie's upright codium   *Codium duthieae*

Thick upright branches; forks sometimes flattened. Some utricles large; tips rounded (172.5a). **Size:** 300 x 10–14 mm. **Biology:** Occurs subtidally and in low intertidal pools.
SIMILAR SPECIES:
172.6 *Codium capitatum* (Port St Johns–Mozambique) is slender and smooth, not hairy: 200 x 6 mm. Utricles capitate – with a globular apex and a neck-like constriction.

172.7 Stephens' codium   *Codium stephensiae*

An encrusting codium with thick flattened lobes that are almost free from the substrate and stick up like masses of contorted ears. **Size:** Individual lobes 100–300 x 5 mm. **Biology:** Common subtidally and often forms extensive growths in rocky areas.

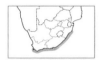

172.8 Flat-lobed codium   *Codium platylobium*

Large, with a basal attachment and broad, strap-shaped, flattened spongy lobes; deep black-green in colour. **Size:** Up to 500 mm long, 70 mm wide and 5 mm thick. **Biology:** Occurs in sandy-bottomed rock pools and gullies. An encrusting red seaweed, *Placophora binderi*, which often grows on *Codium* spp., is evident here.

172.9 Creeping codium   *Codium prostratum*

Spongy, creeping, with cylindrical closely forking branches that overlap, anastomose (fuse) and cling to the substrate. Utricles small. Dark green. **Size:** Stiff clumps up to 100 mm in diameter; branches 3–5 mm thick. **Biology:** Occurs in intertidal pools.

172.10 Golf-ball codium   *Codium megalophysum*

Forms regular green balls with a small attachment. Utricles enormous: 5–12 mm long, clearly visible to the naked eye. **Size:** Plants 20–50 mm in diameter. **Biology:** Grows in small groups on shady vertical sides of mid-tide pools and in gullies. SIMILAR SPECIES: *C. papenfussii* (Cape Peninsula–Sodwana) consists of flattened balls with a small attachment. The small utricles are compacted into a continuous surface. *C. pelliculare* (south coast) forms thin, skin-like, hollow sacs about 20 mm wide and 2 mm thick.

172.11 Spongy codium   *Codium spongiosum*

Plants made up of thick spongy cushions that disintegrate easily. Utricles arranged in clusters rather than being individual. **Size:** Plants 50 x 15 mm thick. Utricles large: 3–4 mm long. **Biology:** Grows in intertidal pools.

172.12 Lucas' codium   *Codium lucasii*

Irregular cushions closely attached to the substrate and only free at the margins. The utricles have knob-like tips with a constricted neck. **Size:** Lobes 50 x 5 mm thick. **Biology:** Forms extensive mid-tide lumpy sheets on sand-covered shady rocks.

172.1

172.3

172.5

Hairs

172.1a

Utricle

Spores

172.2

172.3a

172.4

Rounded tips

Constriction

172.5a

172.6

172.8

172.7

172.9

172.10

172.11

172.12

PLATE 173

173.1 False codium — *Pseudocodium devriesii*

Plant erect; cylindrical branches with constrictions at irregular intervals. Surface utricles are not separable by tearing or squashing, unlike the situation in *Codium* spp. Grass-green. **Size:** 100 mm long by about 2.5 mm wide. **Biology:** Common in low-tide rock pools and the shallow subtidal zone. Compare with *Codium* spp. (Plate 172).

173.2 Wedge weed — *Halimeda cuneata*

A series of flat calcified discs linked together with flexible joints to form a distinctive, dark green plant resembling a miniature prickly-pear cactus. Each segment is supported by a short stalk; the stalk zone consists of filaments and may include a small round cushion. **Size:** 150 mm tall. **Biology:** Common on subtidal rocky ledges and in pools and sandy gullies. Survives periodic inundation by sand. **SIMILAR SPECIES:** *H. gracilis* is a sprawling, deep-water tropical species with grass-green calcified segments that are connected directly to one another without any distinct stalk zone.

173.3 Green fan — *Udotea orientalis*

A tough, flat fan with a short stalk. Fibrous in texture, the fibres fanning outwards from the stalk. Green, often with concentric paler lines. **Size:** 30 mm. **Biology:** Inconspicuous; grows on submerged rocky ledges. Often found on the floors of sand-inundated pools.

173.4 Green balloons — *Valonia macrophysa*

Large, glistening, blackish-green balloon-like sacs that are loosely joined to one another. **Size:** 50 x 20 mm tall; 'balloons' 10 mm diameter. **Biology:** Occurs on the low shore and subtidally, on vertical rocky walls.

173.5 Small green balloons — *Valonia aegagropila*

Shiny, irregular, bubbly cushions, built up from a network of bulbous tubes that are easily separated. Dark grass green. **Size:** Cushion 80 mm wide x 5 mm tall; 'balloons' 2 mm wide. **Biology:** Occurs in rocky crevices near low-tide level and subtidally on coral reefs.

173.6 Bubble cushions — *Dictyosphaeria versluysii*

Solid cushions; hard to the touch and composed of large cells that are not separable by tearing or squashing. Pale greyish green. **Size:** Cushions 10–25 mm, cells 0.8–1.2 mm. **Biology:** Common in low-tide rock pools and down to 12 m deep. **SIMILAR SPECIES:** *D. cavernosa* (Sodwana northwards) has stiff, brittle, hollow dark green cushions 10–15 mm across, composed of a single layer of large polygonal cells. Cushion-like when young, later becoming convoluted and ruptured. Common in intertidal pools.

173.7 Green sticks — *Neomeris vanbosseae*

Grows in small groups. Plant erect, cylindrical or club-shaped and unbranched; base brittle; white due to calcification. Tip often curved and green with whorls of dark green dichotomous hairs. **Size:** Up to 40 mm long, 2–3 mm diameter. **Biology:** Frequent in intertidal pools throughout the tropical Indo-Pacific region.

173.8 Sea brush — *Chamaedoris delphinii*

Resembles a group of dark green paintbrushes with cylindrical annulated stalks, each bearing a terminal tuft of matted branched filaments. The base of the stalk is often calcified. Young plants consist of a transparent annulated tube with a bulbous tip. **Size:** 40 mm tall. **Biology:** Grows subtidally on rocky ledges and pools.

PLATE 174

Brown algae   Ochrophyta

Usually yellowish brown due to their combination of pigments: green chlorophyll a and c together with other pigments such as brown fucoxanthin. Brown algae include membranous forking plants (Plate 174), simple or split fans (Plate 175), complex foliar, tree-like forms such as the kelps (Plate 176), and cushions (Plate 178). Many have a large dominant sporophyte that alternates with a microscopic gametophyte. The Fucales (wracks and sargassums, Plates 176–177) produce sexual gametes in special fertile branches directly on the sporophyte.

Forked brown algae

174.1 Blue dictyota   *Dictyota humifusa*
Short-forked, overlapping, bright blue fronds. **Size:** 20–30 mm long x 5 mm wide. **Biology:** Grows in mid-tide pools, often with *Hypnea viridis* (186.5). **SIMILAR SPECIES:** *D. cervicornis* (see 57.9) is brown, slightly iridescent, narrower, 50 x 2–3 mm. Branches unequal (like antlers), diverging at a wide angle, especially at the tips.

174.2 Spotted dictyota   *Dictyota naevosa*
Fairly robust, forked fronds, expanding in width towards the tip. Light brown with a blue-green sheen and dark spots. **Size:** 150 mm long, blades 5 mm wide. **Biology:** Grows in pools and gullies at and below low-tide level.

174.3 Intricate dictyota   *Dictyota sp.*
Delicate, forked greenish blades with a yellow fringe. **Size:** 50 mm tall; primary branches 4 mm in width, final branches 1–2 mm. **Biology:** Common in rock pools; often grows on other algae. This unnamed species is similar to *D. dichotoma*.

174.4 Banded dictyota   *Dictyota ciliolata*
Crisp, flat, regularly forked fronds; medium brown, slightly iridescent, often with transverse bands. Apices rounded, margins smooth or dentate. Hair tufts common. **Size:** 80 mm long, blades about 6 mm wide. **Biology:** Grows in pools and to depths of 20 m.

174.5 Suhr's dictyota   *Rugulopteryx suhrii*
Frond sparsely dichotomous, medium brown, non-iridescent. Tips rounded, spatula-like; margins smooth. Hair tufts common. **Size:** Blades 90 x about 4 mm. **Biology:** Occurs intertidally on wave-exposed coasts. **SIMILAR SPECIES:** *D. liturata* (see 57.8; Cape Peninsula–KwaZulu-Natal) has fronds with unequally developed forks that taper towards the rounded tips. Brown, non-iridescent. Blades 80–250 x 5 mm wide. Common in pools and down to a depth of 30 m.

174.6 Spatula weed   *Spatoglossum aspersum*
Elongate, thin, leathery blades, irregularly divided into narrow straps with small side branches from the main blades. Yellow-brown. **Size:** 200 mm tall, blades 10–50 mm wide. **Biology:** Grows at depths down to 20 m.

174.7 Smooth-tongued dictyopteris   *Dictyopteris ligulata*
Elongate, thin, leathery blades, forked regularly about every 50 mm. Yellow-brown. Mid-rib distinct; margin smooth. **Size:** 200 x 20 mm. **Biology:** Grows in calm, deep, mid-shore pools. Present but rare on west coast. **SIMILAR SPECIES:** *D. delicatula* (Isipingo–Zululand) has delicate membranous fronds 2–3 mm wide; midrib thin.

174.8 Frilled dictyopteris   *Dictyopteris macrocarpa*
Long, forking blades with discoloured streaks and irregularly split margins. Small leaflets arise from the midrib. Fertile blades have 2–4 rows of dark, oval, spore-bearing patches. **Size:** 200 x 15 mm. **Biology:** Grows on walls of deep rock pools, down to 30 m.

174.9 Serrated dictyopteris   *Dictyopteris serrata*
Elongate blades with serrated margins and delicately oblique veins from the midrib. Scattered dark spots where the spores are borne. **Size:** 200 x 20 mm. **Biology:** Sublittoral fringe and subtidal reefs.

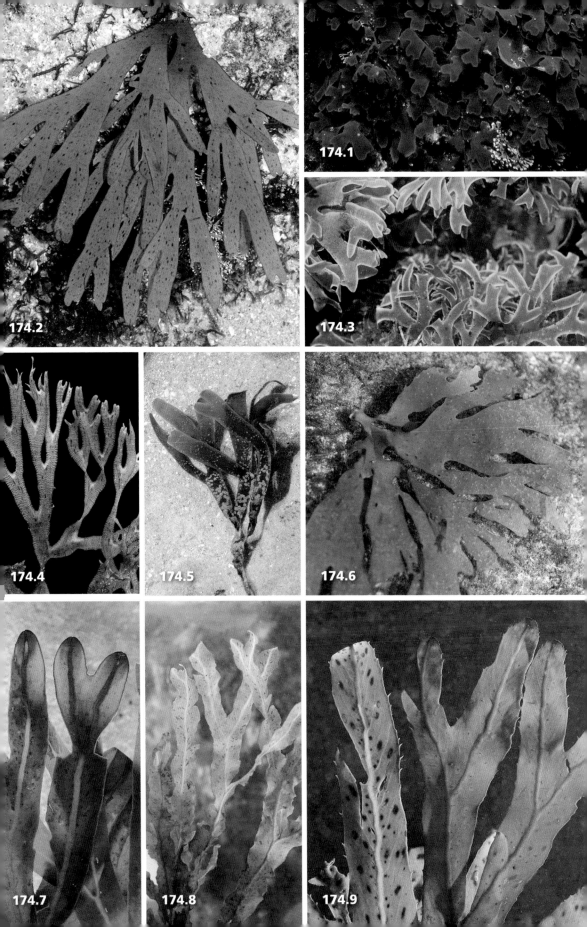

174.1

174.2

174.3

174.4

174.5

174.6

174.7

174.8

174.9

PLATE 175

Fan-shaped brown algae

Brown algae that are fan-shaped, or have flat branches with fanned tips. They grow from a row of dividing cells (the meristem) along the curved rim.

175.1 Acid weed   *Desmarestia firma*

Elongate, flat, thin, leafy fronds. Margin serrated. Midrib narrow; regular angular lateral veins lead into pairs of lateral fronds. Translucent yellowish brown; darker when old. **Size:** Up to 1 m long; blades 30 mm wide. **Biology:** Grows subtidally beneath kelp. Contains sulphuric acid as a deterrent to herbivores and etches patterns on rocks. Stranded plants soon fade and disintegrate.

175.2 Ralfsia   *Ralfsia verrucosa*

Forms flat patches or irregular concentric rings. Brown, grading to khaki; edge pale. **Size:** 1 mm thick; 150 mm wide. **Biology:** Found in 'gardens' of the limpet *Scutellastra longicosta* (72.6). Produces polyphenols that deter grazers by inhibiting digestion. **SIMILAR SPECIES:** *R. expansa* replaces it in KwaZulu-Natal and Mozambique.

175.3 Turkey-tail   *Padina boryana*

Delicate, light brown fans, with concentric light and dark bands, encrusted with lime. Margins rolled inwards to protect the meristem. Tetraspores produced in bands on the ventral surface just distal to the bands of hairs. Blades two cells thick at the edge and three cells at the base. **Size:** Fans about 40 mm. **Biology:** Grows in clusters in mid-tide pools, especially in shallow pools with a thin covering of sand.

175.4 Large turkey-tail   *Padina boergesenii*

Similar to the above species but larger, with up to four cell layers and hair bands on both surfaces. **Size:** Fans 70–140 mm. **Biology:** Common; forms luxuriant growths on the floors of shallow bays and deep intertidal pools.

175.5 Multi-fanned zonaria   *Exallosorus harveyanus*

Short overlapping fans with a few branches. Yellowish brown with pale margins, often with bluish iridescence. Texture smooth; thin but fairly tough and pliable. **Size:** Fans about 30 mm long. **Biology:** Grows low on the shore to depths of at least 5 m. Formerly called *Zonaria multifidus* and *Homoeostrichus multifidus*.

175.6 Articulated zonaria   *Zonaria subarticulata*

Flat and branched; dark yellowish brown with a greyish tinge and discoloured dark spots; pale fan-shaped tips. Lateral margins irregular, interrupted at intervals by dark joints. Texture thin and leathery. Holdfast covered in a mat of hair. **Size:** Plants 200 mm, branches 10 mm wide. **Biology:** Subtidal on rocky shores. **SIMILAR SPECIES:** *Z. tournefortii* (Port Elizabeth–Mozambique) is membranous, undulating, and uniformly yellow-brown with broader overlapping fanned tips.

175.7 Zoned stypopodium   *Stypopodium multipartitum*

Large, irregularly split fans; light yellowish brown with a greenish iridescence and dark concentric bands when young. Older plants dark and corrugated. **Size:** 250 mm. **Biology:** Occurs subtidally on sand-covered rocks and coral reefs down to 20 m. Produces a chemical that repels herbivorous fish. Previously called *S. zonale*.

175.8 Lobe-fan   *Lobophora variegata*

Plants range from loosely attached crusts to semi-erect fans with a narrow stipe. Blades leathery, flattened; margins not rolled inwards, sometimes split. Tufts of hairs in concentric rings on both surfaces. Brown, with a pale margin and bluish iridescence. **Size:** Fan 60 mm diameter. **Biology:** Common in algal turfs in deep pools ; extends to offshore reefs.

175.9 Endarachne   *Endarachne binghamiae*

Several strap-like fronds arise from a discoid holdfast. Fairly thin but opaque; medium brown. **Size:** 100 mm long, blades 10–20 mm wide. **Biology:** Occurs in low-shore pools. **SIMILAR SPECIES:** *Petalonia fascia* (west coast) is almost identical, but has a different internal structure.

175.1

175.2

175.3

175.4

175.5

175.6

175.7

175.8

175.9

PLATE 176

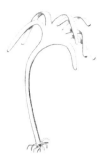

Kelps & wracks

Kelps are the largest and fastest-growing algae, growing up to 13 mm a day. The huge sporophyte plants are long-lived and form extensive underwater forests. They have sturdy, root-like holdfasts and long stalks or stipes that support the blades. Unlike most algae, which have simple cells, the tissues of the kelps are complex, with specialised cells for reproduction, photosynthesis, support and the transport of nutrients. Huge numbers of tiny spores are released from the blades and grow into microscopic male and female gametophyte plants. Kelp is harvested for alginic acid, used as a gel in food products, toothpaste, paint and ink or to stabilise earth embankments and waterproof cement. It is a good fertiliser with a fungicidal action and is rich in mineral salts. Fresh kelp contains growth hormones that dramatically increase the yield of crops such as wheat. Kelp forests create a unique ecosystem. They break the force of the waves and provide a sheltered habitat; many animals graze the kelp plants or consume the fine soup of particles that continually erode from the tips of the fronds.

176.1 Split-fan kelp   *Laminaria pallida*

Stipe solid and stiff, ending in a large fan-shaped blade, irregularly split into fronds. Spores borne in patches on the blade. **Size:** Up to 5 m. **Biology:** Grows under a canopy of *Ecklonia maxima* down to 15 m, but replaces it in deeper water, down to 30 m. The fronds curve over and touch the ocean floor, sweeping away animals such as sea urchins and sea cucumbers that feast on kelp debris and sporelings. Young plants grow around adults, so clumps develop. *L. pallida* becomes the dominant kelp on the northwest coast.

176.2 Sea bamboo   *Ecklonia maxima*

The largest of local kelps. Stipe hollow and gas-filled, expanding at the top into a bulb that floats and holds the strap-shaped fronds at the surface. The blades have thickened knobs along their edges and arise from a tongue-like base. Spores are borne in raised patches on the blades. **Size:** Up to 12 m. **Biology:** *E. maxima* is the dominant kelp on the southern west coast. Small plants occur in the shallow water, larger individuals further offshore, down to depths of 10–15 m. Beneath their canopy is a host of other algae and animals such as sea urchins, mussels, rock lobsters and sea cucumbers. Three species of red algae grow epiphytically on *E. maxima*: *Carpoblepharis flaccida* (189.1), *Gelidium vittatum* (185.10) and *Polysiphonia virgata* (189.10). The limpet *Cymbula compressa* (73.6) also lives on it.

176.3 Spined kelp   *Ecklonia radiata*

A small species of kelp with a short solid stipe and irregular prickly fronds. **Size:** Up to 1 m long. **Biology:** Occurs in small numbers in deep pools and shallow gullies. The only southern African kelp that does not occur on the cold west coast.

176.4 Bladder kelp   *Macrocystis angustifolia*

A slender, flowing plant with a long flexible stipe that bears blades at regular intervals. Each rippled blade has a spiny margin, a pointed tip and a gas-filled bladder at its base. At the tip of the plant the new blades are fused together and gradually separate as they grow. The spore-bearing tissue is confined to a few smooth blades at the base of the plant. **Size:** Plant up to 12 m long. **Biology:** The most localised of the west coast kelps, it shelters inshore of kelp forests, inside rocky reefs.

176.5 Hanging wrack   *Bifurcaria brassicaeformis*

Swathes of long, tough, cylindrical axes hang from creeping holdfasts. Colour yellowish brown. Fertile branches arise on either side of mature axes. They are flattened, spear-shaped, and bear two rows of lateral cavities that release gametes along the edges. **Size:** Axes 200 x 3–4 mm. **Biology:** Favours wave-pounded areas; forms glistening carpets on low-shore rocks.

176.6 Upright wrack   *Bifurcariopsis capensis*

A conical, disc-shaped holdfast gives rise to a tough, upright bushy plant with cylindrical axes. Yellow-brown with grey tinges. Fertile branches cylindrical, elongate and pitted with scattered openings. **Size:** Plants up to 200 mm tall. **Biology:** Grows on the floors of deep rock pools and gullies.

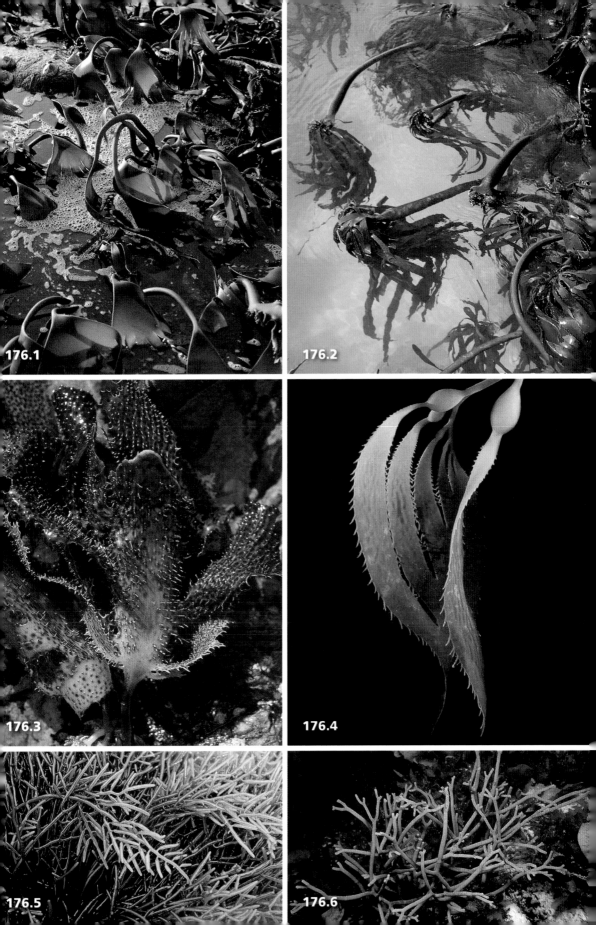

176.1

176.2

176.3

176.4

176.5

176.6

PLATE 177

Sargassum-like brown algae

The Fucales is an order of brown algae that lacks an independent sexual gametophyte. The sporophyte plants produce male and female gametes directly: these fuse and form new sporophytes. Special fertile branches bear the gametes; the extruded eggs form tufts attached to the reproductive branches by mucous threads. They are not washed away: an advantage considering that most species live in heavy surf.

177.1 Ornate turban-weed   *Turbinaria ornata*

Small tufted bushes with a branching holdfast and a tough stem with spined, slightly flattened branches. The unusual fertile branches in the centre are thick and trumpet-shaped with spined margins. Yellow-brown, with a greyish tinge and dark spots on the fertile branches. **Size:** 30 mm tall. **Biology:** Clustered in shallow rock pools from mid-tide level down.

177.2 Double-edged sargassum   *Sargassum crassifolium*

Plants tough with thick ovate toothed branchlets, weakly to strongly turbinate (with a double margin). Yellow-brown with darker spots of hair tufts. Discoid holdfast. Reproductive receptacles in the axes of the branches. **Size:** 50–100 mm, blades about 15 mm wide. **Biology:** Occurs on lower intertidal rocky shores.

177.3 Different-leafed sargassum   *Sargassum incisifolium*

Bushy yellow-brown plants with a triangular stem, small air-floats and two types of blades: the lower 'leaves' oval with smooth edges or occasional dentations; upper fronds small, spear-shaped and often dentate. Fertile branches form inconspicuous tufts like miniature bunches of grapes. **Size:** 250 mm long. **Biology:** Common in gullies and pools; thrives in high-tide pools warmed by the sun. Previously named *S. heterophyllum*.
SIMILAR SPECIES:
177.4 *Sargassum elegans* (south and east coasts) is very similar, but stem cylindrical.

177.5 Long-leafed sargassum   *Anthophycus longifolius*

Tall, with only one type of 'leaf', which is long and spear-shaped, with marginal teeth and spurs. The stem is spirally twisted and knobbly at the base, and flat with leafy wings and a strong midrib in the distal part. Bladders in the axils of the blades are usually topped by a leaflet. The fertile branches are delicate and elongate with tiny, grape-like clusters of receptacles. **Size:** Up to 500 mm; blades 20 mm wide. **Biology:** Occurs in deep gullies and subtidally on rocky reefs.

177.6 Hormophysa   *Hormophysa cuneiformis*

Plants erect, stiff; several axes arise from a conical base. Recognised by the three-winged fronds, which are triangular in section, with dentate margins. The plants have a jointed appearance because the wings are periodically constricted. Orange-brown, darkening with age. **Size:** Axes 200 mm long x 4 mm wide. **Biology:** Grows in low-shore rock pools.

177.7 Fine cystoseira   *Cystoseira trinodis*

Tall slender plants with narrow basal leaf-like blades. Stem densely covered with spines, and the upper side branches of the plant bear smooth bladders in pairs or threes. **Size:** 300–500 mm long; blades 30–50 x 3 mm. **Biology:** Occurs in pools and shallow bays. **SIMILAR SPECIES:** *C. myrica* (northern KwaZuluNatal–Mozambique) is spiny, spruce-like, 70–150 mm tall and completely covered by small spiny branchlets; bladders 2 x 5 mm, covered with spines. Common in shallow, high-shore, sand-inundated pools.

177.8 Constricted axils   *Axillariella constricta*

Axes thick, leathery, with flattened, wing-like expansions, which are irregularly constricted, forming serial triangular shapes. Yellow-brown when young, blackish when old. Paddle-shaped fertile branches are borne along the axes on the upper corners of the triangles. **Size:** Axes 250 mm long. **Biology:** Grows on shallow subtidal rocks among kelp.

177.1

177.2

177.3

177.4

177.5

177.6

177.7

177.8

PLATE 178

Bladders & strings

178.1 Oyster thief
Colpomenia sinuosa

Crinkled yellowish balls with a thin smooth skin and large internal cavity. **Size:** 30 mm wide. **Biology:** Often grows on other algae in low-tide pools or on sheltered rocks. During photosynthesis fills with oxygen and may float to the surface. A nuisance in oyster farms because it grows on and floats away with the oysters – hence 'oyster thief'.

178.2 Brown brains
Leathesia difformis

A thick-walled spongy yellow-brown cushion, with a small central cavity. **Size:** Cushion about 25 mm in diameter. **Biology:** Grows in mid-tide rock pools and subtidally; often epiphytic on other algae or on the reef-worm *Gunnarea capensis* (28.3).

178.3 Starred cushion
Iyengaria stellata

Knobbly yellowish cushions composed of hollow compacted branching tubes. **Size:** Cushions about 50 mm in diameter. **Biology:** Favours sheltered rock platforms and shallow tidal pools. Often washes ashore as it is weakly attached and floats.

178.4 Hydroclathrus
Hydroclathrus clathratus

Irregular, convoluted yellowish cushions, hollow, with numerous perforations when older; stiff but slippery to the touch. **Size:** Cushion about 150 mm in diameter. **Biology:** Favours rock pools and shallow subtidal reefs.

178.5 Sausage skins
Scytosiphon simplicissimus

Hollow brown tubes that are constricted at intervals, several cells thick and have a gas-filled central cavity. Yellow-brown. **Size:** About 150 mm. **Biology:** Attached to rocks in shallow pools and subtidally. **SIMILAR SPECIES:** Compare with *Ulva intestinalis* (169.3).

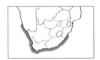

178.6 Dead-man's fingers
Splachnidium rugosum

Swollen yellow-brown finger-like bladders, filled with slimy mucilage. Turgid when wet but becoming withered and wrinkled when dry. Spores are released from pores in the surface skin. **Size:** Branches 80 x 10 mm. **Biology:** Occurs on low-shore rocks. Its mucus protects it against desiccation during low tide.

178.7 Cape cord-weed
Chordariopsis capensis

Stringy plants with a narrow cylindrical central axis and many short side branches that stick out at right-angles in all directions. Yellow-brown to blackish. **Size:** About 150 mm long; strings 1 mm wide. **Biology:** Lies flaccidly on the floors of mid-tide rock pools.

178.8 Bristle-tips
Phloiocaulon suhrii

Axes slender and tough, with delicate bristly feather-like appendages alternating up the branches. Yellow-brown to blackish. **Size:** Axes about 40 mm long and 1 mm wide. **Biology:** Occurs on the sides of high-shore pools and in the shallow subtidal zone.

178.9 Broom-weed
Stypocaulon funiculare

A small tufted plant with numerous small stiff bristle-like branches coming off in all directions but pointing towards the tip, like a 'besom' reedbrush. The bristles are dark brown with a dark terminal cell in fertile plants (see inset). **Size:** 20–30 mm tall. **Biology:** Occurs among short turf in the shallow subtidal zone.

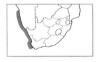

178.10 Furry slime-strings
Chordariaceae

Cylindrical furry brown axes with a few branches. Soft and slippery. **Size:** About 200 mm long; 5–10 mm wide. **Biology:** Seasonally common in mid-tide pools and gullies. **SIMILAR SPECIES:** Members of the family Chordariaceae are very difficult to tell apart without microscopic examination. West coast genera include *Myriogloea*, *Myriocladia* and *Papenfussiella*; *Levringia* extends to Durban.

178.11 Ectocarpus
Ectocarpus sp.

Fine tufts of thin uniseriate filaments; many-chambered sporangia on side branches of reproductive phase (see inset). Yellow-brown. **Size:** Axes 20 mm long, <1 mm wide. **Biology:** Several different species grow on rocks or attached to seaweeds in high-shore pools.

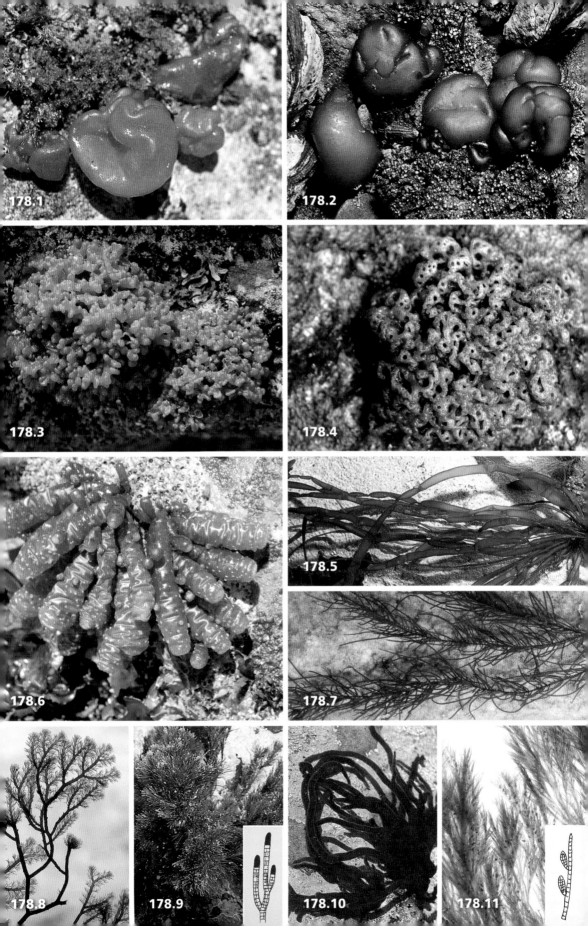

178.1

178.2

178.3

178.4

178.5

178.6

178.7

178.8

178.9

178.10

178.11

PLATE 179

Red algae   Rhodophyta

Phylum Rhodophyta includes the majority of seaweeds – those that contain blue and red pigments (phycobylins) as well as green chlorophyll a. Many, especially deep-water species, are red or purple-red and their phycobylins absorb the blue-green light that penetrates deepest in the water, and transfer the energy to chlorophyll for photosynthesis. Intertidal forms are shades of reddish brown and easily confused with the Phaeophyta. One 'red' alga, *Hypnea spicifera* (186.4), is mainly green. Rhodophyte life cycles usually have distinct phases, complicating identification. Asexual tetrasporophytes produce spores in groups of four, which develop into male and female gametophytes that, typically, form knobbles when mature. Tetrasporophytes and gametophytes can be similar, but in *Gigartina* and *Gymnogongrus* (Plates 182, 183) tetrasporophytes are smooth with groups of spores forming small dark spots, whereas gametophytes are more branched, with surface papillae.

Flat red algae

179.1 **Purple laver**   *Porphyra capensis*
Thin, membranous blades. Slippery when wet, becoming like crumpled black plastic when dry. Dark purplish to purple-green. Margin yellow in male and pink in female. Sporophytes microscopic. **Size:** Blades 150 mm long, 150 µm thick. **Biology:** Occurs high on the shore; able to withstand drying as water is lost from mucus between the cells rather than the cells themselves. Grazers eliminate it lower on the shore. Grows extremely fast. Edible; a related species, 'nori', is cultivated in the Far East. 'Laver bread' is a traditional dish in Wales and the Hebrides, fried with oatmeal. **SIMILAR SPECIES:** *P. saldanhae* (Namibia–Cape Point) is almost identical but its blades are thinner (100 vs 150 µm) and its cells shorter (length 3 x width, vs 4 x width in *P. capensis*).

179.2 **Spotted mazzaella**   *Mazzaella capensis*
Strap-shaped blades. Brown, with dark spots and a rough texture when fertile; not slippery. The blade is channelled and curled inwards where it meets the short stipe. Holdfast tiny and simple. **Size:** Blades about 300 mm long. **Biology:** Common intertidally on rocky shores on the west coast, associated with *Aeodes orbitosa* (179.3). Previously called *Iridaea capensis*.

179.3 **Slippery orbits**   *Aeodes orbitosa*
Blades broadly lobed, tough and extremely slippery; margin simple to finely toothed. Stipe absent; holdfast a thickened disc. Olive-brown or yellowish. **Size:** Blades about 300 mm long. **Biology:** Common on rocks at the mid- to low-tide level on the west coast. Adult plants apparently unpalatable to grazers.

179.4 **Orange sheets**   *Schizymenia apoda*
Flat, irregularly lobed blades: holdfast with short branches. Texture fleshy, with a very finely corrugated surface, horny when dry. Colour characteristic brownish orange and may have black patches caused by a microscopic epiphyte. **Size:** 300 x 150 mm. **Biology:** Occurs on the floors of mid-tide pools and gullies.

179.5 **Rippled ribbon-weed**   *Grateloupia longifolia*
Flaccid, membranous, strap-shaped blades. Margins longer than the central region, so that the frond ripples and coils. Plum-red, shimmering blue underwater. **Size:** 300 mm long, 30 mm wide. **Biology:** Found in sandy gullies and pools, where it ripples in the runnels. **SIMILAR SPECIES:** *Sarcodia dentata* (Cape Point–East London) is purplish red; the blade is haphazardly forked, with a thickened, toothed margin. Texture fleshy.

179.6 **Red rubber-weed**   *Pachymenia carnosa*
Thick, flat, irregularly lobed blade. Margin smooth, stipe flat or cylindrical, holdfast a disc. Texture like rubber inner-tubing, not slimy. Colour orange-red to blood-red. **Size:** Large, 500 mm. **Biology:** Grows in the shallow subtidal zone, near kelp.
SIMILAR SPECIES:
179.7 *Pachymenia cornea* (west coast–East London) has circular purplish-red 200-mm blades of similar texture, but with irregular holes and double-lipped toothed margin.

179.1

179.2

179.3

179.4

179.5

179.6

179.7

PLATE 180

Foliose red algae

180.1 Lance-weed — *Tsengia lanceolata*

Long, narrow, soft, fleshy blades, forking once or twice, with tapering tips. Clear reddish pink in colour. **Size:** Blades 300 mm long and about 20 mm wide. **Biology:** Grows submerged at depths of 1–5 m; often seen growing on the floors of deep pools and gullies and down to at least 8 m depth. Previously called *Nemastoma lanceolata*.

180.2 Split disc-weed — *Thamnophyllis discigera*

Blades thin, translucent pinkish red, arising directly from a disc holdfast without any stipe. Each blade is circular in outline but is much divided and branched, with many smaller truncated lobes at the tips. Texture crisp. **Size:** About 150 mm long. **Biology:** Occurs in sheltered gullies on sand-covered rocks.

180.3 Eyelid-weed — *Calliblepharis fimbriata*

Broad, flat, fleshy, forking once or twice, margins with small papillae and larger proliferations; veins absent. Reddish purple. Arising from a small holdfast and short stipe. **Size:** About 80 mm long; blades 5–15 mm wide. **Biology:** Grows on rocks in the lower intertidal and shallow subtidal zones.

180.4 Comb-tress — *Ptilophora helenae*

Large, distinctive, flowing red to orange plants, with wide, flattened, branching main axes; pinnately branched to four orders, becoming progressively narrower; tips pointed. Holdfast fibrous. **Size:** Up to 600 mm in length; main axes 15 mm wide. **Biology:** Grows subtidally. Uprooted plants often wash ashore. **SIMILAR SPECIES:** *P. pinnatifida* (Port Elizabeth–Durban) is stiffer; axes cylindrical at the base, becoming flattened at the tips; midrib distinct. Often overgrown by a yellow sponge.

180.5 Cape wine-weed — *Rhodymenia capensis*

Narrow flat blades, without veins, more or less dichotomously branched, arising from a disc holdfast and short stipe. Thin, crisp texture. Colour clear wine-red. **Size:** 100 mm long, blades 3–6 mm wide. **Biology:** Grows on exposed rocks at the sublittoral fringe, associated with *Gelidium* and *Plocamium*. Previously named *Epymenia capensis*.

180.6 Palmate roseweed — *Rhodymenia pseudopalmata*

Fan-shaped blade, forking at a wide angle up to eight times. Small disc holdfast and short stipe. Thin, crisp texture. Colour bright red. Firmer and less translucent than *R. capensis*. **Size:** Plants 100 mm tall, blades 5 mm wide. **Biology:** Common along the west coast; frequently overgrown by crustose corallines, bryozoans and sponges.

180.7 Stalked roseweed — *Rhodymenia natalensis*

Narrow, flat, firm, forking fronds borne on a long stalk arising from a creeping stolon. Colour dark red. **Size:** 100 mm tall x 2–3 mm wide. **Biology:** Grows commonly on low-shore rocks and below. Most abundant in KwaZulu-Natal.

180.8 Roseleaf — *Rhodophyllis reptans*

Plants membranous, narrow, flat, branching in a cervicorn manner, like the antlers of a deer. Blades narrow towards the tips. Colour clear wine-red; shimmers iridescent blue underwater. **Size:** About 50 mm tall; blades up to 2 mm wide. **Biology:** Occurs commonly down to depths of about 3 m, often associated with the holdfasts of kelps.

180.1

180.2

180.3

180.4

180.5

180.6

180.7

180.8

PLATE 181

Membranous red algae

181.1 Curled acrosorium   *Acrosorium ciliolatum*

Tiny membranous blades, uniformly narrow with characteristic curling tips and short lateral branchlets; translucent pinkish red. **Size:** 20 x 1.5 mm. **Biology:** Grows epiphytically on other algae. Previously named *Acrosorium uncinatum*.

181.2 Plain acrosorium   *Acrosorium acrospermum*

Small thin blades, forking two or three times. Translucent pinkish red. **Size:** 20 x 4 mm. **Biology:** Grows epiphytically on other algae (see 184.2). **SIMILAR SPECIES:** *A. maculatum* (Namibia–east coast) has rounded tips and is pink with diagnostic white dots on the surface, 20 x 5 mm.

181.3 Frilly broekies   *Delesseria papenfussii*

Small plants with a short stipe ending in a few branches that become the midribs of delicate frilled blades, which have lateral veins. Leaflets arise from the midrib. Margins entire, not serrate. Holdfast a small disc. Transparent brick-red. **Size:** About 50 mm tall; blades about 7 mm. **Biology:** Occurs in intertidal rock pools.

181.4 Broad wine-weed   *Rhodymenia obtusa*

Flat, dichotomising blades with broadly rounded tips and no veins. Texture thin, crisp, not slimy. Colour clear reddish pink. Stipe often forked; holdfast disc-shaped. Fertile blades bear rosettes of tiny leaflets. **Size:** Blades about 90 x 15 mm. **Biology:** Subtidal; often associated with kelp holdfasts. Commonly encrusted by the bryozoan *Jellyella tuberculata* (58.7), and the seaweed ascidian, *Botryllus elegans* (112.2), both of which are visible in this image. Previously placed in the genus *Epymenia*.

181.5 Black spot   *Botryocarpa prolifera*

Flat, thin, leathery blades without a midrib. Colour a distinctive copper-red with blackish discolorations, particularly along the margins. Holdfast a small disc. The stipe is short and may branch. The blades are oval, often with a tattered margin – small blades grow from the surface and the margin. Fertile plants have scattered rosettes of tiny leaflets on the surface of the blades. **Size:** Blades 200 x 40 mm. **Biology:** Subtidal beneath kelp.

181.6 Veined oil-weed   *Hymenena venosa*

Delicate, membranous, irregularly forking, strap-like blades with several parallel veins and a short stipe. Margin rippled. Colour pink, iridescing like oil on water. **Size:** About 150 mm x 20 mm. **Biology:** Subtidal, common in kelp beds and often grows among sponges.

181.7 Veined tongues   *Neuroglossum binderianum*

Membranous leaf-like blades with a thick flattened stipe and midrib that stops near the tip without fanning into veins. Blades appear untidy, and bear lateral leaflets, which are spotted when fertile. Holdfast branching. Transparent red. **Size:** About 200 x 20 mm. **Biology:** Common in the shallows below kelp; favours sheltered, sand-covered rocks.

181.8 Botryoglossum   *Botryoglossum platycarpum*

Neat, delicate membranous blades with a solid midrib at the base that fans out into veins in the tip. The blades are irregularly forked, with rippled margins. Stipe long and narrow. Holdfast a rhizome. Transparent red. **Size:** About 150 x 15 mm. **Biology:** Common in shallow water below kelp.

181.1

181.2

181.3

181.4

181.5

181.6

181.7

181.8

PLATE 182

Balloon & tongue-like red algae

Phases in the life cycle of these algae, although similar in size, may differ in their branching and surface texture, complicating identification. The tetrasporophyte is usually dotted, smoother and has fewer surface papillae than the gametophyte.

182.1 Tongue-weed   *Gigartina polycarpa*
Tough, fleshy, oval blades. Holdfast a small disc. Stem short, blades dark reddish brown. Gametophyte (right of photograph) covered with knobbly papillae, reminiscent of a rough tongue. Tetrasporophyte (left) ear-like with pointed tip, smooth margin, and surface network of ridges and grooves. **Size:** Blades 150 mm long. **Biology:** Common on the low shore. A source of carrageenan, used as a gel. Previously called *G. radula*.

182.2 Red tongue-weed   *Gigartina bracteata*
Blades deep black-red, thick and tough. The gametophyte has a few surface and marginal papillae. The tetrasporophyte is smooth but, when the spores are released, becomes a lacy mass of holes with very short papillae on the margins. The blades are irregularly lobed. **Size:** About 250 mm long. **Biology:** A deep-water species growing beneath kelp.

182.3 Soft tongue-weed   *Gigartina paxillata*
Blades thin, soft and fleshy, margins not thickened. Gametophytes flat with many small papillae and few leaflets. The tetrasporophyte has forked tips and a few large, peg-like papillae that may branch and have black spots. Olive-green to yellow or purple-brown. **Size:** Blades about 100 mm long. **Biology:** Occurs in mid-shore pools and on ledges in the lower intertidal zone.

182.4 Corrugated red alga   *Grateloupia belangeri*
Dark purplish-red blades with disc holdfast and irregular lobes. The surface is coarsely textured, becoming strongly corrugated, tough and pliable as it matures. **Size:** About 200 mm long. **Biology:** A deep-water species that grows beneath kelp.

182.5 Twisted gigartina   *Sarcothalia stiriata*
Both phases rubbery, succulent, with thickened margins, and are yellow to purplish brown. Tetrasporophyte smooth; a narrow stipe expands into an irregularly forked blade. Dark spots mark spore-bearing tissue. Gametophyte contorted, with fleshy leaflets in irregular marginal ranks. **Size:** 60–80 mm. **Biology:** Occurs on wave-washed shores.

182.6 Convoluted mazzaella   *Mazzaella convoluta*
Blades narrow, succulent, deeply channelled, curled inwards and irregularly forked, with small blades arising from the margins near the tips. Brown. The tetrasporophyte is rough, with dark spots marking spore-bearing tissue. Gametophyte is smoother. **Size:** About 100 mm long. **Biology:** Occurs on lower intertidal rocky shores. Western Cape Peninsula only.

182.7 Hedgehog seaweed   *Nothogenia erinacea*
Elongate fronds, yellowish to dark brown, thin and never succulent; become black and papery when dry. Fertile gametophytes covered with numerous short, branched outgrowths. Tetrasporophyte crustose, and can survive prolonged sand-burial. **Size:** Fronds 80–120 mm long, 60 mm wide. **Biology:** Abundant in the upper balanoid zone on flat sheltered rocks, often associated with sand.

182.8 Balloon weed   *Nothogenia ovalis*
Forms groups of dry, oval, gas-filled, balloon-like bladders. Dark spots mark the spore-bearing tissue. Colour light brown. Tetrasporophyte crustose. **Size:** Up to 30 mm long, about 8 mm diameter. **Biology:** Abundant on rocks adjacent to sand or gravel.

182.9 Tattered-rag weed   *Grateloupia capensis*
Fronds narrow, elongate, flat, with many lateral branches of varying lengths, some much longer than the blade width. Thin; papery when dry. Yellow to purple-brown; black when dry. **Size:** Fronds 70 x 4 mm. **Biology:** Common in mid-shore rock pools. Previously called *G. filicina*. **SIMILAR SPECIES:** Compare with ***Chordariopsis capensis*** (178.7).

182.1

182.2

182.3

182.4

182.5

182.6

182.7

182.8

182.9

PLATE 183

Tough branching red algae

183.1 Comb-fan weed
Trematocarpus flabellatus

Small flat comb-like fans; distinctive yellow to purple-brown. Thin, tough, springy, flat, narrow axes forked at close intervals. **Size:** Fans 20–40 mm long, branches 2 mm wide. **Biology:** Forms dense fans on rims of mid-tide pools and gullies. **SIMILAR SPECIES:** *T. fragilis* (Namaqualand): axes thinner and round to oval, not flat.

183.2 Constricted polyopes
Polyopes constrictus

Axes tough, slender, irregularly constricted with forked branching in all directions. Dark purplish brown. **Size:** 60 mm long; branches 2 mm wide. **Biology:** Grows subtidally on rocks.

183.3 Threadlike prionitis
Prionitis filiformis

Crustose holdfast gives rise to densely packed slender axes, 3–4 times dichotomously branched. Greenish to dark purple. **Size:** 150 x 1 mm. **Biology:** Grows on extremely wave-exposed rocks in the low intertidal to shallow subtidal zones.

183.4 Knobbled prionitis
Prionitis nodifera

Tough, constricted axes; coarse, purple-black and knobbly; compressed in parts and contorted. **Size:** Axes maximally 5 mm wide. **Biology:** Grows on the sublittoral fringe in wave-washed areas.

183.5 Fine gymnogongrus
Gymnogongrus polycladus

Axes narrow, cylindrical, tough and twig-like, with pointed tips. Main axis forks repeatedly, but older axes have short, finger-like side branches on one side. **Size:** Axes about 50 mm long and 1–2 mm wide. **Biology:** Grows on rocks at low-tide level. **SIMILAR SPECIES:** *G. vermicularis* (Namaqualand–Cape Town) has similar cylindrical branches, but they are wider (up to 3 mm), less forked, and lack side branches. *Gigartina pistillata* (Cape Point–East London) is also forked and twiggy with many laterals, but these emerge at right angles from the main axis. Branches compressed, up to 4 mm wide, tips tapering sharply. Fertile knobs borne on short laterals.

183.6 Complicated gymnogongrus
Gymnogongrus complicatus

Upright axis tough and forks several times; ultimate branches ribbed and curled like contorted hands. Red-brown in colour with paler tips. **Size:** Axes 40 x 1–3 mm. **Biology:** Occurs in the sublittoral fringe with *Gigartina polycarpa* and *Sarcothalia stiriata*.

183.7 Dilated gymnogongrus
Gymnogongrus dilatatus

Fronds deep plum-red; base channelled but then flattening out and arched back at the tips. Axes fork regularly and become broader; lobes wider than 5 mm. Tips of the branches often truncated and notched and have large, ball-like knobs when fertile. Texture crisp and tough. **Size:** Axes 150 mm tall, more than 5 mm wide. **Biology:** Grows at the low-tide level.

183.8 Tufted gymnogongrus
Gymnogongrus tetrasporifer

Axes compressed, irregularly constricted, dichotomously branched; apices rounded. Swollen fruiting bodies contain chains of tetrasporangia. Wine-red. **Size:** Axes about 50 x 1 mm. **Biology:** Densely branched tufts growing from a common holdfast on edges of pools.

183.9 Clustered gymnogongrus
Gymnogongrus glomeratus

Axes flattened, thin, regularly forked; progressively wider towards the tips, forming overlapping fans. Fertile fronds bear warty knobs. Yellow-brown to purple-brown. **Size:** Axes about 50 x 2–4 mm. **Biology:** Occurs along the sublittoral fringe of rocky shores.

183.10 Forked gigartina
Sarcothalia scutellata

Succulent, twig-like branches that fork at short intervals. Axes compressed, but tips swollen and with a dent at the apex. Purple-brown in colour. Reproductive structures are small balls borne in groups near the tips of special branches. **Size:** Plants 60 x 1–3 mm. **Biology:** Grows in dense stands at low-tide level. Previously called *Gigartina scutellata*.

183.1

183.2

183.3

183.4

183.5

183.6

183.7

183.8

183.9

183.10

PLATE 184

Gelatinous red algae

Many red algae contain agar, which gels. In South Africa, agar from Gelidium *and* Gracilaria *spp. are used in food and as microbiological growth mediums.*

184.1 Abbott's jelly-weed   *Gelidium abbottiorum*

Finely but irregularly branched, giving a tatty appearance. Tough, wiry, maroon-coloured. Main axis bears lateral branches that have secondary branchlets with tertiary branchlets (pinnate to the third degree). Branches emerge at right angles to the axis; secondary branches often bent. Fertile branches spatulate and stalked. **Size:** Axes 150 x 1 mm. **Biology:** Grows on vertical rocks, down to 2 m in wave-beaten areas. Confined to deep pools in the Cape. Often encrusted by the coralline *Polyporolithon patena*.

184.2 Cape jelly-weed   *Gelidium capense*

Dark red-brown, fern-like plants with lateral branches that emerge at right angles to the main axis and then bend towards the tip of the plant; branched to the fifth degree, creating dense bunches. Lower branches often shed. **Size:** 200 mm tall, axes 1 mm width. **Biology:** Occurs from the low shore to the shallow subtidal zone.

184.3 Fern-leafed jelly-weed   *Gelidium pteridifolium*

Coarse, neat, dark red-brown fern-like plants; triangular in outline. Axes flattened. Pinnate; branching to the fourth degree. The branchlets get progressively narrower and shorter towards the tip and are not bent. **Size:** Plants up to 500 mm, axes 2 mm wide. **Biology:** Occurs in the low-shore to subtidal zones, on wave-exposed shores.

184.4 Turf jelly-weed   *Gelidium reptans*

Forms dense mats of short, tongue-like uprights. Irregular pinnate branches. Margins entire, no midrib. Distinctive orange-brown colour. **Size:** Up to 10 mm tall, branches 1 mm wide. **Biology:** High shore; can withstand long periods of exposure.

184.5 Saw-edged jelly-weed   *Gelidium pristoides*

Fronds narrow, flat, with a midrib and serrated margin. Branching irregular; small lateral leaflets often expanded and paler. **Size:** Fronds 60 x 3 mm. **Biology:** A mid-shore dominant. Tufts a scruffy mix of juveniles, sporophytes and gametophytes. Often grows on limpets or barnacles, out of reach of grazers. Harvested commercially. **SIMILAR SPECIES:** *G. micropterum* is much smaller and grows around the pear limpet (see 72.5a).

184.6 Spiny gracilaria   *Gracilaria aculeata*

Stiff, horny, branching bushes, yellow-brown when young, becoming dark reddish brown when old. The branches arise in whorls, and each branch has swollen zones at regular intervals, which are encircled by leathery spines. **Size:** Axes 100 x 3 mm. **Biology:** Forms dense growths on the vertical sides of deep rocky pools and gullies.

184.7 Irregular gracilaria   *Gracilaria corticata*

Axes elongate, stiff, gelatinous, compressed; branching highly variable, with distal parts occasionally bearing fine branchlets. Colour dark purple to greenish red; tips pink. **Size:** Axes 100 x 4 mm. **Biology:** Abundant on the sides of gullies in strong surf.

184.8 Segmented gracilaria   *Gracilaria salicornia*

Cartilaginous, brittle, club-shaped segments, splitting into two or more branches. Pale to dark reddish brown. Arises from creeping axes with discoid holdfasts. **Size:** Axes 60 x 4 mm. **Biology:** On rocks and sand-covered rocks in intertidal pools and subtidal fringe.

184.9 Agar-weed   *Gracilaria gracilis*

Stringy, straw-coloured to red axes with many long cylindrical branches. Holdfast tiny and insignificant; plants often detached. **Size:** Up to 500 mm long; branches 1 mm wide. **Biology:** Grows at and below low-tide level in sheltered sandy bays and lagoons, often lying loose on the bottom. At Saldanha Bay tangled masses wash ashore and are harvested, dried and exported for extraction of agar. Previously called *G. verrucosa*.

184.1

184.2

184.3

184.4

184.5

184.6

184.7

184.8

184.9

PLATE 185

Ribboned & feathery red algae

185.1 Red spirals   *Osmundaria serrata*
Striking plants with a forking stem and elongate forked blades that spiral in a regular manner, with four marginal serrations to each spiral of the blade. Midrib distinct. Colour red to purple. Basal axes cylindrical and woody. **Size:** Plant 150 mm long, blades 8–10 mm wide. **Biology:** Subtidal in rocky areas. Previously named *Vidalia serrata*.

185.2 Plectrum-weed   *Plectrophora natalensis*
Stiff, upright, bushy plants. Dichotomously branched, flat, loosely twisted branches with opposite marginal teeth; curled ventrally at the tips. Dark red. **Size:** Axes 200 x 1 mm. **Biology:** Common on wave-exposed shores attached to rocks and coralline algae. Previously named *Kuetzingia natalensis*.

185.3 Little hands   *Portieria hornemannii*
Soft, fleshy, flattened fronds, branching into a loose fan: branches progressively narrower distally and tips curled under and resembling tiny hands. Orange-red. **Size:** About 120 x 2 mm or less. **Biology:** Occurs in rock pools and to depths of 20 m; rarely exposed.

185.4 Untidy spyridia   *Spyridia hypnoides*
Pliable, densely branched; spiky in appearance. The main branches get progressively shorter towards the apex of the plant and are surrounded by pointed and finely striped branchlets (see inset). Conspicuous holdfast. Brownish red with orangy tips. **Size:** 200 mm. **Biology:** Common; hangs from walls of intertidal pools and gullies.
SIMILAR SPECIES:
185.5 *Spyridia cupressina* (Eastern Cape–southern KwaZulu-Natal) is stiff and spiky, with rigid axes bearing evenly spaced hooked branchlets in four rows (see inset). Holdfast cone-shaped. Medium red to brownish. Common in intertidal pools.

185.6 Aristocratic plume-weed   *Aristothamnion collabens*
Delicate, purple-red, intricately branching plants. Main branches progressively shorter towards the apex of the plant, and are themselves finely branched to form bottlebrush-like fronds. **Size:** 20–30 mm. **Biology:** Grows epiphytically on other algae in pools.

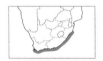

185.7 Iridescent plume-weed   *Callithamnion stuposum*
Forms small, soft untidy clumps; finely branched, plumed and tree-shaped, but the filaments twist together and trap sand. Purple to deep-green with iridescent blue tips. **Size:** 20–30 mm. **Biology:** Common. Hangs from rocks in the low-tide zone.

185.8 Bottlebrush   *Dasya scoparia*
Delicate pinkish-red bottlebrush-like plants composed of irregularly branched cylindrical axes surrounded by spirals of fine branchlets, each intricately branching and incurved. **Size:** Plant about 20 mm tall. **Biology:** Common in algal turf in the wave-exposed subtidal fringe.

185.9 Veined toothweed   *Neurymenia nigricans*
Crisp, foliose blades with a distinct midrib and lateral veins. Branches predominantly from the margins. Margins, midrib and veins all bear teeth. Brownish red. Holdfast discoid and stipe short. **Size:** Plant 60 mm long, blades 5–9 mm wide. **Biology:** Occurs in rocky areas in the intertidal to shallow subtidal zones. **SIMILAR SPECIES:** *N. fraxinifolia* (Sodwana northwards) is similar, but the blades branch from the midrib and have branched teeth and deeply incised apices; 50 x 6–12 mm. *Osmundaria melvillii* (Sodwana northwards) lacks lateral veins; numerous lateral branches arise from the margins or midrib.

185.10 Red ribbons   *Gelidium vittatum*
Long, ribbon-like, sparsely branched fronds with a distinct midrib, and a frill of delicate leaflets along the margin. They are often spiralled and have a few branches. Purple-red. **Size:** Fronds 200 x 10 mm. **Biology:** Grows on the kelp *Ecklonia maxima*. Can be boiled in water to extract the agar, which is added to flavouring and sugar to make jelly puddings. Previously called *Suhria vittata*.

PLATE 186

Spiky & iridescent red algae

186.1 Straight-tipped hypnea
Hypnea ecklonii

Main axis extends along whole length of plant from base to apex; side branches are flanked with numerous very short branchlets. Tips straight, not hooked. Dark red. **Size:** 20 cm tall; axes 0.5 mm wide. **Biology:** Subtidal; usually grows on other algae.

186.2 Rosy curled hypnea
Hypnea rosea

A loose tangle of red axes with short spiky branches arising in all directions. Tips characteristically curled. **Size:** Plants 20–30 x 1.5 mm. **Biology:** Occurs in low-shore pools and the shallow subtidal zone. Grows epiphytically on other algae, particularly *Gelidium* spp., at low-tide level, entwining itself with its host plant.

186.3 Fine hypnea
Hypnea tenuis

A loose tangle of delicate axes, branching irregularly or from one side of the axes; tips hooked. Orange to dark red. **Size:** Plants 20–40 mm tall; branches 0.25 mm wide. **Biology:** Grows epiphytically on other algae, particularly *Gelidium* spp., low on wave-exposed shores.

186.4 Green tips
Hypnea spicifera

Creeping rhizomes giving rise to stiff green axes with spiked branches in their upper half. Fertile plants are densely covered with short branchlets. Green, except for the base of the plant, which is purplish, giving the only clue that it contains the red pigments diagnostic of the red algae. **Size:** Axes 200 x 2 mm. **Biology:** In KwaZulu-Natal and the southern Cape it forms a vivid-green band exposed at low spring tide. It is less common, and a dirty dark green colour, on the west coast. Has potential commercial importance for carrageenan extraction.

186.5 Iridescent hypnea
Hypnea viridis

Fine axes with short pointed branches that are intertwined into a loosely tangled turf. Iridescent purple-blue. **Size:** Turf 20 mm tall; branches 0.5 mm wide. **Biology:** Common amid small *Dictyota* spp. and corallines in mid-tide pools and the shallow subtidal zone.

186.6 Spiky turf-weed
Caulacanthus ustulatus

A low turf of tangled wiry axes with short spiny branches. Light yellow in colour, with maroon tinges. **Size:** Turf 20 mm tall; axes 1 mm wide. **Biology:** A common component of mixed algal turfs on exposed wave-washed rocks in the lower balanoid zone. Often found growing on reef-worm tubes, apparently protected there from grazers.

186.7 Chylocladia
Chylocladia capensis

Low-growing cylindrical succulent axes with constricted segments that are longer than wide. Short branches arise at the joints and are often arranged in whorls. Dark reddish purple, often dusted with iridescent green. **Size:** Plants 12 mm tall; axes 2 mm wide. **Biology:** A common component of intertidal turfs.

186.8 Earthworm champia
Champia lumbricalis

Upright, reddish-brown axes arise from branching rhizomes and look like stiff earthworms, being cylindrical and divided into segments by septa, which are clearly visible against the light. The axes bear bunches of branches. **Size:** Axes about 150 mm long x 4 mm wide. **Biology:** Grows abundantly on sloping rocks in wave-beaten areas at the low-tide and shallow subtidal levels, where it is often the dominant seaweed.

186.9 Compressed champia
Champia compressa

A dainty plant with short compressed axes, rounded tips and regular segments that are wider than long. Lateral branches arise in one plane, with the branches becoming progressively shorter towards the tip. Pinkish red, often with a brilliant iridescent green gloss. **Size:** Axes 25 x 3–4 mm. **Biology:** Grows subtidally among corallines in clean pools and gullies.

PLATE 187

Branching red algae

187.1 Cape chondria — *Chondria capensis*

Plants have a small base and well-spaced stiff branches. Tips swollen, bearing bunches of small spindle-shaped branchlets ornamented with apical hairs. Purplish brown. **Size:** Plants about 200 mm tall. **Biology:** Common in the sublittoral fringe in exposed localities, with *Hypnea spicifera*. Endemic to South Africa.

187.2 Pink chondria — *Chondria armata*

Forms dense cushions of closely packed upright axes, which branch radially and bear small tapering branchlets. Tips acute with a prominent apical cell. Tetrasporangia borne on ultimate branchlets. Pale pink. **Size:** Plants 20 mm tall. **Biology:** Common; forms extensive patches in low intertidal pools and the shallow subtidal zone.

187.3 Asparagopsis — *Asparagopsis taxiformis*

Small, soft, plumose axes arising from a branched stolon. Each axis tree-shaped and has a bare stalk and a densely branched top. Pinkish grey. **Size:** About 50 mm tall. **Biology:** Forms extensive pinkish-grey patches on shallow subtidal rocks.

187.4 Flattened laurencia — *Laurencia complanata*

Fronds resemble thick, fleshy, purplish-red feathers. Axes broad and compressed with branches bearing bunches of short pinnae that become swollen when fertile. **Size:** Plants 60–80 mm long; axes 4 mm wide. **Biology:** Grows in pools and on subtidal rocks.

187.5 Red-tipped laurencia — *Laurencia natalensis*

Small bunched plants with numerous cylindrical branches in all directions. Dull green with bright-red tips. **Size:** Fronds 30–40 x 1 mm wide. **Biology:** Common in rock pools and on sand-covered rocks.

187.6 Grape laurencia — *Laurencia glomerata*

Plants uniformly purple-brown. Cylindrical branches and branchlets are densely crowded and swollen, giving an outline like an inverted cone or bunch of grapes. **Size:** 50 mm tall; branches 2 mm wide. **Biology:** Subtidal or in pools.

187.7 Flexuose laurencia — *Laurencia flexuosa*

Crisp, fleshy, pinkish-red plants with narrow, slightly flattened, much-branched axes and truncated tips. The branches arise neatly on both sides, mainly in one plane. **Size:** Plants about 50 mm tall, branches 2 mm wide. **Biology:** Common in rock pools, in the cochlear zone and in the subtidal fringe on moderately sheltered shores.

187.8 Dwarf laurencia — *Laurencia pumila*

A small flattened species, with a few short branches in all directions. Fertile axes end in stubby clumps of branches. Greenish with purple tips. **Size:** Less than 30 mm tall. **Biology:** Forms small, distinct cushions at mid-tide level on wave-exposed shores.

187.9 Spine-stalk — *Acanthophora spicifera*

Plants crisp, brittle, cylindrical, with short, spirally arranged spiny branchlets. Purple to straw yellow. **Size:** Plants about 100 mm tall, branches about 2 mm wide. **Biology:** Occurs in sheltered to moderately exposed pools.

187.10 Bostrychia — *Bostrychia tenella*

Mats of dark purple to brown feather-like fronds, with 3–4 orders of alternating branches. **Size:** Fronds 15 x 10 mm wide. **Biology:** Grows as black patches on shaded high-tide rocks. **SIMILAR SPECIES:** Several species of *Bostrychia* are found high on the shore. *B. intricata* (Saldanha–Mossel Bay) is smaller, black; simple curled fronds. *B. moritziana* and *B. harveyi* grow on the aerial roots of mangroves.

187.1

187.2

187.3

187.4

187.5

187.6

187.7

187.8

187.9

187.10

PLATE 188

Elegant red algae

Plocamium *spp. have curved branches that arise in groups of two or three, which alternate on the two sides of the main axis (see 188.8a). The branches of* Pterosiphonia *alternate singly up the axes and side branches.*

188.1 Elegant net fan
Martensia elegans

Beautiful, soft, iridescent mauve fans, attached by a small disc; the outer third of each fan forms a delicate mesh of fine tubes. Warty reproductive bodies dot the bars of the mesh. **Size:** Fans 20–30 mm. **Biology:** Common in shallow pools and gullies at mid-tide level. Usually associated with *Hypnea viridis*, *Dictyota* spp. and corallines.

188.2 Camouflaged net fan
Martensia flabelliformis

Camouflaged fans shaded green, yellow and brown (but not iridescent blue), and attached by a short stipe; the outer third of each forms a delicate mesh of fine tubes. Warty reproductive bodies occur on the bars of the mesh. **Size:** Fans up to 40 mm. **Biology:** Occurs in intertidal pools and down to depths of 20 m on coral reefs.

188.3 Red feather-weed
Pterosiphonia cloiophylla

Small, dark, opaque, brownish-red fern-like axes. Branchlets narrow and pointed. Main axis microscopically divided into segments. **Size:** Fronds 40 mm long, axes 1 mm wide. **Biology:** Occurs on wave-swept sublittoral fringe with plocamiums. **SIMILAR SPECIES:** *P. complanata* (Namibia) nearly identical, but side branches slightly wider (bases spanning 4–6 segments of the main axis, compared to 2–3 in *P. cloiophylla*). **188.4** *Pterosiphonia stangerii* (southwest–KwaZulu-Natal) has broader, fan-like branches.

188.5 Coral plocamium
Plocamium corallorhiza

A beautiful deep pink, iridescing blue-purple underwater. Fronds broad and flattened, bearing claw-like leaflets with marginal teeth that are themselves serrated. Leaflets arranged in alternating pairs of a large and simple lower leaflet and a branched upper one. Reproductive bodies form rosettes of tiny leaflets. **Size:** Fronds 150 mm, claws 10 mm wide. **Biology:** Subtidal fringe down to 5 m, often in exposed, wave-pounded positions.

188.6 Becker's plocamium
Plocamium beckeri

Plants pink, small, flat and more delicate than *P. rigidum*. Branchlets occur in series of three in all parts of the plant; sporangial branches simple. **Size:** 10–20 mm tall. **Biology:** Found in mid- to low-tide pools, growing on other algae, and in the shallow subtidal zone.

188.7 Rigid plocamium
Plocamium rigidum

Plant small and neat, branches in series of two near the base and three near the tips; Sporangial branches clustered; red in colour. **Size:** 30 mm tall. **Biology:** Common in the sublittoral zone.

188.8 Suhr's plocamium
Plocamium suhrii

Resembles *P. corallorhiza* (188.4) but more delicate and the claws have simple marginal teeth that are not serrated. Deep pink. Reproductive structures form minute axillary branchlets (188.8a). **Size:** 30 mm long, claws 5 mm wide. **Biology:** Occurs in low-shore pools and down to depths of 5 m. Can be confused with *Portieria hornemannii* (185.3).

188.9 Horny plocamium
Plocamium cornutum

Coarse, untidy, brownish red. Crowded, cylindrical branchlets in series of not more than two. **Size:** Fronds 70 mm, claws about 1 mm wide. **Biology:** Abundant on rocks at low-tide level and characteristic of areas exposed to heavy surf.

188.10 Brush weed
Halopithys subopaca

Plants with stiff erect axes, compressed distally, with curved, spirally arranged branchlets; dark red-black. **Size:** Up to 100 mm tall, branchlets 8 x 0.5 mm. **Biology:** Grows in low intertidal pools and in gullies; accumulates sand. **SIMILAR SPECIES:** *Digenia simplex* (Zululand northwards) is similar, but the axes are up to 40 mm tall, cylindrical, dichotomously branched and more densely covered with smaller branchlets.

188.1

188.2

188.3

188.4

188.5

188.6

188.7

188.8a

188.8

188.9

188.10

PLATE 189

Epiphytic & fine red algae

189.1 Flaccid kelp-weed   *Carpoblepharis flaccida*

Long, narrow, flattened main axes with haphazardly placed lateral branches. Numerous tiny branchlets, creating a frilled margin. Soft, fleshy, purplish brown. **Size:** Fronds 200 mm long; axes 2 mm wide. **Biology:** A common epiphyte on the kelp *Ecklonia maxima*. SIMILAR SPECIES: *Carpoblepharis minima* is similar but grows on *Laminaria*.

189.2 Beaded ceramium   *Ceramium arenarium*

Delicate filaments branching in all directions, with incurved, claw-like tips. Each filament has a single row of long transparent central cells surrounded by bands of small red cortical cells, resembling beads, just visible to the naked eye. Round spore bodies borne on the branches. **Size:** Axes 20–30 mm long, 0.5 mm wide. **Biology:** Epiphytic on other algae. Several closely related species.

189.3 Cape ceramium   *Ceramium capense*

Axes whip-like, branching in all directions, usually in whorls. There are large and small branchlets along the axes. Tips form unequal pairs of slightly incurved claws. Axes opaque, purple, with only a suggestion of beading. **Size:** 50 mm long, less than 0.5 mm wide. **Biology:** Epiphytic on other algae.

189.4 Black-red ceramium   *Ceramium atrorubescens*

Axes delicate, dichotomously branched, with small branchlets from the inside of the forks. Tips form equal pairs of strongly incurved claws. Axes beaded, with blackish-red bands. **Size:** 50 mm long, up to 0.5 mm wide. **Biology:** Grows on rocks and algae.

189.5 Coarse ceramium   *Ceramium obsoletum*

One of the larger ceramiums. The branches fork regularly, diverge at a wide angle and have short secondary branches along the inner sides of the forks; tips of branches short. Axes opaque and purple; not beaded. **Size:** 200 mm long. **Biology:** Epiphytic on algae.

189.6 Flat-fern ceramium   *Ceramium planum*

Perhaps the most beautiful of the delicate red algae. Flat fern-like purplish-red fronds with a neat pinnate branching. Axes not beaded **Size:** Fronds 100–200 mm long. **Biology:** Grows on other algae, notably *Codium* spp. Also recorded in Mozambique.

189.7 Rhodomelopsis   *Rhodomelopsis africana*

Bushy, composed of a stolon and upright axes. Axes cylindrical, with lateral branches arching over the apex. Tetrasporangia in grouped branchlets at the tips, forming tufts. Colour black-purple. **Size:** Up to 100 mm. **Biology:** On rocks in deep intertidal pools.

189.8 Curl-claw   *Centroceras clavulatum*

Forms tufts of filaments that are jointed, not beaded. Terminal joints have a ring of microscopic spines. Tips of the branches form pairs of strongly incurved claws. Blackish brown. **Size:** Fronds 40–80 mm. **Biology:** Not epiphytic; grows intertidally.

189.9 Tayloriella   *Tayloriella tenebrosa*

Bushy, composed of a stolon and upright axes with short awl-shaped alternating branches, simple or rebranched. Axes of rows of cells; tetrasporangia buried in swollen side branches (see inset). Blackish. **Size:** Up to 50 mm. **Biology:** Common in intertidal turf.

189.10 Kelp fern   *Polysiphonia virgata*

Fine, whip-like axes that branch in all directions. The axes are made up of several rows of microscopic cells, and rows of tetrasporangia are buried in the swollen ends of the branches. Round spore-bearing cysts form on short branches. Dark purple-black. **Size:** Axes 20–300 mm. **Biology:** Grows epiphytically on the kelp *Ecklonia maxima*. SIMILAR SPECIES:

189.11 *Polysiphonia urbana* (southern Namibia–Cape Agulhas) is one of several much finer *Polysiphonia* spp. with the same characteristic multicellular structure (see inset).

189.1

189.2

189.3

189.4

189.5

189.6

189.7

189.8

189.9

189.10

189.11

PLATE 190

Lightly calcified red algae

190.1 Common galaxaura — *Dichotomaria diesingiana*

Axes unsegmented, flat, pliable, with a lime-impregnated skin. Pinkish red with spatulate red tips. Attached by rhizoids; base cylindrical and often hairy. **Size:** Axes 120 x 2–5 mm wide, branching dichotomously at 7–14 mm intervals. **Biology:** Grows on low-shore and subtidal wave-exposed rocks. Previously named *Galaxaura diesingiana*.

190.2 Segmented galaxaura — *Galaxaura obtusata*

Axes segmented, cylindrical, pulpy, with a tough lime-impregnated skin. Segments about 10 mm long. Deep pink in colour. **Size:** Axes 200 mm long x 2–4 mm wide, forked every 8–30 mm. **Biology:** Grows on the sides of deeper pools and gullies down to 30 m.

190.3 Flat galaxaura — *Dichotomaria tenera*

Axes unsegmented, flat, fleshy, with a lime-impregnated skin. Pink to purplish red with light banding. Attached by rhizoids; base cylindrical, often hairy. **Size:** Axes 90 x 2–5 mm, forked every 3–8 mm. **Biology:** Grows in low-tide pools and down to about 40 m.

190.4 Hairy galaxaura — *Galaxaura rugosa*

Forms dense hemispherical tufts. Axes unsegmented, cylindrical, pulpy, with a tough lime-impregnated skin. Forked branching. Gametophytes (190.4) pink to yellowish with bleached tips, slightly hairy at the base. Tetrasporophytes dark red, densely covered with hairy filaments; often arranged in distinct whorls near the tips (190.4a). **Size:** Axes 90 mm long x 2–3 mm wide. **Biology:** Grows on the sides of intertidal pools and down to 12 m.

190.5 Tricleocarpa — *Tricleocarpa fragilis*

Thallus erect, segmented; segments slightly rounded at both ends, heavily calcified. Pale pinkish white. **Size:** Up to 70 mm long; branches 0.8 mm wide, forking at a narrow angle every 3–8 mm. **Biology:** Forms brittle tufts on intertidal and shallow subtidal rocks.

190.6 Ramrod weed — *Scinaia salicornioides*

Axes cylindrical, forking two or three times; constricted at the forks. Not calcified. Discoid holdfast. Tips swollen, covered with fine, red hairs. Dark red. **Size:** Axes about 150 mm long, 1–4 mm wide. **Biology:** Occasionally found on rocks in pools and gullies.

190.7 Epiphytic liagora — *Liagora divaricata*

Small bush comprised of unsegmented, cylindrical, non-mucilaginous branches; moderately calcified. Branches fork at a wide angle; additional lateral branches. Purplish red. **Size:** 50 mm tall; branches 1 mm wide, forking every 5–8 mm. **Biology:** Epiphytic on the seagrass *Thalassodendron ciliatum* (195.3); occurs in deep pools and subtidally.

190.8 Slimy liagora — *Liagora ceranoides*

Thallus erect, unsegmented, forming bushes of cylindrical, forking, mucilaginous branches that are lightly calcified. Often with additional lateral branches. White with pink to purplish tips. **Size:** 60 mm tall, branches 1 mm wide, forking every 2–3 mm. **Biology:** Grows in low-shore intertidal pools and on subtidal rocks.

190.1

190.2

190.3

190.4

190.4a

190.5

190.6

190.7

190.8

PLATE 191

Upright coralline algae

Upright coralline algae have jointed stems, the segments of which are impregnated with lime to deter grazers. The type of branching and position and structure of fertile segments are diagnostic for the genera.

191.1 Finely forked coralline   *Jania adhaerens*
Slender cylindrical axes with symmetrical forked branching at an angle >45°; joints marked by a narrow line. Grey to pink. Swollen fertile segments are subterminal with a distal pore (191.1a). **Size:** Axes usually 20–30 mm long; segments five times longer than broad. **Biology:** Forms low turfs on rocks and in pools.
SIMILAR SPECIES:
191.2 *Jania verrucosa* (False Bay eastwards) pale reddish brown, 1–5 segments between dichotomies, branching angle <30°, segments 1–3 times longer than broad. *J. intermedia* (KwaZulu-Natal northwards) greyish pink, 1–15 segments between dichotomies, branching angle <30°, segments 10 times longer than broad.

191.3 Nodular coralline   *Amphiroa bowerbankii*
Segments rectangular, flat with thin edges; chalky pink. Large joints with nodules. Branching forked; ultimate joints have pale rounded tips. Surface of segments covered with warty reproductive capsules, (191.3a). **Size:** Axes 50 mm, joints 5–8 x 2–4 mm. **Biology:** Grows in low-shore pools and the shallow subtidal zone.

191.4 Horsetail coralline   *Amphiroa ephedraea*
Segments elongate, cylindrical or slightly flattened, with smooth ends; purplish pink. Joints black, 1 mm wide. Branching forked. Surface of segments covered with warty reproductive capsules. **Size:** Axes 150 mm long, segments 7–10 x 1–2 mm. **Biology:** Forms large hanging clumps on low-shore and subtidal rocks.
SIMILAR SPECIES:
191.5 *Amphiroa anceps* (Cape Agulhas–Durban) has narrow flattened segments with lateral shoulders at the joints, which are less obvious.
191.6 *Amphiroa capensis* (Cape Peninsula) is much smaller and forked at each joint, forming a fan about 50 mm long. Segments cylindrical, 3 x 1 mm; joints obvious in the centre but narrow at the sides (191.6a). *A. beauvoisii* (Cape Hangklip–East Africa) is greyish red or violet and densely bushy; segments cylindrical, up to 5 mm long, with thin joints that are not black.

191.7 Arrowhead coralline   *Cheilosporum cultratum*
Segments arrowhead-shaped, with irregular, toothed edges and separated by thin joints. Branching sparse, forking every 4–10 joints. Deep pink; 1–3 spore capsules on the distal lip of segments. Two varieties exist (191.7a, 191.7b). **Size:** Axes 50 mm long; segments 2 mm long, 3–6 mm wide. **Biology:** Low-shore to shallow subtidal zone.
SIMILAR SPECIES:
191.8 *Cheilosporum sagittatum* (Cape Town–Durban) is delicate, smooth, mauve, with acute arrowheads (191.8a); 1.5 mm long x 1.5 mm wide. One spore capsule per wing.

191.9 Feather coralline   *Corallina officinalis*
Bushy clumps of jointed axes, branching pinnately (feather-like) with two or three orders of laterals. Conceptacles club-shaped, on the ends of laterals (191.9a). **Size:** About 50 mm. Segments 0.5–1 x 0.5–1.5 mm. **Biology:** Widespread; abundant on exposed coasts in the lower intertidal zone and on limpet shells.
SIMILAR SPECIES:
191.10 *Haliptilon* sp. (Sodwana northwards) is pinnately branched from every joint, with additional branches resulting in irregular whorls of branches distally. The reproductive conceptacles bear lateral branchlets or have a whorl of branchlets.

191.11 Hinged corallines   *Arthrocardia* spp.
Axes stout, oval in section; up to four branches at a joint; segments are flattened irregular wedges. Deep pink, bleaching white. Fertile fronds fork distally. Spore capsule with terminal pore and a branch on either side (191. 11a). **Size:** 50–80 mm. **Biology:** Close-set tufts grow from mid-shore downwards. Several difficult to distinguish species.

191.1

191.2

191.1a

191.3a

191.3

191.4

191.5

191.6a

191.6

191.7

191.7a

191.7b

191.8a

191.8

191.9

191.10

191.9a

191.11a

191.11

PLATE 192

Encrusting algae

Some seaweeds form flat crusts. Notable are the encrusting corallines, which are laden with lime, a putative deterrent to grazers. They are diverse, but accurate identification requires microscopic examination of their tissues and reproductive bodies (conceptacles). Generally, thicker crusts are good competitors, overgrowing thinner ones, but are slower-growing and less tolerant of grazing.

192.1 Seagrass collars   *Pneophyllum amplexifrons*

Forms distinctive calcareous, trumpet-shaped collars enveloping the stems of the seagrass *Thalassodendron ciliatum*; colour greyish, pinkish or dark purple, usually with small red spots. **Size:** Fans about 10 mm long. **Biology:** Epiphytic on seagrass and *Codium*.

192.2 Red fan-weed   *Peyssonnelia capensis*

Flat, overlapping, leathery fans; white below and purplish red above, with yellowish or green margins. Attached to rocks by a central holdfast, but its fans are raised from the substrate. **Size:** Fans about 40 mm. **Biology:** Grows on the walls of deep pools or gullies, often in caves and overhangs, down to 20 m. **SIMILAR SPECIES:** *P. atropurpurea* is dark red-black.

192.3 Tar crust   *Hildenbrandia lecanellierii*

Forms irregular, gnarled crusts that lift at the margins. Purple-black. **Size:** 20–100 mm wide; 1–4 mm thick. **Biology:** Encrusts crevices low on the shore and in pools. **SIMILAR SPECIES:** *H. rubra* (Cape Point–Zululand) forms thin, smooth encrustations in relatively regular circles; resembles red bloodstains. *Placophora binderi* (Cape Point–Mozambique) forms crusts on *Codium* (see 172.8).

192.4 Cochlear coralline crust   *Spongites yendoi*

Relatively thin. Chalky white; mauve if shaded. Lumpy, or has small upright knobs. Conceptacles pimple-like, uniporate. **Size:** 0.5 mm thick. **Biology:** Abundant on the southwest coast; usually grows on or near the limpet *Scutellastra cochlear* (72.5). **SIMILAR SPECIES:** *Pneophyllum keatsii* comprises thin, circular grey crusts that grow on kelps. *Synarthrophyton eckloniae* is thicker, pink and multiporate; also grows on kelps.

192.5 Scrolled coralline crust   *Spongites impar*

Moderately thick. Chalky or beige with a pale margin. Produces twisted ridges where two colonies meet. Conceptacles uniporate. **Size:** 1 mm thick; ridges 10 mm high. **Biology:** Occupies mid to low shore; common where wave action is strong. Weakly attached and intolerant of grazing. Overgrows *S. yendoi* unless grazed by *Scutellastra cochlear*.

192.6 Velvety coralline crust   *Heydrichia woelkerlingii*

Thick, flat or lobed; surface smooth, glossy, velvety to the touch. Deep purple-pink and white-edged. Asexual conceptacles uniporate. **Size:** 3–15 mm thick; 50–300 mm wide. **Biology:** Aggressively overgrows all other crusts in the shallow subtidal zone, but held at bay by grazing limpets. Often bored by the polychaetes *Polydora* and *Dodecaceria* (see 27.5).

192.7 Thin coralline crust   *Leptophytum foveatum*

Thin, paint-like, smooth. Brownish pink, with pale squiggles. Edges white. Asexual conceptacles multiporate. **Size:** 0.5 mm thick. **Biology:** Forms sheets at or below low-tide level. Tolerates grazing, but susceptible to desiccation. Generates new margins to combat overgrowth. Often associated with the limpet *Scutellastra argenvillei*.
SIMILAR SPECIES:
192.8 *Leptophytum acervatum* (Cape Point–KwaZulu-Natal) is almost identical but brighter pink; surface often pocked. Grows on pebbles, not rock faces.
192.9 *Leptophytum ferox*, 'Packman' (Namaqualand–Mozambique), is 5–10 mm thick, with upright pillars, often capped by slits bordered with 'lips'.
192.10 *Mesophyllum engelhartii* (Namibia–East London) is purple-brown, thin, white-edged, 1–2 mm thick; it has bumps that erode to form white caps. Occurs on the low shore.

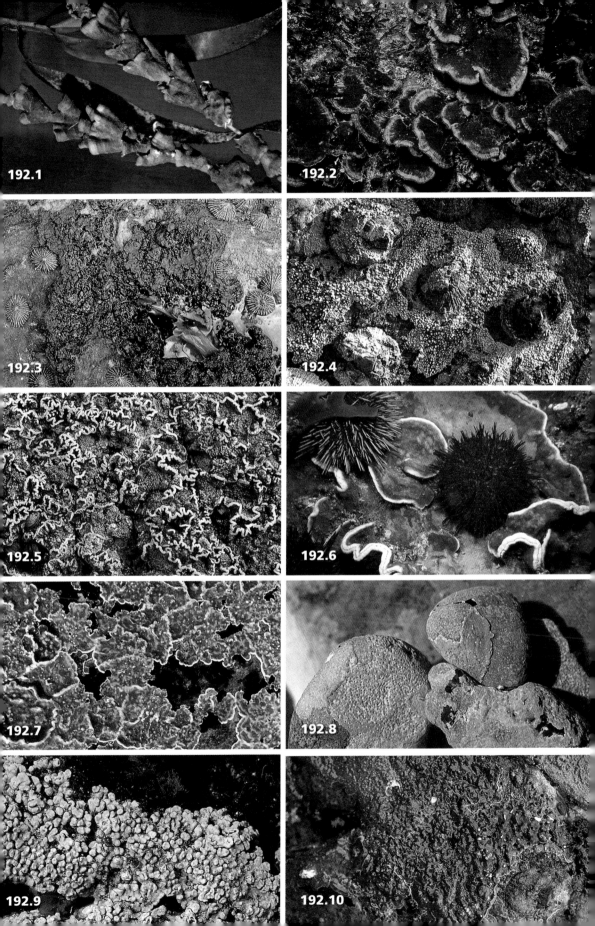

192.1

192.2

192.3

192.4

192.5

192.6

192.7

192.8

192.9

192.10

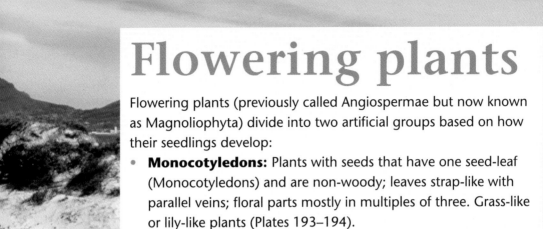

Flowering plants

Flowering plants (previously called Angiospermae but now known as Magnoliophyta) divide into two artificial groups based on how their seedlings develop:

- **Monocotyledons:** Plants with seeds that have one seed-leaf (Monocotyledons) and are non-woody; leaves strap-like with parallel veins; floral parts mostly in multiples of three. Grass-like or lily-like plants (Plates 193–194).
- **Dicotyledons:** Plants with two seed-leaves (Dicotyledons); often woody; leaves net-veined, often broad; floral parts mostly in multiples of four or five (Plates 195–201).

Flowering plants are adapted to several unique interfaces with the ocean – salt marshes, mangrove swamps, coastal cliffs, dunes and dune thickets and forests. Stressed by salt spray and wind, the plants often have succulent, hairy or waxy leaves to reduce water loss. Dune vegetation is vulnerable to disturbance, and its destabilisation by coastal development should be avoided.

PLATE 193

Monocotyledons
Reeds, rushes, sedges & grasses in dunes & estuaries

Liliopsida

193.1 Thatching reed, Dekriet
Thamnochortus insignis

Stems clumped, cylindrical, smooth and green. Dry brown bracts at nodes typify family Restionaceae. Female flowerheads (right) erect, stiff spikelets; male (left) has drooping, softer spikelets. **Size:** 2 m tall. **Biology:** Coastal dunes. Important for thatching.

193.2 Dune slack sharp rush
Juncus kraussii

Long, sharply pointed, cylindrical stems that lack nodes. Leaves cylindrical and sharply pointed. Flowers and cylindrical fruits in terminal tufts. **Size:** 40 cm. **Biology:** Dominates low-salinity salt marshes; often extends into dunes. Widely used for weaving mats.

193.3 Tufted dune sedge
Ficinia lateralis

Forms low dense tufts of weeping blue-green leaves; clusters of 5–10 brown flowerheads near the tips. **Size:** Tufts 15 cm tall, 25 cm wide. **Biology:** A pioneer in secondary dunes and dry dune slacks. **SIMILAR SPECIES:** *F. nodosa* has solid leafless stems with spiny points, and tight, single, round cluster of flowerheads below a sharp terminal bract.

193.4 Giant sedge
Cyperus crassipes

Triangular solid stems with underground stolons; basal tuft of rough curved leaves. Flowerheads tightly clustered or on short apical branches above long, leaf-like bracts. **Size:** 40 cm tall. **Biology:** Common in dune slacks and around estuaries.

193.5 Sedge-stemmed love grass
Cladoraphis cyperoides

Cylindrical stems with side shoots that end in spiky points. Flowerheads in dense clusters that spiral up the stem. **Size:** 35 cm tall. **Biology:** A pioneer of primary and secondary dunes. **SIMILAR SPECIES:** *C. spinosa* (west coast) has many lateral spines on flowerhead.

193.6 Sea wheat
Thinopyrum distichum

Long narrow leaves ensheath the stems. Flowerhead has large straw-coloured spikelets. **Size:** 50 cm tall. **Biology:** A pioneer of foredunes, with creeping rhizomes. Both this species and the introduced marram grass, *Ammophila arenaria*, are used to stabilise loose sand, but this can cause disappearance of beaches by starving them of sand.

193.7 Brakgras
Sporobolus virginicus

Long underground runners with erect shoots bearing stiff, upwardly pointing curved leaves. Flowers and seeds densely packed on a single spike. **Size:** 25 cm tall. **Biology:** Common on dunes, dune-slacks and edges of salt marshes.

193.8 Swamp-reed
Phragmites australis

Reeds with long, hollow, jointed stems. Flowerhead forms a large terminal feathery plume. **Size:** 1.5–3 m tall. **Biology:** Cosmopolitan on riverbanks and the upper ends of estuaries where there is freshwater seepage. Previously named *Phragmites communis*.

Alien

193.9 Cord grass
Spartina maritima

Long thin rough leaves arise near the base of the plant, taper gradually, and are rolled inwards. Inflorescence usually with two branches. **Size:** 25–50 cm tall. **Biology:** Stabilises sediment in the upper shore of estuaries. Alien; established here in 1840.

193.10 Bulrush
Typha capensis

Leaves long, strap-shaped and hairless. Unmistakable cylinder of female flowers bursts when ripe, releasing copious fluffy seeds. Male flowers borne on a terminal rod and soon drop off. **Size:** 2 m tall. **Biology:** Forms dense perennial beds along streams and marshes.

193.11 Arrowgrass
Triglochin bulbosa

Flower spike ensheathed by thin upright leaves (left). Fruits slender, 5–10 mm long (centre). **Size:** 15 cm. **Biology:** Occupies high-shore salt marshes. **SIMILAR SPECIES:**
193.12 *Triglochin striata* (right of picture): flowers more dense; fruits round, 0.2 cm in diameter; leaves splay sideways and curve up. Distribution and habitat as for *T. bulbosa*.

193.1

193.2

193.3

193.4

193.5

193.6

193.7

193.8

193.9

193.10

193.11

193.12

PLATE 194

Bulbs & lilies in secondary dunes

Secondary dunes are less stressful and have a greater variety of plants. Many have underground 'bulbs' for storage to survive the dry season.

194.1 Dune starlily, Duine kool — *Trachyandra divaricata*

A robust perennial, forming clumps of narrow, smooth, fleshy leaves with papery brown sheaths at the base. Star-like scented white flowers on a wide branching inflorescence. Six petals strongly curled back; only a few open each day. **Size:** Plant 1 m; flowers 2 cm long. **Biology:** Grows on coastal sands and dunes. **SIMILAR SPECIES:** There are several coastal species of *Trachyandra*. *T. falcata*, the Namaqua starlily (Orange River–Cape Town), has a closely packed cylindrical floral spike. The young shoots are eaten like asparagus. *T. ciliata* (Namibia–Port Elizabeth) has hairy leaves; flowers in a long trailing spike.

194.2 Soldier-in-the-box — *Albuca grandis*

A large bulbous geophyte with soft erect leaves. Flower spike with nodding yellow flowers with a green median stripe; slightly fragrant. **Size:** Leaves 40 x 1–3 cm long; flowers 3 cm long. **Biology:** Fairly common on sandy coastal flats. Most *Albuca* and *Ornithogalum* spp., such as the chincherinchee, contain poisonous glycosides.

194.3 Sand lily — *Veltheimia bracteata*

A bulbous perennial with glossy green leaves. Flower spike a dense raceme with nodding tubular pink flowers. **Size:** Leaves 40 cm long; flowers 3 cm long. **Biology:** Forms patches on coastal cliffs. **SIMILAR SPECIES:** *V. capensis* (Namaqualand–Mossel Bay) has crinkly matt bluish leaves, and speckled pinkish flowers.

194.4 Candelabra lily — *Brunsvigia orientalis*

A geophyte with an oval bulb; 2–6 narrow velvety leaves lie flat on the ground. Flowerhead a distinctive reddish-pink ball; flowers stalked and curve up; petals curl back. **Size:** Flower ball 30 cm. **Biology:** Grows on sandy flats. Dry flowerheads break free and are wind-tumbled, scattering the seeds. Flowers in March; leaves appear in May.

194.5 Sand lily, Rooibobbejaantjie — *Babiana hirsute*

A robust perennial with short horizontal branches and stiff pleated leaves with minute hairs. The two-lipped red flowers are borne on the side branches and face the tip of the spike. **Size:** Plant 50 cm; flowers 1.5–2 cm. **Biology:** Common on coastal sandflats and dunes. Flowers July–October. Previously named *B. thunbergii*. **SIMILAR SPECIES:** *B. ringens* (Columbine–Mossel Bay). Known as the 'rotstert' because the main stem is sterile and sticks up like a rat's tail. Sunbirds perch on the stem to feed from the two-lipped red and yellow flowers growing on short side branches at ground level.

194.6 April fool — *Haemanthus coccineus*

A geophyte with a large flattened bulb. Two or three broad leathery hairless leaves appear after flowering. Flower stalk white to red, with red spots; up to nine red bracts surround the group of small red flowers. Bears many bright red berries. **Size:** Leaves 70 cm long; flowerhead 7 cm. **Biology:** Widespread; flowers in March. **SIMILAR SPECIES:** *H. sanguineus* (Clanwilliam–Port Elizabeth) has almost round leaves and a plain red flower stalk. *H. pubescens* (Namibia–Cape Town) has narrow, slightly hairy leaves and a red flower stalk, sometimes mottled. Confined to coastal plain. *H. albiflos* (Eastern Cape) has white flowers.

194.7 Arum lily — *Zantedeschia aethiopica*

Large arrowhead-shaped leaves with a soft fleshy stalk arise from a swollen rhizome. A distinctive white bract curls elegantly around the central yellow inflorescence, which has male flowers near the top and female flowers in the lower part. **Size:** 50 cm tall. **Biology:** Forms mass displays in spring, in damp, often sandy, coastal flats. Sap slimy, contains irritant oxalic acid, and stains clothing. Valuable commercial flower.

194.8 Flame lily — *Gloriosa superba*

Tuber slender, white, often V–shaped. Stems pliable; leaves end in a tendril that twines around other vegetation. Six flame-coloured petals curve back to expose the stiff style and stamens. **Size:** Flower 7 cm; plant 1.5 m tall. **Biology:** Common in coastal bush. A related species is the national flower of Zimbabwe.

194.1

194.2

194.3

194.4

194.5

194.6

194.7

194.8

PLATE 195

Dicotyledons
Submerged & salt marsh plants

Magnoliopsida

195.1 Cape eelgrass
Zostera capensis

Creeping rhizomes. Leaves narrow, flat; tips rounded, faintly notched; about eight parallel veins and periodic crossbars (see 74.10). **Size:** Blades 10–30 cm, 1–2 mm wide. **Biology:** Occurs in lagoons and estuaries. Binds sediment, shelters small fish, and yields detrital food. **SIMILAR SPECIES:** *Halodule uninervis* (St Lucia northwards) has leaf tips with three points.

195.2 Syringe seagrass
Syringodium isoetifolium

Upright flexible plants with a few long, narrow, grooved, almost cylindrical leaves, arising from a creeping buried rhizome. Flowers arranged in a sickle-shaped cyme. **Size:** 18 cm tall. **Biology:** Grows at the low-tide boundary of muddy flats and along channels down to 6 m, often mixed with other seagrasses. Tropical Indo-Pacific.

195.3 Stalked seagrass
Thalassodendron ciliatum

Leaves broad (8–12 mm) and strap-like, with numerous parallel veins and finely spined margins; bundled at the ends of long bare woody stalks borne on a creeping stem. **Size:** 25 cm tall. **Biology:** Abundant in sheltered lagoons, the shallow subtidal zone and deep rock pools. **SIMILAR SPECIES:** Several short-stemmed species share the same habitat and region. *Cymodocea rotundata* has 2–4 mm wide leaves; tips smooth and veins parallel. When old leaves are shed, they leave ragged scars around the base of the short stem. *C. serrulata* has 4–9 mm leaves, tips serrated; clean leaf scars on stems. *Thalassia hemprichii* has 5–7 mm wide leaves, smooth-edged with net veins; old leaf sheaths persist around base of short stem, giving it a shaggy appearance.

195.4 Sago pondweed
Stuckenia pectinatus

Stems and leaves thin, grass-like and tangled; flowers clustered along a spike (195.4a). **Size:** Stems 1 m long, 1 mm wide. **Biology:** Prolific in low salinities at the top of estuaries. Always submerged; forms dense mats cursed by boatmen. Retards waterflow, increasing sedimentation. Previously named *Potamogeton pectinatus*.
SIMILAR SPECIES:
195.5 *Ruppia maritima*, the estuarine pondweed (Walvis Bay–Mozambique), has flowers grouped at the tip of a short straight flower stalk. See also 124.4.
195.6 *Ruppia cirrhosa* (widespread) has a characteristically coiled flower stalk.

195.7 Oval saltweed
Halophila ovalis

Develops from underground creeping rhizomes that bear pairs of single flat oval leaves with long slender stalks. **Size:** 4 cm tall; leaves 1 cm wide. **Biology:** Occupies estuarine sandbanks down to 12 m. Favours brackish water (*halophila* means 'salt-lover').

195.8 Coastal samphire
Sarcocornia littorea

Bushy perennial with a thick woody stem; terminal branches succulent, jointed, lacking leaves. **Size:** 60 cm tall. **Biology:** On rocky shores above high-tide mark.
SIMILAR SPECIES:
195.9 *Sarcocornia pillansii* (whole coast) forms shrubs at the upper levels of salt marshes. Stems thick, flat; each joint ends in a gondola-like tip.

195.10 Glasswort samphire
Sarcocornia perennis

A sprawling succulent perennial with underground rhizomes; stems cylindrical, fleshy jointed, with no obvious leaves. Flowers tiny, arranged in threes at stem nodes (195.10a, b). **Size:** 3 cm tall. **Biology:** Forms creeping mats low on estuarine salt marshes. Becomes red when salt-stressed (195.10).

195.11 Marsh samphire
Salicornia meyeriana

A bushy annual with upright succulent jointed stems (195.11), slender woody lower branches, and a short taproot; no obvious leaves; small flowers arranged in threes with a larger central flower (195.11b). **Size:** Low bushes 50 cm. **Biology:** Grows in the upper zones of estuarine marshes. Greyish green, becoming red when salt-stressed (195.11a).

195.1

195.2

195.3

195.4

195.7

195.4a

195.5

195.6

195.8

195.10

195.10a

195.9

Large central flower

Flowers

195.10b

195.11b

195.11a

195.11

PLATE 196

Dune pioneer plants

Several plants are important colonisers of primary dunes. They stabilise shifting sands and allow other plants to establish themselves. Growing in a hostile, desiccating environment with salt spray and shifting sands, colonists often have prostrate stems and tough or succulent leaves.

196.1 Salt bush, Seeplakkie   *Scaevola plumieri*

Small woody evergreen shrub with clusters of tough waxy oval leaves. Flowers small white and fan-shaped. Fruits small and globular (196.1a), purple when ripe. **Size:** Leaves 4 cm; shrub 1 m tall. **Biology:** Stabilises shifting sands with its extensive roots, building small hummocks. The thick waxy layer on its leaves reduces water loss. **SIMILAR SPECIES:** *Scaevola sericea* (Indo-Pacific) has pinkish flowers, and fruits with 10 ribs.

196.2 Goat's foot   *Ipomoea pes-caprae*

A sprawling creeper; long runners bear pairs of bilobed leaves (resembling a goat's cloven hoof). Flowers trumpet-shaped, bright purple. **Size:** Leaves 6 cm; stems metres long. **Biology:** Important early coloniser of seashore dunes. Widely distributed, as its seeds disperse in ocean currents. Previously named *I. brasiliensis*. **SIMILAR SPECIES:** *I. cairica* (Eastern Cape) has leaves with 5–7 lanceolate leaflets; flowers pale mauve. *I. ficifolia*, the wild morning glory (Eastern Cape–KwaZulu-Natal), has three-lobed hairy leaves, red stems and pale mauve flowers. Common in coastal scrub.

196.3 Dune-pea   *Sophora inhambanensis*

A prostrate plant with hairy grey compound leaves with 8–10 paired leaflets. Pink pea flowers. Fruits are elongate, hairy, pea-like pods. **Size:** Leaves 6 cm long; pods 5 cm. **Biology:** A coloniser of foredunes in Mozambique.

196.4 Bay bean   *Canavalia rosea*

A creeping dune coloniser with shiny green compound leaves with three leaflets; has small purple flowers resembling those of a pea plant. Long, smooth, bean-like pod with a ridged edge. **Size:** Leaves 3 cm; pods 8 cm. **Biology:** Coloniser of dunes.

196.5 Dune creeper   *Hydrophylax carnosa*

Long prostrate succulent stems, square in section, green tinged with pink. Leaves opposite, small, fleshy and light green. Solitary small white flowers with four petals occur in the axils of the leaves. **Size:** Stems 30 cm long, 0.3 cm wide. **Biology:** A pioneer of foredunes.

196.6 Dune rosette   *Launaea sarmentosa*

A perennial prostrate runner with succulent stems rooting at the nodes, and a rosette of slightly succulent blue-green leaves. Yellow daisy flowerhead. **Size:** Leaves 4 cm; flowerhead 1.5 cm diameter. **Biology:** A pioneer species in salt-spray zones. Also found in East Africa, Egypt, India and China.

196.7 Dune cat's tail   *Hebenstretia cordata*

Shrublet with upright branches closely packed with overlapping heart-shaped waxy leaves that alternate neatly up the stem. Dense spikes of white flowers with a corolla that is split down the front; upper lip four-lobed. **Size:** Plant 30 cm, leaves 0.5 cm long. **Biology:** Hardy plants adapted to survive wind and sand inundation on coastal dunes.

196.8 Brineweed   *Salsola nollothensis*

A low-growing shrub with a tough woody stem; pink twigs tightly packed with small silvery leaves. **Size:** Bushes 10–30 cm across. **Biology:** The most important pioneer plant on coastal dunes in Namibia, where it has to survive water shortage, salt spray, heat and shifting sands.

196.1

196.1a

196.2

196.3

196.4

196.5

196.6

196.7

196.8

PLATE 197

Succulents of cliffs, dunes & salt marshes
Succulent, or with hairy or waxy leaves to handle salt spray and wind.

197.1 Ice plant *Mesembryanthemum crystallinum*
Sprawling annual with paddle-shaped, succulent, reddish leaves, covered with glistening bladder-like cells. Flowers small, white to pink. Fruits with five segments. **Size:** Flowers 2 cm. **Biology:** Confined to coastal sands. Flowers November and December.

197.2 Sour fig *Carpobrotus edulis*
Creeping plants. Paired, succulent, three-angled leaves. Flowers yellow, ageing pink; single central style. **Size:** Leaves 0.8–1.8 cm wide; flowers 5–8 cm. **Biology:** Flowers August–October. Fruits fleshy; used to make jam. Sap antiseptic and soothes sunburn. **SIMILAR SPECIES:** *Carpobrotus* spp. are used worldwide to stabilise shifting sands.
197.3 *Carpobrotus acinaciformis* (Yzerfontein–Mossel Bay) has robust, sabre-shaped leaves, 1.5–2.5 cm diameter. Flowers purple, 7–10 cm in diameter. Colonises coastal dunes (see p. 420). Flowers August–December. *C. quadrifidus*, formerly named *C. sauerae* (coastal Namaqualand–Saldanha), has the largest flowers, 12–15 cm across, magenta with a yellow centre. *C. mellei* has smaller pinkish-purple flowers; stamens shorter than stigma.

197.4 Dewplant *Disphyma crassifolium*
Stem creeping and fleshy; leaves cylindrical to triangular. Flowers glistening white, pink or magenta. Fruit a dried capsule. **Size:** Leaves 1.5 cm long; flowers 2 cm. **Biology:** Common in brackish soils fringing salt marshes or rocky shores. Flowers July–October.

197.5 Shoreline seapurslane *Sesuvium portulacastrum*
A succulent perennial herb with trailing red stems and opposite, oval, fleshy green leaves. The flowers consist of a star-shaped pink calyx and no petals. **Size:** Leaves 2–3 cm. **Biology:** Tropical coasts, often among upper-shore mangroves. Cooked as a vegetable.

197.6 Green-eyed desert primrose *Grielum grandiflorum*
A creeping, woolly annual. Leaves finely divided with pointed lobes. Glistening yellow flowers with a green eye make a dazzling impact in spring. Fruits flat and thorny, with a winged edge. **Size:** Flowers 2.5 cm. **Biology:** Forms mats on sandy coastal flats.

197.7 Maerbos *Roepera flexuosa*
Shrub with sessile leaves divided into two succulent leaflets. Five yellow petals with reddish markings. Fruits globular, with five sutures. **Size:** Shrub 70 cm, flowers 2 cm. **Biology:** On sand and limestone. **SIMILAR SPECIES:** *R. morgsana* has four petals, and four-winged fruits.

197.8 Hairy plantago *Plantago crassifolia*
A perennial with narrow, hairy, succulent leaves. Tiny green flowers borne on a dense flower spike. **Size:** 15 cm tall. **Biology:** Common in the upper edges of salt marshes and on exposed cliffs near the sea.

197.9 Sprawling duneweed *Tetragonia decumbens*
A sprawling succulent, glistening with swollen cells. Stem red, leaves oval, curled under. Flowers tiny, yellow, crowned with yellow stamens, clustered in leaf axils and shorter than the leaves. Fruits three or four-winged. **Size:** Leaves 4 cm. **Biology:** Abundant foredune coloniser. Grazed by stock. **SIMILAR SPECIES:** *T. fruticosa* (Namaqualand–Port Elizabeth) bears larger flowers on terminal branches longer than the long thin leaves, and held above them. Fruits larger, always four-winged. Occurs on dunes and in coastal scrub.

197.10 Soutbossie *Chenolea diffusa*
Reddish branches surrounded by velvety, succulent slightly silvery, grey-green leaves. Flowers tiny; 1–2 per leaf axil. **Size:** 10 cm. **Biology:** Coastal and estuarine, above high-tide level. **SIMILAR SPECIES:** *Suaeda caespitosa*, seablite (Eastern Cape), is taller; leaves longer and pale green, never silvery. Flowers and fruits larger and bunched (4–6 per leaf axil).

PLATE 198

Dune daisies   Asteraceae

Over 200 daisy species occur in South Africa. Flowerhead comprises many small flowers (florets), but only those on the edge form 'petals'.

198.1 Woolly everlasting   *Helichrysum crispum*
Straggling shrublet; stem and oval, upturned leaves covered with woolly white hairs. Flowerheads tightly packed; flowers papery yellow. **Size:** 15 cm tall. **Biology:** One of several *Helichrysum* spp. Flowers November–December. Traditionally used to repel insects.

198.2 Bushtick berry, Bietou   *Osteospermum moniliferum*
Large bushes. Leaves simple, spirally arranged, ovate; edges serrated. Flowers yellow. Cobwebby hairs on young leaves and shoots. Only South African daisy that has berries: black when ripe; arranged in a ring. Edible. **Size:** Bushes 1–6 m tall; flowerhead 3 cm. **Biology:** Stabilises dunes. Invasive in Australia. Formerly named *Chrysanthemoides*.

198.3 Dune daisy   *Didelta carnosa*
Rounded, perennial, fleshy shrublet. Leaves narrow, margins rolled; smooth or felted with grey hairs. Flowers yellow. Fruit prickly; splits into five winged 'seeds'. **Size:** 1 m tall; flowerheads 4–7 cm. **Biology:** Abundant on dunes. Flowers July–October. SIMILAR SPECIES: *D. spinosa* (Namaqualand) has oval to elliptical sharp-pointed leaves.

198.4 Sea pumpkin   *Arctotheca populifolia*
Leaves grey: simple and oval or lobed; coated with white reflective hairs that reduce air movement and water loss. Flowers pale yellow. **Size:** Leaves 3 cm wide, flowerhead 2.5 cm. **Biology:** A common occupant of coastal foredunes, creating small hummocks.

198.5 Dune gazania, Gousblom   *Gazania rigens*
Perennial herb with trailing stem; leaves shiny dark green above and woolly below. Flowerheads large, solitary; ray and disc florets yellow. **Size:** Flowerheads 4 cm. **Biology:** A common pioneer of foredunes and rocky outcrops. Forms lush stands in salt marshes.

198.6 Wild cineraria   *Senecio elegans*
Stems and leaves roughly hairy. Leaves deeply incised; margins rolled under. Disc yellow; ray florets pinkish purple. Black-tipped bracts on buds and flower base. **Size:** 30 cm tall. **Biology:** One of several common annual *Senecio* spp. Flowers July–March. SIMILAR SPECIES:
198.7 *Senecio maritimus* (Saldanha–Agulhas) has uniformly yellow flowers; leaves slightly succulent with lightly toothed margins, hairy below.

198.8 Salt marsh cotula   *Cotula coronopifolia*
Erect or creeping succulent. Leaves flat, fleshy; margin entire or lobed. Papery white leaf-base sheaths. Flowerhead yellow, button-shaped; no large petals; cupped by 14–18 bracts. **Size:** Plant 15 cm; flowerhead 0.8 cm. **Biology:** Common annual in seeps and salt marshes. Flowers May–February. SIMILAR SPECIES: *C. vulgaris* has thread-like leaves; flowerheads with 8–12 bracts. *C. lineariloba* has finely pinnate, fern-like leaves.

198.9 White bristle bush, Blombos   *Metalasia muricata*
Small spiky leaves, tightly clustered on branches; green above, whitish below and thinly cobwebby. Leaves curved or hooked at the tips. Numerous small, stalked flowerheads clustered at ends of branches. Flowers with greenish-white bracts. **Size:** Bushes 1.5 m tall, leaves 0.8 cm. **Biology:** A dominant coastal-dune shrub. Flowers April–September.

198.10 Wild rosemary, Kapokbossie   *Eriocephalus africanus*
Silvery shrub. Leaves small, hairy, aromatic. Flowers with 2–3 conspicuous white ray florets. Seeds fluffy, white. **Size:** Bush 1 m tall, flowers 1 cm. **Biology:** Widespread in coastal clays. Leaves used as a herb. Flowers May–September. SIMILAR SPECIES: *E. racemosa* (Lüderitz–East London) seeds also fluffy, but flowers lack white petals.

198.11 Ericoid phylica   *Phylica ericoides*
A compact shrublet, with narrow leaves and the margins curled under. Flowers white with a hairy calyx, in small rounded heads, petals hooded. Not a daisy. **Size:** Bush 1 m tall, leaves 0.5–0.8 cm. **Biology:** Grows on coastal slopes and secondary dunes.

198.1

198.2

198.3

198.4

198.5

198.6

198.7

198.8

198.9

198.10

198.11

PLATE 199

Salt-marsh & secondary-dune plants

199.1 Sea rose   *Orphium frutescens*

Leaves opposite or spiral up stem; lance-shaped, slightly fleshy. Flowers terminal, shiny pink. Anthers twisted, with an apical pore. **Size:** Shrub 60 cm; flower 3 cm. **Biology:** Perennial in sands and salt marshes. Bumblebees buzz the anthers to release pollen. **SIMILAR SPECIES:** *Chironia* spp. have similar pink (but non-shiny) silver-backed flowers.

199.2 Paper flower   *Limonium purpuratum*

Small shrub. Leaves basal, paddle-shaped, 8 x 2 cm. Flowers papery, in flattened sprays. **Size:** 50 cm tall. Flowers 1–2 cm. **Biology:** Grows in coastal sands; flowers October–February. **SIMILAR SPECIES:** *L. capense* (Cape Columbine) has leaves that run up stems; six times longer than broad. *L. longifolium* (west coast) has basal leaves, 10–20 times longer than broad. *L. perigrinum* (west coast) has leaves at branch tips; length four times width.

199.3 Sea lavender   *Limonium scabrum*

Tufts with a basal rosette of oval leaves. Stems and inflorescence much-branched. Flowers have a long corolla tube and five apically-notched petals. Calyx rust-coloured. **Size:** 20 cm tall. Flowers 5 mm. **Biology:** Brack soil on cliffs and salt marshes.

199.4 Coastal pelargonium   *Pelargonium capitatum*

Low woody shrub, coated with hairs. Leaves with 3–5 lobes, crinkled and serrated; aromatic. Flowers grouped, pink: two larger striped upper petals; three smaller lower petals. **Size:** Flower 2 cm. **Biology:** Abundant on dunes. Flowers spring–summer. **SIMILAR SPECIES:** South Africa has over 400 pelargonium species; widely used in perfumes.

199.5 *Pelargonium suburbanum* (Cape Peninsula–Eastern Cape coastal dunes) upper two petals wide, lower ones often reduced to a pair. Leaves once- or twice-divided.

199.6 Geranium, Bergtee   *Geranium incanum*

Leaves delicate, finely divided. Flowers pink to mauve with five equal petals. Geranium means 'crane's head', referring to the fruit, which splits into a distinctive 'maypole' with the five seeds attached by curling threads. **Size:** Flower 15–30 mm. **Biology:** On sandy and stony coastal soils. Flowers July–December. Popular garden plant; used for herbal tea.

199.7 Purple gorse, Skilpadbessie   *Muraltia spinosa*

Shrub with stiff, spine-like lateral branches. Leaves small, oblong. Flowers purplish, inner two sepals large, twisted and petal-like; lower petal keeled, with a crest. Fleshy yellow-to-red fruits. **Size:** Flower 10 mm. **Biology:** Common on sandy and rocky slopes.

199.8 Drumsticks   *Zaluzianskya villosa*

Leaves narrow, hairy, with scattered teeth. Flowers with five heart-shaped petals on a long tube; white to lilac: yellow 'eye' turns red after pollination. **Size:** Flower 1 cm. **Biology:** Common annual on sand. Flowers August–October. **SIMILAR SPECIES:** *Z. affinis* has sharper, less hairy, leaves and replaces it in the northwest.

199.9 Dune celery   *Dasyspermum suffruticosum*

Straggling annual with frilly, dissected, carrot-like leaves on a smooth main stem. The flower inflorescence is an umbel of many small white flowers. **Size:** Plant 30 cm. **Biology:** Frequent on stable dunes and sand flats. Flowers September–November.

199.10 Chinese violet   *Asystasia gangetica*

Low growing. Leaves crisp, oval, notched at tip. Tubular white flowers with purple spots on lower lip. **Size:** Leaves 2 cm long, flowers 2 cm. **Biology:** Endemic to South Africa and Asia but an invasive weed in Australia. Used as a traditional vegetable and has a high mineral content. Leaves used to treat asthma in Nigerian folk medicine.

199.11 Beach salvia, Bruinsalie   *Salvia africana-lutea*

Grey shrub. Leaves finely-hairy. Flowers golden to red-brown (*S. lanceolata* is rose-pink); long upper petals hooded. Calyx flower-like; persistent. **Size:** Flower 3–5 cm. **Biology:** Coastal dunes and arid fynbos. Leaves smell of lemon-pepper; used in cooking.

199.1

199.2

199.3

199.4

199.5

199.6

199.7

199.8

199.9

199.10

199.11

PLATE 200

Dune thickets & forests

Coastal shrubs and dune forests occur on stabilised dunes in the southeast, where summer rainfall is high. Most have waxy or hairy leaves and berries. Mined dune forests are slow to recover.

200.1 Wild banana, Coastal strelitzia　　　　　*Strelitzia nicolai*

Easy to identify, with large splitting leaves arranged in two ranks. A boat-like blue spathe houses the 'crane' flowers. Flower has three long white tepals and two blue petals that fuse into a stiff, arrow-like structure: birds landing on this perch open a central groove to expose the stamens. Seeds black, with a furry orange cap. **Size:** Leaves 2 m long. **Biology:** Common in coastal forests.

200.2 Coastal silver oak　　　　　　　　*Brachylaena discolor*

Leathery 'two-tone' leaves are green above, silvery white with dense hairs below, hence '*discolor*'. Thistle-like flowerheads cupped by 7–10 rows of bracts. Bristly tuft on fruit. Separate male and female trees. **Size:** Tree 4–20 m; leaves 5–12 cm. **Biology:** Common. **SIMILAR SPECIES:**
200.3 *Tarchonanthus littoralis*, camphor bush (southeast and south coasts), has aromatic 'two-tone' leaves with obvious net-venation. Flower cup with 1–2 rows of bracts.

200.4 White milkwood　　　　　　　　*Sideroxylon inerme*

Dense tree with milky latex. Leaves shiny, dark green, oval; midrib distinct. Young twigs and leaves bear rusty hairs. Flowers in leaf axils; small, scented, greenish white. Berries fleshy, ripening purplish black (200.4a); single-seeded. **Size:** 10 m tall; leaves 4–12 cm. **Biology:** Protected; the 'Post Office Tree' (Mossel Bay), 'Treaty Tree' (Cape Town), and 'Fingo Milkwood' (Peddie) are ancient national monuments. **SIMILAR SPECIES:** *Mimusops caffra*, coastal red milkwood (Port Alfred–Mozambique), is a 'walking tree' that blows over and roots where its branches touch the ground. Fruits red, edible, two-seeded.

200.5 Coastal tannin-bush　　　　　　　*Osyris compressa*

A small bushy tree. Bluish-green leaves opposite, oval, with a fine tip; yellow margin rolled under; petiole continues down the stem. Small greenish flowers. Black-red fruit fleshy, oval. **Size:** Tree 3 m tall, leaf 2 cm. **Biology:** Common on coastal dunes and rocks.

200.6 Dune crowberry　　　　　　　　　*Rhus crenata*

Dense shrub or small tree with trifoliate leaves, the upper margins of the leaflets scalloped. Small, white flowers in terminal heads. Fruits fleshy, round, dark bluish. **Size:** Tree 3–5 m tall, leaflet 1–2.5 cm. **Biology:** Common in coastal dunes. One of many *Rhus* spp. All have trifoliate leaves, lenticels (pores) on the stem and smell of apples when crushed.

200.7 Dune star-apple　　　　　　　*Diospyros rotundifolia*

Young branches grey with reddish hairs. Leaves spirally arranged, oval, leathery, glossy, hairless. Flowers creamy white. Red 'apple' with persistent winged calyx. **Size:** Shrub 2–9 m, leaves 0.2–0.6 cm long; fruit 2 cm. **Biology:** Common in dune scrub and forests.

200.8 Big num num, Natal plum　　　　　*Carissa macrocarpa*

Thorns once or twice forked. Leaves leathery, glossy; apical bristle. Flowers star-shaped, corolla tubular. Edible fleshy red berry. **Size:** Shrub 4 m; leaves 2–3 cm. **Biology:** Forms dune-thickets. **SIMILAR SPECIES:** *C. bispinosa* flowers 1 cm; clustered. *Acokanthera oblongifolia*, dune poison-bush, lacks thorns and has oval red fruits that are deadly.

200.9 Christmas berry, Dune string　　　　*Passerina ericoides*

A willowy shrublet with small oblong leaves in four ranks, pressed closely to the woolly stem. Flowers yellow to pink, in spikes, each a small flask with protruding anthers. Fruit a red berry. **Size:** Shrub 1 m; leaf 0.2–0.3 cm. **Biology:** A dominant shrub on coastal dunes. **SIMILAR SPECIES:** *P. rigida* has smaller, triangular leaves; Eastern Cape dunes.

200.10 Slangbos　　　　　　　　　　　*Stoebe plumosa*

Much-branched shrub with tiny silvery-grey leaves that are tightly pressed against side branches. Small golden-brown flowers form in the axils of leaves on the upper branches. **Size:** Bushes 1.5 m tall, leaves 0.2 cm. **Biology:** Abundant in coastal dunes but extends inland; can form dense stands. Flowers April–July. Bulbous white insect galls common.

200.1

200.2

200.3

200.4a

200.4

200.5

200.6

200.7

200.8

200.9

200.10

PLATE 201

Mangroves

Mangroves are trees that grow in saltwater on intertidal mudflats, in estuaries or even on sheltered coasts. Their roots consolidate and trap fine mud; sediments associated with them are rich in organics but lack oxygen, and are laden with hydrogen sulphide produced by sulphur bacteria. Mangroves support several species of animals that are seldom found elsewhere, including two snails, Cerithidea *(80.6) and* Terebralia *(80.7), and the mudskipper* Periophthalmus *(151.4). Mangrove roots are shallow and have above-ground pneumatophores to allow them to breathe, exchanging carbon dioxide for oxygen from the air.*

201.1 White mangrove   *Avicennia marina*

Trees of considerable stature, with a grey-white bark and lance-shaped silvery, grey-green leaves. Distinctive mats of vertical pneumatophores ('pencil roots') project from the mud beneath them. Fruits egg-shaped with a pointed tip (201.1a). **Size:** 12 m tall, leaves 6.5 cm long, fruit 2.5 cm long. **Biology:** The most abundant mangrove in southern Africa, and an early pioneer in the establishment of mangrove swamps, stabilising the sediment with its fine roots and providing a shaded 'nursery' for other, less hardy mangroves. Its roots exclude much of the salt in seawater, and its leaves have specialised salt glands that expel salt from the plant. Its leaves contribute substantially to the detritus available as a source of food for animals, and are particularly important for the mangrove crab (50.5).

201.2 Black mangrove   *Bruguiera gymnorrhiza*

A tall tree with a rough red-brown bark, buttress-roots around the trunk, and knee-like, above-ground pneumatophores. Leaves dark green, yellowing with age, smooth and shiny, roughly oval but with a pointed tip. The fruit has a star-shaped basal calyx from which a cigar-shaped hypocotyl develops (201.2a). **Size:** 18 m tall, leaves 12 cm long, fruit 18 cm long. **Biology:** Common, but cannot establish new stands of mangroves on its own: grows in the middle of reedbeds or *Avicennia* stands, often outcompeting *Avicennia*. Its roots efficiently prevent most salt from entering the tissues as they draw up water from the surrounding seawater. Its leaves accumulate salt, and regular loss of leaves helps rid the plant of excess salt. Mature flowers remain tightly shut until touched by an insect, when they explosively burst open, showering the insect with pollen. Mature fruits drop off and plunge into the mud, where they grow beneath the parent plant.

201.3 Red mangrove   *Rhizophora mucronata*

A moderate-sized tree with reddish to dark brown bark, and obvious characteristic prop (or 'stilt') roots that arch down from the main stem. Leaves elliptical with an abruptly spiked tip (*mucro* = 'point'). The fruits have a pear-shaped basal calyx and a long, thin, sharply pointed hypocotyl (201.3a). **Size:** 8 m tall, leaves 10 cm long, fruit 30 cm long. **Biology:** Forms thick hedges along the edges of creeks running through well-established mangrove swamps, to which *Rhizophora* is restricted.

201.4 Tagal mangrove   *Ceriops tagal*

A relatively small tree with light-grey bark, buttress-roots at the base of the trunk, and a small number of 'knee roots' and 'prop roots'. Leaves bright yellowish green, rigidly stiff, oval with a rounded or notched tip. Fruit similar to that of *Rhizophora*, with a pear-shaped calyx and very long slender hypocotyls. Fruits fall from the tree and become embedded in the mud, where they sprout to form seedlings (201.4a). **Size:** 6 m tall, leaves 7 cm, fruit 30 cm. **Biology:** Rare in South Africa, isolated specimens occurring in Kosi Bay, but common in Mozambique. Grows high on the shore among landward thickets of *Avicennia*.

201.1

201.1a

201.2a

201.2

201.3a

201.3

201.4a

201.4

Glossary

Acontia – threads laden with stinging cells that are ejected as a defence by sea anemones.
Adipose – containing fat layers, which act as an energy reserve and provide insulation and protection.
Androgynous – describing hermaphrodites that are first male and then female.
Annulated – beaded in appearance, or with a series of rings.
Aperture – opening or mouth (as of a gastropod shell).
Avicularia – individual bryozoans that have beaks and snap at intruding organisms.
Axil – angle between a leaf or branch and the axis from which it originates.

Balanoid zone – the middle of the intertidal zone, usually dominated by barnacles.
Barbel – fleshy projection near the mouth used for taste or smell.
Benthic – living on sediment or rocks on the seafloor.
Brachidium – internal skeleton supporting the lophophore in brachiopods.
Byssus – anchoring threads produced by a gland in the foot of many bivalves.

Calcareous – made of calcium carbonate or chalk (hence opaque white in appearance).
Callus – area of thickened shiny shell material on the inner lip of a gastropod shell.
Canine – long pointed tooth for grasping and piercing.
Carapace – outer case that covers all or part of the body.
Cephalothorax – fused head and thorax, as in crustaceans.
Cerata – finger-like projections on the backs of nudibranchs that act as gills.
Cervicorn – forking with one branch larger than the other; antler-like.
Chelipeds – nipper-bearing first pair of legs.
Chitin – horny organic material forming part of the skeleton of many invertebrates.
Circumtropical – occurring in all the tropical seas of the world.
Cirrus (-i) – slender flexible appendage for feather-star attachment or barnacle feeding.
Coenenchyme – tissue connecting adjoining polyps in a colony of cnidarians.
Column – trunk or main part of body of a sea anemone.

Commensal – living together with another species but doing it little or no harm.
Conceptacle – cavity or swelling containing reproductive organs.
Corallite – portion of a coral skeleton housing an individual polyp.

Dactylozooid – cnidarian individual modified into a tentacle for capturing prey.
Demersal – living close to the seabed.
Detritus – particles of decaying plant or animal material.
Diatoms – unicellular algae with walls impregnated with silica.
Dichotomous – regularly forking into pairs of branches.
Dicotyledon – flowering plant with two seed-leaves (cotyledons) and a net of leaf veins.
Distal – towards the tip or end of a structure.

Endemic – limited to a specific region.
Epiphytic – growing on other plants or animals.

Foliar – leaf-like, with flat blades.
Frond – flattened, leaf-like portion of an alga.
Fusiform – spindle-shaped or tapering at both ends.

Gametophyte – sexual or gamete-producing phase of a plant with alternating generations.
Gastrozooid – an individual specialised for feeding in a cnidarian colony.
Geophyte – plant with an underground storage organ that re-sprouts annually.
Girdle – thickened mantle surrounding shell plates of a chiton.
Gnathopods – first two pairs of thoracic limbs in amphipods: usually ending in nippers.
Gonophore – structure bearing reproductive individuals in a hydroid colony.
Gonotheca (-ae) – skeletal container of reproductive body of a hydroid.
Gonozooid – reproductive individual in a cnidarian colony.

Hectocotylus – arm of a male cephalopod specialised to transmit sperm to the female.
Hermaphrodite – individual that has both male and female organs.
Holdfast – the (often root-like) attachment organ of a seaweed.
Home scar – scar on a rock to which a limpet repeatedly returns after feeding.

Hydrotheca (-ae) – cup-like, skeletal structure protecting a hydroid polyp.
Hypocotyl – part of a seedling projecting below the seed-leaves; elongate in mangroves.

Intertidal – between the high-tide and the low-tide levels on the shore.
Introvert – tubular anterior process that can be protruded or drawn back into the body.

Lappet – lobe or flap of flesh.
Lateral line – line along the side of the body of a fish, responsible for detecting vibrations.
Leptocephali – long thin transparent eel larvae.
Ligament – elastic hinge joining valves of a bivalve shell, or the fibrous tissue joining bones.
Lophophore – horseshoe-shaped organ supporting feeding tentacles.
Lunate – crescent-shaped, like a new moon.

Mantle – outgrowth of the body wall that lines and secretes the shell of molluscs.
Manubrium – structure hanging below the bell of a jellyfish and ending in the mouth(s).
Marsupium – pouch-like structure in which young develop.
Medusa – jellyfish-like, umbrella-shaped individual in the life cycle of cnidarians.
Meristem – the part of a plant where growth takes place.
Mid-rib – central thickening of a leaf or frond of a plant.
Mid-water – middle depths of the water column.
Molar – rounded grinding tooth.
Monocotyledon – flowering plant with one seed-leaf (cotyledon) and parallel leaf veins.
Monotypic – classification group that has only a single representative species.
Mucilage – slimy substance produced in cell walls of certain plants.
Multiporate – having many pores, like a pepper pot.
Muscle scar – scar marking muscle attachment to a shell or bone.

Notochord – rod supporting the dorsal nerve cord in primitive chordates.

Operculum – protective lid closing a shell or a tube, or the gill cover of a fish.
Opisthosoma – hind part, or abdomen, of a spider.

Osculum (-a) – chimney-like opening, through which water leaves the body.
Ovicell – structure containing developing eggs of a bryozoan.

Palp – sensory appendage attached to the head.
Papilla (-ae) – small, blunt, conical projection.
Paragnath (-es) – tiny tooth on the pharynx of certain polychaete worms.
Parapodium (-a) – leg-like locomotory appendage on the body segments of worms, or the pair of dorsal flaps that covers the gills in sea slugs.
Pectoral – related to the breast or chest region or limbs, anterior to the belly.
Pedicel – stalk or stem-like attachment of a brachiopod.
Pedicellaria – minute pincer-like structures studding the surface of certain echinoderms.
Peduncle – slender base of the tail fin of fishes; stalk supporting the body in ascidians.
Pelagic – living in the waters of the open ocean.
Pelvic – related to the pelvis or hind limbs, posterior to the belly.
Pereiopods – thoracic 'walking' limbs in crustaceans.
Periostracum – outer horny layer of a mollusc shell (often eroded or shed after death).
Perisarc – tough outer skeletal covering of the stem of a hydroid.
Peristomium – the first cylindrical segment of a worm, bearing the mouth.
Pharynx – section of the gut immediately behind the mouth; gullet.
Phytoplankton – minute plants that float in the water.
Pinnate – with branches on either side of an axis, like a feather.
Pinnules – side branches of a plume-like structure.
Planktivorous – feeding on plankton
Plankton – tiny plants or animals that float in the water.
Pleon – abdomen of a crustacean.
Pleopods – abdominal 'swimming' limbs in crustaceans.
Pleotelson – one or more abdominal segments fused to the telson in crustaceans.
Pneumatophore – above-ground root of a mangrove, used for gas exchange.
Polyp – cylindrical individual with upward-facing tentacles in the cnidarian life cycle.
Preoperculum – large flat bone lying on top of the operculum or gill cover of fish.
Proboscis – tubular snout or projection of the head, usually extensible.

Prosoma – front part of the body of a spider, bearing feeding appendages and the legs.
Prostomium – anterior lobe of a worm's head, usually bearing sensory appendages.
Protandrous – being initially male, then becoming female.
Protogynous – being initially female and later becoming male.
Protrusible – capable of being projected or thrust forward.
Proximal – towards the base of a structure.
Pseudofaeces – material processed by the gills of bivalves but discarded before ingestion.

Radial shields – pairs of plates on the upper surface of brittlestars near base of each arm.
Radula – ribbon-like tongue bearing rows of teeth in a mollusc.
Raptorial – adapted for seizing prey.
Ray – flexible, soft, jointed, cartilaginous element supporting the fin of a fish.
Resilial ridge – band on the internal surface of a bivalve shell next to the ligament.
Rhinophore – second sensory pair of tentacles on the top of the head of some molluscs.
Rhizome – creeping horizontal stem sending out shoots above and roots below.
Rostrum – beak-like process, or a pointed projection between the eyes.

Scutes – modified fish scales with keels or spines on them.
Septum (-a) – partition separating two cavities or bodies of tissue.
Sessile – attached or incapable of shifting position.
Seta (-ae) – bristle, particularly on the body of a worm or arthropod.
Siphon – tube through which water is drawn into or expelled from the body.
Spat – newly settled juveniles of bivalve molluscs.
Spatulate – flat and round-tipped, like a spatula or miniature spade.
Spherules – small spherical bodies at the top of the column of certain sea anemones.
Spicules – tiny spines or granules in the body walls of sponges, soft-corals, sea cucumbers.
Spination – the pattern of spines on a body.
Spire – coiled portion of a shell above the aperture.
Sporophyte – phase in the life cycle of algae that produces asexual spores.
Statocyst – organ of balance consisting of a sac containing granules of lime or sand.

Stipe – stalk- or stem-like portion of an alga.
Stridulation – production of a rasping sound by rubbing two rough surfaces together.
Substratum (-a) – rock or sediment to which an animal or plant can attach or into which it can burrow.
Subtidal – below the lowest level on the shore exposed by the tides.
Suture – groove that spirals around a gastropod shell; where one whorl meets the next.
Symbiosis – intimate relationship between two organisms that is of mutual benefit.
Synapticulum (-a) – skeletal bar connecting adjacent septa in a coral.

Telson – the 'tail' at the end of a crustacean's abdomen.
Test – hard outer tunic in ascidians, or the outer 'shell' in sea urchins.
Tetrasporophyte – sporophytes that produce asexual spores in batches of four.
Thallus – body of an alga that is undifferentiated into a holdfast, stipe or fronds.
Truncated – cut-off or ending abruptly.
Tubefeet – cylindrical limbs with an apical sucker, used by echinoderms for locomotion.
Tubercle – conical projection or small hump.

Umbilicus – open end of a spiral hollow running up the central axis of a gastropod shell.
Uniporate – having a single pore, like a salt cellar.
Uniseriate – consisting of a single series or row (of cells).
Uropods – appendages on either side of the telson in crustaceans; part of the tail fan.
Utricle – swollen, bladder-like tip of a cellular filament in certain green algae.

Valve – one of the pair of shells of a bivalve, or one of the eight plates of a chiton shell.
Vesicle – hollow, bladder-like body usually filled with fluid.

Whorl – one coil of a gastropod shell, or a circle of parts arising from one point.

Zooecium (-a) – chamber enclosing a single individual or zooid of a bryozoan colony.
Zooid – individual forming part of a colonial organism.
Zooplankton – small animals that swim or float in the water column.
Zooxanthellae – microscopic unicellular algae symbiotic in the bodies of some animals.

References

GENERAL WORKS

Branch G & Branch M. 1981. *The Living Shores of Southern Africa*. C. Struik, Cape Town.

Branch M. 1998. *Explore the Seashore of South Africa*. Cambridge University Press, Cambridge.

Day JH. 1974. *A Guide to Marine Life on South African Shores*. AA Balkema, Cape Town.

Griffiths C, Griffiths R & Thorpe D. 1988. *Seashore Life*. Struik Publishers, Cape Town.

Jones G. 2008. *A Field Guide to the Marine Animals of the Cape Peninsula*. Southern Underwater Research Group, Cape Town.

Kalk M (Ed.). 1995. *A Natural History of Inhaca Island, Mozambique* (3rd ed). Witwatersrand University Press, Johannesburg.

Lubke R & De Moore I (Eds). 1998. *Field Guide to the Eastern and Southern Cape Coasts*. University of Cape Town, Cape Town.

Payne AIL, Crawford RJM & van Dalsen A. 1989. *Oceans of Life off Southern Africa*. Vlaeberg Publishers, Cape Town.

Richmond MD (Ed.). 2002. *A Guide to the Seashores of Eastern Africa and the Western Indian Ocean Islands* (2nd ed). SIDA/SAREC-UDSM.

GUIDES TO SPECIFIC GROUPS

Sponges

Samaai T & Gibbons MJ. 2005. Demospongiae taxonomy and biodiversity of the Benguela region on the west coast of South Africa. *Afr. Nat. Hist.* 1: 1–96.

Cnidarians

Carlgren O. 1938. South African Actiniaria and Zoantharia. *Kungl. Svensk. Vet.-Ahad. Hatidl.* (Series 3) 17(3): 1–148.

Kramp PL. 1961. Synopsis of the medusae of the world. *J. Mar. Biol. Assoc. U.K.* 40: 1–469.

Millard NAH. 1975. Monograph on the Hydroida of southern Africa. *Ann. S. Afr. Mus.* 68: 1–513.

Pages S, Gili JM & Bouillin J. 1992. Planktonic cnidarians of the Benguela Current. *Scientia Marina* 56 (Suppl. 1): 1–144.

Riegl B. 1995. A revision of the hard coral genus *Acropora* Oken, 1815 (Scleractinia: Astrocoeniina: Acroporidae) in south-east Africa. *Zool. J. Linn. Soc.* 113: 249–288.

Riegl B. 1996. Corals of the south-west Indian Ocean. IV. The hard coral family Faviidae Gregory, 1900 (Scleractinia: Faviina). *Invesl Rept., Oceanogr. Res. Inst. Durban* 70: 1–47.

Veron JEN. 1986. *Corals of Australia and the Indo-Pacific*. Angus and Robertson, North Ryde, Australia.

Williams GC. 1990. The Pennatulacea of southern Africa (Coelenterata, Anthozoa). *Ann. S. Afr. Mus.* 99: 31–119.

Williams GC. 1992. The Alcyonacea of southern Africa. Stoloniferous octocorals and soft corals (Coelenterata, Anthozoa). *Ann. S. Afr. Mus.* 100: 249–358.

Williams GC. 1992. The Alcyonacea of southern Africa. Gorgonian octocorals (Coelenterata, Anthozoa). *Ann. S. Afr. Mus.* 101: 181–296.

Worms & kin

Day JH. 1967. *A Monograph on the Polychaeta of Southern Africa*. British Museum (Natural History), London.

Newman LJ & Cannon LRJ. 2003. *Marine Flatworms: the World of Polyclads*. CSIRO, Collingwood, Victoria.

Wesenberg-Lund E. 1963. South African sipunculids and echiuroids from coastal waters. *Vidensk. Medd. Dansk. Naturh. Foren.* 126: 101–146.

Arthropods

Barnard KH. 1950. Descriptive catalogue of South African decapod Crustacea (crabs and shrimps). *Ann. S. Afr. Mus.* 38: 1–837.

Barnard KH. 1950. Descriptive list of South African stomatopod Crustacea (Mantis shrimps). *Ann. S. Afr. Mus.* 38: 838–864.

Barnard KH. 1954. South African Pycnogonida. *Ann. S. Afr. Mus.* 41: 81–159.

Boden BP. 1954. The euphausiid crustaceans of southern African waters. *Trans. Roy. Soc. S. Afr.* 34: 181–234.

Debelius H. 1999. *Crustacea Guide of the World*. IKAN-Unterwasserarchiv, Frankfurt.

De Freitas AT. 1985. The Penaeoidea of southern Africa 1. The study area and key to the southern African species. *Investl Rep. Oceanogr. Res. Inst. Durban* 56: 1–31.

Griffiths CL. 1976. *Guide to the Benthic Marine Amphipods of Southern Africa*. South African Museum, Cape Town.

Kensley B. 1972. *Shrimps and Prawns of Southern Africa*. South African Museum, Cape Town.

Kensley B. 1978. *Guide to the Marine Isopods of Southern Africa*. South African Museum, Cape Town.

Bryozoans

Florence WK, Hayward PJ & Gibbons MJ. 2007. Taxonomy of shallow-water Bryozoa from the west coast of South Africa. *Afr. Nat. Hist.* 3: 1–58.

Lamp shells & molluscs

Debelius H. 1998. *Nudibranchs and Sea Snails Indo-Pacific Field Guide*. IKAN-Unterwasserarchiv, Frankfurt.

Gosliner T. 1987. *Nudibranchs of Southern Africa – A Guide to Opisthobranch Molluscs of Southern Africa*. Sea Challengers, Monterey.

Gosliner TM, Barnard DW & Valdes A. 2008. *Indo-Pacific Nudibranchs and Sea Slugs – a Guide to the World's Most Diverse Fauna*. Sea Challengers. Monterey.

Hiller N. 1991. The southern African recent brachiopod fauna. In: *Brachiopods through Time* (Eds DI McKinnon, DE Lee and JD Campbell), pp. 439–445. AA Balkema, Rotterdam.

Jackson JW. 1952. A revision of some South African Brachiopoda, with descriptions of new species. *Ann. S. Afr. Mus.* 41: 1–40.

Kaas P & van Belle RA. 1985–1991. *Monograph of Living Chitons* (in 4 volumes). EJ Brill, Leiden.

Kensley B. 1973. *Sea-shells of southern Africa*. Maskew Miller, Cape Town.

Kilburn R & Rippey E. 1982. *Sea Shells of Southern Africa*. Macmillan South Africa, Johannesburg.

Liltved WR. 1989. *Cowries and their Relatives of Southern Africa. A Study of the Southern African Cypraeacean and Velutinacean Gastropod Fauna*. Gordon Verhoef, Seacomber Publications.

Norman M. 2000. *Cephalopods a World Guide*. ConchBooks, Hackenheim.

Richards D. 1981. *Shells of Southern Africa – A Concise Guide for Collectors*. Struik Publishers, Cape Town.

Steyn DW & Lussi M. 1998. *Marine shells of South Africa: an illustrated collector's guide to beached shells*. Ekogilde Publishers, Hartebeespoort, South Africa.

Zsilavecz G. 2007. *Nudibranchs of the Cape Peninsula and False Bay*. Southern Underwater Research Group Press, Cape Town.

Echinoderms

Balinsky JB. 1957. The Ophiuroidea of Inhaca Island. *Ann. Natal Mus.* 14: 1–33.

Clark AM & Courtman-Stock J. 1976. *The Echinoderms of Southern Africa*. British Museum (Natural History), London.

Coleman N. 2007. *Sea Stars: Echinoderms of the Asia/Indo-Pacific*. Neville Coleman's Underwater Geographic, Springwood, Australia.

Thandar AS. 1989. The sclerodactylid holothurians of southern Africa, with erection of one new subfamily and two new genera (Echinodermata: Holothuroidea). *S. Afr. J. Zool.* 24: 290–304.

Thandar AS. 1990. The phyllophorid holothurians of southern Africa with the erection of a new genus. *S. Afr. J. Zool.* 25: 207–223.

Sea squirts & kin

Monniot C, Monniot F, Griffiths CL & Schleyer M. 2001. South African ascidians. *Ann. S. Afr. Mus.* 108: 1–141.

Fishes

Compagno LJV, Ebert DA & Smale MJ. 1989. *Guide to the Sharks and Rays of Southern Africa*. Struik Publishers, Cape Town.

Heemstra P & Heemstra E. 2003. *Coastal Fishes of South Africa*. NISC and SAIAB, Grahamstown.

King, D. 1996. *Reef Fishes and Corals, East Coast of Southern Africa*. Struik Publishers, Cape Town.

King D & Fraser V. 2002. *More Reef Fishes and Nudibranchs*. Struik Publishers, Cape Town.

Smith MM & Heemstra PC. 2003. *Smiths' Sea Fishes*. Struik Publishers, Cape Town.

Van der Elst R. 1993. *A Guide to the Common Sea Fishes of Southern Africa* (3rd ed). Struik Publishers, Cape Town.

Zsilavecz G. 2005. *Coastal fishes of the Cape Peninsula and False Bay*. Southern Underwater Research Group, Cape Town.

Reptiles & birds

Branch WR. 1998. Marine reptiles. In: *Field Guide to the Eastern and Southern Cape Coast* (Eds R Lubke & I de Moore), pp. 156–159. University of Cape Town Press, Cape Town.

Hockey PAR, Dean WRJ & Ryan PG. 2005. *Roberts Birds of Southern Africa* (7th ed). John Voelcker Bird Book Fund, Cape Town.

Newman K. 2002. *Newman's Birds of Southern Africa* (8th ed). Struik, London.

Sinclair JC, Hockey PAR & Tarboton WR. 2002. *Sasol Birds of Southern Africa* (3rd ed.). Struik, Cape Town.

Mammals

Best PB. 2007. *Whales and Dolphins of the Southern Africa Subregion*. Cambridge University Press, Cambridge.

Skinner JD & Smithers RHN. 2005. *The Mammals of the Southern African Subregion*. Cambridge University Press, Cape Town.

Seahorse, Sodwana Bay.

Seaweeds

De Clerck O, Bolton JJ, Anderson RJ & Copperjans E. 2002. Guide to the Seaweeds of KwaZulu-Natal. *Scripta Botanica Belgica* 33: 1–294.

Lluch JR. 2002. Marine benthic algae of Namibia. *Scientia Marina* 66 (Suppl. 3): 5–256.

Lubke RA & Siegrief SC. 1998. Marine algae. In: *Field guide to the Eastern and Southern Cape Coast*. (Eds R Lubke & I de Moore); pp. 65–116. University of Cape Town Press.

Stegenga H, Bolton J & Anderson R. 1997. Seaweeds of the South African West Coast. *Contrib. Bolus Herbarium* 18: 1–655.

Flowering plants

Berjak P, Campbell GK, Huckett BI & Pammenter NW. 1977. *The Mangroves of Southern Africa*. Natal Branch of the Wildlife Society of Southern Africa.

Lubke RA & van Wyk K. 1998. Estuarine plants. In: *Field Guide to the Eastern and Southern Cape Coasts* (2nd ed). (Eds) R Lubke and I de Moore; pp 187–197. University of Cape Town.

Lubke RA & van Wyk K. 1998. Terrestrial plants and coastal vegetation. In: *Field Guide to the Eastern and Southern Cape Coasts* (2nd ed). (Eds R Lubke and I de Moore); pp 289–342. University of Cape Town.

Manning J. 2008. *Field Guide to Fynbos*. Struik Publishers, Cape Town.

Scientific index

The gaudy amphipod Hoplopleon

Detail of a sea-urchin 'shell'.

General index

All numbers refer to **page numbers**.

Flamingos grace a sunset at Skeleton Coast National Park, Namibia.

About the authors

PROFESSOR GEORGE BRANCH is world renowned for his research on marine ecology. Together with his wife, Margo, he wrote *The Living Shores of Southern Africa,* a best-selling book on the ecology of marine life that won the UCT book award. He is an NRF A-rated scientist and has received Fellowships from the University of Cape Town and the Royal Society of South Africa, the Gilchrist Medal for marine science, the Gold Medal of the Zoological Society, a Distinguished Teachers' Award and the International Temperate Reef Lifetime Award for his contributions to marine science and education, which span coastal ecology, fisheries policy, subsistence fisheries, and Marine Protected Areas. His photographs have been widely published and exhibited.

LYNNATH BECKLEY is an Associate Professor of Marine Science at Murdoch University, Western Australia. She completed her PhD at the University of Cape Town and was Principal Scientist at the Oceanographic Research Institute in Durban for several years. She has broad interests in fisheries science, biological oceanography and marine conservation in the Indian Ocean. She has published widely on the biology of fishes and is a co-author of *Seychelles: the Bradt travel guide.*

PROFESSOR CHARLES GRIFFITHS is Director of the Marine Biology Research Centre at the University of Cape Town and is internationally known for his research on African marine biodiversity and marine invasive species. He is the author of over 120 research publications and of papers describing more than 100 species new to science. He is a co-author, with his wife and D. Thorpe, of the Struik pocket guide *Seashore Life,* and with M. Picker and A. Weaving of the best-selling *Field Guide to the Insects of South Africa.* Over 2 000 of his natural history photographs have been published in books and magazines around the world.

MARGO BRANCH is a biologist with wide interests in research, interpretation and education. She has written or illustrated many scientific papers and numerous books including *Trees of Southern Africa, Seaweeds of South Africa, A Field Guide to the Mushrooms of South Africa,* and the junior *Explore the Seashore* and *Explore the Cape Flora and Fauna.* She was a member of the team that produced the award-winning Coastcare Interpretive Poster Series and Fact Sheets and the interpretive signage and teaching aids for the Two Oceans Aquarium, Table Mountain National Park and Addo Elephant National Park. She is a recipient of the Stevenson-Hamilton Silver Medal for contributions to zoology and a Lifetime Marine Communicator Award.

George and Margo Branch, Charles Griffiths and Lynnath Beckley (left to right) at home in their natural habitat.